Criminal Justice and Law Enforcement Books

of

WEST PUBLISHING COMPANY

St. Paul, Minnesota 55102

December, 1977

CONSTITUTIONAL LAW

Maddex's Cases and Comments on Constitutional Law by James L. Maddex, Professor of Criminal Justice, Georgia State University, 816 pages, 1974. Maddex's 1976 Supplement.

CORRECTIONS

Burns' Corrections—Organization and Administration by Henry Burns, Jr., Professor of Criminal Justice, University of Missouri–St. Louis, 578 pages, 1975.

Kerper and Kerper's Legal Rights of the Convicted by Hazel B. Kerper, Late Professor of Sociology and Criminal Law, Sam Houston State University and Janeen Kerper, Attorney, San Diego, Calif., 677 pages, 1974.

Killinger and Cromwell's Selected Readings on Corrections in the Community, 2nd Edition by George G. Killinger, Chairman, Board of Pardons and Paroles, Texas and Paul F. Cromwell, Jr., Director of Juvenile Services, Tarrant County, Texas, 357 pages, 1978.

Killinger and Cromwell's Readings on Penology—The Evolution of Corrections in America by George G. Killinger and Paul F. Cromwell, Jr., 426 pages, 1973.

Killinger and Cromwell's Selected Readings on Introduction to Corrections by George G. Killinger and Paul F. Cromwell, Jr., about 450 pages, 1978.

Killinger, Cromwell and Cromwell's Selected Readings on Issues in Corrections and Administration by George G. Killinger, Paul F. Cromwell, Jr. and Bonnie J. Cromwell, San Antonio College, 644 pages, 1976.

Killinger, Kerper and Cromwell's Probation and Parole in the Criminal Justice System by George G. Killinger, Hazel B. Kerper and Paul F. Cromwell, Jr., 374 pages, 1976.

Krantz' The Law of Corrections and Prisoners' Rights in a Nutshell by Sheldon Krantz, Professor of Law and Director, Center for Criminal Justice, Boston University, 353 pages, 1976.

Rubin's Law of Criminal Correction, 2nd Edition (Student Edition) by Sol Rubin, Counsel Emeritus, Council on Crime and Delinquency, 873 pages, 1973.
Rubin's 1977 Supplement.

CRIMINAL JUSTICE BOOKS

CORRECTIONS—Continued

Smith & Berlin's Introduction to Probation and Parole by Alexander B. Smith, Professor of Sociology, John Jay College of Criminal Justice and Louis Berlin, Chief, Training Branch, New York City Dept. of Probation, 250 pages, 1975.

CRIMINAL JUSTICE SYSTEM

Kerper's Introduction to the Criminal Justice System by Hazel B. Kerper, 558 pages, 1972.

Senna and Siegel's Introduction to Criminal Justice by Joseph J. Senna and Larry J. Siegel, both Professors of Criminal Justice, Northeastern University, 540 pages, 1978.

Study Guide to accompany Senna and Siegel's Introduction to Criminal Justice by Roy R. Roberg, Professor of Criminal Justice, University of Nebraska-Lincoln, 187 pages, 1978.

CRIMINAL LAW

Dix and Sharlot's Cases and Materials on Basic Criminal Law by George E. Dix, Professor of Law, University of Texas and M. Michael Sharlot, Professor of Law, University of Texas, 649 pages, 1974.

Ferguson's Readings on Concepts of Criminal Law by Robert W. Ferguson, Administration of Justice Dept. Director, Saddleback College, 560 pages, 1975.

Gardner and Manian's Principles, Cases and Readings on Criminal Law by Thomas J. Gardner, Professor of Criminal Justice, Milwaukee Area Technical College and Victor Manian, Milwaukee County Judge, 782 pages, 1975.

Heymann and Kenety—The Murder Trial of Wilbur Jackson: A Homicide in the Family by Philip Heymann, Professor of Law, Harvard University and William Kenety, Instructor, Catholic University Law School, 340 pages, 1975.

LaFave's Principles of Criminal Law by Wayne R. LaFave, Professor of Law, University of Illinois, about 600 pages, 1978.

Loewy's Criminal Law in a Nutshell by Arnold H. Loewy, Professor of Law. University of North Carolina, 302 pages, 1975.

CRIMINAL PROCEDURE

Davis' Police Discretion by Kenneth Culp Davis, Professor of Law, University of Chicago, 176 pages, 1975.

Dowling's Teaching Materials on Criminal Procedure by Jerry L. Dowling, Professor of Criminal Justice, Sam Houston State University, 544 pages, 1976.

Ferdico's Criminal Procedure for the Law Enforcement Officer by John N. Ferdico, Assistant Attorney General, State of Maine, 372 pages, 1975.

Israel and LaFave's Criminal Procedure in a Nutshell, 2nd Edition by Jerold H. Israel and Wayne R. LaFave, 372 pages, 1975.

Johnson's Cases, Materials and Text on The Elements of Criminal Due Process by Phillip E. Johnson, Professor of Law, University of California, Berkeley, 324 pages, 1975.

CRIMINAL JUSTICE BOOKS

CRIMINAL PROCEDURE—Continued

Kamisar, LaFave and Israel's Cases, Comments and Questions on Basic Criminal Procedure, 4th Edition by Yale Kamisar, Professor of Law, University of Michigan, Wayne R. LaFave, Professor of Law, University of Illinois and Jerold H. Israel, Professor of Law, University of Michigan, 790 pages, 1974. Supplement Annually.

EVIDENCE

Gardner's Criminal Evidence by Thomas J. Gardner, Professor of Criminal Justice, Milwaukee Area Technical College, about 640 pages, 1978.

Klein's Law of Evidence for Police, 2nd Edition by Irving J. Klein, Professor of Law and Police Science, John Jay College of Criminal Justice, about 600 pages, 1978.

Markle's Criminal Investigation and Presentation of Evidence by Arnold Markle, The State's Attorney, New Haven County, Connecticut, 344 pages, 1976.

INTRODUCTION TO LAW ENFORCEMENT

More's The American Police—Text and Readings by Harry W. More, Jr., Professor of Administration of Justice, California State University at San Jose, 278 pages, 1976.

Police Tactics in Hazardous Situations by the San Diego, California Police Department, 228 pages, 1976.

Schwartz and Goldstein's Law Enforcement Handbook for Police by Louis B. Schwartz, Professor of Law, University of Pennsylvania and Stephen R. Goldstein, Professor of Law, University of Pennsylvania, 333 pages, 1970.

Sutor's Police Operations—Tactical Approaches to Crimes in Progress by Inspector Andrew Sutor, Philadelphia, Pennsylvania Police Department, 329 pages, 1976.

JUVENILE JUSTICE

Cromwell, Killinger, Sarri and Solomon's Text and Selected Readings on Introduction to Juvenile Delinquency by Paul F. Cromwell, Jr., George G. Killinger, Rosemary C. Sarri, Professor, School of Social Work, The University of Michigan and H. N. Solomon, Professor of Criminal Justice, Nova University, 502 pages, 1978.

Faust and Brantingham's Juvenile Justice Philosophy: Readings, Cases and Comments by Frederic L. Faust, Professor of Criminology, Florida State University and Paul J. Brantingham, Professor of Criminology, Florida State University, 600 pages, 1974.

Fox's Law of Juvenile Courts in a Nutshell by Sanford J. Fox, Professor of Law, Boston College, 286 pages, 1971.

Johnson's Introduction to the Juvenile Justice System by Thomas A. Johnson, Professor of Criminal Justice, Washington State University, 492 pages, 1975.

Senna and Siegel's Cases and Comments on Juvenile Law by Joseph J. Senna, Professor of Criminal Justice, Northeastern University and Larry J. Siegel, Professor of Criminal Justice, Northeastern University, 543 pages, 1976.

CRIMINAL JUSTICE BOOKS

MANAGEMENT AND SUPERVISION

Gaines and Ricks' Selected Readings on Managing the Police Organization by Larry K. Gaines and Truett A. Ricks, both Professors of Criminal Justice, Eastern Kentucky University, about 500 pages, 1978.

More's Criminal Justice Management: Text and Readings, by Harry W. More, Jr., 377 pages, 1977.

Souryal's Police Administration and Management by Sam S. Souryal, Professor of Criminal Justice, Sam Houston State University, 462 pages, 1977.

Wadman, Paxman and Bentley's Law Enforcement Supervision—A Case Study Approach by Robert C. Wadman, Rio Hondo Community College, Monroe J. Paxman, Brigham Young University and Marion T. Bentley, Utah State University, 224 pages, 1975.

POLICE-COMMUNITY RELATIONS

Cromwell and Keefer's Readings on Police-Community Relations, 2nd Edition by Paul F. Cromwell, Jr., and George Keefer, Professor of Criminal Justice, Southwest Texas State University, 506 pages, 1978.

PSYCHOLOGY

Parker and Meier's Interpersonal Psychology for Law Enforcement and Corrections by L. Craig Parker, Jr., Criminal Justice Dept. Director, University of New Haven and Robert D. Meier, Professor of Criminal Justice, University of New Haven, 290 pages, 1975.

VICE CONTROL

Ferguson's the Nature of Vice Control in the Administration of Justice by Robert W. Ferguson, 509 pages, 1974.

Uelman and Haddox' Cases, Text and Materials on Drug Abuse Law by Gerald F. Uelman, Professor of Law, Loyola University, Los Angeles and Victor G. Haddox, Professor of Criminology, California State University at Long Beach and Clinical Professor of Psychiatry, Law and Behavioral Sciences, University of Southern California School of Medicine, 564 pages, 1974.

MANAGING

THE

POLICE ORGANIZATION:

SELECTED READINGS

By

LARRY K. GAINES

Professor of the College of Law Enforcement,
Eastern Kentucky University

and

TRUETT A. RICKS

Professor of the College of Law Enforcement,
Eastern Kentucky University

CRIMINAL JUSTICE SERIES

WEST PUBLISHING CO.
St. Paul • New York • Los Angeles • San Francisco
1978

Library of Congress Cataloging in Publication Data

Main entry under title:

Managing the police organization.

    (Criminal justice series)

    1. Police administration—Addresses, essays, lectures. I. Gaines, Larry K.
II. Ricks, Truett A. III. Series.
HV7935.M35   363.2   78–1270
ISBN 0–8299–0163–9

Gaines & Ricks—Man.Pol.Org.Pamph.

PREFACE

The readings in this text represent both the traditional concepts of police administration and the contemporary, innovative issues which have come to light over the last several years. The text presents the reader background material on the status of police administration today, and suggests new directions which police agencies may take to improve the quality of law enforcement. Basically, contemporary policing can be characterized as being quasi-military or classically organized. The authors of the various articles contained in this text have gone to great lengths to repute the successfulness and utility of this style of administration. The authors also focus upon two alternatives to this classical organizational arrangement. First, the human-relations perspective is presented. (This alternative is represented by John E. Angell and others.) This administrative style focuses upon decentralization, participative-democratic leadership and decision-making. This perspective also entails the redefining of the role of police in society. The second perspective presented here is the systems approach to administration. (This alternative is represented by John Hudzik, Harry P. Hatry, and others.) This administrative style is characterized by the introduction of data systems, identification of goals, and control and coordination based to a large degree on data analysis.

This text was designed to fill a significant void in the police administration literature. Heretofore, the majority of the literature has dealt with police administration at an extremely infantile level. If one were to compare the state of the art of police administration, as depicted in the literature, to business administration or general public administration, one would find that police administration is possibly twenty years behind the other administrative disciplines. This volume delves into those organizational and managerial issues which have traditionally been neglected. Moreover, the reader is expected to possess a cursory knowledge of police administration, and this text will build upon such a foundation and introduce the reader to new innovative techniques in the management and organization of police departments.

Basically, the text is divided into five specific areas: (1) Perspectives on the Role of the police and police administration; (2) The police organization; (3) Organizational behavior in police systems; (4) Control processes in the police organization; and (5) Changing the police organization. These five areas represent the most crucial areas of study in police administration. Briefly, the role of the police and police administration represents one of the most critical issues in society. In order for our police to be effective, their role must be clearly defined. This problem is intrinsic to police administration since police administrators must devise and introduce strategies for goal accomplishment. Presently, this process is impossible to undertake due to the lack of agreement as to the proper role of police in society. Effectiveness and efficiency in administration is based upon the pursuit of goals. A hierarchy of goals must be discovered in order for the police to become successful.

The second area, police organization, has become one of the most discussed issues in criminal justice. Organization is the structuring of people, offices and units within the police department. Many contemporary theorists and practitioners have come to the realization that present police organizations and management structures possess out-dated and dysfunctional qualities—new administrative matrices must be devised and considered. The human-relations and systems approaches represent new administrative matrices that warrant consideration within the police setting.

The third area, organizational behavior in the police organization, includes an analysis of all facets of behavior within the police organization. In order for the organization to reach its maximum effectiveness and efficiency, the behavior of the organizational membership must be controlled. Within the police setting, control has traditionally consisted of authoritarian leadership; however, participative and democratic styles of leadership are now being considered. Basically, control of behavior will come about only if behavior is understood, and once this understanding is achieved, administrators can start developing appropriate leadership styles.

The fourth area, control processes in the police organization, represents the managerial functions and processes which take place within the police organization. The articles in this section focus upon the systems approach to police administration. Basically, this managerial perspective entails the quantification and subsequent analysis of activities within the police organization. Management becomes an empirical science as opposed to an art.

The final section, changing the police organization, examines various issues surrounding change theory as it relates to police administration. Today, we are beginning to understand and recognize change within the police structure as being extremely difficult to accomplish, and must be approached from a cautious and deliberate

PREFACE

standpoint. Hopefully, this text will provide its reader with a complete understanding of its complex subject.

Finally, we would like to acknowledge and offer our sincere appreciation to the authors and publishers who granted us permission to reprint their material in this text.

LARRY K. GAINES
TRUETT A. RICKS

Richmond, Kentucky
February, 1978

*

TABLE OF CONTENTS

TABLE OF CONTENTS

†

MANAGING THE POLICE ORGANIZATION: SELECTED READINGS

PART I

PERSPECTIVES ON THE ROLE OF THE POLICE AND POLICE MANAGEMENT

The identification of the proper role and goals of the police in our society is one of the most critical and perplexing issues in criminal justice. Society, the police, nor academia have come to a common agreement as to what purpose our police should serve. Upon examining the police related literature, one finds numerous authorities presenting their impressions as to the functions, goals, and roles of the police; however, activities range from provision of miscellaneous services to the community to law enforcement or "crook catching" activities with little agreement as to which activities are most important.

Numerous lists of police roles have been generated. For example, John P. Kenney stated that the roles of the police are:

Coercive Activities	Criminal Law Enforcement
	Traffic Law Enforcement
	Juvenile Law Enforcement
	Keeping the Peace
	Intelligence Gathering
Noncoercive Activities	Social Service
	Crime Prevention
	Creation of an Environment of Security and Stability
	Provision of Service
	Protection of Personal Liberty and Civil Rights [1]

1. John P. Kenney, *Police Administration*, Springfield, Ill.: Charles C. Thomas, Publisher, 1972: pp. 32–44.

1

The American Bar Association has detailed the current responsibilities of the police as:

(1) to identify criminal offenders and criminal activity and, when appropriate, to apprehend offenders and participate in subsequent court proceedings;

(2) to reduce the opportunities for the commission of some crimes through preventive patrol and other measures;

(3) to aid individuals who are in danger of physical harm;

(4) to protect constitutional guarantees;

(5) to facilitate the movement of people and vehicles;

(6) to assist those who cannot care for themselves;

(7) to resolve conflict;

(8) to identify problems that are potentially serious law enforcement or government problems;

(9) to create and maintain a feeling of security in the community;

(10) to promote and preserve civil order; and

(11) to provide other services on an emergency basis.[2]

Kenney and the American Bar Association, more or less, exemplify the current thinking as to what functions our police should serve.

Although functions and goals for the police are explicitly stated, it is not possible to discern that which the police should be doing. Most role or goal statements and lists of functions are all inclusive which make it impossible for the line police officer to discern his responsibilities to society. For example, considering Kenney's statement of roles, one finds that the statements are generic and could possibly include any activities that a police officer selected to perform. On the other hand, the American Bar Association's responsibilities are more specific in detailing police functions; however, the functions are too inclusive. They cover far too many activities. Moreover, which activities are most important? Successful goal accomplishment can come only if resources are expended toward those needs which are most important. By not setting priorities, it is impossible to determine what the police should be doing. Police, like other government agencies, operate under strict budgetary constraints. Given the present level of government funding, it is impossible for the police to achieve all of the aforementioned goals. Therefore, the police must either concentrate on a few goals with the real-

---

2. American Bar Association, *Comparative Analysis of Standards and Goals of the National Advisory Commission on Criminal Justice Standards and Goals with Standards for Criminal Justice of the American Bar Association,* Washington: American Bar Association, 1976: p. 8.

ization that the best possible results will be mediocracy. Goal selection and the means of accomplishing goals are ultimately left to the police, and the subsequent process of selection falls under the preview of police discretion. The police tend to select the goals and means for goal accomplishment which they perceive to be the most important at the time.

This current method of police direction setting is not effective nor efficient. Too often the police select goals which are impossible to achieve. For example, most police see themselves as "crook catchers" whose principle function in society is to eliminate crime. However, crime is a social-cultural phenomenon of which the police have little or no control. At best, all the police can hope to accomplish is to displace crime from their jurisdiction to another. Our society and police must come to a realization as to which police functions are realistic and concentrate on those functions. The police are ineffective in terms of catching crooks, but the police are somewhat more efficient and can improve in maintaining order.[3] Most police officers view family disorders as a mundane duty, whereas, a crime in progress is an extremely important assignment even though more citizens and police officers are killed or injured as a result of family disorders. The point is, we must determine those functions which are most important and which the police can perform successfully and guide our police accordingly.

Goals become an extremely important concept in police administration. Goals establish a parameter for all other activities in the police organization. Goals:

(1) present the general purpose and ideology of the organization;

(2) guide and support organizational decision-making;

(3) help in developing and maintaining a useful information system;

(4) perform a control function;

(5) aid in motivating the organizational membership;

(6) delegate and fix responsibility;

(7) integrate the activities between the operating subunits with the organization; and

(8) aid in the planning process [4]

Since goals serve many vital purposes in organizations, it becomes extremely important that clear-cut goals are formulated.

3. See James Q. Wilson, "Dilemmas of Police Administration". *Public Administration Review* (September/October, 1968). pp. 407–416.

4. Paul M. Whisenand and R. Fred Ferguson, *The Managing of Police Organizations,* Englewood Cliffs, N.J.: Prentice-Hall, Inc., 1973. p. 88.

The readings in this first section examine the problem of police goals. The authors present their impressions as to what the goals or role of the police should be. Not only is it important to understand police goals, it is also extremely important to understand the technology or means of accomplishing goals and the probability of goal attainment. Too often police administrators or society mandate goals which are impossible to attain. If goals are unrealistic, then it becomes impossible to properly direct the police organization within prescribed parameters. These are a few of the problems associated with the selection of goals. The preceeding readings will objectively examine the state of the art regarding police organizational goals and future implications.

Objectives of Part I

1. Identify the various roles of police in society.
2. Identify the strategies utilized or proposed in order to fulfill the police roles.
3. Identify the degree of success and future-possibility of success of police agencies fulfilling the various police roles.
4. Identify the various perceptions of the role of the police by the various elements within our society.

CRIME CONTROL MANAGEMENT AND THE POLICE * †

Broad strategic questions such as "What are the goals and objectives of this business?" and "How can the available resources be best utilized to achieve these goals and objectives?" should be applied to the management of public institutions as well as that of corporations. In this article, Professor Reppetto raises the strategic issues of crime control management and discusses the role of the police. He notes that although the management of crime control is fragmented, police strategies are the center of the effort. The limitations of these strategies are analyzed in terms of police resource allocation and criminal behavior. The author suggests that the key defect in current crime control methods has been the overreliance on a single strategy, and hypothesizes that more effective crime control would result from a broader strategic posture.

* This article is based upon a paper on street robbery presented at the 4th National Symposium on Law Enforcement, Science, and Technology, Washington, D.C., May 1971.

† Source: Reppetto, Thomas A., "Crime Control Management and the Police," *Sloan Management Review*, Winter 1972–73, pp. 45–53.

INTRODUCTION

In 1970 there were 5,568,000 index crimes recorded in the United States, an increase of 11 percent from the previous year and 176 percent over 1960.[1] Probably two to three times this amount were not recorded.[2] Beyond the bare figures, attitude surveys consistently find index type crime ranked as the most serious domestic problem and report that in some cities 40 to 50 percent of respondents feel unsafe walking around their own neighborhoods at night.[3] So sober a source as the financial page of the *New York Times* offers a grim account of contemporary urban life:

"The large American city has become like an armed camp. Shop keepers and ordinary citizens fight gun duels with hold-up men and intruders in their homes. The streets are empty at night, cab drivers huddle behind their bullet-proof shields and some of the world's largest corporations protect their property and employees as though they were under seige." [4]

The institution most immediately concerned with reducing the incidence of index crime is the criminal justice system of police, courts, and corrections. In recent years the manpower and other resources of these agencies have been increased substantially. In addition, since the creation in 1968 of the Federal Law Enforcement Assistance Administration (LEAA), the criminal justice system, particularly the police, has had considerable advice and assistance from academic and private expertise. To date, these efforts have not yielded major results. It is the intent of this article to suggest that the criminal justice system can be made more effective in reducing index-type offenses. An analysis will be presented of the present police-management strategy for controlling crime, with suggestions regarding its possible refinement and supplementation.

THE MANAGEMENT OF CRIME CONTROL

If one seeks to determine what anti-crime strategies are in use in a particular metropolitan area, there is no single source of information. The criminal justice system is an amalgam of federal, state, and local police, prosecutorial, judicial, probation, and parole agencies which occasionally are augmented by private security forces. Normally each maintains its own records and devises its own goals and

---

1. Index Crimes include murder, rape, robbery, aggravated assault, burglary, larceny over $50, and auto theft. The first five are predatory in nature and constitute the heart of so-called "crime in the streets." See FBI [6], p. 6.

2. See President's Commission on Law Enforcement and Administration of Justice [13], p. 17.

3. See [1], p. 44.

4. *New York Times*, January 24, 1972, p. 59.

work methods. Perhaps, then, the first apparent weakness in the management of crime control is that there is no overall crime control agency within any coherent geographical, social, and economic unit, such as a standard metropolitan statistical area (SMSA).

Probably the nearest equivalent is a central city police department. The police, by the mandate of law, are charged with the investigation of all reported crimes and the legal processing of offenders and victims. Courts and correctional agencies in large measure must wait for police initiative. Normally the central city is where the bulk of crime occurs, and its police force performs a coordinating function for smaller police agencies in the area. In essence, central city police strategies constitute the core of the criminal justice system's efforts to control crime.

The basic police anti-crime strategy may be modeled as follows.[5] The major assumption is that common index crimes arise from a union of desire and opportunity; for a crime to occur there must be individuals who are motivated to engage in criminal behavior and opportunities for them to do so. The model posits crime control as the central task of the police and sees its achievement through the application of specific techniques designed to repress criminal behavior. Among the chief techniques are:

Omnipresence

This involves projecting to the maximum extent a belief by potential offenders in the high probability of police presence at any given point in time and space. This heightens the offender's perception of risk.

Aggressive Patrol

This requires that police seek to interdict crime by locating and challenging suspicious persons through methods sometimes referred to as stop and frisk, or field interrogation.

Rapid Response

Police strive to develop the capability of responding quickly to citizen emergency calls in order that criminals may be apprehended in the act.

Follow-up Investigation

Police utilize optimum investigative techniques in order to maximize the possibility that offenders who manage to flee successfully from crime scenes will be apprehended at a later date.

5. See Eastman [5], pp. 77–78 and Goodman et al. [7], pp. 12–13.

In essence, the police strategy seeks to *deter* or prevent crimes from occurring, *detect* crimes when they do occur, and *apprehend* crime perpetrators. This strategy is usually abbreviated as deterrence, detection and apprehension (DDA).

An examination of the allocation of resources within a typical police department illustrates the reliance placed on the DDA strategy. Most police officers (50 to 75 percent) are assigned to the uniformed patrol division where they are dispersed on a time and area basis according to anticipated workload. Officers patrolling in vehicles or on foot are the prime means of projecting omnipresence and effecting arrests. The detective division, normally utilizing 10 to 12 percent of total strength, is charged with conducting follow-up investigations which lead to apprehensions.

In the management area emphasis on application of technique has led to adoption of a military type of organizational structure designed to ensure that operating personnel adhere to procedural regulations. In turn, this has led to emphasis on centralized control and close supervision.

The major impact of federally funded technical assistance has been to support the DDA strategy. Police communications centers have installed command and control systems designed to reduce to the minimum the period of delay between citizen call and police response. The planning units now utilize operations research techniques in order to deploy manpower and to optimize DDA capabilities. Computers which primarily contain on-line data base information useful for apprehension purposes (e. g., names of wanted persons and lists of stolen vehicles or property) have been installed at all levels from the local police force up to the FBI National Crime Information Center (NCIC).

LIMITATIONS ON THE DDA STRATEGY

While the tenets of the DDA strategy have been widely accepted in the law enforcement field, recent research has cast doubt on its efficacy. When subjected to close analysis, DDA's major methods and assumptions appear questionable. Its chief difficulties are discussed here.

The Nature of Criminal Behavior

The model essentially requires the typical criminal offender to be a rational decision maker. Index offenders who are apprehended tend to be young and to represent disproportionately the lower levels of educational and economic achievements—segments of the population where rational decision making is not a highly developed skill.[6]

6. See FBI [6], pp. 126–127, and President's Commission on Law Enforcement and Administration of Justice [12], p. 44.

Motivations also tend to vary greatly within the index categories. Murder, rape, and assault often result from uncontrolled passion, whereas robbery, burglary, and larceny may be more calculated offenses. Even in the latter category there are some offenders (drug addicts, for example) whose needs may be so compelling that cost factors are outweighed by immediate benefits. A Washington, D.C. study of property offenders (robbers, burglars, and thieves) indicat-

Table 1   Arrest for Index Crimes *

Crime	Cases	Arrest Index
Homicide	338	.7130
Rape	906	.4834
Robbery	15,847	.1327
Assault	13,392	.4599
Burglary	67,028	.0434
Grand Larceny	40,822	.0420
Motor Vehicle Theft	20,792	.0810

* For further detail, see Greenwood [8], p. 24.

Table 2   Victimization Rates (per 100,000 population)*

Crime	NORC Survey	UCR
Willful Homicide	3.0	5.1
Forcible Rape	42.5	11.6
Robbery	94.0	61.4
Aggravated Assault	218.3	106.6
Burglary	949.1	299.6
Grand Larceny	606.5	267.4
Motor Vehicle Theft	206.2	226.0

* For further detail see President's Commission on Law Enforcement and Administration of Justice [12], p. 21.

ed they were not highly rational, were not fearful of consequences or, at the time of committing the crime, were able to block out the fear.[7] A study of robbery offenders in Boston concluded that one-third did not fear capture, one-third blocked out the fear, and one-third thought chances of capture were minimal.[8]

The Operational Effectiveness of Law Enforcement

There is evidence that the minority of offenders who do calculate risks are correct in their assessment that the chances of capture are

7. See Goodman et al. [7], p. 56.   8. See Conklin [2], p. 134.

minimal.   Table 1 presents the findings of a 1970 Rand Corporation study of the New York City Police Department (NYCPD) apprehension activities in the area of index crime.

If the New York figures are typical it would appear that the police arrest about 50 percent of the offenders versus person and five percent of the offenders versus property.   However, the true situation may be even worse since many crimes are not reported.   Table 2 presents a comparison of crime experience reported in a victimization survey conducted by the National Opinion Research Center (NORC) and official Uniform Crime Report (UCR) figures.   Viewed in conjunction with the Rand data, Table 2 suggests that for person crimes the true arrest figure may be close to 25 percent, and for property crimes 2.5 percent.

Of those arrested only a minority are convicted and an even lesser number incarcerated.   A presidential commission calculated that less than 10 percent of all persons arrested for index crimes actually are sentenced to prison.[9]   On the other hand, given the tendency of property offenders to commit multiple offenses, it is likely that statistical probabilities catch up to them over a period of time.   Thus virtually all routine offenders are arrested, and if they continue their crime careers, eventually are incarcerated.[10]   It was the conclusion of the Washington offender study, however, that the DDA strategy had no greater impact on criminal careers than it did on criminal acts.[11]

Resource Allocation and Police Methods

A consideration of police task allocations serves to explain their relative ineffectiveness in controlling index crime.   First, it is clear that although police departments' central concern may be serious crime, it is not their central task.   Studies of municipal police departments usually find that about 80 percent of the typical uniformed patrolman's case assignments involve order maintenance, i. e., settling family, street corner, and barroom disputes, or rendering miscellaneous services such as rounding up stray animals.[12]

Further, although police management texts place great reliance on patrol methods, it is doubtful that this type of activity is especially productive.[13]   A typical American city with one half million population is likely to have only 40 one-man patrol cars on duty at any given time, of which a fair number will be on assignment and there-

9.   See President's Commission on Law Enforcement and Administration of Justice [12], pp. 262–63.

10.   See Conklin [2], pp. 101, 177.

11.   See Goodman et al. [7], p. 57.

12.   See Livermore [9], Webster [20], and Wilson [21], pp. 17–19.

13.   See Wilson and McLaren [22], p. 418.

fore unavailable.[14]   This leaves a relatively small force for preventive patrol and response.

A common crime of stealth such as burglary (typically breaking and entering a structure whose occupants are away) for practical purposes is relatively invisible to patrolling police.   In contrast, street robbery is highly visible but comparatively rare.   The relationship among manpower resources, number of potential crime targets, and frequency of criminal attack is illustrated by a presidential commission calculation that in the city of Los Angeles, a patrolling policeman's chances of encountering a robbery in progress are once in 14 years.[15]

A close study of patrol activities in three major cities found that the mobilization of police is largely dependent upon the extent to which the police are summoned by the public.   The study also found that the number of criminal arrests and overall police-citizen cooperation are chiefly a function of whether or not police intervention is citizen initiated.   Few criminal arrests resulted from police initiated contacts.   The study, therefore, concluded that patrol activity was ineffective in controlling crime.[16]

Given the competing demands of necessary noncrime tasks, it is difficult to envision ways in which police manpower for crime control can be increased substantially.   Indeed, uncritical additions along conventional DDA lines might cause serious difficulties in the larger criminal justice system.   The courts and correctional institutions might either collapse from overcrowding or be forced to employ plea bargaining methods to such an extent that it would make the connection between crime and correction meaningless.[17]

TOWARD A BROADER STRATEGIC APPROACH

The fact that most police time is not spent on index crime, that citizen support is crucial to police effectiveness, that traditional methods to a large extent are ineffective or even counterproductive, and that increased attention is being given to community relations problems, has led to the development of a model of policing which emphasizes close involvement between police and citizens.   This model stresses prevention and community service rather than repressive

14. See President's Commission on Law Enforcement and Administration of Justice [15], p. 11.

15. See President's Commission on Law Enforcement and Administration of Justice [15], p. 12.

16. See Reiss [17], pp. 94–96.

17. Plea bargaining involves negotiations for a lesser sentence in return for a plea of guilty. See President's Commission on Law Enforcement and Administration of Justice [14], pp. 9–13.

tactics. The concrete manifestations of this are found in the operation of neighborhood police teams in several cities in the United States. Here, the emphasis is on close integration between local police and citizens. The new model of police service is essentially a reaction to the shortcomings of the old, but as yet it has developed no coherent strategy akin to the DDA.

The strategic concept of crime as a function of desire plus opportunity is a useful one. The shortcoming has been an overreliance on repressing desire (temporarily) by apparent foreclosure of opportunity. Were the concepts of desire and opportunity analyzed separately, more useful alternative strategies might evolve. The remainder of this article will suggest two possible strategic approaches and a refinement of the DDA strategy.

Opportunity Minimizing Strategies

Police efforts toward securing potential crime targets traditionally have not gone beyond patrol activities. Since resources are limited, targets numerous, and a significant portion of criminal activity nonvisible, it seems logical to attempt to secure targets by other than patrol measures. High risk targets often can be predicted in advance because there is a sufficient patterning of crimes. Opportunity minimizing requires active partnerships among police, private persons, and organizations. Examples of this include educational programs designed to acquaint households with the proper locks to use on their doors, the organization of citizen patrol groups with walkie-talkies to monitor street conditions, and major physical design programs to channel commercial and social activity in the interest of increased security from crime.

On one hand, adoption of this strategy is difficult for police management since it tends to shift a major aspect of anticrime activity outside the confines of the police service with attendant lessening of professional autonomy. On the other hand, some professional groups display similar reluctance to include security factors in their own planning. For example, there is a natural conflict between police and builders over the inclusion of alleys in new residential or commercial developments. The builders see alleys as cost effective avenues for refuse removal and other useful functions while the police regard them as crime hazards which simply add to the linear miles on a patrol route.

An almost totally neglected opportunity minimization approach is the nature of the crime victim. Industry has long recognized that some workers are accident prone. There is reason to believe that the same holds true for certain crime victims. Even police departments with extensive information retrieval systems, however, rarely attempt to identify multiple victims, though some people through carelessness, provocative behavior, or occupational role invite criminal attack.[18] For example, the elderly are disproportionately victims of street robbery.[19] One possible means of countering this would be to provide low cost or subsidized checking accounts for older persons, thus eliminating their need to carry cash.

Recently some police departments have established crime prevention units which conduct inspections of various premises in order to assist in designing appropriate security measures.[20] In some cities they even have assisted in developing model building codes. Several police departments engage in educational programs to enlighten the general public on counter-crime measures. Most such units number less than one percent of the total police strength, and thus their efforts are limited. The basic problem, however, is that they lack a well-articulated management policy regarding the manner and extent to which crime prevention or opportunity minimizing programs will be carried out.

Desire Lessening Strategies

The index offender population for the most part is geographically concentrated, and is known to the police because of frequent arrests. In any community the number of offenders is a relatively small percentage of the population.[21] Therefore, it would seem appropriate to work with the source of the crime problem rather than its multitudinous effects. In the past this approach has been seen as social work and therefore beyond the purview of the police. Similarly the social welfare bureaucracy has not sought a close alliance with law enforcement.

The DDA strategy may repress criminal desire but does not remove it. The only police efforts directed toward this more positive objective have been in the juvenile delinquency area, and these efforts have been limited. The typical police youth division is less than five percent the size of the combined patrol and detective field force.

While it is not clear what factors motivate crime in a given individual, most offenders tend to come from low income or minority groups, and in many instances possess a drug habit. This suggests that social, economic, and medical programs offer a possibility of reducing the offender population or at least the extent to which some individual offenders engage in criminal behavior.

Currently, the most promising desire minimizing programs center around youth service bureaus, community treatment centers, and crisis intervention training for police. The first two involve multi-faceted agencies operating at the neighborhood level, designed to of-

---

18. See, for example, Schafer [18].

19. See Conklin [2], pp. 89–90.

20. See Church [3].

21. See Singer [19], pp. 8–9.

fer under one aegis a variety of services ranging from job counseling to drug treatment. Such programs envision the police role to be one of close cooperation.[22]   Crisis intervention provides special training for selected officers in order to equip them to deal with emotional disturbances.   In a New York City experiment, it was reported that the presence of a family crisis intervention unit (FCIU) in a precinct led to a significant reduction in the incidence of family related homicides and assaults, compared with a control precinct of similar characteristics which had not employed an FCIU.[23]

Refining the DDA Strategy

If supplemental strategies were instituted, the traditional DDA activities of the police could be concentrated against highly visible crimes like street robbery and refined to deal more effectively with calculated property crimes. The police methods currently used to implement the DDA strategy are largely tactical and individualistic rather than strategically oriented. For example, criminal investigation is conducted on a case method basis and intelligence activities are directed at individual offenders or groups. Success in police work is measured by the arrest of a burglary gang and the clearance of a number of cases. This is a futile process given the volume of crime in relation to control resources.

A more productive approach would be to consider the entire problem of burglary from a systems standpoint and attempt to determine its nature with a view toward making it a cost ineffective undertaking. For example, most items taken in burglaries have no intrinsic value to the thief but must be converted into cash by sale to others. In some instances this may be a criminal receiver or so-called "fence." Sometimes the goods may be moved through an informal network of acquaintances. In both instances, commercial establishments such as taverns, stores, and gas stations are utilized as outlets. The number of such locations is much smaller and more stationary than the number of burglars. Logically, the place to dam the stream of stolen goods is at its narrowest point. A concerted effort to identify receiver outlets and deprive them of their business licenses might produce a major reduction in burglary loss.

CONCLUSION

This article has attempted to demonstrate that, although the management of crime control is fragmented, police strategies are at the core of such efforts. In this respect the DDA strategy is the one on which the criminal justice system has relied almost exclusively for

22. See President's Commission on   23. See Clark [4], pp. 124–126.
  Law Enforcement and Administration
  of Justice [16], pp. 48–49.

the control of index crime. The limits of the DDA strategy in terms of criminal behavior and police resources have been identified. More importantly, it has been shown that the strategy does not deal adequately with criminal motivation or crime opportunity factors.

The article has suggested that the key defect in crime control management has been the overreliance on a single strategy. It has been hypothesized that more effective crime control would result from a broader strategic posture that emphasized social service techniques which address criminal motivation, technological approaches directed toward identifiable crime hazards, and a refinement of the DDA strategy to make it more systematic and cost effective.

1. "City Taxes and Services: Citizens Speak Out," *Nations Cities*, Vol. 9 (November 1971), pp. 37–52.

2. Conklin, J. *Robbery and the Criminal Justice System*. Philadelphia, Lippincott, 1972.

3. Church O. "Crime Prevention: A Stitch in Time," *The Police Chief*, Vol. 37 (March 1970), pp. 52–54.

4. Clark, R. *Crime in America*. New York, Pocket Books, 1971.

5. Eastman, G. E. (ed.). *Municipal Police Administration*, 7th ed. Washington, ICMA, 1971.

6. FBI. *Uniform Crime Reports 1970*. Washington, Government Printing Office, 1971.

7. Goodman, L. H., Miller, T., and DeForrest, P. *A Study of the Deterrent Value of Crime Prevention Measures as Perceived by Criminal Offenders*. Washington, Bureau of Social Science Research, 1966.

8. Greenwood, P. W. *An Analysis of the Apprehension Activities of the New York City Police Department*. New York, Rand Institute, 1970.

9. Livermore, J. M. "Policing," *Minnesota Law Review*, Vol. 55 (March 1971), pp. 649–729.

10. Luedtke, G. *Crime and the Physical City*. Detroit, Luedtke Associates, undated.

11. Marx, G. T. and Archer, D. "Citizen Involvement in the Law Enforcement Process: The Case of Community Patrols," *American Behavioral Scientist*, Vol. 15, no. 1 (1970), pp. 52–72.

12. President's Commission on Law Enforcement and Administration of Justice. *The Challenge of Crime in a Free Society*. Washington, Government Printing Office, 1967.

13. President's Commission on Law Enforcement and Administration of Justice. *Task Force Report: Crime and Its Impact, An Assessment*. Washington, Government Printing Office, 1967.

14. President's Commission on Law Enforcement and Administration of Justice. *The Courts*. Washington, Government Printing Office, 1967.

15. President's Commission on Law Enforcement and Administration of Justice. *Science and Technology*. Washington, Government Printing Office, 1967.

16. President's Commission on Law Enforcement and Administration of Justice. *Juvenile Delinquency and Youth Crime.* Washington, Government Printing Office, 1967.

THE POLICE: MANDATE, STRATEGIES, AND APPEARANCES *

I. INTRODUCTION

All societies have their share of persistent, chronic problems—problems of life, of death, problems of property and security, problems of man's relationship to what he consecrates. And because societies have their quota of troubles, they have developed ways in which to distribute responsibility for dealing with them. The division of labor that results is not only an allocation of functions and rewards, it is a moral division as well. In exchange for money, goods, or services, these groups—such as lawyers or barbers or clergymen or pharmacists—have a *license* to carry out certain activities that others may not. This license is a legally defined right, and no other group or groups may encroach upon it.[1]

The right to perform an occupation may entail the permission to pick up garbage or to cut open human bodies and transfer organs from one to another. What it always involves, however, is a series of tasks and associated attitudes and values that set apart a specialized occupational group from all the others. Further, the licensed right to perform an occupation may include a claim to the right to define the proper conduct of others toward matters concerned with the work. The claim, if granted, is the occupation's *mandate*. The mandate may vary from a right to live dangerously to the right to define the conditions of work and functions of related personnel.

The professional mandate is not easily won, of course, for clients are often unwilling to accept the professional definition of their problem. Professions claim a body of theory and practice to justify their right to discover, define, and deal with problems. The medical profession, for example, is usually considered the model of a vocation with a secure license and mandate. Yet even in medicine the client may refuse to accept the diagnosis; he may change physicians or fail to follow doctor's orders or insist upon defining his troubles as the

---

* Source: Manning, Peter K. "The Police: Mandate, Strategies, and Appearances," Edited by Jack D. Douglas in *Crime and Justice in American Society*, New York: The Bobbs-Merrill Co., 1971: 149–194. Peter K. Manning has recently expanded this work, *Police Work*, Cambridge: MIT Press, 1977.

1. See Everett C. Hughes, *Men and Their Work* (New York: The Free Press, 1958), chap. 6; idem, "The Study of Occupations," in *Sociology Today*, ed. R. K. Merton, Leonard Broom, and L. S. Cottrell (New York: Basic Books, 1959), pp. 442–458.

product of a malady best cured by hot lemonade or prayer. The contraction and expansion of an occupation's mandate reflects the concerns society has with the services it provides, with its organization, and with its effectiveness. In times of crisis, it is the professions that are questioned first.[2]

Some occupations are not as fortunate as others in their ability to delimit a societal "trouble" and deal with it systematically. The more power and authority a profession has, the better able it is to gain and maintain control over the symbolic meanings with which it is associated in the public's mind. As we have become less concerned with devils and witches as causes of mental illness, clergymen have lost ground to psychiatrists who have laid claim to a secular cure for madness; in this sense, mental illness is a product of the definitions supplied by psychiatry. A profession, therefore, must not only compete with its clientele's definitions, it must also defend itself against the definitions of competing groups. Is a backache better treated by a Christian Scientist, an osteopath, a chiropractor, a masseuse, or an M.D.? Professional groups whose tools are less well-developed, whose theory is jerry-built or unproved, and who are unable to produce results in our consumer-oriented society will be beset with public doubt, concern, and agitation. In other words, these are the groups that have been unable to define their mandate for solving social "troubles" in such a way that it can be accomplished with ease and to the satisfaction of those they intend to serve.

The police have trouble. Among the many occupations now in crisis, they best symbolize the shifts and strains in our changing socio-political order. They have been assigned the task of crime prevention, crime detection, and the apprehension of criminals. Based on their legal monopoly of violence, they have staked out a mandate that claims to include the efficient, apolitical, and professional enforcement of the law. It is the contention of this essay that the police have staked out a vast and unmanageable social domain. And what has happened as a result of their inability to accomplish their self-proclaimed mandate is that the police have resorted to the manipulation of *appearances*.

We shall attempt to outline the nature of the police mandate, or their definition of social trouble, their methods of coping with this trouble, and the consequences of their efforts. After developing a sociological analysis of the paradoxes of police work and discussing the heroic attempts—*strategies*—by police to untangle these paradoxes, we shall also consider the recommendations of the President's crime

2. Hughes, *Men and Their Work.*

commission [3] and assess their value as a means of altering and improving the practical art of managing public order.

To turn for the moment to "practical matters," the same matters to which we shall return before concluding, the troubles of the police, the problems and paradoxes of their mandate in modern society, have become more and more intense. Police today may be more efficient in handling their problems than were the first bobbies who began to patrol London in 1829. Or they may not be. There may or may not be more crime. Individual rights may or may not be greatly threatened by crime or crime-fighters, and the enforcement of law in view of recent Supreme Court decisions may or may not be a critical issue in crime control. The police may or may not have enough resources to do their job, and they may or may not be allocating them properly. Peace-keeping rather than law enforcement may or may not be the prime need in black communities, and the police may or may not need greater discretionary powers in making an arrest. But however these troubles are regarded, they exist. They are rooted deeply in the mandate of the police.

Some Sociological Assumptions

This essay makes several assumptions about occupations, about people as they execute occupational roles, about organizations as loci or structures for occupational activities, and about the nature of society. Not all activity taking place "on the job" can be construed as "work"; goldbricking is not unknown in American society and some professionals have even been known to use their places of work to conduct business somewhat outside the mandate of their organization. An individual's "organizational" behavior varies with what the organization is said to require or permit, with his particular place in the organizational hierarchy, and with the degree of congruence between the individual's personal definition of his role and the organization's definition of his role. In a given situation, then, organizational rules and regulations may be important sources of meanings ("He's working hard"), or other criteria may provide more relevant meanings of behavior ("He can't be expected to work. His wife just had a baby"). The ways in which people explain or account for their own organizational activities and those of others are problematic. How do people refer to their organizational roles and activities? How do they construct their moral obligations to the organization? What do they think they owe the organization? How does this sense

3. The President's Commission on Law Enforcement and Administration of Justice (hereafter cited as President's Commission), *The Challenge of Crime in a Free Society* (Washington, D.C.: United States Government Printing Office, 1967); and idem, *Task Force Report: The Police* (Washington, D. C.: United States Government Printing Office, 1967).

of obligation and commitment pattern or constrain them in another role—the role of golfer or father or politician?

People as they perform their roles are actors. They are alert to the small cues that indicate meaning and intention—the wink, the scowl, the raised eyebrow. Those who attend to these behavioral clues are the audience. All actors try to maximize the positive impression they make on others, and both experience and socialization provide them with a repertoire of devices to manage their appearance.

People as actors in roles must also make assumptions about their audience. The politician, for example, must make certain assumptions about his constituency, the lawyer certain assumptions about clients. Assumptions are an important part of urban life. Some actors with white faces, for instance, may make certain assumptions about others with black faces, that they will be ill-mannered or badly educated and that any request for directions is a prelude to a holdup. Assumptions are not simply individual in nature; they are shared, patterned, and passed on from one social group to the next.

One of the most important aspects of assumptions, however, is that they are the basis for strategies.[4] Strategies arise from the need of organizations and individuals to cope with persistent social problems about which assumptions have been made. Strategies are often a means of survival in a competitive environment; they can be inferred from the allocation of resources or from the behavior and pronouncements of an organization. In short, strategies assist any organization within the society in managing its appearance and in controlling the behavior of its audience.

All organizations and individuals, we assume, are bent on maximizing their impressions in order to gain control over an audience.[5] The audience for the police is diverse; it should be considered many audiences. For the police must convince the politicians that they have used their allocated resources efficiently; they must persuade the criminals that they are effective crime-fighters; they must assure the broader public that they are controlling crime. Rather than a single rhetoric—the "use of words to form attitudes or induce actions in other human agents"[6]—directed toward convincing one audience, the police must develop many rhetorics. Linguistic strategies to control audiences are only one of many ploys used by the police organiza-

4. The important, sociological notions of "strategy" and "tactics" come from military theory and game theory. See, for example, Erving Goffman, *The Presentation of Self in Everyday Life* (Garden City, N.Y.: Doubleday, 1956).

5. Ibid.

6. Kenneth Burke, *A Grammar of Motives and a Rhetoric of Motives* (New York: Meridian Books, 1962), p. 565.

tion to manage its impression. Not all the results of the use of rhetorics are intended; the consequence of the rhetorical "war on crime" in Detroit in the fall of 1969, to cite one example, was a continued advance in the city's downtown crime rate. Moreover, rhetoric can take on different meanings even within the organizational hierarchy. To patrolmen, the term "professionalism" means control over hours and salary and protection from arbitrary punishment from "upstairs"; to the chief and the higher administrators, it relates to the public-administration notions of efficiency, technological expertise, and standards of excellence in recruitment and training.

Tactics are the means by which a strategy is implemented. If the strategy is to mount a war on crime, then one tactic might be to flood the downtown area with scooter-mounted patrolmen. Tactics, in other words, are the ways in which one group of people deals with others in face-to-face encounters. How does the policeman handle a family quarrel in which the wife has the butcher knife and the husband already knows how sharp it is? Strategies pertain to general forms of action or rhetoric while tactics refer to the specific action or the specific words used to best meet a specific, problematic situation.[7] The tactic of flattery may be far more effective—and safer—in wresting the butcher knife than a leap over the kitchen table.

All occupations possess strategies and tactics, by means of which they attempt to control their most significant audiences. However, our analysis must do more than describe the existence of such means of creating impressions. So far as the police are concerned, impression management, or the construction of appearances, cannot substitute for significant control of crime. To maintain the dramaturgic metaphor, we suggest that there are significant flaws and contradictions in the performance of the police that cast a serious doubt on the credibility of their occupational mandate.

The mandate of the police is fraught with difficulties, many of them, we shall argue, self-created. They have defined their task in such a way that they cannot, because of the nature of American social organization, hope to honor it to the satisfaction of the public. We will argue that the appearances that the police create—that they control crime and that they attain a high level of efficiency—are transparent on close examination, that they may, in fact, be created as a sop to satisfy the public's impossible expectations for police performance. By utilizing the rhetoric of crime control, the police claim the responsibility for the social processes that beget the illegal acts. They cannot control these social processes that are embedded in

7. D. W. Ball makes this distinction between rhetoric and what he terms "situated vocabularies" in "The Problematics of Respectability" in *Deviance and Respectability*, ed. Jack D. Douglas (New York: Basic Books, 1970).

American values, norms, and cultural traditions. Creating the appearance of controlling them is only a temporizing policy; it is not the basis for a sound, honorable mandate.

The police mandate and the problems it creates in American society are our central concern. We will rely on the concepts of actor, organization, and audience, of mandate, and of strategy and appearances. We will show that the police mandate, as presently defined, is full of contradictions. We will further demonstrate that the strategies and tactics of the American police are failing in a serious way to meet the need of controlling crime.

The Occupational Culture of the Police

Before beginning an analysis of the police mandate, a brief comment is necessary about the occupational culture of our law enforcers. The American police act in accord with their assumptions about the nature of social life, and their most important assumptions originate with their need to maintain control over both their mandate and their self-esteem. The policeman's self is an amalgam of evaluations made by the many audiences before whom he, as social actor, must perform: his peers, his family, his immediate superiors and the higher administrators, his friends on and off duty. His most meaningful standards of performance are the ideals of his *occupational culture*. The policeman judges himself against the ideal policeman as described in police occupational lore and imagery. What a "good policeman" does is an omnipresent standard. The occupational culture, however, contains more than the definition of a good policeman. It contains the typical values, norms, attitudes, and material paraphernalia of an occupational group.

An occupational culture also prompts the *assumptions* about everyday life that become the basis for organizational strategies and tactics. Recent studies of the occupational culture of the police allow the formulation of the following postulates or assumptions, all of which are the basis for police strategies to be discussed later:

1. People cannot be trusted; they are dangerous.
2. Experience is better than abstract rules.
3. You must make people respect you.
4. Everyone hates a cop.
5. The legal system is untrustworthy; policemen make the best decisions about guilt or innocence.
6. People who are not controlled will break laws.
7. Policemen must appear respectable and be efficient.
8. Policemen can most accurately identify crime and criminals.

9. The major jobs of the policeman are to prevent crime and to enforce the laws.

10. Stronger punishment will deter criminals from repeating their errors.[8]

Some qualifications about these postulates are in order. They apply primarily to the American noncollege-educated patrolman. They are less applicable to administrators of urban police departments and to members of minority groups within these departments. Nor do they apply accurately to nonurban, state, and federal policemen.

We shall now describe the paradoxes of the police mandate, the strategies of the police in dealing with their troubles, and some of the findings and recommendations of the President's crime commission as they bear on the current attempt by the police to make a running adjustment to their problems.

II. THE "IMPOSSIBLE" MANDATE

The police in modern society are in agreement with their audiences—which include their professional interpreters, the American family, criminals, and politicians—in at least one respect: they have an "impossible" task. Certainly, all professionals have impossible tasks insofar as they try to surmount the problems of collective life that resist easy solutions. The most "successful" occupations, however, have managed to construct a mandate in terms of their own vision of the world. The policeman's mandate, on the other hand, is defined largely by his public—not, at least at the formal level, in his own terms.

Several rather serious consequences result from the public's image of the police. The public is aware of the dramatic nature of a small portion of police work, but it ascribes the element of excitement to all police activities. To much of the public, the police are seen as

8. These postulates have been drawn from the work of Michael Banton, *The Policeman in the Community* (New York: Basic Books, 1965); the articles in *The Police: Six Sociological Essays,* ed. David Bordua (New York: John Wiley & Sons, 1967), esp. those by Albert J. Reiss and David Bordua, and John H. McNamara; Arthur Niederhoffer, *Behind the Shield* (Garden City, N.Y.: Doubleday, 1967); Jerome Skolnick, *Justice Without Trial* (New York: John Wiley & Sons, 1966); and William A. Westley, "Violence and the Police," *American Journal of Sociology* 59 (July 1953), pp. 34–41; idem, "Secre-cy and the Police," *Social Forces* 34 (March 1956), pp. 254–257; idem, "The Police: Law, Custom and Morality," in *The Study of Society,* ed. Peter I. Rose (New York: Random House, 1967). See also James Q. Wilson, *Varieties of Police Behavior: The Management of Law and Order in Eight Communities* (Cambridge: Harvard University Press, 1968); idem, "The Police and Their Problems: A Theory," *Public Policy* 12 (1963), pp. 189–216; idem, "Generational and Ethnic Differences Among Police Officers," *American Journal of Sociology* 69 (March 1964), pp. 522–528.

alertly ready to respond to citizen demands, as crime-fighters, as an efficient, bureaucratic, highly organized force that keeps society from falling into chaos. The policeman himself considers the essence of his role to be the dangerous and heroic enterprise of crook-catching and the watchful prevention of crimes.[9] The system of positive and negative sanctions from the public and within the department encourages this heroic conception. The public wants crime prevented and controlled; that is, it wants criminals caught. Headlines herald the accomplishments of G-Men and F.B.I. agents who often do catch dangerous men, and the reputation of these federal authorities not infrequently rubs off on local policemen who are much less adept at catching criminals.

In an effort to gain the public's confidence in their ability, and to insure thereby the solidity of their mandate, the police have encouraged the public to continue thinking of them and their work in idealized terms, terms, that is, which grossly exaggerate the actual work done by police. They do engage in chases, in gunfights, in careful sleuthing. But these are rare events. Most police work resembles any other kind of work: it is boring, tiresome, sometimes dirty, sometimes technically demanding, but it is rarely dangerous. Yet the occasional chase, the occasional shoot-out, the occasional triumph of some extraordinary detective work have been seized upon by the police and played up to the public. The public's response has been to demand even more dramatic crook-catching and crime prevention, and this demand for arrests has been converted into an index for measuring how well the police accomplish their mandate. The public's definitions have been converted by the police organization into distorted criteria for promotion, success, and security. Most police departments promote men from patrol to detective work, a generally more desirable duty, for "good pinches"—arrests that are most likely to result in convictions.[10] The protection of the public welfare, however, including personal and property safety, the prevention of crime, and the preservation of individual civil rights, is hardly achieved by a high pinch rate. On the contrary, it might well be argued that protection of the public welfare could best be indexed by a low arrest

9. Although the imagery of the police and their own self-definition coincide on the dangers of being a policeman, at least one study has found that many other occupations are more dangerous. Policemen kill six times as many people as policemen are killed in the line of duty. In 1955, Robin found that the rate of police fatalities on duty, including accidents, was 33 per 100,000, less than the rate for mining (94), agriculture (55), construction (76), and transportation (44). Between 1950 and 1960, an average of 240 persons were killed each year by policemen—approximately six times the number of policemen killed by criminals. Gerald D. Robin, "Justifiable Homicide by Police Officers," *Journal of Criminal Law, Criminology and Police Science* 54 (1963), pp. 225–231.

10. Niederhoffer, *Behind the Shield*, p. 221.

rate. Because their mandate automatically entails mutually contradictory ends—protecting both public order and individual rights—the police resort to managing their public image and the indexes of their accomplishment. And the ways in which the police manage their appearance are consistent with the assumptions of their occupational culture, with the public's view of the police as a social-control agency, and with the ambiguous nature of our criminal law.

The Problematic Nature of Law and Order

The criminal law is one among many instrumentalities of social control. It is an explicit set of rules created by political authority; it contains provisions for punishment by officials designated with the responsibility to interpret and enforce the rules which should be uniformly applied to all persons within a politically defined territory.[11] This section discusses the relationships between the laws and the mores of a society, the effect of the growth of civilized society on law enforcement, and the problematic nature of crime in an advanced society. The differential nature of enforcement will be considered as an aspect of peace-keeping, and will lead to the discussion of the police in the larger political system.

A society's laws, it is often said, reflect its customs; it can also be said that the growth of the criminal law is proportionate to the decline in the consistency and binding nature of these mores. In simpler societies, where the codes and rules of behavior were well known and homogeneous, sanctions were enforced with much greater uniformity and predictability. Social control was isomorphic with one's obligations to family, clan, and age group, and the political system of the tribe. In a modern, differentiated society, a minimal number of values and norms are shared. And because the fundamental, taken-for-granted consensus on what is proper and respectable has been blurred or shattered, or, indeed, never existed, criminal law becomes a basis of social control. As Quinney writes, "Where correct conduct cannot be agreed upon, the criminal law serves to control the behavior of all persons within a political jurisdiction." [12]

Social control through the criminal law predominates in a society only when other means of control have failed. When it does predominate, it no longer reflects the mores of the society. It more accurately reflects the interests of shifting power groups within the society.

11. See Richard Quinney, "Is Criminal Behavior Deviant Behavior?" *British Journal of Criminology* 5 (April 1965), p. 133. The following two pages draw heavily from Quinney. See also R. C. Fuller, "Morals and the Criminal Law," *Journal of Criminal Law, Criminology and Police Science* 32 (March-April 1942), pp. 624–630.

12. Quinney, "Criminal Behavior," p. 133.

As a result, the police, as the designated enforcers of a system of criminal laws, are undercut by circumstances that accentuate the growing differences between the moral order and the legal order.

One of these complicating circumstances is simply the matter of social changes, which further stretch the bond between the moral and the legal. The law frequently lags behind the changes in what society deems acceptable and unacceptable practice. At other times, it induces changes, such as those pertaining to civil rights, thereby anticipating acceptable practice. The definition of crime, then, is a product of the relationship between social structure and the law. Crime, to put it another way, is not a homogeneous entity.

The perspective of the patrolman as he goes about his daily rounds is a legalistic one. The law and the administrative actions of his department provide him with a frame of reference for exercising the mandate of the police. The citizen, on the other hand, does not live his life in accordance with a legalistic framework; he defines his acts in accordance with a moral or ethical code provided him by his family, his religion, his social class. For the most part, he sees law enforcement as an intervention in his private affairs.

No matter what the basis for actions of private citizens may be, however, the patrolman's job is one of practical decision-making within a legalistic pattern. His decisions are expected to include an understanding of the law as a system of formal rules, the enforcement practices emphasized by his department, and a knowledge of the specific facts of an allegedly illegal situation. The law includes little formal recognition of the variation in the private arrangement of lives. Even so, the policeman is expected to take these into account also. No policeman can ever be provided with a handbook that could tell him, at a moment's notice, just what standards to apply in enforcing the law and in maintaining order. Wilson summarizes the difficulty inherent in law enforcement as follows:

> Most criminal laws define *acts* (murder, rape, speeding, possessing narcotics), which are held to be illegal; people may disagree as to whether the act should be illegal, as they do with respect to narcotics, for example, but there is little disagreement as to what the behavior in question consists of. Laws regarding disorderly conduct and the like assert, usually by implication, that there is a condition ("public order") that can be diminished by various actions. The difficulty, of course, is that public order is nowhere defined and can never be defined unambiguously because what constitutes order is a matter of opinion and convention, not a state of nature. (An unmurdered person, an unraped woman, and an unpossessed narcotic can be defined so as to be

recognizable to any reasonable person.) An additional difficulty, a corollary of the first, is the impossibility of specifying, except in the extreme case, what degree of disorder is
intolerable and who is to be held culpable for that degree.
A suburban street is quiet and pleasant; a big city street is
noisy and (to some) offensive; what degree of noise and offense, and produced by whom, constitutes "disorderly
conduct"?[13]

The complexity of law enforcement stems from both the problem
of police "discretion" and the inherent tensions between the maintenance of order and individual rights. The law contains rules on how
to maintain order; it contains substantive definitions of crime, penalties for violations, and the conditions under which the commission of
a crime is said to have been intended.[14] Further, the law contains
procedures for the administration of justice and for the protection of
the individual. The complexities of law enforcement notwithstanding, however, the modern policeman is frequently faced with the instant problem of defining an action as either legal or illegal, of deciding, in other words, whether to intervene and, if so, what tactic to
use. He moves in a dense web of social action and social meanings,
burdened by a problematic, complex array of ever-changing laws.
Sometimes the policeman must quickly decide very abstract matters.
Though a practitioner of the legal arts, his tools at hand are largely
obscure, ill-developed, and crude. With little formal training, the
rookie must learn his role by absorbing the theories, traditions, and
personal whims of experienced patrolmen.

Police Work as Peace-Keeping [15]
The thesis of two recent major works on the police, Wilson's *The
Varieties of Police Behavior* and Skolnick's *Justice Without Trial*,
can be paraphrased as follows: the policeman must exercise discretion in matters involving life and death, honor and dishonor, and he
must do so in an environment that he perceives as threatening, dangerous, hostile, and volatile. He sees his efficiency constrained by
the law and by the police organization. Yet, he must effectively

13. Wilson, *Varieties of Police Behavior*, pp. 21–22.

14. Skolnick, *Justice Without Trial*,
pp. 7–8, 9.

15. This perspective on police work is
emphasized by Wilson, *Varieties of
Police Behavior;* Banton, *The Policeman in the Community;* and Skolnick, *Justice Without Trial.* In addition, see the more legalistically oriented work of Wayne R. LaFave, *Arrest,* ed. F. J. Remington (Boston:
Little, Brown, 1965); Joseph Goldstein, "Police Discretion Not to Invoke the Legal Process: Low-Visibili-
ty Decisions in the Administration of
Justice," *Yale Law Journal* 69 (1960),
pp. 543–594; and Herman Goldstein,
"Police Discretion: The Ideal Versus
the Real," *Public Administration Review* 23 (September 1963), pp. 140–
148.

manage "disorder" in a variety of unspecified ways, through methods usually learned and practiced on the job. As a result of these conditions, the policeman, in enforcing his conception of order, often violates the rights of citizens.

Many observers of police work regard the primary function of a policeman as that of a *peace-keeper,* not a *law enforcer.* According to this view, police spend most of their time attending to order-maintaining functions, such as finding lost children, substituting as ambulance drivers, or interceding in quarrels of one sort or another. To these observers, the police spend as little as 10 to 15 per cent of their time on law enforcement—responding to burglary calls or trying to find stolen cars. The large-scale riots and disorders of recent years accounted for few police man-hours. Wilson illustrates the peace-keeping (order maintenance) and law-enforcement distinction this way:

> The difference between order maintenance and law enforcement is not simply the difference between "little stuff" and "real crime" or between misdemeanors and felonies. The distinction is fundamental to the police role, for the two functions involve quite dissimilar police actions and judgments. Order maintenance arises out of a dispute among citizens who accuse each other of being at fault; law enforcement arises out of the victimization of an innocent party by a person whose guilt must be proved. Handling a disorderly situation requires the officer to make a judgment about what constitutes an appropriate standard of behavior; law enforcement requires him only to compare a person's behavior with a clear legal standard. Murder or theft is defined, unambiguously, by statutes; public peace is not. Order maintenance rarely leads to an arrest; law enforcement (if the suspect can be found) typically does. Citizens quarreling usually want the officer to "do something," but they rarely want him to make an arrest (after all, the disputants are usually known or related to each other). Furthermore, whatever law is broken in a quarrel is usually a misdemeanor, and in most states, an officer cannot make a misdemeanor arrest unless one party or the other will swear out a formal complaint (which is even rarer).[16]

The complexity of the law and the difficulty in obtaining a complainant combine to tend to make the policeman underenforce the law—to overlook, ignore, dismiss, or otherwise erase the existence of many enforceable breaches of the law.

16. James Q. Wilson, "What Makes a Better Policeman?" *Atlantic* 223 (March 1969), p. 131.

Some researchers and legalists have begun to piece together a pattern of the conditions under which policemen have a tendency not to enforce the law. From a study of police in three Midwestern states, LaFave has concluded that two considerations characterize a decision not to arrest. The first is that the crime is unlikely to reach public attention—for example, that it is of a private nature or of low visibility—and the second is that underenforcement is unlikely to be detected or challenged.[17] Generally, the conditions under which policemen are less likely to enforce the law are those in which they perceive little public consensus on the law, or in which the law is ambiguous. LaFave found that policemen are not apt to enforce rigorously laws that are viewed by the public as dated, or that are used on the rare occasions when the public order is being threatened.

There is a certain Benthamic calculus involved in all arrests, a calculus that is based on pragmatic considerations such as those enumerated by LaFave. Sex, age, class, and race might also enter into the calculus of whether the law should be enforced. In a case study of the policeman assigned to skid row, Bittner illustrates the great degree of discretion exercised by the policeman. Yet the law, often reified by the policeman, is rarely a clear guide to action—despite the number of routine actions that might be termed "typical situations that policemen perceive as *demand conditions* for action without arrest."[18]

In the exercise of discretion, in the decision to enforce the law or to underenforce, the protection of individual rights is often at stake. But individual rights are frequently in opposition to the preservation of order, as a totalitarian state exemplifies in the extreme. The police try to manage these two contradictory demands by emphasizing their peace-keeping functions. This emphasis succeeds only when a consensus exists on the nature of the order (peace) to be preserved. The greater the difference in viewpoint between the police and the public on the degree and kind of order to be preserved, the greater will be antagonism between the two; the inevitable result of this hostility will be "law breaking."

The resolution of the contradictions and complexities inherent in the police mandate, including the problems of police discretion, of individual rights, of law enforcement and peace-keeping, is not helped, however, by the involvement of police in politics. Politics only further complicates the police mandate. The law itself is a political phenomenon, and at the practical level of enforcing it, the local political system is yet another source of confusion.

17. LaFave, *Arrest.*

18. Egon Bittner, "The Police on Skid-Row: A Study of Peace-Keep-   ing," *American Sociological Review* 32 (October 1967), pp. 699–715.

The Police in the Political System

In theory, the American police are apolitical. Their own political values and political aims are supposed to be secondary to the institutional objective of law enforcement. In practice, however, police organizations function in a political context; they operate in a public political arena and their mandate is defined politically. They may develop strategies to create and maintain the appearance of being apolitical in order to protect their organizational autonomy, but they are nonetheless a component of American political machinery. There are three reasons why the police are inextricably involved in the political system, the first and most obvious being that the vast majority of the police in this nation are locally controlled.

> [Among the 40,000 law-enforcement agencies in the United States], there are only 50 . . . on the federal level . . . 200 on the state level. The remaining 39,750 agencies are dispersed throughout the many counties, cities, towns, and villages that form our local governments. . . . Only 3,050 agencies are located in counties and 3,700 in cities. The great majority of the police forces—33,000—are distributed throughout boroughs, towns, and villages.[19]

In 1966 there were 420,000 full- and part-time law-enforcement officers and civilians employed by police agencies in the United States. Most of them—371,000—were full-time employees; about 11 per cent—46,000—were civilians. Of the full-timers, 23,000 served at the federal level of government, 40,000 at the state level, and the remaining 308,000, or 83 per cent of the total, were divided between county and local political jurisdictions. Of the 308,000, somewhat more than 197,000 were employees of counties, cities under 250,000, townships, boroughs, and villages; the balance of 110,500 served in the 55 American cities with populations of more than 250,000. The number of police personnel in any one type of political division varied widely, of course. For example, on the county level of government, the roster of the 3,050 sheriff's offices in the United States ranged from a one-man force in Putnam County, Georgia, to a 5,515-man force in Los Angeles County.

What all these figures indicate is the massive dispersal of police authority—and political authority—throughout the nation. What these figures also indicate is the existence of overlapping laws governing law enforcement. Further, they show that the responsibility for maintaining public order in America is decentralized, and that

19. President's Commission, *Task Force Report: The Police*, pp. 7, 8–9.

law-enforcement officers are largely under the immediate control of local political authorities.

The second reason why the police are an integral part of the political system is this: law is a political entity, and the administration of criminal law unavoidably encompasses political values and political ends. The police are directly related to a political system that develops and defines the law, itself a product of interpretations of what is right and proper from the perspective of different politically powerful segments within the community.

The third reason why the police are tied to the political system emanates from the second: the police must administer the law. Many factors pattern this enforcement, but they all reflect the political organization of society. The distribution of power and authority, for example, rather than the striving for justice, or equal treatment under the law, can have a direct bearing on enforcement.

Because law enforcement is for the most part locally controlled, sensitivity to local political trends remains an important element in police practice. Since the police are legally prohibited from being publicly political, they often appeal to different community groups, and participate sub rosa in others, in order to influence the determination of public policy. Community policy, whether made by the town council or the mayor or the city manager, affects pay scales, operating budgets, personnel, administrative decisions, and, to some extent, organizational structure. The police administrator must, therefore, be responsive to these controls, and he must deal with them in an understanding way. He must be sensitive to the demands of the local politicians—even while maintaining the loyalty of the lower ranks through a defense of their interests.

There are several direct effects of the political nature of the police mandate. One is that many policemen become alienated; they lose interest in their role as enforcers and in the law as a believable criterion. The pressures of politics also erode loyalty to the police organization and not infrequently lead to collusion with criminals and organized crime.

The policeman's exposure to danger, his social background, low pay, low morale, his vulnerability in a repressive bureaucracy all conspire to make him susceptible to the lures of the underhanded and the appeals of the political. Studies summarized by Skolnick [20] reveal a political profile of the policeman as a conservative, perhaps reactionary, person of lower-class or lower-middle-class origin, often a supporter of radical right causes, often prejudiced and repressive, often

20. Jerome Skolnick, ed., *The Politics of Protest* (New York: Simon & Schuster, 1969), pp. 252–253.

extremely ambivalent about the rights of others. The postulates or assumptions of the police culture, the suspiciousness, fear, low self-esteem, and distrust of others are almost diametrically opposed to the usual conception of the desirable democratic man.

Thus, the enforcement of some laws is personally distasteful. Civil-rights legislation, for example, can be anathema. Or truculence can be the reaction to an order relaxing controls in ghettos during the summer months. It is the ambivalence of policemen toward certain laws and toward certain local policies that fragments loyalty within a department and causes alienation.

There is another consequence of the political nature of the police mandate: the police are tempted. They are tempted not to enforce the law by organized crime, by the operators of illegal businesses such as prostitution, and by fine "law-abiding," illegally parked citizens. All too frequently, the police submit to temptations, becoming in the process exemplars of the corruption typical of modern society, where the demand for "criminal services" goes on at the station house.[21]

Police and politics within the community are tightly interlocked. The sensitivity of the police to their political audiences, their operation within the political system of criminal justice, and their own personal political attitudes undermine their efforts to fulfill their contradictory mandate and to appear politically neutral.

The Efficient, Symptom-Oriented Organization

The Wickersham report, the Hoover administration's report on crime and law enforcement in the United States, was published in 1931. This precursor of the Johnson administration's *The Challenge of Crime in a Free Society* became a rallying point for advocates of police reform. One of its central themes was the lack of "professionalism" among the police of the time—their lack of special training, their corruption, their brutality, and their use of illegal procedures in law enforcement. And one of its results was that the police, partly in order to demonstrate their concern with scientific data gathering on crime and partly to indicate their capacity to "control" crime itself, began to stress crime statistics as a major component of professional police work.

Crime statistics, therefore—and let this point be emphasized—became a police construction. The actual amount of crime committed in a society is unknown—and probably unknowable, given the private

21. There are several popular treatments of police corruption, none of them very good. Ralph L. Smith, *The Tarnished Badge* (New York: Thomas Y. Crowell, 1965); Ed Cray, *The Big Blue Line* (New York: Coward-McCann, 1967).

nature of most crime. The *crime rate*, consequently, is simply a construction of police activities. That is, the crime rate pertains only to
"crimes known to the police," crimes that have been reported to or
observed by the police and for which adequate grounds exist for assuming that a violation of the law has, in fact, taken place. (The
difference between the *actual* and *known crimes* is often called the
"dark figure of crime.") Of course, the construction of a crime rate
placed the police in a logically weak position in which they still find
themselves. If the crime rate is rising, they argue that more police
support is needed to fight the war against crime; if the crime rate is
stable or declining, they argue that they have successfully combated
the crime menace—a heads-I-win-tails-you-lose proposition.

In spite of their inability to control the commission of illegal acts
(roughly, the actual rate), since they do not know about all crime, the
police have claimed responsibility for crime control, using the crime
rate as an index of their success. This use of the crime rate to measure success is somewhat analogous to their use of a patrolman's arrest rate as an indication of his personal success in law enforcement.
Questions about the actual amount of crime and the degree of control
exercised are thus bypassed in favor of an index that offers great potential for organizational or bureaucratic control. Instead of grap-
pling with the difficult issue of defining the ends of police work and
an operational means for accomplishing them, the police have opted
for "efficient" law-enforcement defined in terms of fluctuations of
the crime rate. They have transformed concern with undefined ends
into concern with available means. Their inability to cope with the
causes of crime—which might offer them a basis for defining their
ends—shifts their "organizational focus" into symptomatic concerns,
that is, into a preoccupation with the rate of crime, not its reasons.

This preoccupation with the symptoms of a problem rather than
with the problem itself is typical of all bureaucracies. For one characteristic of a bureaucracy is goal-displacement. Bureaucratic organizations tend to lose track of their goals and engage in ritual behavior, substituting means for ends. As a whole, bureaucracies become
so engrossed in pursuing, defending, reacting to, and, even, in creating immediate problems that their objective is forgotten. This tendency to displace goals is accelerated by the one value dear to all bureaucracies—efficiency. Efficiency is the be-all and end-all of bureaucratic organizations. Thus, they can expend great effort without
any genuine accomplishment.

The police are burdened with the "efficiency problem." They
claim to be an efficient bureaucratic organization, but they are unable to define for themselves and others precisely what it is they are
being efficient about. In this respect, they do not differ from other
paper-shuffling organizations. The police's problem is that the na-

ture of their work is uncertain and negatively defined. It is uncertain in the absence of a consensus not only between the police and the public but also among themselves as to what the goals of a police department should be. It is defined in the negative because the organization punishes its members—patrolmen—for violating departmental procedures but offers no specifications on what they should do or how they should do it.

What do the police do about the problematic nature of law, about the problems arising from their involvement with politics, about their preoccupation with the symptoms of crime rather than the causes? Do they selectively adopt some strategies at the expense of others? Do they vacillate? Are the roles of the organization's members blurred? Before answering these questions, let us examine how the police, through various strategies, manage their appearance before the public. The questions will then be easier to answer.

III. MAJOR STRATEGIES OF THE POLICE

The responsibilities of the police lead them to pursue contradictory and unattainable ends. They share with all organizations and occupations, however, the ability to avoid solving their problems. Instead, they concentrate on managing them through strategies. Rather than resolving their dilemmas, the police have manipulated them with a professional eye on just how well the public accepts their dexterity. Thus, law enforcement becomes a self-justifying system. It becomes more responsive to its own needs, goals, and procedures than to serving society. In this section, we will show the ways in which the police have followed the course of most other bureaucratic institutions in society, responding to their problems by merely giving the appearance of facing them while simultaneously promoting the trained incapacity to do otherwise.

The two primary aims of most bureaucracies, the police included, are the maintenance of their organizational autonomy and the security of their members. To accomplish these aims, they adopt a pattern of institutional action that can best be described as "professionalism." This word, with its many connotations and definitions, cloaks all the many kinds of actions carried out by the police.

The guise of professionalism embodied in a bureaucratic organization is the most important strategy employed by the police to defend their mandate and thereby to build self-esteem, organizational autonomy, and occupational solidarity or cohesiveness. The professionalization drives of the police are no more suspect than the campaigns of other striving, upwardly mobile occupational groups. However, since the police have a monopoly on legal violence, since they are the active enforcers of the public will, serving theoretically in the best interests of the public, the consequences of their yearnings for prestige and power are imbued with far greater social ramifications than the relatively harmless attempts of florists, funeral directors, and accountants to attain public stature.   Disinterested law enforcement through bureaucratic means is an essential in our society and in any democracy, and the American police are certainly closer to attaining this ideal than they were in 1931 at the time of the Wickersham report.   Professionalism qua professionalism is unquestionably desirable in the police.   But if in striving for the heights of prestige they fail to serve the altruistic values of professionalism, if their professionalism means that a faulty portrait of the social reality of crime is being painted, if their professionalism conceals more than it reveals about the true nature of their operations, then a close analysis of police professionalism is in order.

Police professionalism cannot be easily separated in practice from the bureaucratic ideal epitomized in modern police practice. The bureaucratic ideal is established as a means of obtaining a commitment from personnel to organizational and occupational norms. This bureaucratic commitment is designed to supersede commitments to competing norms, such as obligations to friends or kin or members of the same racial or ethnic group.   Unlike medicine and law, professions that developed outside the context of bureaucracies, policing has always been carried out, if done on a full-time basis, as a bureaucratic function.

Modern police bureaucracy and modern police professionalism are highly articulated, although they contain some inherent stresses that are not our present concern.   The strategies employed by the police to manage their public appearance develop from their adaptation of the bureaucratic ideal.   These strategies incorporate the utilization of *technology* and *official statistics* in law enforcement, of *styles of patrol* that attempt to accommodate the community's desire for public order with the police department's preoccupation with bureaucratic procedures, of *secrecy* as a means of controlling the public's response to their operations, of *collaboration* with criminal elements to foster the appearance of a smoothly run, law-abiding community, and of a *symbiotic relationship* with the criminal justice system that minimizes public knowledge of the flaws within this largely privately operated system.

Professionalism

To say that a type of work can only be carried out by professionals is to make both it and them immediately acceptable.   The need of the police to proclaim themselves professionals arises out of their need to control both the public and their own organization.   Externally, professionalism functions to define the nature of the client, to maintain social distance with the clientele, and to define the purposes, the conventions, and the motivations of the practitioners; internally, it functions to unify the diverse interests and elements that exist within any occupational or organizational group. This view sees professionalism as an ideology. Habenstein has described it as follows:

> Certain groups, claiming special functions, have been able to arrogate to themselves, or command increased power over, the conditions of members' livelihood. . . . "Profession" is, basically, an ideology, a set of rationalizations about the worth and necessity of certain areas of work, which, when internalized, gives the practitioners a moral justification for privilege, if not license. . . .[22]

Efforts toward the professionalization of any occupation are, above all, efforts to achieve power and authority. In police work, professionalization serves the self-esteem of all practitioners, from patrolman to commissioner, by gilding the entire enterprise with the symbols, prerequisites, tradition, power, and authority of the most respected occupations in American society.

The Bureaucratic Ideal

The organizational *ideal* of the "professional" police department is a rational, efficient, scientifically organized, technologically sophisticated bureaucracy. This is the way Niederhoffer depicts a modern police organization:

> Large urban police departments are bureaucracies. Members of the force sometimes lose their bearings in the labyrinth of hierarchy, specialization, competitive examinations, red tape, promotion based on seniority, impersonality, rationality, rules and regulations, channels of communication, and massive files.[23]

They are bureaucracies because the bureaucratic organization is perceived by the police as the best way to solve their problems. To them, a bureaucracy is the best device for managing appearances and the best method of working out a running adjustment to the pressing nature of their problems. And bureaucratic rhetoric, with its reverence for science and professionalism, is accurately assessed as the most powerful source of legitimation in American society. All modern bureaucratic organizations claim to be efficient and all strive in

22. Robert W. Habenstein, "Critique of 'Profession' as a Sociological Category," *Sociological Quarterly* 4 (November 1963), p. 297. This notion follows H. S. Becker's in "The Nature of a Profession," in *Yearbook of the Na-*
tional Society for the Study of Education (Chicago: National Society for the Study of Education, 1961).

23. Niederhoffer, *Behind the Shield*, p. 11.

varying degrees to become more efficient. Understandably, they inevitably fail because the organizational rules under which the bureaucrats work are never able to cover all contingencies.

Technology

One of the strategies employed by the police to appear professional and bureaucratically efficient is the use of technology. Again quoting from Niederhoffer:

> The modern police specialist requires a wide range of technical and scientific skills. Experts are needed to operate radar, photographic equipment, electronic listening devices, instruments for analysis of evidence, computers, complex office machines, radio, television, airplanes, and helicopters. The scientific devices used in detective investigations have created a corps of specialists, quasi-scientists, [and] technicians. . . .[24]

All these devices illustrate the technological strategy and are related to the police assumptions that if they have more information more quickly, more visibility, more policemen, more firepower, and better allocation of resources, all organized around technology, they will be able to efficiently prevent and deter crime. These assumptions are also manifested in the President's crime commission report. The police have brought a scientific perspective to crime prevention, elaborating on the means of obtaining more information more quickly, and on methods of more efficiently allocating men, material, and more potent weapons. Technology, of course, does not deal with the great difficulties in obtaining information.

Official Statistics

Another strategy used by police to convey the appearance of efficiency is their pursuit of "official statistics." Nothing sells easier than a statistic, no matter what it says, and the police use them not only for self-justification and organizational survival but for enhancement of community relations. All bureaucracies ply the official-statistics strategy, and insofar as the police are concerned, they "very often corrupt the statistics," as Jack Douglas has pointed out.[25]

The police construct and utilize official statistics, such as the clearance rate and the crime index, to manage the impression of efficiency. The clearance rate, so popular among professionalized police departments, is a measure of a patrolman's or a detective's efficiency.

24. Ibid., pp. 17–18.

25. Jack D. Douglas, "Deviance and Order in a Pluralistic Society," in *Theoretical Sociology: Perspectives and Development*, ed. Edward A. Tiryakian and John C. McKinney (New York: Appleton-Century-Crofts, 1970).

Offenses categorized as "solved" become part of the clearance rate. The police ignore all unreported crimes and all crimes without victims where no complainant is required; these crimes, therefore, are never "cleared"—they never become part of the clearance rate. As for the index of crime being an index of efficiency, no mandatory, centralized crime-reporting system exists, although many police departments have adopted and report on the basis of the F.B.I. index of crimes: murder, aggravated assault, rape, burglary, robbery, larceny over $50, and auto theft. Needless to say, the more the police enforce the laws, the higher the crime rate. Because there has been very little in the way of standard reporting and investigation practices, the police have been able to control the crime rate to a large degree by controlling aspects of enforcement.

The use of technology and official statistics as strategies, in the context of professionalism, is related to patrol strategies adapted by departments in their efforts to resolve the "problematic nature of the law." Styles of patrol, or modes of law enforcement by patrolmen, characterize departments as a whole. They represent a means of integrating community norms and expectations with the legal and procedural rules of the community and the police department.

Styles of Patrol

Patrol strategies, to the police at least, are an aspect of bureaucratic efficiency. They are closely related to the differential enforcement of the law. Enforcement must be differential because if it were not, "we would all," in Dodson's often quoted remark, "be in jail before the end of the first day. The laws which are selected for enforcement are those which the power structure of the community wants enforced." [26]

The tasks absorbed by the police have burgeoned in recent years —along with the demands for their services. The police have tried to answer these demands of their environment by three distinct types of patrol—what Wilson describes as the *watchman, legalistic,* and *service* styles.[27] The watchman style is the classic mode of policing urban areas and is still used in some degree in most cities. It is a style of patrol that emphasizes maintenance of public order rather than enforcement of the law. The policeman is instructed to be sensitive to the interests of groups within his beat and to overlook many of the minor offenses connected with juvenile infractions, traffic violations, vice, and gambling. A legalistic style, on the other hand, rests heavily upon enforcement of the law to control the routine situations encountered by the patrolman. The police using this style of patrol are

---

26. Daniel Dodson, as quoted in Niederhoffer, *Behind the Shield,* p. 12.

27. Wilson, *Varieties of Police Behavior,* pp. 140–141.

instructed to act as if a single level of order was desirable in all settings and for all groups, and to enforce the law to that end. The service style, Wilson's third type of patrol, is "market-oriented," that is, it is designed to meet the fairly well-articulated demand of "homogeneous middle-class communities." The police respond to and take seriously all calls for police action (unlike the watchman style which ignores certain kinds of demands for intervention), but (unlike the legalistic style which it more closely resembles) the police seldom use the law to control the situation. They prefer informal action to law enforcement.

The value of these varied styles to the police is the survival potential they provide. They allow the police administrator a certain leeway in trying to control his men in line with the demands of the most powerful interests in the community and to mitigate the strain between preserving individual liberty and protecting the collective social enterprise.

Secrecy and Public Complaints

No matter what the level of operation of a police force, it will generate citizen complaints. It will generate complaints because the role of the policeman is to restrain and control, not to advise and remedy. While advice and solutions are usually welcome, restraint is not. For a substantial proportion of the population, the policeman is an adversary; he issues summonses, makes arrests, conducts inquiries, searches homes and people, stops cars, testifies in court, and keeps a jail. For the police, threats from outside, such as citizens' complaints and political moves to control police policy, are efforts to destroy their organization. One strategy used by police to withstand these threats is to keep all information they obtain secret.

The shared secrets possessed by the police assist them in creating internal cohesion. Information is concealed for the additional reason that the police fear and dislike their clients—the various segments of the public. Westley, one of the first and most profound sociological analysts of the police culture, here describes the occupational perspective of the policeman and the centrality of secrecy:

> The policeman finds his most pressing problems in his relationships to the public. His is a service occupation but of an incongruous kind, since he must discipline those whom he serves. He is regarded as corrupt and inefficient by, and meets with hostility and criticism from, the public. He regards the public as his enemy, feels his occupation to be in conflict with the community, and regards himself to be a pariah. The experience and the feeling give rise to a collective emphasis on secrecy, an attempt to coerce respect from

the public, and a belief that almost any means are legitimate
in completing an important arrest. These are for the policeman basic occupational values. They arise from his experience, take precedence over his legal responsibilities, [and]
are central to an understanding of his conduct. . . .[28]

Most observers of the police have noted their penchant for secrecy as a strategy used for their own protection. Secrecy helps keep
the public at arm's length; further, it helps the police to maintain
their power. Indeed, its very existence suggests power. One aspect
of the strategy of secrecy is that it deliberately mystifies, and mysti-
fication has always been a means of sustaining respect and awe. As
a strategy, then, secrecy is one of the most effective sources of power
that the police have over their audiences.

One aspect of the secrecy strategy is that it constrains many citizens from making complaints about police misconduct. No adequate
records are kept on police malfeasance. While the misconduct of the
citizen—his law-breaking activities—are closely monitored and recorded, little attempt is made by most departments to maintain publicly available records of police wrongdoing. Certainly, few cities
have bureaus that make systematic examinations of police activities
for public assessment. Many efforts by citizens to set up public files
on police services or to create civilian review boards have failed. The
police have in every instance opposed moves to establish evaluational
mechanisms; they have continued to prefer losing most citizens' complaints in an endless tangle of red tape. The battle with crime thus
goes on largely unmonitored by the public at large.

Collaboration, The Strategy of Corruption

In dealing with the demands of certain segments of their criminal audience, some police departments find that the most expedient
policy is simply to acquiesce. This is a strategy adopted by corrupt
departments. It is a strategy that reduces the pressures of organized
crime against the department and that minimizes the chances of organized crime deliberately and publicly embarrassing the police in order to control police activities. As a strategy, it is the least common
used by police to manage their appearance of efficient crime-fighters.
What it amounts to is that the police collaborate with the criminal element by taking the line of least resistance: they enter into the vice,
gambling, and protection rackets themselves or in concert with organized crime. Because the police have resorted to secrecy and the frac-
tionalization of public demands, they have at times been free enough
from the constraints of justice to engage in full-scale lawlessness.

28. Westley, "Violence and the Police," p. 35.

This strategy, although relatively infrequent for entire departments, involves selective enforcement of the law together with the encouragement of a lack of consensus on enforcing certain laws, particularly those pertaining to gambling, prostitution, homosexuality, and abortion. Of course, an alliance with organized crime for the purpose of receiving payoffs is involved, too. Complicity with the criminal element is sometimes also necessary in order to obtain information that can be used against those who are not in league with the police and their allies. The corruption strategy is ultimately a self-defeating strategy, but to those in our police forces who are corrupt, this is a relatively unimportant matter.

Symbiosis and Justice

The relationship between the police and our system of criminal justice is symbiotic—each is dependent upon the other for support. One of the reasons why the professionalized police department is so concerned with its public image originates with its inability to control the conviction process. Because the courts control the process, the police are eager to make the "good pinch," the one that will result in a conviction. To the police, failure to obtain a conviction is a failure of their mandate.

The symbiotic relationship between law enforcement and our system of criminal justice is largely sustained through the abrogation of the right of due process. This is accomplished through the simple expedient of what has been termed "bargain justice." Under the bargain-justice system, accused persons are persuaded to plead guilty to a lesser offense than the one with which they are charged, thereby forgoing their right to a trial by jury. But the complicity of the police in this system allows them to maintain their rate of good pinches. At the same time, it permits the prosecutor's office to preserve its conviction rates and it allows the courts to meet production quotas.

The system works on the assumption that all accused persons are guilty and that almost all of them, whether they are or not, will plead guilty. As Skolnick and Blumberg have shown, the assumption of guilt is the oil that lubricates an otherwise outdated, overworked, inadequate system of justice.[29]

Complicity in bargain justice is one more strategy employed by our police departments in their efforts to manage a troublesome mandate. In the second part of this essay the major problems of the police were outlined under the general themes of the problematic nature of the law and law enforcement, the political context of police work, and the symptomatic quality of their occupational tasks. In the pre-

29. Skolnick, *Justice Without Trial*, and Abraham Blumberg, *Criminal*   *Justice* (Chicago: Quadrangle Press, 1967).

ceding section, we focused on the major strategies the police have used to manage their troublesome mandate. In the following section, we will assess the relative efficacy of police strategies in battling crime in American society.

IV. THE EFFECTIVENESS OF POLICE STRATEGIES

The police have developed and utilized the strategies outlined above for the purpose of creating, as we have said, the appearance of managing their troublesome mandate. To a large extent, they are facilitated in the use of these strategies, in being able to project a favorable impression, by a public that has always been apathetic about police activity. Moreover, what activity the public does observe is filtered through the media with its own special devices for creating a version of reality. The public's meaning of police action is rarely gathered from first-hand experience, but from the constructed imagery of the media—which, in turn, rely upon official police sources for their presentation of the news. The police for their part, understandably, manipulate public appearances as much as they possibly can in order to gain and maintain public support.

The specific strategies used by the police to create a publicly suitable image were described in Section III: the guise of professionalism; the implementation of the bureaucratic ideal of organization; the use of technology, official statistics, and various styles of patrol; secrecy; collaboration with corrupt elements; and the establishment of a symbiotic relationship with the courts. This section will present evidence by which to evaluate these strategies. The term "effectiveness" is used only in the context of how well these devices accomplish the ends which the public and the police themselves publicly espouse; the recommendations and evaluations of the President's crime commission will be central in making judgments of police effectiveness. This appraisal of how well the police manipulate their appearance will also be a guideline for evaluating the recommendations of the commission's task force report on the police.

Professionalism and the Bureaucratic Ideal

The assumptions of professionalism and of a bureaucratic organization include a devotion to rational principles and ends that may then be translated into specific work routines having predictable outcomes. The police are organized in a military command fashion, with rigid rules and a hierarchy governing operations. However, the patrolman, the lowest man in the hierarchy—and usually the least well-trained and educated—is in the key position of exercising the greatest amount of discretion on criminal or possibly criminal activities. Especially in his peace-keeping role and in dealing with minor infractions (misdemeanors), the patrolman has wide discretionary power concerning if, when, why, and how to intervene in private affairs.

Police work must both rely on discretion and control it. Excessive inattention and excessive attention to infractions of the law are equally damaging to a community. However, the complexity of the law, its dynamic and changing properties, the extensiveness of police department regulations, policies, and procedures, and the equivocal, relativistic nature of crime in regard to certain situations, settings, persons, and groups make it impossible to create a job description that would eliminate the almost boundless uncertainty in police patrol.

Neither professionals nor bureaucrats, however, have yet found an effective means of controlling discretion. If an organization cannot control those of its members with the greatest opportunity to exercise discretion, it flounders in its attempts to accomplish its stated purposes. Two general principles suggest why the police have not been able to control discretion. The first has to do with the general problem of control and the second with the specific nature of police work.

Men are unwilling to submit completely to the will of their organizational superiors. Men will always attempt to define and control their own work. Control means the right to set the pace, to define mistakes, to develop standards of "good" production and efficiency. But as surely as superiors seek to control the quality and the extent of work performed by their subordinates in a hierarchy, just as surely will they meet with attempts to reshape and subvert these controls.

In the specific instance of police bureaucracies, the patrolman conceives of himself as a man able to make on-the-spot decisions of guilt or innocence. He does not think of himself as a bureaucratic functionary nor as a professional. Further, since the police organization itself has become far more interested in efficiency than in purpose, since it is unable to specify its overall objectives, the patrolman finds it difficult, if not impossible, to demonstrate that necessary devotion to rational ends required of professionalism and bureaucratic organizations. Until police departments are able to control the amount and kind of discretion exercised by their members, and until the police are able, with the help of lawyers and other citizens, to develop positive means of motivation and reward in line with clear, overall policy directives, the failure of what we have called the professionalism-bureaucracy strategy is an absolute certainty.

Technology, Statistics, and the Crime Rate

This section will evaluate the strategy of technology in the control and prevention of crime, the use of statistics, and the significance of the so-called crime rate. Given the sociological nature of crime, let it be said immediately that present technology deals with unimportant crime and that the F.B.I. index of crimes, by which we base judgments of police effectiveness, is biased and an unrealistic reflection of the actual crime rate.

One of the striking aspects of the President's crime commission report is the thoroughly sociological nature of the document. The discussion of the causes of crime in the first two chapters points to the growth of urbanism, anonymity, the breakdown in social control, and the increasing numbers of frustrated and dissatisfied youth who have always constituted the majority of known lawbreakers. There are no labels such as "evil people," "emotionally disturbed," "mentally ill," or "criminally insane." The first set of recommendations under prevention in the summary pages of the report are "sociological": strengthen the family, improve slum schools, provide employment, reduce segregation, construct housing. All these matters are patently and by definition out of the control of the police.

There is every evidence that the police themselves subscribe to a thoroughly social, if not sociological, definition of the causes of crime —that is, that crime is the manifestation of long-established social patterns and structures which ensnare and implicate the police and the criminals as well as the general public. And they are doubtless correct.

Surveys done by the President's crime commission revealed that there are always contingencies in the information police receive about a crime even before they are able to investigate it. These contingencies involve such matters as the nature of the relationship between the victim and the offender and whether or not the victim believes the police are competent to investigate and solve the crime. Computer technology depends on informational "input." On that point, the police seem both unable to define what sort of information would be useful and unable to obtain, and probably never can obtain in a democratic society, information that would make them better able to enforce the law.

The facts in the problem of "crime prevention" overwhelmingly doom the present professionally based notion that the application of science and technology will begin to ease the distress the police feel as they face the escalating demands of their audiences. Also, it would be easier to assess the value of the technology strategy if we were able to define exactly to what end the technology would be applied and in what ways it could be expected to work.

Styles of Patrol

Police strategy is subject to many contingencies. It is a basic principle of public administration that policy made at the higher echelons of an organization will be effective only if each successively lower level of the organization complies with that policy and is capable of carrying it out. It is also a truism that participants at the lowest level in the hierarchy are the most "difficult" to mobilize and integrate into the organization. A style of patrol is basically the manner in which an administrative police policy is executed. The policy may prescribe that the patrolman overlook certain types of illegal acts; it may order that he minimally enforce particular laws or be sensitive to and strictly enforce others. If the administrative order setting a patrol style does not win the cooperation of the patrolman it is certain to fail. Thus, the success of any high-echelon policy that involves the performance of the patrolman is contingent upon his compliance with that policy. If the administrator's orders are not binding on the patrolman, no distinctive style of patrol will result; all that will be demonstrated will be the responses of the patrolman to other aspects of his social environment, especially, how his fellow patrolmen perform.

The success of this strategy is dependent upon the capacity of the administrator to create loyalty to his internal policies. With the rise of police unions, the discontent of the black patrolman, low pay, and relatively less security for the policeman, organizational control is a major problem in all the large police departments of the country —with Los Angeles possibly the single exception.

The effectiveness of the watchman, legalistic, and service styles of patrol will also depend on the degree of political consensus among the community groups patrolled, the clarity of the boundaries of community neighborhoods, competition between the police and self-help or vigilante groups, and the relative importance of nonoccupational norms in enforcement practices—that is, the importance of racial or ethnic similarities between the patrolman and the people in his neighborhood. If a clear social consensus on the meaning of the law and what is expected of the police can be established within a community, a well-directed policy of control over police patrol is the most logical and rational approach to police work. In some communities, largely suburban and middle-class, the police can carry out what their public demands and a degree of harmony exists. This consensus is absent in our inner cities.

Secrecy and Collaboration

The use of secrecy by the police is, as we have pointed out, a strategy employed not only to assist them in maintaining the appearance of political neutrality but to protect themselves against public complaints. Secrecy also helps to forestall public efforts to achieve better police service and to secure political accountability for police policy. Police collaboration with criminal elements—corruption, in other words—has much the same effect since it decreases the pressure to enforce "unenforceable" laws against certain segments of the police's clientele.

These two strategies were among the major concerns of the President's crime commission task force on police. The task force's report devoted major attention to the fact that political forces influence police actions and policies. The report affirmed the political nature of police work; what concerned the writers of the report was the nature and type of political influence on police actions. Their recommendations, furthermore, were based on their recognition of the fact that the police have been fairly successful in managing the appearance of being apolitical.

There are several reasons why the police strategies of secrecy and collaboration will continue in force: (1) as long as the client—the public—is seen as the enemy, the police will treasure their secrecy and use it to engineer public consent to their policies and practices; (2) as long as a new political consensus is not formed on the nature and type of police control necessary in society as a whole, the organized, self-serving survival aims of police organizations will emerge victorious. Any well-organized consensual, secretive organization can resist the efforts of an unorganized public, managed by rhetoric and appearances, to reform it; (3) as long as there remains a lack of consensus on the enforcement of many of our "moralistic" laws, police corruption and selective law enforcement will continue. Collaboration to reduce adversary relationships with the criminal segment of society will always be an effective strategy—providing a sudden upsurge in public morality doesn't temporarily subject the police to a full-scale "housecleaning." Replacements would, of course, be subject to the same pressures and would, in all likelihood, eventually take the same line of least resistance.

One solution to corruption is said to be better educated, more professional policemen. By recruiting better educated men, the more professionalized police departments also seek to diminish the expression of political attitudes on the job and the tendency of policemen to form political power groups based on their occupation. These are also assumptions made by the crime commission's task force on police. There is, however, no evidence that college-educated or better-paid policemen are "better policemen"; nor is there any evidence that "better men" alone will solve the essentially structural problems of the occupation.

We can tentatively conclude from this review that corruption will remain with us as long as laws remain which stipulate punishments for actions on which a low public consensus exists. It will remain when there is likely to be a low visibility of police performance, and it will remain while there is a high public demand for illegal services—gambling, prostitution, abortion—and the concomitant need of the police for information on these services from the practitioners themselves.

Symbiosis and Justice

Although the police have the principal discretion in the field with reference to the detection, surveillance, and appraisal of alleged offenders, the final disposition of a criminal case must be made in the courts. The police are thus dependent on the courts in a very special way for their successes. The ideal model of the criminal-justice system makes the police essentially the fact gatherers and apprehenders, while the courts are to be the decision-makers.

The police attempt to appear efficient has led them, as we have noted before, to seek the good pinch, the arrest that will stand up in court. With victimless crimes, such as those involving gambling or drugs or prostitution, the police control the situation since they alone decide whether an offense has been committed and whether they have a legal case against the offender. To control the success rate in these cases, the police create a gaggle of informants, many of whom are compelled to give the police evidence in order to stay free of a potential charge against themselves for a violation similar to the one they are providing information about. In the case of more serious crimes, the problems are more complex; in these cases the police must rely on other informants, and their discretion on arrests and charges are more often exercised by administrators and prosecuting attorneys.

In the prosecution stage, the bureaucratic demands of the court system are paramount. Abraham Blumberg describes these demands and the tension between efficiency and "due process":

> The dilemma is frequently resolved through bureaucratically ordained shortcuts, deviations and outright rule violations by the members of the courts, from judges to stenographers, in order to meet production norms. Because they fear criticism on ethical as well as legal grounds, all the significant participants in the court's social structure are bound into an organized system of complicity. Patterned, covert, informal breaches, and evasions of "due process" are accepted as routine—they are institutionalized—but are nevertheless denied to exist.[30]

The net effect of this strain within the court system is to produce a higher rate of convictions by means of encouraging a plea of guilty to a lesser charge. As far as the police are concerned, then, the strategy of symbiosis is sound.

There are several undesirable effects of this symbiosis. First, it encourages corruption by permitting the police to make decisions about the freedom of their informants; it gives them an illegal hold

---

30. Blumberg, *Criminal Justice*, p. 69.

and power over them, and thus it undercuts the rule of law. Second, many offenders with long criminal records are either granted their freedom as informants or allowed to plead guilty to lesser charges in return for the dismissal of a more serious charge. Skolnick calls this the "reversal of the hierarchy of penalties," because the more serious crimes of habitual criminals are prosecuted less zealously than the minor violations of first offenders. Third, it helps blur the distinction between the apprehension and prosecution aspects of our criminal-justice system.

V. CONCLUSIONS AND PROPOSED REFORMS

The allocation of rewards in a society represents both its division of labor and its configuration of problems. Ironically, the allocation of rewards is also the allocation of societal trouble. Societal trouble in a differentiated society is occupational trouble. The ebb and flow of rewards emanating from the division of labor becomes structured into persistent patterns that are sustained by continuous transactions among organizations and occupational groups. Occupational structures reflect societal structures, but they reflect them in ways that have been negotiated over time. The negotiation is based upon the universal human proclivity to differentiate roles, organizations, and occupations. The more dependent an organization is upon its environment for rewards, the more likely it is to rely on the management and presentation of strategies to establish the appearance of autonomy.

Organizations without a high degree of autonomy in the environments in which they operate are greatly constrained by the internal pressure of competing aims and roles of members. The agreement on problems, goals, values, and self-concepts that emerges from occupational socialization and functioning is a strong basis for influencing organizational direction. The occupational standards in this case subvert the rule of law as a system of norms outside the informal norms of the occupation. The policeman's view of his role and his occupational culture are very influential in determining the nature of policing. The basic source of police trouble is the inability of the police to define a mandate that will minimize the inconsistent nature of their self-expectations and the expectations of those they serve.

The problems derived from a contradictory mandate remain unaffected by the efforts of the institution to solve them; they do, however, take the shape into which they have been cast by institutional functionaries. Cooley long ago discussed the process of institutional ossification, the process by which institutions stray from serving the needs of their members and their publics, thereby losing the loyalty of those within and the support of those without. The consequences of institutional ossification as related to the police are twofold.

First, the police begin to search for a so-called higher order of legitimacy; they make appeals to morality, to patriotism, to "Americanism," and to "law and order" to shore up eroded institutional charters and to accelerate their attempts to control and manipulate their members and clients. Second, the police, as they develop a far greater potential for controlling those they serve through their presentational strategies, come to serve themselves better than ever before.

The problem of the police is, essentially, the problem of the democratic society, and until the central values and social structures of our society are modified (and I think we are seeing such a modification), there can be no real change in the operation of social control. The needed changes are, by and large, not those dealt with in the crime commission report. And this is telling. For an eminently sociological document, it did not focus on the heart of the problem: our anachronistic, moralistic laws, with which the police are burdened, and our dated political system, which is unable to bring political units into a state of civil accountability. The focus of the report and recommendations was predictably on symptoms of crime, not on causes of crime. The "managerial focus" of the report, or its public-administration bias, outlined needed reforms, but not ways in which to implement them, and the problem of efficiency was never really faced.

Not surprisingly for a political document having a variety of public functions, the report has little to say about the nature of the present criminal laws. It dwells, like the police themselves, on means, not ends. As Isidore Silver points out in a critique of the report, more than one-half the crimes committed do not harm anyone: more than one-third are for drunkenness, and a small but important portion are for other "crimes without victims." Most crimes are committed by juveniles who inexplicably "grow out" of their criminality. In 1965, 50 per cent of the known burglaries and larcenies were committed by youths under 18.[31] The report does note what was a central point of our discussion of the political nature of crime, that police corruption is, in almost every instance, a consequence of trying to enforce admittedly unenforceable laws. The demand for services provided by homosexuals, by gamblers, prostitutes, and abortionists is high, and the supply is legally made unavailable to anyone who wants to remain in the so-called "law-abiding" category. The laws, in effect, create the crime and the criminals.

Changes in laws to reduce their absolutistic element and to free people who deviate with little harm to others from the onus of cri-

31. Isidore Silver, "Introduction" to *The Challenge of Crime in a Free Society* (New York: Avon Books, 1968), p. 25. The President's Commission, *Task Force Report: The Courts*, discusses substantive criminal law, however, and does make some suggestions for legal change.

minalization cannot be accomplished without a parallel change in the nature of police accountability. As we have seen, the strategies of secrecy and rhetoric used by the police play on the fears of society and provide a basis for police control. The managerial reforms contained in the task force report—more public debate on and greater internal and external control over police actions—are needed. Even more urgently required are specific ways in which the cities can control the police and make them strictly accountable for their actions—methods, that is, which go a good deal further than merely disposing of the chief or convening a judicial review board. To give city governments this kind of control over the police, however, entails the reorganization of police departments themselves so that their goals are clear and defined and so that the occupational rewards within the police organization are aligned with public goals.

Three interrelated organizational changes must be made to insure that police attend to the job of maintaining public order. One is to reorganize police departments along functional lines aimed at peacekeeping rather than law enforcement; the second is to allocate rewards for keeping the peace rather than for enforcing the law; the third is to decentralize police functions to reflect community control without the diffusion of responsibility and accountability to a central headquarters.

Present police departments are organized in a military fashion; orders move down the line from the chief to departmental sections assigned law-enforcement functions. These sections usually include such divisions as traffic, patrol, records, detective, juvenile, intelligence, crime-lab, and communications. The principal basis for the assignment of functions, however, is law enforcement,[32] what is needed is a new set of organizational premises so that the basis for the assignment of functions is not law enforcement but the maintenance of order. As Wilson explains:

> If order were the central mission of the department, there might be a "family disturbance squad," a "drunk and derelict squad," a "riot control squad," and a "juvenile squad"; law enforcement matters would be left to a "felony squad." Instead, there is a detective division organized, in the larger departments, into units specializing in homicide, burglary, auto theft, narcotics, vice, robbery, and the like. The undifferentiated patrol division gets everything else. Only juveniles tend to be treated by specialized units under both schemes, partly because the law requires or encourages

32. President's   Commission,   *Task Force Report: The Police*, charts on pp. 46–47.

such specialization.   The law enforcement orientation of most departments means that new specialized units are created for every offense about which the public expresses concern or for which some special technology is required.[33]

What is called for, then, is a new organizational pattern that will provide a domestic unit (as is now being tried in New York City), a juvenile unit, and a drunk unit with a detoxification center, all with a peace-keeping orientation and peace-keeping functions.   Only a felony squad and perhaps a riot squad should be used to enforce the law.

One of the obvious ways in which to improve the morale of the patrolman is to let him do a greater amount of investigative work and to take on the responsibility for "solving" some of the crimes originating with his patrol.   Rewards could then be allocated in accord with the more limited ends of peace-keeping—for instance, in rewarding a patrolman for a decline in the number of drunks who reappear in court.   Since no comprehensive policy can be imagined to guide order maintenance, limited ends for various departments must be developed and subjected to public review.   The key is to allow the policeman to develop judgment about the motives and future intentions of people with whom he comes in contact, and to reward him for peace-keeping, not "good pinches" alone.

This reappraisal of the allocation of rewards means, of course, that there must be greater coordination of police and other agencies within the criminal-justice system in order to increase the benefits to the client (the offender or the criminal) and break down the isolation of the police.[34]   To allow the policeman to assume greater peace-keeping responsibilities would allow him to play a functional role parallel to that of the better general practitioner of medicine: the referral specialist, the coordinator of family health, the source of records and information, and the family friend and counselor.   Such an organizational change in the policeman's function would, naturally enough, make community control of the police a greater possibility.   It would begin to bridge the chasm between the police and many hostile segments within the public, a process that could be facilitated by the creation of a community-relations division within police departments.

The third needed modification of the present structure of police work is the development of decentralized operations.   One of the major social trends of the last ten years has been the increase in the lack of attachment people have for their major institutions.   Police today

33. Wilson, *Varieties of Police Behavior,* p. 69.

34. See John P. Clark, "The Isolation of the Police: A Comparison of the British and American Situations," in *Readings in Social Problems,* ed. John Scanzoni (Boston: Allyn and Bacon, 1967), pp. 384–410.   See also David Bordua, "Comments on Police-Community Relations," mimeographed (Urbana: University of Illinois, n. d.).

suffer from a crisis of legitimacy, and this crisis is heightened by their failure to promote a sense of commitment to their operations by the citizens they serve. One way in which to introduce commitment and a sense of control over the police by members of a community is to make the police more accessible. St. Louis, for example, has experimented with "storefront" police stations, staffed by a few men who are available as advisers, counselors, protectors, and friends of the people in the immediate neighborhood. If the police should begin to differentiate the role of the patrolman to include the functions of a peace-keeping community agent, the control of these agents should reside in the community. Thus, public participation in the decision-making processes of the police would begin at the precinct or neighborhood level; it would not be simply in the form of a punitive civilian review board or a token citizen board at headquarters.

We began with the notion of trouble, police trouble, the troublesome mandate of the policeman. There will be little succor for him as long as our social structure remains fraught with contradictory value premises, with fragmented political power and the consequent inadequate control of the police, with the transformation of public trusts into institutional rights. There will be little succor for him as long as our political agencies resist moving to de-moralize our criminal laws. As it is, we can expect that the management of crime through police strategies and appearances will continue to be a disruptive element in American society.

THE POLICE: IN SEARCH OF DIRECTION *

INTRODUCTION

One of the most critical issues facing the criminal justice system today is the definition of the police role in a modern and urban democratic society. Until that role is defined, both for the present and the future, we shall never effectively resolve the pressing problems with which the police are confronted.

The 1960's were years of great strife, fear, and discord. We are all haunted by the possibility that the violence we saw in the last decade might only be a prologue to the events that might occur in the present decade. The responsibility of preventing this from occurring has been placed on the police. In the 1960's the police were severely tried and found to be desperately wanting. The 1970's, although devoid from the violence such as was witnessed in the 1960's, has not kept the police free from criticism.

* Source: "The Police: In Search of Direction." An original article by Merlyn D. Moore of the Institute of Contemporary Corrections and the Behavioral Sciences, Sam Houston State University.

Louis Radelet, Professor of Criminal Justice at Michigan State University, suggests that the most critical issue concerning the police in recent years is their relationship with the community,[1] and the National Advisory Commission on Criminal Justice Standards and Goals in their *Report on Police* assessed the current relationship between the police and the public in most communities as being "not entirely satisfactory."[2]

Current discussions on this problem of the American police seem fraught with paradox. However, most agree that the criticisms of the police arise out of the radically different conceptions of the police function.

VIEWPOINTS ON THE POLICE FUNCTION

Generally there have been two broad schools of thought concerning the police function. Some police scholars, practitioners, and members of the community feel that the role of the police in today's society should be primarily one of "law enforcement". Conversely, others feel that the "peace-keeping" role should be emphasized more than the "law enforcement" role.

Attributes of the "law enforcement" school of thought are: (1) emphasis placed on criminal apprehension and deterrence; (2) training oriented towards crime detection and adherence to the rule of law; (3) image portrayed as "crime fighters" and "crook catchers"; and (4) organizationally following the "legalistic" style of policing.[3]

Attributes of the "peace-keeping" school of thought are: (1) emphasis placed on crime prevention; (2) training oriented towards dealing with people and adherence to maintaining order; (3) image portrayed as "peace keepers" and "problem solvers", and (4) organizationally following the "watchman" and "service" styles of policing.[4]

While it is generally assumed that civilian policing in the United States has followed the British model of "peace-keeping" and "crime prevention", the relationship has actually been more theoretical than real. In this country, the functions of peace keeping and crime pre-

1. Louis Radelet. *The Police and the Community.* Beverly Hills: Glencoe Press, 1973. (Anyone who is seriously interested in the role of police in modern society should read this volume [second edition, 1977] in its entirety.)

2. National Advisory Commission on Criminal Justice Standards and Goals. *Report on Police.* Washington, D.C.: U.S. Government Printing Office, 1973, p. 9.

3. See James Q. Wilson. *Varieties of Police Behavior: The Management of Law and Order in Eight Communities.* Cambridge: Harvard University Press, 1968, Chapter 6, pp. 172–199 for an in-depth discussion of the "legalistic" style.

4. See James Q. Wilson, op. cit., Chapter 5, pp. 140–171 and Chapter 7, pp. 200–226 for an in-depth discussion of the "watchman" and "service" styles.

vention have not been emphasized as they are in the British system. The primary concern of the police for the last forty-five years has been criminal apprehension and law enforcement activities. Any attempts to improve the police have centered around this goal. Most departmental policies are designed to provide guidelines for the officer in a criminal situation. But the role of the police has expanded greatly as society has become more complex. Many and varied demands have been made upon the police because of their unique authority and position.[5] Dealing with alcoholics and the mentally ill, providing ambulance service, and a myriad of other "peace-keeping" and "social service" activities are the rule rather than the exception. Thus the police have found that the majority of incidents encountered are not situations which deal with crime, but rather situations in which the officer must settle a dispute or provide a service. These situations deal primarily with the "peace-keeping" aspects of his function. In these situations, the departmental procedures do not provide adequate guidelines for directing the officer's actions. A partial explanation of this deficiency is the lack of "organizational commitment"[6] regarding the "peace-keeping" function. Emphasis upon the "law enforcement" function has led to a tendency on the part of both the public and the police to underestimate the range and complexity of the total police task.

A CLOSER LOOK AT THE PROBLEM

Collectively, the police are the largest and most pervasive of all criminal justice components. The police, as the first and activating element of the system, are confronted with many problems, most of which are found throughout the system. Central to these problems is one basic issue—the administration of the police service (essentially police behavior) and its relationship with the community.

In its purest form, the problem is one of a lack of consensus on the part of both the police and the public on what the proper function of the police should be. The solution to this problem can only come about through a resolution of the police role. Recognition of this fact is found throughout police literature.

Richard H. Ward suggests:[7]

The policeman's role has come under considerable scrutiny in the past few years   .   .   .   a major failing has been

5. See Peter K. Manning's discussion of this in his scholarly work "The Police: Mandate, Strategies, and Appearances" in Jack D. Douglas (ed.), *Crime and Justice in American Society.* New York: Bobbs-Merrill Company, Inc., pp. 149–193.

6. See Radelet's excellent discussion of this in *The Police and The Community,* 1973, pp. 596–627.

7. Richard H. Ward. "The Police Role: A Case of Diversity". In *Issues in Law Enforcement,* George G. Killinger and Paul F. Cromwell, Jr., (eds.). Boston: Holbrook Press, 1975, p. 211.

the lack of adequate definition, and this has led to much confusion.

Egon Bittner describes the dilemma in *The Function of the Police in Modern Society*.[8]

> The formulation of criteria for judging any kind of institutional practice, including the police, rather obviously calls for the solution of a logically prior problem. Clearly, it is necessary that it be known what needs to be done before anyone can venture to say how it is to be done well. In the case of the police, this sets up the requirement of specifying the police role in society. Simple as this demand may seem on first glance, it presents difficulties that are more commonly avoided than addressed.

And, Campbell, Sahid, and Stang state: [9]

> The policeman lives on the guiding edge of social conflict without a well-defined, well-understood notion of what he is supposed to be doing there.

Jerome Skolnick believes that the traditional solution to problems involving the police has been one of improving the quality of the police through more education and training, coupled with technological advances. He states:[10]

> It is rarely recognized that the conduct of the police may be related to the character and goals of the institution itself— the duties police are called on to perform, associated with the assumptions of the system of legal justice—that it may not be the men who are good or bad, so much as the processes and design of the system in which they find themselves.

Skolnick's point is very important when considering the future direction of American policing. It is quite possible that "professionalizing" the police through more education and training may only give an outward appearance of professionalization. Centainly the quality of the educational and training package is important, but what seems

8. Egon Bittner. *The Functions of the Police in Modern Society.* Washington, D.C.: U.S. Government Printing Office, 1970, p. 2.

9. James S. Campbell, Joseph R. Sahid, and David P. Stang. *Law and Order Reconsidered—Report of the Task Force on Law and Law Enforcement to the National Commission on* the Causes and Prevention of Violence. Washington, D.C.: U.S. Government Printing Office, 1969; Bantam Books, 1970, p. 291.

10. Jerome K. Skolnick. *Justice Without Trial: Law Enforcement in Democratic Society.* 2nd ed., New York: John Wiley & Sons, 1975, p. 5.

even more important is the philosophy of the organization. If the philosophy of the police is traditional (mechanistic) as opposed to contemporary (humanistic), the resulting change agent that was the hope of the 1970's may be only a shadow of himself.[11]

It would seem that to improve police effectiveness in today's complex society the philosophy of policing is going to have to change in the direction (emphasis) of the peace-keeping aspects of that function. Many suggest this would be a radical departure (even un-American) from what the police function has historically been. But what are the historical facts concerning the role and philosophy of the American police?

ORIGIN OF THE MODERN POLICE DEPARTMENT

The origin of our modern municipal police department dates back to 1829, when Sir Robert Peel managed to secure approval by an apprehensive English Parliament of his Bill for a Metropolitan Police. But Peel did not have an easy time of it. His first attempt to establish a police force, in 1823, was rejected by a Police Committee of Parliament. The criminal law reformers of this time felt that a police force was unnecessary, because crime could be solved by proposing more humane laws. This was based on the assumption that the laws were self-enforcing. Also it was believed that such a force might become a mechanism of political tyranny. It was felt that forfeiture or curtailment of individual liberty, which the creation of an effective police system would bring with it, would be too great a sacrifice on behalf of improvements in police or facilities in detection of crime.[12] In 1825, England was faced with a severe economic depression. Lack of employment and reduced wages, together with hunger and misery, led to a wave of social unrest and disorder. Mobs began to make their appearance in various parts of the country. Riots began in Lancashire in April of 1826 and then spread on to other major English cities. Various methods were tried by the Government to stem the tide of violence, but without success. The Government considered the Army as a last resort, but realized that this would increase public resentment and create more serious problems. Parliament was shocked into the realization that no civil authority existed that was capable of quelling such social unrest. In light of these conditions, Peel's bill, "A Bill for Improving the Police in and near the Metropolis," was approved by Parliament on September 29, 1829. It

11. See this writer's discussion of this dilemma in "A Study of the Placement and Utilization Patterns and Views of the Criminal Justice Graduate of Michigan State University,"

unpublished Ph.D. dissertation, East Lansing Michigan, 1972.

12. Charles Reith. *A New Study of Police History*. London: Oliver and Boyd LTD., 1956.

was with the passage of this bill that modern policing as it is known today originated.

Peel's basic principles of law enforcement, as set forth in his Bill for Improving the Police, laid the basic foundation for the relationships and obligations that were to exist between the police and citizens and which still exist today in England. Peel realized the importance of winning public support and acceptance and stressed that successful police work depends on the cooperation of the people and the police. "From its inception, the essential civilian character of the police was stressed; public service, self-control, and the importance of gaining the public's trust were emphasized."[13] "Further, in a democratic society every citizen has a serious obligation to do police work and the existence of a paid police force does not alter his duty." This idea contrasts with the modern misconception that "the police are paid to do what civilians would prefer not to do."[14]

As suggested by Peel's principles "the primary function of the police was the preservation of the Queen's peace and the prevention of crime. Other functions were regarded as ancillary."[15] These two objectives still remain the prime function of the British police today.

The major significance of the new police lay in its example as a model for subsequent national police reform. The new police proved that an efficient organization could lessen the need for the use of troops against civilians. Also it could maintain all three police objectives, crime prevention, protection of life and property, and apprehension of offenders. Finally, it showed that the new police could be compatible with the English constitutional concepts and philosophy of liberty.[16]

IMPLICATIONS OF PEELIAN REFORM ON THE AMERICAN EXPERIENCE IN LAW ENFORCEMENT

Peelian Reform implied three distinct points[17] for the formulation of American police management and administration of police services:

1. Since in a democratic society the police are the public and the public are the police, the police accurately reflect the general culture of the society they represent. This is not to be confused with

13. J. L. Hyman. "The Metropolitan Police Act of 1829: An Analysis of Certain Events Influencing the Passage and Character of the Metropolitan Police Act in England." In *Issues in Law Enforcement*, George G. Killinger and Paul F. Cromwell, Jr., (eds.). Boston: Holbrook Press, 1975, p. 36.

14. Radelet, op. cit., p. 3–4.

15. Ibid., p. 34.

16. William H. Hewitt. *British Police Administration*, Springfield, Illinois: Charles C. Thomas, 1965.

17. Radelet, op. cit., pp. 6–7.

the cultural style of political policing which enforces local mores enshrined in public statutes. In this type of situation, the police are influenced by the dominant political power in a community, no matter how wrong it may be when judged by other standards. Instead, this point refers to "situational policing" which occurs when the specific goals and priorities which the police establish within the limits of legislatively-granted authority are determined to a large extent by community desires. Some examples of this might be (a) elements of the community might urge increased patrols around schools; (b) stricter enforcement of policing regulations in congested areas; (c) reduced enforcement activities against violations of certain crimes.[18]

2.   In a democratic society, unlike totalitarian systems, the police function depends on a considerable amount of self-policing by every citizen. This system involves personal citizen responsibility which emphasizes the fact that the police are a part of, and not apart from, the community they serve. This point suggests that the police cannot be effective alone. Citizen response, rather than public apathy, must become the rule rather than the exception.

3.   The police in a democratic society are viewed as a living expression of the democratic process which purports equal justice for all. What the police officer does and how he does it is a critical measure of the worth of the democratic process. The reason for this is that for many people, contact with the criminal justice system has a lot to do with their seeing the democratic process as credible. If democratic law is to be credible and ethical to the citizenry, with standards of fairness, reasonableness, and human decency, it will be so to the extent that police behavior reflects such qualities. The premise behind this point is that the role of the policeman in any society is to enforce a non-political law. But today's society demands that police officers enforce the rules of the political system rather than the laws of equal justice. This is often referred to as "political policing" and is what the Wickersham Commission had in mind when it spoke of "taking the police out of politics." The crucial issue is what *style* of political policing will be introduced to deal with the political world that the police are very much a part.[19]

DEVELOPMENT OF THE POLICE ROLE IN AMERICA

In America, as in England, it was the increasing incidence of civil disorder and not the rising crime rates that brought about the establishment of the modern municipal police force. New York, in 1844, was the first city in the United States to adopt Peel's plan of

18. National Advisory Commission on Criminal Justice Standards and Goals, *Report on Police*, op. cit., pp. 9–10.

19. See Radelet's excellent discussion of this in *The Police and the Community*, 1973, pp. 488–519.

police organization. During the ensuing ten years, similar organizational patterns appeared in Chicago, Philadelphia, and Boston. By 1870, the main features of the London Metropolitan Police were firmly established in this country.[20] At this time, the primary function of the American municipal police forces was, as in England, that of maintaining order.

Oscar Handlin, in an article entitled "Community Organization as a Solution to Police Community Problems" observed that "early American police forces had 'undifferentiated functions.' They were public servants with duties pertaining to public health, welfare, and all sorts of odds and ends."[21] Until after 1900, the most important aspects of police work, as modern American police now see it, were not performed by the police. Various private agencies took care of apprehending criminals.

Jack E. Whitehouse in his article, "Historical Perspectives on the Police Community Service Function," discussed some of the duties of the municipal policeman in the nineteenth and early twentieth centuries.[22] Policemen in Boston, in the late 1800's, were always instructed "to remove objects from the streets and sidewalks, to put out fires, test doors and to turn off running water." It was also the patrolman's duty to serve as the eyes and ears of other city departments and note broken lamps, strange odors, and the like. As today, it was also the nineteenth century policeman's duty to handle drunks and family disturbances. In 1853, 506 drunken Boston citizens were taken home and 539 family quarrels were handled by the police. It was also the duty of the policeman at this time to deal with matters pertaining to health. In 1834, in Boston, the officers had to check every house in the city daily for cholera. They were also required to keep a list of physicians who were registered in the precinct in order to refer them to those needing medical assistance. The cells and floors of the police station often served as a temporary hospital for the critically ill. In the 1880's, the police officers inspected all tenement and lodging homes to determine sanitary conditions. The police also inspected steam boilers and tested licensed steam boiler operators. In the area of social welfare, the police in Boston administered the relief funds provided by the municipality as well as provided coal for needy families. It was the patrolman's responsibility to assist people in

20. Raymond B. Fosdick, American Police Systems. Montclair, N.J.: Patterson Smith, 1969.

21. Oscar Handlin. "Community Organization as a Solution to Police Community Problems". *Police and the Changing Community—Selected Readings.* Nelson A. Watson, ed.,

Washington, D.C.: International Association of Chiefs of Police, 1965, p. 107.

22. Jack E. Whitehouse. "Historical Perspectives on the Police Community Service Function". *Journal of Police Science and Administration.* Vol. I. March, 1973, pp. 87–92.

need of shelter and relief by directing them to the proper agency. On some occasions, the police provided overnight lodging for the poor in the police station. According to A. E. Costello, in 1885, New York City had a similar program.[23] In a span of nine years (1861–1869), 880,161 persons were furnished lodgings by New York City police. This figure equaled the number of persons arrested during the same time period.

At the beginning of the twentieth century, the police still emphasized the involvement and commitment to public services as their primary function. The commissioner of police in New York City at that time noted that policemen on the beat probably come more intimately into contact with the life of the people than any other class of men, and their wide opportunities for observation can be harnessed into various forms of constructive social work. Fosdick, in his book *American Police Systems*, emphasized the importance of the patrolman being a referral agent. Police work cannot be isolated from other welfare agencies of the community concerned with social problems. It cannot be divorced from all the organizing influences, such as attempts to improve conditions in city life. The policing demands a type of officer interested and trained in social service.[24]

During the early 1900's, the New York City Police Department initiated a number of community service activities designed to help the youth of the community. In January of 1917, carefully chosen patrolmen were assigned the specific duty of looking after young people who seemed to be going wrong. Many of these cases involved destitute home conditions which could be corrected by referral to certain welfare agencies. The police were instrumental in establishing new city playgrounds, especially in the high crime neighborhoods. Uniformed police officers were assigned to talk to children in public schools, so as to establish a better relationship between the police and the youth.

In 1916, the New York City Police Department initiated a program in which needy children were provided clothes and toys. The patrolmen in each precinct made up a list of the deprived families and on Christmas Day 40,000 youths received such gifts. This program was soon copied by other major cities throughout the nation. In 1917, the New York department established the system of Junior Police. Approximately 6,000 boys between the ages of 11 and 16 were given uniforms, drilled, and given classes in safety, first aid, traffic safety and law. The boys also participated in athletic competition. It was felt that this program had a favorable effect on the boys because there was a marked decrease in juvenile delinquency.

23. A. E. Costello. *Our Police Protec-*
        tors. New York: C. F. Roper, 1885,
        pp. 233–234.

24. Fosdick, op. cit., p. 371.

In addition, when unemployment was at its peak, the police considered themselves to be an employment agency for the large number of people out of work. Frequently, the police created jobs where none existed, such as litter control and street cleaning. From 1914 to 1917, over 3,000 people were employed by the police in one capacity or another. About the time of World War I, the New York City Police Department was finding employment for ex-convicts. They felt that by helping these men get jobs, they might earn a living to support their families, thus preventing crime. During this same time period, many New York police officers were extensively used as parole and probation officers. Eighty-four sergeants were assigned to look after men released from jails, penitentiaries, and workhouses with the purpose of getting the parolee a job and assuring him that the police department stood ready to assist him. The St. Louis and Los Angeles Police Departments also maintained such services within their agencies.

After reading accounts of the 19th century police practices, one can only wonder why some present day policemen seem to be under the impression that the peace-keeping (community service) function is a newly-acquired activity. As can be observed, it is not. The police of yesterday performed a variety of health, welfare, and other social service functions. These duties were considered commonplace and essential. These policemen had no conflict over being termed "social workers." There is no indication that there was a problem with what today's social scientists call "role conflict." They did not have the advantage of sociologists talking to them about incompatibility of roles or role conflict. Some modern police officers, having had these advantages, seem to believe that it is beneath their dignity, or not their duty, to perform service-related activities.[25]

As a result of the peace-keeping aspects of their function, there were few community relations problems because the community and the police saw the police function primarily from the same vantage point.[26]

THE 20TH CENTURY—THE CHANGING OF
THE POLICE ROLE

At the turn of the century, the maintenance of order was still the paramount function of the American police. But several early twentieth century influences shifted emphasis away from maintaining order to that of enforcing law. The first of these influences was the passage by Congress of the Eighteenth Amendment, commonly

25. Whitehouse, op. cit., p. 92.

26. Roger Lane. *Policing the City— Boston 1822–1885*. Cambridge, Massachusetts: Harvard University Press, 1967, p. 160.

called the Volstead Act, on January 16, 1920. This Amendment banned the manufacture, sale, and transportation of all intoxicating beverages. This Amendment was passed in an attempt to regulate public morals. But many people objected to such an attempt by Congress, thus there was still a great public demand for alcoholic beverages. This demand enabled organized crime syndicates to make vast profits from the illegal manufacture of alcoholic beverages. Prohibition caused the underworld to gain a measure of respectability never before attained by becoming the exclusive suppliers of a commodity that the public avidly desired. Despite this great public demand, it was the job of police departments to enforce the Eighteenth Amendment. Traditionally it was the job of the patrolman to take a broad view of his role, exercise initiative and independence, and learn his beat and work with the people on it. But, James Q. Wilson states that Prohibition placed the patrolman into an "adversary relationship" with his beat.[27] That is, for the first time the policeman was supposed to do things that many citizens did not want done. Law enforcement officials were viewed as villians, not only by the lower class elements of society, but also by many middle and upper class citizens who until that time had been respectful, law-abiding citizens.

Public disagreement as to the legitimate use of police discretion and public concern over the officer's capacity to use it honestly and without favoritism led to its progressive curtailment. Prohibition created the opportunity for large scale corruption in police departments. Many policemen, rather than trying to enforce an unpopular law and realizing it was impossible to curtail the manufacture and consumption of all alcohol, took monetary bribes. There are numerous known cases where law enforcement officials accepted large amounts of money from underworld syndicates to allow such illegal practices to continue. Prohibition put the police in a position of choosing between corruption and making a nuisance of themselves.

Another influence which shifted emphasis away from maintaining order to that of enforcing the law was the Depression of the 1930's. In this era, the public attention focused on the escapades of such well-known bank robbers as Bonnie and Clyde Barrow, Baby Face Nelson, John Dillinger, and others. During this era, the crime rate was rising and the public focused their attention on the law enforcement officials' attempts to apprehend these notorious criminals. Therefore, the public saw the primary function of the police as "crook catchers." Wilson stated that:[28]

> Police venality and rising crime rates coincided in the public mind, though in fact they had somewhat different

27. James Q. Wilson. "What Makes A Better Policeman?" *Atlantic Monthly,* March, 1969, pp. 129–135.

28. Ibid., p. 133.

causes. The watchman function of the police was lost sight of; their law enforcement function, and their apparent failure to exercise it, were emphasized.

In essence, the law enforcement function overtook the peacekeeping function in terms of emphasis both within the police department and in the minds of the public.

Because of the public focus on the rising crime rate, President Herbert Hoover, in 1929, appointed the National Commission on Law Observance and Law Enforcement, popularly known as the Wickersham Commission. The Commission reported its findings to President Hoover in 1931. The report clearly placed the blame of the rising crime rates on the police:[29]

> The general failure of the police to detect and arrest criminals guilty of the many murders, spectacular bank, payroll and other holdups, sensational robberies with guns, frequently resulting in the death of the robbed victim, has caused a loss of public confidence in the police of our country.

It was felt that if the job of the police is to catch crooks, then the police have a technical responsibility in which discretion plays little part. Since no one is likely to disagree on the value of the objective, then there is little reason to expose the police to the decision-making processes of city government.[30]

The Commission saw the primary function of the police as "crook catchers" and all ancillary police services were questioned because they were not "real police work." The Commission recommended many reforms in dealing with crime and order problems, one of which was providing training for the police. Of course, with the primary function of the police being viewed as criminal apprehension, this training placed its major emphasis on techniques dealing with crime deterrence. But Wilson stresses that it was this view of police work that really didn't correspond with reality. The patrolman knew that he was still handling family disturbances and troublesome teenagers. The police were also aware that they alone could not prevent crime. Many police departments turned to manipulating crime records, to make things look better from a public standpoint.

---

29. National Commission on Law Observance and Enforcement. *Report on Police.* Vol. IV, No. 14. Washington, D.C.: U.S. Government Printing Office, 1931, p. 1.

30. Wilson, op. cit., p. 133 (This is certainly a different viewpoint from National Advisory Commission on Criminal Justice Standard and Goals, *Report on Police,* 1973, pp. 9–10, where in it is stated—"police officers are decisionmakers".

Organizational rewards and promotions were based on criminal apprehension.

The police operated along the guidelines proposed by the Wickersham Commission. The police saw their primary function as law enforcement and all training and education was aimed towards this end. But the crime rate was not being reduced. Police officers, characterized as crime fighters, were still spending the majority of their time handling order maintenance incidents. As a result, officers were being judged by a goal they could not attain.

The impact of the Wickersham Commission on American policing could be summed up as follows:[31]

(1) The law enforcement function became uppermost in the minds of the police and the public.

(2) The police were given sole responsibility for the reduction of crime.

(3) The police used unethical means to meet the public's expectations of crime reduction—i. e., the manipulation of crime statistics.

(4) The peace-keeping (community service) functions (soup kitchens, providing lodging, referral agents, etc.) became looked upon as not "real police work."

(5) The policeman, in effect, took on an adversarial relationship with the public.

(6) The number of arrests by a police officer became the criteria for promotion.

(7) The public looked upon the policeman as mainly involved in crime fighting and doing very little in the way of peace-keeping (order maintenance or community service).

During the 1940's and 1950's, the police viewed their primary role as law enforcement and all training and education was aimed toward this end. The public was more concerned about World War II than the problems at home with crime and the police. Despite fairly widespread violations of the war measure, the great mass of American citizens obeyed the law, displayed a remarkable tolerance for the rights of others, contributed to the war effort, and supported law enforcement.[32] Thus, the dilemma of the patrolman, whether his primary role was law enforcement or peace-keeping, was not apparent during this period.

31. Ibid., p. 133–134.

32. William J. Bopp and Donald O. Schultz. *A Short History of American Law Enforcement.* Springfield, Illinois: Charles C. Thomas Company, 1972, p. 120.

But, the 1960's brought fear and civil disorder to our nation. The United States experienced mass disorders with unprecedented frequency and simultaneously witnessed harsh and sometimes lethal reactions by the police. Several commission reports[33], studying the violence and civil disorders of the 1960's, reported a common finding: the police were not equipped and trained to handle mass disorders and, in most cases, police action taken tended to precipitate or escalate the level of violence. Yet, the public had turned to the police for protection and a restoration of order, and found instead a very ineffective and insensitive organization unable to achieve this end.

Many realized that a redefinition of the police role was necessary if our society hoped to achieve the long-forgotten Peelian Reform. It was also plain to see that the police, functioning alone, could not solve the problem. Attention refocused on the police role. The President's Commission on Crime and Administration of Justice (1967) recognized the role dilemma and stated:[34]

> The current widespread concern with crime and violence, particularly in large cities, *commands* a *rethinking* of the *function* of the police in American society.

In addition, it was recognized that crime prevention was the responsibility of every part of society, thus relieving the police from being solely responsible for crime.

THE ROLE QUESTION TODAY

As previously stated, the role of the police in today's society is considered one of the central most perplexing problems affecting the effectiveness of the police and their relationship to the community. The question of police role is being examined by many analysts. In 1968, the National Advisory Commission on Civil Disorders, also known as the Kerner Commission, dealt with this problem in its chapter on police and the community.[35]

> The policeman in the ghetto is a symbol of increasingly bitter social debate over law enforcement. One side, disturbed and perplexed by sharp rises in crime and urban violence, exerts extreme pressure on police for tougher law en-

33. U.S. National Advisory Commission on Civil Disorders. *Report of the National Advisory Commission on Civil Disorders* (Kerner Report). Washington, D.C., Government Printing Office, 1968; U.S. National Commission on Causes and Prevention of Violence. *Violence in America: Historical and Comparative Perspectives*, Vols. 1 and 2, 1969.

34. U.S., President's Commission on Law Enforcement and Administration of Justice. *Task Force Report: The Police*. Washington, D.C.: U.S. Government Printing Office, 1968, p. 13. (emphasis added)

35. U.S. National Advisory Commission on Civil Disorders. (Kerner Report), op. cit., pp. 299–300.

forcement. Another group, inflamed against police as agents of repression, tends toward defiance of what it regards as order maintained at the expense of justice.

Perhaps the landmark event concerning the redirection or change in emphasis of the police role was the 1967 report of the President's Commission on Law Enforcement and Administration of Justice. The Commission recommended a greater emphasis be placed in the peace-keeping aspects of the police function that mainly fell outside the traditional law enforcement pattern. The Commission was quite critical of the organizational focus being almost entirely on the apprehension and prosecution of criminals when, what a policeman does, or should do, instead of making an arrest or in order to avoid making an arrest, or in a situation in which he may not make an arrest, was rarely discussed. The peace-keeping and service activities, which consumed the majority of police time, were not given adequate attention.[36]

Herman Goldstein, former assistant to O. W. Wilson when he was with the Chicago Police Department, and a noted police expert, argues that the police must become more, not less, involved in non-criminal activities if they are to be effective in dealing with the complex problems facing them in the future. Goldstein observes:[37]

> The police function is in two worlds. They play an integral part, along with the prosecutor, the courts, and correctional agencies, in the operation of the criminal justice system. As the first agency in the system, their primary responsibility is to initiate a criminal action against those who violate the law. This is a highly structured role, defined by statutes and court decisions and subjected to strict controls.
>
> The second world is less easily defined. It comprises all aspects of police functioning that are unrelated to the processing of an accused person through the criminal justice system. Within this world a police department seeks to prevent crimes, abate nuisances, resolve disputes, control traffic and crowds, furnish information, and provide a wide range of other miscellaneous services to the citizenry. In carrying out these functions, officers frequently make use of the authority which is theirs by virtue of their role in the

36. U.S. President's Commission on Law Enforcement and Administration of Justice. *The Challenge of Crime in a Free Society.* Washington, D.C.: U.S. Government Printing Office, 1967, p. 92.

37. Herman Goldstein. "Police Response to Urban Crises." *Public Administration Review.* September-October, 1968, p. 407.

criminal process . . . Police spend most of their time functioning in the second of these two worlds . . . Despite this distribution of activity, police agencies are geared primarily to deal with crime.

Goldstein, along with Frank Remington, in the Task Force Report—*The Police* (1967), suggested two ways the police can respond to both current and future problems:[38]

1. The police can continue doing what they are doing by the process known as "unarticulated improvisation." This would be reacting to a crisis after the crisis has already happened. This would be similar to the "after-the-fact" approach to problem solving. This is the comfortable approach, requiring neither the police nor the community to face regularly the difficult social issues which are involved until after a crisis occurs.

2. The second alternative would be to recognize the importance of prior planning. This process anticipates social problems and adapts to meet them before a crisis situation arises. This would be similar to the "before-the-fact" approach to problem solving.

Unfortunately, the first alternative is the approach utilized by most police departments today. Goldstein and Remington stressed the importance of the second response if the police are to be effective in preventing and controlling crime and developing a positive relationship with the community.

Role theorists studying the police role dilemma advocate that the role concept involves four functional categories. They are:[39]

1. Law Enforcement—"crook catching" and the application of legal sanctions.

2. Order Maintenance—"peace-keeping" or conflict management.

3. Crime Prevention—"the before-the-fact" approach to crime, reducing opportunities.

4. Social Services—police assume a "referral agent" role in solving an individual problem.

Bruce Terris clearly suggests that emphasis should be placed on the last three categories. As Terris phrases it:[40]

. . . the situations in which police officers most frequently find themselves do not require the expert aim of a

38. U.S. President's Commission on Law Enforcement and Administration of Justice. *Task Force Report: The Police.* op. cit., p. 18.

39. James Q. Wilson. "Dilemmas of Police Administration." *Public Ad-* *ministration Review.* September-October, 1968, p. 407.

40. Bruce J. Terris. "The Role of the Police". *The Annals,* November, 1967, p. 67.

marksman, the cunningness of a private eye, or the toughness of a stereotyped Irish policeman. Instead they demand knowledge of human beings and the personal, as opposed to official, authority to influence people without the use or even the threat of force. These characteristics are not commonly found in police officers because police departments do not consider these values as paramount. As a result, persons with these abilities are not attracted to police work nor rewarded by promotion or other incentive if they happen to enter a department.

The basic premise of those favoring the order maintenance, crime prevention, and social service functions is that the police are in a unique position to fulfill a vital role in coping with certain types of social problems. They contend that the police should not discontinue their present task of law enforcement, but rather enhance their ability to deal with the social crisis before the fact. This will, in effect, increase the officer's ability to function as a mediator, preventor, and referral agent.

And yet there are many who feel that the law enforcement function is the only appropriate role and that other more appropriate social agencies should deal with the remaining functional role categories.

Their major premise is that becoming involved in miscellaneous "social service" functions severely hampers the police in the performance of their "law enforcement" function and is indirectly responsible for at least part of the failure of police agencies to *control* traditional crime. Some of the problems raised by "diluting" the police function are seen as:[41]

1. Inflation of the police budget and distortion of the apparent cost of *crime control;*

2. Prevention of professionalism in the police career group;

3. Dilution of police attention to their primary assignment, combatting violation of traditional criminal laws.

4. Prevention of more satisfactory performance of the service functions by an especially constituted agency.

This position assumes erroneously that the sharp delineation of function will free the police from the dilemma of being accountable for developing policies and making decisions on matters that don't concern them. The problem of this viewpoint in limiting police responsibility to deal with "real" crime is twofold. First, it ignores the "so-

41. Harry More. *Critical Issues of Law Enforcement.* Cincinnati: The   W. H. Anderson Co., 1975, p. 31. [emphasis added]

cial reality of crime"[42] thus severely limiting an effective response to crime and, secondly, it ignores the fundamental fact that the police operate within a larger social milieu requiring coordination and cooperation between the police and other social forces of the community.

The supportive role of the police has been well documented.[43] Some of these supportive services include: (1) requests for health services, (2) assistance of incapacitated persons, (3) assistance regarding personal disputes and quarrels, and (4) assistance regarding missing persons and behavior of juveniles.

While common knowledge to policemen, this obvious fact is cleverly disguised by organizational mythology and the "macho" personality of the police subculture. However it can be concluded that the police do perform many actions that are not directly related to enforcement of the law per se, but are instead supportive of other aspects of the welfare of the community.

This point is crucial, for in effect the narrow definition of the police role as a "law enforcer" tends to isolate the police from the community as a whole and exemplifies the fragmentation and diffusion that characterizes the ineffectual approach to crime and rising public disorder that is one of the major problems of the criminal justice system.[44] (Or possibly better phrased "the criminal justice *non-system*").

In addition, this narrow viewpoint ignores the context or environment of the police-community relationship. Sources of variation in the behavior of police are to a large extent determined by the expectations in different kinds of communities.[45] Probably the most significant characteristic that accounts for differences in community expectations of the police is the extent to which the community is homogeneous or heterogeneous. In a homogeneous community one can expect fairly well-defined expectations and a relatively easy time of it for the police. On the other hand, a heterogeneous community, by comparison, makes the job of the police much more difficult. What should be emphasized here though is that no matter how the community is comprised, the police carry out their functions within the con-

---

42. See Richard Quinney's *The Social Reality of Crime*, Boston: Little, Brown and Company, 1970.

43. See Lawrence W. Sherman, "The Sociology and the Social Reform of the American Police: 1950–1973". *The Journal of Police Science and Administration*. September, 1974, pp. 256–259.

44. Merlyn D. Moore, "Crime and Criminal Justice in the Year 2000",

paper presented at Quality of Life Conference, Sam Houston State University, February, 1977.

45. A synthesis of Albert Reiss, *The Police and the Public*, 1971; James Q. Wilson, *Varieties of Police Behavior*, 1968. Jerome Skolnick, *Justice Without Trial*, 1975; Michael Banton, *The Police and the Community*, 1964.

text or environment of the community, rather than following the abstract principles of the narrowly conceived "law enforcement" function.

Finally, some specific observations on the problems encountered by "dilution" of the police function. The disadvantage of the inflation of the police budget and resulting distortion of the cost of *crime control* is a very simplistic one. Possibly if one is thinking about short-term costs this inflationary consideration might be correct. But in terms of long-range costs, rather than increasing the police budget, the opposite should occur. (And distorting the cost of *crime control* suggests by the phraseology the reactive nature of this stance).

Also, the suggestion that broadening the police function prevents professionalism in the police career group suggests a very traditional viewpoint of police professionalism and ignores the special significance of professionalizing the police from a police-community standpoint. A profession serves needs, not wants, thus pointing out a dilemma that many police experts have failed to grasp. Although the police have indeed "professionalized" they have done so by improved "tools" and "hardware", and traditional training and educational methodologies—yet they are still heavily criticized. Why is this so? Radelet poses this answer:[46]

> . . . There is more to professionalism than efficiency and hardware—or perhaps it is that police professionalism *without a human dimension* is not a very significant goal after all.

Jerome Skolnick in *The Police and the Urban Ghetto,* concurs. He feels that the problem of policing in a democratic society is not merely a matter of obtaining newer police cars or more sophisticated equipment, or of recruiting men who have more education. Skolnick feels that a significant alteration in the philosophy of policing is necessary so that police professionalization rests upon the values of society and the democratic process rather than the notion of technical proficiency in enforcing the law. He goes on to suggest the conflict between productivity demands and the concept of accountability has caused the police to adopt "a philosophy of professionalism based upon managerial efficiency, with the hope that advancing technology will somehow resolve their dilemma."[47]

Skolnick suggests that technological advances in the form of wiretaps, eavesdropping equipment, surveillance cameras, and so

46. Radelet, op. cit., p. 63.

47. Jerome Skolnick. *Justice Without Trial: Law Enforcement in Democrat-* ic Society. 2nd ed., New York: John Wiley & Sons, 1975, p. 243.

forth only make the police more competent to interfere with individual liberty.   Modern day police administration would do well to take
heed of what Skolnick is saying.   Increased efficiency in police work
is certainly laudable, but only as a means to an end, not as an end in
itself.   If the latter occurs, a community is often faced with a police
department that is not responsive to community needs.

While it is reasonable for the police to benefit personally from
their professional efforts, their work must be directed primarily to
benefitting the community on a whole.   Two concepts of organizational theory are pertinent here :[48]

1.   The "prime beneficiary" concept which states that the intended recipient of an organization's activities must be identified—
in the case of the police this can only mean to serve the people.   (What
they "ought" to do.)

2.   The "goal displacement" concept which involves directing
benefits of the organization from those for whom they were intended
to the organization itself.   (In the case of the police considering themselves before the public.)

Unfortunately, present day policing methods suggest the police
are following the latter organizational concept in far too many instances.   (Narcotic enforcement activities may be one example of
this.)

CAN THE POLICE ROLE DILEMMA BE RESOLVED?

Radelet sheds some light on the dilemma by stating :[49]

It is necessary to recognize that the debate is not over
whether the police should be relieved of either of their principal functions.   That is, the question is not one of law enforcement versus order maintenance.[50]   It is recognized that
the police must work both functions.   The debate pertains to
which function should be emphasized.

If the police spend the majority of their time performing the order maintenance function, then they should be organized in such a
manner that the performance of this function will be enhanced.   The
question might be posed: why should police officers be trained as if

48.   California Commission on Police
Officer's   Standards   and   Training.
*Project Star—Systems Training Anal-
ysis of Requirements for Criminal
Justice Participants*, Santa Cruz, California: Davis Publishing Company,
1974, p. 25.

49.   Radelet, op. cit., p. 39.

50.   In this context "order maintenance" would be a collectivity of the
order maintenance, crime prevention
and social service functions.

most of their time were spent catching crooks, when most of their time is not spent in this way?

Although there is no consensus, it is generally believed that the police should recognize that order maintenance is their central function. The problem, however, is how to bring about this recognition. This is especially so because of the public interest in crime in the streets which is leading many (including the police) to emphasize the law enforcement function as the principal role function.

James Q. Wilson sums up this dilemma as follows:[51]

> The simultaneous emergence of a popular concern for both crime and order does put in focus the choices that will have to be made in the next generation of police reforms. In effect, municipal police departments are two organizations in one serving two related but not identical functions. The strategy appropriate for strengthening their ability to serve one role tends to weaken their ability to serve the other
>
> . . .

Efforts to resolve this dilemma have taken several different forms. One of these involves training the police officer in the various roles he is expected to perform. The content of their training was developed by a research project known as PROJECT STAR. It involved a 39-month effort involving four states: California, Michigan, New Jersey, and Texas. PROJECT STAR was designed for the purpose of "developing attitudes and behavior which will enable criminal justice personnel and the public to achieve the goals and objectives of the criminal justice system more effectively."[52]

One of the interesting observations of the overall research effort was that PROJECT STAR emphasized heavily the order maintenance, crime prevention and social service functions over that of law enforcement. The research effort suggested that some police officers may reject this emphasis in favor of the perspective portrayed by doing "real police work" or "fighting the war against crime". However police officers were seen as being responsible for solving problems for citizens that may or may not be crime related. In this way the public are truly the prime benefactor of police actions. Responding to appropriate observed or requested non-crime services enables the police to fulfill a much needed function in society which does not seem to be available through other private or public services.[53]

51. James Q. Wilson, "What Makes A Better Policeman", op. cit., p. 135.

52. California Commission on Police Officer's Standards and Training, op. cit., p. 4.

53. Ibid., Module 3, pp. 2–3.

James Q. Wilson, in his most recent book, *Thinking About Crime*, agrees with the above observation and makes this enlightened statement:[54]

> It is easy to misunderstand the problem. What is necessary is not to replace training for police work with training for social work, not to separate order maintenance and law enforcement responsibilities, not to substitute 'human relations skills' for the ability to make an arrest or take charge of a situation. The debate over the role of the policeman has tended to obscure the fact that the patrolman does all of these things most of the time . . . . The argument about whether 'cops' should be turned into 'social workers' is a false one, for it implies that society can exercise some meaningful choice over the role the patrolman should play. Except at the margin, it cannot; what it can do is attempt to purpose officers for the complex role they now perform.

PROJECT STAR is an attempt at bringing about this change.

TOWARD A NEW POTENTIAL

Social change, in the sense of altered people-to-people relationships and community attitudes, has changed the dynamics of social control in society to involving a reappraisal on restructuring of the relationship between the police and the policed.

Police departments throughout America are in a challenging period. The past decade has been marked by rising crime rates, growing urban tensions, and increasing street violence. Unfortunately, long-range forecasts [55] suggest these trends are highly probable in the remainder of the twentieth century.

Because of this the predictable response has been for "stricter" more efficient law enforcement. At the same time, there is the growing belief that much of the police work in America has been wasteful and ineffective as a result of following the above response. Accordingly, there have been many suggestions that have stated the need for instituting essential reforms (new problems require new responses) all seemingly centering on the question of police role.

The role of the police officer is changing as more emphasis is being placed on order maintenance, crime prevention, and community services which only indirectly have to do with law enforcement. In-

54. James Q. Wilson. *Thinking About Crime.* New York: Basic Books, Inc., 1975, p. 121.

55. For an excellent account of this see *PROJECT STAR: The Impact of Social Trends on Crime and Criminal Justice,* Cincinnati: Anderson Publishing Company, 1976.

creasingly, the public has come to question the kind and quality of services provided when they "call a cop".

CONCLUDING THOUGHTS

Implied, but not stated in this paper, was the conclusion that significant improvements of the police cannot occur without significant improvement of the criminal justice system of which it is a part; this does not preclude improvements within policing itself, but is merely a restatement that the police cannot do the job of maintaining public order or public confidence alone. Emile Durkheim suggested long ago that crime and disorder is an indication of the progress that society has made in meeting the needs of its members. Perhaps the police and the system as a whole should take heed of Durkheim and examine what their role is and why it is what it is (e. g., central to the role dilemma, regardless of its philosophical origin, is the question of its utility or productiveness).

Apropos of the message in this paper and a fitting finale is the following quote attributed to the late John F. Kennedy :[56]

> You see things; and you say why? 'But I dream things that never were [or perhaps even things that once were[57]]; and I say why not?

Areas for Discussion for Part I

1. If society determines that the primary role of the police should in fact be order maintenance provision of services, then who should be held responsible for the crime problem?

2. Assuming that the police are held responsible for societies crime problems, what alternatives are available to the police in coping with this increasing crime problem?

3. Evaluate the probability of success of the roles imposed upon the police by various elements within our society.

4. What are some alternative roles and/or strategies for the police?

56. William Manchester. *The Glory and the Dream: A Narrative History of America 1932–1972*. Boston: Little, Brown and Company, 1974, p. 1208.

57. Additional thought and emphasis by author.

PART II

THE POLICE ORGANIZATION

Police administration encompasses two distinct areas, organizing the police department and the managerial processes which transpire within the organization. Organization refers to structure, or the arrangement between and within the various bureaus, sections, and units within the police department. This includes chain of command or hierarchy, span of control, and division of labor or specialization. Managerial processes refer to actions which take place within the organization such as decision-making, goal setting and ordering, power and authority, lines of communications, etc. The organization of the police department will affect the managerial processes. If the department is decentralized, has an increased span of control and utilizes a shorter chain of command, and utilizes a generalist approach as opposed to a specialist approach, there will be a distinct difference in managerial processes as compared to a centralized police department. Decision-making, goal setting will take place at lower levels in the organization, informal communications will be utilized, and power and authority will become less a factor within the organization. Thus, organization is extremely important in the management of the police department.

In organizing the police department, the police administrator's goal is to integrate and satisfy the goals of the police organization and the individual goals of the employee. Police organizational goals; order maintenance, provision of services, crime prevention, and law enforcement, provide the foundation for which police departments, are established. Police departments must strive to accomplish these goals in order to justify their existence. On the other hand, police organizational goal achievement is dependent upon the police manager's ability to gain the support and cooperation of the individual officers. Thus, it becomes necessary for management to consider and include individual employee goals in the overall organizational scheme. These goals include material rewards, ego needs, and the need to belong or identify with the organization. It may be that individual needs and organizational needs are incongruent, and the police administrator may have to make sacrifices in both areas to reach an optional state. Regardless, the police administrator must constantly strive toward the accomplishment of organizational and individual goals.

This portion of the text focuses upon organizing the police department. Law enforcement is in a transitional period where emphasis is being placed upon adherence to a decentralized model as op-

73

posed to the classical or quasi-military model.[1] The crux of this section is the analysis of the contributions management science has made toward the improvement of police organizations—this improvement refers to enabling police departments to successfully strive for goals as a result in changes in organizational philosophy. Historically, police organizations have adhered to a classical organizational model. This centralized structure has greatly impaired goal attainment. Management science has aptly identified the reason for the lack of success; the quasi-military organized department has not been able to obtain the cooperation of the employee in the pursuit of organizational goals. A decentralized organizational model, to the contrary, has been more successful due to the involvement of employees in decision-making, goal setting and ordering, communicating, etc.[2] When the employee has an interest in the organization as a result of his involvement, he will probably be a more effective employee.

The articles contained in this section of the text represent the current thoughts on decentralization or employee-centered management in law enforcement. This is not to say that this philosophy has been widely accepted by police administrators—to the contrary, most police organizations still adhere to the classical police organizational arrangement. However, there has been a great deal of experimentation with other models,[3] and academia and practitioners are generating a number of publications exploring and advocating the usage of alternative organizational arrangements.

Moreover, the authors feel that police management is now considering a third administrative path, the systems approach (this approach is, more or less, detailed in Part IV of this text). The emphasis in this approach is the quantification of activities, analysis, and reaction to present and future problems. This philosophy is greatly dependent upon the development of information technology. Finally, the authors advocate the marriage between this decentralized model and systems model of police management and organization. The future of policing is dependent upon the ability of police departments to rally its personnel and its ability to correctly identify, analyze, and find solutions to problems.

1. This appears to be the major thrust in the literature; however, actual application of these principles has not dominated applied police management.

2. For example see. Rensis Likert, *The Human Organization,* New York: McGraw-Hill Book Co., 1967.

3. For examples of police innovative structure see. Robert B. Koverman, "Team Policing: An Alternative to Traditional Law Enforcement Techniques." *Journal of Police Science and Administration,* Vol. 2, No. 1 (March 1974): 15–19. Peter B. Block and David Specht, *Neighborhood Team Policing,* Washington: Government Printing Office, 1973.

Objectives of Part II

1. Identify the three organizational philosophies.

2. Identify the managerial concepts associated with the organizational philosophies.

3. Identify some of the problems associated with the organizational philosophies.

4. Identify some of the innovative managerial techniques which are being proposed for police administration.

5. Identify the democratic model of team-policing, and the problems associated with it.

6. Identify the state of the art of organizational theory as it applies to police administration.

POLICE ORGANIZATIONS: THEIR CHANGING INTERNAL AND EXTERNAL RELATIONSHIPS * †

The axiom that the internal management structure of a large-scale organization determines to a great extent the style in which that organization interacts with its clients is nowhere more dramatically illustrated than in the field of law enforcement.

For two years, the authors have had an opportunity to participate first-hand at a policy input level in the largest law enforcement agency in the world. Our positions have allowed us to observe changing directions in police work. The developments which have commenced in New York City are just one part of a series of attempted changes occurring in progressive police departments throughout the country.

THE PARA-MILITARY ORGANIZATION STYLE

When police agencies are defined, they are most frequently characterized as para-military organizations. As such, they typically consist of: centralized command structure; one-way downward communications in the form of orders; rigid superior-subordinate relationships defined by prerogatives of rank; impersonality; obedience; and stress on the repressive nature of the work. The purpose of such a structure is to produce strict and unquestioned discipline for rapid mobilization in the emergency and crisis situations with which police

* This paper was originally presented at the annual meeting of the Eastern Sociological Society, Philadelphia, Pennsylvania, in April 1974.

† Source: Sandler, Georgette Bennett and Mintz, Ellen, "Police Organizations: Their Changing Internal and External Relationships," *Journal of Police Science and Administration*, Vol. 2, No. 4, 1974, pp. 458–463.

typically deal. At the same time, it is a structure designed to reduce inefficiency as created by the personal/emotional involvement so easily generated by the many non-ordinary situations to which police are exposed.

All this is well and good as a rationale. However, it results in several serious negative consequences both within and without the organization. Within the organization a para-military structure tends to create a sense of demoralization and powerlessness at the lower ranks. One-way communication creates a perception of the top command as being arbitrary in its actions. Not having had input into top management decisions and being deprived of access to its rationales results in cynicism among middle management as well as the rank and file. It is a cynicism exacerbated by the fact that top command decisions are perceived as unrealistic by the time they reach the level of execution. The end result is the fortification of a "we-they" feeling which creates an almost unbridgable gap between the administrative and operational levels of the organization. Given this gap, management is deprived of necessary information from the field and the field is left with alienation and cynicism.

The price paid for this state of affairs is rigidity in the organization as expressed through various blockages to change. Not having participated in the development of department programs, lower ranking members have no stake in their success. Thus, programs are often sabotaged at the level of execution. Not having received communication from that level, top management is often not aware that programs and policies have been implemented only on paper.

Even more important, however, is the stifling of innovation produced by the organizational structure. First, the rigidity of the chain of command tends to block the upward flow of ideas at the middle management level (sergeants and lieutenants). Second, there is a tendency to "cover yourself" by acting only when so ordered. This manifests itself as an overdependence on authority and produces a chronic fear of the risk-taking which is so essential to good management. Because actions of superiors and top command are viewed as arbitrary, members anticipate a lack of support for any risks they do take. It is small wonder that most police officers will deny the existence of discretion in their jobs. Yet, given the crucial impact which effective use of discretion has upon policing specifically, and the functioning of the criminal justice system in general, it is easy to see why such an attitude can be devastating.

Other serious problems arise from the para-military form of organizational structure. For one, the member of the organization is exposed to a conflicting set of expectations. On the one hand, outside the organization, he is constantly making on-the-spot decisions, carries deadly weapons and is capable of power over life and death. On the other hand, within the organization he experiences himself as being treated like a child who is not even permitted to decide on his own which uniform to wear when the weather changes! Apart from such a dilemma, the organization itself suffers from the vast human resource which is left untapped by the para-military form of decision-making and communication. Under this form of organization, it is precisely those members who are in direct contact with clients and who control implementation of policy who are eliminated from the process.

The role relationships and processes within the organization establish a model for interactions with the public. Here, too, problems arise which may ultimately lead to less effective police practice. First, in terms of the police image, which constitutes a crucial aspect of police-community relations, the military model carries a connotation of war and conflict. Hence, police are often viewed as an occupying army in ghetto communities. Indeed, police often view themselves as meriting "combat pay" for their role as the "thin blue line" separating the lawful from the lawless.[1] On a more general level, the militaristic approach sets rigid boundaries which create police-community distance and reinforce a "we-they" orientation. Drawing such boundaries encourages conflict rather than cooperative relationships.

At the same time, one-to-one relationships with the public may be affected. The military model produces many in-house frustrations which may be expressed in police-citizen interactions. For example, the authoritarian structure of the organization becomes translated into a similar style of dealing with the public. Along with authoritarianism comes a need for deference. A lack of deference becomes a psychological threat and is often viewed as a justification for use of force.[2] Even in the absence of force, however, the approach to the public tends to be procedural, technically oriented, and legalistic. This "by the book" style often leaves clients feeling vaguely dissatisfied and alienated. The result of the alienation is a lack of coopera-

1. See, for example, Alex, Nicholas, *Black in Blue* (1969) 3–19.

2. In her book, *Women in Policing* (1972) 28, Catherine Milton cites a statistic in Paul Chevigny's *Police Power*, showing that 36% of one New York City recruit class felt that defiance of police was enough provocation to use force. She further cites Albert Riess as saying, "The subculture of officers has been shown to carry with it a fairly strong belief that the officer who ignores the challenges from citizens loses the respect of the citizenry and makes it difficult for other officers to work in the precinct." See also, Piliavin, Irving, *Police—Community Alienation: Its Structural Roots and a Proposed Remedy* (1973) 8–11.

tion and withholding of information potentially relevant for crime prevention or investigation.[3]

Despite the problems cited in this admittedly one-sided exploration of para-military organization structure as it affects style, many police officers and departments continue to cling to it. One may hypothesize any of a number of appeals.[4] However, that is not the purpose of this paper. Nor is it the purpose to establish a false dichotomy of styles. Rather, it seeks to connect certain modifications of structure with new demands of law enforcement.

NEW DEMANDS OF LAW ENFORCEMENT

In the 1960s, the nature of police work did not actually change. However, perspectives on the job did. It became recognized that 80–90 percent of the work is not directly related to law enforcement. Rather, it consists of helping services and order maintenance. Police represent the first line of government when dealing with personal emotional crises of individual citizens. They provide aided services, make referrals, maintain peace and order, and provide short term solutions to insoluble social problems.[5]

Nor was the cry for "law and order" a sufficient guide for police style.[6] The demonstrations and riots of the 60s demonstrated that to enforce the law is sometimes to create disorder. To maintain order is sometimes to violate the law.[7] What these civil actions also indicated was a need for a cooperative rather than a conflict-oriented model of policing.[8]

What all this pointed out is that a technical, procedural, legalistic approach to the job is not sufficient. Rather, the job requires a whole set of human relations and problem-solving skills that can be applied to the wide range of complex situations which police confront daily.

3. Detectives working in the Rape Investigation and Analysis Unit, NYCPD, for example, claim that using techniques such as solicitude toward the victim and allowing victims to ventilate their feelings, they are obtaining information which is not usually forthcoming in this type of situation. This information is making possible the detection of patterns which ultimately aid in the apprehension of perpetrators.

4. See Niederhoffer, Arthur, *Behind the Shield: The Police in Urban Society* (1969) 109–161, for one possible hypothesis relating to the authoritarian personality.

5. Task Force on the Police, The President's Commission on Law Enforcement and Administration of Justice. *Task Force Report: The Police* (1967) 13–14.

6. Footnote 5, 145. Also, Marx, Gary, "Some Sources of the Police Problem and Problems of Police", from *Police, Community and Conflict* (forthcoming). (Revised version of paper delivered at Eastern Sociological Society meetings 1972).

7. Skolnick, Jerome, *Justice Without Trial* (1966) 7–9.

8. Footnote 4, 29.

It also became clear that "orders" could not begin to cover the broad discretionary areas in which individual judgment has to be exercised.

The achievement of this style of policing requires a modification of those aspects of a militaristic approach which alienate the community as well as the organizational membership, interfere with the development of the aforementioned skills, and encourage a "cops and robbers" approach to the job.

INDICATIONS OF CHANGE IN THE STRUCTURE

Major indications of change include breaking down the rigidity of the organization, "humanizing" its image, and reducing distance between administration and operations, police and civilians. Often, the first area in which change manifests itself is in nomenclature. In the New York City Police Department, for example, the organization is no longer referred to as a police "force," but rather as the police "service." Following in this non-military vocabulary, the patrol function is now referred to as "field services." The title "patrolman" has been changed to "police officer," "inspector" has been dropped from the highest department ranks, and the "chief inspector" is called a "chief of operations." The precinct commanding officer was for awhile viewed as a precinct manager. Orders are subsumed under the rubric "management directives." Similarly, in Simi Valley, California, the chief is now called a community safety administrator. Captains and lieutenants are referred to as supervisors and police officers are now community safety officers. While all of the above may be seen as nothing more than euphemisms, language is an important component of change in that it screens perceptions and molds thought processes. It is clear from the new nomenclature that attempts are being made to alter the perception of some police departments as militaristic organizations.

Further evidence of attempts at change are found with regard to symbols of the organization as expressed in uniforms and equipment. In New York, uniforms are being de-emphasized in the training division and staff positions. Also, more out-of-uniform functions, such as community relations, are emerging. At the same time, though currently tied up in legal suit, the use of name tags by police officers is being mandated. Simi Valley's and Menlo Park's offices have substituted blazers for uniforms. Simi Valley has also removed the word "police" from their patrol cars and substituted a "community safety" logo. In New York, new patrol cars have been painted in "friendly" colors and most of the numbers and writing have been removed. Thus, many of the visible reinforcers of police-civilian distance are being modified.

More significant is the access to legitimate use of force and weapons which characterizes military organizations. While it is true that police still retain both rights, the focus is on restraint rather than reliance on weapons.[9] Training increasingly stresses alternatives to deadly physical force and the development of verbal modes of settling issues. Among them are transactional analysis and family crisis intervention training.[10]

One major thrust for modification of the para-military structure is the civilianization of many department functions. New York City, for example, now has a civilian director of police personnel and civilians occupy top advisory positions, while Chicago and Boston have civilianized the directorship of their academies. This is not to mention all the clerical, communications and traffic functions which are being infused with civilians.

Another major countervailing force to a military structure is the ever-increasing power of police unions. These serve to curtail the top-down actions of the top command and allow lower ranks to exert some influence on the system.

Most important, however, are the indications that the "battle line" ideology is being attacked. Attempts are being made to substitute a collaborative model of law enforcement in which police and the community work together. For example, in New York City, the community relations function has been upgraded through the application of financial rewards as well as commendations. Community dialogue programs have emerged. Precinct facilities have often been opened up for community use. There exist expanded liaison efforts by crime prevention units with "block watchers" and other citizen groups. Cambridge, Massachusetts, has gone as far as to directly involve citizens in the development of its police policy manual.[11] The Dallas police department has expanded its function to include formal referral services and follow-ups.

Collaborative relationships within the organization are similarly being encouraged. Such devices as conference workshops bring ranks in direct contact with each other and enable members to bypass the often crippling chain of command. At the same time, the "think tank" approach has had some dramatic success in law enforcement.

9. Footnote 4, 28. See also T.O.P. 237, s. 72, New York City Police Department, which specifies the limitations on use of force.

10. See, for example, Bard, Morton, "The Study and Modification of Intra-Familial Violence", in Singer, J. L. (ed.), *Cognitive and Physiological Factors in Violence and Aggression* (New York, Academic Press), Preparatory Phase. Also, Geis, Jon, "The Policeman of the Future: A Psycho Therapist's View of Tomorrow's Policeman as Human Relations Expert and Psychologically Skilled Interventionist-Activist", presented at Second Inter-American Congress of Criminology, November, 1972.

11. MacDonald, Lloyd, *Preparing a New Police Policy Manual: The Cambridge Experience* (1972) 1.

Finally, the introduction of women into the full range of police duties has important implications for the development of alternate styles in law enforcement. Cultural stereotypes and socialization patterns define women as "humanizing" forces who are empathetic, service-oriented, and inclined to settle issues verbally rather than physically. This is almost a direct opposite of the masculine stereotype of which military structures are the ultimate manifestation (e. g., the association with war, aggression, force, action, toughness, detachedness).[12]

PARTICIPATIVE MANAGEMENT

While all of the aforementioned factors are indicators of modifications in the para-military foundations of police organizations, it appears that a new over-all management philosophy is emerging. The philosophy, participative management, has long existed in the private sector. Generally defined, it is a method of improving services by utilizing the abilities, experience, and talents of *all* personnel levels by soliciting their inputs and permitting decision-making at the lowest possible level. The Theory Y of motivation, which is its underpinning, manifests itself in a "fluid, non-hierarchical structure, wide-scale participation in decision-making, situational leadership, goal-oriented management, leadership oriented to helping rather than controlling the individual."[13] In a word, the structure is very much the antithesis of, though not necessarily incompatible with, a military form of organization.[14] Some have argued that Theory Y has come to police departments.

The key to this development in New York City is the attempt to decentralize authority, accountability, and input to the level of sergeant and police officer. Structurally, this attempt manifests itself in four major media: team policing, functional management, management conferences, and peer panels.

Team policing has its origins in the Detroit and Syracuse police departments. It is a model in which officers and supervisors operate as a team in which they work the same charts, use conference techniques to secure team-wide input into operational decisions, assign responsibility, and permit flexibility in the exercise of that responsibility. In New York City, Neighborhood Police Team members are gen-

---

12. See Milton, Catherine and Laura Crites, "Women in Law Enforcement", *Management Information Service* (International City Management Association), September 1973, Vol. 5, No. 9. Sandler, Georgette and Ellen Mintz, "Policemen, Policewomen and the Masculine Ethic", presented at annual meetings of the New York State Psychological Association, New York City, April 1973.

13. Berkley, George, "Theory Y Comes to the Police," presented to annual convention of the American Society for Public Administrators, April 2, 1973, Los Angeles, California, 1–2.

14. Footnote 13, and Footnote 4, 29.

erally permitted greater flexibility than other officers and supervisors, thereby reducing the role of rules and regulations. In theory, at
least, they are supposed to make their own decisions. The teams
stress personal development for members and interaction with the
community for more effective crime control.[15] The operations of the
teams have been uneven, but for those defined as successful, crime
rates have dropped and community relations appear to have improved.

The expansion of team policing principles to precinct-wide practice is found in the functional management concept once implemented,
but now abandoned, in many New York precincts.[16] This concept allo-
cates fixed resources to the precinct manager, who uses them as he
sees fit. From there, authority is further decentralized on a division
of labor basis. That is, the precinct is organized in terms of the
functions it must perform. Within these functions, responsibility is
fixed on a geographical and temporal basis.

A third vehicle for participative management is the establishing
of management retreat conference programs in the New York City
Police Department. In this program, participants selected from all
ranks in the department meet for several days, to "think-tank" solutions to problems of importance to the department's administrators.
This program reduces the gap between headquarters and the field in
several ways. First, it gives members direct access to top command.
In this way, policy inputs and other communications move upward in
the hierarchy, thereby reducing the insulation of top command from
"what's really going on" in the field. Similarly, top command has an
opportunity to directly disseminate policy downwards without the
distortions that occur as it passes through the chain of command.
An added payoff exists because this channel cuts down some of the
arbitrariness associated with top command. This is because it is now
given the opportunity to dispel rumors and explain the rationales for
management decision. It is important to note that in this setting, unlike the military model, informality and dispensing with ranks are
stressed.

A fourth important vehicle for participative management is the
utilization of the peer group. Based on a model developed in the
Oakland, California Police Department, New York City has attempted to develop various kinds of peer panels. While the attempts have
been hampered by legal and labor problems, some panels have nonetheless been developed. Among these are: action review panels, in
which peers locate and retrain violence-prone officers; safety review

15. Footnote 13. Also, Murphy, Patrick, "The Beat Commander", *Police
Chief* (May 1970).

16. Bayer, William, "Functional Management", Conference paper NYCPD
(May 1974).

panels, which do the same for accident-prone officers; precinct advisory councils, which assist precinct managers with local problems; and panels that provide peer input into selection of field training officers and awarding of extra compensation.[17]

In all fairness, it must be pointed out that all of the above procedures are as yet unrefined and have often run into severe logistical, political and union problems. Nonetheless, they do provide rudimentary models for dealing with some of the problems of para-military organizations. It is hoped that by modifying some of the internal and external relationships of police departments, these relationships can become more responsive to the needs of the citizens they serve.

Ultimately, however, the military structure rests upon the rigid rank hierarchy and the ingrained self-image of the organization and its members as crime fighters. The effect can be modified by programs such as those that have been mentioned. However, a rational transition to becoming a full service agency functioning in cooperation with its community cannot occur without significant modifications in the internal structure of the organization. The elimination of ranks, the actual decentralization of authority, and a reorientation of the police image to one of social service officer are all prerequisites to significant alteration of the style and value system of any police agency.

SOCIAL PSYCHOLOGICAL CONTRIBUTIONS TO THE MANAGEMENT OF LAW ENFORCEMENT AGENCIES * †

To what set of conditions can such a thing as criminal behavior among police be attributed? Are poor management practices, working conditions, and low morale related to this management problem in law enforcement agencies? How can the performance and over all effectiveness of police be improved? While public concern for reform in time of trouble is quick to be reflected in the press, few references to actual programs of workable reform also appear at such times. It has, therefore, usually been easier for many people to criti-

---

17. The Action Review Panels for Oakland were developed by Hans Toch of S.U.N.Y. Albany, who also consulted in New York City's efforts. For details of their operations see his book, *Men of Violence*.

* Based on a recent symposium held at the American Psychological Association annual meeting, Philadelphia,

1963. The author wishes to thank Dr. Arnold Tannenbaum for his contribution to this paper.

† Source: Reprinted by special permission of the Journal of Criminal Law, Criminology and Police Science, Copyright © 1965 by Northwestern University School of Law, Vol. 56, No. 3.

cize than to find workable solutions to this and other problems of police management.

In what other directions may one expect to find possible answers to this complex problem and related problems of management and administration? We can be reasonably sure now that the solution, if one exists at all, is not just a matter of better personnel selection, weeding out undesirable members of a department, increasing salaries, and more discipline. In part, a management philosophy is at fault. A case can be made that all kinds of delinquent behavior, large or small, ranging from theft to the simplest possible broken regulation, goes well beyond these factors to include all that falls under the heading of organizational mismanagement of human resources. This is fostered in part by neglect of important psychological needs which all people have. It is also fostered by a lack of awareness of the important principle that a balance is necessary between organizational needs and individual needs.

THE INDIVIDUAL IN THE ORGANIZATION

A traditional aspect of police management is that it occurs within a quasi-military organization. The military model is very old and is easily recognized by its reliance upon direct hierarchical control, rigid superior-supervisor relationships in an ascending order from the lowest ranks to the highest which, in contrast to the lower ranks, contain most of the decision making power.

The principle of span of control tends to be inflexibly applied. Supervision is usually based upon a pattern of downward communication from higher ranking members to lower ranking members, with less opportunity for lower ranking members to communicate upward other than to acknowledge receiving an order to carry out. Such organizations seem to have a permanent moratorium on expression of grievances from below, and an absence of a flexible mechanism by which communication from below to higher positions can occur with the ease and frequency often needed. In another sense, grievances in such organizations can be said to exist because of the absence of appropriate informal adjudication procedures between superiors and subordinates.

A familiar argument is, or course, that the war against crime requires a military type of organization geared to the resolution of the unending crises precipitated by criminal behavior. It has often been argued that is a "war." This point of view is familiar and popular, but not easily defended by existing facts or the historical record. For the concerted attack on crime has *not* been wholly successful in spite of the widespread use of the military model of police organization. One can safely ask, if it is so good then why has it not worked better?

What may be missing in this model? How does that which is missing relate to such important things as morale, productive effort in pursuit of a public good, and general organizational effectiveness? Is there an alternative model for a law enforcement organization which might increase effectively the level of performance of police, reduce delinquency among them, and perhaps even increase measurably the so-called "war" on criminal behavior? A tentative answer to these questions is suggested by an emerging theory of organizational behavior based upon recent social psychological research. The theory is not yet complete; but some important elements in it are now known, and others are emerging as research continues. Our argument here will be by analogy the strength of which rests on the fact that all organizations are similar in structure although different in purpose. They are, for example, all inhabited by people, possess identifiable structures such as goals, communication networks, reward systems, and a distribution of social power and control which affects in a profound way the behavior of all members of the organization. Certain extrapolations are here made from research in the neighboring field of business and industry to the field of police work.[1] While these extrapolations are not intended as a substitute for actual empirical studies of police organizations which eventually must be done, they will allow us to make several important points clearly and forcefully. Also it will be apparent that many of these points are not new by any means. Nor were they invented in the twentieth century.

INSIGHTS FROM OTHER FIELDS

Every social organization, be it a business or industrial organization, government agency, or other, has a problem of internal law enforcement. We infrequently talk about such law enforcement with respect to organizations, and usually view it as enforcing rules and regulations, and official standards or norms. Whatever words we choose to use to describe this phenomenon we have to agree that some effort is required on the part of any organization to assure that too many rules are not broken, and that minimum standards are maintained. It is always revealing that some organizations seem to be more successful in this process than others. What role should the organization play in this process?

It is now common knowledge that achieving "law enforcement" in organizations of any kind, or for that matter in society as a whole, is partly a problem of motivation and of identification with organizational goals on the part of members of social groups within an organ-

1. While the research findings used as examples in this paper were taken from one source, they are confirmed by other publications examples of which are cited in the bibliography in this paper.

ization or society.   Motivation is always involved because the individual has to see law-abiding behavior as a source of some material or psychological reward.   There has to be something in it for him or it will not work.   It cannot be all give and no take.   Identification is involved because people need to connect their personal goals with the goals held by the organization, and they can do this best when they can see their way clear to achieving the rewards available for good behavior in the organization.   A person's self-image, or self-concept, reflects his own norms and values about that which is either good or bad in life, and these need to be lined up with the values which exist within the organization and are part of its rules for living in it.   If the relationship between the individual and organization is such that only a few values held by the individual match those values held by the organization, then little incentive for "good" behavior will exist, and conflict between the individual and the organization will result. When organizational norms and personal norms are far apart there is a significantly greater chance that the person will engage in behavior that will be seen by agents and caretakers of the organization, its "police" so to speak, as "misbehavior."   It is not incorrect, or fruitless, occasionally to ask, therefore, when a law is broken whose law is it that is being broken?   The organization's law or the individual's law?

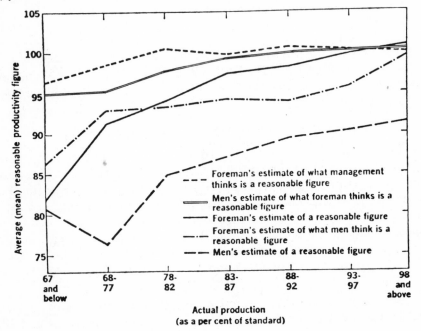

Figure 1

Productivity increases when foremen and men agree in estimates of reasonable productivity.   (From *New Patterns of Management* by Rensis Likert.   Copyright 1961.   McGraw-Hill Book Company.   Figure used by permission.)   [B7267]

We are now beginning to learn that it is a good idea for managers in any organization to ask: Do the personal goals of the members of the organization have any relation to the goals established by the organization as its formal rules of operation? This is a problem area where recent social psychological research on organizations can be helpful in pointing out the importance of understanding the needs of both the individual and the organization.

Let us take an employee's ideas about reasonable productivity as an example. If both the employee and the company man, a foreman, see eye to eye about production rates, then ideally we might expect conflictless effort on the part of the employee and also acceptable productivity by company standards. In other words, the employee's needs under these "ideal" conditions are in line with management's needs as conveyed by the foreman. Is this what actually tends to happen in real organizations? Results from recent research say yes. Look, for example, at figure 1 which summarizes findings in a large manufacturing company.

Notice that the actual production of employees increases when foreman and men agree about that form of activity which constitutes reasonable output, or productivity. As the estimates converge at the right hand side of the figure actual production is higher than before when they disagreed in their estimates (left hand side of figure). It is a short step in thought from the shop floor to the police department where, instead of foremen and men, there are patrolmen, sergeants, lieutenants, and captains interacting with one another. Do the principles illustrated in figure 1 have any application to police management? A fair answer is that they probably do apply just as they applied on the shop floor.

INFLUENCE AND CONTROL OVER OTHERS

Like all military forces (and some industrial units), many police organizations have power, authority, influence, status, prestige, privilege, and personal rights distributed throughout the organization in a particular way. In many police departments, there is more of all of these things at the top than at the bottom of the organization. So we have the ironic and possibly significant fact that the policeman who symbolizes power and authority to the man on the street may share little of this in his own department. Little, if any, systematic research has been done on this subject in police departments.

But surveys in other organizations indicate that rank and file members are often psychologically deprived persons who would like to have more say in what goes on in their organizations. When they do receive such influence upward they seem to be more satisfied with their jobs, with their supervisors and managers, and they are more likely to express an identification with their organization and feel a sense of responsibility for meeting organizational goals. Actual cases can be documented in which control and influence were more evenly distributed throughout the organization that substantiate such results. What happens in such organizations when employees throughout the organization are allowed more say about their own specific work and related decisions? An answer is suggested by the research findings in figure 2.

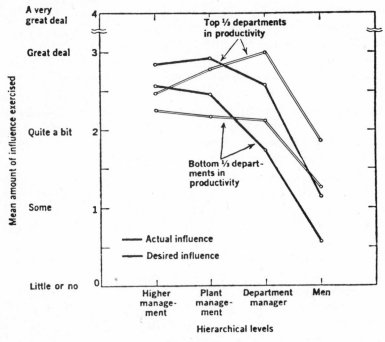

Figure 2

Relation of department productivity to average amount of influence and control actually exercised by different hierarchical levels and to average amount of desired influence (as seen by nonsupervisory employees). (From *New Patterns of Management* by Rensis Likert. Copyright 1961. McGraw-Hill Book Company. Figure used by permission.)   [B7270]

The slope of the curves in figure 2 reflect the amount of influence exercised by the different ranks in the organization starting with top management at the left and ending with the men at the right of the figure in descending order of their organizational responsibility. Notice especially the curve for the departments which are in the top one-third in productivity. Contrast this curve with the one for the departments in the bottom one-third in their productivity. The most productive departments seem to have a greater distribution of influence and control among employees.

An important point in this set of findings is that even though the control and influence are more evenly distributed with respect to some activities, the status hierarchy *still remains intact* and is actually strengthened because more influence on the part of employees leads to greater identification with the organization. It is interesting to note that the curve for desired influence is *not* "revolutionary" in the sense that employees want complete control. There will always be a need for a division of labor and responsibility in any organization. There seems to be no radical departure from reasonable expectations, and the men do not expect, or even want, to do management's job. This suggests that a "fair share" principle seems to be at work. People want as much freedom as possible to do their *own* jobs and not necessarily their bosses' jobs. Paradoxically then, giving up control over others does not always mean losing control over them in the organization.

These points are clarified further by a closer look at supervision in organizations. Supervision is an activity which reflects closely the way in which control and influence are distributed. Supervision is, after all, another form of police activity in the broadest sense of the term. As experienced supervisors know, there are many ways to "police" the work of an employee. An alternative to close supervision is shown in figure 3. When close supervision is the rule, and employees are "over-policed" a result is usually lowered productivity. Higher productivity is associated with general supervision in which the employee receives appropriate guidance and support, but is not closely supervised by a superior in the fashion common in military organizations. Under the latter form of supervision there is maximum freedom to perform a job within the broad limits of a personal style and job requirements.

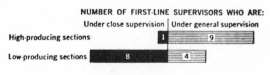

Figure 3

Low-production section heads are more closely supervised than high-production section heads. (From *New Patterns of Management* by Rensis Likert. Copyright 1961. McGraw-Hill Book Company. Figure used by permission.)

[B7268]

Personal recognition for work done and attention are two cardinal requirements in good supervision. There must be recognition of important human needs in others, and more than a token kind of attention has to be paid to these needs in order to produce in others an incentive to work well. When emphasis in supervision is only upon work activities to the neglect of important human needs on the job then a result is often to create a job environment in which starvation of such needs invariably leads to lowered personal effectiveness and productivity. A balance between production needs of the organization and the human needs of employees seems to lead directly to increases in on-the-job effectiveness and productivity whether the productivity is creating some material object or performing a service for another person or group as in police work. The results of several studies in figure 3 make a telling point about on-the-job supervision which leads to higher productivity. The studies show that "Employee-centered" supervisors tend to be higher producers than "job-centered" supervisors.

ALTERNATIVES

The weathered veteran of police work might well ask by what alternative form of organization are police administrators to achieve the kinds of improvements which the research findings cited above suggest are possible? If the traditional pattern in figure 4 with its predominately downward and isolating pattern of communication is not the best available model then what form of organization is?

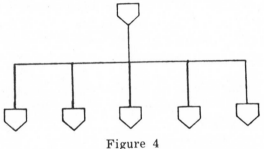

Figure 4

A traditional organization chart

[B7269]

An organizational structure which allows meaningful and constant exchanges between superiors and subordinates is part of the answer. Essentially, all ranks require an opportunity to influence one another about their individual functions within the organization. Verbal commitment is, however, usually not enough. Administrators need to go to greater lengths to insure that the organization has mechanisms by which a variety of important psychological conditions are met in daily routine activities, not just when crises occur and immediate mobilization of effort required "to put out fires" created by poor management of human affairs.

Likert [2] has used the term "linking pin" function to characterize the supervisor or manager in that form of organization which gives such staff members influence upward and downward to enable them to handle effectively problems which involve their own well being and the well being of their subordinates.   In the overlapping structures of such an organization each hierarchical level has its functioning "linking pin" personnel, usually a supervisor, who are there to insure that channels of communication between levels of the organization remain open and operating continuously.   In this way top men in the organization do not lose touch with the daily needs of subordinates, and avenues are open for upward communication and adjustment about employee needs and job associated problems.   This organizational concept is illustrated in figure 5.

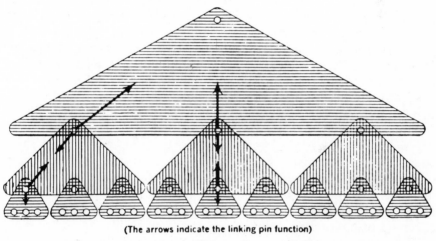

(The arrows indicate the linking pin function)

Figure 5

The "linking pin" organizational pattern.   (From *New Patterns of Management* by Rensis Likert.   Copyright 1961.   McGraw-Hill Book Company.   Figure used by permission.)

[B7271]

An important functional aspect of this kind of organizational pattern is the system of interaction and influence which operates through formal groups in the organization called organizational families.   Each "family" is made up of a supervisor and his subordinates. A function of the groups is to meet regularly to talk fully and freely about work problems, and then for the supervisor to communicate on-going problems upward to higher levels so that remedial action and adjustment can take place at the appropriate level of decision

2.   R. Likert, New Patterns of Management, McGraw-Hill, New York, 1961.

making in the organization. Downward communication and action can then take place rapidly and on the basis of full information.

Informal groups will always exist among employees. It is often hard for an administrator to tell if such groups are beneficial or harmful to the organization. As some police departments have learned too late, informal groups which exist among rank and file members of the police organization who are dissatisfied and unhappy may lead to criminal behavior. Under the open system of communication this form of behavior is less likely to occur, and if it does tend to arise, corrective measures can be taken early before real damage is done. It is not surprising under the older form of organization to learn that the chief of police is often the last person to learn about important specific problems at the patrolmen's level of the organization. Just an improvement in upward and downward communication would be of considerable assistance to the police chief and to other administrators in a department.

The patrolman on a beat is required to take initiative and to act independently. He is required by his role to do this much more than many other kinds of employees. Few will argue that to perform this role effectively he requires frequent consultation with others in the police department who are guiding its policies and mandates. When, for example, should a foot patrolman use his discretionary powers? Their use is recognized as complex and each new application of them requires special consideration based on the merits of the individual case. Few can argue with the wisdom of providing a law enforcement officer with ample opportunity to discuss his problems of interpreting his role in such cases. Apprehending a criminal in a clearly defined act of aggression against society is certainly difficult and often perilous, but the actual decision to act against the criminal may not be hard to make. The crime is underway and the law enforcement officer intervenes to stop it. But the decision to act officially in a case where a crime is *suspect,* but where the patrolman is *uncertain* about the guilty party is of another order of complexity. Here the task becomes much more complex requiring even closer coordination with other officials in a department.

This example brings up an underlying problem in all organizations which can be stated as a continuing need on the part of the organization to reduce role conflict in job performance. To the extent that role conflict is acted out by policemen in the conduct of important police activities one can then be reasonably certain that supervisory and other organizational problems will also tend to increase. Conflict and uncertainty about one's role as a policeman would appear to be especially serious because of the important place occupied by the law enforcement function in society.

SUMMARY

To remain effective public servants law enforcement personnel may require a re-evaluation of the organizations in which they are working members. This paper has discussed an alternative approach to police management in contrast to the traditional military organizational model which has been the rule in police departments. While the manifest goals of organizations will vary widely, their internal structure and the patterns of human relations in them have many things in common. In this paper research findings from business and industry have been discussed in terms of police management. This social psychological research on organizations suggests that many facets of police management can be improved leading to increased on-the-job effectiveness, improved communication, and better morale among members of the police organization. The job of achieving these things is not easy, but the return of investments in these newer approaches in other organizations suggests that police organizations will benefit from them also.

REFERENCES

Argyris, C. Personalty and Organization. New York: Harper, 1957.

Coch, L., and French, J. R. P., Jr. Overcoming resistance to change. Human Relat., 1(4):512–532 (1948).

Haire, M. (Ed.) Modern Organization Theory. New York: Wiley, 1959.

Herzberg, F., Mausner, B., and Snyderman, B. The Motivation to Work. (2d ed.) New York: Wiley, 1959.

Kahn, R. L. Productivity and job satisfaction. Personnel Psychol., 13(3):-275–278 (1960).

Kahn, R. L. and Katz, D. Leadership practices in relation to productivity and morale. In D. Cartwright and A. Zander (Eds.), Group Dynamics: Research and Theory. (2d ed.) Evanston, Ill.: Row, Peterson, 1960. Pp. 554–571.

Likert, R. New Patterns of Management. New York: McGraw-Hill, 1961.

McGregor, D. Human Side of Enterprise. New York: McGraw-Hill, 1960.

Morse, N. and Reimer, E. The experimental change of a major organizational variable. J. Abnorm. Soc. Psychol., 52:120–129 (1956).

Morse, N. and Weiss, R. The function and meaning of work and the job. Amer. Soc. Rev. 20(2):191–198 (1955).

Patchen, M. Absence and employee feelings about fair treatment. Personnel Psychol., 13(3):349–360 (1960).

Ross, I. C. and Zander, A. Need satisfactions and employee turnover. Personnel Psychol., 10(3):327–338 (1957).

Tannenbaum, A. and Georgopolous, B. S. The distribution of control in formal organizations. Soc. Forces, *36*(1):44–50 (1957).

White, R. and Lippitt, R. Autocracy and Democracy: An Experimental Inquiry. New York: Harper, 1960.

PARTICIPATION IN POLICING *

We have presently reached the point of development in a competitive society where continuous change is the norm.[1] A paradoxical situation has resulted from this continuous transition in that we must enact and effectively enforce more controls as the population increases, while, simultaneously, the American people demand more individual freedoms. Since increased power of individuals has been exemplified through initiation of special interest groups, additional segments of society are able to induce influence in government, causing the role of public servants to become increasingly difficult.

Constant change is present in areas other than the citizen's role with government. Technologically, we continue to surpass past accomplishments at an alarming pace. Freeways are obsolete, automobiles are a burden, and moon trips are passé—all in the era in which they were initiated. In addition, our population continues to shift and redistribute itself.[2]

Police agencies are directly affected by change. The new demands of citizens are mandates to which police must respond. For the past ten years, police have been faced with continuous adjustments to maintain a continuity with the public norms.

Legally, police procedures have been altered to ensure increased protection of individual rights. Police administrators who have experienced dynamic changes in search and seizure or interrogation and reporting methods are finding their organizations shocked by new requirements. Many agencies have never accepted the movement and continue to resist desires of the people they serve.

Socially, police are faced with demands of service from a diversified society. Never before have communities required attention to their needs as they are now doing. The agency which is responsive to local needs and, at the same time, is geared for continuing change is unusual.

Internally, police departments are encountering additional problems that are related to individual differences. Some Americans now

---

* Reproduced from *The Police Chief* magazine, December, 1974 issue, with permission of the International Association of Chiefs of Police.

1. W. Bennis, *Changing Organizations* (1966), p. 19 (hereafter cited as W. Bennis).

2. C. Reich, *The Greening of America* (1971), or A. Toffler, *Future Shock* (1972).

require jobs which offer more than a weekly paycheck. They respond to positions of responsibility and growth rather than security.

As administrators face changes internally and externally, pressure to alter traditional organizational structures increases. The standard organization approach has been the law enforcement model for many years. Before a change in this model takes place, a review of the police function is necessary. Along with responsiveness to community needs and employee desires, police must retain their roles as our primary emergency unit and crime-fighting force.

To cope with the changing society and the changing employee, participatory management models have been suggested. While these experiments in police management have served to modify antiquated systems, they have not supplied complete answers to a complex situation. In order to assess what management model works best in practice, it is essential to evaluate the impact of traditional and participatory models as they interact with community needs, personnel demands, and crime control functions.

TRADITIONAL POLICE ORGANIZATION

Standard police agencies mimic the following principles of organization:[3]

1. Sound and clear-cut allocation of responsibilities.
2. Equitable distribution of work loads among elements and individuals.
3. Clear and unequivocal lines of authority.
4. Authority adequate to discharge assigned responsibilities.
5. Reasonable spans of control for administrative, command, and supervision officers.
6. Unity of command.
7. Coordination of effort.
8. Administrative control.

These principles closely follow Frederick Taylor's "Principles of Scientific Management."[4] Taylor's innovative approach originated in the late 1880s when organizations were first required to consider problems of inefficiency. The employee's status during this period was considered excellent if it included longevity and security. The principles were easily adapted to a police structure since a constant

3. E. Nelson and C. Lovell, *Developing Correctional Administrators* (1969), p. 10.

4. Frederick Taylor, *Principles of Scientific Management* (New York, Norton, 1967).

concern of law enforcers is efficiency. The efficiency requirements are encompassed in two basic categories:

1. Police agencies are usually the largest departments of city governments and they receive intense financial scrutiny.

2. Police departments will never have enough men or equipment to control crime completely so an efficient course of action is necessary.

George Eastman supports the efficiency approach in his statement: "Organization on the basis of purpose provides for consolidation and centralization on a functional basis for better direction and control and increased efficiency and economy."[5]

When the organization/crime control interface is considered, the principles of organization appear to be excellent guidelines. The result is a hierarchical structure which is capable of transmitting policy and orders downward to well-controlled employees. Clear and unequivocal lines of authority, unity of command, and administrative controls all take part in forming the following police organizational outline:

ADMINISTRATION

SUPERVISORS

OFFICERS

Downward flow of communication and control

The structure is ideal for handling emergency situations and ensuring efficiency in the criminal enforcement pattern. Every officer has a supervisor who is able to direct his actions. Each situation is within administrative reach of an authority-designated official. The officer's only concern is to perform his appointed tasks in a satisfactory manner. As reacting to emergency or crime control requests demands cooperative execution by all individuals involved, the far-reaching control by supervisors in the traditional model predicts successful task completions.

A basic drawback of the traditional model is its rigidity in responding to reactions of the organization/community interface. Police departments often display this rigidity through increases in citizen complaints. The downward flow of information, controlled by the hierarchy of command, negates the organization's ability to receive community feedback from patrolmen who are in the best position to monitor community feelings.

Trist[6] calls the traditional structure a "closed" system. He states that "thinking in terms of a 'closed' system . . . is to regard

5. G. Eastman, Supra note 2, p. 21.

6. E. Trist, "On Socio-Technical Systems," in *The Planning of Change*, W. Bennis, K. Benne, and R. Chin, eds. (1969), pp. 269–82 (hereafter known as E. Trist).

the enterprise as sufficiently independent to allow most of its problems to be analyzed with reference to its internal structure and without reference to its external environment."[7]

Police agencies must realize that they are directly connected to community needs if they are to respond properly to changing norms. An unresponsive police department often reflects an unhappy community. A rigid status is in direct conflict with the proposal that law enforcement agencies must be structured in a manner as to cope with our continually changing society.

We will discover additional problems with the traditional structure when we examine the organization/employee interface. Policemen have displayed unusual abilities in accepting salient responsibilities. Among their ranks exist men requiring satisfaction of high-order human needs.

Argyris, Maslow, and McGregor recognize these needs in their development of motivational assumptions which have been labeled "self-actualizing man." [8] Maslow theorizes that,[9]

> Man's needs are arranged in a hierarchy—needs for safety or survival, social needs, needs for self-esteem, needs for autonomy, and needs for self-actualization. . . . As the lower-level needs (safety and social, etc.) are satisfied, man becomes interested in satisfying the higher-order needs, autonomy and self-actualization. . . . The problem, according to this view, is that while man ultimately seeks independence and self-actualization, the organizational context places him in a position of depending and constraint which prevents him from satisfying these high-order needs.

The traditional style of management was devised at a time when the American people were concerned primarily about their lower-level needs. The system, based on monetary rewards in exchange for work accomplished, satisfied the basic and safety needs of physical comfort, available money, good working conditions, and security. As Maslow has predicted, the American people have outgrown the limits of the "scientific management" approach, and they now demand independence and autonomy rewards from their employment. The police officer may be in this position as increased salaries, more benefits, and higher education levels will satisfy the lower-level needs. This would indicate that he is ready to take the responsibility of assuming a more independent position in the operation of police services.

7. Ibid., p. 270.   9. Ibid., p. 64.

8. P. Lawrence and J. Lorsch, *Developing Organizations: Diagnosis and Action* (1969), p. 63.

The traditional police department, through its organizational behavior and structure, has demonstrated that the higher-order needs have not been recognized. In the traditional pyramid, everyone's assignment is under observation of a higher authority. Sergeants, lieutenants, and captains are all available to maintain this direct control. When administrators and supervisors assume that patrolmen have little ambition, they attempt to ensure efficiency through the use of strictly enforced internal controls. The chief, in his paternal role of manager, assumes full responsibility for his employee's decisions and, thusly, justifies the direct control procedures.

This interface shows that the organization is working against itself through its inevitable alienation of employees. It appears that gains the traditional police organization model realizes from efficiency in crime control are neutralized through losses in the community and employee interfaces.

POLICE AND PARTICIPATORY MANAGEMENT

A basic movement from the traditional police organization structure is exemplified by the democratic model as proposed by John Angell.[10]

A brief summary of this model is as follows:

1. The decision-making source is decentralized. The patrolman works in policy-making and problem-solving teams and, thusly, is the actual decision maker of his organization.

2. The patrolman is viewed as a "generalist." He is responsible for completing criminal investigations from start to finish. The police specialist still exists, but he is relegated to being solely a support for the patrolman.

3. The patrolman is able to advance himself while retaining his basic position. No longer is promotion or advancement based upon the hierarchical structure.

4. Heavy emphasis is placed on the patrolman's contact with the community. He is viewed as the source of information which reflects community attitudes and needs.

This model changes the flow of communications from a one-way downward flow to a two-way exchange of information between administration and employee structure and allows coordination of information concerning employees, community, and crime. (See *Figure 1*.)

In the proposed model, the individual officer is allowed freedom to experience self-satisfying tasks through self-direction. The team

10. J. Angell, "Toward an Alternative to the Classical Police Organization Arrangements: A Democratic Model," *Criminology*, Vol. 9.

is also a natural arrangement for subordinate-superior collaboration. This joint decision-making process develops the employee's creativity and intellectual potentialities while committing him to the goals of the organization.

McGregor,[11] in his Theory "Y" concept, emphasizes that the employee, when motivated by his independence needs, will operate by the concepts of self-control, collaboration and integration. Theory "Y" emphasizes the need for organization and product with which he works. The theory does not state that people need to be secure in their jobs but that they be allowed to have an important part in the organization.

McGregor reasons that "the manager also cannot provide people with a sense of achievement, or with knowledge or with prestige, but he can provide the opportunities for them to obtain these satisfactions through efforts directed toward organizational goals."[12] He places the responsibility for inducing employee's motivation directly on the management. "If employees are lazy, indifferent, unwilling to take responsibility, intransigent, uncreative, uncooperative, Theory "Y" implies that the causes lie in management's methods of organization and control."[13]

By allowing the team officer to assume the function of the specialists, the employee is further integrated into the organization and he has a direct influence on the finished product. From his studies of coal miners, Trist has denounced the overemphasis on specialists. He states, "The only justification for a rigid division of labor is a technology which demands specialized nonsubstitute skills and which is, moreover, sufficiently superior as a technology, to offset the losses due to rigidity."[14]

This theory recognizes the value of the specialists' expertise but places their importance in the proper context. By reversing the supportive roles between specialists and patrolman, the team officer regains a prestige and status equal to his responsibility in the organization.

Considering these well-based theories, the democratic model has recognized and challenged the salient problems inherent in the organization/employee interface. Through this proposal, the employee should find satisfaction of his needs in the same goals as those

11. D. McGregor, "Theory X and Theory Y," *Organizational Behavior and the Practice of Management,* D. Hampton, C. Summer, and R. Webber, eds. (1968), p. 132 (hereafter cited as D. McGregor).

12. D. McGregor, *Leadership and Motivation* (1966), p. 45.

13. D. McGregor, Supra note 10, p. 137.

14. E. Trist, Supra note 5, p. 276.

of the organization. Employee and organization are in contact in a cooperative effort instead of a conflict situation.

Another basis of the team model is supported by Trist's open system concept. In the open system, the organization maintains a constant interaction with the environment. To gain this advantage, the organizational structure must be flexible to change and must keep an open communication flow.

Trist reports that organizations of this type "manage to achieve a steady state while doing work. They achieve a quasi-stationary, equilibrium in which the enterprise as a whole remains constant, with a continuous 'throughout,' despite a considerable range of external changes."[15] The teams are in the position of monitoring the community's needs through their daily interactions and their planned evaluations. The participatory approach of the team-management collaboration effort ensures that the flow of information is properly and accurately directed to and from the organization. This communicative ability allows the organization to maintain its "steady state" with the environment without sacrificing its operating effectiveness.

In regards to the manager's role in the organization/community interface, Trist reports, "If the vision of the task is locked up in a single man or is the subject of dissension in top management, it will be subject to great risk of distortion and susceptible to violent fluctuations."[16]

The outline of the organization/community interface is obvious. There must be a method of continually testing and examining community attitudes and needs. The democratic model offers this opportunity by allowing two-way communications. If the police manager accepts this mandate, he must also alter his approach of organizational leadership. Thus, a change in leadership style could solve problems involving organization/community interface resulting from rigidity of the traditional structure. Similarly, it progressively approaches the problems of the organization/employee interface.

The organization/crime control interface is improved through the following occurrences:

1. The patrolman has more interest in completing his goal, so more crimes should be solved.

2. The community has a better concept of policemen so there is more community-police cooperation. Crime prevention is a factor of this cooperation.

3. The specialists of the department are utilized more efficiently.

15. Ibid., p. 271.   16. Ibid., p. 281.

4. Departments are able cooperatively to utilize crime-specific teams to attack increased crime incidents.

These proposals are exemplified by the Holyoke Police Department team policing project[17] in which there were numerous incidents of community assistance in crime control. Effects of crime-specific teams are positively examined in the Syracuse team policing research reports.[18]

Since the democratic model successfully deals with the three basic interfaces of a police department, it makes it worthwhile to fully explore utilization of the model in our changing society.

Experiments and critics of the police democratic model, however, report many problems and failures. The following list is an example of hazards facing participation projects:

1. Community interaction projects develop into the function of a few "community-relations" officers. This eliminates necessary contacts between regular street officers and their area residents on an informal basis.

2. Special team policing units respond to experiments positively because of a "Hawthorne effect." (They make the project a success because they are part of an experiment.)

3. Because of time and financial demands, team meetings are not conducted. This failure to complete the democratic process destroys group dynamics and eliminates coordination efforts necessary to complete the crime control function.

4. Teams are controlled by supervisors in the traditional manner. Many departments view the team proposal as being solely a crime-specific unit. They tend to ignore the participatory management benefits of a police unit.

GROUP DYNAMICS AND POLICING

Our concern has been society's rapid and continuous change. Innovative police organization must reflect an adaptation to this phenomenon. The democratic model is such a solution, but only if it includes patrolman participation in departmental decision making. Attempts and experimentations with participatory management under the guise of team policing, unit-beat policing, or crime-specific policing have often failed to recognize the importance of patrolman interaction in group processes.

17. J. Angell, R. Gavin, and M. O'Neil, *Evaluation Report on the Model Cities Team Policing Unit of the Holyoke Police Department* (1972), pp. 1–100.

18. J. Elliot and T. Sardino, *The Crime Control Team, An Element of an Offensively Deployed Municipal Police Department*, General Electric Corporating Technical Information Series (1970), pp. 1–166.

Toch [19] has demonstrated that group problem solving by police officers is a potent influence in increasing self-esteem and producing salient solutions to police problems. Officers have displayed a desire to formulate innovative answers to situations that police management has been unable to solve through its traditional methods.

Several researchers, Elton Mayo[20] being a prime example, have emphasized the importance of including employees in decision making in their work environment. They have succeeded in proving that workers participating in group problem solving become committed to the decisions of the group. Along with a group commitment to formulate goals is successful completion of the goals.

To ensure that a true participation atmosphere exists for the policeman group, the supervisor-subordinate relationship must be equalized. Bennis[21] lists the requirements necessary for an effective democratic approach:

1. Full and free communication, regardless of rank and power.

2. A reliance on consensus, rather than on coercion or compromise, to manage conflict.

3. The idea that influence is based on technical knowledge rather than the vagaries of personal whims or prerogatives of power.

4. An atmosphere that permits and even encourages emotional expression as well as task-oriented acts.

5. A basically human bias, one which accepts the inevitability of conflict between the organization and the individual but which is willing to cope with and mediate this conflict on rational grounds.

SUMMARY

Our initial concern was to explore answers to problems of continuous change. Police departments are directly involved with several dimensions of organization change. Employees, functions, and the community are salient areas to be considered before successful solutions may be formulated. The major premise is that the traditional structure should be altered to allow proper change analysis to take place. The democratic model or participatory management model has been suggested as an organizational design that will solve these new problems.

19. H. Toch, "Change Through Participation (and vice versa)," *Journal of Research in Crime and Delinquency* (1970), p. 199.

20. F. Nigro, *Modern Public Administration* (1970).

21. W. Bennis, Supra note 1, p. 19.

In the proposed model, the employee's position is improved through recognition of his basic needs and motivations. The organization, via a democratic model, allows employees direct participation in important decision making. This style of leadership not only raises the individual's self-esteem and importance, but it also commits the employee to organizational goals.

Crime control functions and service functions are improved through the democratic model as employees have a greater stake in successful completion of company objectives. These functions are facilitated in two ways. First, officers are able to finish activities they previously initiated. This ensures an interest in successful task completion. Secondly, officers involved in goal setting and decision making become personally responsible for their successful completion.

The salient attribute of a democratic model is its ability to allow two-way communication within the organization. By opening communication between patrolmen and administrators, new changes in community attitudes will be tested. The patrolman is literally the "man on the street," and he has direct daily contact with community members. A responsible, hard-working officer should be able to judge community needs on a continuous basis. Participation in the management scheme by officers should open communication channels between top administrators and the public to be served.

As the approach considers the areas of employees, functions, and environment as being equally important to the health of the organization, a considered change in organizational style is necessary if the rigidity of the traditional model is to be overcome.

Although a democratic model may be difficult to implement, its potential should be fully explored. One vexing question must be faced: Has the traditional, bureaucratic model of policing served the needs of the public? For in the final analysis, this is the reason for government and the police.

TOWARD AN ALTERNATIVE TO THE CLASSIC POLICE ORGANIZATIONAL ARRANGEMENTS *

Theories are developed to facilitate understanding; however, social science theories, unlike theories of the physical sciences, are complicated by the fact that their subjects think and act. Human decisions and actions have a multiplicity of causations including past experiences, influences of culture, and expectations about the future.

* Source: "Toward an Alternative to the Classic Police Organizational Arrangements: A Democratic Model," by John E. Angell is reprinted from *Criminology* Vol. 9, Nos. 2 & 3 (Aug./Nov. 1971) pp. 185–206 by permission of the Publisher, Sage Publications, Inc.

Consequently, social theories are particularistic. Their usefulness is restricted by specific values and perceptions that determine the characteristics of behavioral patterns and rationality.

Social science theory about the organization and management of bureaucracies is no exception; it is also particularistic and must be situationally conditioned. Therefore, since rationality is culturally or normatively determined, conclusions about "proper" or "improper," "right" or "wrong," and "good" or "bad" organizational arrangements cannot be absolute. The values and expectations of the social system within which the organization exists will define the norms and boundaries for organizational arrangements and managerial practices.

The structural model most frequently advocated and utilized in American police endeavors were first implemented in the Anglo-Saxon world by the Metropolitan Police Act, which established the London "bobbies" in 1829. This model follows closely the tenets of the classic organizational theory, which is an ideal-type based on pre-twentieth-century organizations. In spite of the tremendous changes in society, its culture and values, no significant changes have occurred in the approach to police organization and management since 1829. However, just as it took the traumatic realities of Panzer warfare in World War II to cause the United States Army to abandon the horse cavalry and horse-drawn artillery, the inability of the police to deal effectively with the social problems of the past decade has alerted perceptive people to the need for changes in police administration.

CHARACTERISTICS OF THE EXISTING POLICE STRUCTURES

The structures of modern American police organizations are rationalized, hierarchical arrangements that reflect the influence of classic organizational theory as promulgated by Max Weber (Bendix, 1962; Gerth and Mills, 1958: 196–244; Henderson and Parsons, 1947: 329–340). The most salient characteristics of these departments, as with all organizations that are based upon classic theory, are:

1. formal structures are defined by a centralized hierarchy of authority;

2. labor is divided into functional specialties;

3. activities are conducted according to standardized operating procedures;

4. career routes are well established and have a common entry point; promotions are based on impersonal evaluations by superiors;

5. management proceeds through a monocratic system of routinized superior-subordinate relationships;

6. status among employees is directly related to their positions (jobs) and ranks.

These characteristics result in a firmly established, impersonal system in which most of the employees and clients are powerless to initiate changes or arrest the system's motions. While this organizational arrangement has generally been afforded high esteem among prescriptive authors in the police field, questions are increasingly being raised concerning its adequacy (Kimble, 1969; Myren, 1960).

PROBLEMS OF CLASSIC THEORY

Classic Bureaucracies in General

Criticisms of classic bureaucracies in general and police organizations in particular are plentiful (Bennis, 1966). The most common criticisms fall into four categories (Argyris, 1957: 1–24; Bennis and Slater, 1964).

1. *Classic theory and concepts are culture bound.* Weber's normative conclusions about organizations were founded on his observation and studies of early military organizations, the Catholic church, and the Prussian army. Therefore, his theoretical concepts quite naturally reflect the authoritarian biases of such systems.

2. *Classic theory and concepts mandate that attitudes toward employees and clients be inconsistent with the humanistic democratic values of the United States.* Managers in organizations adhering to classic philosophy are expected to view employees and clients of the organization as "cogs" that can be relatively easily replaced. The individual value of each person, a fundamental assumption of American democracy, is foreign to classic organizational concepts.

3. *Classic structured organizations demand and support employees who demonstrate immature personality traits.* Employees of classic organizations are analogous to children in a family—they are expected to obey orders and carry out assignments. This situation is best illustrated by traditionalists among military officers who are fond of telling their enlisted subordinates, "You're not paid to think, you're to do as you're ordered." Employees who do not question, but blindly obey every regulation and order are rewarded, whereas the mature person who raises legitimate questions about the organization and its activities is often ostracized and punished. Such behavior discourages attitudes of inde-

pendence that are characteristic of a mature adult personality.

4. *Classic organizations are unable to cope with environmental changes; therefore, they eventually become obsolete and dysfunctional.* The hierarchical organizational structure and related classic theory power arrangements stifle communications and restrict information about both the internal and external environments of the organization; therefore, they find it difficult to detect and respond to changes. In addition, the emphasis upon routinization of organizational activities creates inflexibility in employee and organizational behavior and reduces the organization's ability to adapt to change.

These criticisms are as relevant to police departments as other bureaucracies. In addition, police departments have specific problems that are peculiar to their operations and can be traced to classic organizational concepts.

Problems Related to Police Bureaucracies

Although many police organizational problems can be related to the basic bureaucratic theory as operationalized by police managers, three of the most significant are appropriate as illustrations. These problems are: (1) the state of police and community relations where well-developed police bureaucracies exist, (2) the state of morale among police employees, and (3) the lack of communication and control in law enforcement agencies (President's Commission on Law Enforcement and Administration of Justice, 1967).

Police and Community Relations. Since increased efficiency is a basic goal of classic organization theory, consolidating small organizations and centralizing control over them is always at least rationally justified. Their concern for efficiency and economy has caused police administrators to develop a myopia to side effects that accompany increased centralization of police departments. For example, consider the side effects from attempting to develop the one "best" procedure for enforcing an abandoned vehicle law in a large jurisdiction with an economically heterogeneous population. Assume that those who have the greatest economic advantage and the most political influence feel a need to eliminate inoperable vehicles from the city. Since they are politically powerful they have no difficulty impressing upon the equally middle-class police management the importance of enforcing this law. According to classic theory a uniform policy is developed and officers are instructed to enforce the law in a nondiscriminatory fashion (that is, they cannot make exceptions to the enforcement policy), and they carry out the policy in a highly impersonal manner.

Although not blatantly apparent, this kind of enforcement is highly discriminatory. First, the lower-income citizens are generally the only people who have inoperable vehicles where the police can detect them; second, lower-income people cannot afford to maintain their cars in as good a state of repair as can higher-income people; and, third, lower-income people need the parts from their inoperable autos to repair the ones they are currently driving. In addition, an abandoned vehicle law has no social utility for people with lower incomes if they are not disturbed by the presence of inoperable cars. The value of having such a vehicle may be greater to them than a tidy backyard.

The centralized authority and responsibility of the police to develop a policy facilitate their manipulation by the powerful persons and groups, while it precludes other less powerful groups from legitimately influencing these policies. In other words, classic organization concepts do not facilitate adequate policy flexibility. If the police adhere to classic principles, they cannot develop their policies to meet legitimate needs and values of individual subcultures or groups —even when these variations might improve justice, as in the preceding example. This inflexibility is detrimental to police-community relations.

Classic theory also supports police reformers who insist that police departments be isolated from politics. As police departments become more refined and move nearer this goal, they move further away from another basic goal of democracy—guaranteeing every citizen access to and influence with governmental agencies. Under a highly developed police bureaucracy, nearly all citizens view their police department as essentially beyond their understanding and control. Where the police department is a highly developed traditional bureaucracy, its structure and its philosophical underpinnings will eventually cause the organization to become socially irrelevant and ineffective. This situation in turn will have a profoundly damaging effect upon police and community relations.

Once a negative police-community relationship begins to develop, communications problems increase and may worsen geometrically. The classic organization impedes improvements by further restricting communications and by failing to facilitate personalized attention to subgroup problems. This situation makes it impossible to develop a significant level of role consensus between minority groups and the police.

Police Employee Morale. The classic organization model appears to support a perpetual state of low morale among employees of bureaucracies. Max Weber is quoted as having condemned this aspect of bureaucracy (Bendix, 1962: 464):

It is horrible to think that the world could one day be filled with nothing but these little cogs, little men clinging to little jobs and striving toward bigger ones—a state of affairs which is to be seen once more, as in Egyptian records, playing an ever-increasing part in the spirit of our present administrative system, and especially of its offspring the students. This passion for bureaucracy is enough to drive one to despair. It is as if in politics we were deliberately to become men who need "order" and nothing but order, who become nervous and cowardly if for one moment this order wavers, and helpless if they are torn away from their total incorporate in it. That the world should know men but these, it is in such an evolution that we are already caught up, and the great question is therefore not how we can promote and hasten it, but what can we oppose to this machinery in order to keep a portion of mankind free from this parcelling out of the soul, from this supreme mastery of bureaucratic way of life.

If employees in a democratic environment are to be satisfied, they must be more valuable than cogs in a machine. Their jobs must be challenging and rewarding enough so that they have a sense of pride and self-importance in performing them.

The division of labor and organization structure should be such that an employee can be content doing his job well. A good patrolman or specialist should not be dependent on a promotion to a supervisory position for increases in pay or status. It is irrational to train and coach an officer until he obtains a high degree of competence in performing his specialty, and then promote him into a supervisory position where his skills will be useless to him (Peter and Hull, 1969). Yet in a police department employees are hired for one level but they are expected to strive for promotions to completely different kinds of jobs in supervisory positions. Consideration is seldom given to the fact that a good patrolman may be a poor manager. In fact, under classic concepts it is improper to reward a patrolman with a salary equal to that of a top administrator even though both may be equally important to the successful operation of the organization.

Another major cause of poor morale among police employees is the conflict between generalists and specialists (Wilson, 1963). In police organizations the most important people in the organizations, the generalists or patrolmen, tend to become nursemaids to the specialized officers such as investigators, and juvenile and traffic officers. This situation creates tension between police generalists and police specialists, and results in a lack of cooperation toward the accomplishment of common goals. The reason for this conflict is apparent. The patrolman's duties mandate that he be highly skilled and knowledgeable in handling a wide range of human behavior. However, he is accorded low status and pay, whereas the specialist receives much more of both. Patrolmen often believe the public thinks that detectives solve large numbers of serious crimes (in fact they usually have a far lower arrest rate than patrolmen and a large percentage of their arrests are based upon information provided by patrol officers) ; and that juvenile specialists are the only police officers who are concerned about helping children. On the other hand, they believe that the public credits uniformed patrolmen only with victimizing citizens and starting riots. These perceptions may so affect the motivation of the generalists that they shunt responsibility onto the specialist at every opportunity.

In addition, low morale among police employees is also caused by feelings about their inability to affect their own working conditions. As the educational level of police employees rises, they insist that they have a right to be involved in decision-making processes of the police organization. Educated officers believe that they have the ability to make decisions about their jobs. Police activism has increased and a number of jurisdictions have recognized the legitimacy of police employees' groups and unions. Such recognition is contrary to the tenets of monocratic, classic theory, which holds that the ultimate decision-making authority rests with the chief of police and flows from the top of the hierarchy to the positions at the bottom; however, the trend toward employee involvement in decision-making processes is not likely to cease. The continued utilization of classic autocratic managerial techniques by traditional managers only increases employee hostility and dissatisfaction.

Communication and Control. According to the postulates of classic organization theory the chief administrator is responsible for controlling the personnel of the organization. It is surprising that although students have noticed that certain types of control are almost always absent, they have failed to deduce the basic weaknesses in the theoretical foundation of the existing organization structures (Angell, 1967). Apparently, a chief of police of a large department cannot remain loyal to classic principles and at the same time exercise informed control. The explanation for this situation can be traced back to a long recognized problem of bureaucracies—communication.

The hierarchy of authority through which communications travel distorts and filters communications both deliberately and unintentionally (Tullock, 1965). The chief administrator seldom gets a true picture of what is occurring in his department. When he issues a directive to correct a situation (which he probably has already perceived inaccurately), his communication will most likely be distorted as it travels through the hierarchy; therefore, it will not have the impact he originally intended.   Even with improved communication, the assumption that formal authority to command can force compliance from subordinates appears to be questionable.   As Chester Barnard (1968) pointed out many years ago, authority rests with the subordinates rather than with the supervisor.   In other words, if the subordinates are not disposed to accept them, orders will receive little or no compliance.

Various functional supervision units established to guarantee employee compliance with departmental expectations have not been notably successful (Angell, 1967).   Therefore, it is questionable whether in our culture, traditional bureaucratic principles can accomplish the objective of adequate control.

Conclusion

Weber's concepts of organization may not be adequate for organizing police departments in the United States.   The police problems appear to indicate that gaps in expectations and role perceptions exist between actors who are significantly related to police organizations. Further application of the tenets of classic theory at this time in this society would serve only to heighten tension and increase conflict. Therefore, the basic hope for correcting the dysfunctional trends of American police organizations lies in the development of a new model that will be compatible with the values and needs of American society.

THE PROPOSED ALTERNATIVE

The following model is an attempt to develop a flexible, participatory, science-based structure that will accommodate change.   It is designed for effectiveness in serving the needs of citizens rather than autocratic rationality of operation.   It is democratic in that it requires and facilitates the involvement of citizens rather than autocratic rationality of operation.   It is democratic in that it requires and facilitates the involvement of citizens and employees in its processes.   It is designed to improve decision-making and role consensus among citizens and employees by increasing the exchanges of information and influence among the people who are related to the organization.

Overview of the Structure

The basic model is an organization with three primary sections: (1) General Services Section, (2) Coordination and Information Section, and (3) Specialized Services Section.   This arrangement would not be structured in a hierarchical fashion with formal ranks and formal supervisors. In order to improve communication and increase the flexibility of the organization all supervisory positions, as they have been traditionally defined, have been abolished. Similarly, military titles and ranks are not used.

The controls in this system are varied, in contrast with the single chain of command control required by classic concepts. Although the control responsibilities will be well defined, no single section or individual will be totally responsible for controlling the entire organization. The control system is defined as a system of checks and balances in which one section of the organization has authority in one instance, another section of the organization has authority in a second instance, and the third section in the third. The General Services Section would consist of teams of generalists decentralized to work in a small geographic area. On the other hand, the Coordination and Information Section would be centralized and might even include many jurisdictions (e. g., a regional or state level). Within the Coordination and Information Section would be those activities related to the coordination of activities and housekeeping of the organization (e. g., those activities presently called administrative and staff functions). The Specialized Services Section would contain those specilized activities currently classified as line units (e. g., investigative, juvenile, and traffic functions).

General Services Section. The General Services Section of the organization would consist entirely of police generalists, who would have equal rank and would have no formally assigned supervisor. The leadership is expected to develop situationally as the circumstances dictate. In other words, team members can determine who will lead them, and the person who occupies the leadership role may change as the situation changes.[1]

Officers will be assigned in teams of five positions by the Coordination Section to work within an assigned geographic area.[2] Ex-

1. This approach to leadership is not new. According to Maslow (1965: 123), "The Blackfoot Indians tended not to have general leaders with general power . . . but rather different leaders for different functions. For instance, the leader in a war party was the one whom everyone thought to be the best person to lead a war party, and the one most respected or the leader in raising stock was the man best suited for that. So one person might be elected leader in one group and be very last in the second group." Caudill (1963: 39) points out that Confederate soldiers often elected their officers during the Civil War. In addition, it is common practice in small hospitals for surgical teams composed of the same members to shift the leadership role for different types of operations. Finally, there is considerable research which suggests many advantages to functional leadership (Katz and Kahn, 1960: 554–570; Coch and French, 1948: 512–532; and Cloward, 1959).

2. Teams of five positions have been chosen because a total of approximately 25 officers would be required to staff five positions on a 24-hour-a-day basis when days off and holidays are considered. Since informal

cept for broad guidelines that would prevent extreme or deviant behavior by the generalists, no procedural guidelines will be imposed on these teams by administrators in the organization. The freedom from rules is intended to permit: (1) the local teams to adopt goals and policies consistent with the needs and desires of the people in their community, and (2) the teams to develop their own methods for handling the problems within their geographic area.[3] However, the goals, policies, and procedures established by the teams could be registered with the Coordination and Information Section.

A team will be expected to work closely with the community of its area. Each team should be responsible for maintaining a community office that will be its local headquarters. Informal meetings involving team and community members should be held periodically to discuss the policies, procedures, problems, and conduct of the community and police. Attempts should be made in these meetings to get consensus on various police responsibilities and procedures.

The teams are also expected to involve specialists from the other sections of the organization in these community meetings. These specialists will be able to provide additional information that can be used to identify and solve community problems as well as serve as communication links with their fellow specialists.

Team members should also attend intraorganizational communications and training programs and meetings. These activities will be designed to eliminate organizational conflicts and misconceptions and to improve the abilities of team members. In addition, study and supervision groups that include team members may be established, ad hoc or permanently.

The officers on each team will have considerable flexibility in deciding when to utilize the services of the Coordination and Information Section and the Specialized Services Section of the organization. In other words, the generalists within each area will be expected to decide how far to go in each particular situation. For example, they will have the right to decide when they will call an investigator to assist in the investigation of a crime. However, no organizationwide regulations will prohibit them from completing an investigation alone. If, on the other hand, a team member decides that he needs the assistance it will be available. This freedom from organizationwide policies does not prohibit individual teams from establishing guidelines for their own members.

communications among officers is essential, the team must be kept as small as possible to facilitate face-to-face communications and solidify the team.

3. The research indicates that placing such responsibility on employees results in higher worker satisfaction (Katz and Kahn, 1960).

The evaluation of these teams could be multiphased such as :

1. team evaluation whereby each member of the team would evaluate all other members of the team;

2. evaluation by Coordination and Information Section, which could determine whether the teams are adequately accomplishing the organizational objectives: this section probably should not evaluate the procedures that the team uses in doing the job, but rather it would assess how far the team has gone in adequately meeting its obligations and accomplishing its goals;

3. evaluation by the community served by a team;

4. functional evaluation by specialists in their areas of expertise.

Coordination and Information Section. The Coordination and Information Section of the organization will be made up of functional supervision units (including an ethics unit to ensure that the teams meet the established standards), a planning unit that will provide assistance for the teams, and certain other support units such as detention, records, communications, and training. In other words this section will contain units that are concerned not with policy development, but essentially with providing coordination, support, and minimal supervision for the other sections of the organization.

One of the most important responsibilities of this section is the definition of communities and the assignment of team members to them. This activity involves determining areas where the citizens have relatively homogeneous value systems and assigning teams to these areas in such a way that their workloads are equal.

In the assignment of team members, this section should attempt to provide each team with generalist members who have complementary skills and attitudes. Every team should be monitored and evaluated constantly, so that improperly assigned officers can be reassigned to other teams and areas where they can perform better. When evaluation reveals that the teams as a whole are not meeting their objectives or not complying with standards, the Coordination Section should be responsible for breaking up the team and reassigning the members. A new team must then be selected and assigned to the area.

The Chief Coordinator of this section should play a role analogous to that of a hospital administrator. It will be his job to:

1. represent the organization on occasions when a spokesman for the entire organization is needed;

2. oversee the continual updating of the organizational philosophies and long-range objectives;

3. coordinate the activities of the various segments of the organization and settle conflicts and duplications of efforts;

4. provide employees and teams with maximum, yet equal, support within organization resources.

This official should be selected for the job because of his expertise and abilities in coordinating and managing human organizations. He should have a contract for a definite number of years and be considered for reappointment at the end of his term. Members of the organization as well as the public should be involved in his selection and evaluation. Obviously, his success will depend on his ability to maintain the system.

Specialized Services Section. The third branch of the organization, the Specialized Services Section, will employ and house specialists such as investigators, juvenile specialists, and traffic specialists. These specialists will be available to support and assist generalists. The generalists will have the freedom to establish their own team policy regarding the utilization of specialists. Their police may leave such decisions up to the individual generalist.

When called by a member of the General Services Section, a specialist will serve at the pleasure of the generalist or team who called him. He is responsible for performing his particular speciality without interference from the generalist in much the same way as an X-ray technician or other medical specialist performs services for a doctor. Therefore, while a specialist will work at the discretion of and as an assistant to the generalist, he is nevertheless responsible for doing a professional job. Once he has completed his work his only responsibility is the submission of a report to the generalist who requested his service. Decisions regarding further action are the responsibility of the generalist.

Specialists may be evaluated by their fellow specialists, functional supervision units in the Coordination and Information Section, the generalists or teams for whom they work, or any combination of the preceding. If they are not performing adequately, the authority for retraining lies with the Coordination and Information Section; however, these people should have received most of their professional education and training prior to their employment. This procedure will permit the hiring of skilled specialists who are already qualified professionals.

In addition to the traditional specializations of police work, new specialties could be developed to improve the quality of policing. For example, if a decision to disarm the General Service officers were made, a specialized unit might be established to assist the generalists in situations involving explosives or firearms. Such a unit could be kept on reserve in much the same way as firemen are kept ready. Members of this unit could be highly trained and adequately equipped to respond immediately anywhere in the jurisdiction. The potential for such specialization is limited only by the imagination.

Although the specialists will have a considerable amount of freedom to perform as they see fit, it should be reemphasized that they will be working for the generalists rather than for an independent supervisor as they do now. On the other hand, these specialists may be expected to evaluate the quality of the activities performed by generalists in their area of expertise (e. g., investigators might evaluate the quality of investigations performed by the various teams).

EXPECTED ADVANTAGES OF THIS MODEL

This organizational arrangement offers the potential for solving many of the problems that elude solution under the classic police organizational arrangements. First, by eliminating formally assigned supervision and by providing officers with more control over their own jobs, it should increase the morale and effectiveness of employees. In addition, it should result in improvement in the ability of the groups to establish and achieve goals.

The decentralization of these groups will give citizens more influence in policy decision. This influence should provide the generalists with more direction than police officers currently have for the establishment of socially relevant enforcement policies as well as the exercise of discretion. It will also provide more flexibility in policy, so that the various segments of the population will receive more appropriate police service. These factors should improve the relationships between the public and police officers, and thereby improve the effectiveness of the police.

This organizational structure increases the professional standing and prestige of the generalist without damaging the status of the specialist. It recognizes that the generalist is important and has the intelligence needed to make decisions about his job. On the other hand, the importance of the specialist is recognized and rewarded. Since this plan permits hiring from outside the organization, highly skilled persons could be selected for specialized jobs, thus saving the organization training expenses.

In essence this organizational structure destroys the formal classic hierarchy. It establishes a system of checks and balances somewhat like that of the federal government. Some aspects of this arrangement are analogous to a hospital situation, and other features are very similar to those used in universities. It provides for increased communications and more adequate information about perceptions and expectations of the various actors in the system. It provides employees with the authority and responsibility necessary for attaining professional status. It facilitates citizen involvement and organizational responsiveness, the hallmarks of democratic institutions. And it should encourage the development of more mature employees and citizens.

RELATED CHANGES

In order for this model to work substantial changes in aspects of management other than the organization per se will be necessary. One of the most important of these changes will be the modification of police training programs. The traditional training method utilized in police academies—the lecture—is inadequate to prepare employees for the decision-making responsibilities they will encounter in this type of organization. For this sytem to function properly personnel must have a broad education that emphasizes improving their decision-making abilities. The generalists will, because of structure, have to be well versed in human relations and dealing with people, politics, management, and a broad range of other activities, with which they are not too familiar at the present time. Training activities for General Services officers may utilize techniques such as the crisis intervention program that has been developed by Mort Bard in New York City (Bard, 1969) and the community-based training program that has been implemented in Dayton, Ohio (Igleburger and Wasserman, 1970). The training of the specialists will be facilitated because people can be hired from outside into these positions; therefore, they will be trained to perform at a high level of efficiency before they enter the organization. The Coordination and Information Section can be staffed by management specialists, planners and other specialists who have the appropriate training and education. Many such positions might be staffed by students, researchers, and educators to increase the relevance of higher education and draw on the ideals of its personnel.

A second area where changes may be necessary is salary. Under this organizational structure there should be no significant differences among the salaries of the various people. A patrolman or a generalist is equally important in his particular area as an administrator is in his area, and the investigator is as important as an administrator or a police generalist. Therefore, the starting salaries might be in the neighborhood of $9,000 or $10,000 with merit increases to about $20,000 a year. Since the work of people in all three areas is equally important, they should also receive merit and seniority salary increases up to the same maximum. Such salaries would eliminate the need for patrolmen to be promoted to a supervisory position for salary increases, and it would improve efficiency by allowing employees to concentrate exclusively on their jobs.

A third important activity that might be necessary is the establishment of an ethics committee. This committee might consist of employees and citizens who would hear complaints regarding the behavior and decisions of various members in sensitive, well-defined areas. It would have the power to take certain kinds of action to correct misbehavior and improper decisions by professionals within the organization. Part of the value of this unit would be in the information it would provide for decision about training and organizational improvements. Although this unit might be part of the Coordination and Information Section of the organization, it does not necessarily have to be located in this section. Other arrangements, such as an independent unit outside the organization, may be equally desirable.

However, the most important change necessary is in attitudes. Police executives will need to place more confidence in their officers, and the officers will have to accept increased responsibility and deal with it realistically. Executives will be tempted to impose their values about how things should be done on the teams and they will have to resist this temptation and evaluate teams on their results. Team officers will be constantly frustrated by the ambiguous, unstructured, insecure nature of their jobs and they will need to learn to accept and deal with the problems inherent in such an environment. Naturally, people currently holding middle-management positions will have the biggest adjustment to make in order to understand why their positions are unnecessary. Members of the organization and many citizens will have difficulty adjusting to this arrangement. Democratic ways are never tension-free or easy.

CONCLUSIONS

The problems related to the utilization of the military or classic model for municipal police organizations that have heavy service goals are numerous. I have attempted to present an alternative organizational model which I believe would be an improvement on the existing approach to police organization. This model is democratic in that it rejects the dictatorial, classic approach and facilitates the involvement of many people in its decision-making processes. On the other hand, it also provides for control of its employees and coordination of their activities. It provides methods for making policy differentials as well as for maintaining organizational efficiency. Significantly, it increases the probability of the police officer's job becoming a full-fledged profession.

Implementation of the recommendations should be well planned and tied to a program of evaluation. A department might be reorganized to continue the existing approach in all but two experimental areas where teams constructed along the lines recommended would be implemented. The communities where these experimental units are implemented could be subjected to pre- and postevaluations. Comparisons of attitudes and changes related to the operation would be essential. Such evaluation would require an extensive interdisciplinary research effort of a caliber never before undertaken in the police field.

REFERENCES

Angell, J. E. (1967) "The adequacy of the internal processing of complaints by police departments." M.A. thesis, School of Police Administration and Public Safety, Michigan State University.

Argyris, C. (1957) "The individual and organization: some problems of mutual adjustment." Administrative Sci.Q. (June): 1–24.

Bendix, R. (1962) Max Weber. An Intellectual Portrait. Garden City, N.Y.: Doubleday.

Bard, M. (1969) "Alternatives to traditional law enforcement." Presented before the 77th annual convention of the American Psychological Association. Washington, D.C.

Barnard, C. (1968) The Functions of the Executive. Cambridge, Mass.: Harvard Univ.Press.

Bennis, W. (1966) Changing Organizations. New York: McGraw-Hill.

—— and P. Slater (1964) "Democracy is inevitable." Harvard Business Rev. (March-April): 51–59.

Brown, J. A. C. (1954) The Social Psychology of Industry. Baltimore, Penguin.

Caudill, H. M. (1963) Night Comes to the Cumberlands. Boston: Little, Brown.

Cloward, R. (1959) "Social control and anomie: a study of a prison community." Ph.D. dissertation. Columbia University.

Coch, L. and J. French (1948) "Overcoming resistance to change." Human Relations 1, 4: 512–532.

Gerth, H. H. and C. W. Mills [eds.] (1958) From Max Weber: Essays in Sociology. New York: Oxford Univ.Press.

Igleburger, E. and R. Wasserman (1970) "The incorporation of community-base field training into a police recruit training curriculum." Presented at the Third National Symposium on Law Enforcement Science and Technology. Chicago.

Katz, D. and R. Kahn (1960) "Leadership practices in relation to productivity and morale," in D. Cartwright and A. Zander (eds.) Group Dynamics, Research and Theory. New York: Harper & Row.

Kimble, J. (1969) "Daydreams, dogma and dinosaurs." Police Chief 36, 4:12–15.

Maslow, A. H. (1965) Eupsychian Management. Homewood, Ill.: Dorsey.

Myren, R. (1960) "A crisis in police management." J. of Criminal Law, Criminology and Police Sci. 50, 6: 600–605.

Peter, L. and R. Hull (1969) The Peter Principle. New York: Morrow.

President's Commission on Law Enforcement and Administration of Justice (1967) Task Force Report: The Police. Washington, D.C.: Government Printing Office.

Tullock, G. (1965) The Politics of Bureaucracy. Washington: Public Affairs Press.

Weber, M. (1958) "Bureaucracy," in H. H. Gerth and C. W. Mills (eds.) From Max Weber: Essays in Sociology. New York: Oxford Univ. Press.

—— (1947) "The essentials of bureaucratic organization: an ideal-type construction," in H. Henderson and T. Parsons (eds.) The Theory of Social and Economic Organization. New York: Oxford Univ.Press.

Wilson, O. (1963) Police Administration. New York: McGraw-Hill.

MIDDLE MANAGEMENT AND POLICE DEMOCRATIZATION: A REPLY TO JOHN E. ANGELL *

John Angell's democratic model of police organization (1971), in the three years since it was published in this journal, has been widely discussed in the field of law enforcement. Police administrators have been attracted to many of the model's features: decentralization of decision-making authority to locally autonomous police teams, merging all operational functions into those teams, and evaluating the performance of those teams with a central research unit. But the Angell model as a whole is often dismissed out of hand because of a single feature: the abolition of middle management.

In a study of seven team-policing programs similar to the model Angell suggests (Sherman et al., 1973), middle management was found to be a universal obstacle to the implementation of more democratic structures of policing. But the conclusion of that study was not that mid-management must be abolished in order to change police departments, but that the change processes had failed to treat mid-management "democratically" enough in the planning stages.

This paper will review the response of police mid-management to team policing, and suggest that the response was not inevitable. Rather than supporting Angell's position, the team-policing experience shows how important middle management is in organizational change.

* Source: "Middle Management and Police Democratization: A Reply to John E. Angell," by Lawrence W. Sherman is reprinted from *Criminology* Vol. 12, No. 4 (Feb. 1975) pp. 363–377 by permission of the Publisher, Sage Publications, Inc.

THE OBSTRUCTIONS OF MIDDLE MANAGEMENT

Police executives implementing team policing generally bypassed the middle level of the management-lieutenants, captains, and similar ranks. By fiat from the top, the bottom—patrol officers and sergeants—was given authority and discretion that had traditionally been reserved for, though rarely used by, the middle levels. In the perception of middle managers, team policing was a form of decentralization that gave them less control than any previous attempts at rigid centralization. The consequence was a multitude of attempts to block the proper implementation of team programs.

Middle management subversion took three main forms: (1) sins of omission, (2) sins of commission, and (3) active disagreement openly expressed to their superiors.

Sins of Omission

Middle management's sins of omission were their failures to deal with, or even pay attention to, conflicts and problems arising out of team experiments under their command. For example, friction often developed between team leaders and the rank immediately above them over questions of deployment. This problem surfaced almost immediately in England, the birthplace of the team concept. Despite the role definitions of sergeants as tacticians and inspectors as strategists, one home office study found that both ranks found their functions overlapping (U.K. Home Office, 1967). Moreover, the operational middle managers—chief inspectors—did little about it.

In the Detroit Beat Commander project the formal chain of command bypassed the next rank above the team leader, going directly to the precinct commander. Not role confusion, but anger resulted as the lieutenants sought to reestablish their supremacy over the team leader-sergeant. The precinct commander who had helped plan the experiment refused the demand, but he was soon transferred. His replacement shared the lieutenant's distaste for the new arrangement, and immediately reinstituted the old chain of command. More important, he looked the other way as the lieutenants countermanded the innovative patrol tactics developed by the beat team.

When New York began a team program, its lieutenants were virtually unaffected. Traditionally restricted to the clerical supervision of a stationhouse desk, they had almost no involvement in field operations. Their only function was to ensure that all actions were properly recorded. Several months after the initiation of the Neighborhood Police Team (NPT) program, though, a different experiment began to put lieutenants out in the street. The "lieutenant-operations officer" experiment was, at first, restricted to precincts without

NPTs. But when the two programs were combined in one precinct, it was immediately apparent that the team sergeant and the operations lieutenant had been given the same power: to deploy manpower as they saw fit. From their differing perspectives, differing deployment strategies arose. The team sergeant tried to meet the needs of his subprecinct on a 24-hour-a-day basis; the operations lieutenant tried to meet the needs of the entire precinct during his 8-hour tour. The upshot was tension and the frequent occurrence of the lieutenants not only redeploying team manpower within the team area, but also sending team officers out of their area—both in contradiction to the team sergeant's orders. Yet despite heated statements by both sergeants and lieutenants, their captain, in separate meetings, denied that a problem existed.

Both Dayton and Syracuse avoided a clash between lieutenants and sergeants by building lieutenants into the team structure from the outset. In both cities the lieutenants coordinated several teams headed by sergeants. All of the area under the command of the lieutenant was organized on a team basis, and his responsibilities, like the sergeants', were on a 24-hour-a-day basis, instead of just one watch. When both had this broader perspective on the needs of the team area, the relations between those two ranks went more smoothly (though both these cities failed to implement other important aspects of their team programs).

In Los Angeles the Basic Car Plan (BCP) confused staff and line functions with a resultant confusion of appropriate rank roles, yet the captains ignored the problem there as elsewhere. The BCP teams were supervised on patrol by the watch commander lieutenants and at their monthly community meetings by the (staff) community relations lieutenants. Attempts to follow through on community meetings during patrol operations were opposed by the watch commanders, since they had no part in the meetings. An internal seminar on the problem concluded that captains had not given sufficient guidance, but the problem remained. (The LAPD has developed a different form of team policing since my 1971 visit; see Sherman et al., 1973: 45–57.)

A similar, yet distinct problem that middle managers often ignored was the relationship between the team leaders and men of equal rank who were not team leaders. In New York this problem was almost written into the plan by having other sergeants "cover" an NPT area when the team sergeant was not on duty. Even though the team sergeant was accountable for everything that happened in his area, he could count on his orders being followed only as long as he was physically present. If he was successful in persuading other precinct sergeants to accept his deployment policies, little conflict appeared. But those sergeants who resented the team program often took the opportunity of the team sergeant's absence to redeploy the team out of its area, or to otherwise contradict team policies. "I don't care what 'your' sergeant told you; follow my orders or I'll write up a complaint on you!" The team commander who heard of such incidents had little recourse besides complaining to his captain. If the captain was unsympathetic—as he often was—the problem remained.

Due to the small size of the Holyoke Police Department, the chief there may be considered the equivalent of a middle manager and the mayor, the top manager. While the chief was out sick during the first months of their team program, considerable friction developed between the team captain and the other captains in that department. The result was the virtual secession of the team-policing unit from the rest of the department. All calls from the team area received at headquarters were transferred to the team storefront, and the attitude of the shift captain was "good riddance." While this total lack of interference (or imvolvement) from the rest of the force was a blessing for the team captain, it guaranteed the future opposition of the other captains to expanding the team concept to other areas of the city. By the time the chief (middle manager) returned from sick leave, the polarization was fixed.

Sins of Commission

The problems discussed above were only permitted to persist by mid-managers; they did not start them. They did, however, start other problems, some of which were even more successful in blocking the implementation of team programs.

The most effective torpedo was simple bad-mouthing: sending the word out through the grapevine that the team idea was no good. The feudal nature of many police departments results in the precinct commander becoming someone whose word was more important than the word from headquarters. In Detroit the Beat Commander project was announced at roll calls with such prefatory remarks as "listen to this shit!"

In Dayton such language was equally shrill and damaging. Shortly after the team policing program was announced, the captains circulated rumors that it was a communist conspiracy, manipulated via federal funding to get the police to cease law enforcement. Team patrolmen complained that the captains would tell the director of police what a great idea the team program was, then turn around and tell their men that the program would destroy the department.

Syracuse, like Dayton, was plagued with bad-mouthing of the Crime-Control Team (CCT) by captains in other units. Unlike any other city, however, the CCT lieutenant was formally subject to orders from no one save the chief. This arrangement was announced only through departmental memoranda, and not in any face-to-face sessions between the chief and his commanders. The captains felt their loss of status so strongly that their bad-mouthing was expanded into harassment and persecution. The team leader was still a lieutenant as far as they were concerned and, in total disregard for the CCT's independent status, patrol captains came into the team area and gave orders to the lieutenant and his team. Though at first reluctant to complain to the chief, the CCT lieutenant finally requested that all captains and above be called into a meeting with the chief in order to have the new chain of command restated. The meeting had some impact, but the CCT leader complained that the problem was not really solved until he was promoted to captain himself.

In larger team programs, mid-managers often selected low-caliber personnel as team leaders. Rumors circulated in New York that captains were using "hoople" (stupid) sergeants. One particularly unqualified sergeant had such little understanding of the NPT program that a visit to his precinct when the team was a month old revealed that team patrolmen did not know who the other members of their team were.

Undercutting the operational freedom of the team commanders was a third form of sabotage. In Detroit where the team precinct was commanded by three different men during the life of the Beat Commander project, the latter two mid-managers countermanded almost every visible innovation of the team: a plan to not wear hats as a means of mitigating the militaristic image, a plan to use police reserves for surveillance, and backyard driveway anti-burglary patrols. These small thwartings of operational discretion were not appropriate for appeals to a higher level, such as the police commissioner. At the same time, though, they effectively defeated the program's goal of innovative team response to local conditions. Thus, the information block posed by the middle prevented the top from ensuring that the bottom could, in fact, exercise its increased formal authority and discretion. (A former Detroit precinct commander observed that the guidelines gave the beat commander as much authority as the precinct commander, but he never used it. "The sergeant was a practical man," he explained.)

Formally Expressed Opposition

This third form of mid-management resistance to change was the most honest: frank complaints about the programs to top management. It often occurred simultaneously with other forms of resistance, but it usually addressed policy matters that the middle managers could not overrule without attracting attention.

In the guidelines for the Beat Commander program, the sergeant had the power to call in—or keep out—Detroit's tactical (riot control and crime suppression) unit. Never had this authority been given to even precinct commanders, nor was it allowed them during the life of the Beat Commander project. The justification for giving a sergeant such extraordinary powers was the need of the evaluation design to keep the team area free of large, erratic influxes of manpower that would contaminate the study of how effective the men in the beat command were. Nonetheless, the (later) precinct commander argued that the beat command area could not be sacrificed to statistical purity. Formally raising this issue through the chain of command, he managed to have the beat commander's authority on this issue revoked.

USES OF MIDDLE MANAGEMENT

The essential weakness of team-policing experiments was the continued definition of mid-management's function solely in terms of *control*, and not in any terms of *support* of the bottom. The foregoing suggests that if middle managers had helped to iron out implementation problems, guided rather than vetoed innovations, and agreed to guidelines in advance, then they would have supported rather than obstructed change. The reality was the opposite for "democratization" reduced their control functions without increasing their support tasks.

Moreover, as long as the command hierarchy was maintained, it was almost impossible to successfully reduce mid-management's control. The policies of the top notwithstanding, a man of higher rank was still permitted to give orders to an officer of lower rank, unless countermanded by an even higher-ranking officer on the scene. Police administrators must also rely largely on middle management for information about field performance. As Angell (1971) rightly argues, information is filtered as it goes up the hierarchy, each level filtering out that which reflects poorly upon it. Thus it was easy for precinct commanders and higher to pay lip-service to team policing while ignoring it or working for its demise. It does not necessarily follow, however, that mid-management should be abolished.

Angell (1971) suggests that middle management could not obstruct change if they were abolished—although they would clearly seek to obstruct his proposal. According to his model of democratic police organization, a central coordination staff would keep each democratically run team apprised of other teams' activities, while advising and evaluating all teams. Freed from the restrictions of rank chain of command, and rules and procedures, the teams would, according to Angell, develop a sense of pride and professional responsibility which would be a more valuable motivation than the fear of middle management's sanctions.

It is interesting to note that the industrial experiments in factory democracy, the most advanced of which are in Sweden, have not seen fit to abolish middle management (Jenkins, 1973).   Rather, those experiments have placed the foremen and supervisors largely in the role of securing production materials and coordinating overall production schedules on behalf of the work teams that they "supervise."   Control is still exercised, but only in a prosecutorial sense—supervisors must bring their charge of wrongdoing to a board comprised mainly of workers.   As a single example, the Swedish case can be given strong theoretical backing as an alternative way of making police organization more democratic.

First, Lipset (1960) has argued that it is difficult to create and maintain a new system "if the status of major conservative groups is threatened during the period of structural change."   Speaking about countries that have changed from monarchy to democracy, a change not unlike that sought by team policing for police organization, Lipset (1960: 65) suggests,

> If, however, the status of major conservative groups and symbols is not threatened during this transitional period, even though they lose much of their power, democracy seems to be much more secure.   And thus we have the absurd fact that ten out of the twelve European and English-speaking democracies are monarchies.

Lipset's reasoning extended to police bureaucracy suggests that any attempt to abolish the positions of middle management while retaining the people who had occupied those positions—a necessity under most civil service laws—would produce a level of conflict rendering the new structure ineffective—regardless of its merits. If, however, mid-management positions are retained, despite a decrease in their power, the legitimacy of a new system will be easier to obtain and its effectiveness more easily demonstrated.

Further, decreasing the power of middle management is not a necessary requirement of decentralization.   Much recent literature in organization theory suggests that there is not a fixed supply of power to be allocated among the different levels of an organization.   Rather, it may be possible to expand the power of each level simultaneously with benefits for the entire organization.

Tannenbaum has developed this point in his *Control in Organizations* (1968: 12):

> Traditional analyses of social power assume that the total amount of power in a social system is a fixed quantity and that leaders and followers are engaged in a "zero-sum game": increasing the power of one party must be accompanied by a corresponding decrease in the power of the other.

Some social scientists are now inclined to question the generality of this assumption. . . . The total amount of power in a social system may grow, and leaders and followers may therefore enhance their power jointly. Total power may also decline, and all groups within the system may suffer corresponding decreases.

Tannenbaum notes two classes of conditions under which organizations may expand their power: (1) external expansion into the organization's environment, and (2) internal conditions of structure and motivation. In team policing the two classes are interrelated. The goal of each team is to expand the effectiveness of the police in the community: talking to more people, establishing positive communication links, apprehending more criminals, and providing more and better services. This expanded external role is ideally accompanied by a new internal structure: the followers (patrol officers) must do more leading of themselves, and the leaders must lead in new and different ways. Mid-managers must analyze the increased flow of information and obtain more resources to support the expanded role of their men, e. g., liaison with social service agencies, traffic, and sanitation departments.

The human relations school of organization theory which Tannenbaum represents holds that the consequence of an expanded job role is that the job becomes a more important part of one's life, producing higher levels of motivation and effort on the job. But if this premise is valid for workers on the bottom of an organization, it should be equally valid for those in the middle.

Tannenbaum uses graphs to explain his thesis.

Figure 1 illustrates some standard organizational possibilities.

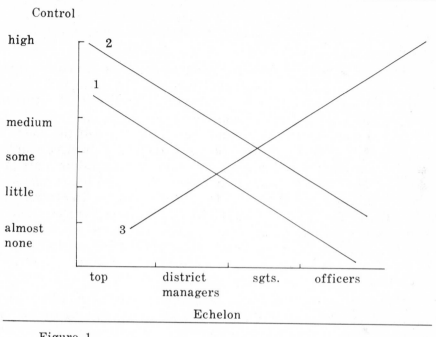

Figure 1

[B7265]

Line 1 is the traditional bureaucratic pyramid, with a tight, even, span of control all the way down the line. Line 2 describes the modern, centralized police organization, which recognizes the legal authority of the patrol officer, and the increasing authority of those above him to direct his activities. Line 3 describes a decentralized beat-cop department with weak leadership on the laissez-faire pattern, so the closer one sits to field operations, the more control one has. Taken together, lines 1 and 2 could describe a before 1 and after 2 picture of an organization that has enlarged its role in its external environment while expanding the amount of control at each internal level. And in all of these examples, control comes to mean both veto control and initiating control, which was called support above.

Figure 2 illustrates some organizational possibilities for democratized police departments.

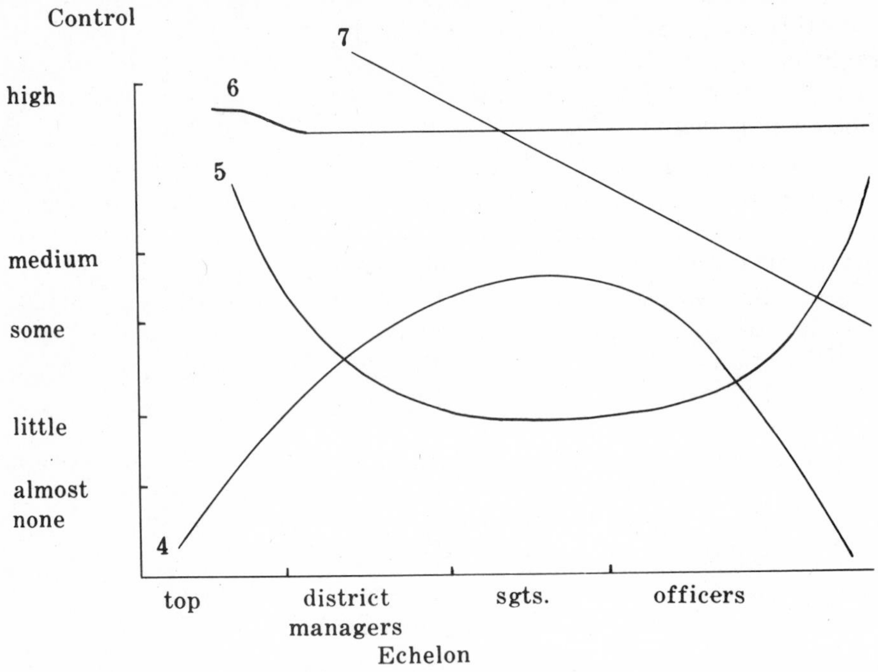

Figure 2

[B7024]

Line 4 describes older, eastern police forces, where most of the control was held by precinct commanders. The perpetuation of this pattern his meant that team policing took this, rather than line 1, as a starting point, requiring a complete turn-around described by line 5: the top and the bottom in charge with the middle left out.

Line 6 describes Angell's model (1971) of police organization. This model abolishes all supervisory levels save the top, which becomes central coordination and evaluation. Veto control is replaced entirely by initiating control or support. And seemingly, the model meets Wilson's requirements (1968: 291) that a "decentralized, neighborhood-oriented, order-maintenance patrol force requires a central command to insure a reasonably common definition of appropriate order, a reduction in the opportunities for corruption and favoritism, and the protection of civil liberties of suspects and witnesses."

Most police administrators, however, would find the central command in Angell's model inadequate and would prefer line 7 to 6 as a team-policing model for two reasons. First, it would be politically impossible to loosen central veto control to the degree implied by line 6—if not immediately, then as soon as something goes wrong, "tighten the controls!" will be heard from the public. Second, the technical and staff assistance functions that Angell acknowledges a need for might be better performed in a vertical structure, given the intense nature of competition between horizontally arranged units in extant police departments.

The size and social environment of the police organization obviously needs to be considered as well when choosing between lines 6 and 7. A small police organization—50–150 officers—in a small, homogeneous community might feasibly adopt line 6. Such a community would be well aware of its rights and quick to complain about inappropriate police behavior; members of such small forces, each knowing the others and aware of the central evaluation unit, might develop adequate self-regulation (though the opposite is equally conceivable). In a large city, however, there is no question that loose systems of control are full of dangers. The great corruption opportunities of big gambling and drug operations require strict internal controls, and politically inefficacious groups need protection from aggressive patrol tactics. A patrol force like New York's, divided into eight hundred teams, would be impossible to monitor and evaluate without middle management.

In a city of any substantial size, then, decentralization of police operations needs middle management—not just to refrain from obstructing change, or to retain minimal veto controls, but to help implement change as well. The question then becomes how their support can be elicited. Kansas City, Missouri is one successful precedent for involving mid-managers, and all other levels, in a comprehensive planning process to improve the department. A task force of two patrolmen, two sergeants, two captains (there are no lieutenants there), and a major was established in each patrol division in order to identify community and organizational problems and develop programs to solve them. A constant effort was made to communicate with all other officers in the divisions, soliciting their suggestions and reactions to preliminary plans. While it is too soon to determine the impact of the programs they developed, the important thing is that the programs *were* implemented, which is more than most team-policing programs can say.

Yet there is no simple formula for enlisting mid-management's support for democratization, or any other kind of change. Indeed, this paper has left many implications and problems of police democratization totally unexamined in order to concentrate on one central issue. It may be that democratizing the police is simply a bad idea, but that question is here left open. If one assumes that it is an end well worth pursuing, the means necessary for implementing it must include middle management. For only if policemen at all levels can feel that this is "our" way of doing things, rather than the boss's pet project, will democratization of any sort have a chance.

REFERENCES

Angell, J. E. (1971) "Towards an alternative to classical police organizational arrangements." Criminology 19.

Jenkins, D. (1973) Job Power; Blue and White Collar Democracy. New York: Doubleday.

Lipset, S. M. (1960) Political Man. New York: Doubleday.

Sherman, L. W., C. H. Milton, and T. Kelly (1973) Team Policing: Seven Case Studies. Washington, D.C.: Police Foundation.

Tannenbaum, A. S. (1968) Control in Organizations. New York: McGraw-Hill.

Wilson, J. Q. (1968) Varieties of Police Behavior. Cambridge: Harvard Univ.Press.

ORGANIZING POLICE FOR THE FUTURE: AN UPDATE OF THE DEMOCRATIC MODEL * †

INTRODUCTION

In the monograph, "Toward an Alternative to the Classical Police Organizational Arrangements: A Democratic Model," I suggested the conventional police organizational design has been responsible for problems in the areas of (1) police and community relations, (2) police employee morale, and (3) coordination and control of police operations (Angell, 1971). As an alternative to traditional arrangements, I proposed a participatory community-based, collegial, police organizational structure called the "Democratic Model."

THE DEMOCRATIC MODEL

Traditionally police operations have been organized in a manner consistent with bureaucratic or classical organizational theory (Eastman & Eastman, 1969; Leonard, 1971; Wilson & McLaren, 1972).

* I would like to acknowledge my gratitude to my good friends and colleagues, Professor Raymond T. Galvin, University of Missouri at St. Louis, and Dr. Michael W. O'Neill, Criminal Justice Research, Mill Valley, California, who offered excellent criticism of an earlier draft of this article. I am also indebted to Donald Clark, Commission Chairman of Multnomah County, Oregon, whose leadership and progressive ideas in police administration contributed substantially to this paper.

† Source: Angell, John E. "Organizing Police For the Future: An Update of the Democratic Model," *Criminal Justice Review*, Vol. 1, No. 2, (Fall, 1976): pp. 35–51.

The Democratic Model is structured to alleviate the specific problems mentioned above which seem to be a consequence of rigid adherence to these classical organizational principles (Bittner, 1970; Bordua, 1967; Clark & Dykes, 1974; Pursley, 1971; Radelet, 1973; Whisenand & Ferguson, 1973). In the organization of the Democratic Model, the horizontal differentiation (Lawrence & Lorsch, 1970) of police functions provides three basic divisions of labor or component sections—General Services, Specialized Services, and Coordination and Information (Angell, 1971).

The General Services Section is responsible for delivery of street-level police operations. This Section consists of teams of police officers with general police responsibilities, assigned to well-defined neighborhood areas (Shalala & Merget, 1974; Whitaker, 1971; Note 2; Note 3). Each team would be responsible for a joint effort with people from the neighborhood to establish police priorities and policies, and provide police services which are appropriate for the neighborhood. In place of traditional, formal supervisory arrangements, the supervisory structure of the teams would be based on flexible, situational group leadership (Bekrin & Meeland, 1958; Fiedler, O'Brien & Ilgen, 1969; Lange, et al, 1958; Little, 1955; Stone, 1946). The designation of team leadership would rest with team members in contrast to the traditional reservation of this function as a management prerogative. Under situational arrangements leaders will be identified through informal group processes. They can be changed by a team as situations require different leadership. The evaluation of the teams and team members would include citizen and peer group input.

The Specialized Services Section would consist of skilled specialists responsible for supporting generalist team officers in a manner analogous to a radiologist's relationship with a general medical practitioner (Goss, 1963; Perrow, 1960). This arrangement contrasts with current police practices wherein generalist patrol officers merely conduct preliminary investigations (i. e., respond to dispatches and initiate preliminary reports) and specialists are responsible for follow-up investigations and the final disposition of cases.

Under the Democratic Model, generalist police officers would have complete responsibility for cases they initiate—including the supervision of specialized police employees. This supervisory responsibility entails an obligation to decide when and under what conditions specialist investigators will be called into a case. Hence, a specialist would commence work at the request of a generalist team officer, and would turn the results of the work over to the generalist. The generalist responsible for a case would evaluate the work performed on the case by a specialist, integrate it with available information and make decisions about the disposition of cases.

The Coordination and Information Section would consist of a collection of centralized staff units and individuals for performing administrative staff, housekeeping and coordination functions for the police operations. This section would be responsible for defining team areas, for developing and assigning generalist teams, for establishing appropriate specialized line and staff support units, and for providing activities such as dispatching, records, data processing, planning, citizen complaints processing, corruption investigation, laboratory services, and training. The top administrator of the Coordination and Information Section would perform management duties analogous to those of a hospital administrator for the police agency.

Although aspects of the Model have been controversial (O'Malley, 1973; Sherman, 1975), many of its features have been tested in "team police" experiments in urban communities over the past few years (Angell, 1975). Evaluative data from these experiments seem to support the conclusion that the Model has potential for improving community relations, employee morale, and effectiveness of the police (Angell, Galvin, & O'Neill, 1972; Bloch & Specht, 1973; Elliott & Sardino, 1972; Fink & Sealy, 1974; O'Malley, 1973; Patterson, 1964; Phelps & Harmon, 1972; Schwartz & Clarren, 1974; Sherman, Milton & Kelley, 1973; Tortoriello & Blatt, 1973).

However, as Sherman (1975) has suggested, changing from a Classical bureaucratic organizational design to the Democratic Model entails disruption of established, well-entrenched power arrangements and practices. Resistance in some quarters to the implementation of the Model has been both active and intense. Therefore, as part of this paper updating the Democratic Model, I will offer suggestions which may facilitate future efforts at model implementation.

PROBLEM AREAS

Despite the purported successes of team-type police organizational arrangements, the ultimate potential of the police will remain unrealized if police organizations continue to ignore two basic problems. First, traditional police operations are organized consistent with the assumption that police are primarily in the "criminal apprehension" business. Adherence to this "role" concept restricts the potential of police. Second, police agencies are basically organized as self-contained agencies which operate autonomously from other units of government. This independence reduces the potential utility of police. Both of these problems and their implications merit review.

Role of Police

In spite of numerous polemics urging otherwise, many police authorities still assume that *the* primary police responsibility is investigation of crime and apprehension of criminals. This assumption is reflected by police structures where 30% to 40% of the resources is allocated to investigative and apprehension operations (Angell, Hagedorn & Egger, 1974). It is reflected in police dispatch priorities which frequently rank crime as more important than situations that are a threat to human life.

In reality, local police agencies were not established to be, nor have they traditionally been, primarily law enforcement agencies (Whitehouse, 1973). Citizens in urban areas of the United States originally supported the establishment of local police agencies to provide 24-hour emergency services to all members of the public. Local police agencies have often been charged with performing such activities and service functions as street cleaning, watching for fires, dispensing relief for the poor, advising their communities of the time and weather during hours of darkness, waking travelers, lighting street lamps, assisting probationers, and maintaining public order (Fosdick, 1920; Whitehouse, 1973). These responsibilities are consistent with the dictionary definition of "police" as ". . . the department of government concerned primarily with maintenance of public order, safety, and health and enforcement of laws."

Even though over the years the responsibility for some of these service functions has been assigned to other governmental agencies, citizens in need of emergency assistance still expect police to perform non-enforcement services and emergency functions which cannot be conveniently obtained from other agencies. Police workload studies conducted in a variety of police agencies throughout the United States reveal crime-related requests for police assistance actually comprise a *minority* of all requests for police action (Angell, Hagedorn & Egger, 1974; Misner & Hoffman, 1967; Press, 1971; Webster, 1973; Yaden, 1974).

People with problems apparently turn to the police when they do not know where else to obtain assistance (Galvin, Angell & O'Neill, 1969). Perhaps they call the police in time of need because police provide the only readily available 24-hour operations that will respond promptly during any part of day or night. Regardless of their reason for calling, when police do not respond, the citizens who call are usually distressed and often angry. As public service organizations, police should be receptive to performing those functions needed and demanded by their clients. To devote police resources exclusively to criminal apprehension ignores the wishes of a majority of those who seek police services (Galvin, Angell & O'Neill, 1969).

Not only is a criminal apprehension-oriented role definition inconsistent with client expectations as reflected by citizen requests, public service oriented policing seems to have more potential than apprehension-oriented policing in reducing some types of crime. There is considerable research and theory to support the conclusion that many serious crimes with which local police frequently deal, result largely from mental stress, attitudes toward economic and social inequalities, interpersonal conflicts, and perceptions of unfair treatment (Bloch & Geis, 1970; Clark, 1970; Gibbons, 1968; Sutherland & Cressey, 1970).

Regardless of the legitimacy of their feelings, abused or frustrated people may reach a point where changing their situations by whatever means is more important than the threat of arrest, prosecution, or incarceration. These people may conclude that deviant behavior is their most rational option. When this is the case, deviance will be prevented only by adequate treatment of underlying socio-psychological precursors of deviance—either by the police or some other agent. Identification, arrest, and prosecution of people who have adopted deviate methods after perceiving legitimate options as unproductive, has more limited utility than other strategies available to the police.

The value of legal action as an effective deterrent to crime is further diminished by the ineffectiveness of courts and corrections in finding treatment which will rehabilitate offenders (Glasser, 1964; Kassebaum, Ward & Wilner, 1971; Martinson, 1975; Wilkens, 1968). Nationwide, fewer than three percent of the people who commit criminal acts are ultimately convicted of the acts they commit. Those people who are processed through court and correctional agencies frequently return to society in worse financial and mental condition than before they were arrested, thereby perpetuating their dependence on crime (President's Commission, 1967). Hence, arrests and subsequent processing by criminal justice agencies may ultimately be counter-productive.

August Vollmer (1964) once said, "I have spent my life enforcing the laws. It is a stupid procedure and has not, nor will it ever solve the problem unless it is supplemented by preventive measures" (p. 246).

The irony is that if police had a broader role definition, at least a partial solution would be close at hand. In this society a multitude of human service organizations are responsible for performing functions that will prevent deviancy and crime. These agencies exist in every urban area, but they are frequently disregarded by apprehension-oriented police. Many predeviates and deviates who are ignored or funneled into the courts by police could likely receive assistance which would prevent the continuation of their behavior if they were referred to welfare, mental health or other public service organizations (Bard & Berkowitz, 1967; Note 1). Closer organizational ties between the police and other human service agencies should increase the social utility of police. Crime prevention would be increased and

social justice would be enhanced. Such alignment should further produce greater effectiveness on the part of other human service agencies.

One major obstacle to police adoption of a broader role definition
and the improvement of police and human service relationships is the
arbitrary classification of police as the major component of the so
called "criminal justice system." So long as the police conceive of
themselves as the key agency in a system dedicated to arresting and
punishing criminals, they will probably be shackled to a criminal apprehension approach to handling crime. They are likely to continue
to devote their resources to criminal investigation at the expense of
crime prevention and public service activities. Jailing violators of
the criminal code will continue to seem more important than the
long-range deviancy reduction or social improvement activities.

Police Autonomy

Theoretically, police operations should be consistent with the
broad policies and priorities of their superordinate governments. In
many instances they are not. The organizational independence of police from other segments of government is certainly one of the major
factors contributing to this inconsistency (Angell, Hagedorn & Egger, 1974).

Unlike most governmental agencies, police organizations have
staff units which duplicate the activities of similar units at the governmental level. For example, most governmental agencies rely on
the legal department of their superordinate government (e. g. city law
department or county attorney's office) for legal advice. However,
police departments frequently have their own legal advisors. Personnel and training services are provided by a general staff organization
for nearly all government agencies (e. g. city or county personnel and
training department), but the police maintain their own personnel
and training units (Angell & Gilson, 1973; Hagedorn & Angell,
1975).

As a result of such independence, police tend to have less than
optimal information about the problems and plans of their government. Police planning units are usually not aware of planning efforts occurring at the governmental level; and even when they are,
the police seldom participate actively in these planning activities.
Changes planned by local governments fail to consider the potential
impact on police. Police training usually fails to prepare police managers in the same way managers in other agencies are trained.
Therefore, police may not be prepared to participate in carrying out
city-developed plans.

These situations not only produce policy inconsistencies between
the police and other agencies of government, they also reduce the full

realization of the preventive potential in such areas as street light locations, building codes, street designs, and neighborhood organizations. As a result of their lack of information, police fail to seek expert advice and support from personnel and training professionals at
the city level. The opportunities for efficiencies of scale within a
jurisdiction are not realized. In many instances, the problem goes
deeper than a mere duplication of efforts and costs—police have been
known to directly oppose the policies and work of other governmental
agencies and even their superordinate governmental officials. The
result is reduced governmental effectiveness and increased cost.

PROPOSALS FOR IMPROVING ORIGINAL MODEL

In light of the preceding information, the effectiveness of the
Democratic Model could be improved by four courses of action.
First, a more accurate, human service oriented police role should be
developed and formally adopted by the police department. Second,
the police agency should be viewed as an integral part of a "human
service" rather than "criminal justice" system. Third, the General
Services Section of the Democratic Model should be integrated with
the other human service agencies of government. Fourth, functions
of the Coordination and Information Section should be reorganized in
government-wide units which serve a broad range of agencies rather
than simply the police.

Police Role Definition

As previously discussed, improvements in the effectiveness of police in a democratic society are dependent on the acceptance of a
broad human service role for the police. Police must not be confined
by a formal role definition which restricts them, psychologically or
otherwise, primarily to conducting criminal investigations and initiating arrests. The public expects, and the police are in a better position than any other governmental agency to provide, a broad range of
public safety and human services to citizens.

The following are premises about the police which can be used as
boundaries for the development of an appropriate role statement for
a specific police agency (Angell, Hagedorn & Egger, 1974):

1. The preservation of human life is *the* most important police
   responsibility.

2. The police responsibility for maintaining social order is conditioned by a responsibility for protecting individual rights
   and ensuring social justice. Therefore, the maintenance of
   order clearly does not obligate or authorize the police to regi-
   ment society. In our society, the police are expected to protect the right of citizens to behave in individualistic, even so-

cially deviant ways if such individualism and deviance do not injure others or deprive others of the right to just treatment.

3. Police organizations are in a unique position to support other governmental agencies with information about citizen problems and needs that should be addressed.

4. Law enforcement is an important function of the police; however, physical arrest is only one strategy that police use to enforce laws. In most areas, police are required to *enforce* the criminal code, but they are not specifically directed to *arrest* every person who violates a law. Therefore, police officers can legitimately exercise discretion if it results in the enforcement of laws (Radelet, 1973).

5. Police should work with and for citizens as much as they serve the government. Police should strive to assist citizens in developing communities that are livable places where people do not have to be afraid of being abused, attacked, placed in jeopardy of injury, or denied fair treatment. Police methods should stress cooperation with the public based on trust rather than fear, and they must emphasize prevention rather than suppression. Police should be concerned about obtaining voluntary rather than forced compliance with laws. The authority and effectiveness of police depend on public approval of police existence, actions, and behavior, and in general, on the police ability to secure and maintain public respect (Radelet, 1973).

Acceptance of these role parameters would facilitate improvement in the operation of the Democratic Model. These parameters will establish a human service prevention-oriented philosophical perspective, thereby permitting police to maximize their socially useful functions. Such a philosophical perspective in the United States is not new—it is a basic element which helps distinguish policing that is supportive of democracy from policing of more authoritarian, totalitarian forms of government.

Reclassification of Police

The community-based, participatory team organizational structure of the Democratic Model is consistent with a human service oriented role definition for police. However, if police were to be classified as a human service rather than a criminal justice agency it would exert tremendous additional influence to change officer attitudes and philosophy from an apprehension to a service orientation. Therefore, police officials should take steps to present their agencies as a part of the human service system. Such a classification would further legitimize police responsibilities for performing public services, which when performed would likely reduce citizen frustrations and interpersonal conflicts.   Acceptance of these responsibilities by police agencies will facilitate more effective crime prevention activities by police officers.

Police who accept the responsibility for becoming involved in solving domestic and other interpersonal disputes will likely prevent assaults and homicides.   Economic problems and discrimination could, through the efforts of the police, receive governmental attention before these problems become motivation for robberies and burglaries.   People with educational or mental deficiencies could receive sympathetic police assistance and referrals to assistance before they feel it necessary to resort to deviance.

The reclassification of the police would not only be psychologically supportive of crime prevention efforts by police, it legitimizes more efficient organizational interfaces.   As previously mentioned, the human service resources available in most urban communities are extensive.   However, the biggest weakness of the current human service system is the absence of a comprehensive coordinating or "gatekeeping" agency which can refer citizens in need to the appropriate service agency (Silverman, 1970).   The classification of police in the human service system places them in a position to effectively perform this duty.   Police are currently available to respond at any time; citizens are already inclined to seek emergency assistance from the police department; and police officers are already generally familiar with the variety of human problems existing in their communities.   Police agencies are presently in the unique position not only of having access to many private service groups and officials, they are also able to communicate directly with all levels of governmental agencies and field personnel.   Therefore, police are the logical gatekeepers for the human service functions of government.

The classification of police forces as human service agencies would in no way detract from their effectiveness as law enforcement operations.   As stated in the role parameters, while most police agencies are legally obligated to "enforce" the criminal laws, physical arrest is only one strategy for law enforcement.   Verbal warnings, direct assistance, and referrals to other social service agencies are all legitimate methods of ensuring compliance with the law.   The classification of police as a human service agency should increase the number of enforcement strategies available to an officer.   Nonetheless police must continue to make referrals to the criminal justice system (e. g., prosecutors, courts, probation and parole agencies, and correctional institutions) when such actions are necessary for the protection of other members of society and in those instances where incarceration is essential to rehabilitation.

The movement of police from a criminal justice to a human service system has other obvious implications for police operations and procedures. As an entry point of the human service system, the first responsibility of police officers when responding to a citizen problem will be to stabilize the situation sufficiently to obtain information needed for a gross diagnosis of the problem. Upon completion of the diagnosis, the officers can decide on the most appropriate course of action to alleviate a problem and prevent its recurrence. For instance, in handling a domestic dispute, the police officer may decide that the key problem is underlying financial difficulties, in which case the officer can assume responsibility for establishing a relationship between the participants in the dispute and the appropriate family financial planning, unemployment, or welfare agency. In some instances, police administrators may go even further than simple referrals. Some departments have already established specialized units such as the Portland, Oregon, Police Sunshine Unit, to provide emergency, temporary relief to people in need.

Establishing Police/Human Service Teams

Consistent with classification of police in the human service system, the General Service Section of the Democratic Model should be expanded to include people from other human service agencies as members of the community teams (Handbook of Organization and Decentralization, 1974). Such expansion would mean that in addition to sworn police officers, a team might include health officers, nurses, nutritionists or home economists, family counselors, welfare or public assistance experts, lawyers, and others familiar with all varieties of human services including veterans' assistance, welfare programs, community action programs, human relations assistance, and other areas relating to the health, safety and welfare of citizens.

The organization and operation of these teams should follow the basic format of the original Democratic Model. Each team should be organized in a well-defined geographic area with enough common characteristics to be considered a community. The specific membership composition of each team should be based on the characteristics, problems and needs of its specific community. Each team would work closely with the citizens and clients to define problems, needs and preferences, and to provide appropriate social and police services for the community.

Teams could be made of people with complementary skills which are appropriate for the needs of the community served. The team members would be generalist-specialists; that is, every member should be knowledgeable in the general area of human services but at the same time have highly developed skills in a specific area. Teams so organized could have a variety of experts among their members to provide consultation and functional supervision for the team. This would give every team the ability to handle expeditiously the variety of human problems coming to its attention.

Teams should be required to observe common ethical and legal standards. Financial support for the teams should be based on a single equitable system for allocation of resources among teams. However, within broadly established limits, internal team management should be the responsibility of the team. Team objectives, priorities, and procedures should be the joint responsibility of team members and community people. Even the specific work assignments and schedules of team members could be within the authority of the team rather than a central management responsibility. Teams should be evaluated by the extent to which each achieves its own objectives rather than, as is the case in traditional police bureaucracies, the extent to which police officers follow agency-wide internal rules or standard operating procedures.

Such a decentralized human service team arrangement should reinforce the philosophical orientation of the previously suggested police role parameters by increasing police contact both with citizens and with other human service professionals. It should facilitate police cooperation with other human service personnel in a manner that will serve the best specific interest and preferences of individual neighborhoods and people. The decentralization of policy development should improve police flexibility and conformance to local neighborhood needs. The maintenance of limited centralized control in broad policy areas should serve to prevent discrimination against minorities and people from other neighborhoods.

Contrary to the contentions of some people, sound decentralization does not entail simply turning control of the police and other human services over to local groups or neighborhood boards (Freund, 1969; Waskow, 1969). Such approaches have been notably unsuccessful in the past. Decentralization should ensure community participation in priority identification and service delivery procedure development; however, at the same time, there must be adequate jurisdiction-wide policy, control, and coordination over all teams to ensure a consistent quality of policing efforts across all neighborhoods. Such centralized coordination is necessary to prevent abuses such as discrimination by police in one community against people who live in another and to guard against the disjointed, fragmented approaches that are common under some decentralized arrangements.

Reorganizing Staff Services

The inadequate interface of police operations with the other parts of government can be corrected by a reorganization of the Coordination and Information Section (Angell, Hagedorn & Egger, 1974; Hagedorn & Angell, 1975). The staff responsibilities of this Section should be separated into two categories—"administrative staff activities" and "support staff activities." Administrative staff activities are those which are directly involved with policy development and implementation such as planning, training, personnel, internal affairs, inspections, financial administration, public information and legal services.   Support staff activities are those which merely assist police by providing an ancillary service such as communication, records, data processing, criminalistics, evidence and property control, detention, identification and photography, facility and equipment maintenance, and property acquisition.   As proposed in the original discussion of the Democratic Model, these functions should all be organizationally centralized.   However, the specific level of centralization is the factor most critical to their effective performance.

Since administrative activities involve broad, but local, policy matters, they should be integrated with the administrative units of the superordinate local government (e. g., police planning should be integrated with city planning, police training should be merged with a city training unit, police inspectional activities should be a part of a city inspectional unit, etc.).

Such an arrangement will not only reduce unnecessary duplications and the cost of local government, it should improve the quality of overall guidance for the police.   It will increase channels of communication between the police and their superordinate government, thereby improving the exchange of information.   The impact of police actions on other units of government can be more adequately assessed and vice versa.   Crime prevention and other governmental responsibilities can be approached from a wider, more effective perspective.   Decisions about street lighting, road design and building codes will be sounder as a result of police participation in the planning processes.   Effective coordination and management of both decentralized teams and the entire local government will be facilitated by such organizational arrangement.

Support staff activities can be standardized and efficiently performed in a routinized fashion.   Since these functions require extensive capital investment, the "economies of scale" principle makes it imperative that they be consolidated to serve the maximum number of agencies consistent with the limits of technology and time.   Due to the high capital investment requirement, a communications center that serves many agencies should be less expensive than several independent communications centers for individual organizations.   A crime laboratory which is independent of any police department and serves many agencies should be able to provide more services and a higher quality of work than several laboratories, each attached to an individual police force.

Support staff activities should be organized on a county, regional or state level to serve as broad a range of agencies as possible.   For example, a communications center might provide services for police, fire, mental health, animal control, and street maintenance agencies. A crime laboratory could serve police, prosecutors, courts, consumer protection agencies, and public defenders. The precise level of centralization of a support staff unit should be based on considerations of technological limitations, variations in the support staff requirements of user agencies, limitations on the ability effectively to control the operations, and time constraints on service performance.

Anticipated Impact of Proposals

The preceding proposals should facilitate more effective operation of the Democratic Model. Redefining the police role and categorizing the police in the human service system rather than the criminal justice system should have a substantial impact on police officer attitudes about their responsibilities. These actions should facilitate legitimization of (1) police provision of general services, (2) police performance of more effective crime prevention functions, and (3) police interface with other social service agencies. On the other hand, these changes will not detract from the police ability to exercise their powers of arrest and prosecution of offenders when the exercise of such power is in the best interest of society.

The inclusion of police and other human service professionals in the same community-based teams should facilitate more effective follow-ups in those situations where additional rapid delivery of special human services are needed by police clientele. The improved communication arrangements should also result in better cooperation on social improvement between police officers and other social service professionals. Regularly scheduled, public team meetings should result in police priorities and policies which better address neighborhood needs.

The merger of police administrative staff units with those of the superordinate government should reduce duplication and costs, and improve the overall coordination of all decentralized human service teams. It should keep the police operation more consistent with the overall policies and procedures of local government. Changes throughout the government should be based on broader information; therefore, such changes will be more rational. Since plans will be more comprehensive, the probability of their successful implementation will be increased.

Finally, the organization of support staff on a county, regional or state level should ensure economies of scale and more efficient achievement of mechanistically performed support functions. Dispatching can be provided not only for the police, but also for other agencies such as fire, animal control, mental health, medical examiners, and even street maintenance agencies. Citizens could receive practically any type of emergency service from government simply by calling a single number. Crime laboratory services would be organized as readily available to a broad range of criminal justice people including police, prosecutors, public defenders, and judges.   This would facilitate increased quantity and quality of criminalistics work. Large-scale purchasing and maintenance of police equipment by a regional operation should provide additional economies of scale. Since the support staff activities can be performed by civilians, rather than sworn police officers, the personnel cost of performing these duties may be substantially reduced.

As with the original Democratic Model, a major constraint on implementation is human resistance to changing such a fundamental institution as police (Sayre & Kaufman, 1960; Sherman, 1975). In most instances, administrators who want to initiate changes along the preceding lines will have to concern themselves not only with the normal planning of organizational structure and procedures, they must also take steps to modify the broader organizational environment in order to enhance receptivity to the necessary changes.

SUGGESTIONS ON IMPLEMENTING PROPOSED CHANGES

Organizational modifications needed to convert a classical police bureaucracy to the Democratic Model require a thorough understanding of social behavior and the ability to conceptionalize and carry out complex administrative strategies (Igleburger, Pence & Angell, 1973). Stated another way, administrators must not only know *why* the organizational changes are desirable, they must also have an understanding of *how* to ensure that the appropriate restructuring of the police agency will occur.

The Democratic Model implementation will disrupt established practices and power arrangements—both in the agencies affected and the broader community (Sherman, 1975). The element most critical to an administrator's ability to successfully implement the Democratic Model is attitudes—attitudes of the public, of higher officials, of subordinate managers and of other employees. Simply because an administrator has the formal authority to initiate organizational changes does not mean he has sufficient power. The key to a chief's power lies in those attitudes that determine the extent of resistance, apathy, or support for changes in the police organization.

If the Holyoke, Massachusetts Democratic Team Police experiment was an indication of what can be expected in other places, lower level police officers who become members of a team arrangement quickly adopt supportive stances (Angell, Galvin & O'Neill, 1972; Fink & Sealy, 1974). Further, those aspects of the Model which facilitate increased police-citizen contact and which enhance communication between the police and the public seem to result in improvements in the attitudes of both citizens and police toward each other. The potential of support from these areas must be recognized and fully utilized by the administrator.

In regard to dealing with other people, it is essential that a majority of those affected by changes must have supportive or neutral attitudes toward the changes. Therefore, officials who wish to implement the Democratic Model and related organizational changes must take steps to cultivate such support or neutrality.

The cultivation and maintenance of necessary support is more an art than a science. It is difficult to define universally applicable strategies for building support. However, some of the methods which appear to have facilitated organizational changes similar to those proposed are as follows.

First, in order for the public to support such changes in the police, citizens must be at least vaguely dissatisfied with the existing police arrangements and convinced that the administrator sincerely intends to improve the organization. Given citizen attitudes toward goverment, such dissatisfaction may well exist naturally.

An administrator can actively cultivate public support for implementing the Democratic Model by exposing and displaying a concern for the public and the needs of police clients. This concern can be reflected both in statements and in actions. The administrator can walk the streets in neighborhoods and particularly ghetto areas, attend community meetings, talk with all varieties of citizens, attempt to facilitate the resolution of citizens' problems which come to attention, and encourage managers of other human service agencies and police employees to cheerfully follow the example. In addition, the administrator should provide police employees with direct exposure to public demands and take steps to educate officers to their clients' needs. Police officers can be encouraged to attend meetings of neighborhood groups to spend on-duty time visiting with people as well as talking with people who have complained about police behavior. Officers should be urged to visit shut-ins and invalids, and to associate with people throughout their area of assignment.

These actions should make it apparent that the administrator is dedicated to an organization based on a philosophy of providing useful services to people who need such services. The message can be reinforced with news releases, public statements and speeches, and policy enactments which give the philosophy constant visibility.

In addition to displaying concern for citizens and public needs, the chief administrator can also take specific steps to establish an internal organizational environment that will support progressive organizational changes. Such actions might include:

1. Removing the traditional secrecy surrounding the police organization and opening the police agency and its operations up to inspection by interested officers and citizens.

2. Establishing tolerance within the organization by such moves as rescinding policies which force all police to look and behave alike, and by deliberately recruiting and hiring all varieties of minorities and atypical people.

3. Reducing reliance on formal authority and commands directed at forcing subordinate conformity to arbitrarily established behavioral patterns. This includes providing employees and citizens with opportunities to participate in a meaningful way in police policy decisions that affect their lives and work activity (i.e., the development of reorganization plans, the writing of police procedures).

4. Improving communications through informational documents, open staff meetings, employee involvement in planning and implementation activities; expanding the use of communications technology such as closed circuit television to all sections of the agency; establishing more rational assignment and transfer policies; increasing the opportunities for meetings among personnel of all ranks to discuss work-related activities; and allocating more resources to training and in-service education.

5. Reducing organizational rigidity by such techniques as temporary planning task forces and special-purpose units made up of citizens and employees (Igleburger, Pence & Angell, 1973).

The major source of internal resistance to the revised structure has been management personnel and specialists—particularly traffic officers and detectives. Employees in both of these groups, rightly or wrongly, perceive themselves as suffering substantial losses of prestige and power under the Democratic arrangements. Their resistance and their ability to articulate arguments against the Democratic arrangements seem to increase as time passes.

Managers at times create problems by playing on the insecurity of generalist officers in performing major investigations. They may attempt to create dissention by neglecting to perform coordinating and informational functions which would increase subordinate confidence and smooth the implementation process.

Investigators tend to play up the initial problems which occur in the preparation of felony cases and the processing of these cases through the courts. They can usually produce evidence of an initial decrease in convictions, particularly in homicides, to support contentions of a decrease in police effectiveness. Prosecuting officials, who are effected by changes in procedures, often support the contentions of the specialists.

The resistance of managers should be anticipated and addressed early by expanding their responsibility for the development of efficient teams. Managers who are to be assigned key positions in the system should be sympathetic to the changes and well prepared to handle collegial organizational methods prior to any implementation moves. They should be aware of their accountability for the success of the component for which they have ultimate responsibility.

Resistance from specialists can be handled by (1) establishing with the prosecutorial officials sound plans for efficiently processing major cases, (2) reassigning investigators to teams at the outset of geographic reorganization, (3) providing team officers with uncomplicated procedures for processing cases and adequate training concerning the new problems they will encounter, and (4) implementing the initial reorganization jurisdiction-wide in an expeditious fashion.

These actions should reduce the prosecutorial support for specialists, reduce the efficiency of the specialists communication system, enhance generalists security and confidence, and reduce the time available for resistance to build and solidify.

An administrator also has other, more traditional devices which can be used to neutralize resistance among police employees. Among these tools are indoctrination, rewards, punishment, cooptation, transfer, camouflage, and diversionary tactics. Both the ethics and possible unanticipated consequences of each of these strategies should be given careful consideration prior to their use. Actions which can be interpreted as reflecting to employees or citizens a lack of integrity on the part of the administrator should be avoided. Commitment to the realization of the changes must be accompanied by fairness and mutual trust relationships. Fairness and trustworthiness does not preclude an administrator from playing a strong and active management role. In fact, they will enhance the administrator's ability to maintain his leadership position.

One final comment on implementation. One of the must crucial elements in the successful achievement of implementation is the ability of the administrator to present and defend with clarity the changes for the managers of other related agencies, superiors, legislative officials, and the press. To do this the administrator must have strong, aggressive, and competent staff support. Perhaps the most important positions in this regard are inspections, planning, training, and press relations. The people assigned to these positions should be carefully selected and closely aligned with the administrator prior to the initiation of planning for the changes.

The variables affecting the ultimate success or failure of organizational change are such that, in spite of the methods utilized, failures will occur. Even the best conceived planning will likely fall short of administrative desires. In fact, success may never be total.

CONCLUSION

The original Democratic Model provided the framework for an alternative to classical police organizational arrangements. Where attempted, modifications in police organizational arrangements that are consistent with the Democratic Model appear to have been accompanied by improvements in community relations, employee morale, and police operational effectiveness. The original Model was not promulgated as the apex of police organizational design. Its effectiveness can be increased by (1) formally establishing a more service and prevention-oriented definition of the police role, (2) characterizing the police as a human service agency rather than a criminal justice agency, (3) integrating team police officers and human service workers in community teams assigned to neighborhoods, and (4) centralizing and merging police staff services with non-police governmental staff services at the local government or regional level.

In implementation efforts to date, police administrators have encountered problems implementing aspects of the Democratic Model. Experience reflects the major resistance will start with management and specialized officers. In the future, police executives who undertake substantial organizational modification will have to use more systematic and sophisticated analysis and change strategies to counter resistance. These methods will have to be directed both toward cultivating a good environment for specific modifications and toward guiding the changes.

The preceding observations and proposals do not change the basic structure of the Democratic Model. Rather, the original structure provides a sound foundation for these improvements. Future experience and research, which will hopefully be sounder than past research, will no doubt reveal the need for further rethinking and additional up-dating.

1. Brostoff, P. H. *The Police Connection: A New Way to Get Information and Referral Services to the Elderly.* Paper presented to the National Conference on Crime Against the Elderly, Washington, D. C., June 6, 1975.

2. Ostrom, E., & Whitaker, G. P. *Black Citizens and the Police: Some Effects of Community Control.* Paper presented to the Annual Meeting of the American Political Science Association, 1971.

3. Ostrom, E., & Whitaker, G. P. *Does Community Control of Police Make a Difference?* Paper presented to Western Political Science Association, 1971.

REFERENCES

Angell, J. E. Toward An Alternative to the Classic Organizational Arrangements: A Democratic Model. *Criminology*, 1971, *9*, 186–206.

Angell, J. E. *An Exploratory Study of Changes Accompanying the Implementation of a Community-Based Participatory Team Police Organizational Model.* Unpublished doctoral dissertation, Michigan State University, 1975.

Angell, J. E., Galvin, R. T., & O'Neill, N. W. *An Evaluation of Holyoke Team Policing.* Holyoke, Mass.: Holyoke Model Cities Agency, 1972.

Angell, J. E., & Gilson, J. A Systematic Approach to Criminal Justice Personnel Development. *Ohio Cities and Villages*, February 1973, pp. 7–10.

Angell, J. E., Hagedorn, F., & Egger, S. A. *Staff Report—Police Consolidation Project.* Portland: Portland—Multnomah County, 1974.

Bard, H., & Berkowitz, B. Training Police as Specialists in Family Crisis Intervention. *Community Mental Health Journal*, 1967, *3*, 315–317.

Bekrin, M., & Meeland, T. Sociometric Effects of Race and Combat Performance. *Sociometry*, 1958, *21*, 145–149.

Bittner, E. *The Functions of the Police in Modern Society.* Washington, D. C.: Government Printing Office, 1970.

Bloch, H. A., & Geis, G. *Man, Crime, and Society* (2nd Ed.), New York: Random House, 1970.

Bloch, P. B., & Specht, D. *Neighborhood Team Policing.* Washington, D. C.: Government Printing Office, 1973.

Bordua, D. J. (Ed.) *The Police: Six Sociological Essays.* New York: Wiley and Sons, 1967.

Clark, J. P., & Sykes, R. Some Determinants of Police Organization and Practice in a Modern Industrial Society. In D. Glasser (Ed.), *Handbook of Criminology.* New York: McNally College Publishing Co., 1974.

Clark, R. *Crime in America.* New York: Simon and Schuster, 1970.

Eastman, G. D., & Eastman, E. M. (Eds.). *Municipal Police Administration* (6th Ed.). Washington, D.C.: International City Management Association, 1969.

Elliott, J. T. & Sardino, T. J. *Crime Control Team.* Springfield, Ill.: Charles C. Thomas, 1972.

Fiedler, F. E., O'Brien, G., & Ilgen, D. The Effect of Leadership Styles Upon the Performance and Adjustment of Volunteer Teams Operating in a Stressful Foreign Environment. *Human Relations*, 1969, *22*, 503–514.

Fink, J., & Sealy, L. G. *The Community and the Police—Conflict or Cooperation?* New York: Wiley and Sons, 1974.

Fosdick, R. *American Police Systems.* New York: Century, 1920.

Freund, J. R. Neighborhood Police Districts: A Constitutional Analysis. *California Law Review,* 1969, *57,* 907–947.

Galvin, R. T., Angell, J. E., & O'Neill, M. W. *Survey of Public Attitudes Toward Police Services.* New Haven: City Plan Commission, 1969.

Gibbons, D. C. *Society, Crime and Criminal Careers.* Englewood Cliffs: Prentice-Hall, 1968.

Glasser, D. *Effectiveness of a Prison and Parole System.* New York: Random House, 1974.

Goss, M. E. Patterns of Bureaucracy Among Hospital Staff Physicians. In E. Friedson (Ed.), *The Hospital and Modern Society.* New York: The Free Press, 1963.

Hagedorn, F. & Angell, J. E. A Proposal for Reorganizing Police Training. In *Concept Papers: Police Consolidation.* Portland: Portland—Multnomah County, 1975.

Handbook of Organization and Decentralization. Portland: Multnomah County, 1974.

Igleburger, R. M., Pence, G., & Angell, J. E. Changing Urban Police: Practitioners' View. In *Innovation in Law Enforcement.* Washington, D.C.: Government Printing Office, 1973.

Kassebaum, G., Ward, D., & Wilner, D. *Prison Treatment and Parole Procedure.* New York: Wiley and Sons, 1971.

Lange, C. T., et al. *A Study of Leadership in Infantry Platoons.* Washington, D.C.: George Washington University, 1958.

Lawrence, P., & Lorsch, J. *Studies in Organizational Design.* Homewood, Ill.: Richard D. Irwin, 1970.

Leonard, V. A. *Police Organization.* Brooklyn: Foundation Press, 1971.

Little, R. W. *A Study of the Relationship Between Collective Solidarity and Combat Performance.* Unpublished doctoral dissertation, Michigan State University, 1955.

Martinson, R. *The Effectiveness of Correctional Treatment.* New York: Praeger, 1975.

Misner, G., & Hoffman, R. *Police Resource Allocation.* Berkeley: University of California, 1967.

O'Malley, H. C. *Evaluation Report on the Holyoke Team Police Experiment.* Holyoke, Mass.: Holyoke Police Department, 1973.

Patterson, A. M. The Salford Method of Team Policing. In S. G. Chapman (Ed.), *Police Patrol Readings.* Springfield, Ill.: Charles C. Thomas, 1964.

Perrow, C. *Authority, Goals and Prestige in a General Hospital.* Unpublished doctoral dissertation, University of California, 1960.

Phelps, L., & Harmon, L. Team Policing: Four Years Later. *FBI Law Enforcement Bulletin,* February 1972, pp. 2–5; 8.

President's Commission on Law Enforcement and Administration of Justice. *Crime in a Free Society.* Washington, D.C.: Government Printing Office, 1967.

Press, S. M. *Some Effects of an Increase in Police Manpower in the 20th Precinct of New York City.* New York: NYC Rand Institute, 1971.

Pursley, R. D. Traditional Police Organization: A Portent of Failure? *Police*, October 1971, pp. 29–30.

Radelet, L. A. *The Police and the Community: Studies.* Beverly Hills: Glencoe Press, 1973.

Sayre, W. S., & Kaufman, H. *Governing New York City.* New York: Russell Sage, 1960.

Schwartz, A., & Clarren, S. *Evaluation of Cincinnati's Community Sector Team Policing Program.* New York: Urban Institute, 1974.

Shalala, D. E., & Merget, A. E. Decentralization Plans. In T. P. Murphy and C. R. Warren, *Organizing Public Services in Metropolitan America.* Lexington, Mass.: Lexington Books, 1974.

Sherman, L. Middle Management and Team Policing. *Criminology*, 1974, *11*, 363–377.

Sherman, L., Milton, C., & Kelly, T. *Team Policing: Seven Case Studies.* Washington, D.C.: Police Foundation, 1973.

Silverman, S. B. *A Model for Police-Social Service Cooperation: Project ACORN.* Dayton, Ohio: U.S. Department of Justice, 1970.

Stone, R. C. Status and Leadership in a Combat Fighter Squadron. *American Journal of Sociology*, 1946, *51*, 388–394.

Sutherland, E. M., & Cressey, D. R. *Principles of Criminology.* Philadelphia: J. P. Lippincott, 1970.

Tortortiello, T., & Blatt, S. *Community Centered Team Policing: A Second-Year Evaluation.* Dayton, Ohio: Dayton—Montgomery County Criminal Justice Center, 1973.

Vollmer, A. Community Coordination. In V. A. Leonard, *Police Organization and Management* (2nd Ed.). Brooklyn: Foundation Press, 1964.

Waskow, A. I. Community Control of Police. *Transaction*, December 1969, pp. 4–7.

Webster, J. A. *The Realities of Police Work.* Dubuque, Iowa: Kendall—Hunt Publishing, 1973.

Whisenand, P., & Ferguson, R. F. *The Managing of Police Organizations.* Englewood Cliffs: Prentice-Hall, 1973.

Whitaker, G. *Urban Police Forces: Size and Scale in Relation to Service.* Published doctoral dissertation, University of Indiana, 1971.

Whitehouse, J. E. Historical Perspectives on Police Community Service Functions. *Journal of Public Science and Administration*, 1973, *1*, 87–93.

Wilkens, L. *Evolution of Penal Measures.* New York: Random House, 1968.

Wilson, O. W., & McLaren, R. D. *Police Administration* (3rd Ed.). New York: McGraw-Hill Book Company, 1972.

Yaden and Associates. *Consultant Report: Police Clientele Inventory.* Portland: Police Consolidation Project, 1974.

OVERVIEW OF ORGANIZATIONAL THEORY AND ITS RELATION TO POLICE ADMINISTRATION *

The purpose of this paper is to provide an overview of organizational theory and the theories' implications and impact upon police administration. Previous selections within this text have alluded to or directly discussed these theories. Here, the organizational theories will be discussed in detail to facilitate an understanding of the relationships between and within them. Once this understanding is achieved, the various management processes and their problems and implications will become discernable and thus enable the administrator to manipulate the various managerial processes to introduce change within the police organization. One qualification concerning organizational theory must be made at this point to ensure that organizational theory and management practices are not misunderstood. Organizational theory does not control the behavior within the organization, but the behavior within the organization constitutes the particular theory. In order for an administrator to change his organization from an authoritarian organization to a more humanistic or decentralized organization, he must alter the management processes or behavior within the organization. Too often administrators state changes, but effectually, changes are not made since the behavior of the organizational membership is not changed. Thus, in order to identify an organization's operational organizational theory, the management processes must be identified and examined.

PURPOSE OF ORGANIZATIONS

First, what is an organization? Organizations are contrived social groupings which pursue specific goals via a concerted effort on the part of the organizational membership. Perhaps the most important aspect regarding organizations is goal attainment. Organizations strive toward some stated goal or goals. Amitai Etzioni points out that corporations, armies, schools, hospitals, churches, and prisons are organizations; tribes, classes, ethnic groups, friendship groups, and families are not organizations since their formation is based on social processes rather than goal attainment. He further states that organizations are sometimes referred to as bureaucracies, formal organizations or institutions.[1]

How an organization accomplishes its goals varies from one organization to another; however, managerial processes; communication processes, decision-making, power, authority, goal setting and or-

---

* Larry K. Gaines, College of Law Enforcement, Eastern Kentucky University.

1. Amitai Etzioni, *Modern Organizations.* Englewood Cliffs, N. J.: Prentice-Hall, 1964, p. 3.

dering, and leadership and motivational forces are general to all organizations. The differences between organizations center around how the managerial processes function, and these differences are indicative of the particular organizational philosophy adhered to by the organization. The primary concerns of organizations are to limit the behavioral alternatives of its members and to enhance the predictability of their behavior. The result is control and coordination of effort toward goal achievement. Organizations limit behavioral alternatives by manipulating managerial processes, and this manipulation determines the organization's particular organizational theory.

Additionally, Paul M. Whisenand and Fred R. Ferguson have stated, "organizational theory is problem centered, the problem being how to construct human groupings that are as rational as possible and simultaneously to produce a maximum of individual job satisfaction." [2] This balance between rationality and individual job satisfaction is the crux of organizational philosophies and creates a frustrating dilemma:

> If personalities could be shaped to fit specific organizational roles, or organizational roles to fit specific personalities, many pressures to displace goals, much of the need to control performance, and a good part of the alienation would disappear . . . But even if all the dilemmas which result from the incomplete articulation of personality and organization were resolved, there still would remain those which are consequences of conflicting tendencies built into the organizational structure. [3]

This relationship between the individual personality and the organizational role becomes critical in police organizations because of the autonomous nature of units within police departments and the individual police officer's discretionary power. An objective of the police organization is to increase officer productivity without disrupting job satisfaction. Job satisfaction is related to productivity. The evolutionary process of organizational theory articulation has been a process by which the employee and the organization have been manipulated in different ways to achieve a balance between organizational goal attainment and employee job satisfaction. This evolutionary process has moved through three distinct phases or philosophies; classical, neo-classical or human relations, and structural/systems organizational theory. The thrust of this paper outlines these philosophies and their impact upon police administration.

2. Paul M. Whisenand and R. Fred Ferguson, *The Managing of Police*   *Organizations.* Englewood Cliffs, N. J.: Prentice-Hall, 1973, p. 151.

3. Etzioni, p. 75.

CLASSICAL ORGANIZATIONAL THEORY

Organizations have existed through the ages, but serious study of organizations is relatively new. The scientific study began with Frederick Taylor in the early 1880's. Taylor was primarily concerned with constructing an outline of the way people in organizations should perform. Max Weber, a contemporary of Taylor has often been credited with the early development of the study of organizations. His major emphasis was the study of bureaucracies. The theories of these two men were the building blocks of the classical school of organizational theory. The study of classical organizational theory can be divided into three broad categories. First, Weber's contribution focuses on rationality and its role in the bureaucratic structure. Second, Taylor's contribution, attempts to maximize efficiency by making management a science. Finally, the "principles" which rely on the works of Gulick, Urwick, Mooney and Reiley, and represent a restatement of Weber and Taylor.

Weber's Bureaucratic Structure

Max Weber was the conceptionalist of "bureaucracy", which means "power of the office". An individual's authority and power emanate from the position he holds within the organization. His impressions of bureaucracy and authority grow out of his observations of the Prussian Civil Service in nineteenth century Germany. His ideal model of complex organizations is of paramount importance today. Many organizations adhere to this model, and the ideal model is the foundation for all organizational theories. Two aspects of Weber's work are especially relevant in the study of complex organizations: his discussions of authority and his discussion of the characteristics of bureaucracy.

Authority is the probability that directives or orders are followed because of the belief that they should be followed; compliance is obtained through the recognition of a superior's position within the hierarchy. Weber described authority as:

> Imperative coordination . . . the probability that certain specific commands (or all commands) from a given source will be obeyed by a given group of persons. It thus does not include every mode of existing "power" or "influence" over other persons. The motives of obedience to commands in this sense can rest on considerations varying over a wide range from case to case; all the way from simple habituation to the most purely rational calculation of advantage. A criterion of every true relation of imperative control, however, is a certain minimum of voluntary submis-

sion; thus an interest (based on ulterior motives or genuine acceptance) in obedience.[4]

Within the confines of this definition, Weber described three pure types of authority.

(1) Traditional authority—authority based on perception that a particular individual or class has a preordained right to rule.

(2) Charismatic authority—individualistic leadership based on the individual leader's personality.

(3) Rational authority—authority resultant from hierarchial position.

Regarding Weber's rational authority, he recognized the bureaucracy as the legitimate authority in an organization. Authority was based upon one's position within the organization, and as one's upward mobility within the hierarchy increased, so did his authority. Rational authority provided the organization with an element of stability and continuity. He felt that traditional authority many times left authority in the hands of those not capable of properly exercising it. With charismatic authority, the organization became too dependent upon the charismatic leader, and when the leader left the organization, the organization was weakened due to a lack of leadership.

Once proper authority was achieved, Weber felt that it would be functional in the proper organization. He described this proper organization as having the following characteristics:

(1) There is the principle of fixed and official jurisdictional areas, which are generally ordered by rules, that is, by laws or administrative regulations.

(2) The principles of office hierarchy and of levels of graded authority mean a firmly ordered system of super-and subordination in which there is a supervision of the lower offices by the higher ones.

(3) The management of the modern office is based on written documents ("the files"), which are preserved in their original or draft forms.

(4) Office management, at least all specialized office management—and such management is distinctly modern—usually presupposes thorough and expert training.

(5) When the office is fully developed, official activity demands the full working capacity of the official, irrespective of the

4. Max Weber, *The Theory of Social and Economic Organization*, trans. A. M. Henderson and Talcott Parsons.   New York: The Free Press, 1947, p. 324.

fact that his obligatory time in the bureau may be firmly de-
limited.

(6) The management of the office follows general rules, which
are more or less stable, more or less exhaustive, and which
can be learned.[5]

Weber's characteristics of a proper organization were not a description of a particular organization, but represented an ideal type, and
as an organization approached this ideal type, it would become more
efficient. It represented a model which emphasized characteristics
which were important and common to organizations. Weber was distinguishing bureaucracies from organizations which were held together by a particular leader. Further, Weber felt that membership
in an organization was a career or vocation, and when individuals entered the organization, they moved up in the structure with little
movement from one organization to another. The principal assumption behind this model was that man was rational or acted rationally,
and from rational man, a rational organization would evolve.

Scientific Management

Frederick W. Taylor and Henri Fayol individually made major
contributions to classical organizational theory in the form of scientific management, which addresses itself to improving the efficiency
of the organization. Taylor characterized the best management of
the time as management of initiative and incentive. This term de-
notes management in which the workmen give their best initiative
and in return receive some special incentive. Taylor attempted to
improve this type of management by the use of scientific management which entailed utilizing scientific principles of job analysis.

> Now, among the various methods and implements used in
> each element of each track there is always one method and
> one implement which is quicker and better than any of the
> rest. And this one best method and best implement can only
> be discovered or developed through a scientific study and
> analysis of all the methods and implements in use, together
> with accurate, minute, motion and time study.[6]

Prior to Taylor, work was somewhat unorganized. The foreman
was assigned a project and his job was to ensure that his men
worked. Generally, workers were engaged in numerous tasks which
the foreman did not comprehend, and it was difficult for the foreman
to supervise or increase worker output. Additionally, job standards

5. Max Weber, "Bureaucracy," in *Or-
ganizations,* Volume I, ed. Joseph A.
Litterer. New York: John Wiley &
Sons, 1969, pp. 29–31.

6. Frederick W. Taylor, *The Principles
of Scientific Management.* New
York: W. W. Norton & Co., 1911, p.
25.

were non-existent.   Most workers learned their particular trade by themselves.   Thus, several men could perform the same task with each man doing it differently with varying degrees of efficiency.

Taylor felt that improvement would come only if management analyzed tasks and assumed more responsibility.   These responsibilities were:

(1) Develop a science for each element of a man's work, which replaces the old rule-of-thumb method.

(2) Scientifically select and train, teach, and develop the workman, whereas in the past he chose his own work and trained himself as best he could.

(3) Heartily cooperate with the men so as to insure all of the work being done in accordance with the principles of the science which has been developed.

(4) There is an almost equal division of the work and the responsibility between the management and the workmen.[7]

These tenets were an attempt to provide an orderly manner to work. Taylor's work suggested job planning which had seldom been utilized, and he attempted to have the worker and the manager cooperate rather than be opposed to each other.

Taylor provided one other element, the concept of functional supervision.   Custom had dictated one foreman per work group.   This work group would be responsible for accomplishing a wide variety of tasks.   Taylor recognized that it was impossible for one foreman to master all the knowledge required to provide adequate supervision for these varied tasks.   Taylor felt there should be a system of functional supervision where the supervisors were specialized and provided specialized supervision to groups of workers.   Each supervisor would master all the knowledge required to provide adequate supervision for this facet among numerous work groups.   This had not been done in the past, because it was believed that workers should be responsible to only one supervisor.   Taylor felt that functional supervision would increase efficiency since all facets of the job would be brought under the eyes of supervisors who possessed expertise in relevant areas.

The result of scientific management was to emphasize method over men.   Again, the assumption that man is rational played a predominant role in Taylor's theory.   If there were mutual benefits, workers and management would cooperate.   If there was cooperation, the principal goal of the theory—increased organizational efficiency —would be met.

Scientific management's other principal contributor, Henri Fayol, focused upon the management of the organization.   He believed

7.   Ibid., pp. 35–7.

there was a universal science of management applicable to all organizations.   Additionally, he recognized that the need for technical knowledge decreased as hierarchical position increased.   Fayol developed five principles which he felt were imperative if an organization was to be successful:

(1) A program of action prepared by means of annual and ten-year forecasts.

(2) An organization chart to guarantee order and assure each man a definite place; careful recruiting and technical, intellectual, moral, administrative training of the personnel in all ranks in order to find the right man for each place.

(3) Observation of the necessary principles in the execution of command (i. e. direction).

(4) Meetings of the departmental heads of every division; conferences of the division heads presided over by the managing director to insure coordination.

(5) Universal control, based on clear accounting data rapidly made available.[8]

Whereas Taylor attempted to increase efficiency by improving managerial supervision, Fayol attempted to provide a system by which management itself would be more efficiently organized.

The Principles

According to this approach, there are certain universal rules applicable to all organizations.   For example, James D. Mooney and Alan C. Reiley proposed four principles that organizations should follow.

(1) The Coordinative Principle which was all-inclusive.   Basically, this principle detailed the need for a supreme authority to direct or coordinate the overall organizational activities.   The other principles were the machinery by which this process occurred.

(2) The Scalar Principle refers to organizational hierarchy with authority appropriate to hierarchial position.   Subprocesses are (1) Leadership or positions of authority, (2) Delegation, the conferring of authority and establishment of leaders throughout the organization, and (3) Functional Definition, the delegation of assignments or duties.

(3) The Functional Principle is the concept of division of labor or specialization.

8. Ernest Dale, *Readings in Management: Landmarks and New Frontiers.*   New York: McGraw-Hill, 1965, p. 148.

(4) Staff and Line Principle is the delineation between the organizational advisors and the line commanders.[9]

Many of the concepts behind the principles came from Weber and Taylor. The principles were only a refinement of the foundations previously discussed. However, this approach did take on new dimensions and expanded earlier ideas. Gulick attempted to define the activities comprising administration. He identified seven activities which have become known by the acronym POSDCORB: planning, organizing, staffing, directing, coordinating, reporting, and budgeting. Gulick reasoned that these areas should be the prime areas of concern for the administrator. Organizational theorists who utilized the principles approach were attempting to identify universals which were applicable to all organizations and expand the knowledge in reference to these universals. Generally, these theorists emphasized the structure of the organization rather than the individuals within the structure.

CLASSICAL THEORY'S IMPACT ON POLICE ORGANIZATIONS

Seemingly, police administration has evolved around the principles of classical organizational theory. The literature is replete with essays prescribing, describing, and critiquing police organizations in terms of classical organizational theory. The President's Commission on Law Enforcement and Administration of Justice stated that police departments' objectives can be achieved more easily, efficiently, and satisfactorily by utilizing the following principles:

(1) The force's work is apportioned among the various individuals and units according to a logical plan.

(2) Lines of authority and responsibility are made as definite and direct as possible.

(3) The number of subordinates who can be effectively supervised by one officer is not exceeded.

(4) There is "unity of command" throughout the organization.

(5) Responsibility, once placed, is accompanied by commensurate authority, and that once delegated, the user is held to account for the use he makes of it.

(6) The efforts of the organizational units and of their component members are coordinated so that all will be directed harmoniously toward the accomplishment of the police pur-

9. John M. Pfiffner and Frank P. Sherwood, *Administrative Organization.* Englewood Cliffs, N.J.: Prentice-Hall, 1960, p. 60.   See James D. Mooney and Alan C. Reiley, *Onward Industry!: The Principles of Organization and Their Significance to Modern Industry.* New York: Harper and Row, 1931.

pose. The components thus coordinated will enable the organization to function as a well-integrated unit.[10]

The above principles are a mirror image of the writings of Taylor, Weber, Fayol, Gulick and Urwick, and Mooney and Reiley. Additionally, The National Advisory Commission on Criminal Justice Standards and Goals states, "the traditional principles or organization should be a guide to administrators and supervisors, but should be by-passed if agency goals can be achieved by less traditional means." [11]

Classical organizational theory has been able to persist as a viable philosophy for several reasons: [12] (1) It persists because it is pro-management. It fits with an authoritarian attitude which is still prevalent in law enforcement. (2) The principles are simplistic and ordered; they are generally few in number and uncluttered by jargon. (3) The principles are formulated in a prescriptive manner. Prescription saves time for the manager, and provides him with something outside himself upon which he can depend. This prescription also has an aura of certainty for the manager. This is particularly important since most police administrators are police officers by trade as opposed to being trained administrators. (4) Classical theory is impersonal; emotions are difficult and are avoided by managers. Classical theory provides the manager with a dogma which tells him that if he adheres to it he will be successful. Finally, the classical approach to organizational theory has been successful on many occasions, and in cases of failure, it has not been the fault of the theory, but the people who attempted to operationalize it; so claim the advocates of classical organizational theory.

Criticism of Classical Theory

In essence, the criticisms that have been made of classical theory fall into two classes, those which attack the inconsistencies and lack of sophistication of the formulations of classical theorists and those which take issue with the pro-management bias of classical theory.

The principle critic of classical theory's inconsistencies has been Herbert Simon.

It is a fatal defect of the current principles of administration that, like proverbs, they occur in pairs. For almost every principle one can find an equally plausible and accepta-

10. The President's Commission on Law Enforcement and Administration of Justice. Report of the Commission. *Task Force Report: The Police.* Washington, D.C.: Government Printing Office, 1967, p. 46.

11. National Advisory Commission on Criminal Justice Standards and Goals,

Report of the Commission: *Police.* Washington, D.C.: Government Printing Office, 1973, p. 46.

12. This discussion is based on, T. E. Stephenson, "The Longevity of Classical Theory." *Management International Review,* Vol. 8, No. 6 (June, 1968): 77–83.

ble contradictory principle. Although the two principles of the pair will lead to exactly opposite organizational recommendations, there is nothing in the theory to indicate which is the proper one to apply.[13]

V.   Subramanian examines the principles in the same vein:

For example, according to the principle of span of control the number of subordinates whom a superior can efficiently supervise is limited to, say six. By adopting this in a large organization one would create more levels in the hierarchy than if a larger number, say twelve, was placed under each supervisor. At the same time, there is a contradictory principle which enunciates that administration efficiency is enhanced by keeping at a minimum the number of organizational levels through which a matter must pass. It is obvious that whenever one seeks to increase efficiency according to the former principle it automatically decreases according to the latter, but there is nothing in the statement of these two principles to indicate which one is to be preferred on a given occasion or how the two considerations are to be balanced. Simon goes on to show that all the other principles occur in such contradictory pairs. Thus the principle of unity of command is opposed by the principle of function foremanship, and the principle of departmentalization by purpose is opposed by the principle of departmentalization by process.[14]

From these criticisms, Simon surmises that the principles are not administrative principles, but only criteria for describing and diagnosing administrative situations.

Much of the classical theory criticism stems from its pro-management bias. Chris Argyris states that the chain of command principle tends to make individuals dependent upon, passive toward, and subordinate to their leader.[15] This is substantiated by Georgette Bennett Sandler and Ellen Mintz, who state, "within the organization (police) a para-military structure tends to create a sense of demoralization and powerlessness at the lower ranks."[16] Argyris attacks the

13. Herbert Simon, *Administrative Behavior*. New York: The Free Press, 1945, p. 20.

14. V. Subramanian, "The Classical Organization Theory and its Critics." *Public Administration*, Vol. 44, (Winter, 1966): 435–446.

15. For a complete examination of this topic see, Chris Argyris. *Personality*

and Organization. New York: Harper & Row, 1957.

16. Georgette Bennett Sandler and Ellen Mintz, "Police Organizations: Their Changing Internal and External Relationships." *Journal of Police Science and Administration*, Vol. 2, No. 4 (December, 1974): 458–463.

principle of unity of direction, because it substantially inhibits individual psychological success. The individual is forced to pursue prescribed goals via prescribed means. The individual generally has no input into these goals and modes. This lack of input is a violation of a basic principle of personality; that is, a mature individual is expected to act immaturely by being subservient. Additionally, by not participating in the development of programs (goals), lower ranking individuals have no stake in their success; therefore, it becomes doubtful if the individuals will exert an appreciable amount of effort toward the realization of those goals. The span-of-control principle is largely criticized because it increases the administrative distance between individuals.[17] Additionally, strict adherence to this principle increases communication problems as the number of levels of authority increase. By limiting the number of subordinates to a minimum, there is greater emphasis on close supervision which, in turn, tends to increase the subordinate's feelings of dependence and stifle his innovation. Subramanian sums up the pro-management criticism:

> Even its (classical organizational theory) earliest proponents, Taylor and Fayol, were already faced with the facts of worker's dissatisfaction and worker's organizations and the need for the worker's cooperation. The classicalist's sin was not really unawareness of the "managed part" of the organization; rather did it consist in the confusing way they dealt with it in their theory, its inconsistencies and vagueness.[18]

Finally, Pursley notes that the traditional police organization will fail for two reasons. First, society's ever changing nature and power to redefine the police role necessitates that the police must alter their goals and methods of achieving these goals. If classically organized, the police will not be able to stay abreast of society's needs. Second, there is a rising level of expectation and self-concept among some police officers due to the recruitment of better educated officers.[19] This in itself will force change, and classical organizations are incapable of radical change.

THE HUMAN RELATIONS PHILOSOPHY

The human relations philosophy was a reaction to the mechanistic organizational prescriptions of the classical era. The human relationists focus on the human elements of the organization which were of little concern to the classicalists. The human relations approach

17. For a complete critique of the "Principles of Management" See Simon, pp. 20–60.

18. Subramanian, p. 441.

19. Robert D. Pursley, "Traditional Police Organization: A Portent of Failure?" *Police*. (October, 1971): 29–30.

evolved from the discovery that workers tend to form informal groups or organizations within the formal organization which influence the formal structure. The human relationists emphasize multidirectional communication and shared decision-making and leadership. The origins of the human relations philosophy are usually associated with the Hawthorne studies and the writings of such authors as Elton Mayo, Mary Parker Follett, Kurt Lewin, and Douglas McGregor.

The Hawthorne Studies

These studies were conducted at the Western Electric Company's Hawthorne Works in Chicago from 1927 to 1932. They initially attempted to verify a principle of scientific management, that better illumination would result in increased productivity. The investigators were unable to find such a relationship. In a later experiment, workers were segregated in a room and the effects of fatigue were examined. Rest breaks were given to the workers, and as the rest breaks were given, production increased. However, production did not increase proportionally with the rest breaks. Even when rest breaks were decreased and finally eliminated, production continued to increase. After examination of the results, researchers hypothesized that increased production resulted from modifications of the social arrangements of the workers; the workers were receiving psychological satisfaction due to their being arranged in a small work group and to the increased attention which they received as a result of the experiment. The results of the Hawthorne studies questioned the assumptions of scientific management and classical theory in general. Additionally, the studies provided a foundation for the ideological assault upon the classical principles by theorists who believed that the worker should be included in the overall scheme.

Mary Parker Follett, initiated a great deal of the early philosophy surrounding the human relations approach. Follett's thesis was that man's behavior is based upon group behavior, and the individual cannot be understood without considering the individual in an environmental context. Additionally, she emphasized that man is only productive via cooperation and control within his work group.[20]

Concerning cooperation, Follett hypothesized that conflict could be resolved by four methods: (1) voluntary submission of one side; (2) struggle and the victory of one side; (3) compromise; or (4) in-

---

20. Regarding the discussion on cooperation. See Mary Parker Follett, *Creative Experience*. London: Longmans, Green and Company, 1924, p. 156. Regarding the discussion on Control. See Mary Parker Follett, "The Process of Control" in *Papers on the Science of Administration*. ed. Luther Gulick and L. Urwick. New York: Institute of Public Administration, Columbia University, 1937, pp. 159–170.

tegration of interests. The former two methods were unsatisfactory since they involved the dysfunctional utilization of power, and compromise was unacceptable since it only postponed the dispute. Integration of interests involved the identification of a solution which was mutually satisfactory. This mode of conflict resolution becomes particularly important when the conflict involves management and the managed. Only integration of interests could effectively resolve a conflict without producing alienation which would detract from the operating effectiveness of the organization.

Regarding organizational control, Follett examined two facets. First, control within the organization should focus upon the situation, facet-control, as opposed to management control when management is concerned with controlling employee behavior. Regarding facet-control, Follett emphasized that management should base its action, not upon the managed, but upon the situation confronting the manager and the managed. The specific situation generated the desired control factors, not individuals, since the situation, not the individuals, dictates the necessary actions to be taken. Parker's second facet was concerned with correlation of organizational control as opposed to superimposed control. Again, due to the increased complexity of modern management, it becomes improbable that a centralized power center could adequately control the organization through a centralized effort. Therefore, rather than attempting to centrally control the organization, management should attempt to correlate control by delegating and instituting various control processes throughout the organization and attempt to correlate or coordinate these sub-control processes.

Chester Barnard, in his analysis of formal organizations came to a conclusion similar to Mary Follett's. In essence, Barnard's thesis was that people exert various amounts of effort toward the achievement of objectives within the organization. The organization must secure the organizational membership's cooperation to become more productive, and financial incentive is not the most effective manner to secure the cooperation. The willingness of subordinates to accept directives from leaders is the true measure of an individual's authority. Consequently, authority is delegated upward rather than downward in the organization, and the web of authority is maintained by effective communications and managerial support which is by the individual in the organization. The individual or the organizational society becomes the principle component of organizational authority.[21]

21. Chester Barnard, *The Functions of
the Executive.* Cambridge, Mass.:
Harvard University Press, 1938.

The role of subordinates' acceptance of their leader's authority is an essential aspect of the organization. F. J. Roethlisberger and William J. Dickson state:

> The industrial concern is continually confronted . . . with two sets of major problems: (1) problems of external balance, and (2) problems of internal equilibrium. The problems of external balance are generally assumed to be economic; that is problems of competition, adjusting the organization to meet changing price levels, etc. The problems of internal equilibrium are chiefly concerned with the maintenance of a kind of social organization in which individuals and groups through working together can satisfy their own desires.[22]

The type of social structure within the organization has definite impact upon the organization's efficiency. Within the organization, employee interactions cause individual and group associations and certain patterns of relationships to be formed. Groups and individuals interacting within these patterns come to accept and react to them. Additionally, each of these groups has its own value system which in total, result in a matrix of values and norms which exert definite influence on the day-to-day operations of the organization. Traditionally, management tends to classify this influence of group collaboration under the technical problems of production and efficiency, and by disregarding the informal organization and its influence, management detracts from its operational efficiency.

The Dynamics of Groups and Individuals

The human relations philosophy is built around group dynamics, and Kurt Lewin in many respects was the creator of group dynamics which has had a profound effect upon the theories of authority and motivation. Lewin's major contribution was his Field Theory. The key elements in the Field Theory were the groups of which an individual was a member or to which he aspired. These groups were the bases for his perceptions, feelings, and actions. A group was never at a steady state, but was in a continual process of adaptation; consequently, the group is dynamic rather than static. Lewin saw behavior as a function of an individual and his environment, and the interaction between the environment and the group to which the individual belonged could be utilized as a vehicle for changing the individual. Lewin surmised that if you want to change the attitudes of a group, you allow the group to make the changes by providing support and the direction of change. Lewin's work formed the foundation for

22. Fritz J. Roethlisberger and William J. Dickson, *Management and the Worker*. Cambridge, Mass.: Harvard University Press, 1939, p. 552.

sensitivity training which attempts to aid individuals to understand the attitudes, feelings, and behavior of others. Over the last several years, sensitivity training has been utilized extensively in managerial development and the study of groups.[23]

These influencial or reference groups are formed and serve several of an individual's needs.[24] First, the group provides companionship to the worker which is necessary for man to be effective. Individual isolation breeds discontent, employee turnover, and poor efficiency. Second, the group provides a source of identification. Basically people want to belong, and fulfill this need through the group. Third, the group provides a guide for acceptable and non-acceptable behavior. This may be in conjunction with or in violation of the formal structure. Fourth, since many jobs are monotonous or boring, the group provides the individual opportunities for initiative and creativity. The group becomes a vehicle to combat boredom. Fifth, the group provides the individual with help in solving problems both technically and personally. Finally, the group provides the individual a degree of protection from management. Once a group is formed, bonds between individuals within the group enhance its solidarity. From this analysis, it becomes apparent that the group becomes a primary motivator of individual behavior.

In 1943, Abraham Maslow identified a multidimensional approach to an individual's motivation. Classical organizational theory had assumed that man is rational; that is, if you pay the employee enough money, he will provide the organization with his work services. The key to motivation was financial incentive. Maslow recognized that financial incentive was an important motivating factor; however, he recognized that there were other sources of particular importance in motivating man in his work environment.[25] In his theoretical hierarchy of man's needs, Maslow identified five levels of needs:

(1) Physiological needs

(2) Safety needs

(3) Love needs

(4) Esteem needs

(5) Self-Actualization needs

23. Daniel A. Wren, *The Evolution of Management Thought.* New York; The Ronald Press, 1972, pp. 324–325.

24. Leonard R. Sayles and George Strauss, *Human Behavior in Organi-* zations. Englewood Cliffs, N. J.: Prentice-Hall, 1966, pp. 83–87.

25. A. H. Maslow, "A Theory of Human Motivation," *Psychological Review,* Vol. 50 (1943): 370–396.

These needs are related to each other and are arranged in a hierarchy. According to Maslow, only the unsatisfied needs are sources of motivation, and when one need is satisfied, the individual progresses up the hierarchy. The theory states that man's first needs are his physiological needs, food and shelter, and as these are satisfied, he progresses to his safety needs. Safety needs are job security, pension plans, etc. and once satisfied, man progresses to the love needs. This process continues until man self-actualizes which involves improving one's self-concept and receiving personal satisfaction from one's job and life in general. Once a need is fulfilled, it no longer motivates behavior.

The essence of Maslow's theory attacked a major premise of the classical school, that man was rational and his sole motivator was economic needs. Maslow's theory states that once physiological and safety needs are met, money is no longer the primary motivator; man's social environment becomes his source of primary motivation. Additionally, when the formal organization fails to fulfill man's social needs, he turns to the informal organization for fulfillment of these needs. The human relationists point out that this primary identification with the informal structure is dysfunctional to the organization unless the informal group is able to provide input into the organization's administration.

Human relationists proposed that if management wanted to improve the efficiency of the organization, it must fulfill the higher needs of its employees. There are two methods by which management could succeed in this task, job enlargement and participative or employee-centered management. Job enlargement entails expanding the duties of the individual employee by giving him a wide variety of tasks which theoretically are more challenging and more interesting. Additionally, job enlargement gives the individual more responsibility which is psychologically satisfying and enables the individual to cope with job boredom and monotony. Research points out that employee satisfaction increases as work becomes more complex and skilled.[26] Job rotation is another tool used to enlarge the activities of the employee. This activity produces a more skilled and better adjusted employee. Human relationists have deemed job enlargement more effective as a motivating device than wages or security.

Participatory management entails:

Widespread delegation of responsibility and authority, considerable managerial freedom in decision-making, a free interchange of ideas at all levels, and the corollary acceptance of the fact that managers grow by having the freedom to fail.[27]

26. For a complete discussion of research on job enlargement. See, Argyris, pp. 177–187.

27. Wren, p. 332.

Theoretically, if the individual is given a chance to provide input into the organization at the level which the organization interfaces with him, he will become more committed to the organization's goals and objectives; hence, he will become a more efficient employee.

Regarding employee centered leadership, Katz found effective supervisors tend to (1) pay more attention to the long range direction of their group, (2) spend more time on motivational problems, and (3) increase the employee's feelings of freedom and self-responsibility by not supervising too closely and by increasing the degree of participation of employees in decisions related to problems affecting their real world.[28]   Human relationists contend that problem-solving by the group, if it is not formally structured, provides more effective solutions.   The essence of this philosophy is delegation, the delegation of responsibility and authority to the lowest levels—the work group.

The Crux of the Human Relations Philosophy

Human relations has been defined as, "the integration of people into a work situation in a way that motivates them to work together productively, cooperatively, and with economic, psychological, and social satisfaction." [29]   In essence, there are two facets to the human relations philosophy: one concerns understanding, describing, and identifying causes and effects of human behavior through empirical investigation, while the other facet is the application of this knowledge into operational situations.   This line of thought combines the economic and psychological aspects with the social aspects of man.

Douglas McGregor sums up the human relations approach in contrast to the classical approach in his Theory X and Theory Y.[30] Theory X which is representative of the classical philosophy includes the following propositions:

(1) Management is responsible for organizing the elements of productive enterprise—money, materials, equipment, people —in the interest of economic ends.

(2) With respect to people, this is a process of directing their efforts, motivating them, controlling their actions, modifying their behavior to fit the needs of the organization.

(3) Without this active intervention by management, people would be passive—even resistant—to organizational needs.

28. Katz, Daniel. "An Overview of the Human Relations Programs. "Groups, Leadership, and Men. ed. Guetzkow.   Pittsburgh: Carnegie Press, 1951, pp. 68–85.

29. Keith Davis, Human Relations in Business.   New York: McGraw-Hill, 1957, p. 4.

30. Douglas McGregor, "The Human Side of Enterprise." Leadership and Motivation.   ed. Warren G. Bennis and Edger H. Schein.   Cambridge, Mass.: MIT Press, 1966, pp. 5–16.

They must therefore be persuaded, rewarded, punished, controlled—their activities must be directed. This is management's tasks—in managing subordinate managers or workers. We often sum it up by saying that management consists of getting things done through other people.

(4) The average man is by nature indolent—he works as little as possible.

(5) He lacks ambition, dislikes responsibility, prefers to be led.

(6) He is inherently self-centered, indifferent to organizational needs.

(7) He is by nature resistant to change.

(8) He is gullible, not very bright, the ready dupe of the charlatan and demagogue.

In contrast, Theory Y proposes that:

(1) Management is responsible for organizing the elements of productive enterprise—money, materials, equipment, people —in the interest of economic ends.

(2) People are not passive or resistant to organizational needs. They have become so as a result of experience in organizations.

(3) The motivation, the potential for development, the capacity for assuming responsibility, the readiness to direct behavior toward organizational goals are all present in people. Management does not end there. It is a responsibility of management to make it possible for people to recognize and develop these human characteristics for themselves.

(4) The essential task of management is to arrange organizational conditions and methods of operations so that people can achieve their own goals best by directing their own efforts toward organizational objectives.

The human relations approach emphasizes the needs of the individual and the informal organization, and if these needs are not satisfied, human relationists postulate that the organization will be ineffective.

The Human Relations Effect on the Police

The human relations philosophy has had little effect upon the administration of police agencies in this country. The literature suggests that, by and large, police administrators adhere to the classical principles of management. However, there are isolated cases in the literature where police departments have attempted to venture away from the classical model.

In several departments, administrators have attempted to provide job enlargement for the lower ranks. The technique usually employed is the establishment of the police generalist as opposed to the police specialist. The Simi Valley, California, Police Department utilizes such a technique. In Simi Valley:

> There is no detective, traffic, or other bureau in the organization. The individual officer is responsible for all patrol activity, traffic enforcement, investigation of burglaries, robberies, homicides, and other police-related matters in his assigned area. In addition, he must devote time to juvenile delinquency and the mediation of neighbor disputes.[31]

The second dimension of the human relations movement, participative management, has had limited impact upon police administration. Participative management entails decentralization with the organizational membership at all levels providing input into decision-making. Theoretically, if the organizational member were able to provide input into decisions affecting him, there is a higher probability that he will be committed to those decisions. The formal leader serves as a facilitor rather than decision mandator. Numerous forms of participative management have supposedly been implemented in police departments; however, only occasionally has a true form of participative management been installed in the management structure. The general case is management soliciting employee input into policy issues after-the-fact; that is, the administrator asks his subordinates their opinions after the policy has been formulated and implemented. Etzioni charges that participative management is sometimes used as a manipulative device creating more problems than authoritative decision-making.[32] Etzioni found that solicitation of employee input which will not be utilized tends to alienate subordinates and creates distrust and resistance toward management.

However, the advent of police employee organizations is providing the impetus for the institution of participative management in police organizations. The union is a major countervailing force to the semi-military structure and serves to curtail the top-down actions of the top administrators and allow lower ranks to exert some influence on the organization. It has been suggested that the police union promotes democratization in a police force since the union is able to force the administration to consider issues the rank and file feel are important or face the consequences of collective dissatisfaction.[33]

31. Frank C. Barnes, "A Unique Approach to Law Enforcement, Delinquency, and Community Relations." *Police Chief.* (Feb., 1973): 58–63.

32. Etzioni, pp. 44–5.

33. George E. Berkley, *The Democratic Policeman.* Boston: Beacon Press, 1969, pp. 46–52.

Team policing which has been sporadically utilized has in some cases taken on the dimension of the "total" group and attempted to utilize job enlargement and participative management within the overall managerial scheme. Dayton, Ohio initiated an experimental program, the Community Oriented Team Policing Project, which was designed to provide job enlargement and officer input into the line management.[34] In Dayton, one district was used to test the concept. The district was policed by 36 team members and four team leaders who were elected by the team members. These officers had total responsibility for their district and did not rely on specialists for support. In essence, it was hoped the generalist approach would be more effective, produce a community centered police structure, and alter the police bureaucratic structure away from the para-military model. This particular model was an attempt to institute job enlargement and participative management within the department.

John E. Angell advocates the utilization of a human relations form of team policing as implemented in Dayton.[35] He promotes the use of police generalists, all of equivalent rank and with no formally assigned supervisor. Such a move, to a large part, eliminates job specialization, hierarchy, and close supervision. The emphasis would be on the work group as opposed to work task. Leadership would develop situationally, that is, each team would choose its own leader in accordance with the particular situation confronting the team. This would allow the individual with the greatest expertise to control the situation. This makes control more viable since, in many instances, a police supervisor does not know any more about the problem at hand than does the officer who is confronted with the problem. The supervisor takes control of the situation because that is his job, not because he knows more about the problem. Additionally, except for broad guidelines to prevent extreme or deviant behavior by the generalists, there would be no procedural guidelines imposed by the administration. Problems and individual evaluation would be handled on a peer level. Again, the essence of this type organization is job enlargement and participative management. If administrators intend to retain the quality police officer, the officer should be placed in a work environment where he feels he has definite input into the department. Angell felt that his model of team policing would provide the atmosphere to attract and retain competent educated police officers.

34. Robert B. Koverman, "Team Policing" An Alternative to Traditional Law Enforcement Techniques." *Journal of Police Science and Administration*, Vol. 2, No. 1, (March 1974): 15–19.

35. John Angell. "Toward an Alternative to the Classic Police Organizational Arrangements: A Democratic Model." *Criminology*, (August/November, 1971): 185–206.

In conclusion, the human relations approach has had little effect upon the managerial processes of most police departments. There are isolated cases where departments have formally incorporated human relation philosophies into their structure; however, this is a rarity. What may be more interesting, however, is the extent to which there is an informal organization and its influence within the police department. It may be that while departments ascribe to a classical organizational philosophy, the informal organization may have significant influence which alters the implementation of the classical philosophy at the operational level.

Criticisms of the Human Relations Approach

In essence, the human relations philosophy states, "once a cohesive primary work group is seen as a motivating force, a managerial elite may become obsolete, and the work group itself becomes the decision-maker".[36] The classical approach emphasized an organization without people; the human relations approach advocated people without an organization. That is, the human relationists in their philosophy have completely disregarded the organization as the initiator of existence. More contemporary writers, the structuralists, advocate that there must be an integration of the people and the organization.

Herbert G. Wilcox suggests that human relationists want to abandon hierarchy and the principles of organization; however, they do not propose any viable alternatives. Additionally, hierarchy is important because it corresponds to the role expectations of those involved within the organization and is a part of all relationships in society.[37]

To a large extent, the humanist attack on the principles is based on Maslow's theory of motivation. Man does not work for money alone, but there is a need to receive psychological satisfaction from the job. There is only theoretical, not empirical evidence to support this contention. Frank K. Gibson and Clyde E. Teasley attempted a review of all the empirical evaluations of Maslow's hierarchy of needs.[38] Their conclusion was that the theory was too simplistic and did not permit the consideration for complex organizational, situational, and personal variables that affect the individual and the or-

36. Warren G. Bennis, "Beyond Bureaucracy. *American Bureaucracy.* ed. Warren G. Bennis. Chicago: Transaction Books, 1970, p. 8.

37. Herbert G. Wilcox. "Hierarchy, Human Nature, and the Participative Panacea." *Public Administration Review.* (Jan./Feb. 1969): 53–64.

38. Frank K. Gibson and Clyde E. Teasley, "The Humanistic Model of Organizational Motivation: A Review of Research Support." *Public Administration Review* (Jan./Feb. 1973); 89–96.

ganization. Additionally, it may be that people use money from their jobs to pursue those higher psychological needs. Proponents of classical theory argue that at least the principles of classical theory work; when there is failure, it is due to the administrator who improperly applies the principles rather than the principles themselves. And, there is very little known about the feasibility of the new theory; there is no proof that the new theory will be any more or less effective than the principles.

There seems to be little data to support the human relations philosophy. However, there has been a wide acceptance of the human relations philosophy in private enterprise throughout this country. This acceptance had its impetus from the labor movement which had gained strength and forced managerial concessions. Managers found that the classical principles were not working; all managers could do was attempt to endure their problems, or incorporate the new managerial style into their organizations. The acceptance of the human relations philosophy was due to the failures of classical organizational theory rather than the accomplishments of the human relations movement.

THE STRUCTURALIST PHILOSOPHY

The structuralist philosophy was a reaction to the human relations model. The structuralists felt that the human relationists were paying far too much credence to the informal group and its influence on the organization. Etzioni identified five areas where structuralists disagreed with the human relationists:

(1) Formal and informal. Human relationists devote full attention to informal relations negating the formal relationships and their effects on informal relations.

(2) The scope of informal groups. Human relationists' total emphasis is the informal group, however, structuralists have found that informal work groups are uncommon and the majority of workers do not belong to such a group.

(3) The organization and its environment. Human relation studies examine the informal group in a void; they fail to examine environment effects upon the group or the total organization.

(4) Material and social reward. The structuralists view the reward systems of human relations as segmental, that is, monetary rewards are just as, if not more important than social rewards. Both rewards systems must be considered.

(5) Factories, churches, prisons, and schools. Whereas, the humanists focused on industrial organizations, the structural-

ists have expanded to include all organizations in hopes of generating universalist theories.[39]

These areas of conflict have prompted the structuralists to push into the structural era of management which incorporates the formal organization and group theory.

One of the early structuralists, Herbert A. Simon, vehemently attacked the classical principles and advocated an integration between the worker and the organization. He felt the central concern of the organization was the boundary between the rational and the nonrational aspects of human social behavior. In essence, he realized the influence of the individual/group upon the organization and vice versa, and that management must consider these influences in order to be effective. However, the great majority of Simon's contemporaries lost sight of the organization and emphasized the informal group.[40]

William Foote Whyte noted that during the human relations era, we learned that which was not true about organizational behavior rather than that which was true. This observation provided an impetus for the rethinking of organizational theory and prompted the structuralist era. Whyte further stated that the structuralists have expanded the human relations philosophy in three general areas; approaches to incentive, accent on face-to-face relations, and the re-entering of the formal organization.[41]

In the approaches to incentive, structuralists found that money is still a prime motivator among employees. Human relationists had postulated that money was secondary to social influence and often could be disregarded. Structuralists find that economic incentive and human relations fit together in a motivational matrix. This fitting together, the proportional relationship of economic needs and human relations needs is constantly changing. Also, the economic/human relations system is constantly disrupting the internal equilibrium of the organization; various groups within the organization vie for economic/human relations rewards. A change in either area, economic raises or job positions receiving more prestige, causes a disruption within the social organization which in turn affects the efficiency of the organization. Finally, structuralists have found that an organization-wide incentive program as opposed to individual, departmental, or sectional incentive plans does not upset the balance of the economic-human relations system.

In the area of face-to-face relations, the structuralists differ from the human relationists in several areas. First, the structural-

39. Etzioni, pp. 45–49.

40. Simon, pp. 20–44.

41. William Foote Whyte, "Human Relations Theory—A Progress Report." *Harvard Business Review*, Vol. 34, (May 1956): 125–132.

ists found that there are misleading conclusions drawn from Hawthorne studies; i. e., there are certain forces operating that are more powerful than the human relations techniques of individual union leaders or management. Additionally, there are numerous groups within an organization; some of these groups are permanent, others are temporary, and an individual may belong to several groups. This premise goes beyond the basic work group concept of the human relationists. Group pressures are multidimensional which entail examination from an organizational perspective rather than the limited individual-group concept. The individual's belonging to several groups tends to dilute the impact of the work group on the individual. Finally, the human relationists left the direction and leadership in the hands of the group. Structuralists are committed to a systems approach, that is, there are numerous work groups within the organization, all receiving some direction from an authority center, but having appropriate input in the policy formulation process.

The third area of disagreement between the structuralists and human relationists is the revitalization of the formal organization. Human relationists emphasized that informal groups are the organization, however, structuralists argue that the structure (formal) and the groups (informal) within the organization should be integrated into a general organizational theory. The focal point of this integration of the group and the formal structure is the supervisor and his role. Structuralists have attempted to keep a formal structure with superiors at key points. At these points the emphasis has changed from close supervision to supportive relationships ensuring cooperative relationships rather than superior-subordinate relationships. Generally, research tends to support this hypothesis, that is, general supervision rather than close supervision increases productivity.[42] Additionally, general and light supervision is ensured by decentralization, that is, increase the span of control in order to allow for job enlargement. This, in effect, forces an interface between management and the informal structure. Further, this form of decentralization is accomplished by planning the structure for its human relations qualities rather than its structural qualities.

Rensis Likert identified four managerial systems, ranging from classical to structural.[43] He endorsed a system where management's primary goal is to coordinate the workers. To a large degree there is a formal structure; however, a great deal of the decision-making and input into policy formulation is delegated to the group. The major emphasis of this approach is management's control of tasks rather than people. In essence, the group controls the people. The founda-

42. Rensis Likert, *New Patterns of Management*. New York: McGraw-Hill Book Co., 1961, Chapter 2.

43. Rensis Likert, *The Human Organization*, New York: McGraw-Hill Book Co., 1967.

tion of this approach is cooperation within and between the various groups toward the achievement of tasks. Management's task is to facilitate and coordinate the various organizational groups.

From these early beginnings of attempting to fit the psychological and organizational variables into the structure, the structuralists have advanced into the systems era. The systems approach is the integration of quantitative measures and human behavior toward specific goals. The essence of the systems era of organizational theory is the attempt to predict the outcomes of interactions between the employee and the organization. This becomes possible because the organization does not operate in a vacuum but is a part of one or several super-systems. Specific behaviors within the organization become reactions to other behaviors or manipulations within the super-system. Patterns develop within the structure, and given specific conditions, it becomes possible to predict behavior with the system.

Systems theory had its origin with Ludwig von Bertalanffy who noted there were characteristics similar in all sciences: (1) the studying of an organism as a whole, (2) organisms tend to strive for a state of equilibrium, and (3) the organism is affected by its environment and the organisms affect the environment.[44] The systems approach complemented cybernetics, the science of control through communications.[45] The study of cybernetics has shown that systems could be designed to control themselves through communications loops which allow the organization to adjust to its environment. The principles of cybernetics and the similar characteristics of organisms have become the foundation of the systems approach.

Daniel Katz and Robert L. Kahn have identified nine common characteristics of open systems.

(1) All systems import energy from their environments. A system must draw energy from other institutions, people, or material environment. No social structure is self-supporting.

(2) The open system transforms or processes energy available to it into a new product (through-put).

(3) Every open system exerts influence (outputs) on its environment.

(4) The pattern of activities of the energy exchange has a cyclic character which enhances study and control.

44. Ludwig von Bertalanffy, "General Systems Theory: A New Approach to the Unity of Science," *Human Biology.* Vol. 23 (December 1951): 302–361.

45. Wiener, Norbert, *Cybernetics.* Cambridge, Mass.: MIT Press, 1948.

(5) There must be negative entropy, that is, open systems must store energy for use during a crisis or during periods which it expends more energy than it absorbs from its environment.

(6) In open systems, input and its conversion process is monitored to provide input or feedback as to how the system is operating.

(7) Open systems have a functional steady state which is not motionless or a dynamic homeostasis. An open system is constantly involved in a given process for which it constantly monitors and adjusts.

(8) Open systems move in a direction of differentiation and elaboration, that is, they are constantly moving toward multiplication and elaboration of roles with greater specialization of function.

(9) An open system is characterized by equifinality. A system can reach the same final state via a variety of paths. As open systems move toward regulatory procedures they satisfy this principle.[46]

The open system concept is a framework which is utilized to explain behavior within an organization. In order to examine the system, its cyclic process must be identified and traced. Human organizations are open systems since the organization is dependent upon its environment for people and materials. Although the organization is constantly in a state of change, each member of the organization has various roles which enhances identification of the organization's cyclic process. Within the general cyclical process, there are various subsystems at work in the same manner as the general system. Hence, in order to understand a particular organization, its subsystems must be understood. This approach differs from earlier theories in that early theorists believed the system was closed and did not consider the interaction between organization, man, and his environment; however, an organization cannot survive as a closed system, but must adjust to its internal and external environments. The systems approach is a theoretical foundation which attempts to enable an organization to cope with its environment. The systems approach admits that there is no universal theory to explain the interworkings of all organizations, but the systems approach does attempt to identify a super structure by which all organizations operate. The human and material interfaces will vary from one organization to another, but the overall structure will remain the same.

46. Daniel Katz and Robert L. Kahn, *The Social Psychology of Organiza-* *tions.* New York: John Wiley & Sons, 1966, pp. 19–26.

Structuralist Effect Upon the Police

Traditionally, there are two models of administration in police organizations, the classical model and the structural model. Police organizations predominately abide by the former model. This has occurred because the classical model fits in with the authoritarian attitudes of management, it is simple, since police administrators by and large are professional police officers rather than professional administrators, it is more easily grasped, and finally, it removes personality from administration.[47] However, a few police agencies are beginning to utilize structuralist philosophies.

One area where the structuralists have had influence is in information systems. One of the main building blocks of the systems concept is the gathering of data in order to adequately analyze a situation. In this vein, police agencies are beginning to construct massive data retrieval and analysis systems. Police administrators utilize this information to predict crime and disperse their personnel. Due to federal involvement many police departments in the nation are affected by this structuralist innovation.

Very few departments have progressed beyond this point. There are isolated cases where departments are attempting to use programs such as Management by Objectives (MBO), Program Evaluation and Review Techniques (PERT), and Planning-Program-Budgeting Systems (PPBS). These programs attempt to systemize various aspects of the police endeavor. James J. Hennessy argues that if police administrators utilize PPBS, it will enable them to utilize more information in their decision-making and hence, arrive at better decisions.[48] In the same vein, others have argued for the use of structuralist innovations to improve the efficiency of police. Hoover advocates the systematization of programming in police departments.[49] Although the police literature tends to advocate a structuralist approach to police administration, the structuralist approach is practiced in only a few departments. Thus far, classical theory seems to be the predominant mode of management; however, the structuralist approach may be beginning to erode this old philosophy.

Criticisms of Structuralist Theory

Structuralist theory is relatively new, consequently there are only sporadic criticisms. The human relationists are generally opposed to the structuralist theory, because it reincorporates the formal

47. Stephenson, pp. 77–83.

48. James J. Hennessy, "PPBS & Police Management." *The Police Chief.* (July 1972): 62–67.

49. Larry T. Hoover, "Planning-Programming-Budgeting Systems: Problems of Implementation for Police Management." *Journal of Police Science and Administration,* (March 1974): 82–93.

organization. Another criticism of the structuralists questions the availability of needed data. The structuralist programs are dependent on data. Augustus Turnbull in an analysis of PPBS noted that the program would be of great benefit to the manager; however, it is difficult if not impossible to accurately accumulate the required data.[50] Additionally, decisions have to be made within time frames; many times there is not enough time to adequately analyze the data. Hoover joins in those criticisms, but recommends that alternatives such as programmatic budgets be utilized because research has not provided adequate information to compare alternative police programs.[51]

Etzioni was critical of the open systems approach because it was exacting and expensive.[52] Due to the very nature of the theory, it is difficult to apply and is applicable to some organizations, but not to others. Additionally, Richard Hall points out that due to the scope of the open systems approach, program research becomes exacting and expensive.[53] Few researchers have the tools or the ability to take all the components which should be examined into account. Finally, Herbert Simon and James March have stated that decision-making is based on bounded rationality, even with the aid of computers it becomes difficult for the decision-makers to grasp all the information to make a rational decision under the systems model.[54]

In conclusion, the structuralist philosophy is relatively new. Only recently have organizations attempted to adapt to this new model. Lawrence Sherman after studying team policing in America, notes that it's extremely difficult to change, especially something as monumental as the organizational model.[55] This inability to change is a major drawback to the adaptation of the structuralist philosophy in police organizations. However, in business where the model has been successfully adopted by the organization, results show improvements in the efficiency of the organization. The systems approach will ultimately increase the knowledge about the criminal justice system and improve the practice of the profession.

50. Augustus B. Turnbull, "PPBS in Perspective," *Public Administration.* ed. Robert T. Golembiewski, et al., Chicago: Rand McNally & Co., 1972, pp. 598–605.

51. Hoover, pp. 82–93.

52. Etzioni, p. 17.

53. Richard H. Hall, *Organizations: Structure and Process,* Englewood Cliffs, N. J.; Prentice-Hall, 1972, p. 25.

54. Ibid.

55. Lawrence W. Sherman, "Middle Management and Police Democratization: A Reply to John E. Angell." *Criminology* (February 1975): 363–377.

THE APPLICATION OF ORGANIZATIONAL THEORY TO THE PROBLEM OF POLICE RESISTANCE TO POLICE COMMUNITY RELATIONS *

In the past 10 years, millions of dollars have been spent on the problem of improving police community relations within our urban municipal police departments. We have seen gimmicks emerge out of frustrated attempts to make police departments more palatable to the people they serve. We have seen countless innovative programs developed, including neighborhood block committees, police athletic leagues, and family crisis intervention programs. Policemen have received an increased amount of training, ranging from sensitivity sessions to college academic programs. Unfortunately, in spite of this massive attempt to reduce the polarity that exists between the policeman and the community, mutual hostility and distrust still abound.

In view of the fact that the tone of police-community relations has not been appreciably altered, and still remains one of our nation's most pressing dilemmas, it is remarkable that the basic structure and function of our municipal police departments have not changed in the last 10 years, if not the last 70 years. Moreover, it seems astounding that with all the recent experimentation in municipal police departments, there have been so few attempts at redesigning the basic structure of the police organization itself.

Because of the absence of structural change within police organizations, it is appropriate to pose the following questions:

1. Do police administrators view the problem of police-community relations as restricted to the patrolmen or line level?

2. Are municipal police departments impossible to redesign because of their very size?

3. Is there a virtual vacuum of reasoning when considering the police-community relations problem from an organizational point of view?

4. Do police administrators themselves resist changes that improved community public relations would require?

The answers to the above questions may indicate why structural change has not occurred. However, the important point now is to familiarize future police administrators with the value of organiza-

* Source: Johnson, Thomas Alfred, "The Application of Organizational Theory to the Problem of Police Resistance to Police Community Rela- tions." *Journal of Police Science and Administration*, Vol. 3, No. 1 (1975): pp. 84–94.

tional theory and its application to police problems in something more than the traditional sense of improving methodologies of efficiency. Future police administrators must now be equipped to think in terms of effectiveness and design measures of performance that include, not exclude, the community at large. At the same time, the community must face up to its responsibilities in the area of improving police community relations programming.

This paper is based on the postulate that police community relations can indeed be improved if police administrators use and develop a greater appreciation of organizational theory and its application to the structure of their organizations, not only the problems their organizations encounter.

ORGANIZATIONAL CONCEPTS

In an analysis of the structural characteristics of an urban police organization, or, for that matter, any typical large organization, the following structural characteristics can be observed: large size, specialization, hierarchy, status anxiety, oligarchy, cooptation, efficiency, and rationality.[1] Out of these structural characteristics, organization theory has for the most part directed itself toward two dominant organizational objectives: productive efficiency and management control.[2]

Further clarification of the focus of organizational theory can be found in Koontz and O'Donnell's definition of organization. The task of organizing is to establish a system of activity groupings and authority relationships in which people can know what their tasks are, how their tasks relate to one another, and where authority for decisions needed to accomplish these tasks rests.[3]

The literature on organization centers upon such topical areas as: the span of management control, decentralization, line and staff relationships, authority, responsibility, delegation, functions, specialization, and coordination.

Perhaps one of the better conceptualizations of organizational theory in which the aforementioned topic areas were discussed was contributed in a monograph by William G. Scott. Essentially, Scott analyzes organization theory in terms of the following three subdivisions: classical theory, neoclassical theory, and modern organizational theory.

1. Presthus, *The Organizational Society: An Analysis and A Theory* (1962) 27.

2. Greenwood, *Management and Organizational Behavior Theories: An Interdisciplinary Approach* (1965) 437.

3. Koontz & O'Donnell, *Management: A Book of Readings* (1964) 174.

The classical organization theory position is built around four key pillars:

1. The division of labor is without doubt the cornerstone of the four elements.

2. The scalar and functional processes, scalar referring to the growth of the chain of command and the functional process referring to the evolution of the line and staff relationship.

3. Structure implies system and pattern, and is the logical relationship of functions in an organization, arranged to accomplish the objectives of the company efficiently.

4. The span of control relates to the number of subordinates a manager can effectively supervise.[4]

While the classical organization theorists have had relevant insights into the nature of organizations, the classical position is severely limited by its narrow concentration on the formal anatomy of organization. March and Simon indicate that the authors or theorists most associated with the classical school are Taylor, Gulick, Ulbreck, Fayal, Reiley, Mooney, and Haldone.[5]

The neoclassical theory of organization attempted to overcome the deficiencies of the classical doctrine. In so doing, the neoclassical position was to modify the "four pillars" of the classical theory by suggesting that these "four pillars" also were acted upon within the context of the informal organization. However, the main contribution of the neoclassical theory was the introduction of behavioral sciences in an integrated fashion into the theory of organization. The neoclassical approach was a systematic treatment of the informal organization, showing its influence on the formal structure.

The third major division, modern organization theory, shifts the conceptual level of organization theory beyond the classical and neoclassical schools in that its focus is on a series of related questions not considered by the classical or neoclassical theories. As examples of these questions and the orientation of the modern organization theorists position, the following questions are representative of the approach:

1. What are the strategic parts of the system?

2. What is the nature of their mutual dependency?

3. What are the main processes in the system which link the parts together and facilitate their adjustment to each other?

4. What are the goals sought by systems?[6]

4. Scott, *Organization Theory: A Behavioral Analysis for Management* (1967).

5. March & Simon, *Organizations* (1958) 12–22.

6. Scott, *Organization Theory: A Behavioral Analysis for Management* (1967).

Books that are representative of this area are March and Simons, *Organizations,* and Mason Haire, *Modern Organization Theory.*

Mason Haire puts forth the following two questions as being essential to organization theory: "What are we trying to do with the organization?" and "How do the various aspects of the organization structure affect the various goals?" [7]

Also illustrative of the contribution of systems approach to modern organization theory is the following framework provided by Professor C. West Churchman:

1. What are the problems the system faces?

2. What are the limits of the system?

3. In what areas, methods, or means would you pursue these weaknesses of the system?

4. What is it we are really trying to accomplish? How are we going about doing it? [8]

Scott's conceptualization of organization theory into three basic components—classical, neoclassical and modern organization theory —provides us with a framework for suggesting that there are structural and organizational deficiencies conducive to police resistance to police-community relations. With the background of the three theories, the ramifications of the structural approach to police community relation problems can be more fully comprehended. For example, the neoclassical theorists discovered that the informal organization resists change, but the approach suggested in this paper goes back to the classical theorist's position as to why the structural approach is again important for the analysis of organizations.

The classical theorists have long ago placed heavy emphasis on such structural factors as command, discipline, and authority in their organizational design. Since the role of authority in organizations has been diminishing because of decentralization, professionalism, coordination, communication, and participative management philosophies, the structural approach in addressing many of our organizational problems has been largely ignored. Or as Leavitt suggests:

> The great early emphasis of structural people on authority
> led us for a while toward rejecting the whole structural approach. We tended, as we so often do, to want to throw out
> the baby with the bath water. Recently, however, we have
> begun to come back to structural questions from very different angles. We have come back to structure largely because
> we have been forced to—because it has become so patently

7. Haire, *Organization Theory in In-*   8. Churchman, *The Systems Approach*
    dustrial Practice (1962) 2.   (1968) 28–48.

obvious that structure is an organizational dimension (1) that we can manipulate, and (2) that has direct effects on problem solving. If we decentralize, things happen. Maybe not all the things we wanted to have happen, but things happen. If we change the definitions of roles of members of our organization, things happen. If we change communication lines by removing telephones or separating people, or making some people more accessible to others, things happen. . . . Yet there is an important limiting factor in the structured approach. The structure of an organization makes some things possible, but it does not guarantee that they will happen.[9]

Furthermore, the importance of organizational design is increasingly gaining attention because of the work on role conflict and the increasing use of computers which has forced us to make room for new kinds of people and new kinds of relationships. These two developments, rather than killing off the idea of organizational structure, are putting it back into the spotlight, making us ask ourselves again, what is the ideal structural design for an organization aimed at performing a particular task?

One of the main theses of this research has been that there are structural and organizational deficiencies that are not only conducive to police resistance to police-community relations programs, but that remedial action might well be accomplished by changing the structure of police organizations. Leavitt reinforces this thesis by suggesting the following:

But we are really just beginning to reattack the structural problem after leaving it alone for many years. It is an important issue to attack, both because it is clear that the structure we work in has a great deal to do with how we behave, and also because structure is susceptible to relatively easy manipulation and change. If we could learn more about what effects we would get from particular manipulations, we might be able to answer a key question in applied organizational theory: "What organizational designs are appropriate for what task?"[10]

Finally, organization is viewed by many as a vehicle for accomplishing goals and objectives. As useful as this approach is, it does tend to obscure the inner workings of the organization. It is these inner workings, particularly when they manifest resistance to change,

9. Leavitt, *Managerial Psychology: An Introduction to Individuals, Pairs, and Groups in Organizations* (1965) 382–383.

10. Footnote 9, p. 385.

that this paper is most concerned with in this area of organizational theory. Therefore, the main thrust of the review of the organizational literature will be in the area of resistance to change, since it plays such an integral part in the problem of police organizations accepting the concept of police-community relations programs.

The resistance to change literature is but one small component part of the literature on organizational change. Therefore, to put the resistance to change concept in its proper perspective, a very cursory examination of the literature on organizational change will first be presented.

ORGANIZATIONAL CHANGE

All organizations, and police organizations in particular, should change. Frederick Mosher perhaps best identifies the reasons for this in his study which focuses on governmental reorganizations. Mosher lists the following reasons why change is necessary:

A number of different and identifiable factors may over the course of time make major structural change within an agency desirable or even mandatory. All are manifestations of organizational obsolescence. One of the most pervasive of these in a growing society is simply growth in size, consequent upon growth in clientele or population serviced, with or without change in nature of services or techniques.

.   .   .   A second factor contributing to the need for reorganization is changes in problems and needs and therefore in organizational programs and responsibilities.

.   .   .   A third factor   .   .   .   is a changing philosophy as to the proper responsibilities of government.

.   .   .   A fourth factor is a consequence of new technology, new equipment, and advancing knowledge.

.   .   .   A fifth factor is the changing—and usually rising —qualifications of personnel in fields of specialization used in the agency's work.

.   .   .   Finally organizations of lower levels may in effect become obsolescent because of actions taken above them in their department or government or higher levels of government.[11]

11. Mosher, *Government Reorganizations: Cases and Commentary* (1967) 494–496.

Perhaps the strongest reason for organizational change is simply to keep the police department or any organization more responsive to the needs of its clientele.

A social agency cannot immunize itself from the social situation—the community—in which it operates. It can for a time be unresponsive to new situations and new needs. But eventually, it must react and respond to situational forces, or decline in influence and in time pass out of existence.[12]

An excellent thumbnail sketch of what is involved in the management of change is presented in Irwin and Langham's article "The Change Seekers," in which the authors list 10 crucial stages in an organizational change:

1. Recognizing the forces of change affecting you and your business.
2. Determining your ability to change.
3. Establishing a climate for change.
4. Involving people in change.
5. Organizing for change.
6. Generating action.
7. Planning change.
8. Implementing change.
9. Minimizing risks and conflicts.
10. Providing leadership.[13]

In a most perceptive discussion of analyzing organized change which at the same time presents a very precise review of the literature on organizational change, Harold Leavitt suggests four potential strategies for analyzing organizational change within the following four variables:

Task—refers, of course, to the industrial organization's *raisons d'être:* the production of goods and services, including the large numbers of different but operationally meaningful subtasks that may exist in complex organizations.

Actors—refers chiefly to people, but with the qualifications that acts executed by people at some time or place need not remain exclusively in the human domain.

Technology—refers to direct problem solving inventions like work measurement techniques, or computers, or drill press-

12. Johns, *Confronting Organizational Change* (1963) 60–61.

13. Irwin & Langham, "The Change Seekers," *Harv. Business Rev.*, Vol. 44, pp. 81–82 (1966).

es. Note that both machines and programs may be included in this category.

Structure—means systems of communication, systems of authority (or other roles), and systems of work flows.[14]

Leavitt maintains that each of these four variables represent a particular strategy for addressing the problem of organization change, and that each strategy in turn attracts specialists who develop expertise in employing the particular variable of their change strategy for improving the organization's performance. For example, the "people" approaches attempt to change organizations by changing the behavior of the organization's members. The more outstanding contributions to the literature on human aspects of organizational change are: Lippett, Watson, and Westley's *The Dynamics of Planned Change*, Lawrence's *The Changing of Organizational Behavior Patterns*, Guest's *Organizational Change*, Ginzberg and Reilly's *Effecting Change in Large Organizations* and Bennis, Benne and Chin's *The Planning of Change*.[15]

In contrast, technological and structural approaches focus on problem-solving mechanisms, while overlooking the internal operations of the organization. However, there are variations, as some of the structural approaches are not aimed directly at the task but at people, in the hope that by changing structure to change people one improves task performance.[16] Similarly, some of the people approaches seek to change people in order to change structure and to change or improve the task performance. Authors representative of this approach are Chris Argyris and Rensis Likert.[17]

Greiner's unpublished 1965 Ph.D. dissertation, "Organizational Change and Development" reviewed the literature on organization change and identified and categorized the most commonly used approaches to organizational change as falling within seven basic categories as follows:

1. The Decree Approach. A one-way announcement originating with a person with high formal authority and passed on to those in lower positions (e. g., Taylor, 1911; Gouldner, 1954).

2. The Replacement Approach. Individuals in one or more key organizational positions are replaced by other individuals. The basic assumption is that organizational changes are a

14. Leavitt, "Applied Organizational Change in Industry: Structural, Technological and Humanistic Approaches," in March (ed.), *Handbook of Organizations* (1965).

15. Footnote 14, 1151.

16. Chapple and Sayle, *The Measure of Management.*

17. Footnote 14.

function of personnel changes (e. g., Gouldner, 1954; Guest, 1962).

3. The Structural Approach. Instead of decreeing or injecting new blood into work relationships, management changes the required relationships of subordinates working in the situation. By changing the structure or organizational relationships, organizational behavior is also presumably affected (e. g., Burns and Stother, 1962; Chapple and Sayles, 1961; Woodward, 1958; Doltar, Barnes, and Zalennik, 1966).

4. The Group Decision Approach. Participation by group members in implementing alternatives specified by others. This approach involves neither problem identification nor problem solving, but emphasizes the obtaining of group agreement on a predetermined course (e. g., Coch and French, 1948; Lewin, 1958).

5. The Data Discussion Approach. Presentation and feedback of relevant data to the client system by either a change catalyst or by change agents within the company. Organizational members are encouraged to develop their own analysis of the data which has been given to them in the form of case materials, survey findings or data reports (e. g., Main, 1957; Andrews, 1953).

6. The Group Problem Solving Approach. Problem identification and problem solving through group discussion with the help of an outsider. This would be one type of "planned change" (e. g., Sofer, 1961).

7. The T-Group Approach. Training in sensitivity to the processes of individual and group behavior. Changes in work patterns and relationships are assumed to follow from changes in interpersonal relationships. T-Group approaches focus upon the interpersonal relationships first, then work towards improvements in work performance (e. g., Argyres, 1962; Foundation for Research on Human Behavior, 1960).[18]

The preceding discussion on organizational change was presented as background for a more detailed discussion of resistance to change, especially as it applies to police organizations.

RESISTANCE TO CHANGE

A most appropriate method of introducing a discussion on police resistance to police-community relations, or on resistance to change itself, is to follow the Lippitt, Watson and Westley example of classi-

18. Barnes, "Approaches to Organizational Change," in Benne & Chin   (eds.), *The Planning of Change* (1969) 82–83.

fying forces that are either conducive to resistance or conducive to change. In other words, it is not only important to identify both forces pushing for change or retarding change, but it is also important to identify at what levels, stages, or times these forces manifest themselves. Furthermore, it should be stressed that these forces will emerge irrespective of any formal change process occurring.[19]

While resistance to change may emerge at any point in the continuum of a change process—at the beginning, while it is under way, or later on in the program—there are specific points at which various types of resistance occur. If these types of resistance are anticipated, remedial action can be taken to reduce their impact on the particular change being fostered. Although these types of resistance are in response to formal programs of organizational change, they nevertheless will be highly useful in explaining some of the rationale for police resistance to police-community relations, which more often than not occurs quite informally.

Awareness of Problem

The most logical area for resistance to emerge is when the need for help or the awareness that a problem exists is not realized.[20] In many cases, this certainly is the situation regarding police resistance to police-community relations. A variation on this theme is that if we do have a problem, and we aren't entirely convinced we do, then it is beyond our capabilities of resolving the problem.

However, even if the problem is recognized, specifically in the case of police-community relations, there still may well be reasons for resistance emerging. For example, there may be a reluctance to admit a weakness or fear of failure in trying to initiate a new practice, or a fatalistic expectation of failure instilled by previous unsuccessful attempts to improve the police and community relationship.

Opposition to Change

One form of resistance most likely to occur at the beginning of a change process is the opposition to any type or kind of change. There are many explanations for this initial type of resistance. It can be founded on fear or ignorance or a combination of both. Insofar as police organizations are concerned, most resistance to police-community relations emerges because accepting this role implies change or innovative thinking. As Bayley and Mendelsohn suggested, police are more aligned with the status quo, since that is what their job is essentially all about, and there are few innovative-orient-

19. Lippitt, Watson & Westley, *The Dynamics of Planned Change* (1958) 71–72.

20. Footnote 19, p. 131.

ed people attracted to police work. Nevertheless, fear and ignorance could also initiate police resistance to police-community relations. The police department may fear that it would be unable to successfully shift its orientation to police-community relations, or that if it did, this change would require things of the police department that its individual members were unable to deliver.

Opposition to Change Objective

However, in all fairness to police organizations, it must not be assumed that resistance is always organized against change, for the resistance might be focused more accurately against a particular objective of change.[21] An excellent example of this occurs within the police-community relations area, where resistance might be manifested, not because police are against maintaining a sound relationship with the community, but because police consider police-community relations as irrelevant to their perception of their basic mission, which is law enforcement.

Opposition Because of Tradition

Resistance to police-community relations can emerge because the police department is reluctant to give up traditional types of satisfaction which might include the traditional manner of getting reward, which is certainly not amenable to police-community relations programs, as James O. Wilson's writings have indicated. Other traditional satisfactions that might cause resistance are the familiar ways of avoiding pain or anxiety, and especially the ways one conceives of his role. One's conception of himself and his external view of the world is especially crucial.

Mistrust of Change Agent

Police resistance to police-community relations is also centered in the relationship that exists between the police department and that segment of the community that is acting as a change agent in its demands for increasing police sensitivity to police-community relations. Lippitt suggests that when resistance between the client system and change agent occurs, it might well be because of the unfamiliarity and suspiciousness each has of the other.[22] There can be no doubt about similar feelings of mistrust and incompatibility existing between the police department and the community. This certainly accounts for a portion of police resistance to police-community relations.

21. Footnote 19, p. 83.   **22.** Footnote 19, p. 85.

Dissatisfaction with Community

Additional points of resistance that might emerge out of this relationship between the police and the community could center around the dissatisfaction each group has with the other. For example, police resistance to police-community relations may well intensify after the police department has made a definite commitment to improving police-community relations, but the response of the community is still characterized by avoiding any responsibility to facilitate this change. To the police this might well be considered as a rational reason for not taking seriously the demands of the community that police-community relations be improved. Another variation of this same theme occurs when factors which were considered of small consequence in the initial change phase later become major obstacles to change, such as the community demand for improved police-community relations without an attendant commitment to provide the police department with the budget, men, materials, and consultant help necessary to achieve this improved police-community relationship. In essence, the community is avoiding responsibility again by its failure to make any commitment towards involvement in the entire problem. Whenever the loss of support or help becomes imminent, especially in such a sensitive area as police-community relations, resistance to change may dramatically increase.

Resistance can also be observed when there is a faulty internal distribution of power, with the power being either too diffused or too concentrated within the police department.

This is especially the case when one considers that the patrolmen are a subculture within a subculture. Subcultures naturally possess different values and mores; thus, one source of power to the patrolman subculture is its ability to resist change that the administration considers necessary.

Defective Communication

Resistance might well be manifested when pathologically defective communication arises both within the hierarchial structure of the police organization and between the organization and the community. Police organizations are particularly vulnerable to communication problems, because no formal structure exists for maintaining a dialogue with members of the community.

Perceived Expectations

Lippitt suggests that, "The client system learns that the change agent expects certain things of it and these expectations constitute a force of change. The influence of the desires and expectations of the change agent will increase in accordance with the esteem and liking for him felt by the client system." [23] The corollary of this is equally important, especially in terms of police resistance to police-community relations. There can be little doubt that the police sense the expectations of the community toward improving police-community relations. However, these expectations cannot be considered as a force for change, because the police do not feel they are held in high esteem by the community, and segments of the community do not feel the police regard them with any degree of respect or esteem. When one's worth is being questioned, there will be little movement toward making significant change; thus, another rationale is developed for resisting change.

Community Hypocrisy

Another explanation of police resistance to police-community relations can be observed when a subsystem of society or the administration of justice is given a problem and it is unable to change because there is resistance originating outside the subsystem, or coming from the larger system in which the subsystem is embedded. In other words, the police department has long ago acknowledged the hypocrisy of the total community. A community insists on improved police-community relations but tolerates inadequate housing, inferior education, wholesale unemployment, and worst of all, maintains the very ghettos and slums of the city. The police response is a very understandable one: "How can we improve police-community relations when the overriding attitude of the majority community towards minority groups has not only remained constant, but shows little sign of changing?" In short, what is the utility of the police improving their relationship with the community when the community itself cannot live in harmony? Moreover, how can the police improve their relationship with the community when other parts of the administration of justice system and the community itself degrades this relationship by the very process of their interaction?

Impartiality Challenged

Resistance can also be expected when a proposed change offers benefits to one part of the organization's clientele at the expense of other portions of the clientele. The defensive reaction, especially in police organizations which are committed to impartiality of service, is to oppose the change automatically. This certainly exemplifies the dilemma of the police organization in the area of police-community relations. Therefore, resistance may emerge because individual members of the department feel their ideals on impartiality are being tampered with.

23.   Footnote 19, p. 76.

Dissipation of Authority

Another traditional value—in fact, almost a religious belief of a police organization—is the idea that productivity and organizational authority will dissipate somewhat if community relations programs are adopted. Again, the point is not so much police resistance to police-community relations as it is to the accompanying change that may reveal latent forms of conflict that might challenge the hierarchical authority structure. Furthermore, police organizations, like almost all organizations, are geared to productivity, and any organizational change either formally or informally might well be viewed as lowering the productivity of the police department.

Anxieties from Nonspecific Programs

Another source of resistance to police-community relations might reside in the anxiety the police organization feels over whether the department will be competent to effectively assume this sensitive responsibility of improving police-community relations.

Alvin Zander indicates that "resistance can be expected if the nature of the change is not made clear to the people who are going to be influenced by the change." [24] This is certainly applicable to police resistance to police-community relations. Police officers often express their frustration by asking, "What does the community expect from us? What do they want us to do?" Not knowing what is expected certainly can generate misgivings about accepting any program or making any change.

Implication of Perceived Failure

Resistance to police-community relations from the line personnel may be more pronounced if they perceive that the change is being made on personal grounds. A person working on what he considers to be an important job usually comes to see his job performance as being consistent with the type of person he considers himself to be.[25] Therefore, with the suggestion that police-community relations need improvement, the policeman is required to change his conception of his job and role, and, more importantly, his conception of himself. Perhaps we should be more surprised by an absence of resistance than by the resistance that is manifested towards police-community relations.

Ignoring Police Institutions

Resistance can also be expected in the area of police-community relations if the change ignores the already established institutions in

24. Johns, *Confronting Organizational Change* (1963) 117.

25. Mann & Neff, *Managing Major Change in Organizations* (1961).

the group or organization. The police have, of course, long maintained that the issue of police review, so directly involved in improving police-community relations, is irrelevant. Many police see the
proper grievance procedures for handling complaints already in existence in their own police department or in some structure closely associated with the administration of justice such as a district attorney,
the Federal Bureau of Investigation, etc. Therefore, there is resistance to many police-community relation proposals on this count alone.

Unawareness of Change Responsibilities

Perhaps one potential cause of resistance to police-community relations is simply that some policemen are unaware that they are expected to make efforts to strengthen the police-community relationship. Mann and Neff suggest that in some cases the need for change
must be made explicit, so that the person is confronted with the difference between his present behavior and the specific new behavior
required of him. Part of the resistance problem in the area of police-community relations is that police are asking, "What specific behavior do you expect of us?" The question is quite broad and can
only be answered in generalities, whereas the policeman expects a
specific reply. When the specific reply is not forthcoming, many policemen conclude, "You're expecting me to change, but you can't tell
me what to change to. Forget it!"

Group Pressures

Again forcusing on the police department as a subculture, perhaps one the major causes of police resistance to change is related to
the extreme group pressures on conformity to norms. Pfiffner and
Sherwood comment on the police as a subculture and the attendant
management and organizational problems this creates, as follows:

> The nature of the work helps to erect an institutional sub-
> culture. This is especially true where the organization is
> relatively homogeneous and where there is relatively little
> opportunity for employment mobility . . . Police have
> highly irregular hours, reducing the possibility of normal
> social intercourse; furthermore the demands of their work
> have caused many police officers to develop a perception of
> incompatibility with other segments of society . . .
> The kind of organization and management required for this
> institutional subculture must differ markedly from that re-
> quired in a newspaper office where individual initiative and
> creativity remain important.[26]

26. Pfiffner & Sherwood, *Administra-*
tive Organization (1960) 266.

There will be certain forces that structure a police organization and that make it more susceptible to resistance to change, simply because it is an institutional subculture.

Perhaps the leading study to document the impact of group cohesiveness to resistance to change was Coch and French's study of the Harwood Pajama Manufacturing Company.[27]   While the group norms in their study were high in terms of their correlation to cohesiveness, the cohesiveness nowhere near approached that found in most police departments because police departments are more or less institutional subcultures.

Patrolmen's Socialization Process

While considering the police as an institutional subculture, an analogy from an anthropologist's examination of resistance to change is appropriate. Edward Bruner suggests the following:

> That which was traditionally learned and internalized in infancy and early childhood tends to be most resistant to change in contact situations. This suggests that we view a culture from the perspective of cultural transmission, the process by which the content of culture is learned by and communicated to members of the society.[28]

Under Bruner's view, a patrolman's infancy begins when he is a recruit. The cultural transmission occurs in his recruit training from the police academy, while a far greater part is learned on the job. If Bruner is accurate in his hypothesis that what is traditionally learned and internalized in infancy tends to be most resistant to change, the rookie's association with older officers should be examined.

Organizational Attractiveness

Another explanation for police resistance to police-community relations can be found in William Starbuck's observation that "members may be attracted by the organization's goals; they may be attracted by the activities which they perform in the organization's task structure or they may be attracted by the interactions experienced in the organization's social structure." [29]   Consequently, any changes that would alter what attracted the particular member of the organization will in all probability be resisted. The problem present-

---

27. Coch & French, "Overcoming Resistance to Change," in Cartwright and Zander (eds.), *Group Dynamics: Research and Theory* (1953) 263.

28. Bruner, "Resistance to Change: Cultural Transmission and Cultural Change," in Smelser & Smelser (eds.), *Personality and Social Systems* (1963) 483.

29. Starbuck, "Organizational Growth and Development," in March (ed.), *Handbook of Organizations* (1965).

ed by police-community relations is that few people are motivated to join a police department to strengthen the police-community relationship. Police-community relations proposals would seem to alter some of the basic elements Starbuck suggests have attracted members to the organization. The problem, of course, resides in the fact that when organizational change seems to threaten an individual's goals, that change will be highly resisted.

Priorities

Lippitt suggests that it is quite important to distinguish between resistance and interference, as it can make a considerable difference in how one would address organizational change. Essentially, resistance forces originate in regard to the objective of the organizational change, whereas interference forces are not directly related to the objectives of the change process:

> Sometimes, however, the change process may run into difficulty not because of opposing forces but because of competing forces. Thus, for example, a proposal to build a new city hall might be defeated not because of opposition to such a building, but because it seemed that a new school building was ever more urgent.[30]

Therefore, a great deal of what initially appears to be police resistance to community relations is really not resistance but interference. In other words, police might perceive more urgent needs than that of establishing police-community relations programs. Naturally, a great deal of this interference would depend on the role conception of police officers.

FUNCTIONAL ASPECTS OF RESISTANCE

It is also incumbent upon any analysis to look at the functional properties of resistance to change, for all resistance to change is not negative in nature. For example, resistance can be a source of new ideas. Resistance can also force representatives of the police and the community to clarify more sharply the purposes of change. Resistance also forces both sides to look at the unanticipated or dysfunctional consequences of too fast a change. Finally, resistance not only discloses inadequate communication channels but also inadequate problem-solving processes. Perhaps in this manner it then allows both the organization and the community to measure whether or not the relevant involvement of persons and groups has been secured.

30. Lippitt, Watson, & Westley, *The Dynamics of Planned Change* (1958).

SUMMARY

To briefly recapitulate, most consultants and communities have suggested that police improve the police-community relationship by focusing on the police department, while largely ignoring the environment in which the police department functions. Secondly, as Leavitt suggests, the "people approach" has been used, in which consultants attempt to sensitize the personnel, particularly line officers, to the need and importance of police-community relations. This approach has been most dysfunctional, primarily because the attendant structural changes were not made along with the people approach.

In fact, there is every reason to believe that the sensitivity approach alone has intensified police resistance to police-community relations. The literature documents two reasons for this. First, to provide training to one group of men, like patrolmen, but not to provide the same training to their superiors, means that the superiors still retain their same expectations for the patrolman's behavior patterns and will supervise accordingly. Thus, all the training really accomplished was to frustrate the line officers by presenting them with incongruities and conflict situations. Secondly, as Leavitt points out, any attempt to give power equalizations via sensitivity training in a police organization, rather than power differentiation, represents a clear confrontation with the traditional hierarchical structure of the police organization. The certain outcome of this incongruity is first frustration, then resistance.

We would be well advised to take note of Donald Cressey's observation that in correctional work, management is an end, not a means, and that the management hierarchies extend to the lowest level employee:

> The correctional worker in other words is both a manager and a worker. He is managed in a system of controls and regulations from above, but he also manages the inmates, probationers, or parolees in his charge . . . Because he is a manager, he cannot be ordered to accept a proposed innovation, as a turret lathe operator can be ordered. He can only be persuaded to do so.[31]

The patrolman is a low line manager, and therefore he, too, must be persuaded to change, not simply ordered to do so, even though this does appear incongruent to the authority hierarchy within a police organization. The patrolman does manage situations and does rely on discretion to facilitate his management. He must be approached

31. Cressey, "Sources of Resistance to the Use of Ex-Offenders in the Correctional Process," in Joint Commission on Correctional Manpower and Training, *Offenders as a Correctional Manpower Resource* (1968).

in a persuasive manner, that is, if one wishes to minimize resistance to organizational change.

The significance of this observation suggests what Leavitt has maintained for any organizational change, namely that to accomplish the change with least resistance it would be well to broaden our scope and use structural, humanistic, and technological approaches as opposed to relying on one approach at the expense of the others. Furthermore, if any one variable is manipulated, one must be aware of the concomitant effect it will have on the others, as well as the task.

Merton makes the point even more vividly with his general theorem:

> The social functions of an organization help determine the structure (including the recruitment of personnel involved in the structure), just as the structure helps determine the effectiveness with which the functions are fulfilled .   .   . Structure affects function and function affects structure.[32]

It is imperative to approach police-community relation problems with more than a structural approach. The two (structure and function), however, might be a perfect marriage in any attempt to either improve police-community relations or to reduce police resistance to police-community relations.

Areas for discussion for Part II

1. Regarding the role of the police in society, discuss the relationships of the various roles to the various organizational philosophies.

2. What are the pros and cons for instituting a particular organizational philosophy with the police organization?

3. Discuss the probability for increasing police effectiveness by instituting some of the innovative managerial concepts which have been outlined.

4. What are the major differences between John E. Angell's perception of police management and contemporary police management?

5. What are the major problems associated with the democratic model of team-policing?

---

32. Merton, "Occupational Roles: Bureaucratic Structure and Personality," in Smelser & Smelser (eds.), *Personality and Social Systems* (1963).

PART III

ORGANIZATIONAL BEHAVIOR IN POLICE SYSTEMS

This section of the text contains readings which address various aspects of police behavior within the organizational context. This section examines the behavioral responses to the police organizational settings which were detailed in the previous section. These organizational settings include two distinct areas, the formal and the informal. The formal organizational setting consists of the organizational structure and managerial processes within the police department. Traditional policing consists of a classical organizational philosophy which is typified by O. W. Wilson and Roy C. McLaren [1] and George and Esther Eastman.[2] However the formal organizational setting would also include a structure as outlined by John E. Angell.[3] The informal organizational setting includes those behavioral determinants resultant from individual behavior, informal group behavior and environmental constraints. Individual employees and groups of employees have specific needs. The pursuit of these needs by the employees has definite impact upon the operation of the organization.

In order for a police organization to reach optimal operating effectiveness, there must be a high degree of compatibility between the formal and the informal organizations. This optimal state within a police organization is where the department is rationally structured, and effectiveness is achieved. Additionally, the personnel within such a department would possess a high level of job satisfaction.[4] Such a state would represent an integration of organizational and personal needs within the police organization. This integration entails the structuring or re-structuring of the formal organizational setting to meet the needs of the organizational membership. Regardless of method used, the goal of such a process should be to optimize departmental effectiveness.

One of the principal indicators of the success of a department toward optimization of organizational and individual goals is the behavior patterns of the organizational participants. Moreover, there

1. O. W. Wilson and Roy C. McLaren. *Police Administration*, New York: McGraw-Hill Book Company, 1972.

2. George D. Eastman and Esther M. Eastman. *Municipal Police Administration*, Washington: International City Management Association, 1969.

3. John E. Angell. "Toward an Alternative to the Classic Police Organizational Arrangements: A Democratic Model." *Criminology*, (August/November, 1971), 185–206, and John E. Angell. "Organizing Police For the Future: An Update of the Democratic Model" *Criminal Justice Review*, (Fall, 1976), 35–51.

4. Paul M. Whisenand and R. Fred Ferguson. *The Managing of Police Organizations*, Englewood Cliffs, N. J.: Prentice-Hall, Inc., 1973, p. 151.

is evidence which tends to indicate that the morale or job satisfaction of the organizational membership is correlated with job productivity.[5] This section of the text endeavors to describe the behavior patterns which exist in most traditional police organizations and examine the etiology of the behavior.

First, the police behavior is examined from its bureaucratic perspective. Most police departments ascribe to a quasi-military model which is highly bureaucratized. Such a model produces a specific behavior matrix by the superior and subordinate officers. This behavior matrix includes many dysfunctional types of behavior. Several of the articles in this section detail this dysfunctional behavior and its causes. Additionally, the reader is referred to the previous section which details the various organizational models. These organizational models are prime sources of organizational behavior constraints.

Second, there is growing concern over the environmental or societal impact upon police behavior. This section contains material which examines the relationship between the police officer and the environment in which he works. Studies have identified environmental factors which contribute to the operating effectiveness of police officers. This material is presented here since the police administrator should consider these environmental factors in his planning efforts so that organizational effectiveness may be maximized.

Finally, several articles are presented which describe some of the behavioral changes which must take place within the police organization if policing is going to become more effective. Basically, these changes evolve around the leaders or superiors within the police department, and emphasize how these leaders may become more successful in optimizing efforts toward achieving organizational and personal needs. The effectiveness of any organization rests with its leadership. Subordinates' behavior is usually a response to or at least influenced by their superiors. In the past leadership in policing has been deficient in comparison to the leadership in other public service agencies.[6]

In summary, the behavioral aspects of police management constitute an important, integral part of police management. The purpose of this section has been to critically examine this behavior, its causes, and possible administrative alternatives which could be utilized to alter current behavior patterns.

5. See Rensis Likert. *The Human Organization*, New York: McGraw-Hill Book Co., 1967.

6. This statement represents an assumption on the authors' part. We feel that even though leadership throughout government may be mediocre, it is usually a substantial improvement over the leadership exhibited in many police organizations.

Objectives of Part III

1. Identify some of the negative and positive behavioral attributes of leaders within the police organization.

2. Identify the behavioral attributes of subordinates within the police organization.

3. Identify some of the areas of conflict between police executives and operational personnel.

4. Identify some of the problems with the traditional police organization, these problems include structural and leadership problems, which negatively impact the operating effectiveness of the police personnel.

5. Identify some of the environmental factors which impact police behavior.

THE QUASI–MILITARY ORGANIZATION OF THE POLICE *

The conception of the police as a quasi-military institution with a war-like mission plays an important part in the structuring of police work in modern American departments. The merits of this conception have never been demonstrated or even argued explicitly. Instead, most authors who make reference to it take it for granted or are critical only of those aspects of it, especially its punitive orientation, that are subject of aspersion even in the military establishment itself.[1] The treatment the topic receives in the Task Force Report on the Police of the President's Commission on Law Enforcement and Administration of Justice is representative of this approach. The authors note that "like all military and semi-military organizations, a police agency is governed in its internal management by a large number of standard operating procedures."[2] This observation is accom-

* Source: Egon Bittner, "The Quasi-Military Organization of The Police," from *The Functions of the Police in Modern Society.* National Institute of Mental Health, Chevy Chase, Maryland, November, 1970, pp. 52–62.

1. Recently some authors have expressed doubts about the merits of organizing the police along military lines. Wilson takes issue with Smith's assertion that the police have "disciplinary requirements of a quasi-military body," at p. 79, n. 24 of his *Varieties of Police Behavior: The Management of Law and Order in Eight Communities,* Cambridge, Mass.: Harvard University Press, 1968. Similarly, A. J. Reiss and D. J. Bordua have questioned the adequacy of the idea of the police as a military organization; see "Environment and Organization: A Perspective on the Police," in Bordua (ed.), *The Police: Six Sociological Essays,* N. Y.: John Wiley & Sons, 1967, at p. 46ff.

2. President's Commission on Law Enforcement and Administration of Justice, *Task Force Report: The Police,* Washington, D.C.: U. S. Government Printing Office, 1967, p. 16.

panied by remarks indicating that the existence of elaborate codes governing the conduct of policemen relative to intra-departmental demands stands in stark contrast to the virtual absence of formulated directives concerning the handling of police problems in the community. The imbalance between proliferation of internal regulation and the neglect of regulations relative to procedures employed in the field leads to the inference that the existing codes must be supplemented by substantive instructions and standards in the latter area. The question whether such an expansion of regulation might not result in a code consisting of incompatible elements is not considered. Instead, it is implicitly assumed that policemen can be instructed how to deal with citizens by regulations that will not affect the existing system of internal disciplinary control.

The lack of appreciation for the possibility that the developments of professional discretionary methods for crime control and peace-keeping may conflict with the enforcement of bureaucratic-military regulations is not merely a naive oversight; more likely, it represents an instance of wishful thinking. For the military model is immensely attractive to police planners, and not without reason. In the first place, there exist some apparent analogies between the military and the police and it does not seem to be wholly unwarranted to expect methods of internal organization that work in one context to work also in the other. Both institutions are instruments of force and for both institutions the occasions for using force are unpredictably distributed. Thus, the personnel in each must be kept in a highly disciplined state of alert preparedness. The formalism that characterizes military organization, the insistence on rules and regulations, on spit and polish, on obedience to superiors, and so on, constitute a permanent rehearsal for "the real thing." What sorts of rules and regulations exist in such a setting are in some ways less important than that there be plenty of them and the personnel be continually aware that they can be harshly called to account for disobeying them.[3] Second, American police departments have been, for the greater part of their history, the football of local politics, and became tainted with sloth and corruption at least partly for this reason. Police reform was literally forced to resort to formidable means of internal discipline to dislodge undesirable attitudes and influences, and the military model seemed to serve such purposes admirably. In fact, it is no

3. The tendency of police departments to adopt outward military rigidities has been frequently emphasized; see *Task Force Report: The Police*, ibid., p. 29; J. D. Lohman and G. E. Misner, *The Police and the Community*, A Report Prepared for the President's Commission on Law Enforcement and Administration of Justice, Washington, D.C.: U. S. Government Printing Office, 1966, Vol. I, p. 152, Vol. II, p. 196; Michael Banton reports that American police chiefs admire Scottish officers who "bore themselves well, and were smartly and uniformly dressed," in *The Policeman in the Community*, N.Y.: Basic Books, 1964, at p. 123.

exaggeration to say that through the 1950s and 1960s the movement to "professionalize" the police concentrated almost exclusively on efforts to eliminate political and venal corruption by means of introducing traits of military discipline. And it must be acknowledged that some American police chiefs, notably the late William Parker of Los Angeles, have achieved truly remarkable results in this respect. The leading aspiration of this reform was to replace the tragicomic figure of the "flatfoot cop on the take" by cadres of personally incorruptible snappy operatives working under the command of bureaucrats-in-uniform. There is little doubt that these reforms succeeded in bringing some semblance of order into many chaotic departments and that in these departments "going by the book" acquired some real meaning.

Finally, the police adopted the military method because they could not avail themselves of any other options to secure internal discipline. For all its effectiveness, the military method is organizationally primitive. At least, the standard part of the method can be well enough approximated with a modicum of administrative sophistication. Moreover, since most of the men who go into police work have some military experience, they need not go to outside resources to obtain help in building a quasi-military order. This is important because a century of experience taught American police forces that outside intervention into their affairs—known as the "shakeup"—was almost always politically inspired. Because the suspicion of high-level chicanery is still very much alive, and not without reasons, the police is the only large scale institution in our society that has not benefited from advances in management science. In the absence of lateral recruitment into supervisory positions and developed technical staff skills, changes had to be achieved mainly by means of rigid enforcement of regulations of internal procedure and by emphasizing external trappings of discipline. In a situation where something had to be done, with little to do it with, this was no mean accomplishment.[4]

Acknowledging that the introduction of methods of military-bureaucratic discipline was not without some justification, and conceding that it helped in eliminating certain gross inadequacies, does not mean, however, that the approach was beneficial in larger and longer range terms. Even where the cure succeeded in suppressing many of the diseases of earlier times, it brought forth obstacles of its own to the development of a model of a professional police role, if by profes-

4. In addition to the rigors of outward discipline, military establishments also rely on "command charisma," a feature observed in American police departments by D. J. Bordua and A. J. Reiss: see their "Command, Control and Charisma: Reflections on Police Bureaucracy," *American Journal of Sociology*, 72 (1966) 68–76. The term indicates a leadership principle in which subordinates are moved to obedience by a high regard for, and trust in, the person in command.

sional role is meant that practice must involve technical skill and fiduciary trust in the practitioner's exercise of discretion. The reason for this is simple. While in early police departments there existed virtually no standards of correct procedure at all and no inducement to do well—since rewards were scant and distributed along lines of personal favoritism—one can now distinguish between good and bad officers, and engaging in what is now defined as correct conduct does carry significant rewards. But since the established standards and the rewards for good behavior relate almost entirely to matters connected with internal discipline, the judgments that are passed have virtually nothing to do with the work of the policeman in the community, with one significant exception. That is, the claims for recognition that have always been denied to the policeman are now respected, but recognition is given for doing well *in* the department, not *outside* where all the real duties are located.

The maintenance of organizational stability and staff morale require that praise and reward, as well as condemnation and punishment, be distributed methodically, i. e., predictably in accordance with explicit rules. Correspondingly, it is exceedingly difficult to assign debits and credits for performances that are not regulated by rule. Because the real work of the policeman is not set forth in the regulations, it does not furnish his superior a basis for judging him.[5] At the same time, there are no strongly compelling reasons for the policeman to do well in ways that do not count in terms of official occupational criteria of value. The greater the weight placed on compliance with internal departmental regulation, the less free is the superior in censoring unregulated work practices he disapproves of, and in rewarding those he admires, for fear that he might jeopardize the loyalty of officers who do well on all scores that officially count—that is, those who present a neat appearance, who conform punctually to bureaucratic routine, who are visibly on the place of their assignment, and so on. In short, those who make life easier for the superior, who in turn is restricted to supervising just those things. In fact, the practical economy of supervisory control requires that the proliferation of intradepartmental restriction be accompanied by increases in license in areas of behavior in unregulated areas. Thus, one who is judged to be a good officer in terms of internal, military-bureaucratic codes will not even be questioned about his conduct outside of it. The message is quite plain: the development of resolutely careful work methods in the community may be nice, but it gets you nowhere!

5. See *Task Force Report: The Police,* op. cit. supra., Note 2 at p. 20; Herman Goldstein at p. 162 of his "Administrative Problems in Controlling the Exercise of Police Authority," *Journal of Criminal Law, Criminology and Police Science,* 58 (1967) 160–172; and Wilson, op. cit. supra., Note 1 at p. 16.

There is one important exception to the priority of intra-departmental quasi-military discipline in the judging of the performances of policemen. Police departments have to produce visible results of their work. The most visible results are arrested persons who keep the courts busy. This demand naturally devolves on individual officers. The question about the expected contribution of individual policemen to the statistical total of crimes cleared, summonses delivered, and arrests made is a matter of heated controversy. The problem is usually addressed as to whether or not there exist quotas officers must meet. Of course, the question can always be so framed that one can answer it truthfully either way.[6] But more fundamentally it is quite clear that individual policemen must contribute to the sum total of visible results, unless they have some special excuse, such as being assigned to a desk job. Moreover, how could any police superior under present conditions of supervision ever know whether the men assigned to the traffic division or to the vice squad are on the job at all, if they did not produce their normal share of citations or arrests?

Clearly, therefore, there is added to the occupational relevance of the military-bureaucratic discipline the demand to produce results.[7] While the emphasis on stringent internal regulation, taken alone, merely discourages the elaboration of careful approaches to work tasks, it exercises in combination with production demands a truly pernicious influence on the nature of police work. There are several reasons for this but the most important is based on the following consideration. Though the explicit departmental regulations contain little more than pious sermonizing about police dealings with citizens, whether they be offenders, an unruly crowd, quarreling spouses, accident victims, or what not, it is possible that a policeman could, despite his discretionary freedom, act in some such way as to actually come into conflict with some stated rule, even though the rule is not topically relevant to the situation at hand. Since he knows that his conduct will be judged solely with respect to this point he must be attuned to it, avoiding the violation even if that involves choosing a course of action that is specifically wrong with respect to the realities of the problem. For example, it is far from unusual that officers decide whether to make an arrest or not on the basis of their desire to live within departmental regulation rather than on the merits of the case at hand. In these situations the military-bureaucratic discipline regulates procedure speciously; it does not provide that in such-and-such a situation such-and-such a course of action is indicated. On the

6. Arthur Niederhoffer, *Behind the Shield: The Police in Urban Society*, N.Y.: Anchor Books, 1969, pp. 68–69.

7. The most illuminating and extensive discussion of "pressures to produce" is contained in J. H. Skolnick, *Justice without Trial: Law Enforcement in Democratic Society*, N.Y.: John Wiley & Sons, 1967, pp. 164–181.

contrary, the regulations are typically silent about such matters; but in insisting on specific ways for officers to keep their noses clean they limit the possibilities of desirable intervention and they encourage transgression. Thus, it has been reported that in the New York Police Department, known for its stringently punitive discipline, officers who violate some official rules of deportment while dealing with citizens simply arrest potential complainants, knowing the complaints of persons charged with crimes are given no credence. Incongruously, while in New York the Police Department is much more likely to discipline an officer for brutalizing a citizen than elsewhere, it in fact rarely gets a chance to do it. For whenever there is a situation in which it is possible that an officer could have an infraction entered in his record, an infraction against an explicit regulation, he will redefine it into an instance of police work that is not regulated. Thus, while citizens everywhere run the risk of receiving a beating when they anger a policeman, in New York they run the added risk of being charged with a crime they did not commit, simply because its officers must keep their records clean.[8]

As long as there are two forms of accounting, one that is explicit and continually audited (internal discipline), and another that is devoid of rules and rarely looked into (dealings with citizens), it must be expected that keeping a positive balance in the first might encourage playing loose with the second. The likelihood of this increases proportionately to pressures to produce. Since it is not enough that policemen be obedient soldier-bureaucrats, but must, to insure favorable consideration for advancement, contribute to the arrest total, they will naturally try to meet this demand in ways that will keep them out of trouble. Thus, to secure the promotion from the uniformed patrol to the detective bureau, which is highly valued and not determined by civil service examinations, officers feel impelled to engage in actions that furnish opportunities for conspicuous display of aggressiveness. John McNamara illustrates this tactic by quoting a dramatic expression of cynicism, "If you want to get 'out of the bag' into the 'bureau' shoot somebody."[9] Leaving the exaggeration aside,

8. Paul Chevigny explains that New York policemen sometimes rebut allegations of brutality by maintaining that they are obviously fabrications since the complainant would have been arrested had the officer laid hands on him. Chevigny reports numerous instances of arrests following altercations with citizens which were ineptly or deviously provoked by policemen, and he comments, "Many lawyers think it a triumph for a felony to be reduced to a mere offence, but the truth is that it requires only two simple ingredients: guiltless clients and infinite patience," at p. 167 of his *Police Power: Police Abuses in New York City*, N.Y.: Pantheon Books, 1969.

9. J. H. McNamara at p. 189 of his "Uncertainties in Police Work: The Relevance of Police Recruits' Background and Training," in Bordua (ed.) op. cit. supra., Note 1 at pp. 163–252.

there is little doubt that emphasis on military-bureaucratic control rewards the appearance of staying out of troubles as far as internal regulations are concerned, combined with strenuous efforts to make "good pinches," i. e., arrests that contain, or can be managed to appear to contain, elements of physical danger. Every officer knows that he will never receive a citation for avoiding a fight but only for prevailing in a fight at the risk of his own safety. Perhaps there is nothing wrong with that rule. But there is surely something wrong with a system in which the combined demands for strict compliance with departmental regulation and for vigorously productive law enforcement can be met simultaneously by displacing the onus of the operatives' own misconduct on citizens. This tends to be the case in departments characterized by strong militaristic-bureaucratic discipline where officers do not merely transgress to make "good pinches," but make "good pinches" to conceal their transgressions.[10]

No matter how elaborate and no matter how stringently enforced codes of internal regulations are, they do not impinge on all segments of police departments with equal force. By and large the highly visible uniformed patrol is exposed to far greater disciplinary pressures than personnel in the detective bureaus, which Arthur Niederhoffer aptly described as "mock bureaucracies."[11] While this situation is viewed as unavoidable, because the conduct of detectives cannot be as closely scrutinized as the conduct of patrolmen, and necessary because detectives need more freedom than patrolmen,[12] it tends to demean uniformed assignments. Because patrolmen perceive military discipline as degrading, ornery, and unjust, the only motive they have for doing well—which, of course, involves, among others, the devious practices we have just described—is to get out of the uniformed assignments.[13] Thus, the uniformed patrol suffers from a constant

10. McNamara cites the following case at p. 171, ibid.: "a patrolman directing traffic in the middle of an intersection . . . fired his revolver and hit an automobile whose driver had not heeded the officer's hand signals. The driver immediately pulled over to the side of the street and stopped the car. The officer realized the inappropriateness of his action and began to wonder what he might offer as an explanation to his supervisor and to the citizen. The patrolman reported that his anxiety was dissipated shortly upon finding that the driver of the car was a person convicted of a number of crimes. The reader should understand that departmental policy did not specify that any person convicted of crimes in New York City thereby became a target for police pistol practice." Nevertheless, as the officer's feeling of relief indicates, the transgression was apparently construable as an instance of aggressive crime control.

11. Niederhoffer, op. cit. supra., Note 6 at p. 85.

12. Wilson notes, however, that this view is probably mistaken. The patrolman deals with matters that are ill defined and ambiguously emergent, while detectives deal with more precisely defined crimes and only after they have been committed; op. cit. supra., Note 1 at pp. 8–9.

13. "A high arrest record reinforces the cynicism that inspired it in the first place, while often establishing a

drain of ambitious and enterprising men, leaving it generally under-staffed and, incidentally, overstaffed with men who are regarded as unsuitable for more demanding tasks. Though by no means all competent personnel take advantage of opportunities to leave the patrol for the detective bureaus, those who remain are dispirited by the conditions under which they are obliged to work and by the invidiously low-level of prestige connected with their performance.[14] In consequence the outwardly snappy appearance of the patrol hides a great deal of discontent, demoralization, and marginal work quality.

Another complex of mischievous consequences arising out of the military bureaucracy relates to the paradoxical fact that while this kind of discipline ordinarily strengthens command authority it has the opposite effect in police departments. This effect is insidious rather than apparent. Because police superiors do not direct the activity of officers in any important sense they are perceived as mere disciplinarians.[15] Not only are they not actually available to give help, advice, and direction in the handling of difficult work problems, but such a role cannot even be projected for them. Contrary to the army officer who is expected to lead his men into battle—even though he may never have a chance to do it—the analogously ranked police official is someone who can only do a great deal *to* his subordinates and very little *for* them. For this reason supervisory personnel are often viewed by the line personnel with distrust and even contempt.[16] It must be understood that this character of command in police departments is not due solely to its administrative incompetence. It is exceedingly rare that a ranking police officer can take positive charge of police action, and even in the cases where this is possible, his power to determine the course of action is limited to giv-

policeman's reputation for initiative and efficiency. His superiors recommend him for assignment to the detective division. This route to promotion appeals to many young policemen who have little hope of passing a written competitive test for promotion, and impels many of them to adopt cynicism as a rational and functional way to advancement." Niederhoffer, op. cit. supra., Note 6 at pp. 76–77.

14. "At present the principal rewards are promotion, which takes a patrolman off the street, or reassignment to a detective or specialized unit, which takes him out of order maintenance altogether; not surprisingly, patrolmen wanting more pay or status tend to do those things

that will earn them those rewards." Wilson, op. cit. supra., Note 2 at pp. 292–293.

15. On the pervasiveness of purely punitive discipline, see McNamara, op. cit. supra., Note 9 at pp. 178–183. Wilson reports that regulations are so framed that they do not instruct but "give the brass plenty of rope with which to hang us," op. cit. supra., Note 1 at p. 279.

16. McNamara, op. cit. supra., Note 9 at pp. 187–188, reports attitudes of patrolmen towards their superiors and concludes, "Regardless of their accuracy, these assertions strongly support the feeling that the 'bosses' of the department do not deserve the respect which the organization requires or demands."

ing the most general kinds of directions.[17]   But like all superiors, police superiors, do depend on the good will of the subordinates, if only to protect their own employee interests within the institution.   Thus, they are forced to resort to the only means available to insure a modicum of loyalty, namely, covering mistakes.   The more blatantly an officer's transgression violates an explicit departmental regulation the less likely it is that his superior will be able to conceal it.   Therefore, to be helpful, as they must try to be, superiors must confine themselves to white-washing bad practices involving relatively unregulated conduct, that is, those dealings with citizens that lead up to arrests. In other words, to gain compliance with explicit regulations, where failings could be acutely embarrassing, command must yield in unregulated or little regulated areas of practice.   It is almost as if patrolmen were told, "Don't let anyone catch you sleeping on the job; if they do I'll get it in the neck and you will too.   So, please, keep walking; in return I'll cover for you if you make a false arrest."   Superiors, needless to say, do not speak in such terms.   They probably do not even communicate the message covertly.   Indeed, it is quite likely that most police officials would honestly view the suggestion with contempt.   But this is the way things work out and the more a department is organized along military-bureaucratic lines the more likely it is that they will work out this way.   Naturally, the situation is not conducive to the development of relations of genuine trust, respect, and loyalty.

Finally, emphasis on elaborate codes of internal regulation of a military kind tends to subvert police training, at least wherever this training is administered in departments, as is commonly the case.   In the very best existing training programs instruction consists of three parts.   There are some lectures concerning criminology, criminal law, human relations, mental health, etc., given by visiting social scientists and lawyers.   The second part consists largely of homilies about the social importance and dignity of police work, which emphasize that the occupation makes the highest demands on integrity, wisdom, and courage.   The third part, to which the bulk of instructional time is devoted, relates to the teaching of department regulation.   Since this is the only practical part of the course of instruction, it is abundantly clear that the overall purpose of the training is to turn tyros into compliant soldier-bureaucrats rather than competent practitioners of the craft of peacekeeping and crime control.[18]   But since there exist

17. Banton views the absence of instructions and supervision as a main characteristic distinguishing American police from their British counterpart, op. cit. supra., Note 3 at pp. 115–116. The absence of supervision is frequently noted; see McNamara,

op. cit. supra., Note 9 at p. 183; and *Task Force Report: The Police,* op. cit. supra., Note 2 at pp. 28, 52, et passim.

18. McNamara speaks about the dilemma, "whether to emphasize training

no direct relation between knowing the regulations and maintaining the appearance of complying with them, the first thing graduates learn on their first assignment is that they must forget everything they have been taught in the academy. The immediate effect of the "reality shock" is a massive increase in the attitude of cynicism among first year policemen, not surprisingly since their introduction to the occupation was not only inadequate as far as their work duties are concerned, but also misleading.[19]

It could be said, of course, that the argument proposed thus far merely shows that efforts to professionalize police work by means of importing traits of outward military discipline is apt to create tendencies to displace misconduct into unregulated areas because the pertinent regulations have not yet been formulated. In time, these areas too will come under the scope of the existing discipline. It is our view that it is exceedingly unlikely that this development will take place. The charting of realistic methods of peacekeeping and crime control is profoundly incompatible with the style of current regulations of internal discipline. One simply cannot bring under the same system of control rules relating to dress and bureaucratic formalities, on the one hand, and norms governing the discretionary process of handling an instance of disorderly conduct on the streets, on the other. Emphasis on the first defeats care for the other. This does not imply that all presently existing regulations must be rescinded to encourage a methodical approach to police work tasks. Quite the contrary, the majority of present expectations will probably retain value in any alternative system of control. But their relevance, mode of presentation, and enforcement will have to be made subsidiary to a system of procedure that charts professionally responsible decision-making under conditions of uncertainty. In simplest terms, if policemen can be induced to face problems in the community and to deal with citizens in ways that meet, at once, criteria of purposeful efficiency and will correspond to the expectations of public trust commonly associated with the exercise of professional expertise, then there will be no need to treat them like soldier-bureaucrats. Correspondingly, as long as policemen will be treated like soldier-bureaucrats, they cannot be expected to develop professional acumen, nor value its possession.

strategies aimed at the development of self-directed and autonomous personnel or to emphasize strategies aimed at developing personnel over whom the organization can readily exercise control. It appears that the second strategy is the one most emphasized," op. cit. supra., Note 9 at p. 251. Niederhoffer similarly states that, "At the Academy he [the recruit] masters and simultaneously succumbs to, the web of protocol and ceremony that characterizes any quasi-military hierarchy," op. cit. supra., Note 6 at p. 45.

19. Niederhoffer, ibid., speaks about the "reality shock" and documents the rapid rise of cynicism among first year policemen; see especially p. 239.

It must be said, however, that the true professionalization of police work, in and of itself, is no weapon against sloth and corruption, no more than in the case of medicine, the ministry, law, teaching, and social work. That is, the professionalization of police work still leaves open the matter of its control. But if we are not willing to settle for having physicians who are merely honest, and who would frankly admit that in curing diseases and dealing with patients they have to rely entirely on "playing by ear," it is difficult to see why we would devote all our energies to trying to make the police honest without any concern whatever for whether or not they know, in a technical sense, how to do what they are supposed to do. Some people say it is foolish to demand technical proficiency and professional ethics where none exists. This view is certainly premature and probably wrong. We know far too little about the way police work is actually done to say with assurance that what we desire does not exist. What we know is that policemen have not written any scholarly tracts about it. We also know that presently good and bad work practices are not distinguishable, or, more precisely, are not distinguished. Worst of all, we have good reasons to suspect that if some men are possessed by and act with professional acumen, they might possibly find it wiser to keep it to themselves lest they will be found to be in conflict with some departmental regulation. The pending task, therefore, has less to do with putting external resources of scholarship at the disposal of the *police departments*, than with discovering those good qualities of police work that already exist in the skills of *individual practitioners*. It is not enough to discover them, however, they must be liberated and allowed to take their proper place in the scheme of police organization. By making the possession and use of such skills the controlling consideration in the distribution of rewards, we will have a beginning of a professional system for controlling police practices. The prospect of such a control is in strict competition with presently existing methods of military-bureaucratic regulation.[20]

20. The competitive nature of ideals of military discipline and methodical discretion has been noted in a survey of the Boston police department undertaken in 1934: "Too often the military aspect of organization pushes the essentially individual character of police work into the background." cited in *Task Force Report: The Police*, op. cit. supra., Note 2 at p. 136.

COMMAND, CONTROL, AND CHARISMA: REFLECTIONS ON POLICE BUREAUCRACY *

Bureaucratization can be regarded as an organizational technique whereby civic pressures are neutralized from the standpoint of the governing regime. In the development of the modern police, bureaucratization has been a major device to commit members to the occupational organization, to the occupational community, and to its norms of subordination and service to a degree where these commitments take precedence over extra-occupational ones to family and community.

The political neutrality and legal reliability of the police in modern societies are less a matter of the social sources of their recruitment than of the nature of internal organization, training, and control. While this, of course, is true for all government organizations under a civil service or tenure system, it is true for the police not primarily because they are civil servants in the restricted sense but because of their allegiance to an occupationally organized community that sets itself apart. The situation is particularly crucial for the police since they often are called upon to enforce laws that are unpopular with the public or for which they have no personal sympathy, while at the same time they are armed and organized. Perhaps this fundamental significance of police bureaucratization can be seen by the fact that given a well-organized, well-disciplined, and internally well-regulated police, civil authorities can count on the police if they are assured of the political loyalty or neutrality of the commander. Indeed, the modern police emerged under conditions whereby they were an organized source of stability between the elites and the masses, serving to draw hostility from the elites to themselves and thereby permitting more orderly relations among the elites and the masses.[1]

COMMAND SYSTEMS

To our knowledge, there is no detailed empirical description of command processes in a police department. It is necessary, therefore, to rely largely on published discourses that give information on

* Source: Bordua, David J. and Reiss, Albert J., Jr. "Command, Control, and Charisma: Reflections on Police Bureaucracy." *American Journal of Sociology*, 72 (July, 1966) pp. 68–76. Reprinted with permission of the University of Chicago Press and the Author.

1. Alan Silver, "On the Demand for Order in Civil Society: A Review of Some Themes in the History of Urban Crime, Police and Riot in England" (to be published in David J. Bordua [ed.], *The Police* [New York: John Wiley & Sons, 1966]), p. 11.

the rhetoric of command and control and that are of variable and unknown validity as descriptions of behavior.[2]

Police literature emphasizes the quasi-military nature of police-command relations, and casual observation in metropolitan police departments indicates that police officials are highly sensitive to "orders from above" and to probabilities of official disapproval of behavior. In principle and in rhetoric, a police organization is one characterized by strict subordination, by a rigid chain of command, by accountability of command, and more doubtfully, by a lack of formal provision for consultation between ranks.

Before accepting this description of its structure uncritically, it is necessary to say that such statements are meaningful only by comparison. We have relatively little data comparing the operating as opposed to the rhetorical nature of command in different types of organizations. In many ways, policing is a highly decentralized operation involving the deployment of large numbers of men alone or in small units where control by actual command, that is, by issuing orders, is difficult. This problem is generally recognized by top police administrators, leading to their stressing the importance of accountability of command to achieve control. O. W. Wilson puts it this way:

> Authority is delegated by some form of command; responsibility is effectively placed by some form of control. . . .
> The effective placing of responsibility or the act of holding accountable involves an evaluation of the manner in which the authority was exercised, hence the rule of control: *He who gives an order must ascertain that it has been properly executed.*
>
> It is relatively easy to delegate authority by giving a command, but to ascertain the manner in which the order was carried out so that the subordinate may be held responsible is often difficult.[3]

Other evidence from the police literature suggests that the description is overdrawn, that both internal and external transactions structure the effective range of command and control. Moreover, as J. Q. Wilson points out, it seems clear that the variations between "system-oriented" as opposed to "professionalized" departments includes fundamental differences in styles of control.[4]

2. See, for example, Bruce Smith, *Police Systems in the United States* (2d rev. ed.; New York: Harper & Brothers, 1960), esp. chaps. vii–ix.

3. O. W. Wilson, *Police Administration* (New York: McGraw-Hill Book Co., 1950), p. 59.

4. James Q. Wilson, "The Police and Their Problems: A Theory," in Carl J. Friedrich and Seymour E. Harris (eds.), *Public Policy, XII* (Cambridge, Mass.: Harvard University Press, 1963), pp. 189–216.

Historical changes in the nature of police work and organization have increased the importance of more subtle and perhaps more important developments in methods of control.   In the dialectic of dispersion versus centralization of command, every development in the technology for police control of the population is accompanied by changes in the capacity of the organization to control its members. Originally the bell, creaker, or rattle watches were limited in summoning help to the effective range of their "noise"; the addition of "calling the hours" served to monitor the behavior of the patrol (quite generally open to question).[5]   Here we see evidence of a classic and continuing dilemma in organizations—that to control subordinates they must be required to make themselves visible.   For the police, this means that when they become visible they likewise become more calculable to potential violators.   Control of the dispersed police was really difficult before the call box that simultaneously enabled patrolmen to summon help and enabled commanders to issue calls and require periodic reporting.[6]   The cruising car with two-way radio enabled still greater dispersion and flexibility in the allocation of patrols, while at the same time bringing the patrolman or team more nearly within the range of constant control.   It is now a fundamental duty of the radio patrol officer to remain "in contact," that is, controllable.

More important, perhaps, is the fact that a centralized radio communication system, where telephoned complaints are received and commands given, makes it possible for top management to have independent knowledge of complaints and of who is assigned to them before either subordinate commanders or the patrol team does.   A minimum of centralized control is available, then, not simply by the direct issuance of commands from superior to subordinate but by means of a paper-matching process whereby the complaint board's written record can be matched with the written record the patrolman is required to generate.   This pattern of control by centralized communication and internal organizational audit is highly dependent upon the distribution of telephones in the population.   The citizen's telephone enables the police commander to enlist the complainant—on a routine basis—as part of the apparatus for control of the policeman.   A citizen's opportunity to mobilize the police is intricately balanced with that of the commander.

5. Selden D. Bacon, "The Early Development of American Municipal Police: A Study of the Evolution of Formal Controls in a Changing Society" (unpublished Ph.D. dissertation, Yale University, 1939).

6. The innovation of the police patrol and signal service in Chicago in 1880 brought forth considerable resistance and indignation from the police patrol precisely because it made possible closer supervision of the patrol (see John Joseph Flynn, *History of the Chicago Police: From the Settlement of the Community to the Present Time* [Chicago: Police Book Fund, 1887], chap. xx).

Added to these matters of task organization, in large police departments, the chief's power to command and control is limited by a complex system of "due process" that protects subordinates. This, of course, is true of all civil service organizations. The strong interest in keeping the police "out of politics" coupled with the interest of the rank and file in job security, however, creates a situation where, formally, the department head must contend with legally empowered authorities in the selection, promotion, and discharge of personnel. Even in matters of internal assignment and definition of task, decisions may impinge on the civil service classification system. Police employee organizations, likewise, are quite effective in seeing to it that the system of "due process" continues to protect them. The individual officer, furthermore, when accused of wrongdoing or a crime, demands all the legal safeguards he may deny to those whom he accuses of committing a crime.

Not all police operations are constituted in the fashion of this highly oversimplified picture of so-called routine patrol. Detectives, for example, are less subject to such control. But these considerations of due-process barriers to centralized command and historical changes in control procedures that rely less on actual command as a form of control are intended to raise questions about the sociological meaning of the stress generally placed on command and to lay the ground for a somewhat more systematic analysis of it.

FORMS OF LEGITIMATION

Thus far, "command" has been used in two senses. In one, "command" refers to a technique of control in organizations that consists of "giving commands." The directive communication between superior and subordinate may be called "a command," or, if more impersonally clothed, "an order." In another sense, however, "command" means neither a specific technique of control nor an instance of its use, but something more general—a principle that legitimates orders, instructions, or rules. Orders, then, are obeyed *because* they are "commanded."

Sociologists are familiar with discussions of this type ever since Weber.[7] In Weberian terms, the police department "as an order" is legitimated by the principel of command. Each form of legitimation, however, as Weber so clearly saw, has a correlative requirement of "attitude" on the part of those subject to its sway. In the case of "an order" legitimated by a rhetoric of command, the correlative expectation is "obedience"—again not as a situational expectation in the case of a given specific command but as a principle relating member to organization. To be "obedient" in this sense carries the same

7. Talcott Parsons (ed.), *Max Weber:*   *Organization* (New York: Oxford
    The Theory of Social and Economic   University Press, 1947), pp. 324 ff.

general sense of principle as in the "poverty, chastity, and obedience" of the monk's vow. In a system so legitimated, we can expect that commitment to obedience will be displayed as a sign of membership.

It is not surprising, then, that social scientists who are based in organizations where independence is legitimated, rehabilitation workers based in those where professional discretion and supportiveness are legitimated, and police who are based in organizations where obedience is legitimated so often fail to communicate with one another when they are engaged in exchanges of ideologies.

We may point out as well that in orders legitimated by command and exacting obedience, the classic status reward is "honor." The morale and public-relations problems of the American police can be more clearly understood as an attempt to substitute public prestige sought in an occupational performance market for the Weberian status regard sought and validated in the "honor market." The American police are denied both, for the public seems unwilling to accord the police status either in the European sense of status honor as representatives of the State or in the more typically American sense of prestige based on a claim to occupational competence.

Command as a basis for legitimacy can be located under any of the three basic types of legitimation discussed by Weber—the rational-legal, the traditional, and the charismatic. Inherently, however, command as a principle focuses on the commander, and the exact nature of the concrete "order" legitimated by the principle of command will depend on the role of the specific commander. Because of this commander focus, the command principle is likely to lead to a mystique of the personal commander and an organizational stress on legitimating specific orders or even general rules as emanating from him.

COMMAND AND TASK ORGANIZATION

To regard a metropolitan police system solely in terms of the classic features of the hierarchically oriented command bureaucracy would be mistaken, however. Although the more traditional police departments in American cities are organized on quasi-military command principles, modernized ones display features of other control systems, particularly those of centralized and professional control structures.

The core of the modern metropolitan police system is the communications center, linking as it does by radio dispatch the telephoned demands of a dispersed population with a dispersed police in mobile units. The technology of the radio, the telephone, the recorder, and the computer permits a high degree of central control of operating units in the field. The more modern police departments, for example, have tape records of all citizen phone complaints, the response of dispatch to them, and the action of mobile units. This technology also makes possible reporting directly to a centralized records unit. Indeed, the more rationalized police-command systems make extensive use of the computer as a centralized intelligence system to which mobile units can make virtually direct inquiry, as a "decision-maker" about which units are to be dispersed for what service, and as a source of intelligence on the output of personnel and units in the department. Such a centralized and direct system of command and control makes it possible to bypass many positions in the hierarchical command structure, particularly those in the station command. More and more, those in the line of authority assume work supervision or informal adjudicatory rather than strictly command roles.

There undeniably is considerable variability among internal units of a police department in the degree to which they are centrally commanded such that routine patrol is more subject to central command than are tactical or investigation units. Yet, all in all, there is a growing tendency for all internal units to operate under programed operations of a central command rather than under local commanders. Orders not only originate with the central command but pass directly from it.

The centralization of command and control is one of the major ways that American police chiefs have for coping with the tendency toward corruption inherent in traditional hierarchically organized departments. Chiefs no longer need rely to the same extent upon the station commander to implement the goals of the department through the exercise of command. Indeed, a major way that corrupt departments are reformed these days is to reduce the command operations of local commanders, replacing them with centralized command and control. Yet it is precisely in those operations where corruption is most likely to occur, namely, the control of vice, that a centralized command is least effective. The main reason for this is that a centralized command lends itself best to a reactive strategy, whereas a professionalized or hierarchically organized command lends itself to a proactive strategy. Vice requires an essentially proactive strategy of policing in the modern metropolis, whereas the citizens' command for service demands an essentially reactive strategy and tactics.

A central command not only bypasses traditional hierarchical command relations but, like the hierarchical command, creates problems for the developing professionalized control in police systems. A professionalized model of control respects a more or less decentralized decision-making system where the central bureaucracy, at best, sets general policy and principles that guide the professional. Indeed, many police tasks and decisions would appear to lend themselves to a professional as well as technical role relationship with the client.

Yet, the institutionalized and legally defined role of the police formally denies professional discretion to them in decisions of prosecution and adjudication, granting them to professional lawyers. The "professionalizing" police, therefore, are formally left only with certain decisions regarding public order, safety, service, and arrest. These formal prohibitions coupled with the new technology and centralized command (developed under the banner of professionalization of the police) both serve to decrease rather than enhance discretionary decision-making by subordinates. Police organizations become "professionalized," not their members.

COMMAND AND OCCUPATIONAL CULTURE

The internal organizational life of American police departments displays features which distinguish the police from other organizations and which have important implications for the nature of organizational command. These features are the familial and/or ethnic inheritance of occupation, the almost exclusive practice of promotion from within, the large number of formal voluntary organizations that cut across organizational membership, and, finally, the existence of legal protections for tenure which inhere in civil service regulations.

Specific police jobs differ; yet it is quite important to recognize that, fundamentally, police status overrides these differentiations. Not only does the basic status override lateral differentiations, but it also tends to override differences in rank. Police occupational culture, unlike the situation in industry, unites rather than divides ranks.

This is perhaps the most fundamental significance of the practice of promoting from within. The fact that all police-command personnel came up through the ranks means not only that there is relatively little class distinction among police but that the sharp differences between managers and workers in industry is less apparent for the police.[8]

In addition to the vertical spread of police occupational culture due to promotion from within, local recruitment tends to entrench any specific department's version of the more general occupational culture. This combination of occupational culture and organizational culture produces what J. Q. Wilson referred to as "system-oriented" departments.[9]

---

8. The more professionalized a police department, however, the more it displays manager-worker differences common in industry. The police in the line symbolize this by referring to those on the staff as "empty holster——." The occupational culture holds, nevertheless, for police personnel in staff and line versus the non-sworn personnel, the latter commonly being referred to as "civilians."

9. James Q. Wilson, op. cit.

Interlinked with the features of local recruitment and internal promotion is the factor of familial and ethnic inheritance of the police occupation.   Many occupations are strongly based in ethnicity, and may organizations have widespread kinship bonds; indeed, some companies advertise the fact.   The consequences, however, are more exaggerated in the police, partly because police culture emphasizes distance between the occupation and the general community but, more importantly we suspect, because of the relative lack of vertical differentiation.   Thus, police corruption can become spread up precisely because of this lack of differentiation.

Finally, the development of civil service can mean that a rather rigid formal, legal shell is erected around occupational and organizational cultures in a way that makes the exercise of command from the top even more difficult that it would otherwise be.   The reform chief must choose his command from among those who began tenure under his predecessors.   And except for retirement, "resignation," or formal dismissal proceedings, he is left with the cadre of the "old department."

It should be noted, however, that occupational and organizational cultures and the reinforcing solidarities provided by formal organizations like the Fraternal Order of Police and by the legal protections of civil service have another side.   They make possible the existence of police systems which function at least moderately well over long periods in a society notoriously inhospitable to police; indeed, they are partially a defensive response to that inhospitability.   While they may inhibit modernization and reform, they do insure that the job will get done somehow.   More importantly, they provide the irreplaceable minimum structural conditions for at least the basic elements of status honor.   They provide the essential precondition for a sense of honor—a relatively closed, secure community (not just organization) of functionaries who can elaborate and apply honor-conferring criteria.

These internal solidarities create special barriers to the effective exercise of command over and above the features of task organization previously discussed.   They become particularly significant in attempts at modernization or reform.   The police commander ignores this internal culture at his peril.   It can confront him with an opposition united from top to bottom.

The modernizing chief is constrained, therefore, to make at least symbolic obeisance to police solidarity by demonstrating that he is a "cop's cop" as well as a devotee of systems analysis and psychological screening of applicants.   One of the ways he does so is by emphasis in his dress and bearing—the policeman's chief social tool—the ability to command personal respect.[10] At least during a period of change, personal charisma and "presence" are of particular significance. He must also make his orders stick, of course.

The reform chief's charisma is of special significance because of the objective uncertainty of obedience but also because reform depends on the co-operation of a cadre of immediate subordinates whose careers may depend upon the chief's success. His certainty becomes their hope.

COMMAND AND CIVIL ACCOUNTABILITY

The structure of command is affected not only by elements of task organization and technology and by the features of occupational and organizational culture discussed above but also by the relationship between the chief and his civil superiors. In the case of the American municipality, police chiefs, at least traditionally, both at law and in practice, are politically accountable officials who ordinarily stand or fall with the fortunes of their civilian superiors (who are lodged in external systems). Given the often controversial nature of police work, and the often "irrational" and unpredictable nature of political fortunes in municipal government, the American police chief who is responsible to a politically elected official comes close to the position of a "patrimonial bureaucrat" in Weber's terms. His tenure as chief, though not necessarily his tenure in the department, depends on continuing acceptability to the elected official(s).

We have alluded to some of the dimensions along which police departments and their command processes seem to vary—using terms like "modernized," "rationalized," "reformed." It would be possible to indicate other dimensions which intersect these by referring to department age, growth rate, and other variables as well as environmental context variables such as variations in civic culture—comparing, for example, Los Angeles and San Francisco. It is not our intention, however, to attempt a systematic comparative scheme. In the case of the problem of civic accountability, however, it is possible to use some of the material presented thus far to begin development of such a scheme.

The relations of police commanders to civil superiors are actually more varied and complex than those depicted above. We shall discuss briefly only the two most important dimensions of variation: the security of tenure of the chief commander and the degree to which he is held strictly accountable by a mayor. Given strict accountability plus insecurity of tenure, we can expect a kind of obsession with command

10. The ability to command respect personally is more necessary in America than in Britain where police command more respect officially (see Michael Banton, *The Policeman in the Community* (New York: Basic Books, 1965).

and a seemingly "irrational" emphasis on the twinned sysmbols of the visibility of the commander and the obedience of the force. Some of the rhetoric of command in the police literature likely arises from an attempt to "protect" the chief by the compulsive effort to "over-control" subordinates, almost any of whom can get him fired. This amounts to saying that as civil superiors increase the formal accountability of the police chief *without changing* the tenure features of the role, the increasing bureaucratization of the American municipal police stressed by J. Q. Wilson leads to the development of an organization animated by a principle of the commanding person.[11] This "personalized subordination" to the "Hero Chief" can become an operating, if not a formal, principle of organization.[12]

Increased professionalization can be another accommodative strategy in such a situation, but this time aimed not at control of the force but at control of the mayor by changing the grounds of accountability. One of the first jobs of the "professionalizing" police chief often is to convince his civil superior that "you can't win 'em all" and that it is irrational and "unprofessional" to dismiss a police chief or commissioner because of failure to solve some particular crime. Perhaps, in the long run, it is hard to have a professionalized police without a professionalized mayor. Perhaps also, this would lead us to expect different kinds of command styles where a professional city manager intervenes between the chief and the mayor.

If the civil superior, for whatever reason, does not demand accountability from the chief, the quasi-formalized obsession with "command" as a principle of control may be replaced by a complex system of feudal loyalties. In this situation, ties of personal political fealty between chief and mayor—or between chief and the local "powers"—may become prominent and "keep your nose clean" the principle of subordination. When this trend goes beyond a certain point, the department is commonly described as politically corrupt. Finally, to the degree that the chief is secure in his tenure, we would expect the obsession with command and the emphasis on personalized subordination to decrease.

11. James Q. Wilson, op. cit.

12. One study reports that, as compared with welfare workers and school teachers, policemen were more likely to personalize authority (Robert L. Peabody, "Perceptions of Organizational Authority: A Comparative Analysis," *Administrative Science Quarterly*, VI [March, 1962], 477–80; see also Elaine Cumming, Ian M. Cumming, and Laura Edell, "Policeman as Philosopher, Guide and Friend," *Social Problems*, XII [Winter, 1965], 276–97).

On the basis of this analysis of command and the position of the chief we may distinguish the four types of departments (Table 1).

Table 1

TYPES OF POLICE DEPARTMENTS

RELATION TO MAYOR	TENURE OF CHIEF	
	Secure	Insecure
Strictly accountable	Command bureaucracy	Personalized command bureaucracy
Feudal allegiance	Command feudality	Personalized "political" feudality

[B7262]

We have consciously chosen words such as "feudality" with outrageously large quotas of surplus meaning since the concern here is to direct attention to features of police organization that receive relatively little attention and to questions of fundamental differences in the consequences of organizational membership between police and other organizations.[13]

A word about two of these types seems in order. The command-feudality type seems a contradiction in terms (and indeed derives from the cross-classification itself). Some small municipal and sheriff's departments, where the tenure of the chief in the local "feudal political structure" is secure, may fall here. Because everyone is secure in a relatively non-bureaucratic system, the operating principle of subordination can be command. Such an arrangement possibly characterizes the exceptionally long-tenure chiefs discovered in Lunden's study in Iowa.[14]

The "personalized command bureaucracy" seems likely to occur where an insecure reform head is in office. To reform successfully he must bureaucratize and rationalize administrative operations. To do this against the inevitable internal resistance he must emphasize the principle of command. To make clear that status quo-oriented

13. This typology owes much to the analysis of labor unions in Harold L. Wilensky, *Intellectuals in Labor Unions* (Glencoe, Ill.: Free Press, 1956).

14. Walter A. Lunden, "The Mobility of Chiefs of Police," *Journal of Criminal Law, Criminology and Police Science*, XLIX (1958), 178–83.

commanders have been superseded he must emphasize *his* command and his *capacity* to command.   In *short,* he must exercise what Selznick defines as one of the crucial functions of leadership in administration.   He must define the emerging character of the institution.[15]

CONCLUSION

We have discussed features of American police systems that may account for variations in and possible changes in command structures and also features that account for both a rhetorical and behavioral emphasis not on one or the other formal command system but on something which seemingly appears as alien and contradictory—the personal charisma of the chief and the emphasis on personalized command as a symbolic, if not actual, principle of order.

Command, obedience, and honor ring strangely in analysis of organizational life in America except, perhaps, for the military.   Yet it seems to us that meaningful analysis of the police must touch upon them as well as upon duty, courage, and restraint.   The self-image of the police is different because of them.   We have already alluded to the fact that the status reward for obedience is honor and that the maintenance of honor requires a status community—not simply a formal organization.[16]

The significance of honor is that it lies at the heart of the necessary police virtues—courage, devotion to duty, restraint, and honesty. In the absence of ritually symbolic auspices such as the European State or the English Crown, the personal charisma of chiefs is a necessary transitional step to an occupationally based community of honor.   In the long run, such status honor, not only occupational prestige, is one fundamental answer to police corruption.[17]   In the short run, it means that successful police commanders must attempt not to have the police reflect the society but transcend it.

15. Philip Selznick, *Leadership in Administration* (New York: Row, Peterson & Co., 1957).

16. Military honor is similarly communal and not just organizational (Morris Janowitz, *The Professional Soldier* [Glencoe, Ill.: Free Press, 1960], esp. chaps. iv and v).

17. M. McMullen, "A Theory of Corruption," *Sociological Review,* IX (1961), 181–201.

CONTROL SYSTEMS, SOCIAL BASES OF POWER AND POWER EXERCISE IN POLICE ORGANIZATIONS * † [1]

This paper analyzes (1) the structural conditions which affect the location of social bases of power in an organizational position; (2) the structural conditions affecting the exercise of power; (3) the necessity of altering these structural conditions if one wishes to increase the power-control of the organization over its boundary-spanning members; and (4) the consequences these organizational structures have on persons handled by the organization's personnel.

The analysis was accomplished through studying and comparing the control systems of five street-contact units of one major city police department. The analysis is intended to provide a strategy for recognizing certain organizational problems, locating their sources, and suggesting organizational changes.

An understanding of control structures, structurally determined power bases, and the exercise of power from these bases is especially critical in organizations wherein highly discretionary activity is required of lower level employees. In many organizations the lower level employees of the organization have considerable power and critically determine the organization's efficacy.[2] Consequently, influencing the behavior of policemen, sales personnel, nurses and aides, teachers, guards, welfare workers and government service workers, in

*   An earlier draft of this paper was presented at the Midwest Sociological Association Meetings. April, 1973. Milwaukee, Wisconsin. The author wishes to thank Professors Dennis Sullivan and Bernard Dolnick for their helpful comments on the earlier draft.

†   Source: Tifft, Larry L. "Control Systems, Social Bases of Power and Power Exercise in Police Organizations." *Journal of Police Science and Administration,* Vol. 3, No. 1 (1975): pp. 66–76.

1.   Research support was provided under the Law Enforcement Assistance Act of 1965 by the U. S. Dept. of Justice, Office of Law Enforcement Assistance Grant #385–266–5215: David J. Bordua, Project Director; Larry L. Tifft, Research Associate; Robert Ford and Ivan Kitzmiller, Research Assistants. As to the methodology involved, see Tifft, *Compara-* *tive Police Supervision Systems: An Organizational Analysis.* Unpublished doctoral dissertation, University of Illinois, Urbana, 1970; Tifft & Bordua, "Police Organization and Future Research", *Research in Crime and Delinquency,* Vol. 6(2), 167–176 (1969); Bordua & Tifft, "Citizen Interviews, Organizational Feedback, and Police-Community Relations Decisions", *Law and Society Rev.,* Vol. 6(2), 155–182 (1971).

2.   Wilson, "Police Morale, Reform, and Citizen Respect: The Chicago Case", in Bordua, (ed.), *The Police: Six Sociological Essays,* 137–162 (1967); Homans, *Social Behavior: Its Elementary Forms,* 336–352 (1961); Wager, "Leadership Style, Hierarchial Influence, and Supervisor Role Obligations", *Admin. Sci. Q.,* Vol. 9, 391–420 (1965); Mechanic, Sources of Power of Lower Participants in Complex Organization", *Admin. Sci. Q.,* Vol. 7, 349–364 (1962).

their interaction with citizens (victims, suspects), customers, patients, students, inmates, welfare recipients, and clients, is critical to the goals of their organizations.

Much of the organizational literature assumes that supervisors are in a position to influence the interaction or the behavior of their subordinates. What has not been adequately studied, however, is the structural contingencies and constraints which differentially affect the location of power bases in an organization—and consequently the potential and actual exercise of power or influence by supervisors.[3]

BACKGROUND AND LITERATURE

Power can be described as "O has power over P to the extent that O can influence P to do something O wants P to do.[4] Raven and French[5] describe five bases of power which O can exert over P: (1) *reward power*, based on P's perception that O has the ability to mediate rewards for him; (2) *coercive power*, based on P's perception that O has the ability to mediate punishments for him; (3) *legitimate power*, based on the perception by P that O has a legitimate right to prescribe behavior for him; (4) *preferent power*, based on P's identification with O; and (5) *expert power*, based on the perception that O has some special knowledge or expertise.[6] These bases of power require perception or cognition on the part of P.[7] Thus, this definition of the concept of power is a perceptual and relational one. Power is in this sense meaningless unless it is exercised. Most researchers have consequently measured the bases of supervisory power by asking subordinates why they comply,[8] what type of compliance is elicited via different types of power,[9] or different combinations of

3. Tannenbaum & Bachman, "Structural Versus Individual Effects", *AJS*, Vol. 69, 585–595 (1964); Tannenbaum & Smith, "Effects of Member Influence in an Organization: Phenomenology versus Organizational Structure", in Tannenbaum, (ed.), *Control in Organizations* 199–211 (1968).

4. Hall, *Organizations: Structure and Process* (1972), Ch. 7.

5. French & Raven, "The Bases of Social Power", in Cartwright & Zander (eds.), *Group Dynamics* (1960).

6. For similar formulations, see Weber, *Theory of Social and Economic Organization* (1947) 324–28; Etzioni, *A Comparative Analysis of Complex Organizations* (1961).

7. Bachman, Bowers, & Marcus. "Bases of Supervisory Power: A Comparative Study in Five Organizational Settings" in Tannenbaum (ed.), *Control in Organizations* 229–238 (1968).

8. Bachman, Smith, & Slesinger, "Control, Performance, and Satisfaction: An Analysis of Structural and Individual Effects", in Tannenbaum, footnote 7, pp. 218–229; Bachman, Bowers, & Marcus, footnote 7; Warren, "Power, Visibility, and Conformity in Formal Organizations", *Amer. Sociol. Rev.*, Vol. 33, 951–970 (1968).

9. Warren, footnote 8, 954.

power,[10] and which structural constraints [11] are associated with these different power bases.

Studies have indicated that (1) that there are numerous types of power;[12] (2) that the type of power system critically affects the way in which people are linked to the organization;[13] (3) that organizations and positions within organizations consist of combinations of types of power; [14] (4) that power is not something that is available in a fixed amount; [15] (5) that compliance, satisfaction, performance and effectiveness are linked to the social bases of power;[16] (6) that the nature of the work required, the training and beliefs of the personnel, and the nature of the clients contacted may affect the social base and/or exercise of power;[17] and (7) that more than one base of power may be located in an organization but not necessarily in the same position.[18] However, these research findings and the general approach tend to assume that superiors have the power base to affect P and exercise it.

Much of the supervision literature suggests that lower level supervisors are the backbone of their organizations, or are, at the very least, in a position of high potential for influencing the subordinate and determining his morale.[19] Police administrators often see sergeants as the backbone of their organizations. In some organization-

10. Warren, footnote 8; Bachman, Bowers, & Marcus, footnote 7; Bachman, Smith, & Slesinger, footnote 8.

11. Warren, footnote 8.

12. Weber, footnote 6; Etzioni, footnote 6; Warren, footnote 8.

13. Etzioni, footnote 6.

14. Bachman, Smith, & Slesinger, footnote 8; Bachman, Bowers, & Marcus, footnote 7.

15. Hall, footnote 4; Perrow, "A Framework for the Comparative Analysis of Organizations", *ASR*. Vol. 32(2), 194–208 (1967); Perrow, *Organizational Analysis: A Sociological View* (1970).

16. Bachman, Smith, & Slesinger, footnote 8; Evan & Zelditch, "A Laboratory Experiment on Bureaucratic Authority", *Amer. Sociol. Rev.*, Vol. 26(6), 883–893.

17. Perrow in ASR, footnote 15; Perrow, *Organizational Analysis: A Sociological View*, footnote 15; Warren, footnote 8; Blau & Scott, *Formal Organizations: A Comparative Approach* (1962).

18. Hall, footnote 4.

19. Wilson, footnote 2. It is pointed out by Ohlin, et al., in "Major Dilemmas of the Social Worker in Probation and Parole", *Nat. Prob. & Parole J.*, Vol. 2, 219 (1956), and by Scott, "Reactions to Supervision in a Heterogenous Professional Organization", *Adm. Sci. Q.*, Vol. 10, 65–81 (1965), that in heteronomous professional organizations the role of the supervisor is that of an educator rather than an administrative authoritative superior. This would seem to be directly applicable to the police. Wilson (footnote 2) also points out that factors such as morale are not determined solely by police management but by such factors as the status and honor of the occupation, the opinions of clients, and by the other organizations in the criminal justice system, especially the courts, who process the products of the police department. Not feeling backed up by the courts is a typical syndrome decreasing morale among policemen.

al contexts it is more probable that clients, depending on the degree of client orientation, significantly affect the morale of the operative employee.[20] Thus, one could argue that students rather than an assistant principal affect teachers' morale; that the parolees rather than the parole officers' supervisor affect the parole officers' morale; and that the citizens, victims, complainants, and suspects, rather than the patrol sergeant, affect the patrolmen's morale.

Whichever the stonger influence on morale, the quality and dynamics of police-citizen interactions are very highly dependent upon, and are products of an intricate and complex set of variables and structures both within and outside a police organization.

In recent years police administrators have felt increasing pressure to control the discretionary behavior of policemen and have often turned to consultants and advisors in the police organization and management field. These consultants have often responded by suggesting such personalistic reforms as better selection of officers, longer training, etc. More frequently, however, they have suggested better and closer supervision, or management human relations programs. Basing their advice on the bulk of the supervision literature,[21] their remedies make the faulty assumption that supervi-

---

20. March & Simon, *Organizations* (1958) 89; Etzioni, footnote 6; Blau & Scott, *Formal Organizations: A Comparative Approach* (1962) 77. Note that recently there is an attempt at some community control of police departments and schools, student attempts to organize to influence universities, and welfare recipients forming unions, all to gain a position of more than an "object" of these extended bureaucracies. For other references see Black & Reiss, "Patterns of Behavior in Police-Citizen Transactions", *Studies in Crime and Law Enforcement in Major Metropolitan Areas*, Field Surveys III, Vol. 2, Sec. 1 (1967); Thomas "Role Conceptions and Organization Size", *Amer. Sociol. Rev.*, Vol. 24, 30–37 (1959); Reissman, "A Study of Role Conceptions in Bureaucracy", *Social Forces*, Vol. 27, 305–310 (1949); Parsons, "Suggestions for a Sociological Approach to the Theory of Organizations", in Etzioni, footnote 6, 39–46; Janowitz & Delany, "The Bureaucrat and the Public: A Study of Informational Perspectives", *Adm. Sci. Q.*, Vol. 2, 141–162 (1957); Clark, "Organizational Adaptation and Precarious Values", *Amer. Sociol. Rev.*, Vol. 21,

327–336 (1956), and Clark, *The Open Door College* (1960). Also see Carlson, "Environmental and Organizational Consequences in the Public School and Its Clients", in *Chicago National Society for the Study of Education, Behavioral Science and Educational Administration* (1964). Carlson demonstrates that schools, like police departments, have little or no control over selection of clientele and likewise the clientele lack options to these organizations. This is especially true in the ghetto where most of the social agencies have been abandoned or do not operate hours other than 9–5. The police are thus called to perform many services and enter many encounters which they feel "are not police work". Bredemeir, "The Socially Handicapped and Their Agencies: A Market Analysis", in Reissman, et al., (ed.), *Mental Health of the Poor* (1964) 88–109; Lefton, & Rosengren, "Organizations and Clients: Lateral and Longitudinal Dimension", *Am. Sociol. Rev.*, Vol. 31, 802–810 (1966); Tifft, footnote 1 (1970 article).

21. For a review and bibliography regarding this literature, see Tifft, footnote 1 (1970 article). Basically these

sors have great power potential, yet varyingly exercise this power to influence their subordinates.

THE STUDY

The information presented in this study was collected by an observational analysis exploring comparative control structures. The research demonstrated the necessity of distinguishing among the specialized organizational units within a police department. In significant ways each organizational unit contained different work roles, control structures, task environment, and clients.[22]

The research focused on observing police-citizen encounters as a means of assessing the efficacy of police behavior under alternate control systems and in different police units. Observation was focused upon officers' everyday "normal" work. Observers systematically recorded information detailing the content and process of police officer encounters with citizens and with supervisors. In addition, observers wrote final reports summarizing their oberservations on each unit.

To analyze the control and power structure of a large differentiated police department and suggest structural changes, it is first

studies can be divided into three different categories: those showing the importance of psychological and relationship factors of supervisors affecting organizational effectiveness; those stressing factors other than the relations between people and situations (as well as the first category) and their effects on organizational effectiveness; and those demonstrating the necessity of exploring the larger system of control in order to assess organizational effectiveness. The first group of studies conclude that productivity, morale, and other effectiveness criteria or variables are dependent on many factors and conditions. Under rather specific conditions productivity and morale can both be high. Yet, morale is dependent, for example, on the experience of the group members and varies with the size of the group. Therefore, large work groups generally have more difficulty identifying with their units and bosses. According to these authors, supervisors are regarded as having an important effect. The second group of studies conclude that the human relations analysts and other psychologists have neglected the complexity of management and dealt, to the exclusion of important factors, with relationship, inferring that organizational effectiveness is a matter of good interpersonal relations and only secondarily a matter of technical skill. These authors found that factors such as planning, discipline, organizing, pressure for production, and not pride in the work group, sympathy, communication, lack of arbitrariness, helpfulness, etc. were significant variables differentiating high and low effective supervisors. The third group of studies conclude that there is a need for exploration of organization effectiveness deeper: (1) than supervisor-subordinate relations; (2) than supervisor traits, manner, and abilities, and (3) than the position of the supervisor and his relationships within the role set, to study different work groups within an organization, between organizations, work groups of white vs. blue collar groups, different sized groups, and groups under differing organizational structures.

22.   Tifft, footnote 1 (1970 article).

necessary to describe the control structures, their environments, and the relative weight and importance of difference tasks,[23] technologies,[24] ideologies,[25] and publics.[26] Secondly, it is necessary to determine the effects which these elements have on the control structures and on the performances of task specific policemen.[27] However, this approach, while focusing on each task specific organizational unit, deemphasizes critical control and power relations between organizational units.[28]

The premise of this study was that the social bases of power of a supervisory position are dependent upon the nature of the work being supervised, including the technology involved,[29] where it is done,[30] the occupational cultural norms of subordinates,[31] the type of work group structure,[32] the phase of the organizational unit's history, and the cul-

23. Perrow, footnote 15; Perrow, *Organizational Analysis*, footnote 15.

24. Goldthorpe, "Technical Organization as a Factor in Supervisor-Worker Conflict", *British J. Sociology*, Vol. 10, 213–230 (1958); Scott, "Reactions to Supervision in a Heteronomous Professional Organization", *Admin. Sci. Q.*, Vol. 10, 65–81 (1965); Thurley & Hamblin, "The Supervisor and His Job", *The Problems of Progress in Industry # 13* (1963); Perrow, footnote 15, 194–208; Litwak, "Models of Organization Which Permit Conflict", *Amer. J. Sociol.*, Vol. 67, 177–184 (1961); Thompson, & Bates, "Technology, Organization and Administration", *Admin. Sci. Q.*, Vol. 2, 325–343 (1957); Gouldner, *Patterns of Industrial Bureaucracy* (1954); Stinchcombe, "Bureaucratic and Craft Administration of Production: A Comparative Study", *Admin. Sci. Q.*, Vol. 4, 168–187 (1959); Stinchcombe, "Comment on Technical and Institutional Factors in Production Organizations", *Amer. J. Sociol.*, Vol. 67, 225–259 (1961); Bell, "Formality Versus Flexibility in Complex Organizations" 97–108 in Bell, (ed.) *Organization and Human Behavior* (1967).

25. Strauss, Schatzmen, Bucher, Ehrlich & Sabshin, *Psychiatric Ideologies and Institutions* (1964).

26. See footnote 20, Piliavin & Briar, "Police Encounters with Juveniles", *Amer. J. Sociol.*, Vol. 70, 206–214 (1964).

27. Thompson, *Organizations in Action* (1967) 70.

28. Hall, footnote 4; Perrow, footnote 15; Perrow, "Departmental Power and Perspective in Industrial Firms", in Zald, ed., *Power in Organizations* (1970) 59–89.

29. Goldthorpe, footnote 24; Woodward, "Management and Technology", *Problems of Progress in Industry, No. 3* (1958); Thurley & Hamblin, footnote 24, Litwak, footnote 24; Perrow, footnote 15; Selznick, "Foundation of the Theory of Organization", *Amer. Sociol. Rev.*, Vol. 13, 25–35 (1948); "Role Specializations in Supervisors", University of Michigan, Microfilms (1957).

30. Stinchcombe, footnote 24; Gouldner, footnote 24; Goldthorpe, footnote 24.

31. Gouldner, footnote 24; Patchen, "Supervisory Methods and Group Performance Norms", *Adm. Sci. Q.*, Vol. 7, 275–294 (1962).

32. Whyte, "Small Groups in Large Organizations", in Rohrer & Sharif (eds.), *Social Psychology at the Crossroads*, (1951), 303–304: "We have tended to think of effective supervision as being a product of a relationship between a good leader and a group on the assumption that the group of subordinates was a constant. In fact, variations in the effectiveness of supervision may be as

ture or environment in which the organization operates.[33] Furthermore, the social bases of power located in a specific supervisory position may be the result of the use of other, alternate mechanisms of control. Past research has indicated that supervision (surveillance) is important and utilized in some organizational contexts, and relatively unutilized and unimportant in other organizational contexts.[34]

Drawing on the research of Bell,[35] Perrow,[36] and Thompson,[37] we hypothesized that the most crucial factor affecting the amount of discretion employed by a specific organizational member is the predictability of the work demands faced by that person. The degree of predictability of the work demands is determined by:

1. the perceived extent (range and magnitude) of unexpected events or unpredictable situational demands (dynamic task environment) ;

2. the degree to which the nature of the task problems are perceived as analyzable; and

3. the perceived degree of uniformness and understandability of the persons (raw material) handled.

much due to inherent differences in the group itself as to the leadership or supervisor's practices exemplified by the supervisor".

33. National Institute of Industrial Psychology, *The Foreman: A Study of Supervisors in British Industry* (1952). The influencing factors of the social, economic, and political milieu in which the organization operates is very important. The supervision of leadership needed in a young struggling organization is different from that needed in an established organization. The organization's market position is crucial as well as its phase of history and organizational form. Thus we consider leadership or effective supervision as not a property of individuals but a set of complex relationships among numerous variables listed in the previous footnotes. Also see Goldthorpe, footnote 24; Stinchcombe, "Social Structure and Organizations", March (ed.), *Handbook of Organizations* (1965) 142–169; "Foundations of the Theory of Organization", *Amer. Sociol. Rev.,* Vol. 13, 25–35, (1948); Selznick, *Leadership in Administration* (1957); Selznick, *TVA and the Grass Roots* (1949); Dill, "An Analysis of Task Environment and Personal Autonomy", Unpublished Ph.D. Dissertation

(1957); Dill, "Desegregation or Integration? Comment about Contemporary Research on Organizations", in Cooper, Leavett, & Shelly II (eds.) *New Perspectives in Organization Research* (1964); Evan, "The Organization Set: Toward a Theory of Interorganizational Relations", in Thompson (ed.), *Approaches to Organizational Design* (1966); Forehand & von Haller, Environmental Variation in Studies of Organizational Behavior", *Psychological Bulletin,* Vol. 62, 361–382 (1964). Also see Clark, "Isolation of the Police: A Comparison of British and American Situations", *J. Crim. L., C., & P. S.,* Vol. 56 (3), 307–319 (1965).

34. Rushing, "Organizational Rules and Surveillance: Propositions in Comparative Organizational Analysis", *Admin. Sci. Q.,* Vol. 10, 423–433 (1966); Warren, footnote 8; Tifft, footnote 1 (1970 article).

35. Bell, footnote 24.

36. Perrow, *A.S.R.* footnote 15; Perrow, *Organizational Analysis,* footnote 15.

37. Thompson, *Organizations in Action,* footnote 27.

We hypothesized that within this highly differentiated police department, in the organizational units where the work demands were highly predictable, we would find:

1. that the discretionary power of the working or processing organization member (subordinate) would be low;

2. that the social bases of power of the supervisor would be relatively few;

3. that the exercise of power or influence by the supervisor would be highly constrained and not significantly affected by style;

4. that the use of other mechanisms of organizational control would be high;

5. that the tasks would be preplanned; and

6. that peer (subordinate) interaction and communication would be centered about the issues of job security, pay, and arbitrary power.

Conversely, in the organizational units where the work demands were highly unpredictable, we hypothesized that we would find:

1. that the discretionary power of the working or processing organization member would be high;

2. that the social bases of power of the supervisor would be relatively numerous;

3. that the exercise of power or influence by the supervisor would be highly interpersonal, contingent, and dependent on style;

4. that the use of other mechanisms of organizational control would be highly problematical, though a peer or professional mechanism might develop;

5. that the tasks would not be preplanned; and

6. that much of the peer interaction and communication would be based on discussions of the work mission, the character of the organization, competency, and the issue of police "professionalization."

FINDINGS

Each of the analyzed organizational units was found to vary considerably with respect to the nature of the work performed by the policeman at the operating level, the nature of the citizens with whom the police officer came into contact, and the variability of the work demands. These elements, as well as other contextual elements, create pressures both in defining the nature of the work (role) expected of a police sergeant in each of the organizational units in determining the structural, social bases of power located in that particular position. These elements consequently had considerable effect on the potential exercise of power by an incumbent of these positions. If the bases of power were not structurally located in the position, the incumbent could not exercise this form of power.

An analysis of the five police units—patrol, traffic, tractical force, detective, and vice—discloses the factors which affect the distribution of the social bases of power in a supervisory position, the factors affecting the exercise of power, the consequences of these conditions, and some suggestions and cautions regarding organizational change.

Patrol: Social Bases of Power

Utilizing the concepts of Raven and French, the sergeant in patrol had some coercive power (the ability to mediate punishments) and some legitimate power (the right to prescribe behavior by virtue of holding the position). Yet he had little reward power (the ability to mediate rewards), expert power (special knowledge or expertise), and few opportunities to develop referent power (influence based on the subordinates' identification with the supervisor). Assessing these bases of power, the patrol sergeant was in a structurally weak position to exercise significant influence on his subordinates.

The first of many elements constructing this weak power position is the nature of the work supervised and its spatial distribution. The patrolman handles a large variety of incidents. These incidents or encounters are likely to range from issuing traffic citations to handling domestic disturbances, suspicious persons, sick persons, kids playing ball, thefts, landlord-tenant problems, and burglaries. In the course of these situations the patrolmen are likely to receive a wide variety of conflicting demands from the persons involved, whether they are "victims," "complainants," "offenders," or ballplayers. Moreover, these encounters vary in the actions they demand for resolution from the extreme routine of crime case report writing to the complex dynamics of family conflict. Patrolmen are disproportionately required to deal with service, order maintenance, and disturbance situations, regarding which there are few departmental discretionary guide lines. For some patrolmen, these "jobs" are outside their definition of police work; for others, the legitimacy of the demands of the persons involved is highly questionable. Others have no clear ends toward which they act, or see that only "temporary resolutions" are possible.

The nature of the task and consequent task demands are such that without departmental or professional guidelines the patrolmen must generally rely on their own judgment, past experiences, and definitions of the persons involved. Resolutions or actions taken in these situations are thus determined by the interaction of the patrolmen's and citizens' perceptions and definitions. Differences, especially cultural differences, in these sets of perceptions and definitions, are at the core of numerous police-citizen conflicts.

In patrol work there is rarely a need for coordination of the officers, since there is little division of labor among the patrolmen in different cars. They are generally dispatched by radio or respond on-view to an event, and there is generally no need to increase the number of policemen handling most calls. Therefore, there is generally little contact among the patrolmen. They are not visible to supervision (surveillance) because they are mobilized in cars and because they interact with citizens in the private space of the citizens' homes or apartments.

The control mechanism of radio dispatch generally yields immediate service, but it precludes the close supervision of actual patrolman-citizen interaction, and controls only the extent of availability and the number of calls handled. This control mechanism has no effect in inducing patrolmen to make uniform, or unique, decisions. It also has no effect on the approach made toward citizens, definitions of situations, missions, or domains. Additionally, the nature of many of these situations often involves the need for instant decision-making and prompt action, making the patrolman's job the most vital, difficult, and dangerous.

The patrol sergeant was expected to enter major crime scenes, to see that the patrolmen made out the correct reports, and to spot-check to see that patrolmen responded to their calls in an acceptable amount of time. In the actual work process of most work situations, the supervisor could be of little assistance to the men. If the sergeant entered a situation involving highly discretionary, "non-crime," disturbance-type encounters, his intrusion was generally resented, as he was believed to have less knowledge or at least less recent experience in handling these situations. Contributing to this situation is the fact that the few available rewards for patrolmen (assignment of beat shift, partner) were distributed by supervisors in organizational positions above sergeant. This consequently reinforced the very strong tendency for patrolmen to see the sergeant as a potential source of trouble rather than a potential source of help. The men tended to avoid and resent contact and communication with the sergeant. We found very few supervisory intrusions into the less clearly defined situations.

The patrol sergeant additionally had few opportunities to get to know the patrolmen both because of the spatial distribution of patrolmen and the fact that sergeants rotated shifts (hours worked) every month and often rotated supervisory beats, while patrolmen generally worked the same hours and beats. Supervisor-subordinate relations were consequently highly impermanent, preventing the contact base necessary for the development of referent power.

Essentially, the patrol supervisor's position had few and weak social bases of power. He was forced out of a significantly influential basis for extracting compliance from his subordinates through the complex interaction of (1) the nature of the work supervised, (2) the impermanence of sergeant-patrolman relations, (3) the environmental "high crime" task demands, (4) the nature of manpower deployment decisions, (5) the lack of executive policy guidelines for handling non-crime incidents, (6) the pressures of subordinates and (7) the nature of his superiors' task expectations.

Those administrators seriously desiring to increase the weight of the organizations' influence over the discretionary behavior of patrolmen via the mechanism of supervision must alter the social bases of power of this position by altering the elements which determine these bases of power. However, only some of the aforementioned elements are amenable to structural manipulation. Reducing supervisor-patrolmen impermanence, restructuring rigid manpower and spatial deployment providing knowledge-based discretionary guidelines, and increasing reward structures could have the effect of increasing the power base in the lower-level supervisory position. This does not mean that all lower-level supervisors would or could develop these power bases, nor does it mean that the persons placed in these positions would have the perceived expertise, charisma, or legitimacy to exercise their power potential. Furthermore, the particular uses and the ends of the behavior which this greater organizational power would take must be carefully examined. Finally, changing the bases of power in one organizational position could result in a renegotiation of power-based relations in other organizational positions, both within the patrol unit and in other organizational units. Increasing the power bases of one position does not necessarily mean a reduction in the power bases of other positions.

Traffic: Social Bases of Power

In the traffic unit the position of the sergeant in the organization was quite similar to the sergeants' position in the patrol unit. The sergeants' power/influence bases were significantly affected and constrained by the nature of the work supervised, departmental task demands, command role conceptions and expectations, impermanence of sergeant-traffic officer relations, the deployment of traffic cars to very large, spatially distanced posts, and the rules and regulations regarding the handling of traffic accidents. As in patrol, the exercise of power was further constrained by the pressures from subordinates not to interfere in their work.

Unlike the patrolman, the traffic man had a constricted area of discretionary action, handling the investigation of accidents and issuing moving traffic violation citations. The radio directed him to accidents, and elaborate procedures, rules, and regulations governed his investigations and reports. The issuing of traffic citations was generally the only other type of encounter entered by these specialized officers. Because of this very limited work activity, the work demands of the traffic man were much less dynamic and varying, and the demands of the citizens involved were more routine and understandable than those experienced by patrolmen. Consequently, the traffic officer was much more tightly controlled via a network of indirect, non-surveillance control mechanisms. Radio dispatch, regularized procedures, highly scrutinized reports, a centralized citation accounting system, and the required issuance of a quota of moving traffic violation citations are examples of these mechanisms.

This work situation seems to produce an organizational structure, similar to many well-controlled industrial production units, in which the first line supervisor lacks the structual social bases for influencing his subordinates. The traffic unit, like these industrial production units, had quite rigid hierarchical lines of authority, minimal vertical communication, and minimal normative supervisor control.

As in patrol, the traffic sergeant had some legitimate power and some, though generally minimal, coercive power, depending on the delegation of this from his immediate superior. He had minimal reward power, as there were relatively few rewards to be distributed to this highly "punishment oriented bureaucracy." Furthermore, minimal expert power was possible in the sense that little investigatory expertise was necessary for handling most accidents. As a consequence of the lack of an expert power base, wide spatial distribution and rotation-impermanency, a minimal referent power base developed in spite of the greater interaction of the men and the brass in these relatively small traffic units.

The contact necessary for the development of a referent power base was observed in one traffic unit, wherein the command personnel were intent on mediating the punishment-inspection-surveillance orientation of the division's centralized superiors. However, the development of this potential power base in this case was drained off into the social sphere, rather than critically affecting trafficman-citizen interactions. This suggests that size, intraorganizational conflict, and ideology may also affect the structural bases of power.

Tactical Force: Social Bases of Power

The sergeants and men in the tactical force worked in two very different work situations. The men and sergeants were organized into squads of 10–16 men on a permanent basis, so that the permanency of the sergeant-officer relationship was generally high. In work situations in which the squad worked as a whole—handling crowds, demonstrations, marches, and school walkouts—the sergeant was thrust into a situation demanding coordination, direction, and strategic knowledge or experience. In these situations the compliance of subordinates is critical and the bases of power which yield attitudinal compliance are most significant. Referent, legitimate, and expert power bases are thus most important, and structurally possible through the squad system. Reward and coercive power have extremely low salience in the heat, confusion, and threat or actuality of danger inherent in these highly unpredictable work situations.

Tactical force officers and district patrolmen were subject to the same rules and regulations. However, these formal rules were applicable to a limited range of the tactical force men's tasks, and specifically operable only with regard to crime and arrest procedures. When the squad members were not working as a squad, but were working on tactical, aggressive preventive patrol (stop and frisk) missions, they were not radio controlled and they were spatially dispersed in two-men cars. Consequently, they were quite invisible to the sergeant.

While these men were generally required to stop and search a specified number of persons per tour, and expected to make a certain number of arrests (points), only in some squads were they affected by the squad sergeant. The sergeant was thus thrust into conflicting work situations regarding the development of power bases and the exercise of power. Consequently, the power base of the sergeant was structurally affected by the proportion of time spent in crowd control squad activities versus aggressive-preventive patrol activities. In our observation, the bulk of tactical force activity was concentrated on the latter work situation. Only in a few instances did this mix of squad work experience place the sergeant in a position in which he directly affected the aggressive-preventive patrol operations of the tactical officers. Few sergeants affected the tactical force officers' definition of mission, type of stimuli responded to, type of stop made, manner of handling these encounters, morale, and commitment to the work. Previous work experience, especially the weak power-based patrol experience, seemed to deter the exercise of power or the development of referent power in this structurally conflicting position. Personal style significantly affected power exercise. Sergeants were in a position to have high reward and coercive power, since they determined who stayed in the squad, who worked together, where they worked, and what type of assignments were worked. They had as much legitimate power as any other sergeant by virtue of an assessment of the promotional system. They had varying opportunities to develop high contact and potential referent based power; and they had some expert power, based on squad-type activity.

Unlike the position of the sergeant in either patrol or traffic, in the tactical force unit development and exercise of socially based power was highly dependent upon whether the sergeant made use of the potential influence opportunities located in his position. Critical for the organization, of course, is how this power is used (if used); and if it is not used, then it is critical for the organization to recognize that these proactive, or crowd-controlling, officers, are virtually uncontrolled by organizational control mechanisms. When the sergeant does not exercise his power, the behavior of the tactical force officer becomes dependent upon his own attitudes and definition of mission, the norms of his coworkers, and possibly upon the attitudes and behavior of the citizens with whom he interacts.

This suggests that supervisors placed into these positions must recognize the dependence of the organization on the exercise of their influence. There must be a careful selection of persons who will fill these positions, and superiors must come to grips with discretionary decisions regarding the ends of crowd control or "preventive patrol." They must guide and direct the types of stops made, the tactics and approaches used, and the handling of persons in these encounters. Special education in the nature of, and control of, mass behavior, social movements, and street psychology is necessary. In crowd control situations, the potential consequences of not developing these social bases of power are the occurrence of uncontrolled police responses, overreactions, and "police riots." In the preventive patrol situation, the consequences are potentially severe citizen hostility, harassment, and abuse.

Detective: Social Bases of Power

In the detective units, the sergeants' and detectives' positions were affected by a combination and interaction of numerous constraints. The type of crime investigated, the type of "offender," the type of work pressures and conditions, case load demands, and the cooperation perceived and received within the specific community, all interact to affect the detective, his definition of mission, commitment, approach, attitudes toward citizens and "productivity." Sergeants were affected by these elements and by organizational task demands such as the number of men assigned to the unit and the volume of administrative tasks required. The position of the sergeant was also greatly affected by the need for field coordination. Because of the seriousness of the offense, possible media coverage, and coordination of investigation demands, sergeants in the robbery or homicide-sex-assault units were required to develop a much more active position than detective sergeants place in other less serious, politically visible, coordinational units.

Administrative demands were critical in determining the power bases of these different detective sergeant positions. As indicated in the foregoing comparisons, robbery and homicide-sex-assault sergeants had a greater opportunity to develop and exercise referent and expert power than did their rank-similars in other detective units. In many detective units the sergeant is required to stay in the office, handle paperwork, review investigation reports, distribute case assignments, and make sure that cases are investigated and reports returned on time. In this position, he could potentially be a consultant, helper, or service coordinator of information for the detectives. He also could function as a decision-maker for the members of the patrol unit, who are required to notify the detective units on cases they think might warrant an immediate investigatory follow-up.

Detectives were rarely controlled by surveillance or by rules and regulations except as they applied to investigative requirements. Rather, they were influenced by production-evaluation controls regarding their "success" in arrest and case-clearance activity. This, of course, was a significant control, in that the detective (not performing) could be transferred back to district patrol with the consequent loss of numerous benefits (money, prestige, soft clothes and other desirable working conditions). The importance of this production-evaluation assessment criterion can be seen when it combines with such organizational elements as minor offenses and great volume to cause the practice of rationing, by which attention was focused on those cases which appeared likely to be resolved successfully, quickly, and with a clearance of some type.

Detective sergeants supervised all of the men in their unit rather than some specified subset. This was a consequence of the admistrative constraints affecting the sergeant's task demands, and the relative smallness of the specific operating units. The detective sergeant thus had some legitimate power, some reward and coercive power, and differential opportunity for the development of referent power and expert power depending on the unit, its task specialization, and consequent demands. The degree of influence the sergeant in the detective units had was largely dependent on contact (work potential), coordination tasks, and the specific knowledge-skill the detective sergeant possessed as an individual. This latter influence-source is, of course, not located in the position, other than in the opportunity for knowledge to be displayed.

The degree of influence or control by the sergeant in the detective units was largely dependent on his knowledge as an expert. If the sergeant was respected for his knowledge of burglars/burglary or robbers/robbery, then he could potentially be used as a consultant, or he could coordinate the detectives into a cooperative group working on their specific crime problem. The significance of this knowledge power source was seen and reflected in our comparison of burglary and general assignments units. Specialized knowledge was generally non-existent in the general assignments units, as they did not specialize in any specific crime, but rather were catch-all, unsegmented units. There was, thus, no reason for the detective in the general assignments unit to interact with the sergeant. The general assignments detective was much more concerned with getting his cases followed up and turned in on time. The general assignments sergeant was well out of the influence system. Contrastingly, burglary sergeants were at least potentially more influential than the general assignments sergeants because of the greater need for coordination, and the possibility of specialized knowledge.

Since knowledge is one of the most crucial variables determining whether or not the detective sergeant will be highly involved in the communication-consultation network of his men, it should be a requisite that detective sergeants be assigned who have had previous detective experience and/or knowledge. Further it is critical that they structure communication between the detectives in their unit regarding suspects, modus operandi, crime patterns, etc. If these bases of power/influence are not developed, the detective is actually quite uncontrolled in his behavior by the organization. On the other hand, extraorganizational sources of control, namely citizens as victims, complainants and witnesses, have considerable control potential, because the detective must, in essence, trade his social skills (civility, politeness, and concern) for information, cooperation and investigatory leads.

Vice-Gambling: Social Bases of Power

In the gambling unit, the sergeant, because of the potential development of multiple social bases of power, was perhaps located in the most potentially powerful position of any of the sergeants' positions studied. The sergeant in this unit was generally assigned to work with and supervise three or four vice men. This meant that direct supervision (surveillance) was designed to be a significant control mechanism. Most significant among the structure-power base defining constraints in this unit were the nature of the work and the potentially disastrous consequences for the department's public image and its leaders' security which might result from corruption or poor discretionary judgment on the part of gambling unit officers. The sergeant, generally thrust into a co-working position, was constrained in exercising power by such factors as his knowledge of gambling operations relative to that of his crew members and interpersonal constraints upon the manner of his control. The sergeant was positioned as legitimately responsible for the actions of his crew members and their productivity, which all tended to make him an active working sergeant and gave him high reward-coercive power. The crew co-working arangement also provided the opportunity for significant development of referent power. However, this social base of power depended on the sergeant's assignment to one specific crew rather than to the position of a coordinator of several crews. When the sergeant was administratively required to coordinate the work of two or more crews, his potential referent power base decreased, as did his contact in general.

When the sergeant position was one of coordinator rather than co-working leader, we witnessed the creation, within the crew, of a "substitute sergeant" team-leader, replacing the non-street working sergeant. This clearly attests to the work demands for direction, co-ordination of activity (i. e., the planning of raids), control over discretionary decisions on the street, and the consequent demand for responsible leadership. Someone was needed to call the shots, to be responsible, to plan the coordinated actions of the members of the crew and also to prevent the ever-present corrupting environment from "getting to" these men. In this position (sergeant or team-leader), knowledge of the operation was crucial. Close contact made personalities significant and referent power was potentially high, out of loyalty if not out of expert knowledge. Other mechanisms of control were virtually nonexistent, though moderate productivity pressures, good working conditions, prestige, and the nature of the work, which encompassed the total range of the police function, made the men highly susceptible to the sergeant's high coercive, reward, and referent power bases.

SUMMARY AND CONCLUSIONS

In summary, supervision is but one of a number of alternate control mechanisms which vary in their relative power or controlling influence over the men as functions of the interaction of numerous constraints defining the context of the sergeant's position and its social bases of power. The nature of the work supervised, including the technology involved, the nature of the enforcement pattern, the spatial context in which it is carried out, the occupational culture norms of the subordinates, the type of group structure involved, environmental constraints affecting the definition of the crime, the constraints of the definition of legitimate intrusion as defined by subordinates, the nature of the citizens in contact and their specific roles, the uniqueness of discretion involved in the work, and the task demands and superior expectations demanded, all interact to constrain and define the position of the sergeant in each specific organizational context vis-a-vis other, alternate, organizational control mechanisms. The environmental-structural context of the position of the sergeant in each specific organizational unit largely determines whether or not supervisors can even potentially have significant influence on the working ideology, orientation, or performance of the operative policeman in that unit. Consequently, we have seen that only under specific, exacting organizational-environmental-structural conditions which affect the social bases of power located in the position of supervisor has the style of the sergeant had a significant effect on the performance of his subordinates.

It is sincerely hoped that, through the analysis of the complexities of control structure, the alternate use of mechanisms of control, the contextual determinates of these alternate mechanisms and the social bases of power located in the position of the lower level supervisor, we have contributed both to the knowledge of complex organizational analysis and to the analysis of elements which affect organizational strategies for change, greater organizational control or influence over member behavior, and greater "effectiveness" of the specific segregated organizational units, especially in their effects on the citizens in contact with these organization members.

The analysis is limited in dealing with a highly differentiated police organization and we caution the reader about the generalizability of our structure-power analysis. Rather, we hope that persons anticipating special programs designed to improve the effectiveness of their employees via greater organizational influence will analyze the nature of the work performed, the task environment, and the social bases of power located in the "influencing" positions within the organization. Our analysis, while limited in the realm of interorganizational consequences and relationships, suggests that each unit within an organization has quite different organizational control problems and solutions. There are no panaceas and no programs applicable to whole organizations (police departments), and often the solutions create new problems.

SOME ORGANIZATIONAL STRESSES ON POLICEMEN *

The policeman today exercises an executive function. With minimal supervision and little opportunity for research or reflection, he is required to make extremely critical decisions, to intervene and resolve a variegated spectrum of human crises. In this capacity he op-

* Source: Reiser, Martin, "Some Organizational Stresses on Policemen." *Journal of Police Science and Administration*, Vol. 2, (1974): pp. 156–159. This article is based upon a paper presented at the August 27, 1973 convention of the American Psychological Association in Montreal. Reprinted by permission of the publisher.

erates with considerable autonomy and authority.[1] But police work is a high stress occupation which affects, shapes, and also scars the individuals and families involved.[2] Some of the typical stresses are related to environmental work factors such as danger, violence, and authority.[3] Organizational and role pressures also routinely impinge on the policeman, contributing to his total stress load.[4]

Behavior related to the policeman's symbolic significance is an often overlooked but important factor that generates stress and operates at a largely unconscious level. His symbolization of authority elicits the dormant or active ambivalence that many people feel toward authority figures perceived as potentially threatening or punitive. Individuals whose conflicts are significant and largely unresolved, typically react to authority symbols with resentment, hostility and aggression.[5] Not only the individual police officer, but the organization as well, signifies and exerts symbolic influence over its own members and others in the community.[6]

The police department represents a family to the individuals working within it. The chief of police is the father figure, with all of the consonant feelings related to power, dependency and independence. The hierarchy involves a pecking order which operates on the principles of seniority and rank within the "family" organization. Traditionally, the chief is all-powerful and rules with an iron, if not despotic, hand. The "brass" are usually older, more powerful "siblings" who behave in a paternal and patronizing way toward the young street policemen who occupy the role of younger siblings striving and competing for recognition, acceptance, and adulthood. This dynamic, profoundly influences the organization in many significant areas such as communication, morale, discipline and professionalism.

In the traditional police organization, authoritarian management approaches predominate, with relatively little attention or concern being given to individual problems or human factors.[7] Typically, the jackass fallacy is operative.[8] This is based on the carrot and stick

1. Skolnick, J., *Justice Without Trial* (1966).

2. Reiser, M., *Practical Psychology for Police Officers* (1973).

3. Wilson, J. Q., *Varieties of Police Behavior* (1968).

4. Neff, W., *Work and Human Behavior* (1968); *Task Force Report: The Police.* The President's Commission on Law Enforcement and the Administration of Justice. U. S. Government Printing Office (1967).

5. Reiser, M., "A Psychologist's View of the Badge", *The Police Chief*, Sept. 1970, pp. 24–26.

6. Sterling, J., *Changes in Role Concepts of Police Officers During Recruit Training.* International Association of Chiefs of Police, June, 1969.

7. Likert, R., *Human Organization* (1967); McGregor, D., *The Human Side of Enterprise* (1960).

8. Levinson, H., *The Great Jackass Fallacy* (1973).

approach to personnel management, which assumes that without either dangling a tasty reward in front of someone's nose or beating him with a stick, he will not move. More enlightened police leadership is aware that management by participation is necessary in order to move from the stifling effect of the pecking order to the energetic involvement and commitment of employees who are actively identified with management.[9] These administrators recognize that organizations are at bottom only people and that without the interest and conscientious enthusiasm of the individuals comprising it, the organization can only limp along ineffectually, fighting both internal and external battles. In implementing participative management concepts, modern police managers are utilizing approaches such as decentralized team policing, territorial responsibility and an open system between policemen, the press and the community.[10]

In the past, job security was rated highest in the police applicant's need hierarchy. However, as the conditions and status of the police profession have improved, the primary motivators on the need hierarchy have advanced to that area on the spectrum related to self-actualizing and ego needs.[11] Job tenure and a livable wage are no longer enough to keep the young policeman happy. Like others in our society who are upwardly mobile, when survival and security needs have been met, he wants to be included in on the organizational action. He wants to know the reasons for actions affecting him and to feel that he has some say in the decision-making process.

Even as police departments slowly move, however, toward more democratic ways of operating, numerous internal pressures and stresses still exist that affect the individual policeman. These include such issues as how he is rated. Will the old numbers game be the basis for his evaluation, or will qualitative factors such as his ability to engage in preventive work and in-service functions be considered more important? Will he be given his assignment of choice or are assignments determined in some capricious or discriminatory fashion? Is the promotion system equitable, especially when he goes before an oral board for evaluation? Can the board be objective and impartial in its assessments? These are some of the common questions usually associated with executives that frequently involve a high level of stress and anxiety.[12]

9. Jacobs, T. O., *Leadership and Exchange in Formal Organizations* (1971).

10. Davis, E. M., "Basic Radio Car Plan", *Yearbook* (1971), pp. 38–43, International Association of Chiefs of Police.

11. Maslow, A., *The Farther Reaches of Human Nature* (1971).

12. Levinson, H., *Executive Stress* (1964).

Policemen tend to be very competitive, and failure of promotion at an anticipated time may result in feelings of alienation from the group, depression and low self-esteem. This loss of group identification may seriously affect functioning ability on the street. There are usually no post-examination sessions scheduled to cope with these reactions. Properly conducted, such sessions could help ameliorate some of the negative feelings and remotivate the individuals for the next exam.[13]

Another common stress factor is related to the internal discipline structure within a police department. The officer often feels that he is in double jeopardy in that he is not only liable criminally and civilly for a misdeed, but, in addition, faces punishment within the organization. He is expected to maintain personal and moral standards at a level higher than would be demanded in the general community.[14] If an officer receives a complaint, an investigation is usually undertaken, and in serious situations which may involve criminal matters or the reputation of the department, all stops are pulled. The officer may be subject to a Polygraph examination, in addition to lengthy interrogations, and a trial board hearing. It is interesting that the feelings of policemen toward the internal investigative branch are somewhat analogous to the feelings of certain citizens toward the police department. This is the assumption of an antagonistic stance and the expectation of unfair treatment and punishment.

Although training also has some bearing on the amount of stress officers will later experience, the formal training programs are often superseded by the informal training and attitudes the officer is exposed to in the field. The police academy attempts to reduce future stress on the recruit by simulating as closely as possible those critical field situations which he is expected to encounter later. This gives him increased coping mechanisms and reduces anxiety through familiarity and experience. However, negative attitudes by training officers or older, more influential policemen in the field can effectively diminish the value of the initial training program.

One of the most profound pressures operating in police organizations is peer group influence. As with adolescents, it is a particularly strong motivator because it has shaping influence on attitudes, values, roles and operational behavior at the street level. Identification with the group as "one of the boys" is a powerful, if not irresistible, force. One of the main reasons for this is that peer group identification serves a necessary defensive function. It bolsters and supports the individual officer's esteem and confidence, which then allows him

13. Reiser, M., *The Police Department Psychologist* (1972).

14. Niederhoffer, A., *Behind the Shield: The Police in Urban Society* (1967).

to tolerate higher levels of anger, hostility and abuse from external sources.

As long as peer group supports are functioning adequately, the feelings of camaraderie and *esprit de corps* dominate. However, when there is internal strife in the organization, with cliques and special interest groups pulling in different directions, feelings of depression, alienation, and low morale tend to emerge. The price that the individual officer pays for the enhanced support and bolstered strength that he gains in identifying with his peer group is a loss of autonomy in the areas of values and attitudes. Group values and attitudes are developed and shared, while guilt feeling resulting from any dissonance are diluted by group apportionment and rationalization. Without the peer group effect, young policemen would find it much more stressful and difficult to survive the initial accultoration process.

The young recruit is typically idealistic, intelligent and eager. One of his primary motivations in entering the police profession is a desire to help in the community. He likes action, wants recognition, and desires to assume responsibility. During his recruit training period he is relatively flexible, open and accepting. However, he very shortly begins to develop what has been called the "John Wayne Syndrome".[15]

The symptoms of this malady are cynicism, over-seriousness, emotional withdrawal and coldness, authoritarian attitudes, and the development of tunnel vision. This is a nonocular condition in which there are only good guys and the bad guys and situations and values become dichotomized into all or nothing. The syndrome appears to develop as a result of shaping influences within the organization, particularly by peer group, but is also part of a developmental process which helps protect the young officer against his own emotions as well as outside dangers while he is maturing and being welded by experience.[16] Frequently, part of this developmental picture involves distancing from his family as the new policeman strongly identifies with his peer group and feels he must choose between the two. He may become emotionally cool and lose some of his "love" for his wife. Consequently, she feels alienated and rejected and reacts in ways that significantly influence their total relationship, including communication, sex, and value systems. The John Wayne syndrome usually lasts for about the first three or four years on the job, with subsequent gradual loosening up, regaining of a sense of humor, and rediscovery of family. Concomitantly, a less bifurcated set of perceptions and values evolves.

15. Supra 2.

16. Niederhoffer, A. and Blumberg, A. S., *The Ambivalent Force: Perspectives on the Police* (1970).

The officer who successfully survives the multiplex influences from within himself, from the organization, and from his working environment benefits from the process. Having been tested and tempered in some of the most difficult crisis situations possible, he has coped, gained maturity, poise, judgment, and increased self-confidence. Authority has replaced authoritarianism. At this point the John Wayne syndrome is no longer predominant because he is now functioning as a professional.[17]

THE POLICEMAN AS ALIENATED LABORER * †

What do a policeman who sleeps in his car and a clerk who sleeps in the stockroom have in common? Is there more than superficial similarity between the patrolman who manhandles a suspect and the assembly line worker who sabotages a new car? All four individuals are responding to a shared problem: alienation from their work roles.

The concept of work alienation has a long, rich and honored tradition in American and European social theory, but recently there has been a resurgence of interest in its theoretical and practical utility. The idea that American workers, with their society's presumed generational and career mobility and its superior working conditions and wage scales, could somehow be as dissatisfied with their jobs as some seem to be has attracted increasing attention. The Department of Health, Education and Welfare commissioned a major study which aroused much comment simply by concluding that most American workers were bored with their jobs.[1] There is reportedly wide discussion among industrial personnel administrators about such schemes as the four-day work week, job enrichment and non-material incentives.[2] Radical theorists have pointed to dissatisfied young workers as ripe targets for leftist organizing.[3] Political philosophers have called for extensions of democracy into the workplace.[4] A best-seller simply recounts, in a powerful, first-person fashion, the daily experiences of American working people.[5]

17. Steadman, R. F., *The Police and the Community* (1972).

* We gratefully acknowledge the comments of our colleague, Eduard Ziegenhagen, on an earlier draft of this manuscript.

† Source: Denyer, Tom, Callender, Robert and Thompson, Dennis L. "The Policeman as Alienated Laborer," *Journal of Police Science and Administration.* Vol. 3, No. 3, (1975): pp. 251–258.

1. Special Task Force to the Secretary of Health, Education, and Welfare,

Work in America (Cambridge, Mass.: M.I.T. Press, no date).

2. Poor, Riva, *4 Days, 40 Hours* (1970).

3. Aronowitz, Stanley, *False Promises: The Shaping of American Working Class Consciousness* (1973) 397–442.

4. Dahl, Robert, *After the Revolution: Authority in a Good Society* (1970).

5. Terkel, Studs, *Working: People Talk About What They Do All Day and How They Feel About What They Do* (1972).

Corporate reaction to worker alienation usually involves repressive managerial policies, psychological manipulation of the workplace, or increased material incentives. In the case of the police, however, the most frequently mentioned panacea is "professionalism." We will attempt to describe the background of police alienation and resultant malpractice and consider the viability of professionalism as a response.

PROFESSIONALISM AND ALIENATION

We take "professionalization" to mean upgraded basic and in-service training, as well as higher formal education attainment, for both rookies and veterans.[6] It is widely assumed that training and education will produce policemen who are not only more efficient and productive, but also less susceptible to corruption and more sensitive to due process and citizens' rights. Presumably, these improvements result from the ennobling effects traditionally associated with education: increased capacity to perform tasks and increased tolerance for different kinds of people. Yet, although we presume education does make some difference, we also know that there are no necessary connections between education and competence or tolerance.[7] Furthermore, it is unrealistic to expect an immediate, massive improvement in the educational credentials of policemen, given labor market conditions, police salaries and the number of available openings.[8] This does not imply that the recruiting of college-educated applicants should be deemphasized, especially if graduates are increasingly drawn to social service occupations and if the undergraduate degree loses its weight in the job market. It does mean, however, that

6. We believe this is the ordinary-language sense in which most persons understand police professionalization. We are not specifically concerned with the more formal, sociological meaning, which involves such criteria as testing, licensing, ethics, associations, etc.

7. For a specific critique of the presumed relationship between education and police professionalism, see Chevigny, Paul, *Police Power* (1969) 273–274. We also have in mind more general works, e. g., Goodman, Paul, *Compulsory Miseducation and the Community of Scholars* (1964); Silberman, Charles E., *Crisis in the Classroom* (1970); Coleman, James S., et al., *Transition to Adulthood: Report of the Panel on Youth of the President's Science Advisory Committee* (1974). For alternative views, see

Saunders, Charles B., Jr., *Upgrading the American Police* (1970) 79–93; Buller, Irving B., "Higher Education and Policemen: Attitudinal Differences between Freshmen and Senior Police College Students", *J. Crim. L., C. & P. S.*, Vol. 63, pp. 396–401 (1972); Jagiello, Robert J., "College Education for the Patrolman—Necessity or Irrelevance?", *J. Crim. L., C. & P. S.*, Vol. 62, pp. 114–21 (1971). Finally, the middle ground is taken in Cohen, Bernard, & Chaiken, Jan M., *Police Background Characteristics and Performance* (1973) 122–23.

8. This conclusion is also reached in a careful study of policies and prospects in the New York City department: *Police Training and Performance Study*, PR 70–4, (Washington, D.C.: U. S. Government Printing Office, 1970), p. 59.

greater emphasis must be placed on the more practical objective of improving the training conducted by police departments themselves. Yet the impact of such training is at least as problematical as that of higher education. What kind of training could possibly be effective? We will suggest an answer to this question after examining the relationship between alienation and malpractice.

If education and training do not comprise an adequate explanation and therefore a means for police professionalization, what does? Obviously, many other factors can be considered: the family backgrounds of police personnel; their unique, individual personalities; departmental priorities and administrative practices; local cultures and political systems. These and similar factors cannot be ignored, but we are more interested in the effects of a process which intervenes between an officer's preparation for the job and his actual performance in the job.[9] That process involves comparing reality encountered on the street with prior expectations; reevaluating and redefining the role of a policeman in light of the demands imposed upon him; and assessing the gap between aspirations and accomplishments. Depending on the result of such determinations, the outcome can be either immense satisfaction in a worthwhile job well done or bitter cynicism about a thankless task. In the latter case, a man who does not take his job seriously cannot be expected to refuse a bribe for not doing what he does not want to do anyway. He cannot be expected to maintain the rigorous discipline demanded by due process if he sees that discipline as complicating tasks already too complex. He cannot be expected to deal tactfully with citizens who resent his authority if he himself resents what he is authorized to do. He cannot be expected to patrol enthusiastically if active patrol merely leads him into more situations in which he is forced to see himself as performing inadequately and becoming dissatisfied with his chosen career.

In short, the contemporary American policeman is a classic prototype of the alienated laborer. He recognizes that he has little control over the means for producing and distributing law enforcement. The means of production are held by other authorities in the political system who decide which behaviors are criminally deviant. Legislators produce statutes and judges and attorneys decide what to do with apprehended suspects. While the policeman does marginally control the distribution of law enforcement through his considerable discretion, he is nevertheless whipsawed between contending forces in our society: whites and blacks, older persons and juveniles, puritans and libertines, conservatives and liberals. These groups make competing demands upon him, and these conflicts are only partially rec-

---

9. Compare footnote 8 at pp. 75–76.

onciled by political authorities and police administrators. The residual conflicts are left for individual patrolmen to mediate personally.

Why should this lack of control matter to the patrolman? After all, if he is paid well, if his work takes him outdoors and puts him into contact with varied individuals, if there is camaraderie on the force, if he can see his occupation portrayed favorably on television, and if he can look forward to promotion opportunities and a retirement pension, why should he complain if he is occasionally abused by the public he serves? We feel his real complaint is one shared by many many men who work: his work fails to make him feel good about himself. He does not derive a sense of developing himself into a person of whom he can be proud.

Conversely, an officer who joins a department with reality firmly in his grasp, whose training has prepared him for the inevitable resentment his role creates, who understands that law enforcement in a society ridden with unresolved conflicts is bound to be difficult— this officer is far more likely to discern the real satisfaction his job offers. He becomes his own best critic and supporter because he knows that only he and his colleagues really understand the problems he confronts. He recognizes that an occasional citation for merit, a routine thankyou from a citizen he has served, a crime scene maintained intact for investigative specialists, a delinquent who identifies him as a father image, a parade that moves through the city smoothly, or a family that is kept viable by his intervention are among the real satisfactions available in police work. The good pinch, the appropriate use of his weapon, or the conviction of an incorrigible are still important, but he does not base his feelings about himself or the worth of police work upon these events exclusively.

How can training be conducted so as to maximize the likelihood that policemen will assume this latter attitude of respect toward themselves and their jobs, instead of cynicism, alienation and rejection of efficiency, honesty, legality and democracy? Our hypothesis is that training which encompasses police humanism as well as police science, police reality as well as police romanticism, and police behavior as well as police rules, will increase the number of officers who are psychologically prepared to pursue their careers without becoming cynical, and subsequently unproductive, dishonest, or undemocratic.

POLICE EFFECTIVENESS AS A CONSEQUENCE OF WORK SATISFACTION

The phenomena we wish to explain can be generally understood as the effectiveness of the individual officer and include productivity, efficiency, honesty, legality, the use of force and fair treatment.[10] These are obviously abstract and value-laden terms, and they are susceptible to precise empirical definition only with difficulty. A comprehensive evaluation of police performance, however, demands that all of these policy goals be examined. By "productivity" we mean simply the amount of work performed over a particular time period, and we have in mind such pedestrian matters as the number of calls responded to, number of incident reports submitted, number of arrests, and time spent on patrol and in court versus time spent in clerical work. By "efficiency" we mean the effective rate of return for the efforts considered under "productivity." The more efficient patrolman or detective, for example, has a higher conviction-to-arrest ratio than one who is less efficient. His intervention in a domestic squabble or neighborhood disturbance controls the situation without making it worse and without leaving the situation unresolved so that it subsequently turns into a more serious problem. The repair record for his vehicles and equipment is less extensive.

Honesty, legality, judicious use of force and fair treatment—all of which are demands dictated by American legal and democratic traditions—are even less easily measured. Measures of behavior consistent with such attitudes are not reported systematically in the literature. We cannot rely solely upon direct observation of instances in which an officer violates a substantive criminal law, fails to proceed within constitutional constraints, uses excessive force, or treats citizens unequally, because the definition of such events is open to phenomenological interpretation by all the parties involved, even relatively objective observers.[11]

The merit of using police cynicism (or, more broadly, work satisfaction) as an explanation of police practice is established by Niederhoffer's study, as well as a large body of literature on work satisfaction generally.[12] Furthermore, alienation has been one of the principal organizing concepts of modern social science, from Durkheim to Maslow.[13] For us, it is the critical intervening variable which determines the efficacy of police training practices.

10. Thus, our basic concern is similar to that of Skolnick, Jerome H., in *Justice Without Trial* (1966). Note, however, that we here tend to downplay the inherent contradiction Skolnick sees between efficiency and legality.

11. An excellent review of studies attempting to measure police effectiveness is in Cohen and Chaiken, footnote 7, at pp. 5–17.

12. Niederhoffer, Arthur, *Behind the Shield* (1967) 90–102; Best, Fred,

(ed), *The Future of Work* (1973); Special Task Force to the Secretary of Health, Education and Welfare, footnote 1; Robinson, John P., Athanasiou, Robert, & Head, Kendra B., *Measures of Occupational Attitudes and Occupational Characteristics* (1969).

13. Durkheim, Emile, *The Division of Labor in Society* (trans. George Simpson, 1964); Maslow, Abraham, *Motivation and Personality* (1954).

We assume that individuals engage in goal-seeking behavior—sometimes learned or "cultural," and sometimes instinctual, or derived from "basic needs." When they encounter obstacles to goal achievement, several possible consequences can be hypothesized. A state of stress or anxiety may develop, followed by aggression to remove the obstacle, or displaced aggression.[14] Or, the individual may erect cognitive defenses, which allow him to reinterpret the obstacle. Such defenses include narrowed perceptions, ignoring the stimuli which lead him to believe an obstacle exists, dogmatism, rationalization, intellectualization, projection, and scapegoating.[15] Another possibility is that the frustrated individual may simply withdraw from the conflict between obstacle and goal. He may feel powerless and inefficacious, disoriented, normless, apathetic. Still another possible response to frustrated goal-seeking is the establishment of alternative, achievable goals.

Our hypothesis is that training can increase the recurrence of this fourth response. The policeman, like any other individual, has been socialized into accepting, comprehending, and retaining some set of values. These values have indicated to him that certain behaviors associated with his work role are acceptable and will be appropriately rewarded. He enters his job with expectations geared to this idealized view of the police role. Then, to his consternation, he finds that the values which predict his rewards in accordance with his role in society are not functioning as they should in his case. He should be paid more, but he is not; his working conditions should be better, but they are not; he should be more respected by the persons with whom he interacts, but he is not. Courts and attorneys should simplify his tasks, but they seem to complicate them. His voice should carry more weight in the political system, but it does not. He may also share the general uncertainty and normlessness which seem to afflict Americans today.[16] If he is black, his upward mobility should be respected by his community, but instead he is rejected because he serves white authority.[17] He perceives some or all of these anomalies, becomes disoriented, and responds in one or the other of the ways previously indicated in order to relieve his sense of incongruence.[18]

14. For example, see Chevigny, Paul, *Police Power* (1969) 136–46; Westley, William A., "Violence and the Police", *Amer. J. Sociol.* Vol. 49, pp. 34–41, (1953); Cray, Ed., *The Enemy in the Streets* (1972) 169–80.

15. Such outcomes are described more specifically in Campbell, James S., Sahid, Joseph R. & Stanz, David P., *Law and Order Reconsidered* (1969) 290–92.

16. See Watts, William, & Free, Lloyd A., (eds.), *State of the Nation* (1973)

35, 116; Cantril, Albert H., & Roll, Charles W., Jr., *Hopes and Fears of the American People* (1971).

17. See Alex, Nicholas, *Black in Blue* (1969) 133. See also, Hughes, John J., "Training Police Recruits for Service in the Urban Ghetto: A Social Worker's Approach," *Crime and Delinq.*, Vol. 18, pp. 176–83 (1972).

18. Our treatment oversimplifies the complexity of the alienation literature. As with most heavily studied topics, the literature is complex and

The satisfaction an officer derives from his work is not simply a consequence of such immediate goals as issuing a summons, correctly completing a report, or asserting authority effectively. He achieves self-fulfillment when the whole pattern of interpersonal and object relationships of which he is a part enables him to respect his role within that network. He releases his energies in ways that are creative yet consistent with the symbolic meanings he attaches to valued referents in his world. When he is alienated, his powers are constricted; he feels controlled by uncomprehended forces; he feels unable to participate actively in the building of his own environment. In short, the alienated officer is one who has concluded that the universe into which he is thrust by his occupational role does not meet his basic human needs.

The utility this view of work psychology has for law enforcement can be examined by considering briefly how the policeman's role meets and fails to meet four needs: physical security, belonging, efficacy, and self-transcendence. Our argument is that because the police role meets the individual's needs in some ways but not in others, he maximizes his satisfactions in those areas he can and is alienated by the rest of his work.[19]

First, the policeman's job might fail to meet his need for physical security because of inadequate pay or dangerous working conditions. While pay could certainly be increased, patrolmen's salaries in most urban departments are nowhere near the poverty level. On the other hand, fear for one's life (whether or not statistically justified) is apparently real for most patrolmen. Yet, despite an occasional statement from national law enforcement leaders, there is no rank-and-file ground swell of support for weapons control. We have to infer either that policemen do not really feel threatened by armed civilians, that they are heavily influenced by right-wing ideology and *machismo* culture, or that they have reasoned that weapons control is unfeasible. Whatever the cause of police apathy on this question, the outcome is the same: alienation from the physcial danger associated with the job.

---

internecine. For example, see Josephson, Eric and Mary (eds.) *Man Alone* (1962); McClosky, Herbert, & Sebaar, John H., "Psychological Dimensions of Anomy," *Amer. Sociol. Rev.*, Vol. 30, pp. 14–40 (1965); Neal, Arthur G., & Rettig, Solomon, "On the Multidimensionality of Alienation," *Amer. Sociol. Rev.*, Vol. 32, pp. 54–64 (1967); Finifter, Ada W., "Dimensions of Political Alienation," *Amer. Pol. Sci. Rev.*, Vol. 64, pp. 389–410 (1970).

19. We agree that the assumption of modal personality type among policemen is presently unwarranted. See Balch, Robert W., "The Police Personality: Fact or Fiction?" *J. Crim. L., C. & P. S.*, Vol. 63, pp. 106–19 (1972). Yet we believe there is enough evidence for the existence of substantial police alienation. Therefore, it is worth tracing the etiology and consequences of that alienation.

Second, with respect to the need for belonging, the existence of the police subculture is well documented. The officer's work group is highly supportive, even clannish and secretive. Here, then, is a behavioral region in which the officer's need is met. Extreme dependence on this type of work satisfaction, however, has had consequences ranging from conspiratorial obstruction of justice to massive acceptance of corruption.[20]

Third, the patrolman's need for efficacy is frustrated since his putative mission is controlling the environment, while he is hopelessly ill-equipped for a task demanding resources far beyond his means.[21] Redefining the policeman's role, either toward or away from social service, is perhaps the most commonly advanced solution for this dilemma. Yet, as in the case of weapons control, a seemingly straightforward proposal seems to go nowhere. Why? One reason is that the myth that law enforcement stops crime is useful to police administrators seeking funds and self-serving candidates campaigning against the defunct Warren Court. Whatever the complete answer, the patrolman internalizes the myth of protecting life and property, instead of understanding that he usually intervenes after life and property have been attacked.[22]

Finally, the policeman, along with each of us, faces the finitude of his own existence and the consequent need for self-transcendence. He must assert a role in the world and an interpretation of reality that permits him to involve himself in creating meaning out of chaos. Some of us turn to religion, others to science, still others deny any need for self-transcendence. For the policeman in his work role, the answer is the law. His actions have a past and a future and are endowed with the highest significance by society. Yet here, too, his efforts are condemned to frustration, for society is very ambiguous about the law. Individual and collective consciousness seem to change constantly and erratically.

20. See, for example, Hersey, John, *The Algiers Motel Incident* (1968); Stoddard, Ellwyn R., "'The Informal Code' of Police Deviancy: A Group Approach to 'Blue-coat Crime,'" *J. Crim. L., C. & P. S.*, Vol. 59, p. 201 (1968); Knapp, Whitman, *et al.*, *Report of the Commission to Investigate Alleged Police Corruption* (1972).

21. See Manning, Peter K., "The Police: Mandate, Strategies, and Ap-

pearances," in Quinney, Richard, (ed.), *Criminal Justice in America* (1974) 170–200; Sutherland, Edwin H., & Cressey, Donald R., *Principles of Criminology* (6th ed. 1960) 331.

22. For a similar view, see McDowell, Charles P., "The Police as Victims of Their Own Misconceptions," *J. Crim. L., C. & P. S.*, Vol. 62, pp. 430–46 (1971).

FACTORS AFFECTING THE IMPACT OF TRAINING

Admittedly, the preceding discussion has presumed that before complete cynicism occurs, other processes have already taken place. Thus, our argument about the significance of police alienation depends on the extrinsic validity of the following propositions. First, the patrolman's training and formal education have raised expectations that cannot be fulfilled by actual police work. Second, his on-the-job experience begins to confirm for him the gap between aspiration and achievement. Third, the satisfactions he derives from other areas of his life (e. g., his family, friends, neighbors, community, nation) are either absent or fail to compensate for the needs unmet by his job. Thus, we maintain that police cynicism is dependent upon the presence or absence of extensive training, and especially training which imparts a realistic perspective on police work; the extent of the officer's formal education; and his alienation from or satisfaction with aspects of his personal identity not related to the work role. To a lesser extent, the etiology of cynicism probably also involves race, family socio-economic background, prior occupational experience, length of service, assignment to units with special functions, type of local political system, and style of departmental administration.[23]

The long-term impact of any training period is problematical, especially when the rookie is thrown into a hostile environment and when he can be expected to identify with veterans who have developed personalized styles. Yet even if these mitigating factors are absent, current training programs could still be questioned.

> Current training programs . . . prepare an officer to perform police work mechanically, but do not prepare him to understand his community, the police role, or the imperfections of the criminal justice system.[24]

This pattern does not appear to be on the verge of change, despite the widespread discussion of police professionalism in recent years.

---

23. See Cohen & Chaiken, footnote 7. Variations in police behavior associated with different types of local political systems and administrative styles are discussed by Wilson, James Q., *Varieties of Police Behavior* (1968). Otto Kirchheimer's discussion of the political trial, in *Political Justice* (1961), 47–53, also suggests ways in which political considerations intrude into law enforcement.

24. President's Commission on Law Enforcement and the Administration of Justice, *Task Force Report: The Police* (1967) 138. In fact there is some evidence that many training programs have deteriorated rather than improved in recent years. See Skolnick, Jerome H., *The Politics of Protest* (1969) 255–58; *Police Training and Performance Study*, footnote 8, pp. 36–37, 136. In fact, large numbers of policemen, especially in smaller agencies, never receive *any* formal recruit training; Saunders, footnote 7, pp. 121–22.

"Innovation" and "professionalism" are the images being presented before the public while police departments, for the most part, still function in an archaic and outmoded fashion, providing less and less service in an environment of increasing demands and decreasing budgets.[25]

. . . the recruit and his instructors seemed to take only the "shell" of professionalism, not its core.[26]

Ideally, realistic training would emphasize "the positive approach to police work."[27] It would not artificially and unnecessarily dichotomize "education" and "training." [28] Such an approach implies an accurate perception of reality to which we have alluded. Much of this reality is compellingly described in social science literature. Yet, while much social science research on police work and related subjects has been done in recent years, we doubt that very much of this knowledge has trickled down to the patrolman, who might benefit from it most. We doubt, for example, that many policemen have followed Ahern's prescription:

> While it is the policeman's task . . . to maintain the notion of individual responsibility, individual integrity, and freedom within society—and to maintain, as a professional, his own individual responsibility for his actions—it is also his task to examine the underlying causes of crime.[29]

In fact, training must go beyond merely discussing elementary criminology; it must include reviews of studies on police attitudes and public perceptions of the police, varying public perceptions of deviance, accounts of police delinquency (i. e., bribery, perjury, burglary), critiques of police malpractice, the influence of local political elites on police policy, and police practices in other nations. This training would also recognize that policemen are jurists in every sense of the word. They deliberate on the justifiability of controversies, the admissibility of evidence, the disposition of defendants, and so on. Realistic training would concede this role to the policeman and clarify it, instead of dissembling or denying it. It is hoped that this type of training would follow McNamara's recommendation:

> . . . rather than conceive of ideal police work as being irreconcilable with many aspects of actual police work, training

25. Ashburn, Franklin G., "Changing the Rhetoric of 'Professionalism,'" in U. S. Department of Justice, *Criminal Justice Monograph: Innovation in Law Enforcement* (1973) 1–2.

26. Harris, Richard N., *The Police Academy: An Inside View* (1973) 161.

27. Berkely, George E., *The Democratic Policeman* (1969) 89.

28. Prout, Robert S., "An Analysis of Associate Degree Programs in Law Enforcement," *J. Crim. L., C. & P. S.*, Vol. 63, pp. 587–89 (1972).

29. Ahern, James F., *Police in Trouble* (1972) 218.

personnel perhaps should make every effort to introduce
what they consider ideal practice into the training in such a
way that it does not call for a major scrapping of what the
men in the field units consider to be "tried and true." [30]

Such training could rectify the discrepancies many policemen see existing between school material and field practice.[31] It would also produce immediate benefits. For example, policemen are reported to believe the public is more hostile than it really is, because they tend to come into contact with the public either at its worst or its most demanding.[32] Prior knowledge that such encounters do not accurately reflect public opinion might reduce the hostilities generated.[33]

CONCLUSIONS

We have deliberately emphasized the case for training based upon everyday reality. Law enforcement reform proposals abound, yet few seem on the verge of general acceptance and implementation. The good intentions of critics will not by themselves lead to college-educated forces, or to the decriminalization of victimless offenses, or to departments which see themselves as antipoverty agencies.[34] Yet despite our apparent cynicism we still retain some enthusiasm for a number of reform possibilities. For example, in recent years there have been a number of proposals for bureaucratic decentralization into task teams which have been adopted to some extent by some police departments and could be by others. Under this organizational structure small, specialized units are formed and assigned distinct, limited goals.[35] Empirical models for such proposals are often taken

30. McNamara, John H., "Uncertainties in Police Work: The Relevance of Police Recruits' Backgrounds and Training," in Bordua, David J., (ed.), *The Police: Six Sociological Essays* (1967) 251–252. See also Burnham, David, "How Police Corruption is Built into the System And a Few Ideas for What to Do About It," reprinted in Sherman, Lawrence W., (ed.), *Police Corruption: A Sociological Perspective* (1974) 313.

31. Priess, Jack I., & Ehrlich, Howard J., *An Examination of Role Theory: The Case of the State Police* (1966) 16.

32. See, for example, Bayley, David H., & Mendelsohn, Harold, *Minorities and the Police* (1969) 37.

33. Of course, knowledge of reliable public support might also encourage police lawlessness. As we acknowl-

edge in our conclusions, our argument implies a number of open empirical questions.

34. Arguments around such proposals can be found in Clark, Ramsey, *Crime in America* (1970); Packer, Herbert L., *The Limits of the Criminal Sanction* (1968); and Schur, Edwin M., *Crimes Without Victims* (1965). Harris makes an argument very similar to ours, footnote 26, pp. 171–72. A good example of wishful thinking and the shotgun approach to police reform is A. C. Germann, "Changing the Police—The Impossible Dream?" *J. Crim. L., C. & P. S.,* Vol. 62, 416–21 (1971).

35. An expanded statement of this argument is contained in Bennis, Warren G. and Slater, Philip, *The Temporary Society* (1968). See also Bennis, Warren G., *Changing Organizations* (1966).

from successful projects in the aerospace industry. In addition to imparting a certain morale, such teams have the advantage of being readily disbanded when they have clearly met or failed to meet their objectives; and their dissolution can be accomplished without unduly upsetting the equilibrium of the parent organization.[36] Unfortunately, when applied to police work, this principle seems to have resulted almost exclusively in bomb squads, riot squads, sharpshooter teams and narcotics investigation units and far less often in suicide prevention teams, rape counselling teams, family crisis intervention units and organized crime strike forces.

Bennis' arguments attempt to show that democratic organization is more efficient than traditional hierarchical bureaucracy. Other reform proposals—namely, the right of policemen to organize and bargain collectively, and the right of the neighborhood to control its policemen—rely on democratic theory exclusively, with less explicit attention to the effect these proposals might have on enforcement efficiency.[37] In our vision of the ideal society, law enforcement would be guided by police-citizen councils, representing the interests of policemen as workers and citizens as victims and offenders. However, not only is this prospect utopian, but its community control component is also clearly unacceptable to the police and the public at this time, and police unionization raises the ancient constitutional quandary of guarding the guardians.

Thus, we have reluctantly placed our hopes for improved law enforcement upon more realistic training. This hypothesis, however, does not leave us without a number of dangling questions which will have to be answered by research and policy experimentation. Do recruits enter training with romanticized images of police work? Does higher formal educational attainment make policemen more or less receptive to training? Does length of service increase or decrease the impact of training? In what ways, if any, does training modify the attitudes of policemen? Does this modification lead to more or less effective law enforcement? In particular, does training which instills expectations consistent with the reality of police work do a better job of preparing policemen than training which omits such considera-

36. The *esprit* effects of special purpose organization and clear cut objectives are alluded to by Skolnick, *Justice*, footnote 10, ch. 7, in his discussion of narcotics enforcement. The narcotics investigator engages in a task that not only results in discernible accomplishment, but also avoids (at least for him) the moral and legal ambiguity afflicting most police work. In a narrow sense, this is the sort of relationship between individual self-interest and societal interest suggested by Maslow's concept of "synergy." See Maslow, Abraham, *Eupsychian Management* (1965).

37. See, for example, Waskow, Arthur I., "Community Control of the Police," *Transaction*, Vol. 7, pp. 4–7 (1969).

tions? What relationship exists between a policeman's work satisfaction and his performance? By suggesting answers to these questions, we have tried to contribute to the dialogue on improving law enforcement during one of its most difficult periods.

THE CHANGING POLICE LEADERSHIP: REACTIVE TO ANTICIPATORY, TOP TO BOTTOM *

I am primarily a policeman turned educator, but I did read about Attica. Reactive leadership (crisis management) has been and continues to be one of the major problems of police service. This problem is manifested in the issues of: type of weapon police carry, to writing philosophy, goals or objectives.

Why should we reflect on leadership? Why did the National Advisory Commission on Criminal Justice Standards and Goals see fit to discuss organizational development, management by objectives, managerial philosophy, organization climate, bureaucratic style of management, technocratic style of management, idiosyncratic style of management, participative style of management and requirements for the future, in the "Report on Corrections"? (pp. 442–453)

What impact will leadership have on the success or failure of police organizations and police systems when we reach the year 2000? Will the practitioner be called a criminal justice officer? We are together today, possibly because someone has directed us to attend. Someone has shown leadership, or has he? What was the objective of your coming? Did you discuss the objectives with your leader before you attended? How will the success or failure of this workshop be measured? What relationship do the answers to these questions have to the measurement of your leader's leadership?

Since my discussion is based partly on management by objectives, I think it only fair that I list a few objectives of this presentation. Hopefully by the end of this hour, we will be able to:

Give a definition of management by objectives, reactive leadership, crisis management, proactive leadership, anticipatory leadership, adaptive leadership, and political statesmen.

Think in broader terms about the reason why you are attending the workshop and possibly develop some objectives or results you would like to achieve by the time the workshop concludes.

* Source: Shanahan, Donald T., "The Changing Police Leadership: Reactive to Anticipatory, Top to Bottom", *Proceedings of the Tenth Annual Intera-* *gency Workshop, June 2–13, 1975.* Sam Houston State University, Huntsville, Texas, 1976.

Apply the leadership and management by objective definition to your profession.

Reflect on the views presented in an academic setting.

Identify one factor which can be used to evaluate the leadership credibility of the person responsible for your being here.

I have attempted up to this point to achieve these objectives; however, knowing my limitations, the caliber of people attending, and the setting, my batting average is somewhat questionable in my mind.

MANAGEMENT BY OBJECTIVES

Management by objectives emphasizes a goal-oriented philosophy and attitude. It focuses on results, with less concern for method as long as it is within acceptable legal and moral limits. It is a strategy of planning and getting results in the direction that management wishes and needs to take, while meeting the goals and satisfaction of its participants.[1] The management essential that has been its historical tap root is coordinated decentralization.

REACTIVE LEADERSHIP AND CRISIS MANAGEMENT

Reactive leadership or crisis management is police leadership which reacts to problems or situations as they arise. The central theme of reactive leadership and crisis management is "after the fact leadership". Crisis management differs slightly because of the seriousness of the situation or the immediacy of response required. The response is based on the situation and the manner in which the crisis manager perceives the situation and usually consequences of response or alternative responses are not considered.

PROACTIVE LEADERSHIP

Proactive leadership is a police leadership which considers the problem at hand and is not stifled by the risk involved in a decision. Innovation and creativity are primary elements of the proactive leader. Ad hoc groups or project management is used to resolve problems. "I made a mistake and will correct it," is part of the proactive leader's vocabulary. The proactive leader borrows from the oriental philosophy of decision making in that the solution to a problem sometimes may be to do nothing. However, this do-nothing solution is, in and of itself, a decision as opposed to possibly being described as indecisiveness. The proactive police leader of today uses research as one of his tools of management.

1. Paul Mali, *Managing by Objectives*,
    Wiley-Interscience, New York 1972,
    p. 2.

ANTICIPATORY LEADERSHIP

Anticipatory leadership is based on intellectual enrichment, effective planning, managing by objectives, selection of alternative, significance and consequences of decision-making internally and externally, and on a regular basis thinking through the answers to such questions as: Who am I? Where am I going? How do I intend to get there? For the organization, questions may be: Why does the organization exist? What is the philosophy of the organization? What are the goals and objectives? How do we intend to achieve these objectives? What type of leadership must be provided which will support the personnel of the organization in achieving the stated objectives?

ADAPTIVE LEADERSHIP

Adaptive leadership is simply the possession of enough flexibility to adapt to the changing society, changing environment, and changing personnel by using a continuum of leadership styles. The continuum extends from dictatorial to democratic and the adaptive leader uses the appropriate style to meet the existing conditions.

POLITICAL STATESMEN

Political expediency is so much a way of American life, it may be equated to the balloon holding water, where the balloon is the political environment and the water splashes around within, rising, falling, pushing, and pulling. Political statesmen, for the effective police leader, may be somewhat intangible almost to the point of being abstract. However, if a police leader were asked the question, "Why is city councilman Doe calling for your resignation over the K9 issue?" the response would probably be, "Well, election time is coming up soon and he wants to keep his name in the headlines." The politically aware police leader understands the external forces which place pressure on him, e. g. government, press, ethnic groups, religious groups, civic and business groups, labor, and professional organizations. He also understands the internal forces of the organization, from the formal group to the subversive militant police union. Each group has what it considers to be an important issue and mission. The skillful police leader is one who is able to use his management abilities to meet the test of the diplomat. He conforms, confronts, compromises, and collaborates in order to achieve his objectives but does nothing illegal, unethical, or immoral to succeed.

The police leader of today and of the future should deliver the product to his community by meeting the challenges in open, honest confrontation. He should accomplish this through continuing personal development and through the development of his staff. The result of this development will be what I call a "Collegiality of Command."

The effective police leader should not be controlled by an authoritarian concept of leadership and should reject a patriarchal attitude on the part of government. The police leader should be considered as a department head intimately involved and concerned about the mainstream of national and local life. Fremont, California, has demonstrated how department heads can cooperatively develop effective and efficient budget and service delivery through this concept. Programs are presented to government collectively and whenever one agency has input which may assist another, it is forthcoming. I consider this to be a "preventive waste approach" which results in more efficient and effective government. For example, if a school superintendent submits a program where a new school is to be constructed, the police are expected to have input from the beginning about the architectural design as it relates to security. This preventive approach may well save thousands of dollars and reduce burglary, vandalism, and general theft. I remember not long ago when a major industry in the United States spent millions of dollars for a new plant and less than one year later decided to install a security system. Cost of the security system at this point was 180 percent more than the preconstruction cost because of having to tear down walls, and remove conduit systems. The impact of crime and its relationship to leadership generally, and to police leadership specifically, must be viewed as a critical issue.

Internally, the skillful police leader views the organization in several ways. First he views resources, (i. e. tapping the total talent of individuals) not based on traditional rank, but on ability and quality of input, understanding that rank does not automatically bring with it additional knowledge or abilities. (A good lawyer one day does not make a good judge the next). Secondly, he views the use of women positively, in assignments which provide maximum productivity for the organization and fulfillment for the individual. He does not say, "We can't use women in this organization because they may get hurt." Thirdly, if sharing power will enhance input, production, effectiveness, participatory management, job satisfaction and organizational and self fulfillment, he is big enough and secure enough to realize that the ultimate decision is his.

The National Advisory Commission on Criminal Justice Standards and Goals' *Report on Police* and *Report on Corrections* have some similarities and differences concerning leadership and management. If we look in the index to find the word "leadership," it is not in either report. If we look in the index for the word "management," we find it in the *Report on Corrections* but not in the *Report on Police*. What we do find is, "management consultant," and "management development program," in the index of the *Report on Police* and the glaring difference of management: "analysis," "development," "distribution of responsibilities," "nature of," "need for coordination," to name a few, in the *Report on Corrections*. Does this mean that police do not need standards and recommendations for leadership or management and corrections does? Or, is it a question of what the staff writing the report thought was most important? In another small comparison, when we review the index we find no mention of the word, "media," for corrections, but in police we observe "media" with several subindices. Does this mean that police need media relations, and corrections does not? Also, if we review the index in the *Report on Courts* we see no mention of leadership, management, as such, and no mention of media. Should judges provide leadership?

In 1974, at this workshop, Paul Weston indicated that one of the four new goals of the future in police management concerns the status and role of the public information officer. He indicated that specifications were not too clear, and there was disagreement over background, whether it should be police or journalism. Do the courts and corrections need a public information officer or something similar? The issue was addressed by the National Advisory Commission on Criminal Justice Standards and Goals' *Report on Police* but not in the *Report on Courts* or the *Report on Corrections*.

Reactive leadership will wait until the issue has exploded in the headlines and then accuse the media of inaccurate reporting. Anticipatory management will address the question now, develop alternatives, select the most appropriate, and understand the risk.

> True leadership must be for the benefit of the followers, not for the enrichment of the leader. In combat, officers eat last! If we had to get the modern equivalent of our founding fathers together today, the first thing they'd do is hire Cresap, McCormick, and Paget to write the constitution for them. Some say these initials stand for "Christ!—More people!"[2]

> Most hierarchies are nowadays so encumbered with rules and tradition, and so bound by public laws, that even high employees do not have to lead anyone anywhere in the sense of pointing out the direction and setting pace. They simply follow precedents, obey regulations, and none move at the head of the crowd. Such employees lead only in the sense that the carved wooden figurehead leads the ship.[3]

2. Robert Townsend, *Up the Organization*, Fawcett Crest N.Y., N.Y.: 1970, p. 80.

3. Ibid p. 81.

There is great significance to what is said in these two quotes as they relate to police organization. Police leadership must set the philosophy, goals, objectives, tone, style, atmosphere, and standards upon which the organization will operate. Management has sometimes been described as getting the most with the least by developing abilities of people to achieve maximum effectiveness. This cannot be done by only administering or managing. It must include leading. As leaders, standards of excellence in: conduct, values, attitudes, objectives, performance, purpose, and direction become the terminology. Administering contains quite a bit of treating people as personnel, while leadership considers people as people. My understanding of the differences between efficiency and effectiveness is somewhat similar to the difference between administering and leading. Administration, we sure do need it, but not in the form of a six to one or a seven to one as defined by Blake and Moutons managerial grid where production is paramount and people are subordinate. What we need is the administration and leadership which will progress toward the necessary results for the organization "and" the individual.

Where will leadership in police organizations come from in the future; the top, or the bottom? Each of you should ask the same question about your organization. There seems to be some disagreement about the answer, especially in some people's minds. An example of the disagreement over leadership in the police organization is illustrated in the city of New York. In the April 21, 1975, issue of the *New York Magazine,* there is an article entitled "The PBA's New Centurion" by Robert Daley. You may recall that Robert Daley is the former New York City Police Department Commissioner for the public information, and also the author of the book entitled *Target Blue,* which discusses the experiences he had while in that position under Commissioner Patrick Murphy.

The article is about officer Ken McFeeley, who is President of New York City Police Department's Patrolmen's Benevolent Association, or as Mr. McFeeley puts it, "eight months ago I was a cop in a radio car. Who am I now? I'm the president of the largest police union in the country—in the world!" The significance of Mr. McFeeley's words should ring out to all police administrators throughout this country. The concept of anticipatory management, environmental awareness, and controlling the rate and direction of change will help police leaders recognize the potential impact on their respective organizations.

McFeeley was speaking to a group of police chiefs and commissioners from around the nation and related the story of a police officer and a problem of his conduct. The story is not important for our discussion but the concluding remarks are thought provoking. McFeeley said: "When management screws up on a management level, when the cop in the street doesn't want to perform anymore, his efficiency goes down. And when his efficiency goes down, the crime goes up. As the morale of cops goes down, the public's morale goes down, who gets the blame for it? You do, Management."

Mr. Daley goes on to say, "Not very subtly, he was accusing the men in that room of a failure of leadership. He saw no strong leadership anywhere in law enforcement. He saw none in the courts or in corrections, none in the attorney general's office, none in the FBI. There was not a single bold leader among the nation's thousands of district attorneys, commissioners, and chiefs. Crime was booming while law enforcement drifted. Where were the ideas, the programs, the decisions? Meanwhile, the cops on the street were being forced to decide matters of life and death in an instant—and usually received no support afterward from their so-called leaders; and . . . he decided he would provide leadership from the bottom that would force meaningful change all the way to the top . . . .

What of the police administrators of the New York Police Department? Mr. Daley goes on to quote from Commissioner Codd and Deputy Commissioner Frank McLoughlin: "Can a mere patrolman make cops want to perform, bring efficiency to crime control, bring order out of chaos in the court?" Maybe, but Commissioner Codd, while acknowledging McFeeley's obvious sincerity, does not think so. Deputy Commissioner Frank McLoughlin calls McFeeley "totally committed, almost boyish in his enthusiasm and belief and faith in his cause." McLoughlin is among those who feel that any man who displays such qualities as these will get ground up, that trust inevitably will be taken for weakness. Commissioner Codd warns: "Trust can't be blind. In addition to trust you must have vigilance."

What about leadership in the criminal justice system? Where will it come from? If a void exists, someone usually fills it. Do we have a void? If so, who will fill it?

These are changing times, and the issues and problems for the police administrator are many. He must deal with budget limitations, philosophy, goals, policy, objectives, criminal justice system, EEOC, recruitment, selection, civil service, press, privacy, labor relations, and all in a changing society. He not only cannot do it alone, but must decide where he is going to get help. The enlightened police administrator realizes that police unions are political organizations and, as such, the leaders are elected and must play to their constituents. Police unions are not a myth. On the contrary, they are growing. (Management should and must have prerogatives.) Police administrators must be able to operate effectively, but effectiveness should not exclude meaningfulness and job fulfillment, adaptive leadership, and the use of talent based on individual input. As a matter of fact, in the environment of police organizations today there is no real effectiveness if these factors are missing. Departments using team policing concepts have found them to be most important. Police officers of today have to be lead, not driven. Is leadership necessary for the rest of the criminal justice personnel?

Help may be forthcoming through a concept of collegiality of command. Because of the complexities of operating as a police chief, the demand on the individual's time, physical abilities, and intellectual capacity, the chief will have to seek help from his staff. He will have to be willing to share power-authority, responsibility and accountability. Does this question the concept of responsibility being delegated? Yes, and it should. In the development of people and their assumption of the seat in the collegiality of command, there must be a commensurate understanding of accountability each has accepted. A self-actualized chief should provide the opportunities for qualified people to occupy a seat and obtain self-actualization through the challenge of performing in the position.

Help may be forthcoming through the enlightened leadership of employee organizations. There are very few police chiefs in the country who can obtain all the resources necessary to accomplish the responsibility society has placed on the police organization. Police unions or de facto unions can assist, possibly as full partners, in achieving the clearly stated and understood objectives of a police organization. Cooperation between police leadership and employee organization leadership can certainly achieve quicker feedback from the officers who are directly responsible for achieving objectives. The managerial essence of this approach will be management by objective, organizational development and by participatory management. Whisenand, Fox, and Chamelin deal with leadership thusly: "Yet, the most important ingredient in any recipe of organizational success is good leadership. And, good leadership means motivating others to form a management team, and then prudently leading the team. Further, good leadership assumes that a police administrator is prepared to devote a substantial portion of his time to effecting change."[4]

It would be naive to believe that any police leader has the power or resources to control completely the rate and direction of change. However, the effective police leader will not let change or its process control him. Some issues of change are: climate of the organization regarding change, organizational capability to change, realistic approaches to change which allow for restrictions on the chief and the organization, goals and priorities which have been set for the police by government and community, reaction to criticism and failure, lateral entry, pressure groups, open versus closed system of personnel

4. Paul Whisenand, Vernon Fox, Neal Chamelin, *Introduction to Criminal*   *Justice*, Englewood Cliffs, N.J. Prentice Hall, N.J.: p. 103.

management, career development, and the fact that it is the nature of policing to be involved in change and crises.[5] Whisenand, Fox, and Chamelin add other issues when they discuss police leadership: "He must convince his supervisory personnel of the necessity for change and elicit their commitment to work for effective implementation. He must seek to develop innovations in police operations and prepare his community and his organization to accept some risks and some failures in experimenting with them." Because of the nature of the police function, the leader of a police agency must exert leadership in the accommodation and mediation of conflicting community interests. He should take the initiative in advancing proposals that serve to reduce conflict.[6] In other words, the police leader must be proactive and anticipatory.

Killinger and Cromwell are addressing the management by objectives concept when they discuss "Future Directions for Service Delivery." They suggest:

> To implement an effective system for delivering services to all probationers, it will be necessary to:
>
> 1. Develop a goal-oriented service delivery system.
>
> 2. Identify service needs of probationers systematically and periodically, and specify measurable objectives based on priorities and needs assessment.
>
> 3. Differentiate between those services that the probation system should provide and those that should be provided by other resources.
>
> 4. Organize the system to deliver services, including purchase of services for probationers, and organize the staff around workloads.
>
> 5. Move probation staff from courthouses to residential areas and develop services centers for probationers.
>
> 6. Redefine the role of probation officer from caseworker to community resources manager.
>
> 7. Provide services to misdemeanants.[7]

One can readily see how 1, 2, 3, 4, and 6 directly relate to the police community and the management by objectives concept. For informational purposes, the characteristics of an objective, simply stated are: (1) clearly stated in language that everyone will understand,

5. Donald T. Shanahan, *Patrol Administration*, Holbrook Press Inc., Boston, Mass.: p. 485.

6. Op. cit. Whisenand, Fox, Chamelin, p. 103.

7. George Killinger, Paul Cromwell, *Alternatives to Imprisonment, Corrections in the Community*, West Publishing Co., St. Paul, Minn.: 1974, p. 184.

(2) challenging so that people will have to reach out and extend their talent and efforts, (3) achievable in terms of the end result (also consider the individual who should see success), (4) realistic in that there is a probability of success and not "just trying to impress," (5) that it be measurable, and (6) that it be written.

We have heard demands for educated, sensitive individuals to be recruited into police organizations from such highly authoritative groups as the President's Commission on Law Enforcement and the Administration of Justice, *Task Force Report: The Police,* and more recently the National Advisory Commission on Criminal Justice Standards and Goals. However, we must remember that this type of individual is not compatible with the presently constructed centralized semi-military police organization. Team policing has possibilities to resolve this incompatibility because of its decentralized nature and the placing of responsibility, authority, and accountability at the lowest possible level within the organization. In some cases college educated entrants are resisted by police unions, and in some cases, by superior officer associations for a variety of reasons: loss of upper level position, possible loss of operational position, resistance to change, abolishing rank structure, and titles. The dilemma with which superior police administrators must now come to grips is how to upgrade recruitment and selection standards on the one hand while strenuously recruiting economically and culturally deprived people on the other, and how to do these things without engaging in selective personnel practices that defeat the very principles of law and justice which progressive police departments have fought so long to implement.[8] Thus, one school of thought argues for the traditional practice of admission to the police service of local residents of minimum qualifications; another favors continuation of the status quo (managerial or employees-centered bureaucracy) via retention of civil service practices; and a third suggests raising standards to the college level and reshaping working procedures to fit professionalism.[9] The success or failure of the American police system in facing the complex challenges of today and tomorrow will be decided by the system's leadership. Conflicts must be faced openly, compromise and cooperation must be used to resolve questions of goals, objectives, performance standards, measurement of standards, and a reward system that is equitable and consistent.

I suggest that the principle of supportive relationships as stated by Rensis Likert is the most appropriate approach for police leader-

8. William J. Bopp, *Police Personnel Administration,* Holbrook Press Inc. Boston, Mass.: 1974, p. 143.

9. Donald T. Shanahan, Ed., *Issues in the Administration of Criminal Justice,* Chap. 4, New Horizons in Police Administration, Thomas A. Reppetto, John Jay College of Criminal Justice.

ship and organization. It states: "The leadership and other processes of the organization must be such as to ensure a maximum probability that in all interactions and all relationships within the organization, each member, in light of his background, values, desires, and expectations, builds and maintains his sense of personal worth and importance."[10]

If I were to compare this principle to the police field I would request police leaders to act as cheerleaders or waterboys, in the sense that in both cases the objective is to remove or eliminate red tape or any obstacle which stands in the way of an officer's ability to achieve stated objectives, to provide support and assistance. There are several police agencies in the country providing this kind of leadership presently, such as St. Louis, Missouri; Cincinnati, Ohio; Kansas City, Missouri; Dade County, Florida; Los Angeles County Sheriff's Department; and Rochester, New York to name a few.

Change is taking place. Proactive leaders are facing organizational change through the use of centralization/decentralization, responsibility, authority, and accountability concepts; citizen involvement in police policy; combining community relations and crime prevention at the beat officer level; and use of traditional and neighborhood police team deployment. There is an increase in cooperation within criminal justice system one, and between criminal justice system one and criminal justice system two. There has also been an exchange program of middle managers between police departments. New approaches to police responsibility have been tried, e. g., allocation and distribution of patrol forces, undercover team, crisis intervention and lateral entry of qualified and needed specialists such as the legal advisor.

In-depth approaches to coping with change are being used in the Kansas City Police Department, e. g., participative problem solving, action review panels, participative decision making, and domestic violence studies. The first step is usually the development of an environment which is enthusiastic for change.

The National Institute of Law Enforcement and Criminal Justice (research center for LEAA) is contributing by funding research in the areas of planning, management, personnel, police operation, forensic science, and equipment. As of March 1975, seventeen major projects were in progress. Some of these projects are: development of management information system for strategic planning, (Buffalo, New York, Police Department) psychiatric standards for police selection, police performance appraisal, response time analysis, role of police

10. Rensis Likert, *The Human Organization*, New York: McGraw-Hill 1967, pp. 3–11.

in a free society, a national project to develop police performance measurement systems, and here in Texas at the University of Houston, Mr. Ben Rhodes is addressing "a main computer system for the solution of the mug file problem." [11]

The Police Foundation has contributed to police research by assisting police departments in such areas as: women in policing and patrol, team policing, field interrogation, (San Diego, California) community profile, and in Sacramento, California an attempt is being made to help victims of crimes by photographing stolen property. The victim will have his property photographed, then it will be returned to him, and the photograph shall be used in court presentation rather than the actual property.

One of the National Institute of Law Enforcement and Criminal Justice's new interests is undertaking a feasibility study of establishing a Bramshill-type capability or its equivalent for police leadership training. I support this unequivocally.

I wish to conclude by suggesting to the police community the use of anticipatory leadership by anticipating the need for an in-house research activity for your agency now. If the police department is too small, then I suggest a sharing of research services for several agencies. The need for a legal advisor in police departments is now a foregone conclusion, however, the time to gear up for the in-house researcher is now. The implementation of this suggestion is not without problems as pointed out by Mr. Farmer of the National Institute when he addresses police reserch. He highlights four: (1) practice and methodology gap, (2) the "experiment interruption" tendency, (3) the data base problem, (4) the significance issue. [12]

Research done in one area of the country does not necessarily mean the findings are representative of all areas of the country or that it can be applied as interpreted in another. Just as the police leader must be able to understand how to use the output from the computer, he also needs to understand how to use the conclusions of research as they apply to his police department.

What about corrections? There are several potential sources which may be used to define research needs, probability of payoff, and priorities. One of these is the missions of the agency. Another is agency requirements for self-maintenance and self-improvement. Still another is the perceived role of corrections in relation to other agencies or systems in the community. Finally, there are such matters as correctional experience, and correctional theory. These areas

11. David J. Farmer, *The Police Chief*, International Association of Chiefs of Police, March 1975, Gaithersburg, Md.: p. 68.

12. Ibid. p. 73.

give the administrator his main clues as to what research is needed and what is likely to yield practical results.[13] Two areas of similarity for police and corrections which are obiviously in need of attention are research and leadership. Without leadership few outstanding programs can ever be realized and without research the decisions of leaders will not be as effective.

Areas for Discussion for Part III

1. What form of leadership is usually associated with the various types of organizations?

2. Given the problem of police officer dissatisfaction and low morale, what organizational changes can be instituted to rectify this problem?

3. Considering the police work environment, what is the probability of effecting change within the police organization?

4. What impact would the institution of John E. Angell's Democratic Model of Team Policing have upon traditional police organizational behavior?

5. What are the similarities between traditional police management and bureaucracies?

13. Stuart Adams, Ph.D., *Evaluative Research in Corrections: A Practical Guide*, U. S. Department of Justice, LEAA, National Institute of Law Enforcement and Criminal Justice, p. 23.

PART IV

CONTROL PROCESSES IN THE POLICE ORGANIZATION

Systems management within the police organization is slowly coming into practice. Recently, police administrators have increasingly looked to management science for solutions by which to solve their complex administrative problems. Historically, there has been an untapped wealth of administrative knowledge within the private sector which could have contributed to increased efficiency and effectiveness in policing. Today, police managers are beginning to tap this valuable resource. Police administrators are implementing Management by Objectives (MBO), Planning-Programming-Budgeting Systems (PPBS), Organizational Development (OD), and participative management. Many of these programs have been successful, others failures, but the trend is toward automation, specification of goals and objectives, and the general use of systems management.

Basically, the range of activities in systems management encompasses planning, programming, and budgeting.[1] Planning entails those managerial activities whereby management attempts to systematically foresee and predict future events and design and implement actions in conjunction with those future events. These activities take place within the parameters of the organization's goals; that is, planning and resultant activities should be a definite attempt by which the organization progresses toward some desired state.

Planning is an activity which takes place throughout the organization. For example, Anthony notes that there are at least three types of planning in complex organizations, strategic planning, management control, and operational control.[2] Strategic planning entails decision-making on goals and resource utilization. Management control entails management's obtaining and usage of resources toward accomplishing objectives. Operational control is the process where management assures that specific tasks are carried out. Due to the very nature of organizations, officials throughout the hierarchy must plan.

The second systems management concept, programming, includes the outcomes of planning. Programming is the result of a rational

1. This is not to be confused with PPBS. Here these activities are considered individually and collectively. PPBS is one method of achieving this consideration. PPBS and other methods are discussed in this section.

2. Robert N. Anthony. *Planning and Control Systems: A Framework For Analysis*, Boston: Harvard University, 1965.

examination of various alternatives and the subsequent selection of one of those alternatives. It represents the organization's decision or strategy in solving a problem or foreseeable problem. Moreover, these planning and programming processes include internal and external problems. The internal problems center around organizational control, and the external problems center around goal achievement.[3] Organizational success dictates consideration in the internal and external areas.

A final managerial process considered is budgeting. Budgeting encompasses the rational allocation of resources within an organization. Budgeting is a control process whereby management controls organizational activities via funding. Through specification of funding, management is able to ensure that the organization is attempting to realize its goals. There are a number of types of budgets, and each budget attempts to perform similar functions in differing manners. Success is dependent upon a number of factors such as organizational complexity, quality of management, etc.

The preceeding paragraphs have been a brief examination of management. The readings in this section examine the issues evolving around management. Admittedly, the material contained herein only briefly discusses the issues; however, the editors feel that these articles represent the most in-depth discussion given the space restraints within this volume.

Moreover, systems management as described in this section represents one of the alternatives which police management may pursue in order to achieve maximum efficiency and effectiveness. This alternative has become more viable with the advent of computerization in criminal justice.

One final note regarding systems management concerns its relationship with another managerial alternative, the utilization of a democratic model in policing (See Part II). Although it would appear that these two models are diametrically opposed, the authors feel that the future of police administration lies somewhere in the integration of these two models.

Objectives of Part IV

1. Identify the process of control and its importance within the police organization.

---

3. The generally accepted functions of management are planning, organizing, directing, controlling, reporting, and budgeting (POSDCORB). See, Luther Gulick, "Notes on the Theory of Organization", in *Papers on the Science of Administration*. Edited by Luther Gulick and L. Urwick, New York: Institute of Public Administration, 1937; reprint ed., Augustus M. Kelley, 1969. The PPBS format encompasses the planning, directing, controlling, and budgeting aspects. Organizing and reporting is discussed under organizational theory.

2. Identify the goal setting procedure and the relevance of goals within the organizational context.

3. Present the reader with an overview of the planning process and the implications of planning in the police organization.

4. Identify the budgetary process and its relationship to organizational goal setting and planning.

5. Present the reader with various methods by which management analyzes and attempts to control organizations.

POLICE MANAGEMENT CONTROLLING *

The management process is a widely used framework for transmitting management knowledge.[1] Management process development involves an identification of the sequential and interacting functions of a manager. Almost all management processes identify the functions of planning, organizing, directing and controlling. Some management processes are more detailed in the functions identified. For example, the traditional POSDCORB[2] identifies the management functions of Planning, Organizing, Staffing, Directing, Coordinating, Reporting and Budgeting. More recently, POSTBECPIRD has been utilized in identifying police administrative activities.[3] The functions of this process include Planning, Organizing, Staffing, Training, Budgeting, Equipment, Coordination, Public Information, Reporting and Directing. Although neither PODSCORB nor POSTBECPIRD list Controlling, several of the functions listed are controlling activities, i. e., reporting, the financial controls inherent in budgeting and the control dimension of directing. However identified, Controlling is an essential function of management.

The managerial function that is perhaps the most closely related to controlling is planning. Planning involves determining what is to be done, how and by whom; Controlling involves determining what was done and if inappropriate, taking corrective action. The purpose of this brief paper is to describe a method that can be used to develop a management controlling system for police agencies.

* Source: Kuykendall, Jack, "Police Management Controlling." *Law and Order Magazine*, (May, 1973).

1. The process approach to management is sometimes called functional or operational management. See David I. Cleland and William R. King, *Management: A Systems Approach* (New York: McGraw-Hill, 1973), p. 118 for an analysis of various process approaches to management.

2. Norman C. Kassoff, *The Police Management System* (Washington, D.C.: International Association of Chiefs of Police, 1967), p. 9 citing Luther Gulick (ed.) "Paper and Science of Administration." *Notes on the Theory of Organization* (New York: Institute of Public Administration, 1937).

3. George D. Eastman (ed.), *Municipal Police Administration*, Sixth Edition (Washington, D.C.: International City Managers Association, 1969), p. 38.

DEFINITIONS OF MANAGEMENT CONTROL

Kassoff defines controlling as " . . . a measuring of what we are actually accomplishing against what we planned to achieve."[4] Stokes says that "Controlling is assuring ourselves that what has been planned is actually happening."[5] Halmann is somewhat more detailed in his definition of controlling. He says that "Control is the process of checking to determine whether or not plans are being adhered to, whether or not proper progress is being made toward the objectives and goals, and acting, if necessary, to correct any deviations. The essence of control is action which adjusts performance to predetermined standards if deviations occur."[6]

The above definitions stress certain essential elements of controlling. These elements are synthesized to build the management controlling system described in this paper.

A Suggested Approach to Developing a Police Management Controlling System [7]

The elements used in building the Controlling System are:

1.   Standard of Performance
2.   Key Indicators of Performance
3.   Methods of Checking Key Indicators
4.   Corrective Action

STANDARDS OF PERFORMANCE

Standards of Performance can be defined by given examples of some typical standards. These include policies, procedures, methods, rules and regulations, and objectives.

1.   A *policy* can be defined as a guide to be used for decision making as to appropriate or inappropriate activity or behavior. An example of a policy is a statement that: "Non-injury traffic accidents will be investigated only if property damage to both vehicles totals more than $100.00. The estimate of damages is to be made by the investigating officer."

4.   Kassoff, *Police Management System*, p. 34.

5.   Paul M. Stokes, *A Total Systems Approach to Management Control* (New York: American Management Association, 1968), p. 14.

6.   Theo. Halmann, *Professional Managements Theory And Practice* (Boston: Houghton Mifflin Co., 1962), p. 485.

7.   The approach used to develop the control system is adopted from Stokes, *A Total Systems Approach to Management Control*. The system is modified to fit police management.

2. A *procedure* can be defined as a specified manner of acting once the decision to act has been made. For example, once the decision was made to investigate a non-injury accident, a procedure should exist to describe how the investigative process should take place.

3. A *method* can be defined as one stage, or step of a procedure. For example a step within the investigative procedure is the method for completing the accident report.

4. A *rule and/or regulation* can be defined as a statement that specifies what will or will not be done. For example, a regulation could exist that all officers *will* wear hats while outside their vehicle during accident investigations.

5. *Objectives* can be defined as statements expressing desired results and behavior. These statements may be either qualitative and/or quantitative. For example, a qualitative objective could be the curious behavior of the officer while investigating the accident. A quantitative objective would be completion of the investigation of each non-injury accident within a specific time period (e. g., 45 minutes).

Each of the above can be considered standards of performance in that they define organizationally expected activity and behavior. The establishment of standards of performance occurs during the planning function of management. Obviously, these standards should be based on the best available knowledge as to what is most effective in accomplishing the overall police mission. Policies, procedures, methods and rules and regulations should be systematically developed in response to the reoccurring activities and problems confronting police departments. Objectives should first be established for the entire organization in the form of broad qualitative statements, i. e., goals. More specific, and if possible, quantifiable objectives should be set for each functional unit of the organization (e. g., patrol, investigations, records, etc.) and for each individual in the organization. Quantification of objectives can be in the form of numbers, percentages, and time. Both qualitative and quantitative objectives should be flexible enough to make allowances for possible exceptions.

KEY INDICATIONS OF PERFORMANCE AND METHODS OF CHECKING

A Key Indicator is a piece of essential information that tells the police manager if the standard of performance is being realized. The method of checking the key indicator is the way in which the essential information is brought to the manager's attention. Key Indicators should be as few as possible because of the importance of a manager's time, yet the indicator should be significant in determining if standards of performances are met. Methods of checking indicators include direct observation by supervisors, managers or through inspection, verbal reports; on-going written reports of various kinds (e. g., case reports, weekly, monthly or quarterly summaries of crime, time on calls, response times, etc.) ; special reports on unique problems and input from community groups and other governmental agencies.

Police managers normally use most, if not all, of the above methods of controlling. The frequency with which certain methods are employed by the manager and the information sought relate to the key indicators. For example, an objective described earlier stated that non-injury accidents might normally be investigated in 45 minutes. A possible key indicator would be the monthly (or some other time period) average time on calls for non-injury accidents.

If this average time was more than a few minutes different from the standard of 45 minutes, corrective action might be required. Of course, the establishment of any such standard assumes systematic research in development of reasonable standards.

A summary of the controlling system suggested in this paper can be illustrated as follows: An objective of no more than 45 minutes to investigate non-injury accidents (standard of performance) that is to be checked by the manager through a monthly written report (method of checking) of the average for that month of time per non-injury accident call (Key Indicator).

CORRECTIVE ACTION

Once a deviation is discovered in a standard of performance, action must be taken. The first step is to determine the cause of the deviation. An initial consideration is the standard itself. Is it appropriate and accepted by employees? If the standard is appropriate then the cause lies within the organization and/or in the employee. Possible examples within the organization include inaccurate information, information incorrectly computed, an unusual number of extensive non-injury accidents, inadequate communication, etc. Employee failure in meeting standards, even when the standard is reasonable, can result from inadequate training, motivation, family problems, etc. It is not within the scope of this paper to be more specific about the analyses of causes of deviations, nor to suggest methods for dealing with such problems.[8] However, both are important considerations for the police manager and must be weighed carefully.

8. For an interesting approach in deviation analysis, see Charles H. Kepner and Benjamin B. Tregoe, *The Rational Manager*, (San Francisco: McGraw-Hill, 1965); for motivation problems see Keith Davis, *Human Behavior at Work*, Fourth Edition (San Francisco: McGraw-Hill, 1972).

INTERNAL AND EXTERNAL CONTROL

A distinction needs to be made between internal and external controls. External controls are illustrated by the system described in this paper and that are extended to the employee. An external control system is necessary for effective police management; however, there are limits to the effectiveness of the external control system on behavior and activity of the employee. All employees have their own internal control systems. This means that employees have a certain degree of personal motivation and commitment. There are numerous situations when employees can engage in activity considered inappropriate by organization standards, and not be discovered. If, however, the employee is highly motivated and committed to the performance standards that are part of the external system, then compliance in the form of appropriate behavior and activity is more likely. The successful police manager needs to give careful consideration to methods of selection, training and employee motivation. Motivation and commitment are often enhanced through employee participation in the establishment of performance standards.[9] Methods to enhance the internal control system need systematic consideration by police managers; however, it is not within the limited scope of this paper to give those methods detailed consideration.

CONCLUSION

This paper describes a method that can be used by police managers to build an external control system. The elements of the system are Standards of Performance, Key Indicators of Performance, Methods of Checking Key Indicators and Corrective Action. Some important points to keep in mind are the importance of having standards of performance that are flexible, that are developed through employee participation and that are based on the best available knowledge about what is effective. Key Indicators should be as few as possible but should, through the Methods of Checking developed, bring to the attention of the manager activity and behavior that may require attention. Corrective Action follows deviation detection and includes a systematic analysis to discover the causes of the deviation, and the methods for dealing with those causes. If the manager is involved in active participation with employees in setting standards and critiquing activity and behavior, both the external and internal control systems will be receiving the constant attention needed.

BIBLIOGRAPHY

Cleland, David I., and William R. King, *Managements: A Systems Approach.* San Francisco: McGraw-Hill, 1972.

Davis, Keith. *Human Behavior at Work.* Fourth Edition. San Francisco: McGraw-Hill, 1972.

9. See Davis, *Human Behavior at Work.*

Eastman, George D. (ed.). *Municipal Police Administration*. Sixth Edition. Washington, D.C.: International City Managers Association, 1969.

Halmann, Theo. *Professional Managements Theory And Practice*. Boston: Houghton Mifflin Co., 1962.

Kassoff, Norman C. *The Police Management System*. Washington, D.C.: International Association of Chiefs of Police, 1967.

Kepner, Charles H., and Benjamin B. Tregoe. *The Rational Manager*. San Francisco: McGraw-Hill, 1965.

Stokes, Paul M. *A Total Systems Approach to Management Control*. New York: American Management Association, 1963.

GOAL SETTING FOR POLICE ORGANIZATIONS *

In today's world of terrorism, disregard for law and order, and increased crime on the streets, the police administrator is faced with a constant call from his community for more and better police service. As he listens to these cries, he also feels very real budget constraints placed upon him by the same community. In order to meet these needs within the limitations that the budget imposes on him, he is constantly searching for methods to solve the many complex problems that he and his department face.

Even with the great advances in science and technology and the findings and contributions of research and development divisions, the police administrator's current problems are mounting. As a result, effective and efficient solutions are constantly being sought. A tool readily available for the police administrator in police problem solving that has a low installation cost is that of *setting goals and objectives*.

While one may think that every police department sets objectives, careful analysis reveals that they are only "pseudo-objectives." These objectives are stated in such general terms that they become vague and undefined when analyzed; they can hardly be called true objectives. By adopting a program of goal setting, the police administrator can solve many of his current problems without assuming a tremendous increase in his present departmental budget.

DEFINITION OF OBJECTIVES

Objectives, or goals, are the ends toward which an activity is aimed. These goals are what a police department is striving for; they are where it wants to be. Divided into subgoals, they permeate throughout the entire police organization, resulting in all personnel

* Source: Reproduced from *The Police Chief* magazine, May, 1974 issue, with permission of the International Association of Chiefs of Police. By Gerald R. Griffin.

from the top administrator to the officer on the street having known and identifiable goals. Objectives are the end points of planning.

Let us take a hypothetical trip for a moment. We are going to travel from City A to City B, and have a choice of several modes of transportation. Our objective or goal is City B, but we do not reach this goal until we actually arrive in City B. Before we leave, we plan our trip by checking road maps (plans, policies, and procedures), and we finally choose the mode of transportation (organizational structure) used to reach our objective.

We use the activities within our organizational structure (divisions and departments) as units in which to carry out the functions of management. Our activities provide motion to our plans; and once the motions have been successfully completed and if we have followed our plans, we will reach our objective (our goal). It should be noted that the overall objective for maximum efficiency of the subdivisions and individuals within the police organization should be compatible with the overall departmental objectives.

POLICE MODELS AND THE CRIMINAL JUSTICE SYSTEM

One important method in planning for police organizations is model building. Great strides have been made in defining and building a model of the criminal justice system as a large overall system with a set of subsystems. The system describes crime and the path the perpetrator of a crime follows once he has been detected. The system, on the whole, concerns itself with only detected crimes (either by police or the public), although it considers the relationship of those that are undetected. The major objective of this large system of police, prosecution, courts, and correction is to calculate what happens to arrested offenders as they flow through the system. The system's objective must become a part of the police organization's objective.

The police as a subsystem of the criminal justice system has been described thoroughly, and many analyses have been made of its subsystems. As of 1972, the police system could be broken down into over 40,000 subsystems at the federal, state, and local levels.

This system as a unit has as a major objective, the protection of life and property. Each individual of the unit generally has the same defined, although not clearly stated, objective. Through individual analysis of these subsystems, significant advances have been made in improving their effectiveness and efficiency, even up to the smallest element of the police department, the individual officer.

The most important element of the whole system is the officer on the street, who has been studied from many points of view by many different sources. He has been studied from a behaviorial point of view in an effort to discover the motivations behind his actions, and functionally, so that his task can be defined better. The duties and tasks he performs have been broken down into separate entities and defined as "functions of police officers." Then they are reversed up the organizational hierarchy into functions of a particular division or function of the organization. Many of the individual tasks that police officers perform cause controversies as to whether or not they are truly a police function, but it can be generally stated that the police perform in the way the community directs them to perform.

Although the importance of realizing what a police officer does or how he acts should not be underestimated, it is not enough for the police administrator to know what the officer does and why he does it. The police administrator must first make certain determinations of what he wants the officer to do and what he wants the department as a whole to do. Without definite objectives, the administrator has no measurement of the officer's effectiveness or the efficiency of the organization. These objectives must be set at all organizational levels.

The question is—how can the tool of setting goals be used to help the police administrator achieve the goal of reducing crime?

GOALS SHOULD BE POSITIVE

Many police administrators are satisfied in setting as their department's objectives a lessening of the rising crime rate, as opposed to reducing the crime rate. They even take pride in the fact that the rise in the crime rate was in one time period less than the rise in the last time period. Although this may be better than an increase in the rise of the crime, it is not as satisfactory as a reduction in the total crime rate. For example, if the burglary rate for 1971 in a city was 350 per 100,000 population and 399 per 100,000 for 1972, this would be an increase of 14 percent. A goal of lowering the increase of burglaries to a 10 percent increase from 1972 (439 per 100,000) would not be as satisfactory as lowering the burglary rate to 385 per 100,000, which would be both a total reduction in crime and in the percentage rise in crime.

While the former may be a sufficient objective for short-range planning purposes, it is not a satisfactory long-range objective. If in the long run, the goal was lessening only the rise in a crime instead of lessening the total number of occurrences of a crime, within a given period of time, the crime rate would reach unbearable proportions. For example, if the present rate for a crime was 600 per 100,000 for a given year (x) and this was a 25 percent increase over the previous, and if our only goal was to reduce the crime rate increase by 5 percent per year, the crime rate by (x + 4 years) would be 955 per 100,000.

With proper planning consisting of both short- and long-range objectives, a truly reachable goal would be somewhere between the short- and long-range goal.

GOALS SHOULD BE DEFINITE

Even with his short-range objective of lessening the rising crime rate, the police administrator seldom says how much he is planning to reduce it. He often makes general statements about the war on crime and police attempts to lower the crime rate. Perhaps, the tendency of the police administrator to set indefinite goals is because he fears criticism by appointed organizations or citizen groups if he does not reach these goals. This objection of public disapproval may have some merit; yet if objectives are set properly and honest analysis is made of the results, there should be no fear of retribution from anyone. Success in this would be facilitated by complete dissemination to the public of where the department is and what resources are at its disposal to reach the new objective.

Clearly, if the police administrator does not know his goals or objectives, he cannot know how to solve any problem; and if he is lacking in this respect, it can be assured that the divisions or departments within the police organization and the individual officers are also lacking definite goals.

If we were to take our hypothetical trip again, we would not say we are going on a trip to *some* place, but we would state *where* we are going and *when* we plan to arrive. Likewise, when we set objectives, we must clearly state *what* they are and *when* they will be reached.

MEASUREMENT OF GOALS

Goals and objectives must be definite and measurable. They must be capable of being achieved even though organizational stretch may be needed, and they must have definite measurement values per time period. For example, if the goal is to reduce the crime of burglary by 5 percent in a given time period, simple statistical analysis can determine if this objective has been met within the set standards. If the burglary rate is 60 per month at the beginning of the time period, then all concerned in the reduction effort should know that the goal is to have 57 or less burglaries at the end of the period.

USING OUR PRESENT SYSTEM

If goals are not met, it is then possible to use the criminal justice system that has already been developed and the individual department organizational structure to meet these objectives. A careful analysis of why the goal was not reached should be made. If the reason for failure is defined as lack of adequate resources (either manpower or equipment), then the police administrator now has facts to show the public how, by granting additional resources, the goal can be reached. Decisions concerning the allocation of government resources now have added meaning. It then can be shown that if a decrease in burglary is wanted, the police department will need "x" amount of increase in its resources. Although upon first implementing this objective-setting program, cost-service relationships may not be completely accurate, development of the program will lead to accurate estimates of the cost of services. Once this information is available, it is then a decision for the community as to whether they want a higher offense rate or an increase in police expenditures. Such a procedure also allows for a positive recognition of what will be gained by an increase in these expenditures. This not only aids the administrator in making the decisions, but also, by giving the community detailed facts instead of generalities, makes them an integral part of the police department and gives them a feeling of true involvement. This additional input of coummunity involvement will also be a great asset to reaching police department objectives.

CAUTIONS TO CONSIDER

It should be noted that goal setting should not be done haphazardly, and short-range goals should be set that are obtainable within that certain degree of stretch. If a department or division is given an objective that is unreasonable in terms of accomplishment, this may result in lower morale and cause an increase in problems. Keep in mind that objectives, or goals, are the ends toward which the activity is aimed and not the means of the activity.

ADVANTAGES OF GOAL SETTING

1. Gives a basis for measuring overall departmental effectiveness.

2. Aids administrators, government officers, and citizens in decision making.

3. Aids in reducing crime rates.

4. Points up weaknesses within the organizations.

5. Aids in budgeting funds.

6. Improves officer morale.

7. Aids in community involvement.

FACTORS TO CONSIDER

Goal setting has tremendous advantages; but it requires one thing of everyone who participates: it requires that the participants be willing to take a risk. If one fails to reach his set objectives, then both he and others know that he has fallen short of his goal. This fact may tend to instill an incentive to reach the objective to avoid personal condemnation. Goal setting must become more than a program; it must become a state of mind.

Businesses have long used objectives as tools in managing their organizations, and they are not afraid to take risks because they know that the road to success is lined with these risks. If this is true of businesses, then why should police departments, which are the greatest risk-takers in terms of physical danger and whose success as an organization is of paramount concern to the whole community, be afraid to take the necessary risk to reach their objectives?

SOURCES

Learned, Edmund P., and Sproat, Audrey T. *Organization, Theory and Policy* "Notes for Analysis." Richard D. Irwin, Inc.: 1966.

Odiorne, George S. *Management by Objectives*. Pitman Publishing Corporation: 1965.

The Challenge of Crime in a Free Society. "A Report by the President's Commission on Law Enforcement and Administration of Justice": 1967.

Task Force Report: The Police. "A Report by the President's Commission on Law Enforcement and Administration of Justice": 1967.

POLICE POLICY FORMULATION: A PROPOSAL FOR IMPROVING POLICE PERFORMANCE *

The police function in this country is much more varied and much more complex than is generally recognized. This is particularly true today in the congested areas of large urban centers where the demand for police services is especially great and where the police are confronted with an increasing variety of difficult situations, many of which stem from dissatisfaction with the economic and social conditions existing in such areas. As law enforcement has become more difficult, it has, for the same reasons, taken on new importance as a function of local government.

Contributing to the major current concern regarding law enforcement is the growing awareness of the fact that the police are simply not equipped to respond adequately to the increasing demands being made upon them. This should not come as a surprise to anyone. Law enforcement agencies, over the years, have never been pro-

* Source: Herman Goldstein, "Police Policy Formulation: A Proposal for Improving Police Performance," *Michigan Law Review*, Vol. 65, No. 6, April, 1967, pp. 1123–1146. Reprinted with permission.

vided with the kind of resources, personnel, education, and leadership which their responsibilities have required.[1]

Substantial progress has been made in recent years, especially when compared with the rate of improvement in the past, but such progress has occurred in an uneven manner and its effect has frequently been diminished by backsliding. Within this period, standards and goals have been significantly increased, but they remain modest when related to the magnitude and complexity of existing problems.

Recent improvements have centered upon providing the police with better equipment, more personnel, higher compensation, increased training, and improved management techniques. All of these measures are badly needed and each contributes to raising police efficiency. But it is becoming increasingly apparent that operating efficiency alone is not enough.

Future progress toward fulfilling the law enforcement function is likely to depend primarily upon the degree to which the police and others effectively respond to the numerous problems involved in employing our legal system to deal with the infinite variety of behavioral situations which confront the police. Many of these situations are obviously beyond the control of the police. Their improvement depends upon the correction of existing social and economic conditions, increased effort on the part of community welfare agencies, and changes in the law, in court procedures, and in the functioning and orientation of correctional agencies. Nevertheless, there remain many problems that are within the capacity of the police themselves to resolve.

The issues that are involved in these aspects of the law enforcement problem with which the police themselves can deal are much more difficult to resolve than those that are raised in the attempt to increase operating efficiency. They relate, for the most part, to the highly sensitive and delicate function of exercising police authority. Their solution, difficult as it may be, is essential if the police are to achieve a system of law enforcement that is not only efficient, but also fair and effective. The degree to which the police succeed in meeting these latter objectives will determine, in the long run, the strength of the law enforcement function in our democratic society.

1. Among the most significant works spanning the past half century that document the absence of adequate resources in law enforcement are: Fosdick, *American Police Systems* (1920); Fuld, *Police Administration* (1910); National Commission on Law Observance and Enforcement, *Report on Police*, No. 14 (1931); Smith, *Police Systems in the United States* (2d ed. 1960).

THE EXISTING POLICY VACUUM

The Nature of the Police Function

The most acute problems confronting the police do not receive the kind of attention that they deserve from persons outside police agencies because of a common lack of understanding of the true nature of the police task. Police officers are daily engaged in handling a wide variety of complex situations, but the nature of such situations is rarely communicated to those outside the police establishment. If the police were to analyze their workload in a systematic manner and to make public the results of their findings, it is likely that several of the most widespread notions regarding the police function would be dispelled.

One common assumption is that the police are primarily engaged in activities relating to the prevention of serious crime and the apprehension and prosecution of criminals. Actually, only a small percentage of the time which an average police officer spends on duty is directly related to the handling of serious offenses. This is especially true in small jurisdictions where few crimes occur. But it is equally true in the most congested areas of our large cities where high crime rates are experienced; for, even in such areas, a police officer, during a typical tour of duty, is occupied with a variety of tasks that are unrelated to the crime problem: assisting the aged and the mentally ill; locating missing persons; providing emergency medical services; mediating disputes between husbands and wives, landlords and tenants, or merchants and their customers; caring for neglected children; providing information about various governmental services and processes; regulating traffic; investigating accidents; and protecting the rights of individuals to live where they want to live and say what they want to say.[2]

Another popular misconception is that the police are a ministerial agency, having no discretion in the exercise of their authority. While this view is occasionally reinforced by a court decision,[3] there is a growing body of literature that cites the degree to which the police are, in fact, required to exercise discretion—such as in deciding which laws to enforce, in selecting from among available techniques for investigating crime, in deciding whom to arrest, and in determin-

2. While it is rare for police agencies to articulate this range of functions, it is even rarer for them to respond directly to such functions in a structured manner. For an interesting example of the latter, see Winston-Salem, N.C. Police Department, *A New Approach to Crime Prevention and Community Service* (mimeo. 1966).

3. See, e. g., Bargain City U.S.A., Inc. v. Dilworth, 407 Pa. 129, 179 A.2d 439 (1960); State v. Lombardi, 8 Wis.2d 421, 99 N.W.2d 829 (1959).

ing how to process a criminal offender.[4] Broad and oftentimes ambiguous statutes defining their power and the limited resources made available to them are the major factors among several that require the police to assume such a discretionary role.

A third widespread notion regarding the police function is that the primary authority available to and used by the police is that of invoking the criminal process—that is, arresting a person for the purpose of prosecuting him for having committed a crime. However, for every time that a police officer arrests a person, he also disposes of scores of incidents by employing a lesser form of authority, such as ordering people to "move on," turning children over to their parents, or separating combatants. Furthermore, when an officer does decide to make an arrest, it is not always with the intention of prosecuting the individual; rather it may be for the much more limited purpose of safeguarding the arrestee or controlling a given type of criminal activity, such as prostitution or gambling.[5]

Finally, it is widely believed that, in the investigation of criminal activity and especially in the identification of offenders, police officers depend primarily upon physical evidence that is subject to scientific analysis. Admittedly, collection and analysis of physical evidence does constitute an important facet of police work; in some cases, it holds the key to identification and is the factor upon which the value of all other evidence depends. But, in the vast majority of cases, the analysis of physical evidence, to the extent that there is any, is merely supportive of evidence acquired through some other means. Despite the major and often fascinating advances that have been made in the scientific detection of crime, primary dependence is still placed upon the work of detectives who, once a crime has been committed, set out in search of motives and bits and pieces of information from victims, witnesses, and various other persons who might have some knowledge that will contribute to the identification of the perpetrator of the crime. It is often a rather tedious and undramatic process that depends, for its success, upon the resourcefulness and

---

4. See, e. g., Banton, *The Policeman in the Community,* 131–46 (1964); LaFave, *Arrest,* 61–161, 490–527 (1965); Skolnick, *Justice Without Trial,* 71–88 (1966); Abernathy, *Police Discretion and Equal Protection,* 14 S.C.L.Q. 472 (1962); Breitel, *Controls in Criminal Law Enforcement,* 27 U.Chi.L.Rev. 427 (1960); H. Goldstein, *Police Discretion: The Ideal Versus the Real,* 23 Pub.Admin.Rev. 140 (1963); J. Goldstein, *Police Discretion Not To Invoke the Criminal Process: Low Visibility Decisions in the Adminis-* *tration of Justice,* 69 Yale L.J. 543 (1960); Kadish, *Legal Norm and Discretion in the Police and Sentencing Processes,* 75 Harv.L.Rev. 904 (1962); LaFave, *The Police and Nonenforcement of the Law* (pts. 1–2), 1962 Wis.L.Rev. 104, 179; Remington, *The Role of Police in a Democratic Society,* 56 J.Crim.L.C. & P.S. 361 (1965); Remington & Rosenblum, *The Criminal Law and the Legislative Process,* 1960 U.Ill.L.F. 481.

5. LaFave, *Arrest,* 437–89 (1965).

perseverance of the investigating officers. Involved in the typical investigative effort are such important practices as the questioning of individuals, the search of private premises, the use of informants, and, in some cases, the employment of a variety of "undercover" techniques to acquire firsthand knowledge of criminal activity.

Absence of Adequate Guidelines

One of the consequences of recognizing the true nature of police activities is that one realizes there are vast areas of the police function which, in the absence of adequate legislative guidelines, are left to the discretion of individual officers. Moreover, even when existing laws are clearly applicable, the police are often required to select from among the various alternative forms of action which exist within the outer limits of the authority prescribed by such laws.

There have been some isolated efforts on the part of the police to fill this gap by providing more detailed guidance for the day-to-day work of their personnel. Such efforts have related primarily to traffic enforcement techniques and the handling of juvenile offenders.[6] The overall picture, however, reflects a reluctance on the part of police administrators to establish policies to fill the existing void. This reluctance is in sharp contrast to the strong tradition within police agencies for promulgating a variety of standard operating procedures to govern the internal management of the police force. The difference in attitude appears to be attributable largely to the real doubts possessed by the police as to the propriety of their assuming a policy-making role that so closely parallels the legislative function.[7]

Confronted each day by frequently recurring situations for which no guidance is provided, the individual officer either develops his own informal criteria for disposing of matters which come to his attention—a kind of pattern of improvisation—or employs informal criteria which have, over a period of years, developed within the agency of which he is a part. While such criteria are neither articulated nor officially recognized, they tend to take on some of the char-

---

6. In the area of traffic enforcement, a number of jurisdictions have developed "tolerance policies" which establish the point above the speed limit at which officers are to warn a motorist or issue a summons to him. Some also provide criteria for making similar decisions with regard to other types of motor vehicle violations. Such policies are most frequently promulgated by state police organizations, and they demonstrate that a need is felt for providing guidelines for the isolated officer who cannot frequently consult with his supervisor or fellow officers. They also reflect a desire on the part of administrators to achieve uniformity in the overall operations of the agency. For a discussion of policies relating to the handling of juveniles, see text accompanying notes 18–10 infra.

7. For a more detailed discussion of this point, see President's Commission on Law Enforcement and Administration of Justice, *Task Force Report: The Police*, ch. 2 (1967).

acteristics of officially promulgated policies. Functioning in this manner and employing their own imagination and resourcefulness, individual police officers often succeed to an amazing degree in muddling their way through: disputes are resolved; dangerous persons are disarmed; people not in control of their capacities are protected; and many individuals are spared what, under some circumstances, would appear to be the undue harshness of the criminal process. Unfortunately, the results are often less satisfactory, primarily because the criteria that are employed emerge largely in response to a variety of pressures to which the police are exposed and are therefore not carefully developed. For example, the high volume of work which an officer must handle dictates a desire to take shortcuts in the processing of minor incidents. The personal conveniences of an officer—in making a court appearance, completing reports, or working beyond a scheduled tour of duty—become important determinants of how a case is handled. The desire to solve crime becomes a dominant consideration.[8] And such indefensible criteria as the status or characteristics of the complainant, the victim, or the offender may often be among the most seriously weighed factors, since an officer, left to function on his own, understandably tends to respond to a given situation on the basis of his personal norms regarding individual or group behavior.

Continuation of current practices, which can perhaps best be characterized as a process of "drift," is clearly not in the interest of effective law enforcement. The potential for arbitrariness inherent in an uncontrolled exercise of discretion is clearly inconsistent with the objective of fairness that constitutes so basic an element in the exercise of any form of governmental power. Nor are current practices desirable from the police standpoint; in the absence of guidelines, police officials are continually vulnerable to criticism for the manner in which an officer chooses to exercise his discretion. They are "damned if they do and damned if they don't." Police administrators, moreover, are without an effective means for controlling the behavior of individual officers. Thus, since effective restraints are lacking, incidents tend to arise that prompt legislatures and courts to step in and take actions which often have repercussions—in the form of curtailment of police powers—far beyond the specific situation that initially served to arouse their interests.

There is an obvious need for some procedure by which an individual police officer can be provided with more detailed guidance to help him decide upon the action he ought to take in dealing with the

---

8. This factor is explored in some detail in Skolnick, *Justice Without Trial*, 164–81 (1966).

wide range of situations which he confronts and in exercising the broad authority with which he is invested. Viewed in somewhat different terms, the challenge is to devise procedures which will result in police officers employing norms acceptable to society, rather than their personal norms, in their exercise of discretion.

Alternative Solutions

There is no single way in which the existing policy vacuum can be filled, nor is it likely or desirable that it can be filled in its entirety.[9] But the width of the existing gap—especially as one views the functioning of the police in our large urban centers—affords ample opportunity for reducing its size.

The police are accustomed to looking toward the legislature and the courts for their guidance. There has, in recent years, been a special focus upon the latter since the appellate courts have undertaken to establish, with increasing specificity, the rules of constitutional, procedural due process.[10] Such judicial activity, especially that of the Supreme Court, has been viewed by one commentator as an action of "desperation," taken because of default on the part of others to fill the existing vacuum.[11] It has been argued that the Court, in taking on this rule-making function, has assumed an uncomfortable role which it is not equipped to fulfill and which constitutes, at best, an awkward and somewhat ineffective process for hammering out detailed rules of criminal procedure.[12] Among the major liabilities which are cited with respect to this approach are the breadth and especially the rigidity of the Court's holdings. In addition, in evaluating the courts as a source of guidance, it must be recognized that many of the most important and perplexing problems encountered by the police never become the subject of court proceedings.

Traditionally, both federal and state legislatures have restricted themselves to providing the police with a minimum set of broadly stated guidelines covering the major elements in criminal procedure.[13] They are often cited as the logical branch of government

---

9. Banton observes that the only long-term solution to the problem of police discretion is for the police and the public to share the same norms of propriety. Banton, *The Police and the Community,* 146 (1966).

10. The most recent and most specific rules are found in Miranda v. Arizona, 384 U.S. 436 (1966).

11. Packer, *Policing the Police: Nine Men Are Not Enough,* New Republic, September 4, 1965, p. 19.

12. Id. at 18. See also Friendly, *The Bill of Rights as a Code of Criminal Procedure,* 53 Calif.L.Rev. 929 (1965); Packer, *Who Can Police the Police?,* the N. Y. Rev. of Books, September 8, 1966, p. 10.

13. See LaFave, *Improving Police Performance Through the Exclusionary Rule—Part II: Defining the Norms and Training the Police,* 30 Mo.L.Rev. 566, 568–79 (1965); Remington & Rosenblum, *The Criminal Law and the Legislative Process,* 1960 U.Ill.L.F. 481.

to remedy the need for additional guidelines since they have the capacity to explore problems on their own initiative, to gather facts, to elicit public opinion, and to act in a manner which is subject to later adjustment.[14]　The recent proposal of the American Law Institute, embodied in its Model Code of Pre-Arraignment Procedure, represented an effort to move in this direction, incorporating, as it did, detailed legislative guidelines for police activity during the period from investigation and arrest to the time the suspect is presentenced in court.[15]　In at least one major area covered by the Model Code, however, the opportunity for careful legislative consideration has since been significantly restricted by the Supreme Court's action in Miranda v. Arizona.

Even if legislatures become active in spelling out guidelines for the police, it must be recognized that there are now, and presumably always will be, many areas—particularly as one gets closer to the day-to-day problems encountered by the police—in which it is neither feasible nor desirable for the legislature to prescribe specific police practices.　Variations in the size of police jurisdictions within a state, changing social conditions, and variations in the nature of the police function, among other factors, require that there be room for administrative flexibility.　It seems apparent that the infinite variety of complex situations which confront the police today makes it essential that the most detailed and specific policies for handling them be formulated at the level closest to that at which they arise.

In light of the above considerations, it seems reasonable that, within legislative boundaries that may in some areas be more detailed than those which now exist, the police themselves be given the responsibility for formulating policies which will serve as guidelines in their effort to achieve effectiveness and fairness in their day-to-day operations, and that there be an explicit recognition by the legislatures of the necessity and desirability of the police operating as an administrative policy-making agency of government.　Obviously, such police-made policies would be subject to challenge if they were not consistent with the general legislative purpose or with such legislative criteria as are provided to guide and control the exercise of administrative discretion.　Subject to appropriate review and control, the exercise of administrative discretion in this manner is likely to be more protective of basic rights than the routine, uncritical application by police of laws which are often necessarily vague or overgeneralized in their language.

---

14. See Packer, *Policing the Police: Nine Men Are Not Enough*, New Republic, Sept. 4, 1965, pp. 20–21.

15. Ali, *A Model Code of Pre-Arraignment Procedure* (Tent. Draft No. 1, 1966).

• THE VALUE IN RECOGNIZING THE POLICE AS AN ADMINISTRATIVE AGENCY HAVING IMPORTANT POLICY-MAKING RESPONSIBILITIES

Police participation in the development of policies to fill the existing vacuum and to cope with rapidly changing social and behavioral conditions would be a valuable contribution to the operation of police agencies, to the professionalization of the police, and to the overall functioning of the criminal justice system. Some of the specific advantages are set forth in detail below.

The Maintenance of Administrative Flexibility

The police have always had a great deal of flexibility in their operations, but this has been primarily as a result of legislative default rather than of deliberate, overt legislative choice. The traditional legislative response with respect to difficult issues like the control of gambling activities or the stopping and questioning of suspects has been either to deal with them by means of an overly generalized statute, as is true with respect to gambling activities, or not to deal with them at all, which has been true, at least until recently, with respect to stopping and questioning suspects. The practical consequence has been to leave police with broad flexibility, but the delegation of responsibility has been implicit at best and police have not taken it as a mandate to develop and articulate proper enforcement policies. The action of appellate courts in setting down increasingly specific rules to govern police conduct is partly a result of this failure. This trend toward judge-made rules is inspired in large part by a prevalent assumption that police are unwilling or unable to develop proper policies and to conform their practices to such policies. The police, by assuming responsibility for the development of appropriate administrative policies, will have the opportunity to reverse the trend and, as a consequence, to preserve the flexibility which they need if they are to meet adequately the wide range of problems which they confront under constantly changing conditions.

A Sound Basis for the Exercise of Discretion

The formulation of administrative policies affords the police an opportunity to establish sound grounds for the exercise of their discretion. Careful analysis of existing practices, which is a necessary step in the formulation of policies, should result in the exposure and rejection of those considerations which, according to standards of fairness and effectiveness, are inappropriate. Development of defensible criteria would, in addition, afford an opportunity to incorporate into police decision-making considerations that are based upon existing knowledge regarding the various forms of behavior with which the police are concerned.   In the long run, the exercise of discretion in accordance with defensible criteria would create greater confidence in the police establishment.   More immediately, it would lead to a reduction in the number of arbitrary actions taken by individual officers, thereby substantially reducing the tensions which such actions often create—particularly in areas in which minority groups are affected.

Acknowledgment of the "Risk Factor" Involved in Policing

Numerous factors contribute to the defensive posture commonly assumed by the police.   Among them is an awareness on their part that members of the public will often question their exercise of discretion in a case in which subsequent developments focus attention upon an officer's decision.   For example, a police officer may locate one under-age youth in a group of young people engaged in a drinking party.   The fact that the youth is only one month under age may prompt the officer to release him with a warning.   However, if the youth subsequently becomes involved in a serious accident, the fact that he was released earlier in the evening will often result in the officer's being castigated by his superior, because the officer has no publicly-acknowledged right to exercise discretion although all agree that it is both necessary and desirable that he do so.

Given the wide range of responsibilities that the police have, they cannot be held to a system of decision-making which involves no risk-taking—any more than could psychiatrists in deciding whether to release a person who has attempted suicide or parole board members in voting upon the release of an inmate.   The formulation of policy and its articulation to the public would, over a period of time, begin to educate the public to recognize that the police must not only exercise discretion, but must also assume a risk in doing so.   Prior statements of policy which "put the community on notice" with regard to police functioning in various areas would afford some relief from the current dilemma in which, in the absence of such policy formulations, the police are subject to both ridicule for not exercising discretion and condemnation for making discretionary judgments when they do not work out.

A Means for Utilizing Police Expertise

Many actions which the police officer takes are based upon the knowledge and experience he has accumulated in his years of service.   In concluding that a crime is being committed, an officer may reach a judgment quite different from that which would be reached by an inexperienced layman or even an experienced trial judge, since the officer may have, for example, the ability to recognize the smell of narcotics or the sound of a press used in printing illegal numbers or policy tickets. There has, however, been little effort made to capitalize upon police experience. In order to do so, the police would necessarily have to attempt to assess its reliability; they would have to distinguish accurate inferences (such as, the sound is that of a gambler's printing press) from inaccurate or improper ones (such as, Negroes are immoral). It would also be necessary for the police to systematize their experience so that it can be effectively communicated to new officers through training programs and to others, like judges, when the propriety of police action is challenged. To the extent that operating criteria reflect police experience, the police are afforded a vehicle in the policy-making process for articulating their expertise.

More Effective Administrative Control Over Police Behavior

While the actions of an individual officer may appear on the surface to be improper, there is often no basis on which his superior can take disciplinary action against him, since his conduct violates neither the law nor any existing departmental policies. In such a situation, the police administrator is caught in a conflict between his desire to be responsive to a citizen who has reason to complain about a policeman's behavior and his fear concerning the reaction of his force to seemingly arbitrary discipline where there is no clear breach of a pre-announced standard of proper conduct.

The reluctance to characterize an officer's conduct as unwise is increased when the administrator feels that to do so will result in either the officer or the municipality being sued for damages. Consideration of this possibility may force the administrator into the position of defending a given action as legal, and thus seemingly "proper," even though it reflected poor judgment on the part of the officer. To minimize the likelihood of similar situations arising in the future, the administrator may urge his subordinates to use "common sense," but such a request is of little value unless he is prepared to spell out precisely what is meant by "common sense."

The promulgation of policies to which police officers are required by regulation to adhere would provide a basis for disciplining those who violate such policies. But, more important, it would serve in a positive way to inform members of a force what is expected of them. Progress in elevating the quality of law enforcement is much more likely to be realized if one views clear and defensible standards as a basis for eliciting a proper response from police officers, rather than considering such standards primarily as the basis for the taking of disciplinary actions against police officers.

The Improvement of Recruit and In-Service Training Programs

Recruit training in police agencies is frequently inadequate because the instruction bears little relationship to what is expected of the officer when he goes to work in the field. In the absence of guidelines that relate to an analysis of police experience, the instructor usually is left with only the formal definition of police authority to communicate to the trainee, and this is often transmitted to the student merely by reading statutory definitions to him. Students are taught that all laws are to be fully enforced. The exercise of police authority is similarly taught in doctrinaire fashion. With this kind of formal training, the new officer finds, upon his assignment to the field, that he has to acquire from the more experienced officers with whom he is initially assigned a knowledge of all the patterns of accommodations and modifications. As he becomes aware of the impracticality and lack of realism of much of what he learned as a student, he unfortunately begins to question the validity of all aspects of his formal training.

Obviously, there is a need for training more directly related to the important problems which the officer will face in the field—training which will not only instruct him on the limits of his formal authority, but also inform him of the department's judgment as to what is the most desirable administrative practice to follow in exercising his authority. Carefully developed administrative policies would serve this important function.

A Basis for the Professionalization of the Police

It is now commonplace to refer to practically any effort that is aimed at improving law enforcement as a contribution to the professionalization of the police. Thus, improved training, application of the computer to police work, adoption of a code of ethics, and increased salaries have all, at one time or another, been cited as contributing to police professionalization.

Certainly, there is much that police do today that would not, under any definition of the term, be viewed as constituting professional work. Directing traffic at a street intersection or enforcing parking restrictions requires stamina, but little knowledge. In sharp contrast to these functions, however, are the responsibilities of a patrolman assigned to police a congested area in which numerous crimes occur; he is called upon to make highly sophisticated judgments having a major impact upon the lives of the individuals involved. Such judgments are not mechanical in nature, but rather are every bit as complicated and difficult to make as are the decisions made by any of the behavioral scientists, and in many instances they are more difficult because they must be made under the pressure of the immediate circumstances.

Development of criteria for dealing with such complex social and behavioral problems will require extensive research, the systematizing of experience and knowledge, and continual testing of the validity of the assumptions and findings upon which the criteria are based. The formulation of such criteria will also require adherence to values relating to the role of the police and law enforcement in a democratic society that are more basic than those values which are involved in a consideration of technical operating efficiency. The making of judgments based upon criteria that are formulated pursuant to extensive experience, research, and experimentation together with a commitment to values that reflect a sense of responsibility to society constitute important elements in the development of a true profession.

A Method for Involving the Police in the Improvement of the System of Which They are a Part

Decisions relating to the enforcement function have traditionally been made for the police by persons outside the police establishment. The police have typically not even been consulted when changes have been contemplated in the substantive or procedural criminal law, despite the fact they clearly have more experience than anyone else in dealing with some of the basic issues. Failure to involve the police in most revision projects is probably due to the fact that police personnel are not considered qualified to deal with the complicated questions involved. But, if it is true that police lack the necessary skill to participate in such efforts, this lack of ability is in large measure attributable to the fact that in the past they have not been involved in the making of important decisions.

There is, today, a strong commitment to the involvement of disadvantaged groups, like the poor and the young, in decisions about their roles in society. This commitment is based on the belief that they will respond most affirmatively if they have a feeling of participation in such decisions. The same need is apparent with respect to the police, for, in this sense at least, they also are a disadvantaged group. Law enforcement personnel are more likely to want to conform and are more likely to develop an ability to conform if they are made a part of the process for making important decisions affecting their function.

ILLUSTRATIONS OF AREAS OF POLICE FUNCTIONING WHICH ARE SUBJECT TO POLICY FORMULATION

Practically every aspect of police functioning gives rise to important and sensitive issues of a kind which can and should be dealt with through the careful and systematic development of policies by a law enforcement agency. The following are merely illustrative of the types of functions that are in need of attention, the difficult issues to which they give rise, and the importance of facing up to them.

The Decision Whether to Invoke the Criminal Process

Whether a criminal prosecution is initiated against an individual depends, in most instances, upon police judgment. Theoretically, this judgment is based upon the statutory definition of the crime, although it is abundantly clear that there are many situations in which a violation has in fact occurred and is known to the police, but in which there is no effort by the police to make an arrest. Among the factors accounting for this discretionary decision not to invoke the criminal process are the volume of violations of a similar nature, the limited resources of the police, the overgeneralization of legislative enactments defining criminal conduct, and the various local pressures reflecting community values and attitudes.

The social gambling situation affords a good example of the dilemma which the police face. In most jurisdictions, all forms of gambling are illegal. Yet it is apparent that legislatures neither intend nor expect that such statutes be fully enforced. The consequence is that local police are left with the responsibility for developing an enforcement policy for their particular community. The policy of a department may, for example, be clear, albeit unwritten, that games of chance at church carnivals will be permitted because of their charitable nature.[16] However, in the same community, the police response to gambling in a private home may vary with the circumstances of the individual case. Whether the police take enforcement action may depend on the answers they obtain to several key questions: is there a complainant and, if so, is he adversely affected by the gambling activity; is the gambling the prime purpose for the group's getting together or is it incidental to some other activity or pastime; is the activity organized; do the participants know each other; were they steered to the location for purposes of engaging in gambling or is the assemblage a gettogether of old friends; what is the amount of money involved; and is there a profit separate from winnings being realized by the individual hosting the activity or by any of the individuals present. The existence of any one of these factors will not necessarily result in an arrest, but the police usually will take action when there is an insistent complainant or when a combination of factors suggests that the gambling activity is commercial in nature. The difficulty is that the employment of such criteria by individual officers may lead to disparity in practice and, even where practice is consistent, may involve basic policy questions which are not raised and thus not considered or resolved. Complaints may originate from neighbors who are disturbed by the noise or from

16. For an interesting case study growing out of an unarticulated policy of nonenforcement against bingo in churches and synagogues, see Logue & Bock, *The Demotion of Deputy Chief Inspector Goldberg* (Inter-University Case Program, No. 78) (1963).

wives who are either concerned over the monetary losses of their spouses or resent their absence from home. Should a police agency allow itself to be "used" under such conditions? Does the fact that enforcement take place only when there is an insistent complainant constitute a desirable pattern of action?

The tests used in practice to determine whether the game is "commercial" rather than "social" also raise important policy questions which have not been resolved. Social gambling in a slum area assumes a different form than does social gambling in a middle-class neighborhood: a number of men commonly get together in a private apartment, placing comparatively small bets on a dice game. Such activity is endemic to such an area. When the police investigate such games they typically find that the participants cannot identify each other. The gambling is therefore viewed as not being "social" and thus is considered properly subject to enforcement. Yet, considering the pattern of life in such an area, is there any reason to characterize this behavior as more reprehensible than that engaged in by a group of men involved in a poker game for some financial stakes at a local country club? Pursuant to present practices, the participants in the dice game will generally be arrested, searched, transported to a lock-up, detained overnight, and brought before a judge the following morning. The net effect of such actions for the police seems obvious: relationships with the residents of the area, which typically are already very strained, are further aggravated.

The police action with regard to the dice game in the slum area is often in response to complaints from neighbors who are disturbed by the game. It may also be a response to the general police concern, based on prior experiences, that dice games in such areas frequently end in fights, which in turn sometimes result in homicides. Intervention by the police therefore is viewed as serving a crime prevention function. But neither the attitude of the community nor the relationship of the dice game to more serious crime is studied and evaluated. As a consequence, the current police practice gives the appearance of being the product of improper class or racial discrimination.

The police treatment of aggravated assaults raises issues of a different character. This type of offense comes to police attention more routinely because it frequently occurs in public, the victim or witnesses seek out the police, there is a desire for police intervention before more harm is done, or simply because the victim desires police assistance in acquiring medical aid. Even though the perpetrator is known to the victim in a high percentage of these cases, however, there frequently is no arrest or, if an arrest is made, it may be followed by release without prosecution. This is especially true in the slum areas of large urban centers and is due primarily to an unwillingness on the part of the victim to cooperate in a prosecution.

If the parties involved are related or are close friends, the victim is frequently unwilling to establish the identity of the assailant, attend show-ups, view photographs, or even answer questions truthfully. If the victim does cooperate at the investigation stage, he may still refuse to testify at trial and may even express a desire that the assaulting relative or acquaintance be set free. Due to the frustrations police officers have experienced in handling such cases, they often take less than the expected degree of interest in pursuing a prosecution when there is any early indication of reluctance on the part of the victim to participate in the prosecution. In some jurisdictions, the accumulated police experience results in an early decision not to prosecute and, in some cases, not to arrest.

It would be possible for the police to prosecute more frequently those persons who commit assaults by resorting to the issuance of a subpoena to compel the attendance of the victim at trial, assuming the judge would be willing to compel the victim to testify. This procedure, however, is seldom used. Given the high volume of cases and the competing demands upon a police agency, the path of least resistance is to acquiesce in the desires of the victim. Such acquiescence is often rationalized on the ground that the injured party was the only person harmed and the community as a whole was not affected by the crime. These cases can be written off statistically as clearances—which are viewed as an index of police efficiency—and thus the most immediate administrative pressure is satisfied.

There is some question about the relationship between current police practice in slum assault cases on the one hand, and the amount of crime and the community's attitude toward police on the other. If the criminal justice process has some deterrent value, why would it not deter assaultive behavior in the slum area? To what degree does an awareness of the attitude of the police toward assaultive conduct result in the formulation of negative attitudes on the part of slum residents toward law and order in general? What is the impact upon the residents of such an area when an attack by a slum resident upon a person residing outside the area results in a vigorous prosecution?

Today, these and other basic policy questions which can be raised are not dealt with by the police. Routine practices are not examined in the light of overall enforcement goals and, as a consequence, may very well serve to complicate rather than solve important social problems. Were the police to review their current practices, they might well conclude that, insofar as assaults, for example, are concerned, it is desirable to base police decisions to arrest on such criteria as the nature of the assault, the seriousness of the injury, and the prior record of the assailant, rather than primarily on the degree to which the victim is willing to cooperate.

Selection of Investigative Methods

In the past few years, increasing attention has been given by legislature and particularly by courts to the propriety of current police detection and investigation methods.[17] Nevertheless, there remain many areas in which the determination as to the investigative technique to be used is left to the police. For example, neither legislatures nor courts have yet reflected much concern with the propriety of police use of "undercover" or "infiltration" techniques, surveillance, or other methods which afford an alleged offender an opportunity to commit a crime in a manner which will make evidence of his offense available to the police. If the present trend toward judicial rule-making continues, it is not at all unlikely that current investigative practices thought by police to be proper and effective will be subject to increasingly specific rules. This has already occurred with respect to in-custody investigation, which is now specifically controlled by the *Miranda* decision. Whether this will occur with respect to other police practices will depend in large measure upon whether the police can develop policies which differentiate the proper from the improper use of particular investigative practices and can see to it that improper methods are not used as a matter of informal departmental policy or by individual officers out of either ignorance or excessive zeal.

Field interrogation is illustrative of important police investigative techniques which may or may not survive attack. Police have generally argued that their right to stop and question people is essential, especially with respect to those persons who are observed in an area in which a crime has just been committed. With several exceptions, however, there has been little effort made to provide individual officers with carefully developed guidelines so as to assure that such interrogation is sparingly and carefully employed under conditions that justify its use.

The use of field interrogation as an investigative technique is complicated by the fact that it is a part of the total preventive patrol program—which is a current response by police in large cities to the demand that the "streets be made safe." Preventive patrol often involves stopping persons using the streets in high-crime areas and making searches of both persons and vehicles. The purpose of this technique is not only to talk with individuals who may be suspected of having recently committed crimes but, more broadly, to find and confiscate dangerous weapons and to create an atmosphere of police

---

17. The extent to which legislatures and courts have addressed themselves to three specific areas of police investigation—the conduct of searches, the use of "encouragement," and the stopping and questioning of suspects—is explored in McIntyre, Teffany & Rotenberg, *Detection of Crime*, 1967.

omnipresence which will dissuade persons from attempting to commit crimes because of the likelihood of their being detected and apprehended.

It is probably true that a program of preventive patrol does reduce the amount of crime on the street, although there has been no careful effort to measure its effectiveness. It is also apparent, however, that some of the practices included in a preventive patrol program contribute to the antagonism toward the police felt by minority groups whose members are subjected to them. A basic issue, never dealt with explicitly by police, is whether, even from a purely law enforcement point of view, the gain in enforcement outweighs the cost of community alienation.

The continuation of field interrogation as a police investigative technique depends upon whether the police are willing to develop policies which carefully distinguish field interrogation from street practices which are clearly illegal and to take administrative steps to demonstrate that a proper field interrogation program can be carried out without it leading also to an indiscriminate stopping and searching of persons.

The Decision Not to Prosecute Individuals Who Have Been Arrested

While in some states it is the practice to take all arrested individuals before a judge, it is standard procedure in others for the police to release some individuals prior to their scheduled court appearance. Drunkards are often given their freedom once they are sober; juveniles are often released after consultation with parents or a social service agency; and in large urban areas, narcotic addicts and small-time peddlers are often released with a grant of immunity in exchange for information leading to the arrest of more serious violators.

Where it is the practice to release some drunkards without charging them, eligibility for release tends to be based upon such factors as appearance, dress, reputation, place of residence, and family ties. The process is generally intended to separate the common drunkard from the intoxicated person who "knows better" but, in the judgment of the police, simply had "one too many." Whether this kind of distinction adequately serves an enforcement or social welfare objective is not entirely clear. Certainly police, who are daily confronted with the problem of the drunkard, ought to give continuing attention to whether defeasible criteria are being employed and, perhaps more important, ought to lend support to and participate in an effort to develop ways of dealing with the alcoholic which are more sensible than the current arrest and release programs.

Criteria have been formulated in some communities to assist police in deciding whether a juvenile offender should be released to his parents, referred to a social agency, or brought before the juvenile court.[18]   In other communities, however, such decisions continue to be made by the police without an articulated basis and the decisions often reflect the use of such indefensible criteria as the color of the child, his attitude toward the police, or the status of his parents in the community.[19]

The practice of releasing some narcotic addicts and peddlers in exchange for information or cooperation raises other complex issues. Persons involved in narcotics control assume that the investigation of narcotics traffic requires the accumulation of knowledge from those who are involved in the distribution or use of such contraband and that convictions cannot be obtained without the help of informants who cooperate in return for immunity.   The potential for abuse in pursuing this practice makes it critically important that the standards for extending an offer for immunity and for measuring cooperation be uniformly and fairly applied.   There is moreover, a need for continual evaluation of the practice to determine whether the gain derived from it really justifies the costs which are involved.

The Issuance of Orders to Individuals Regarding Their Movements, Activities, and Whereabouts

The public, whether as pedestrians or motorists, generally recognizes the authority of the police to direct their movements in traffic. There are many other situations, however, in which police regularly tell people what to do under circumstances where police authority is less clear.   For example, police order people to "keep the noise down" or to stop quarreling—usually in response to a complaint from a neighbor; direct a husband to stay away from his wife when they have had a fight; order a young child found on the streets at night to go home; order troublesome "characters" to stay out of a given area; and tell persons congregated on street corners to disperse.

Police generally assume that congregating on a street corner is likely to give rise to disorderly conduct, especially if such assembling takes place outside of a tavern, if those assembled are intoxicated to varying degrees, and if there is heavy pedestrian traffic which is likely to be blocked by the congregating group.   The technique ordinarily used by police in such a situation is to order the persons to "move on," thus presumably minimizing the risk of a group distur-

18. See, e. g., Chicago Police Department, Youth Division, Manual of Procedure (1965).

19. See, e. g., Piliavin & Briar, *Police Encounters With Juveniles*, 70 Am.J. Sociology 206 (1964); Goldman & Nathan, *The Differential Selection of* *Juvenile Offenders for Court Appearance*, in National Research and Information Center, National Council on Crime and Delinquency (1963).   For an overall view of the police function in the juvenile process, see Wheeler & Cottrell, *Juvenile Delinquency: Its Prevention and Control*, 28–31 (1966).

bance. There is a tendency, however, for this technique to become standard operating procedure as applied to all groups that congregate on sidewalks and street corners, without regard to the varying character of the groups. For example, in some cultural groups, congregating on the streets is the most common form of socializing; and in some congested areas of a city, the corner is used because of the absence of adequate public recreational facilities. For police to respond to these situations in the same manner as they respond to the situation involving an intoxicated group outside a tavern may not serve any real enforcement objective and may instead strain the relationship between the police and the residents of those areas in which the street corner is the place of social and recreational activity.

The practice of ordering people to "move on" is one which has major implications and warrants more careful use. In confronting the question of what should be their proper policy in dealing with congregating groups, the police would have an opportunity to give attention to why groups congregate, to distinguish those congregations which create risk of serious disorder from those which do not, and to relate police work to other community programs designed to create positive social and recreational opportunities for persons who now lack these opportunities.

The Settling of Disputes

A substantial amount of the on-duty time of police officers is devoted to the handling of minor disputes between husbands and wives, neighbors, landlords and tenants, merchants and customers, and taxi-cab drivers and their riders. Relatively little importance is attached to the handling of such matters by police administrators, particularly those in large urban areas. The patrolman who responds to the report of such a disturbance may inform the parties of their right to initiate a prosecution, may undertake to effect a resolution of the dispute by ordering the parties to leave each other alone (as, for example, by advising an intoxicated husband to go to the movies), or may use some other form of on-the-scene counseling. The approach taken in each case is a matter of choice on the part of the individual officer.

Important policy questions are raised with respect to the way the police handle all disputes and, in particular, to the way they handle domestic disturbances. Yet there has been no systematic effort made to measure the results which may be obtained under the alternative methods which police use, nor has there been an effort made to develop more adequate referral resources (such as social agencies) which might, if they existed, provide a basis for a positive police program for dealing with such disputes. In an effort to develop adequate policies to guide the actions of the individual patrolman, police agencies should compile several relevant facts: how often the same families become involved in disturbances that require police intervention; how often the husband or wife swears out a complaint; the disposition of such cases and the impact that varying dispositions have in preventing future disturbances; the number of serious assaults or homicides which result from domestic disturbances and whether these follow a pattern which might enable a patrolman to identify a potentially dangerous situation; and the kinds of cases which can be referred with positive results to existing community resources for dealing with family problems.[20]

Through the process of careful evaluation of existing practices and experience, the police can acquire a competence which should enable them to develop more adequate follow-up procedures in the domestic disturbance case. This added competence should increase the value and effectiveness of the emergency intervention function of the police and should, in the long run, reduce the heavy burden that is presently placed on the police in dealing with this type of recurring social problem.

The Protection of the Right to Free Expression

None of the functions which the police perform illustrates the sensitive and unique role of the police in a democratic society as well as that which is involved in the safeguarding of the constitutional rights of free speech and assembly. Police frequently are called upon to provide adequate protection for a speaker or demonstrating group that wishes to exercise the right to express one's opinions—opinions that are often unpopular and which are often voiced in the presence of a hostile audience.

Many urban police agencies have not developed and formulated policies to guide police action in such situations. Although the issues involved in recent demonstrations reflect many factors which are beyond police control, it is nonetheless a fact that the manner in which police respond to demonstrations will determine, in large measure, whether violence will break out and, if it does, the degree to which the resulting conflict will escalate and spread.

The problem is a particularly difficult one because police officers may themselves identify more with maintaining order in their community, especially to prevent disorder created by outsiders, than with their basic responsibility to protect the right of free expression of social and political views. For example, the officer in a police district

20. The techniques which are used by police in handling domestic disturbances have been the subject of a research project conducted with the cooperation of the Chicago Police Department by Raymond I. Parnas, a graduate student in criminal law at the University of Wisconsin. The results of the study are currently being prepared for publication.

which consists of a white neighborhood may view a Negro march through the neighborhood in favor of open housing as a threat to both public order in his district and the values of the very people in the neighborhood upon whom he depends for support in his day-to-day-work. In rural areas or small cities the population may be relatively homogeneous and thus the police officer can be responsive to all of the local citizens without this producing conflict for him. But a very real conflict may develop for the officer in a large urban area, since such areas are typically made up of communities which differ in economic, racial, religious, or other characteristics. The officer who protects the right of free expression of ideas may find himself protecting an attack upon the very segment of the community with which he identifies.

In order for the police to respond adequately and consistently in the highly tense situations which arise from political and social demonstrations, there obviously must be a careful effort on their part to work out, in advance, policies which will govern their actions. This development of policies must be coupled with an effort to communicate them to individual officers in a way which will give each officer a basis for identifying with the protection of freedom of expression as an important enforcement objective. In addition, an effort must be made to articulate such policies to the affected community so that the public will understand the reasoning behind police actions. This, in itself, can serve to lessen the likelihood of major disorders.

Implementation

Since police agencies do not presently have the capacity to fulfill the kind of policy-making role that has been outlined in this article, implementation of this program will require numerous adjustments in their existing procedures, orientation, and staffing. The nature of these requirements is discussed in detail elsewhere,[21] but their general character will be summarized here.

As a prerequisite, it will be necessary for the police to develop a systematic process for the identification and study of those aspects of their operations which are in need of attention. Police administrators must take the initiative in seeking out the problem areas by analyzing complaints, by observing the results of police activities as reflected in the courts, and by the various other procedures available for analyzing the functioning of their respective departments. It is essential that the police develop a research methodology for exploring

21. See President's Commission on Law Enforcement and Administration of Justice, *Task Force Report: The Police*, ch. 2 (1967). With specific reference to the need for controlling police conduct, see H. Goldstein, *Administrative Problems in Controlling the Exercise of Police Authority*, 58 J.Crim.L.C. & P.S., June, 1967.

the kinds of problems that are likely to be identified—a procedure that equips them to clarify issue, to identify alternatives, to obtain relevant facts, and to analyze these facts in a manner that provides a basis for the development of a departmental policy. The end product must include clearly articulated criteria that will serve as guidelines for police officers and that will be open to public view. Flexibility being one of the major values in administrative policy-making, it is important that provision be made for the periodic reconsideration of those policies which are adopted so that adjustments to new developments can be effected and corrections may be made of deficiencies which become apparent after functioning under existing policies.

A police agency which accepts policy-making responsibility must develop more adequate systems of control than now exist to assure compliance of its personnel with the policies adopted by its administrators. The agency must also expect and should welcome responsible outside review of such policies as a protection against arbitrary policy-making.

Numerous changes will be required in existing patterns of leadership, personnel selection, training, and organization in order to equip the police to fulfill adequately their broader responsibilities. It is important, for example, that police leaders be provided with an education that will allow them to grasp fully the unique function of the police in a democratic society and that will enable them to support the overriding values relating to individual liberty which often conflict with their attempt to achieve the goal of maximum efficiency in the arrest and successful prosecution of offenders. It is important also that patrolmen in their training, be provided with a professional identification that is supportive of the proper role of the police and that aids in developing a willingness on their part to conform with administrative policies.

The progress realized in the law enforcement field in recent years, especially in the area of training and education, contributes significantly to achieving some of these objectives. Such efforts, however, have suffered for lack of an adequate definition of direction and purpose. The potential of current improvement programs would be vastly increased if those programs were related to the need for the police to develop their own capacity to formulate and implement law enforcement policies. Incorporating this requirement as an objective would serve to provide such programs with the kind of focus for which the need has long been apparent.

POLICE PLANNING: A STIMULUS FOR NEEDED
ORGANIZATIONAL CHANGE *

The concept of planning continues to increase in popularity. In fact, there appears to be a growing tendency to accept the notion that many of the problems of police agencies can be solved through use of management techniques which have proved successful in other organizations. As one who accepts the values of planning, I am specifically disturbed by such trends when they are not based upon a healthy skepticism and a reasoned commitment to a particular planning effort. I shall, therefore, examine some negative points before discussing various benefits derivable from a planning effort. Finally, we will look at the planning process itself.

SOME NEGATIVE ASPECTS OF PLANNING

In many ways, police agencies are very different from other organizations. For example, colleges and universities tend to hold that the institution exists to increase the contents of the sets of knowledge, aspirations, values, and mental skills associated with *each* individual involved in the academic process. Thus, we have students undergoing experiences intended to expand their knowledge and we have faculty engaged in research and scholarship to enlarge their own understandings. Even when academic activities are intended to contribute to goals more general than individual growth, these goals tend to be extra-institutional. So we have a physicist working to add to knowledge in his discipline and we have an agronomist seeking methods of overcoming starvation, but such motivations also tend to be highly individualized. These are some of the realities in a number of other professions, but they are not to be found to the same extent in most other public service organizations. Consider industry, for example; the preservation of the integrity and continuity of a company's own purposes are paramount. Individuals may relate to the organization to achieve personal fulfillment, but only in ways which contribute to organizational goals. Exceptions, when discovered, are usually not tolerated for very long.

I am definitely committed to the police and want to make every effort to increase the workability of their organization. This commitment is well worth the income lost by avoiding more lucrative pursuits. Now, suppose that under the struggle for institutional survival we decide to introduce planning and other management techniques. What we must recognize is that planning brings the tendency to focus attention upon institutional goals. It also introduces

* Source: Felkenes, George T. "Police Planning: A Stimulus for Needed Organizational Change." *Police.* (June, 1972), pp. 24–27.

many concepts, activities, and uses for data which are strange in the police environment. By what it carries with it, planning is capable of transforming a police department into a completely new organizational configuration from that which previously existed. Planning is based partly on the new and innovative, often some of which have not been adequately tested and analyzed for workability. By precipitously adopting new ideas as part of the planning processes, the wise administration will always keep in mind that traditional operating methods will change. He must likewise weigh carefully the freedom given by perpetuation of traditionally adequate operations with some uncertainty and temporary restrictions found by adopting the new.

Another way of looking at it is that one purpose of planning itself has side-effects which may create unwanted change. All that can be done is to urge any planner to be constantly critical of what he is doing. In fact, one of the personal frustrations of the planner—namely, an inevitable agency resistance and skepticism—is actually an excellent means of protecting this critical attitude. What may appear to be recalcitrance is often a natural tendency to conserve that which is valued, and the planner should be sensitive enough to ferret out the meaning of such "conservatism."

Another important negative aspect of planning is the tendency to generate a *plan*. This plan is considered a blueprint of the future. It is the *way* the organization will go. Such plans are normally quickly forgotten, except perhaps when resurrected occasionally to demonstrate to outsiders (legislators, civic leaders, and budgetary analysts for example) that the institution *knows* its own purposes and methods of achieving them. While planning should be somewhat predictive, it should be so by revealing future possibilities and by getting people to use their imaginations. It would encourage people to think in terms of alternatives. The plans, rather than being a static blueprint, should be a "roadmap" which reveals numerous paths into the future. Planning should be open and dynamic and it should never tend to preclude the spontaneous creativity which is so important to institutional vitality.

Another danger inherent in some planning systems, such as those built upon computer-based information systems, is that a set of relationships is built into the system, often at great expense. When many thousands of dollars are spent in developing such a system, it is not easy to let go of it. Consequently, there can be a tendency to try to maintain the invariance of the relationships. To illustrate what I mean, take the fictitious overly-simplified example of the formula: "Patrol vehicle = the number of street miles x number of serious crimes in the particular area." In this simple formula you are free to insert a number of street miles and the number of serious crimes in order to determine the required vehicle density. My contention is

that street miles may have some vague statistical meaning for traditional policing, but I would not be able to assign any meaningful value under a drastically modified and highly diverse urban setting.
Now, imagine that the preceding formula has been highly elaborated.
It is still based upon many traditional experiences and assumptions
concerning the forms of relationships in a police agency. It has been
very expensive to develop. Along comes some innovative thinking,
creating new theories which do not fit this elaborate formula. What
goes, the formula or the innovation? Ultimately, the formula will go,
but probably not without some undesirable resistance.

The final point is that planning is hard work and that it creates
new demands for both information and effort. Expansion of personnel and resources to accomplish successful planning may not be possible for many smaller departments, but there is always a price to be
paid. The question to the answer is: "Will the benefits of planning
offset the price?"

SOME BENEFITS OF PLANNING

Only you can answer the preceding question. I can, however, describe some of the possible benefits of planning one police agency is
trying to realize.

In these days of conflict, job pressures, and competition for personnel among various police agencies, it is very easy to lose the silent
people. In losing them, we lose their ideas and energy and the opportunity to give them relevance. A planning system can be designed to
involve these people and to give agency relevance to their thinking
and actions. When you look, you find these people among the students, practitioners, other departments' personnel, and with your own
agency. At the same time, the planning effort can channel the energies and enthusiasms of the more aggressive people and groups within the department.

In focusing attention upon change and potential actions (i. e., because of its future-orientation) planning tends to intellectualize conflict. It gets people together to argue and discuss differences before
they occur. This, it seems, is far superior to having an evolutionary
process create unexpected conflict conditions; and it is also consistent with the traditional organizational commitment to rational processes.

Closely coupled to the aforestated benefit is what might be called
the integrative function of planning. By this, I mean the bringing
together of individuals, groups, efforts, and goals. Planning should
tend to counteract the isolation of groups so common among bureaus,
divisions and sections in a police department. The detective division,
for example, does not communicate with the patrol division. The

command, field, and administration personnel view themselves in separate ways. Distinctions are made between operational goals and administrative goals. Such distinctions may be valuable for some purposes, but they should not prevent people from interacting in meaningful ways. I believe that planning can be designed to remove these barriers.

Another important integrative benefit of planning is related to what we might call the community-relations function. An integrative planning system can contribute to increased understanding of both the organization functions and its external environment. Personnel officers, for example, can be encouraged to remain alert to social changes which may affect the operations of the community relation function as well as remaining aware of innovations in normal work techniques in the particular field of expertise. This process of organizational awareness might also be called a process of "searching the field" for new ideas, techniques and innovations. In an integrated planning program, organizational awareness can easily be made one of the steps in the planning activity. For example, given the opportunity to interact in new ways with command and field persons, the personnel officer can become acquainted with some of the realities of agency needs. Patrol leadership decisions also can lead to a greater appreciation of the personnel selection methods. Thus, operations personnel can be given the chance to develop insight into the fundamental administrative goal of preserving the organizational equilibrium by careful utilization of personnel resources.

One of the principal reasons for planning is to introduce conscious intelligence into the change process. This puts the department in the position of being able to pursue change rather than being pursued by it. Anticipating change means that the agency need not merely react to every chance event, but rather that it can establish a creative balance between intelligent choice and evolution.

Once the alternative departmental plans are developed, they can be used to design various support programs; such as community relations, capital construction, public relations, and personnel development and recruitment. They can also be used for monitoring program activities, for allocating space and for budgeting. In other words, planning can serve the purposes of "effective management:" but "effective management" may be secondary to the opportunities for leadership which can be created by planning.

In conclusion, some of the goals of planning as I see them from the perspective of an educator viewing a police department are:

1. To bring people together in performance of significant actions and, in general, to develop an integrative force within the agency.

2. To provide a basis for monitoring programs, allocating resources and using information.

3. To provide for experiences and exchange of information which serve to create mutual understanding in the various groups within the organization.

4. To associate decisions with people having the information and expertise to best make them.

5. To seek out and solicit the thinking of people from all groups within the department.

6. To create a method for using mathematical and computer techniques in ways which support, not supplant, the full range of human intelligence and aspirations.

7. To provide guidance for future action without destroying the possibility of rapid departmental evolution.

8. To encourage investigation of the behavioral aspects of administration to assist in satisfying human needs, goals, and desires.

THE PLANNING PROCESS—AN OVERVIEW

There are many steps in the planning process as used in most police departments. Details are often described in departmental manuals. However, no attempt is made here to cover the details, but rather to set forth a broad general overview of the planning process.

The first general step is to prepare some of the background information needed for the planning. In most cases, budget projections should be developed, personnel figures for the various divisions projected in detail, and space needs projected. I call these numbers "planning parameters" or "optimal desires." It must be emphasized, however, that many agencies will not have the data base, manpower, or computer capability support to make projections as reliable as those generated in the large police departments. In the system, as envisioned by me, the "shaky" data is not critical, as the developing of alternatives is an answer to incomplete or inaccurate assumptions.

The next step is that of orienting the department to the new concepts, language and processes involved in planning. Most people will have difficulty in appreciating the purpose of planning or the importance of making much effort to understand it. One approach would be to conduct a two or three day workshop for all the command staff and chief administrative personnel. This workshop would include several talks and some simulation of the planning process. Although a fair degree of enthusiasm can be generated during such a workshop, one cannot expect to have communicated full and lasting understanding. If an expectation that something is about to happen is created, and the notion that what is about to happen is not undesirable, label the workshop a success.

The third general step is to organize the personnel into working groups. A central planning committee consisting of key departmental personnel should be formed. This committee sets the parameters, reviews plans and makes recommendations to the Chief. A very important innovation in the planning process is to create a number of sub-planning committees consisting of interest groups within the department, patrol officers, and perhaps, unions. These committees conceivably do the actual program planning. A planning office must also be formed to do the staff work involved in coordinating the planning effort and in making calculations and analyses of plans.

The fourth step is to set up a provocative situation for each of the planning committees and to record the reactions in a uniform way. The provocation (or system perturbation) is amply provided by the parameters given to the committees. Each committee is told that they must design a program which does not generate more departmental resources and use more money or space than the central planning committee says they will have in five years. They may also be given other constraints which are non-quantifiable and are issued as statements, such as: "You cannot plan a public relations program," or "You must develop three general training courses to show the relationship of your division to other divisions in the department." Sometimes I suspect that inadequate data will be an advantage in that it often creates a strong enough reaction for attention to be captured. One important purpose of the planning, however, is to get the committees thinking the terms of *alternatives*. Consequently, they also should be told that they are free to generate as many alternative programs as they wish. This instruction serves both as a means of getting alternatives and also as a safety valve.

The fifth stage is to analyze the plans to put them together in a comprehensible form. During this stage the central planning committee reviews all plans and seeks trustee approval.

The sixth stage, following the approval of the Chief, is to design implementation programs—including the seeking of funds and creation of time schedules.

The final stage is to use the plans a part of the budgeting process and to provide for their annual review and modification.

In the final analysis planning involves a major effort. Since the program budget is becoming more popular as a method of management decision making, it must be remembered that police program planning assimilates into it the budgetary processes. Consequently, by implementing a program planning approach, the former line-item budget is cast into a different mold to permit a more rational decision at the various organizational levels. Basically, the purposes of the program approach (i. e., creating thought stimulation, utilization of intelligence, involvement of outside groups, increased communication, and creation of an orientation toward the future), creates a system oriented toward people as an integral part of planning. As most executives in police work realize, planning is done in an environment of probabilities, possibilities, and uncertainties. Precise information is often non-existent and definite answers are unavailable. To overcome those hindrances, there must be a willingness to intelligently guess and explore alternatives. Program planning permits this and reemphasizes that there is no such thing as *The Plan*.

BIBLIOGRAPHY

Golembiewski, Robert T., and Gibson, Frank: *Managerial Behavior and Organization Demands*. Chicago, Rand McNally, 1967.

Kenney, John P.: *Police Management Planning*. Springfield, Thomas, 1952.

Novick, David, (ed.): *Program Budgeting; Program Analysis and the Federal Budget*. Washington, D.C., U.S. Government Printing Office, 1965.

President's Commission on Law Enforcement and Administration of Justice: *The Challenge of Crime in a Free Society*. Washington, D.C., U.S. Government Printing Office, 1967.

President's Commission on Law Enforcement and Administration of Justice: *Task Force Report: The Police*, Washington, D.C., U.S. Government Printing Office, 1967.

Pfiffner, John M., and Sherwood, Frank P.: *Administrative Organization*. Englewood Cliffs. Prentice-Hall, 1960.

U.S. Bureau of the Budget: *Bulletin No. 66–3*, October 12, 1965.

Wildavsky, Aaron B.: *Politics of the Budgetary Process*. New York, Little-John, 1967.

Wilson, O. W.: *Police Planning*. 2nd ed. Springfield, Thomas, 1958.

Wilson, O. W.: *Police Administration*, 2nd ed. New York. McGraw-Hill, 1963.

A GENERAL MODEL FOR CRIMINAL JUSTICE PLANNING *

In all the recent public clamor about the failure of government to come to grips with pressing urban problems, criminal justice agencies have been singled out for particularly harsh criticism. They are accused by their detractors of being insensitive, unresponsive, and inflexible, while their supporters claim that they are understaffed,

* Source: Nanus, Burt, "A General Model for Criminal Justice Planning", *Journal of Criminal Justice*, Vol. 2, 1974, pp. 345–356.

overworked, and unappreciated for the job they are able to do in the face of some very difficult circumstances. Both positions are correct, but given that crime problems are increasing at a faster rate than the budgets of criminal justice agencies, the situation is almost certain to degrade even further unless more effective means can be found for adapting criminal justice organizations to the new and rapidly changing circumstances in which they must operate. The Omnibus Crime Control and Safe Streets Acts of 1968, which established the Law Enforcement Assistance Administration (LEAA) under the Department of Justice, well recognized this need for improved long-range planning mechanisms. In fact, the national strategy for attacking crime problems specifically recognizes that the key to improving the effectiveness of criminal justice agencies is to institutionalize the process of change in these organizations. It has done this by requiring the formation of state criminal justice planning agencies and regional planning boards. But it should be obvious to everyone by now that the LEAA funding support affects only a small proportion of the total funds spent for law enforcement in this country, and that lasting improvements will require that individual criminal justice agencies learn how to do their own effective long-range planning for the investment of their own local budgets.

The main problem seems to be that individual criminal justice agencies tend to be reactive rather than future-oriented in their decision making and operations. Systematic and comprehensive long-range planning is seldom done because these agencies are constantly being subjected to short-term political pressures; their funding is based on a one-year cycle; and the problems of the moment are often real enough and quite compelling, however, even a totally reactive agency can operate more effectively with a long-range planning perspective, as military strategic planning has often demonstrated. More important, there can be no meaningful regional or systemwide planning without individual agencies first being able to establish their own orderly, systematic, and continuous processes of setting objectives, anticipating the future and bringing these anticipations to bear on critical present decisions. Local criminal justice agencies, however, have very little experience in doing this and very few models to follow. The purpose of this paper is to attempt, in a general way, to lend some structure to efforts to establish planning functions in such agencies.

PLANNING IN THE CRIMINAL JUSTICE SYSTEM

Long-range planning is concerned with the necessity of making today's decisions in the light of an informed anticipation of tomorrow's realities. It is a management process that begins with the setting of objectives; proceeds to the definition of strategies, policies, and detailed plans to achieve them; establishes an organization to implement planning decisions; and includes a review of performance and feedback to introduce a new planning cycle.

Obviously, planning is not new to human organizations. In fact, man is truly a planning animal, since there could be no tools, agriculture, cities, wars, or social projects without it. What is new in the last decade, however, is the following: (1) a new emphasis on planning in all levels of American government; (2) a new awareness of the systems nature of many social problems such as ecology, urban decay, and crime, and a sense of urgency to develop ways to avoid foreseeable crises; (3) a sense of an increasing pace of change in values, technologies, lifestyles, and social structures which create new criminal justice problems as the social fabric tears and is rewoven, and (4) several powerful new methodologies and a growing professionalism in the field of planning itself.

At first, it may seem that planning in a criminal justice agency differs significantly from planning in other types of organization. It has often been suggested, for example, that the so-called "criminal justice system" is a system in name only and that all the agencies operate autonomously with separate charters, perspectives, and constituencies. Nevertheless, all criminal justice agencies are concerned ultimately with a single objective—preserving the peace and protecting the life and property of the citizenry—and the operations of criminal justice agencies are, in fact, very closely related.

In Figure 1, we have attempted to articulate the central mission of each of four types of organizations—criminal justice, corporate, military, and urban. It is obvious that all these missions are complex, only partly quantifiable and are in a constant state of change. Furthermore, all these types of organizations deal with considerable uncertainty in their future and important uncontrollable elements in their present environments; all have large and complex organizations; all operate within severe cost constraints; and all suffer from enormous current pressures and crises that tend to divert attention from the consideration of long-term plans. These similarities may be far more important then the differences between them and, if so, it should be possible to transfer major aspects of planning approaches used in these other contexts to criminal justice agencies.

Figure I

PLANNING OBJECTIVES

Context	Objective
Criminal Justice System Planning	To reduce crime in the long run by preventing, apprehending, and rehabilitating offenders, and to do so in a way that preserves individual rights, equal justice, and human dignity.
Corporate Planning	To achieve an acceptable long-run growth rate in profits while satisfying the diverse needs of employees, managers, customers, the government, and the public.
Military Planning	To prepare for, deter and, if necessary, win military conflicts while preserving democratic values, supporting foreign and domestic policy, and minimizing economic, physical, and human loss to the American people.
Urban Planning	To enhance the quality of life of urban dwellers physically, economically, and spiritually, while preserving democratic values, encouraging diversity, supporting industry and commerce, and maintaining flexibility to adapt to frequent changes in tastes and attitudes.

[B7266]

Planning can serve several important roles for an agency in the criminal justice system. First, as suggested earlier, the process of planning, by requiring the articulation of forecasts and assumptions, and by requiring the formulation of programs and projects involving several areas of jurisdiction, makes *coordination* essential. There is much lip service paid to coordination in the criminal justice system, but in fact, while there may be some informal discussion across agency boundaries, there seems to be very little in the way of systematic coordination between agencies with regard to long-range planning problems. For example, there are many instances where one agency takes a decision with regard to offenders that has enormous implications in terms of requirements for additional services in another agency without informing the second agency that the decision has been taken, let alone offering to jointly examine its implications or consequences. Planning can serve a coordinative role between agencies, but only if each agency has a viable planning process of its own so that it can articulate its own direction and thrust. Similarly, planning can serve a coordinative role inside an agency, provided all levels of management are involved in the planning process.

A second role for a planning process is as a change agent in the organization. The missions and functions of criminal justice agencies are in a state of transition throughout the country, in response to changes in legal requirements, public expectations, technology, and the nature of criminal activity itself. While these changes have resulted in modifications of operational practice, few agencies appear to have made the effort to specify and redefine their missions and objectives in the light of these changes or to make the objective-setting process a periodic and systematic one based upon expectations of future requirements. An effective planning process can serve an important role in forcing the agency to articulate its objectives and to formulate and evaluate alternatives that would not have been explored otherwise. It can do this by helping to define and structure the external environment of the agency, by developing a systematic environmental surveillance framework, and by interpreting external events for their impact on the agency.

A third role for planning in a criminal justice agency is as a framework for resource allocation decisions, most particularly during the budgeting cycle. Making the transition from long-range planning to short-term resource allocation decisions has been one of the most difficult problems facing both corporate and military planners, and it will certainly not be easy in the criminal justice context. However, unless the budget decisions reflect long-range considerations, they will never be optimal, and unless long-range planning reflects financial realities, it can have no real substance. Both short- and long-range planning is essential and the most successful planning operations are those that can produce alternatives for the solution of immediate problems that have long-range implications as well as systematic explorations of long-range issues.

What can be done to make a criminal justice agency more future-oriented? There is no escaping the necessity for making long-range planning responsibilities a clear-cut and well-defined part of the total management process of the agency and a major concern of the chief executive. Beyond this, however, there is a need for a well-designed planning mechanism in the agency. This may include (1) the establishment of a formal planning staff; (2) the appointment of planning task forces or committees; (3) the design of a regular planning cycle to govern the systematic timing and preparation of certain plans; (4) the development of a planning information system; and (5) the institutionalization of a comprehensive planning process or model in the agency. Before proceeding with the organizational aspects, however, we should take a closer look at a planning process that could be used in a wide variety of criminal justice agencies.

THE GENERAL MODEL

A general model for a planning process in a criminal justice agency is shown in Figure 2. Regardless of where the planning takes place—whether at the federal, state, or local level—it is suggested that all five of these distinct and identifiable types of planning should take place in a continuous and systematic fashion. They are discussed briefly below.

Figure II

A GENERAL MODEL FOR A CRIMINAL JUSTICE
PLANNING PROCESS

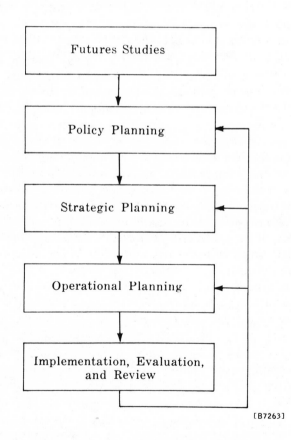

[B7263]

(1) *Futures Studies*—Futures research is a relatively new field which has grown out of the military and corporate planning tradition with strong roots in systems analysis, technology assessment, and mathematical modeling. As one expert defines it, "futures research is a means of discovering and articulating the more important of the alternative futures and estimating the trajectory likely to be produced by contemplated policies. Thus, forecasting is perceived as an aid to decision making in the present . . ." [1]

Futures studies are of considerable importance to the criminal justice planner, particularly in problem identification and analysis. For example, the planner must be able to anticipate crime rates and trends, population and other demographic shifts, changes in values and attitudes toward crime, new legislation and court rulings, new technology that may assist in detecting and apprehending criminals, and a wide variety of other social, demographic, governmental, and economic variables. He needs these forecasts in order to understand and interpret current crime trends as well as to formulate new programs to deal with anticipated developments that may become crises at some future time. There are a wide range of futures research methodologies currently available to assist in this effort. [2]

(2) *Policy Planning*—Policy planning, which is concerned with the determination of the purpose, objectives, and general policy of the agency, is designed to determine what the agency *should do and why*. It should reflect a long-time horizon, perhaps five to seven years or more, and serve as a point of reference for other types of planning. As shown in Figure 3A, it is primarily concerned with establishing objectives, defining problems and opportunities, and elucidating policy guidelines. While policy planning is heavily dependent upon judgments and values, these judgments can be more or less informed in proportion to the effort expended in making systematic forecasts and analyses. In performing these functions, policy planning requires an analysis of the basic mission of the criminal justice system, the strengths and weaknesses of the agency, and crime trends and forecasts of the external environment in which the agency will have to operate.

1. Gordon, Theodore J., "The Current Methods of Futures Research." In *The Futurist*, A. Toffler, ed. Random House, New York, p. 165.

2. For example, see Martino, Joseph P., *Technological Forecasting for Decision Making*, New York: American Elsevier Publishing Company, 1972; Bauer, Raymond A., *Social Indicators*, Cambridge, Mass.: MIT Press, 1966; or recent editions of the journals *Technological Forecasting and Social Change, Futures*, or *The Futurist*.

Figure III

٭   PLANNING INPUTS/OUTPUTS

A. *Policy Planning*

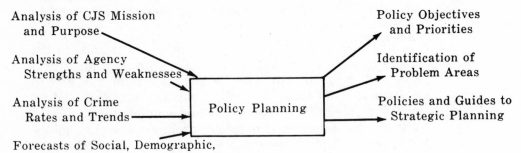

Analysis of CJS Mission
   and Purpose

Analysis of Agency
   Strengths and Weaknesses

Analysis of Crime
   Rates and Trends

Policy Planning

Forecasts of Social, Demographic,
   Technological, and Legislative Futures

Policy Objectives
   and Priorities

Identification of
   Problem Areas

Policies and Guides to
   Strategic Planning

B. *Strategic Planning*

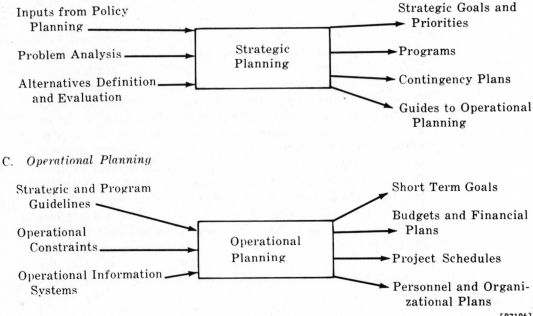

Inputs from Policy
   Planning

Problem Analysis

Alternatives Definition
   and Evaluation

Strategic
Planning

Strategic Goals and
   Priorities

Programs

Contingency Plans

Guides to Operational
   Planning

C. *Operational Planning*

Strategic and Program
   Guidelines

Operational
   Constraints

Operational Information
   Systems

Operational
Planning

Short Term Goals

Budgets and Financial
   Plans

Project Schedules

Personnel and Organi-
   zational Plans

[B71196]

(3) *Strategic Planning*—Strategic planning is generally concerned with developing strategies to deal with particular issues, problems, or opportunities that may arise. It is concerned with what the organization *can do and how*. As opposed to policy planning, strategic planning may be the responsibility of executives who act in a staff capacity for the head of the agency and not infrequently involves the formation of a problem-oriented task force with representation from a number of divisions and bureaus within the agency. As shown in Figure 3B, strategic planning is concerned with the identification of strategic alternatives and their evaluation, the formulation of appropriate programs and contingency plans, and the development of guidelines for tactical or operational planners.

All criminal justice agencies are concerned with strategic plans, whether they formally recognize it or not. One common type of strategic planning is concerned with facilities acquisition; a second is concerned with organizational design; and a third with determining manpower requirements at various levels. In addition, individual agencies may develop strategic plans in problem areas of particular long-range concern such as narcotics, alcoholism, juvenile delinquency, organized crime, etc. Such strategic plans can be developed on an intermediate-term time horizon, perhaps three to five years, and when they are highly structured may involve many bureaus and units within the agency.

Problems of strategic planning in the criminal justice system are often compounded by the fact that many interfacing agencies have an important impact upon the plan. For example, the strategy of a probation department concerning its long-range manpower needs is partially dependent upon the strategy of the courts in sentencing juveniles and the strategies of the law enforcement agencies in apprehension and booking. Where such strategies are heavily interdependent, it is obviously in the best interests of each agency to closely coordinate its strategic plans with those of agencies whose actions can most directly affect its demand for services.

(4) *Operational Planning*—This type of planning, frequently the major responsibility of middle- and lower-level managers, is concerned with the shorter-range plans and activities of organizational units in the agency. That is, it is primarily concerned with what those organizational units *will do and when*. Typically, operational planning is the most highly

structured of all planning in a criminal justice agency, if only because the annual budgeting process demands it. The products of the operational planning process, as shown in Figure 3C, are decisions about the acquisition and deployment of resources and about measures of effectiveness and efficiency in the attainment of short-term goals. This frequently takes the tangible form of a budget, a financial plan, a project schedule, or a manpower recruiting and training plan.

(5) *Implementation, evaluation, and Review*—The culmination of any planning process is a stream of decisions on resource allocation, actions to be taken and goals to be achieved. Needless to say, these must be carefully implemented through the normal chain of command. This is facilitated when an agency uses the increasingly popular, "management by objectives" approach to internal organization development but even without the formal mechanism, a clear-cut process of review and evaluation of the impacts of decisions taken must be made and feedback provided to all the other elements in the planning process.

The model of long-range planning presented here has been kept intentionally broad in order to be adaptable for a wide range of criminal justice agencies. In a very small local agency, many of these functions will be performed by the head of the agency, perhaps with the aid of an administrative assistant. In larger agencies, a more formal and structured approach can be taken. Some of these organizational aspects are discussed in the next section.

ORGANIZATIONAL ASPECTS OF CRIMINAL JUSTICE PLANNING

We may approach the question of organizing for planning by contemplating an "ideal" future-oriented criminal justice agency. First of all, in such an agency, the top management would be committed to long-range planning as the principal vehicle for instituting organizational change and preventing purely reactive management. This implies that there would be a continual effort to clarify and articulate the department's purposes and goals. Second, there would be a permanent staff charged with preparing forecasts and projections of likely futures, facilitating the planning of the various divisions and bureaus in the agencies, and bringing to bear the growing body of new planning techniques to address the long-range problems of the agency. Third, there would be a data base consisting of future-oriented internal and external information for use in decision making in the agency. Fourth, no important decisions would be made without consideration of their possible future effects and without coordinating with other interfacing agencies affected by the decision. Finally, there would be an emphasis upon an on-going research effort to help understand the structure and dynamics of the agency and the way in which it interacts with its environment. Some of these characteristics will be briefly elaborated below.

The head of the agency clearly is a key person in the establishment of a viable planning process in the agency. His support and participation in the process and his use of it as an integral part of his management style is essential to success. Among his specific planning responsibilities are the following:

1. To assure that a planning mechanism for the agency is developed and maintained.

2. To assure that lower level executives bring long-range considerations to bear upon operational problems.

3. To initiate, stimulate, and evaluate the development of strategic and operational planning.

4. To lead the policy planning effort, particularly as regards to the objectives-setting process.

5. To create an environment in which innovation and change is encouraged and rewarded.

Few criminal justice agencies have a formal planning staff, although the number is rapidly increasing. In many agencies, it is still expected that planning will be done by the head of each organizational unit but no effort is made to formalize the process. In others, organized planning is done within certain functional areas, such as facilities or personnel planning, but not in others. In those agencies with a full-time planning executive (e. g., a director of planning) and a small planning staff, their functions may cover a very wide spectrum, including any or all of the following:

1. Provide staff services to the top management of the agency in the development of strategies for achieving the agency's objectives.

    (a) Assist top management in defining long-range and short-range objectives for the agency.

    (b) Analyze strategic alternatives and recommend the best course of action.

    (c) Exercise leadership in the development of a five or ten year plan for the agency.

2. Conduct special planning studies to assist top and middle management of the agency.

    (a) Continuously survey evolving trends in major environmental forces which are likely to influence the demand for agency services. Included are trends in economic, political, social, and technological affairs at the local, state, and national levels.

(b) Analyze local crime trends and patterns, including forecasts on future trends and distribution of crimes.

(c) Forecast the future of the agency on the basis of its current momentum.

(d) Conduct special studies of new methods, techniques, and procedures or systems that might be of long-term benefit to the agency.

(e) Analyze and develop new approaches to achieve strategic goals for the agency. Recommend appropriate allocations of agency resources to support new and continuing programs which promise performance improvement.

(f) Investigate new organizational alternatives and long-term manpower needs.

3. Assist the divisions and bureaus in the agency in the effective development of formal long-term planning for their own functions.

(a) Provide analytical problem-solving skills to these divisions in such areas as forecasting methodology, information systems, and modeling.

(b) Provide scenarios and sets of assumptions that can be used to guide planning in the divisions.

(c) When requested, aid divisions in developing their plans.

(d) Coordinate the plans of the divisions into an overall agency plan and determine the implications of the agency plan for the achievement of agency goals and strategies.

4. Coordinate the planning efforts of the agency with those of interfacing agencies at the federal, state, and local level.

(a) Maintain close relationships with planning staffs of interfacing agencies and regional planning boards.

(b) Prepare action grant applications for the agency to secure state and federal funding for agency projects.

(c) Coordinate the budgeting effort in the agency, insuring its consonance with long-range considerations and represent the agency in its interaction with local administrative and financial officers.

(d) Attend planning conferences to remain abreast of the latest methodologies that can be brought to bear in developing long-range plans.

There is little need to emphasize the fact that effective long-range planning requires considerable information about the current and projected future environments within which the agency functions. Such information varies depending upon the type and level of planning being discussed. For example, information required for policy and strategic planning is primarily analytically oriented, future-oriented, and tailor-made to the particular problem being investigated. On the other hand, information required for operational planning is primarily cyclical and report-oriented, internally oriented, and focused upon performance measures such as budgets and project milestones.

Many criminal justice agencies blame their lack of success in planning on a lack of sufficient information, and there is some justification for such a view.[3] Nevertheless, it is equally true that the requirement for planning information must precede the acquisition of the information itself, and often those agencies that complain of inadequate planning information are also those that have given insufficient attention to their requirements. Actually, there is a great deal of information available to criminal justice agencies from published sources in the government and private sectors (e. g., banks, insurance companies), from unpublished records in local communities, as well as from more traditional court, police, and other criminal records. The problem is that this information is rarely collected and analyzed from a planning perspective. Rosove[4] has shown how this can be done, and great progress is expected in this area in the next few years.

SUMMARY AND CONCLUSIONS

In this article, we have suggested a general planning model that can be used in most criminal justice agencies. How then, can an agency that does not now do very much planning initiate such a process? Some immediate steps can be recommended, none of which are particularly expensive. They include the following:

1. Conduct a planning audit of the agency. The purpose of such an audit would be to determine the effectiveness of the current planning process and where improvements can be

3. For example, see Nanus, Burt and Luther Perry, "A Planning-Oriented Measure of Crime and Delinquency," *Journal of Criminal Justice*, Fall, 1973, p. 259, or Biderman, Albert D., "Crime Rate," in *Social Indicators*, by Raymond A. Bauer, Cambridge, Mass.: MIT Press, p. 111.

4. Rosove, Perry, *The Impact of Social Trends on Crime and Criminal Justice*, Project STAR, Marina del Rey, California, American Justice Institute, 1973.

made. Questions in the audit should be designed to determine the following:

(a) How are agency objectives and strategies determined?

(b) Where is the center of long-range planning responsibility in the agency and how is it organized?

(c) How is planning coordinated with other agencies of the criminal justice system?

(d) What planning documents are prepared regularly and by whom?

(e) What information, either inside or outside the agency, is most useful for planning purposes?

(f) What techniques are used for forecasting analysis, scheduling or evaluation of planning effectiveness?

(g) What problems inhibit the effectiveness of planning in the agency?

2. Set up an information flow on matters relating to the future of the agency. As suggested earlier, there are many organizations that can provide information on trends or likely future developments, often free of charge, including local universities, federal and state government agencies, and commercial organizations such as banks and insurance companies which generate enormous amounts of economic and demographic information. Often this can be done simply by publicizing the agency's interest in certain types of information and getting on the right mailing lists.

3. Develop a planning capability in one or several staff personnel. There are many textbooks in the field of long-range planning (although not in the specific area of criminal justice agencies), and considerable assistance can be found at local universities.

4. Survey planning processes in other criminal justice agencies that are comparable in size and function. This may be done easily by a letter from the head of the agency to his counterpart requesting information.

5. Establish a planning task force or committee to make recommendations on the design of a planning mechanism and the scope of planning responsibilities of the agency. It is important to encourage wide participation in the early stages of such an inquiry so that lower levels in the organization do not feel threatened, but rather see the process as a sign of a growing flexibility in the organization.

With the background and experience provided by these early steps, it should be possible to proceed toward the design of a more formal planning process in the agency. This will be more difficult and there may be mistakes and false starts but in the end, it should lead to a new and much more flexible mode of operation—one in which problems are anticipated and either prevented from occurring or prevented from having deleterious effects. In the long run, a more planning-oriented criminal justice agency should be a much more effective agency.

SYSTEMS ANALYSIS APPLIED TO LAW ENFORCEMENT *

The problem of resource allocation for a police system is similar to that of many other public systems, namely: (1) A lack of agreement regarding the objectives of the system, and their relative importance; (2) A lack of knowledge of alternative means for accomplishing goals, either within or outside the system; (3) A lack of agreement defining the criteria of performance; and (4) A lack of knowledge of transfer functions which would enable the prediction of output from any given set of inputs.

The police system has to be studied as a distinct system within the social structure of society. Optimizing easily quantifiable relationships is likely to obscure the important qualitative aspects.

"The legitimate point (can be made) that police systems can be understood only as institutions in interaction with the rest of the social structure."[1]

IDENTIFICATION OF OBJECTIVES

The Police System objectives are related to law enforcement, order maintenance and public service. Though everyone might agree as to the desirability of the first objective, there is disagreement on what to enforce and how.[2]

"No policeman enforces all the laws of a community. If he did, we would all be in jail before the end of the first day. The laws which are selected for enforcement are those which the power structure of the community wants enforced."[3]

*   Source: Ernst K. Nillsson, "Systems Analysis Applied to Law Enforcement," Allocations of Resources in the Chicago Police Department, Washington: Law Enforcement Assistance Administration, March 1972, pp. 1–12.

1. Arthur Niederhoffer, Behind the Shield: The Police in Urban Society (New York: Anchor Books, 1967), p. 13.

2. Jerome H. Skolnick, Justice Without Trial: Law Enforcement in Democratic Society (New York: John Wilery and Sons, 1966).

3. Dan Dodson, speech delivered at Michigan State University in May, 1955; reported in Proceedings of the Institute on Police Community Relations, May 15–20, 1955 (East Lansing: The School of Police Administration and Public Safety, MSU, 1956), p. 75 and quoted in Niederhoffer, (Ref. 1), p. 12.

The second objective, order maintenance, designates the police system as a buffer for the social system. This is bound to involve conflict situations in which there is no consensus as to what constitutes order and the propriety of the methods of enforcement employed. The function of public service is much less controversial, but constitutes a large drain on police resources. Often these services could be more efficiently performed by other public or private organizations.

Even if an objective such as crime prevention has been agreed upon, it is important to know the alternative methods which can accomplish the objective. Often the most important aspect of improving a system is the generation of good alternatives. In addition, each null alternative has to be investigated. Instead of devoting additional resources to a police system, they might produce better results if allocated to the courts or correctional agencies, or if used for social work or community building. Thus, it is necessary to consider alternatives outside the police system proper.

Criteria of performance represent the means by which a system is to be evaluated. They should provide a way of measuring how well objectives are being accomplished. For example, is an average response time to a call for service a good criterion; is the number of traffic citations issued by each officer a good indicator of traffic management?

Lastly, there is a lack of quantitative descriptions of the police system. This holds true for descriptions of the system and its environment as well as transfer functions for different activities (a transfer function relates inputs to outputs for a given activity). An input-output guide should permit an indication of, for example, the number of policemen needed to control a mob of 200 people or how many police cars must be in service to achieve a certain response time to high priority calls and how response time relates to the probability of arrest.

Answers are sought for the questions posed earlier, and this work has three objectives:

1. To define the Police System (its objectives, its interfaces with other systems, and measures of effectiveness).

2. To develop a new structure for allocating costs (an accounting system). This structure should facilitate the development of production models and the evaluation of benefits.

3. To develop production models for the Response Force in order to evaluate alternatives.

Meeting the first objective is partly solved by the presentation of a conceptual model of the Police System.

The discussion proceeds from the meta-system level down to models of specific activities. First the Police System, its objectives and criteria are defined. Secondly, to make the resource allocation problem manageable, a structure is developed for cost-benefit analysis. This structure is called a Resource Analysis Budget and necessitates a whole new accounting system. The present allocation of resources are calculated for this new accounting structure. Lastly, production models are used to determine efficient combinations of resources.

USING SYSTEMS ANALYSIS

The systems approach is a rational framework for complex problem solving emphasizing hierarchies of systems and their interrelationships. Most often the problem is ill-structured and the objectives are unknown or undefined.

"The systems approach is one in which we fit an individual action or relationship into the bigger system of which it is part, and one in which there is a tendency to represent the system in a formal model."[4]

The systems approach is the methodology used to develop a conceptual model of the police system. The model specifies the objectives and the outputs of the police system and consequently permits determination of output categories (programs) for the Resource Analysis Budget. The systems approach offers a tool for structuring the analysis, and consequently some protection against erroneous suboptimizations.

The Police System as well as the Criminal Justice System is a largely uncharted area. Suboptimizations are ever present hazards; in fact, the optimization of Police System performance is itself a suboptimization.

"A system may be defined as a set of objects, either fixed or mobile, and all relationships that may exist between the objects. All systems are composed of sub-systems and are members of a higher system."[5]

For example, the Police System is in part a member of the Criminal Justice System which is part of the Social System within which our society exists. The Police System, in turn, is a set of sub-systems.

For resource allocation analysis, these sub-systems are a set of mission oriented (output oriented) sub-systems. These sub-systems

4. Charles Zwick, *Systems Analysis and Urban Planning* (Santa Monica: Rand Corp., 1963).

5. Kenneth Heathington and Gustave Rath, "The Systems Approach In Traffic Engineering," *Traffic Engineering*, June, 1967.

are usually called programs. The cost structure of the system, with respect to the given programs, is called The Program Budget. The analyst tries to select a set of sub-systems which:

1. Are consonant with the plan of the decision maker;
2. Have operational objectives and measures of performance;
3. Are as independent as possible;
4. Facilitate cost-effectiveness analysis.

An environment may be defined as a set of objects outside the system. It is the aggregate of external conditions which affect the system.

The systems approach can be succinctly exhibited in a paradigm. The following steps should be considered in drawing a systems analysis. (See figure 1) [6]

Figure 1
SYSTEMS ANALYSIS PARADIGM

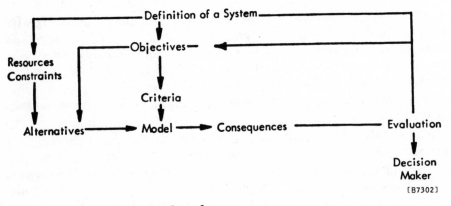

[B7302]

1. Define the desired goals.
2. Develop alternative means for realizing the goals.
3. Develop resource requirements for each alternative.
4. Design a model for determining outputs of each alternative.
5. Establish measurements of effectiveness for evaluating alternatives.

6. For further reading, see: G. H. Fisher, "The Analytical Basis for Systems Analysis," Rand Corp., May 1966, p. 3363; A. Hall, *A Methodology of Systems Engineering* (Princeton, N.J.: D. Van Nostrand Co., Inc., 1962); Van Cort Hare, *Systems Analysis: A Diagnostic Approach* (New York: Harcourt Brace and World, 1967); Charles Hitch and Roland N. McKean, *Economics of Defense in the Nuclear Age* (Cambridge: Harvard Univ. Press, 1963); E. S. Quade *Analysis for Military Decisions* (Chicago: Rand McNally & Co., 1964); E. S. Quade, "Some Problems Associated with Systems Analysis," Rand Corp., June, 1966, p. 3391.

After a system and its environment have been specified, the analyst should consider the objectives of the system and the resources and general constraints which are present. Resources are the total available material which can be allocated. Constraints are limitations imposed on the system.

The objectives express what the system is trying to achieve and to what end resources should be applied. An objective should be defined in such a way that an operational, quantitative measure of performance is possible. It is of little use to have an objective which cannot be quantified.

Equally important are measures of performance. They permit evaluation of how well the objective is being achieved.

ROLE OF ALTERNATIVES

Alternatives offer different means of using resources to achieve objectives. Developing alternatives represents one of the more creative and crucial steps in the systems analysis process. It is here that the analyst seeks to define new alternatives that can provide increased effectiveness over previously considered alternatives.

Once alternatives have been specified, the cost of resources for each alternative has to be determined. This involves considerations of risk, time and different types of costs. To arrive at the benefits of an alternative, a model is necessary. The model determines the output to be derived from a given amount of resources.

Lastly, the cost and benefit of each alternative has to be evaluated to select the optimal alternative. The criterion function relates costs and benefits to system objectives and provides the basis for selection.

"It is my experience that the hardest problems for the systems analyst are not those of analytic techniques .   .   .   . What distinguishes the useful and productive analyst is his ability to formulate (or design) the problem: to choose the appropriate objectives; to define the relevant, important environments or situations in which to test the alternatives, to judge the reliability of his cost and other data, and finally, and not least, his ingenuity in inventing new systems or alternatives to evaluate."[7]

This point cannot be emphasized enough.[8] The great danger in systems analysis lies in not spending enough effort in defining what the system under study should be, and instead seeking to optimize the effectiveness of a given system. The big payoffs are likely to come

7. C. J. Hitch, *Decision Making for Defense* (Berkeley: University of Calif. Press, 1965), p. 54.

8. Lindsey Churchill, "An Evaluation of the Task Force Report on Science and Technology," Russell Sage Foundation mimeograph, 1968.

from a construction of new world views of problems, rather than optimizing current structures.

This point is illustrated in Figure 1 by the arrows drawn from the evaluation phase to the objectives and the alternatives.

AN ART IN INFANCY

The current state of the art, with respect to police resource allocation optimization, is in its infancy. Most research into the Criminal Justice System has dealt exclusively with the social dimensions. Analytical contributions have appeared only during the last five years.

A systems analysis approach was used by the President's Commission on Crime and Law Enforcement to define the scope of the Criminal Justice System problem, possible research approaches, and technology that could be applied.

"Because of the enormous range of research and development possibilities, it is essential to begin not with the technology but with the problem. Technological efforts can then be concentrated in the areas most likely to be productive. Systems analysis is a valuable method for matching the technology to the need."[9]

Blumstein and Larson recently published an article which looks at the flow of people through the Criminal Justice System.[10] It is not a systems analysis as they do not discuss objectives or measures of effectiveness, but rather a descriptive model of the flows. This step is important, however, as it provides a quantitative description of a portion of the real world.

DESCRIBING A POLICE SYSTEM

From a general point of view, a police system is a service organization. Its clientele are people who have broken the law as well as people in need of help. It is a twenty-four hour, city-wide, dual purpose service force.

The police system is not part of the market mechanism. Its output is not a good sold in the market in competition with other enterprises; it is a public service good. The community devotes a certain amount of resources to the system and expects an output, which never is too well defined. Even if the inputs and the outputs of the system were given, the internal process of a police system is difficult to optimize. Very little is known about the transformation of inputs into outputs (the transfer functions). Consequently, tradeoffs be-

9. The President's Commission on Law Enforcement and Administration of Justice, *Task Force Report: Science and Technology* (Washington, D.C.: Govt. Printing Office, 1967) p. 3.

10. A. Blumstein and R. Larson, "Models of a Total Criminal Justice," *Operations Research*, Vol. 17, No. 2 (March-April, 1969).

tween different methods of controlling crime (for example, using more or fewer detectives or using one-man or two-man patrol units) are not known. This is a serious drawback in trying to allocate resources and develop a departmental budget.

The metropolitan police force is usually a paramilitary system. It is characterized by strong internal controls and centralized decision making. Its organizational goals, as pointed out in the Field Study of San Diego,[11] are primarily oriented towards the crime-fighting function.

The Police System does provide two separate services: Crime control and public service. The former is the main focus of activity as will be shown in the Program Budget. This crime control function is part of the efforts of the Criminal Justice System; the public service function is part of the City Government.

The Police System is a set of sub-systems which are part of higher order systems. (See Figure 2) The Police System is a member of the Criminal Justice System (CJS). Its function is preventing criminal events and, failing this, to identify and apprehend the offender. There are other members of the law enforcement agencies in addition to metropolitan police departments; these include federal, state, county and special police, such as Burns, Brinks, etc.

Figure 2
SYSTEMS ANALYSIS OF THE CRIMINAL JUSTICE SYSTEM

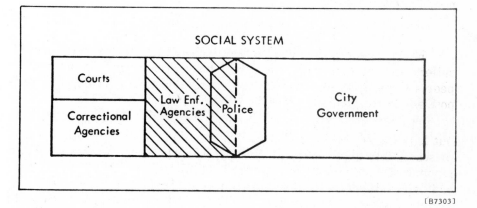

The Police System is also part of the City Government. Its public service mission is a function of the twenty-four hour, city-wide availability of the police force. Part of this function could be carried

11. The President's Commission on Law Enforcement, the Police and the Community, *Field Surveys LV*, Vol. 1 (Berkeley: Univ. of Calif., October, 1966).

out by people with no police training. This function includes actions such as animal rescue, locating missing persons, and ambulance service, all of which could be performed by other city agencies or private groups.

The Police Department has another objective, Community Support. The generation process of individuals who may choose a criminal career is deeply rooted in social, psychological and economic variables over which society has some control. Crime is the responsibility of society, and its control cannot be delegated solely to a Police Department. The Police Department responsibility is to deter and apprehend offenders. The Criminal Justice System can effect deterrence, but this is effective only to the extent that society (or the social group to which the potential offender belongs) disapproves of criminal acts.

Community support implies the willingness of the community to fight crime, both by giving support, help, and resources to the Police Department, and by creating means to affect the crime generation process. Instead of actively seeking community support, police departments have often, in their desire to be professional, tended to become systems isolated from the community. This has had some detrimental effect on police effectiveness.

The investigation of the crime control problem will proceed by first analyzing the Criminal Justice System and then, in more detail, the Police System. This will permit the specification of objectives for the Police System.

CRIMINAL JUSTICE SYSTEM

To help specify the Police System, which is the focal point of the analysis, it is necessary to consider the higher order system. The Criminal Justice System (CJS) has been charged by society to regulate and control certain classes of behavior. These classes of behavior are determined by the legislative branch of government and interpreted by the courts.

The sub-systems of the CJS: The Police, the Courts, and the Correctional Agencies. The police identify misconduct and apprehend the offenders. The courts determine the facts of the case and rule on its disposition. Correctional Agencies administer prisons and supervise the parole system.

How does the CJS affect the generative process of criminal events? The structure of the crime control function is exhibited by a conceptual model. It displays the pertinent sub-systems, decision points and mechanisms for change. It permits an analysis of how the CJS can affect the potential criminal's decision making and how the impact of crime can result in community response.

The model postulates that the forcing function of the crime generation process is a function of social-psychological-economic variable. (See Fig. 3)

Figure 3
CONCEPTUAL MODEL OF THE FORCING FUNCTION

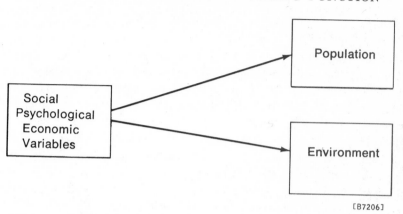

[B7206]

These variables affect the individual's utility function and consequently affect his propensity towards a criminal career. They also affect the distribution of opportunity by altering the generating mechanism. A discussion of the specific mechanisms is outside the scope of this paper.

Welfare programs provide family assistance which gives children a better start, thus reducing the likelihood of their pursuing a criminal career. Job training programs and increased employment opportunities will provide an alternative to crime for an income. For example, people might demand stricter legislation (i. e., cars must have theft proof locks) or elect voluntarily to lock their cars. In either case, the underlying mechanism generating opportunities has been altered.

Two factors are necessary to create a criminal event. There has to be an individual or group of individuals and a specific set of opportunities. A specific opportunity is defined as a factor of:

1. Type of opportunity (theft, robbery, etc. This leaves open the question of the appropriate classification);

2. Gain (usually in dollars);

3. Availability (this dimension measures the probable degree of difficulty of execution associated with the specific opportunity. This permits differentiation between a car that is locked and unlocked, located in the street or in an underground garage);

4.   Location (in space) ;

5.   Time (interval of time when opportunity exists).

For a given type of opportunity, distributions can be generated with respect to location and time.   The set of all opportunities is called Environment.

The population considered in the model is the total population of the community.   It is a set of individuals characterized for our purposes by the following attributes:

1.   The individual's perception of the environment.   The model chooses to maintain an actual environment and vary the individual's knowledge of the actual opportunities.   The value of this attribute would fall between 0 and 1.   That is to say he has incomplete knowledge.

2.   The individual's knowledge of deterrence.   Deterrence is the expected value of negative benefits that the Criminal Justice System contributes to a given type of opportunity.   It is a function of the probability of arrest for a given type of opportunity based on past performance by the police system, the chance of being sentenced, and the length of the consequent jailterm and amount of fine.   Again the value would fall between 0 and 1.   (These benefits would be pure number to which a utility transformation would be applied).

3.   The individual's utility function.   The coefficients of this function are determined by past social-psychological-economic effects.   The utility function concept will permit an explanation of how past states of the individual will influence his present decision-making.   If an offender committed a successful crime (i. e. large monetary reward, not apprehended) one day, he is not likely to attempt another crime the next day.   His attitude towards the risk or estimation of his own abilities may have changed as a result of his success.   The utility concept also permits analysis of "crimes of passion."   The individual puts a low estimation on negative benefits or the positive benefits are very large.   That is, the utility function encompasses, among other things, past experience, needs and behavior towards risk.

The decision making process resulting in a criminal event can be viewed as a two-step decision process.   This allows distinguishing between inputs, which are a function of the past performance of the CJS, and inputs at the moment of execution.

First, the individual is permitted to contemplate the opportunities known to him and make an *a priori* decision to actually commit a specific crime.   The relevant input from the CJS deterrence, as defined above, of which the individual has varying degrees of knowledge. Knowing the individual's utility function, the opportunity having the greatest utility can be determined and a "go, no-go" decision made.

The second decision point is present immediately prior to the execution of the planned criminal event. The potential offender evaluates the actual circumstances of the opportunity and makes a go, no-go decision.

The first stage was an *a priori* decision based on the probable circumstances surrounding the event. The second stage becomes the actual sample reflecting: (1) the juncture of the probable circumstances, and (2) action taken either by private groups, (persons) altering the generation of opportunity distributions and/or their factors, or police actions affecting deterrence or opportunity distributions. For example, a person might decide to break his habit of not locking his car or the police department may employ a new tactic against CTA bus robberies.

For many events, commonly called "crimes of opportunity," the time interval between the decision points is very small. However the interval could be measured in days. Figure 4 summarizes this discussion in pictorial fashion. It has been said that there is a formula for crime: "Desire plus opportunity equal crime."[12]

Figure 4

CONCEPTUAL MODEL OF THE DECISION PHASE

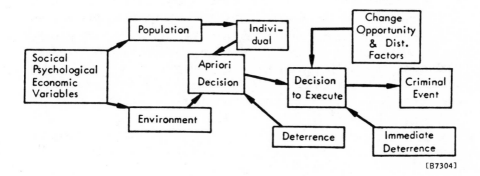

[B7304]

12.   Allen P. Bristow, *Effective Police Manpower Utilization* (Springfield: Thomas Press, 1969).

CRIMINAL JUSTICE SYSTEM RESPONSE

What is the CJS reaction to the criminal event and how can it affect the crime generation process?

The Police sub-system responds to the criminal event seeking to identify and apprehend the offender. Police strategy and tactics can influence the decision to execute.

The generation process of crime is affected by deterrence. Deterrence was defined as the expected value of negative benefits which are a function of the risk of arrest, chance of sentencing, length of jailterm, and fines for different classes of criminal events.

The Courts and Correctional Agencies may either emphasize deterrence or rehabilitation. Rehabilitation is the effect the CJS has on the individual as he is processed through the CJS, resulting in a change in his utility function. The Police contribute through special handling of juvenile offenders, the courts by the sentence they provide, and the correctional agencies by programs which seek to integrate the individual into society.

There is a tradeoff between deterrence and rehabilitation. By rehabilitating the offender the CJS lowers the deterrence effect. The negative payoffs cannot be as large with a satisfactory rehabilitation program.

COMMUNITY RESPONSE

There are usually two parties to a criminal event: the offender and the victim. (The exception is "crimes without victims" such as gambling.) The set of victims represents the impact of crime on the community. This becomes input for private and civic action. Citizens may arm themselves, private group might hire special police to react to criminal events.

The community (individuals, civic groups, businesses) may decide to react through the democratic process. That is, have government legislate new programs to alter social-psychological-economic variables or commit more resources to the CJS. They may, in addition, affect the opportunity distributions through laws (cars shall be locked, banks must have detection cameras) or by their own behavior.

Figure 5 summarizes the Criminal Justice System discussion in an expanded, integrated schematic that approximates the interactions of sub-systems within the Criminal Justice System.

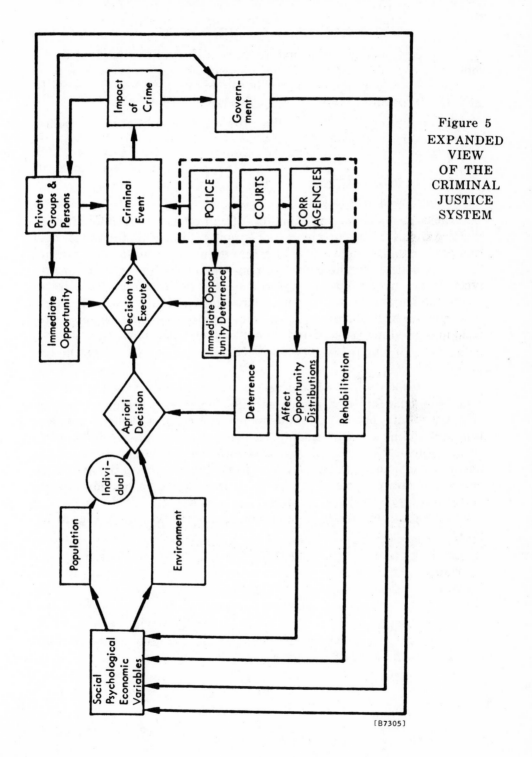

Figure 5
EXPANDED
VIEW
OF THE
CRIMINAL
JUSTICE
SYSTEM

[B7305]

MODEL OF A POLICE SYSTEM

This section focuses in more detail on the police contribution to the crime control function. Police System impact on the crime process occurs at four points: (1) Forcing function, (2) *A priori* decision, (3) Decision to execute, and (4) Criminal event.

It will be convenient to analyze the major activities of the police system in terms of three sub-systems:

- Response Force
- Preventive Force
- Follow-up Force

Police response to a criminal event can be differentiated with respect to the detection process. Detection is defined as the identification of a criminal event. The criminal event detection is by a person or by the police. In the model all non-police detection will be considered as person originating. When a person detects a crime, he initiates a call for service to the police department. If the police, through offensive tactical patrol, detect a crime-in-progress, the person feedback loop need not be actuated. For "crimes without victims" (gambling, etc.), the detection process is carried out by specialized police unit.

The Response Force is defined as the police sub-system which responds to calls for service. These calls for service are generated by criminal events, public service demands and reports of suspicious activities. Public service demands consists of calls such as sick and injured transport, animal rescue and locating missing persons. Reports on suspicious activities are an important factor in being able to detect crime-in-progress. It also is an indicator of community cooperation in fighting crime. Chicago has a campaign called "Operation Crime Stop" to encourage this citizen participation. (See Figure 6)

Figure 6
INPUTS TO THE RESPONSE FORCE

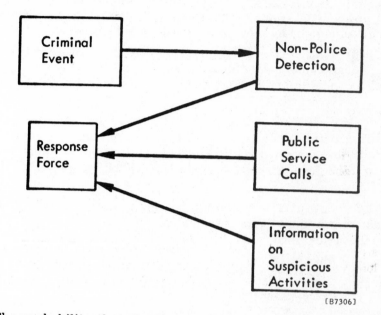

[B7306]

The probability that the Response Force will apprehend the offender is a function of the time elapsed since the crime was committed and the tactic used. The elapsed time consists of:

1. Time until citizen detects event and initiates call to the police department.
2. Processing time by the Communications Center.
3. Travel time for the assigned cars.

It has been shown that the apprehension probability is a decreasing function with respect to elapsed time.

It is possible to initiate campaigns which stimulate citizens to be sensors for the police department and impress upon them the necessity of transmitting the information in a timely manner. This activity might very well have a larger potential payoff than optimization of police detection or response.

Analysis of the effectiveness of the Reactive Force is of great importance. Police departments are being offered hardware such as car locators and computerized communications centers but have presently no means to evaluate the benefits. How much will the proposed hardware decrease response time and how will this affect the probability of apprehension? Finally, how much is an increase of the probability of apprehension worth?

The Preventive Force is the offensive force in the combat against crime. It interacts with the crime process in two ways. It seeks to detect misconduct and apprehend the offender. It also influences the decision to execute a criminal event by affecting the perceived presence of police. For example: have policemen in uniform and marked cars or by otherwise giving the potential offender an impression of police omnipresence.

This can come about through actual presence as a result of successful positioning of forces in time and space or through propaganda.

The Preventive Force also may affect the decision to execute by restricting actual opportunity, either by removing it completely or changing the factor of availability. This would be done through premise check, checking parked cars for valuables, removing drunks from the street, etc.

The Follow-up Force is the third sub-system. Its function is to apprehend criminals through the investigative process. It also includes the actions on a case following the booking of an offender.

Fig. 7 illustrates the interactions of these three forces in police functions.

Figure 7

FURTHER DEVELOPMENT OF POLICE SYSTEMS
INPUTS AND OUTPUTS

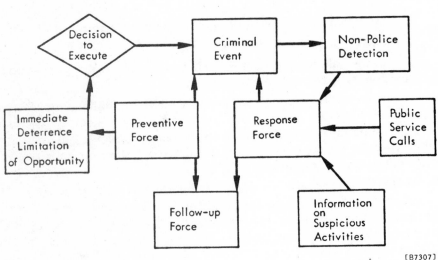

[B7307]

POLICE SYSTEMS OUTPUTS

The outputs of the Reactive Force are arrest and public service. The probability of arrest was expressed as a function of elapsed time and tactics used. The Preventive Force outputs are arrests and impact on the decision to execute. The probability of apprehension is a function of elapsed time, probability of detection (i. e. being at the scene of the event, and recognizing that an event did in fact occur) and tactics used. Follow-up can be characterized by the probability of arrest through investigation. It is dependent on elapsed time and methods used. All of the above functions are also dependent on the type of crime. The tradeoff between the Response and Preventive Forces, given a criminal event, is that the latter may detect an event with a low probability but may have a higher probability of apprehension (due to shorter elapsed time).

Deterrence is an input to the *a priori* decision point. The Police System variable is the probability of arrest for the system (i. e. the combined efforts of all three sub-systems).

The Police System does affect the forcing function by changing the mechanisms generating opportunities. It can also affect an individual's utility functions through rehabilitation measures, mainly with respect to juveniles. This group of offenders is given special attention in order to influence them away from a criminal career. For example, special youth officers handle the cases and often a station adjustment is made.

The conceptual model can account for Community Relations programs. The Police System can influence the crime generation process by devoting resources to communication with private groups and individuals. These measures would influence community support and, hopefully, encourage the community to assist the police in the apprehension process and, even more importantly, affect the generative process of crime. These communication links can be called Human Relations with respect to individuals, and Community Relations with regard to groups.

For a more thorough discussion of these phases of police activity, we recommend "Dilemmas of Police Administration" by James Q. Wilson in the September-October (1968) issue of *Public Administration Review*.[13]

An effective Community Relations program seeks to explain the crime generation process to the community, what the police role is, what it can be expected to do, and what the community can do.

---

13. James Q. Wilson, "Dilemmas of Police Administration," *Public Ad-* *ministration Review,* September-October, 1968.

There is also a link to other branches of Government, for the sake of completeness, to emphasize that police departments have to make other city, state and federal officials cognizant of Police problems, results and limitations.

In summary, the outputs of the Police System are:

1. Apprehension of offenders.
2. Impact of immediate environment on the criminal event.
3. Impact on *a priori* decision.
4. Rehabilitation measures.
5. Changing opportunity distribution.
6. Public service.
7. Community support.

The array of these relationships between the Police System, the larger Criminal Justice System and other governmental systems is illustrated in Fig. 8.

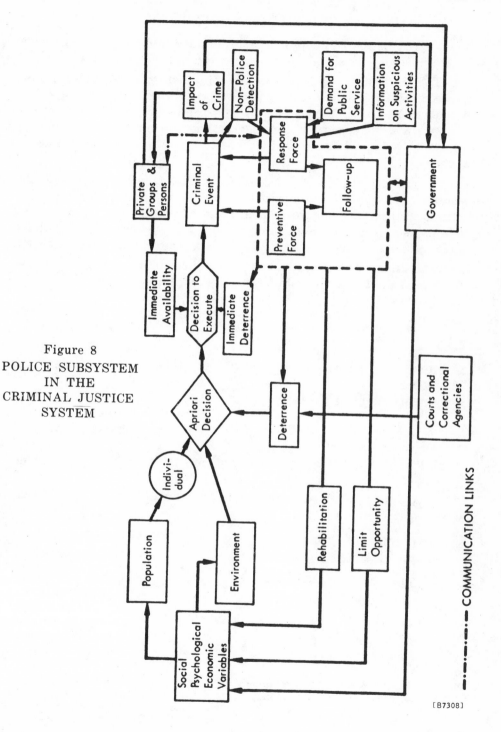

Figure 8
POLICE SUBSYSTEM
IN THE
CRIMINAL JUSTICE
SYSTEM

Impact of Crime

Non-Police Detection

Demand for Public Service

Information on Suspicious Activities

Response Force

Follow-up

Government

Private Groups & Persons

Criminal Event

Preventive Force

Immediate Availability

Decision to Execute

Immediate Deterrence

Courts and Correctional Agencies

Apriori Decision

Deterrence

Individual

Rehabilitation

Limit Opportunity

Population

Environment

Social Psychological Economic Variables

COMMUNICATION LINKS

[B7308]

POLICE SYSTEM OBJECTIVES

Three missions and specific outputs have been identified for the Police System. It remains to specify the objectives of the system.

The first mission is Protection of Life and Property and Maintenance of Peace and Order. It becomes convenient to subdivide the broad notion of crime control into two classes of events as criminal events differ in degree of seriousness and the nature of police response. Crime will be defined as index crimes and hit-and-run accidents.

A second category of misconduct can be called Quasi-Criminal, whose objective contains activities devoted to the enforcement of city ordinances to a large degree. These are crimes of lesser seriousness than index crimes and the maximum sentence is a year in jail and/or a fine. The main offenses are disorderly conduct and drunkenness.

Maintenance of Peace and Order can be subdivided into an objective called Public Peace and one called Traffic Regulation. The Public Service and Community Support objectives conclude the list.

Mission	Objective
Protection of Life and Property	1. Crime Control
Maintenance of Peace and Order	2. Quasi-criminal Control
Public Service	3. Public Peace
Community Support	4. Traffic Regulation
	5. Public Service
	6. Community Support

These objectives can be compared with lists of objectives found in the literature.

The International City Managers Association listed five police objectives: [14]

Prevention of Criminality

Repressions of Crime

Apprehension of Offenders

Recovery of Property

Regulation of Non-criminal Conduct

Another list includes: [15]

Prevention of Crime

14. *Municipal Police Administration* (Chicago: International City Managers Assn., 1961).

15. F. Leahy, *Planning-Programming-Budgeting for Police Departments*

(Hartford: Travelers Research Center, Inc., 1968) from a budgeting workshop sponsored by Florida Institute for Law Enforcement in 1966.

Investigation of Crimes

Apprehension of Violators

Presentation of Criminals for Adjudication

Services to the Public

Enforcement of Non-criminal Ordinances

Regulation of Activity within the Public Way

Peter Szanton defined the following objectives: [16]

1. Control and Reduction of Crime

2. Movement and Control of Traffic

3. Maintenance of Public Order

4. Provision of Public Service

The first two lists are not output-oriented in an independent manner and consequently would be difficult to use in a resource allocation analysis. Szanton's list is excellent but neglects the goodwill aspect. It has been said that a bulldozer is an effective crime fighter. This proposition would be a feasible alternative if there were no objective to represent the social system. For example, repressive police measures might prevent crime, but if individual's rights are destroyed in the process there should be a way of indicating this.

SYSTEMS ANALYSIS IN CONTEMPORARY POLICE MANAGEMENT *

The problem of crime in our society is now recognized as one of the foremost concerns of the nation. In his state-of-the-union address on January 17, 1968, the President of the United States drew his loudest applause from congress with this statement: "The American people have had enough of rising crime and lawlessness."[1]

Crime continues to rise at an alarming rate. Since 1960 major crime has jumped 88 percent while population has only increased 10 percent. This means crime is rising nearly nine times as fast as population.[2]

The police operate within an environment. They cannot accept responsibility for the tremendous problems they face. Social condi-

16. Peter Szanton, "Program Budgeting for Criminal Justice Systems," *Task Force Report: Science and Technology*, see Ref. 9.

* Source: Vernon, Robert L., "Systems Analysis in Contemporary Police Management", *Traffic Digest and Review*, (April and May, 1969), pp. 3–7, 10–17.

1. "Crime Problem—Why It's Not Solved." *U. S. News and World Report*, February 5, 1968, p. 49.

2. Ibid.

tions, the courts, correctional organizations and many other factors greatly influence the situation the police are in today. However, the police must cope with the increasing task they have been assigned.

The function of the police has become more important, its mission more relevant, and its task more difficult than ever before. The President's Commission on Law Enforcement and Administration of Justice recognized the strategic and yet precarious position of the police by making the following remark:

> Since this is a time of increasing crime, increasing social unrest and increasing public sensitivity to both, it is a time when police work is peculiarly important, complicated, conspicuous, and delicate.[3]

At a time when the demands upon the police are increasing, the resources available to them, in the form of personnel, equipment and funds, are remaining static and in some cases are dropping below previous levels. The shortage of man power alone is indeed critical. A recent national survey disclosed a need for 50,000 men just to fill vacancies in the present authorized positions across the country.[4]

Obviously all these facts point to a need for more efficiency on the part of the police—more efficiency in articulating and demonstrating their needs in order to correct inadequate resources; and practically speaking, more efficiency in utilizing present resources, recognizing that planning cannot be based on desires or hopes.

Progress, both in acquiring necessities and in increasing performance with what is presently available, will require changes in many time honored traditions under which police organizations presently function. A fundamental change in attitude may be necessary where resistance to change is prevalent. In some areas outside assistance and advice will be necessary. This, in itself, will be a marked departure from the tradition of isolationism. In many cases a basic re-examination of the entire police command and control function will be necessary.

Generally speaking, the police have not kept pace with the scientific and technological revolution that has so radically changed our way of life. This is especially true at command and administrative levels. Most of the little technological progress that has taken place is related to the application of operational procedures at the lower levels of organizational hierarchies. It appears that one of the greatest needs in police organizations today is a new approach to the process of decision making at the administrative levels. There has been

---

3. Commission on Law Enforcement, Report of the Commission, *The Challenge of Crime in a Free Society* (United States Government Printing Office, Washington, D.C., 1967), p. 91.

4. Commission on Law Enforcement, Report of the Commission, *The Challenge of Crime in a Free Society* (United States Government Printing Office, Washington, D.C., 1967), p. ix.

very little application of the techniques now available that are capable of assisting management in decision making.

In an age when many executives in government and industry, faced with decision making problems, ask the scientific and technical community for independent suggestions on possible alternatives and for objective analysis of possible consequences of their actions, the public officials responsible for establishing and administering the criminal law—the legislators, police, prosecutors, lawyers, judges, and corrections officials—have almost no communication with the scientific and technical community.[5]

One of the seven major recommendations of the President's Commission on Law Enforcement and Administration of Criminal Justice was a call for more operational and basic research.[6] Many police administrators have already recognized the need to not only develop new plans, but to continually review existing plans and operations in order to revise those needing improvement and to eliminate others when necessary.

In the past, command officers could make decisions based on intuitive judgment. Extensive assistance of technological equipment (i. e. computers) or formally organized procedures of examining alternatives was not necessary. Today the police must make the best of everything at their disposal. They *must* apply the principles of optimization—the selection of the best from among a number of possible situations or configurations—if they are to be effective and accomplish their mission. Since this process of optimizing can be a complex task in today's operations, a new approach is needed. Today's decision maker needs assistance.

DEFINING THE METHOD

Basic to the process of decision making is a *rational* choice between the alternatives. A decision maker must either pursue this course or resort to flipping a coin or other random selection. Systems analysis is a formal process of comparing various alternatives that are capable of solving a problem or accomplishing an objective with the intent of selecting the *best* course of action.

Authorities in the field define systems analysis as follows:

Any analytic study designed to assist a decision maker in identifying a preferred choice among possible alternatives.[7]

5. Ibid., p. 245.

6. Ibid., p. vi.

7. E. S. Quade, "Cost Effectiveness," in *Cost—Effectiveness Analysis*, ed. by Thomas A. Goldman (New York: Frederick A. Praeger, Inc., 1967), p. 14.

An attempt to define the most feasible, suitable, and acceptable means for accomplishing a given purpose.[8]

A tool which offers help in choice-of-objective type problems.[9]

Systems analysis is a general term referring to the broad concept of scientifically examining the various alternatives in *any* function. Operations research, although based on the same principle, is a term generally used to describe the application of the science to the analysis of operations per se (i. e. production lines, dispatching systems, search and apprehend operations, etc.). Most authorities agree that it is difficult to arrive at a clear distinction between the two and that they may be used interchangeably. In both applications, a logical sequence of steps is employed to make comparisons systematically in quantitative terms. This, of course, makes it possible for others to follow and verify the process. The decision maker can then compare all of the implications involved and, more or less, forecast the results of each available course of action. Obviously this should sharpen his intention and broaden his basis for judgment. He should be able to make better decisions, more consistently.

Interest in systems analysis, or operations research as it was originally termed, first appeared at the turn of the century. The concept received little attention and remained fairly static until World War II. Necessity often produces progress, and it did in this case. The war effort provided an urgency to develop a scientific process of arriving at optimum procedures.

Teams of scientists began to apply sceintific principles to certain wartime problems. For example, the British Navy employed operations research teams to devise methods of locating and destroying submarines. The "O.R." teams scientifically analyzed all of the alternatives available, considering the resources (ships, planes, instruments, men, etc.), and came up with the best or optimum method, plan or tactic. In many cases the results were astounding.

The modern computer has enlarged the field for operations research, and probably accounts for the massive breakthrough for the discipline in recent years. Today many private firms use the process to continually improve their operations.

Governmental agencies, with the exception of the Armed Forces, have lagged far behind the private sector of our society and have only recently taken advantage of this valuable tool. This is especially true in the law enforcement field.

---

8. Dimitris N. Chorafas, *Systems and Simulation* (New York and London: Academic Press, 1965), p. ix.

9. Gustave J. Rath, "Systems Analysis and Design," class lecture, Northwestern University, January, 1968.

More than two hundred thousand scientists and engineers are helping to solve military problems, but only a handful are helping to control the crimes that injure or frighten millions of Americans each year.[10]

E. S. Quade, a recognized authority on systems analysis, identifies five particular elements of an analysis.[11] Most practitioners and theorists in the field agree generally with his description:

1. The Objective(s)

2. The Alternatives

3. The Costs (Resources)

4. A Model

5. A Criterion

Objectives

Basic to the task of choosing a course of action or item of equipment is a clear understanding of the objectives desired by the decision maker or department. Often the explicit definition of objectives is a valuable by-product of the analysis in itself. Objectives tend to be confused with the means used to accomplish the objectives. For example, traffic citations are a means to accomplish an objective and not, in themselves, the objective.

In the spelling out of the objectives, it is often necessary to work down through an organizational hierarchy, realizing that there exists a hierarchy of objectives.

When the particular objective concerned is clearly understood, it is then possible to evaluate the various strategies, policies or operations under consideration on the basis of how well and how cheaply they can accomplish the objective.

Alternatives

The alternatives are the various means, tactics, policies, operations, equipment, etc., by which the objective may be accomplished. They are often referred to as "systems," which have been defined as: "A group of interdependent elements acting together to accomplish a predetermined task."[12] Hence, the phrase "systems analysis."

10. Commission on Law Enforcement, Report of the Commission, *The Challenge of Crime in a Free Society* (Washington, D.C.: U. S. Government Printing Office, 1967), p. 245.

11. E. S. Quade, "Systems Analysis Techniques For Planning—Programming—Budgeting" (unpublished paper, The Rand Corporation, 1966), pp. 6–8.

12. Dimitris N. Chorafas, *Systems and Simulation* (New York and London: Academic Press, 1965), p. 2.

One of the most important considerations in this step is to be sure that all the good alternatives have been included. Often, as the analysis progresses new alternatives are realized that may have remained unnoticed without the formal process. Some authorities feel that one of the greatest developments in systems analysis is this generation of alternatives.[13]

The alternatives do not necessarily have to be directly interchangeable or perform the same function. For example, the reduction of auto thefts may be approached by computerized roadside license checking, anti-theft vehicle design, public education and/or mandatory isolation of offenders.

Costs

The costs refer to the negative values involved in the analysis. They may be expressed in terms of money or resources; however, occasionally they are difficult to express in tangible quantities. Thus, the image projected by the use of dogs in crowd control may have an effect on relations between the police and certain ethnic groups in a community. This should certainly be considered as a cost of such a system.

Certain costs may be difficult to recognize in an alternative. Although the surface costs of one system may be lower than another, a "spill over" may occur in another system and actually negate the difference in costs.

For example, a police agency considering the purchase of a new fleet of cars for routine plain clothes investigative details may come to the conclusion, on the basis of surface costs alone, that Volkswagens will fill the bill. The initial price is reasonably low and gas mileage is good. A further analysis, however, may reveal a "spill over" cost in another system. Police mechanics may have to receive special training in the maintenance of the vehicles. Police drivers, who are usually above average in size, may be uncomfortable operating the vehicles. The occasional necessity for transporting prisoners must also be considered. In short, there are often hidden costs that must be considered.

Costs in governmental agencies, like police departments, are often referred to as *restraints* by the analysis.

The Model

Probably at the heart of the systematic analysis process is the construction and use of a *model*. The model is a simplified representation of the operation being studied.

In systems analysis a different type of model is constructed that might be envisioned by an individual not familiar with the process.

13. Gustave J. Rath, "Systems Analysis and Design," class lecture, Northwestern University, January, 1968.

Real physical models are used by the aero space industry to test a proposed design under various conditions (i. e. wind tunnel). Through this technique the engineers can predict how the actual aircraft (system) will react.   In a similar manner the model in an analysis performs the function of relating the amount of resources consumed to the degree the objective was accomplished, although not being physical in nature.   In complex systems analysis projects, models are usually expressed by mathematical equations or arranged in the form of a program for a computer.

The basis for judging the value of a model is not its complexity or intricate description of the situation, but in its ability to give better predictions.

According to most authorities the model should be:

1. Simple enough for manipulation and understanding by those who use it.

2. Representative enough in the total range of implications.

3. Complex enough to accurately represent the system.[14]

In the construction of the model, the research worker will analyze the past behavior of the process or system under study by consulting historical data.   Thus, in the case of describing a prisoner transfer system, past data on the frequency and number of prisoners transferred would be some of the facts necessary.   A frequency distribution is often plotted and such factors as the mean, median and standard deviation used to aid in the description.

Once a model is constructed it is tested with past data to see if it approximates the behavior of the real system.   If it does not produce data reasonably close to that produced by the actual system, it is revised until that condition is attained.

Objectives, resources and alternatives are then fed into the model in order to predict the consequences of choosing any system (see Figure 1).   This affords the decision maker the opportunity of viewing predicted results of the various alternatives and their respective trade-offs in costs and efficiency without changing the modeled entity itself.   One can readily see the fantastic advantages of such an arrangement, particularly when a change in the real system would involve great risks.

14. Dimitris N. Chorafas, *Systems and Simulation* (New York and London: Academic Press, 1965), p. 31.

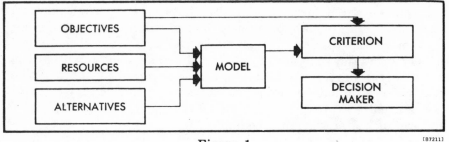

Figure 1

For example, in San Francisco a mathematical model representing the city's dwellings, homebuyers, renters, landlords, builders, and other factors allows municipal planners to evaluate the ramifications of alternative schemes *before* they are put into effect.[15]

Criterion

Simply stated, the criterion is the test by which one alternative is selected over others. The criterion may specify the selection of the system that *most* effectively accomplishes the objective with the least expenditure of resources. However, things are not always that simple. In governmental organizations, due to a limited budget, an agency may be forced to select a less expensive alternative. Quite often the problem is not simply a choice of the most economical alternative, but other factors must come into focus. In many cases the criterion must describe the level of effectiveness desired. For example, in Figure 2 system "B" would probably be the most desirable alternative in situations demanding effectiveness up to 50 percent. However, system "A" would be preferred if effectiveness over 50 percent was required.

15. "Systems Analysis: New Foe of Accidents." *Journal of American In*surance, November-December, 1967, pp. 13–15.

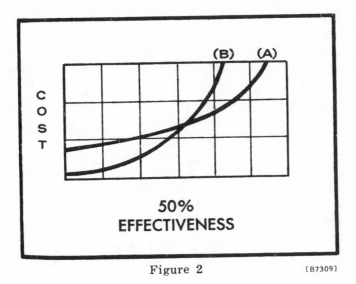

Figure 2   [B7309]

Upon completion of the analysis, weighted alternatives are presented to the decision maker who selects the alternative(s) that best meets the objectives according to his judgment.

There are a number of very practical reasons why today's police administrators need a "systems analysis" approach in the many functions of managing their organizations.

In selecting a course of action, or choosing an item of equipment, the act of making a decision becomes more difficult as alternatives increase. This is especially true when a department is looking for the "best" way or the most efficient piece of equipment. Today's problem for the administrator is not so much to come up with a program, or devise a new technique or procedure, but to choose among a variety of alternatives.

> This approach (systems analysis) today is particularly relevant in today's prolific technology where the problem is less one of producing new devices than of choosing among the many potential opportunities.[16]

With a multitude of ways and devices available and a real need for selecting the "best," not just an efficient one, the decision maker needs help. He can no longer consider *all* the various alternatives with their respective multitudes of implications without some analytical assistance.

16. Commission on Law Enforcement, Task Force Report, *Science and Tech-* nology (Washington, D.C.: U. S. Government Printing Office, 1967), p. 3.

To deal effectively with complex problems of a sophisticated society, police organizations have been organized with a division of responsibility and specialization in varying degrees. Although designed for promoting efficiency, this division of responsibility creates certain problems, some of which should be discussed within this context.

Various functional units within an organization (Police Department) develop objectives of their own. This "hierarchy of objectives" is functional and usually very necessary, but it can create problems. The objectives of certain units within an organization may not always be consistent; in fact they may come into direct conflict with one another. Administrators need a scientific basis for solving problems involving the interaction of components of the organization in the best interest of the organization as a whole.

> A decision which is best for the organization as a whole is
> called an optimum decision; one which is best relative to the
> functions of one or more parts of the organization is called a
> suboptimum decision.[17]

Organizations with a high degree of specialization and division of responsibility are particularly in need of systems analysis for this reason.

Complexity of operations also creates a problem of a decentralization of expertise. In years past it was often possible for the police administrator to have a thorough knowledge of the many operations and functions within his sphere of responsibility. The manager was not always an expert in the various functions, but the non-complexity of the operations allowed him to get by with a shallow knowledge of them.

Specialization has allowed a great deal of progress in the various functions of a police department. Many individuals have become experts in their field. Units have become very sophisticated and developed a high degree of efficiency within their field of responsibility. This condition, although desirable, has complicated the task of top decision makers. No longer can one man have a sufficient degree of insight into all the fields of knowledge required for optimum choices.

> The quantitative relations may involve many different fields
> of technology as well as operational factors, and are some-
> times so intricate that elaborate computations are necessary.
> There is almost never anyone who has an intuitive grasp of
> all the fields of knowledge that are relevant.[18]

17. C. West Churchman, Russell I. Ackoff, and Leonard E. Arnoff, *Introduction to Operations Research* (New York: John Wiley and Sons, Inc., 1957), p. 6.

18. Charles J. Hitch and Roland N. McKean, *The Economics of Defense in the Nuclear Age* (Atheneum, New York: Harvard University Press, 1965), p. 108.

In some cases a group of specialists, who each have an intuitive grasp of the relevant factors, may be assembled to aid administration in attaining a clearer understanding of the implications involved in the decision problem.   But even this technique fails to adequately present an objective view of the various trade-offs, benefits and costs of the various alternatives.   This is especially true when dealing with volumes of data and intricate quantitative comparisons.   The value of a formal objective analysis is that it allows the judgement and intuition of the various experts consulted to be *combined* systematically and efficiently.

For example, if we are comparing a ten passenger prisoner transfer vehicle with a twenty passenger vehicle, it is easy to see that the twenty passenger model would be the most efficient, even though more expensive, if the volume and frequency of prisoner transfers was high enough.   There are several implications that should be considered.   How many ten passenger vehicles could be purchased and maintained on the same budget?   How often do loads exceed ten passengers?   Could a combination of both ten passenger and twenty passenger vehicles be purchased, and if so, in what ratio to fit the need *most* efficiently?

In situations where the choice is not simply between two, as illustrated here, but between many, and the data necessary for a "best" or *optimum* solution is voluminous, systematic quantitative analysis is often mandatory.

Efficient allocation or use of resources has always been of prime importance in private industry.   The competitive market forces individual organizations to arrive at optimum methods of production or the most efficient attainment of objectives.   The profit incentive and the necessity of reducing costs in order to compete has encouraged private firms to use formal analysis techniques.

Progress and increased efficiency will develop in the private sector of the economy even without a formal analytical approach.   However, due to a "natural selection" that takes place, certain companies through trial and error, or just plain chance, will stumble upon a more efficient method or technique.   Other companies competing in the same market will either be forced to copy the innovation or be "plowed under" in this process of "survival-of-the-fittest" selection.

Governmental agencies, and in particular police agencies, do not have this built in optimizing mechanism.   Police agencies are not competing with each other for a consumers market.   They are not required to subscribe to the most efficient methods of operation in order to survive as an organization.   The organization and its membership does not suffer in the same way as private firms from a lack of using optimum ways.   This is another reason why some authorities believe that the formal analysis of alternative actions may be especially rewarding in the public sphere.[19]

The Federal Government recognizes the advantages of operating a formal analysis program and now applies the principles of systems analysis in several of its organizations. The U. S. Bureau of the Budget Bulletin #63–3, dated October 16, 1965, has directed the heads of executive departments to introduce the concept of Planning-Programming-Budgeting (PPBS) into their activities. The bulletin states "whenever applicable this effort will utilize systems analysis, operations research, and other pertinent techniques."[20]

The President's Commission on Law Enforcement and Administration of Justice recommended the employment of systems analysis and operations research techniques by police agencies several times in its report.[21] The task force report on the police specifically urged larger departments to set up operations research groups to study the organization of the department, provide technical guidance to the department management, analyze operations, and assess the effects of all experimentation within the department.

> As an important mechanism for innovation within police agencies, it is urged that police departments of 1,000 or more employees establish an operations research group comprising professionally trained scientists, mathematicians and engineers, including at least one person with a broad statistics background, and at least one person with electronics competence.[22]

Those following the history of Federal influence in local matters may recall that urging and suggestions are usually followed by standards and requirements attached to the disbursement of Federal funds to local agencies. The application of systems analysis techniques may well be a future prerequisite to the availability of Federal funds.

EFFECTIVE BUDGETING

The police are not getting their share of governmental expenditures.

19. Roland N. McKean, *Efficiency in Government Through Systems Analysis* (New York: John Wiley and Sons, Inc., 1958), p. 13.

20. Kenneth W. Heathington and Gustave J. Rath, "The Systems Approach in Traffic Engineering," *Traffic Engineering*, June, 1967.

21. Commission on Law Enforcement, Report of the Commission, *The Challenge of Crime in a Free Society* (Washington, D.C.: U. S. Government Printing Office, 1967), pp. 246, 287.

22. Commission on Law Enforcement, Task Force Report, *The Police* (Washington, D.C.: U. S. Government Printing Office, 1967), p. 61.

Police agencies over the past 65 years have received a declining percentage of increasing total government expenditures. In 1902 for example, police agencies were allotted 4.9 percent of total governmental fiscal outlay. In 1962 this figure declined to 3.5 percent. The percentage of governmental allotments to law enforcement continues to decline even though the cost of enforcing the law has risen.[23]

We are competing for a share of the tax dollar. The police task is increasing. More is expected of the police today than ever before, and yet our resources, on a percentage basis are diminishing. The police *must* effectively present their needs to the appropriate agencies.

History indicates that many police agencies have either failed to rationally allocate their funds or demonstrate that they have. Generally speaking, two methods of budgeting have been utilized by governmental organizations prior to the acceptance of the systems analysis approach.

THE PRIORITIES APPROACH

In this approach a more or less "wishing list" is presented with the most desired items at the top of the list. This method of organizing programs or items according to priority or urgency has several fallacies.

First of all, if it means that items or programs are financed from the top of the list until the money is gone, it either rules out an allocation of various percentages of the total budget to all of the items, or it places the decision for such an allocation upon someone outside the concerned department. Should an individual run his personal affairs with a priority list, the results would be interesting indeed. Imagine a list organized as follows: (1) groceries (2) clothing (3) housing (4) transportation (5) medical needs. What would happen if he ran out of money before arriving at item number 5? Would this mean that he would go without medical attention?

Some would propose that a higher percentage of available funds or resources be devoted to items high on the priority list, with lesser percentages allocated to items further down the list. But this too is unrealistic since an item high on the priority list might only cost a few dollars while an item further down may be worth thousands of dollars.

The priority approach does not measure up as a rational means of appropriating funds.

23. Ibid., p. 11.

THE REQUIREMENT APPROACH

This method approaches a given problem by asking the basic question, "What is required to solve the problem or accomplish the goal?" A plan or system is devised to handle the situation and then is subjected to a feasibility test. If the proposed project or system is "feasible," that is, if it can be arranged and handled within a "reasonable" budget, it is adopted. No effort is made to optimize the system.

The feasibility test rules out grossly inappropriate projects or systems but it does not offer an optimum solution, except perhaps by chance.

Suppose a police agency applied this method of selection while purchasing a quantity of cameras for use in field investigative duties. Occasionally there is a need for colored photos. In certain situations the investigator may be required to have immediate access to prints. The needs alone seem to dictate the purchase of a type of polaroid color camera. However, there are many other considerations that should be made. How many more black and white type cameras could be purchased on the same budget? Could a combination of color polaroid and simple instamatic type cameras be purchased to allow for both instant color and simple black and white reproductions according to need; and if so in what ratio?

In short, it is wise to systematically consider the payoffs and costs of all alternative systems or items. A system or item selected on the basis of need alone may pass the feasibility test but fall much short of being the most efficient solution.

PLANNING, PROGRAMMING, BUDGETING SYSTEM

Many police officials would like to be completely divorced from the function of managing their budget. Some argue that planning a budget is not related to the operation of a police agency, and would have other city officials assume this responsibility. Actually the budget is a very integral part of the planning function and should not be separated from it.

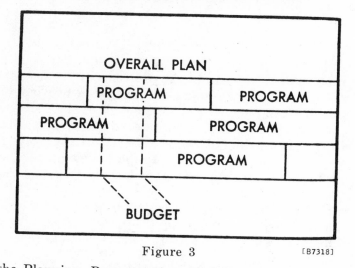

Figure 3   [B7318]

In the Planning, Programming, Budgeting System (PPBS) the budget is appropriately fused in with the overall planning operation (see Figure 3). In this system (PPBS) planning is defined as the establishment of overall goals and objectives, longterm commitments, or the direction the organization is going. Programming has to do with the questions of "HOW." Programming details the components of a plan, the operational schedules, or the *specific* objectives. A program is an activity or set of related activities which produce a common output which is directed toward some particular goal. [24]

Programs within the overall plan have different durations, costs and products.

The budget is a one year slice of the various programs operating within the overall plan. It is actually a translation of programs into fiscal terms for a specific time. Budgets have been defined as plans with a dollar sign attached. As budgets are related to the overall plan and hence the various programs in the plan, individuals responsible for approval of budget requests will be able to logically accept the necessity of requests being made and be more understanding in their appraisals.

In this method of budgeting it is important to analytically relate the reasons that a specific course of action (a program or system) was selected over other alternatives that may have been available. It is important to allow individuals concerned with the costs of programs to be able to follow an orderly, rational process that the administration followed in arriving at the optimal choice of programs. The systems analysis approach fulfills this need.

24. Gustave J. Rath, "Systems Analysis and Design," class lecture, Northwestern University, January, 1968.

LIMITATIONS

At this point one may feel that a panacea has been described that is capable of solving all of the problems of the decision maker. The reader may envision feeding all of his management problems into the "Black Box" and allowing it to make all of the decisions, which will always be the best choice, destined for unfailing success. Of course, this understanding of the role of systems analysis is not a valid one. Systems analysis is an *aid* to the decision maker and not a substitute for him. Its function is primarily to array the various choices before the decision maker in a manner that allows him to compare the costs, results and other implications more realistically. In addition to clearly understanding the proper role of systems analysis, there are other limitations which should be examined.

TESTING DEVICE

Systems analysis may be considered as sort of a testing device. It does not, in itself, manufacture alternatives or even fabricate the best solution. The analyst must determine the scope of the alternatives (it should be recalled, however, that the process often assists the analyst in the generation of alternatives). The decision maker, not the process, must choose the alternative that best fulfills the objectives.

UNMEASURABLE DATA

The model in a systematic analysis deals mainly with quantity and not with quality. The process is limited to working with what can be measured. This poses certain limitations, but does not preclude the assistance of an analysis.

> If the alternatives are arrayed, and a serious attempt made to apply sound criteria in choosing the most efficient ones, decisions are likely to be improved even though the considerations brought to bear are mainly qualitative and intuitive.[25]

In police work, measures of effectiveness may be difficult to express in quantitative terms. For example, the objective of posing a deterrent may have to be expressed in terms of how many arrests will occur. However, even with such a substitute the choice will be facilitated by the system as indicated above.

Decisions at higher levels of the hierarchy within an organization often deal with intangibles and involve quality judgements. In

25. Charles J. Hitch and Roland N. McKean, *The Economics of Defense in the Nuclear Age* (Atheneum, New York: Harvard University Press, 1965), p. 107.

such situations, the definition of a criterion may be particularly difficult and the construction of a model that indicates a *best* decision impossible. However, the use of a model in situations described above will almost always improve the ability of the decision maker to more clearly understand the implications involved and act as an aid even in quality type decisions.

POSSIBILITY OF ERROR

There is always the possibility that the model employed may be in error and therefore predictions obtained from it may be inaccurate. However, one must realize that this possibility exists in practically every human action and particularly when we are planning for the future.

The systems analysis approach has certain limitations. These limitations should be recognized, but should not act as a barrier to prevent the proper applications of a worthwhile technique.

APPLICATION

As previously discussed, the application of systems analysis to the police service should be particularly rewarding. Long range plans and goals should develop as a framework for tying together individual programs. An administrator could experiment with simulated changes of policy, conditions or methods, without the risks inherent in real changes. Organizations could realize the *best* use of manpower and other resources.

In order for a systematic analysis to be relevant, certain characteristics should exist.

1. The objectives of the system should be definable.
2. There should be alternative ways to carry out the task or program.
3. The program, system or whatever is being analyzed should be describable by a model (this may not be readily apparent to one unfamiliar with the technique).
4. Data should be available.
5. There should be room for improvement.

Even the novice will realize that most police systems and programs have these characteristics and should make good subjects of an analysis.

Due to the technical know-how necessary in certain phases of a systematic analysis, it is often necessary to employ or seek assistance from specialists. Most authorities recommend that qualified specialists be included on the research team. Additional help may be solicited from other sources.

. . . for example, certain agencies external to the police may help improve organization, management and operations through research and analysis in collaboration with the police. These include colleges and universities, research institutes, privately funded foundations, and research arms of state criminal justice agencies and the Federal Government.[26]

Although lagging behind private enterprise, governmental agencies are now beginning to apply the principles of systems analysis in their organizations. In 1968 the Chicago Police Department hired an operations research team to work with its own planning unit in optimizing the operations of the Department. The Department is also seeking assistance from systems analysis specialists at the Northwestern University.[27] The Philadelphia Police Department has also recently initiated an operations research project.[28] It is interesting to note that a sizeable portion of both of these programs is being funded by the United States Department of Justice.

The possibilities of the application of the systems analysis approach in police work are practically limitless. Deployment of manpower, purchase and utilization of equipment, and design of overall programs and procedures are just a few of the obvious general applications.

The President's Commission on Law Enforcement and Administration of Justice illustrated the use of systems analysis in its task force report on science and technology. In one example, systems analysis was applied to the task of reducing police response time. Several alternatives were considered including the following:

1. *Public call boxes*—to reduce public access delay
2. *Complaint clerks* —to reduce telephone queue waiting time
3. *Computer control center*—to reduce command and control (including dispatching) time
4. *Automatic car locaters*—to allow for more efficient deployment
5. *Additional one-man police units*—to reduce patrol mobility delay [29]

In this phase of the analysis it was demonstrated that the most attractive alternative, in this case, would be to automate the control

26. Commission on Law Enforcement, Task Force Report, *The Police* (Washington, D.C.: U. S. Government Printing Office, 1967), p. 48.

27. Lt. Walter Valle, private interview held at the Chicago Police Dept., Chicago, Illinois, February, 1968.

28. Philadelphia Police Dept., quarterly progress report, *Operations Research for Crime Prediction*, Philadelphia, 1967. (Mimeographed.)

29. Commission on Law Enforcement, Task Force Report, *Science and Technology* (Washington, D.C.: U. S. Government Printing Office, 1967), p. 11.

center (communication unit) through installation of a computer and other related hardware.

The cost effectiveness phase of the analysis translated dollars allocated into time saved (in terms of seconds) for each of the alternatives considered. The resulting data indicated that automation of the control center would save more seconds of delay per dollar allocated than any of the other systems.

The application of systems analysis and PPBS [30] would allow administrators to experiment with various combinations of men and other resources in attacking an objective. Thus, the operations research team could prepare a model of a particular patrol division, by accumulating data and analyzing its past performance. Perhaps a computer program could be arranged that would simulate the situation and processes involved. Command officers could then feed in different alternatives such as additional men, computerized patrol cars, closed circuit television, computerized dispatching, or different combinations of these, to ascertain which alternative would be most effective. The process could array the various alternatives in terms of their respective costs and projected effectiveness. In other words, the degrees of objective attainment would be shown in terms of cost.

It might develop that in terms of cost effectiveness it would actually be more advantageous to hire only five more officers and equip the entire division with computerized patrol cars rather than hire twenty additional officers.

CONCLUSION

Today, more than ever before, there is a demand for an optimization of all police functions. The increasing task, coupled with diminishing resources, creates a situation that can only be met with the best in law enforcement.

The process of optimizing operations or functions in contemporary police organizations is often difficult and complex. One man rarely has an intuitive grasp of all the information required for selecting the best way. Additionally, there is no built in mechanism in governmental agencies that requires optimization like those inherent in private enterprise. For these and many other reasons, it seems mandatory for today's decision maker to have assistance in gaining insight into the ramifications of the various choices he must make. Systems analysis acts as an aid to the administrator by arraying the different alternatives he must decide between, in a way that allows him to compare the costs with the payoffs. Hence, his job of selecting the best way is facilitated.

---

30. Supra, p. 24, Planning, Programming, Budgeting System.

The police are operating within a society that is experiencing what many scientists refer to as "the knowledge explosion." Man has devised methods and hardware that can assist his own genius in acquiring new knowledge and finding better ways. These advancements in technology and methodology have been used to great advantage by many organizations within our economy. The police should benefit too.

ADDITIONAL REFERENCES

Fredericks, Ward A., "Introduction to Operations Research Techniques," *Physical Distribution Manager Magazine*, January, 1967, pp. 22–28.

Goldman, Thomas A. (ed.), *Cost—Effectiveness Analysis*, Frederick A. Praeger, Inc., New York, Washington, and London, 1967.

Roberts, Edward B., *The Dynamics of Research and Development*, Harper and Row, New York, Evanston, and London, 1964.

CRIMINAL JUSTICE BUDGETING: THE PUBLIC SECTOR CONTEXT *

Criminal justice agencies share with other publically supported agencies the use of tax dollars as their primary source of organizational income. The shared use of tax dollars implies that competition exists among publically supported agencies to secure as much of the tax pie as possible, and it is the budgetary process that plays a central role in determining what the various shares will be.

Criminal justice agencies do not appreciably differ from other publically supported agencies in terms of the basic problems and issues involved in the budgetary process. Furthermore, the centralized power of the legislative and the executive branches to determine agency allocations has meant that numerous uniformities in budgeting procedures have been established for all agencies, whether, for example, police, welfare, sanitation, or fire. The budgetary processes in criminal justice, of necessity, share numerous commonalities with the budgetary activity of other public agencies, and it would thus be a mistake to ignore these commonalities if for no other reason than to maintain a favorable position in the competition for scarce resources.

The discussion that follows places the consideration of criminal justice budgeting within the larger context of the public sector, and is built upon a review of the pertinent conceptual developments in budgeting which have, to a great extent, originated outside the criminal justice community. This is not to suggest that topics of budgeting

* Source: "Criminal Justice Budgeting: The Public Sector Context", an original article by John K. Hudzik, School of Criminal Justice, Michigan State University.

and fiscal administration have been ignored by criminal justice practitioners and theoriticians.   For example, since 1965, when President Johnson ordered the conversion of federal budgetary practices to a planning programming budgeting (PPB) format, there has developed a growing literature relating to the PPB model to criminal justice practices.[1]

At the same time, however, this literature has neglected a systematic treatment of several important underlying issues which touch at the heart of public budgeting in general, and criminal justice agency budgeting specifically.   The purpose of this chapter is to provide an introductory discussion of these underlying issues, with some special references to criminal justice.

DISTINCTIVE FEATURES OF PUBLIC SECTOR BUDGETING:

Budgeting typically encompasses two interrelated operations: the assessment of future or expected income, and the planning of what will be done with that income.   However, budgeting may also be seen as a technique of administrative control, of program evaluation, and of distributing scarce resources.   As such, budgeting becomes a focus for managerial decision making because it provides a common analytical thread by which the three primary functions of management (planning, execution, and evaluation) can be related to one another.   This view implies that the balance sheet, showing items and their costs, or incomes and their sources, is merely a summary of the great deal of budgetary activity preceding it.

Conceptually speaking, the budgetary processes undertaken by private firms and by governmental agencies are similar in the basic concepts described above.   However, important differences exist between the two in the application of these basics.   Perhaps the most important of these differences is that private organizations use profit as a measure for evaluating management decisions, whereas public agencies do not.   The fact is that unlike the private firm, public agencies do not expend resources with the purpose of generating income and subsequent profits.   A police agency does not mount black and white patrols as a means of generating profits for the departmental coffers.   Yet, the encyclopedia salesman has income and prof-

1. For example, Szanton, Peter L., "Program Budgeting for Criminal Justice Systems", *Task Force Report: Science and Technology*, (Washington, D.C., U. S. Government Printing Office, 1967), pp. 83–87.

Leahy, Frank J., Jr., "Planning, Programming Budgeting System", *The Police Chief*, Vol. 35:7 (July, 1968), pp. 16–27.

Hennessy, James J., "PPBS and Police Management", *The Police Chief*, Vol. 39:7 (July, 1972), pp. 62–67.

Hoover, Larry T., "Planning-Programming-Budgeting Systems: Problems of Implementation for Police Management", *Journal of Police Science and Administration*, Vol. 2:1 (1974), pp. 82–93.

it as his primary guiding force and measure of success. There are, of course, exceptions to this distinction on both sides. For example, some police agencies may measure the value of their traffic patrol sections by comparing patrol costs to income produced through ticketing. And as John Kenneth Galbraith suggests, large technocratically controlled firms often supplement their drive for profits with goals related to organizational survival and some pursuance of the public welfare aside from their desire for profit maximization. [2] The fact remains, however, that private firms accrue profits as a means of survival and the pursuance of the public good is used much less as a measure of organizational success than is the attainment of profit.

This fact is both inescapable and unfortunate because the absence of profit as a means for measuring success in public agencies complicates budgetary analyses and program evaluations. Profit is a convenient and relatively simple measurement of effectiveness and efficiency, but measuring the quantity and quality of services rendered by public agencies is a much more difficult way of evaluating expenditures. For example, a large metropolitan police agency may budget millions for a homicide prevention program, but how do we objectively measure the value of this prevention service, even if we can attribute some decline in the homicide rate to the program? How much is a life worth? At what point do expenditures for such a program become too "costly"?

The absence of profit as a measure of effectiveness in public budgeting not only complicates the comparison of dollar return to dollar investment for a single program, but it also complicates comparing the relative merits of expending resources on one program (police, for example) compared to resource expenditures for another program (education, for example). Consider the following view related by Robert Lee and Ronald Johnson:

> "Some further distinctions between private and public sector budgeting provide the rationale for government's undertaking certain functions instead of leaving them to private organizations. Public budgetary decisions, for example, frequently involve allocation of resources among competing programs that are not readily susceptible to measurement in terms of dollar costs and dollar returns. There is no ready means of comparing the net value of a life saved through cancer research and one enemy death on the battlefield; these units simply cannot be equated. The absence of clear-cut measures of profit and loss may be a partial explanation

2. Galbraith, John Kenneth, *The New Industrial State* (Boston, Houghton-Mifflin, 1971).

of why government and not business provides these services." [3]

Many, perhaps most, public service programs cannot be easily equated for purposes of deciding how budget allocations are to be made among them, and many public service programs are intentionally economically inefficient. Few private firms will provide a service that will operate at a loss. Yet society has determined that certain services must be provided to all citizens through public agencies, in part because of a free market economy either will not produce the service or will only offer the service at a rate that only the wealthy can afford. The burgeoning private security field is testimony to the fact that privately funded police services are in demand. Some can afford private security but others cannot, and this inequitable availability of a privately supported service is assumed to speak strongly against any wholesale substitution of publicly supported police service with privately supported security forces.

The public provision of services such as police, corrections, and courts outside the free market pricing mechanism leads to several problems. One of these is to determine if the cost of services rendered meet with public approval. The public exercises no discretion in purchasing such services, they are there and already purchased by virtue of the fact that tax money is allocated to offer the service. This raises one of the most critical questions facing government agencies: In the absence of buyers who have the power not to purchase a service (because all are in effect forced to buy such services) how do government agencies measure the level of demand for their services?

If market pricing and free market buying choices are not exercised, public agencies run a particularly heightened risk of being nonaccountable. Theoretically, private firms are made accountable to the general public in part through the market mechanism and the desire to accumulate profits. Public agencies, especially criminal justice agencies, must measure accountability and be held accountable by other means.

Public budgeting practices originated as a means of holding public agencies and officials accountable. Initially, however, budgetary accountability concerned only whether public funds were being spent for authorized items (legal compliance). Requisition and order forms, personnel position authorizations, quarterly and annual account reports and audits were all developed to ensure that funds purchased proper items. However, the problem developed that such control procedures limited accountability to the input side of public agency

3. Lee, Robert D., Jr. and Ronald W. Johnson, *Public Budgeting Systems,* (Baltimore, University Park Press, 1973), p. 3.

transactions. Inputs may be defined as the objects or resources consumed by an agency; such consumption may be known as costs and expressed in monetary terms. But such measurement and control of inputs alone hardly accounts for the outputs in terms of goods and services delivered by an agency. The problem simply stated is that assuring the proper expenditure of funds does not at the same time guarantee that such expenditures will result in a beneficial delivery of goods and services. For example, although the purchase of twenty new squad cars may be authorized and appropriately purchased, there is no guarantee that these cars will be used efficiently and effectively in the provision of police services.

The necessity of drawing a relationship between inputs and outputs lies at the heart of making public agencies accountable. The response to this accountability dilemma in the public sector has been twofold. First, to maintain accountability within the organization, public agencies have relied heavily on formal rules to guide their personnel, and this may be especially true in police agencies.

> "Bureaus have no direct measures of the value of their outputs, since they cannot engage in voluntary *quid pro quo* transactions. In many cases, members of private firms can shape their behavior on an *ad hoc* basis because they do not need rules to indicate how they can make profits. Similarly, consumers can make spending decisions without elaborate rules, since their own satisfaction provides an immediate guide to the efficacy of their behavior. But whenever there is no clear linkage between the nature of an action and its value or ultimate end, pressure arises for the development of formal rules to help individuals decide their behavior."[4]

The second general response by public agencies to the dilemma of accountability has been to undertake budgetary *cost/benefit analysis*, where costs are the inputs and benefits are the outputs. Cost/benefit analysis involves the construction of ratios comparing the value of inputs to the value of outputs. Budgetary decision making which collects and analyzes input data only, stands no chance of undertaking cost/benefit analysis or of determining the effectiveness and efficiency of resource utilization. Unfortunately, much budgeting in criminal justice today still only considers input data.

Even if both input and output data are collected, however, two analytical problems remain for public agencies in general, and for criminal justice agencies in particular. First, not all outputs are capable of measurement in dollar terms. Borrowing from our previous

4. Downs, Anthony, *Inside Bureaucracy* (Boston, Little, Brown and Company, 1967), p. 59.

example, how does one truly measure the dollar value of lives saved in a traffic enforcement program? Or how do we measure the dollar value of a methadone treatment program? Such questions require an alternative means for quantifying the relationship between costs and benefits. Obviously, costs may still be expressed in dollar terms, but benefits in such cases may only be accurately measured by the amount and kind of goods and services produced (e. g. decrease in Part I crimes, number of complaints cleared, number of offenders successfully reintegrated, decline in juvenile recidivism). The budget ratios between input and output subsequently developed, or *cost/effectiveness analysis*, involve "searching for the lowest cost means of attaining an explicit objective . . ."[5] Thus, where we are unable to attach a dollar value to outputs as in cost/benefit analysis, with this method we compare input costs to the number of outcomes achieved and analyze the unit cost of outcomes (e. g. the dollar cost of successfully rehabilitating each adult drug addict).

The second problem in public budgeting input-output analysis is determining a useful standard for evaluating whether or not costs are acceptable in respect to returns. This problem exists regardless of whether or not we are able to employ cost/benefit analysis. In the absence of profit as a standard, how do we know if costs are acceptable or unacceptable? We may, of course, arbitrarily choose to say that they are acceptable when the dollar return is greater than the dollar costs, but what of the public service program that is intentionally undertaken at a loss? Or, how much money "should" we spend on juvenile programs to decrease recidivism? And ultimately the question will surface: Should we spend more money on adult offender reintegration programs because they may cost only $2,000 per person as compared to juvenile reintegration programs where the costs may be $3,000?

The question of whether public agencies are wisely spending budget resources requires something more than the rationally quantified cost/benefit and cost/effectiveness models of analysis. Indeed, although certain aspects of the budgetary process are always quantifiable, others may never be, for certain decisions will only be reached subjectively, based on value decisions reached in the political arena. The ends or goals of publically funded agencies may ultimately be set by political exigency and there will be limits on how much the budget decision making process relies on a rational, analytical approach to linking expenditures to outputs. Within such subjective limits, however, there is a great deal of room for treating budgeting

5. Haveman, Robert H., "Public Expenditures and Policy Analysis: An Overview", in Robert H. Haveman and Julius Margolis eds., *Public Expenditures and Policy Analysis*, (Chicago, Markham, 1970), p. 6.

as a means of rationally analyzing which goals are possible and what we must do to achieve the goals selected.

THE DEVELOPMENT OF ACCOUNTABILITY THROUGH BUDGETING:

Budgeting, properly conceived and properly undertaken, concerns the analysis of both ends and means. The task that confronts public budgeting is one of devising a system of accountability in respect to ends and means that is also cognizant of the limitations and difficulties caused by the lack of a profit motive and the realities of politics. A functional approach to budgeting will recognize these requirements and limitations. It will, at the same time, serve as a tool of management in reaching decisions.

Budgets rely on the collection of certain critical data that become the elements of analysis. In public budgeting three data elements are critical to effective analysis: (1) resources, (2) activities, and (3) objectives. Resources are the dollars available to an agency translated into the objects or items purchased with these dollars. Dollars purchase buildings, supplies, equipment and personnel, and such resources permit agencies to carry out activities. Activities are the work an agency undertakes and include all tasks, from sweeping out the detention cell to arresting the criminal violator. Activities presumably are undertaken to achieve objectives, and we define an objective as a goal to be attained with respect to some condition of people or the environment.

While these three elements are linked in causal fashion, they are also distinct analytical categories of information or data and should not be confused with one another. The confusion of elements has typically occurred in respect to understanding the difference between activities and objectives. Police departments provide traffic patrol, but traffic patrol is not a purpose or objective of a police agency, but only an activity of it. The purpose of traffic patrol is controlling and reducing accidents. Performing activities produces *outputs* such as road miles patrolled, whereas the achievement of objectives produces *outcomes* such as a decline in the accident rate. The evaluation of outputs represents an attempt to determine whether an agency has performed certain work, whereas the evaluation of outcomes represents an attempt to determine if, and to what degree, agency objectives have been met.

The failure to measure *outcomes* (objectives) leads to incomplete budgetary analysis. Public funds are spent to achieve objectives, not to guarantee police, correctional officers, and others work. Unfortunately, public budgeting, even today, has concentrated on the analysis of resource data and activity data, largely or completely ignoring the gathering and analysis of data on outcomes and objectives. The consequence of this has been to view agency accountability only in terms of the propriety of resource expenditures and the amount of work or activity undertaken. The issue of whether such resource usage and work programs accomplish anything beyond themselves is ignored. The reason for such omission may be traced in part to the historical development of budgeting as a management tool.

Bertram Gross[6], Allen Schick[7] and Nicholas Henry[8] have all characterized the historical development of budgeting in roughly similar fashion, emphasizing a three stage development which gradually shifted analysis from inputs alone to an analysis of the relational aspects of inputs to outputs. The views presented in this chapter concerning the historical developments of public budgeting are roughly parallel to those of these writers.

The first real attempts at public budgeting in this country developed roughly between 1900 and 1921 and were a response to public pressure to control public servants in their use of funds. The budgeting that developed under these pressures was limited to collecting and analyzing resource (input) data. The legislative branch appropriated specified amounts of money to purchase only certain goods and services, and agencies were subsequently audited to determine if their purchases had been authorized through legislative action. This early form of budgeting has been labeled by Allen Schick as control budgeting; more familiarly, it may be known as line-item budgeting in that specific amounts of money were appropriated for certain items. The item categories were general in some instances (personnel, equipment, supplies, etc.) and more highly detailed in others (secretarial, professional, pencils, bullets, etc.). More detailed specifications meant more control, but control and accountability were measured only in terms of resource expenditure. Indeed, such focus leads to little if any consideration of whether an activity is being performed or if objectives are being attained.

The next development in public budgeting was probably forced by Roosevelt's New Deal and the resulting increase in the size of government budgets, and the growth in the number of government agencies and the kinds of services provided. The heyday of laissez faire economics/politics ended with the New Deal, and the philosophy of

6. Gross, Bertram, "The New Systems Budgeting", *Public Administration Review*, Vol. 29 (March-April, 1969), pp. 113–137.

7. Schick, Allen, "The Road to PPB: The Stages of Budget Reform", in Fremont J. Lyden and Ernest G. Miller, eds., *Planning, Programming, Budgeting: A Systems Approach to Management* (Chicago, Markham, 1972), pp. 15–40.

8. Henry, Nicholas, *Public Administration and Public Affairs* (Englewood Cliffs, New Jersey, Prentice-Hall, 1975), pp. 158–183.

active governmental stewardship gained popularity. It no longer seemed sufficient to merely control what resources purchased; rather, resources had to be managed and this meant making agencies accountable not only for their expenditures, but for their work or activity programs as well.

Management or performance budgeting became the successor to control budgeting. The emphasis of this new budgeting form was on whether resources were being spent efficiently, and this meant comparing dollars spent to work performed. Budget data was not only collected on resources but on activities as well. Efficiency comparisons were based on analyses of activity unit costs and budget officers became concerned with matters such as reducing the costs of carrying out specific activities. For example, during budget hearings, a police agency might be asked what the average per mile cost was of patrolling city streets, and why the costs were what they were.

Performance or management budgeting forced a definite change in how public agencies were to be held accountable. Proper expenditure was not the only criteria of accountability; added to it was evaluation of whether expenditures resulted in an appropriate level of work activity and in appropriate activity costs. But a problem still remained: even if resources were expended as authorized, and even if a great deal of work activity was undertaken as a result, there was no guarantee that the work accomplished anything of comparative value.

The need for estimates of accountability in terms of value led to a third development in public budgeting, a development with which we continue to struggle. That development has been labelled PPB, or planning, programming and budgeting. It represents the first serious effort in public budgeting to systematically incorporate data on the attainment of objectives into budgetary analyses. The underlying facet of a planning orientation in budgeting is the connection of present decisions about resource utilization to the attainment of future desirable goals. That is, we develop a plan for using our present resources to attain some future objective. Strictly speaking, a plan requires that we first have a goal in mind and that the means and resources we subsequently choose are dictated by that goal.

The practical effect of public agencies linking resources and activities to goals and objectives is revolutionary. For example, a prison budget would no longer be defended in terms of, "that is what our budget has always been" or "we need that budget to carry out the following activities." Under PPB, the budget justification would be expressed like this: "We need the proposed budget level to do these activities which will help us to achieve these objectives."

Few of us are ever skilled enough to choose the best plan without some consideration of alternative ways to achieve our goals. Indeed, the proper manner of selecting a plan usually proceeds from an analysis of alternative plans at our disposal. Thus, the planning orientation in PPB concerns (1) the linking of means to goals and (2) the analyzing of alternative means to determine which does the best job of achieving our objectives in a cost effective way.

The "programming" portion of PPB refers to the process by which resources, activities, and goals are brought together in a structure or program such as a "welfare program" or a "crime program." Program structures are typically pyramidal with the most general goal at the top and each successive layer less general and more detailed in terms of subgoals, outputs, activities, and subactivities. The lower levels are seen as furthering higher levels, all the way to the top. At a simplified level, for example, motorcycle traffic patrol might be conceptualized as a subactivity of the more general activity of traffic patrol; traffic patrol is an activity meant to further the subgoal or objective of reducing traffic accidents while that subgoal is part of the general police department goal of protecting persons and property. Of course, developing a program structure is, in reality, a great deal more complicated than this. But the critical point exemplified here is that program structure in PPB is meant to explicitly link values to action. Lee and Johnson have succinctly made the point:

> "The purpose is to go from a statement of values that something is deemed good to a statement of fact that activities are contributing to the attainment of that good, to go from nonquantifiable value statements or goals to quantifiable facts relevant to objectives."[9]

It ought to be clear from this discussion of the control, management and PPB budgeting styles that only PPB makes explicit use of all the key data elements of budgeting (i. e. resources, activities, and objectives). But the process of creating a program structure and using it for evaluating agency budget requests and program structure, and program accomplishments is exceedingly complicated, costly, and time consuming. Under PPB a budget officer is not only an accountant who quarterly balances the books. He becomes a policy and a management analyst as well, for under PPB he monitors activity levels and their relationship to resource utilization, and he is intimately concerned with the relationship between program costs and the attainment of program objectives.

The linking of program and financial decision making under PPB leads not only to the most conceptually complete treatment of resources, activities, and objectives, but also raises serious problems

---

9. Lee and Johnson, pp. 161–164.

for budgetary processes, probably because of its attempt at completeness. Presumably under PPB, resources are allocated to programs based on a causal supposition that their use will *cause* some objective to be achieved. Yet, causality is difficult to establish. For example, when a million dollars is appropriated to a Part I crime prevention program, Part I crime decreases. Is there a causal connection? Perhaps, but what if unemployment also decreases during the program period? Is the million dollars the cause or is the drop in the unemployment rate?

Under PPB there is also the great problem of data overload. The dictum to consider all alternative means, their costs and their benefits, their linkages to goals and the like, will require the collection and analysis of great quantities of data by agencies. For this very reason, many budgetary scholars have questioned the practicality of PPB and, indeed, Aaron Wildavsky makes it explicit in *The Politics of the Budgetary Process* that "If you are interested more in being, than in appearing, rational, don't do it!"[10]

One option to considering all alternatives is to consider a limited number, perhaps only the most promising alternatives. Herbert Simon's use of the term "satisficing"[11] represents this limited approach to the analysis of alternatives. The meaning of satisficing may clearly be extended to mean that we search for a satisfactory solution to an agency's problem rather than searching for the optimal one. As related by Charles Lindblom:

> "In the conventional ideal of a rational decision, a decision maker maximizes something—utility or want, satisfaction, income, national security, the general welfare, or some other such value. But, as we have already noted, an exhaustive search for the maximum, for the best of all possible policies, is not usually worth what it costs, and may in fact be impossible of accomplishment. An alternative strategy, therefore, is not to try too hard—to decide instead on some acceptable level of goal accomplishment short of maximization, and then pursue the search until a policy is found that attains that level. One "satisfies" instead of maximizes."[12]

If we take such a limited decision making approach to analyzing alternative means and in setting our objectives, it does not mean, as Wildavsky implies, that we need forsake the basic PPB approach to

10. Wildavsky, Aaron, *The Politics of the Budgetary Process*, (Boston, Little, Brown, 1964), p. 208.

11. Simon, Herbert A., "A Behavioral Model of Rational Choice", *The Quarterly Journal of Economics*, Vol. 69 (February, 1955), pp. 99–118.

12. Lindblom, Charles E., *The Policy Making Process*, (Englewood Cliffs, New Jersey, Prentice-Hall, 1968), p. 24.

budgeting.   Indeed, the only truly basic feature to PPB that we need to keep intact is that planning must link means to ends (or resources and activities to objectives).   Whether we consider all alternatives or only some alternatives is, therefore, less important under a PPB format than is our need to consciously link means to ends.

The thoroughness with which the planning aspect of PPB would be undertaken by an agency depends on the resources (time, skills, and money) available for planning activities.   Some agencies have more such resources available than others and are able to mount more comprehensive PPB type budget planning efforts.   But even where planning resources are extremely limited, it is possible for an agency to undertake some limited PPB approach to budgeting if it is conscious of the need to consider how resources and activities are related to objectives.

This section has concerned development of the key elements in budgetary analysis and their relationship to public agency accountability.   The following points follow from that discussion:

1.   Resources, activities, and objectives are central data elements in budgetary analysis and they are presumed to be linked in causal fashion.   Resources are allocated to agencies to undertake certain work activities and activities are undertaken to accomplish objectives.   Activities are measured as outputs and objectives are measured as outcomes.

2.   When only resource data is collected and analyzed, accountability tends to focus on whether funds are legally spent by agencies.   Agency preparation of the budget takes a balance sheet approach, usually taking last year's appropriation and subtracting or adding dollars to line item categories as the times permit and in terms of what agencies think they can "get away with."

3.   When agencies are held accountable for the level of work activity they undertake with appropriated funds, budgetary accountability begins to emphasize efficiency and performance rather than simple legal compliance in expenditure. Agency budget preparation will include not only filling out forms on line item dollar costs, but also forms asking what and how much activity the agency will undertake as a result.   Justification of budget requests are related to levels of costs for work activities, proposed increases or decreases in those activities, or changes in the costs of carrying out existing service levels.

4.   A budgetary accountability system is most complete when data on the attainment of objectives is related to the expenditure of funds and the undertaking of activities.

Budget forms follow a format of first requesting agencies to list the goals and objectives of their agencies, and then relating funds and activities to outcomes in respect to these objectives. Agency budget requests are justified in terms of measurable objectives to be attained. Increases or decreases in funds are related to the relative priorities assigned to certain objectives, usually by outside powers.

BUDGETING AND MANAGERIAL DECISION MAKING

Managerial decision making encompasses three interrelated functions: (1) program planning, (2) program execution, and (3) program evaluation. These functions should occur in the order listed above; we should have some idea of what we are to do before attempting to do it; and after we have done it, there should be some attempt to assess whether or not we have accomplished what we set out to do. Planning is anticipatory in the sense that we say, "When and if we do X, this or that condition will result". Evaluation, on the other hand, is retrospective in the sense that we learn whether or not our plan anticipated correctly. Evaluation, if conceived properly, supplies feedback data for future planning efforts. Budgeting serves as a linking mechanism among these managerial functions as it can provide a common data analysis framework across all three managerial functions.

It is probably true that how we evaluate a program affects how we plan it. For example, if budget evaluation is limited to issues of legal compliance in expenditures, the emphasis in budgetary planning will usually be on resources and the items to be purchased; data record keeping during the program execution phase will largely be limited to keeping track of what was purchased; data analysis during the evaluation phase will focus on an audit of whether planned and authorized expenditures for items matched actual expenditures.

To exemplify how budgeting can more fully link the three functions of planning, execution and evaluation, it is useful to consider an example where managerial decision making considers data related to resources, activities and objectives. Under such a management orientation, as we have seen, evaluation will focus on how resource utilization is related to the undertaking of activities or work (outputs) and in turn, how it is related to the attainment of objectives (outcomes). Data requirements for such evaluation analyses include information on funds spent, items purchased, work undertaken and impact on intended outcomes. The program plan should be conceptualized in similar categories identifying intended or preferred outcomes, isolating the activities or work that presumably will lead to attainment of objectives, and determining resources required to undertake the work program. During program execution, actual operational data is collected across these same categories and the stage is then set to analyze whether what we presumed would take place did indeed come to pass.

Budgeting conceptualized and undertaken in this fashion *is* managerial decision making and it is the type of decision making that anticipates the need to build in measures of accountability. In the example above, accountability ultimately rests on measurement of outcomes, but it also includes measurement for outputs and of legal compliance in expenditures.

Conceptualizing a managerial approach to budgeting is one thing, but operationalizing it in terms of concrete data collection and analysis is another, and rather difficult. Developing operational measures for resources, activities and objectives, and finding the time and money for agencies to collect the data is far from a simple task. Figure 1 is a hypothetical and limited example showing some of the data categories necessary for a police department's traffic enforcement program. Figure 1 only displays types of data that need collection, it does not make explicit what should be done in collecting and analyzing data on such matters. For example, a question might arise during budget planning concerning how many resources have been applied in the past to motorcycle patrol. Being able to answer this will depend on whether past data collection efforts have identified which of the total resources allotted to the traffic enforcement program (salary costs, equipment costs, maintenance costs, etc.) have been applied to motorcycle patrol. A further question might arise as to what motorcycle patrol actually did as a result of obtaining these resources, and this will mean developing concrete work unit measures. The work units might be road miles patrolled, traffic stops made, NCIC checks undertaken, etc. By itself the term "motorcycle patrol" measures little, but as we develop quantifiable, operational work units associated with the term, we begin to clarify what the activity is and how much of it is taking place. Similar work unit and resource data collected on car patrol would eventually facilitate cost comparisons between motorcycle and car patrol activities. Such comparisons are useful not only for budgeting specifically, but for management decision making in general.

Figure 1

SAMPLE RESOURCES, ACTIVITIES, AND OBJECTIVES
DATA CATEGORIES

Traffic Program Resources	Sample Traffic Program Activities	Sample Traffic Program Target Objectives
Salaries	Motorcycle Patrol	Traffic Deaths
Equipment	Car Patrol	Traffic Injuries
Supplies	Radar Surveillance	Property Damage
Maintenance	Car Safety Inspection	
Training	School & Community Safety Clinics	
	Records Maintenance	
	Program Administration	

[B7261]

Ultimately, both the planning and the evaluation of the Figure 1 traffic program will depend on collecting data on traffic objectives. But actual data collection efforts will require more detail data on the measurement of objectives than is indicated in Figure 1. For example, suppose during the budget planning process the proposal is made to double the number of cars inspected annually. This may mean more resources for safety inspection efforts, but it may also mean reallocating less resources to other traffic activities. Should inspections be double and what effect will it have on the overall objective of decreasing traffic deaths, injuries and property damage? It may have considerable effect if some significant portion of accidents are attributable to equipment failure, but the accuracy of this supposition will rely on data collected in the past on the causes of accidents.

Questions concerning the allocation of scarce resources among competing claims, such as in the example above, strikes to the heart of the relationship between budgeting and managerial decision making. Budgeting is concerned with allocating scarce resources and so is management. Both rely on an effective identification of problems to be addressed and on some preliminary understanding of either the causes of the problems or of how to deal with them.

The allocation of resources to carry out certain activities implies that two very important decisions have been reached: (1) carrying out the activity will have a favorable impact on the target problem or objective and (2) the target objective is relatively worth attacking in that manner. In the example concerning doubling the inspection program, the problem or objective it seeks to attack (traffic deaths, injuries and property damage) may or may not be served better by such a move. What if, for example, less than one percent of all accidents are attributable to equipment failure while over 30 percent are attributable to alcohol intoxication. Doubling the inspection program may not have as much effect on the total traffic problem as spending those resources on a new program to detect and dispose of the drunken driver.

The kinds of managerial questions and decisions above require data for resolution and a great portion of that data must be collected at its source. This is particularly true for activity data where actual knowledge of tasks performed and the time and resources it takes to do them is best recorded by the individuals doing the activity. Log books, dispatch records and the like can serve such data collection functions in police agencies, but the problem has been that many of these departments do not centrally aggregate such activity data in order to draw an accurate map of departmental activities. Part of the reason this is not done is due to the complicated nature of activity and task analysis, as well as the data management costs themselves. But such problems need to be overcome if departments are ever to draw a clear picture of the costs of their activities.

It has been noted that a complete budget planning process will consider at least all likely alternatives for pursuing a given objective. Such a requirement further complicates the time and resource costs of collecting the kinds of necessary data discussed above. The mix of activities to be undertaken is not a given in the planning process, and ideally the relative cost/benefit data should be collected on a great many of them before a specific alternative for activity and resource mix is chosen. The burden of such calculations has often been lightened as a practical matter by agency analysts considering only incremental adjustments in program mixes in any given year.[13] By considering only portions of the entire agency program in any given budget year, data analyses of only certain alternatives, concerned with limited aspects of agency activity, need to be dwelled upon.

There is, of course, always the possibility that managerial approaches to cost/benefit analysis will lead to the decision that certain objectives are either unattainable or too costly to be pursued. This may especially be true under a PPB approach to budgeting where both initial planning and future evaluation are intimately concerned with the attainment of objectives, rather than merely with the efficient performance of work or legal compliance in the expenditure of funds. Thus, the consideration of action alternatives in meeting objectives may, after analysis, conclude with the decision not to ex-

13. Lindblom, Charles E., "Incremental Decision-Making", in Robert T. Golembiewski and Jack Rabin, eds. *Public Budgeting and Finance: Readings* *in Theory and Practice*, (Itasca, Illinois, F. E. Peacock, 1975), pp. 161–162.

pend resources to carry out certain activities because the objectives will not be attained. Such a decision may mean terminating a program, even though resources will be legally spent and even though a great deal of work will be accomplished.

When there is the possibility of program termination for reasons of failure to meet objectives, we begin to approach the kind of accountability parallel to the concerns raised earlier in this chapter. But if the general public exercises little actual discretion in determining whether public services and goods are produced, then we are faced with the unpleasant task of insisting that the public producers themselves exercise such discretion. The accomplishment of this requires two things: (1) that public agencies develop mechanisms that determine when programs should be terminated, and (2) that when termination is indicated, it happens. The first is easier to accomplish than the second.

Zero Base Budgeting (a variant of PPB) has been offered by some as an answer to the problem of resistance to termination, and certainly President Carter's 1976 campaign did much to popularize this notion. Traditionally, agency budget requests for next year are considered in terms of minor adjustments to the present year's budget. Under zero base budgeting, however, the existing budget offers no base, and theoretically, agency managers must justify all fund requests afresh each year. The process of justification involves the identification of agency programs and purposes and the attachment of price tags to each program. The agency then prioritizes the relative importance of its various programs and a budget is proposed beginning with the costs of the most important program and then adding on the costs of the next most important program and so forth.

The problem is, however, that zero base budgeting will not itself necessarily lead to much change with respect to legislative and executive review of budget requests. A zero base approach only details specific programmatic costs and the relative agency assigned priorities given these programs. There is nothing in the process itself to require significant reductions or additions to established budget base levels.

The decision to terminate or drastically alter an agency's authorization level carries heavy political overtones, and it will ultimately fall to political institutions to reach such decisions. The only thing accomplished under a zero base format is to remove the idea of a necessarily "safe" budget base regardless of justification, and it places agency administrators on notice that all expenditures must be yearly rejustified. This difference can be immensely important but only if political decision makers take proper notice of inappropriate or nonsupportable justifications.

BUDGETING AND EVALUATION

Traditionally, the preparation of the next year's budget request has depended on a firm understanding of budgets for the present and past years. Indeed, it is probably a matter of reality that even under a PPB format, budget authorizations for future years will closely parallel previous patterns of authorization. Thus, executive and legislative approval will start (and may end) with a review of present appropriation levels. This kind of approach to budgeting introduces a strong conservative bias against any large scale change from one year to the next, and we are all familiar with the popular dictum that public programs, once started never terminate.

The bias toward resisting large scale change in any one year hardly means that significant change does not take place in agencies over a longer period. However the movement toward change, whether radical or incremental, the need for evaluation of proposed agency budgets and evaluation of past agency expenditures and accomplishments is hardly questionable.

At base, any budget evaluation effort should be concerned with determining the appropriateness and adequacy of agency programs. Indeed, the first step in evaluating an agency budget request (or the first step for an agency preparing its request) ought to be consideration of the appropriateness of target objectives selected and of the adequacy with which these target objectives are to be pursued by the agency. The measurement of appropriateness is a value laden process for it involves determining the relative value of choosing one objective over another. The process of choosing is, of course, made simple in those cases where we know certain objectives cannot be attained no matter what we do. Expending resources on the attainment of these objectives is ludicrous and we presumably eliminate them from consideration. There are, however, few such easy cases. Typically, public agencies are confronted with a myriad of potential objectives and subjectives that all could be pursued except that resources are limited and choices and priorities must be set.

Strictly speaking, determinations of appropriateness rely on setting priorities, which is largely a political process not readily amenable to objective, value-free determinations. Agencies must face the fact and take as given that they are not free to decide which objectives are appropriate to undertake. Some objectives are mandated by legislation, others are informally mandated by the vote swapping that takes place during the budget approval sessions with the executive and legislative committees, and only a few objectives are set by agency inhouse determinations of what is appropriate or what is needed.

The measurement of adequacy will, of course, influence what we come to accept as an appropriate objective. For example, in the absence of our ability to adequately enforce alcohol prohibition, it is quite probable that this nation decided that it was an inappropriate objective to pursue with public funds. "Ideally, objectives are oriented toward [total] elimination of the problem . . . but various constraints may necessitate reducing the scope of an objective from focus on complete solution of a problem to a more modest scope of reducing a problem by a specific amount. . . ." [14] If we have made the determination that, relatively speaking, an objective is appropriate, the next question asks whether what we are able to do is enough to make doing anything at all worthwhile.

Determinations of adequacy are only partially value-free processes. We can make objective determinations of the cost/effectiveness ratios of pursuing some objectives. For example, we can hypothesize, or know from previous experience, that an annual expenditure of a million dollars on stepped-up foot patrol in the downtown business area will reduce breaking and entering (B & E) there by 20 percent. But is this an adequate "return" for the expenditure involved? Perhaps we might answer yes if that 20 percent decrease represents something over a million dollar decrease in property loss. Or perhaps the answer may be yes if the stepped-up foot patrol results in increased consumer confidence concerning their personal safety in shopping the downtown area, thereby increasing commerce. Of course, the problem may still remain that we have not really reduced crime, but have merely displaced it to the suburbs.

As we have seen, however, measuring return is rarely so simple and will be made even more complicated when scarce resources must be allocated in respect to politically competing program demands. Perhaps spending the million dollars on new intelligence and S.W.A. T. units will successfully reduce terrorist activities by 40 percent. Is the return on such units more or less adequate than the B & E program return? Even if the dollar value return of decreasing terrorist activities is half that of the B & E program, the public hue and cry may insist on terrorist control expenditures instead of increased foot patrol. Thus, the definition of "adequate" may often depend on political factors having little to do with quantifiable cost/effectiveness or cost/benefit analysis.

If budget allocation evaluation begins with essentially subjective determinations of program appropriateness and adequacy, what is left that may be evaluated relatively objectively? In taking a composite of themes frequently encountered in the evaluation literature, five

14. Deniston, O. Lynn, Irwin M. Rosenstock, William Welch and V. A. Getting, "Evaluation of Program Effectiveness and Program Efficiency", in Lyden and Miller, footnote 7, p. 142.

major concepts of evaluation emerge as most important.[15] They include:

1. *Effort Evaluation*: The determination of what an agency did in terms of resource expenditure and activities undertaken, and a comparison of that to a norm such as what the agency promised to do or was authorized to do with respect to resources and activities.

2. *Efficiency Evaluation*: The determination through cost/benefit or cost/effectiveness ratios of the unit cost of activities undertaken and/or the costs of attaining objectives.

3. *Effect Evaluation*: Determinations of what objectives (outcomes or end products) have been achieved as a result of agency programs, and the comparison of that to a norm.

4. *Impact Evaluation*: Determination of what portion of the total problem under attack was successfully attained by the program outcomes or effects.

5. *Process Evaluation*: Determination of whether the effects produced are causally attributable to the program.

Effort and efficiency evaluation are the most easily undertaken because they are relatively susceptible to concrete quantitative measurement. A post-evaluation of agency effort, for example, can fairly easily establish (assuming the data has been collected) whether funds have been spent as authorized and whether activity was undertaken as specified in an agency's budget proposal. Such an evaluation would produce findings related to dollars spent and items purchased (*financial audit*), activities undertaken (*activities audit*), and activity unit cost data (*performance audit*).

Effect, impact, and process evaluation are much more difficult to determine and in some instances they are literally impossible to do. All three of these forms of evaluation require accurate data collection concerning the attainment of objectives. Collecting such data is particularly problematic in criminal justice because outcomes are frequently measured in terms of effects on crime rates, and our existing

---

15. For example, Struening, Elmer L., and Marcia Guttentag, eds. *Handbook of Evaluation Research*, Volumes I & II, (Beverly Hills, Sage, 1976).

Hatry, Harry P., Richard E. Winnie and Donald M. Fisk, *Practical Program Evaluation for State and Local Government Officials*, (The Urban Institute, 1973).

Sudman, E. A., *Evaluation Research: Principles and Practices in Public Service and Social Action Programs*, (New York, Russell Sage Foundation, 1967).

Weiss, C. H., *Evaluation Research: Methods of Assessing Program Effectiveness*, (Englewood Cliffs, New Jersey, Prentice-Hall, 1972).

crime rata data has been shown to be suspect as a result of the advent of victimization studies.[16]

Even if we are able to collect accurate effect and impact data, we must be careful to separate those effects attributable to program activities from those effects caused by other forces. Deniston, et al., in a discussion of effectiveness, defines planned objective as, "the net attainment desired less the status that would have existed in the absence of the program."[17] Many public programs are not the only forces actively working in a given problem area. Insofar as these other forces may be presumed to have some effect on the problem, their effects must be separated from the effects attributable to the program under evaluation. During the course of a new traffic enforcement program, for example, accidents may drop 20 percent, but new, lower speed laws initiated at the same time may account for the great majority of that decline. Planning for a net effect and measuring the net effect obtained would require making some attempt at determining what the lower speed limit itself accomplished.

Determining what causes what is the domain of process evaluation. Establishing causality remains one of the most difficult undertakings in research for although it is a relatively easy chore to determine whether two variables covary with one another, it is quite another matter to determine if, and to what degree, one variable influences another. The problem is to determine "whether there is an inherent link between the independent variable and the dependent variables (e. g., resources/activities and objectives) or whether it is based on an accidental connection with some associated variable." [18]

Public programs in particular must not be too quick to assume that measurable effects are necessarily attributable to program activities. They may well be, but a minimally adequate process evaluation would require considering whether non-program related events were at least likely to have affected the problem area.

Making public agencies accountable must ultimately focus on effect, impact and process evaluation if we are to measure whether agency programs are producing anything of value beyond creating jobs for agency personnel. And whether an agency budgets under a control, management, or PPB format will, to a large degree, determine which forms of evaluation are attempted or undertaken either by the agency itself, or by outside review agents such as comptrollers, budget bureaus, legislative committees, etc. (See Figure 2)

16. Kalish, Carol B., *Crimes and Victims: A Report on the Dayton-San Jose Pilot Survey of Victimization*, LEAA, U. S. Department of Justice, (Washington D.C., U. S. Government Printing Office, June, 1974).

17. Deniston et al., p. 157.

18. Rosenberg, Morris, *The Logic of Survey Analysis*, (New York, Basic Books, 1968), p. 28.

Figure 2

THE RELATIONSHIP OF BUDGETING AND EVALUATION FORMATS

Evaluation Formats

	Effort	Efficiency	Effect	Impact	Process
Control	X				
Management	X	X			
PPB	X	X	X	X	X

[B71194]

As indicated in Figure 2, control budgeting will usually focus formal evaluation inquiry on effort only and many times only on resource expenditure rather than activity undertaken. This is not surprising as the data collected under a control budget format is usually limited to records of expenditures. In the absence of activity and objective data, none of the other forms of evaluation can take place.

Management budgeting will, however, usually collect activity data in addition to resource data, thereby allowing (but not guaranteeing) that effort evaluation may extend to work activity. Management budgeting further allows for the limited form of efficiency evaluation that relates costs to activity. The problem is that neither control nor management formats, as defined here, collect data on objectives. Thus, both methods largely limit formal evaluation efforts to internal organizational happenings. Such evaluation of internals is hardly sufficient to determine public agency accountability in terms of what should finally be measured, namely, what the agency does to or for the external public.

Therefore, it is perhaps useful to categorize the five major evaluation types into two groups: (1) the evaluation of internal, enabling matters (i. e. effort and efficiency) and (2) the evaluation of external, goal achievement matters (i. e. effect, impact and process). Insofar as resources and activities enable the attainment of objectives, the evaluation of them unto themselves (Group 1), is merely an operation of determining to what extent and how well the stage has been set to perform a public service.

A complete preevaluation of public agency budget requests should usually involve a review of both prior budgets and the budget request itself, with a view in the first instance toward establishing what the agency's track record has been and how the request for the new budget relates to that history. How the track record looks may do much in determining how friendly a reception the budget request receives. Depending on the budget format employed, and on the modes of evaluation chosen, an agency with unexplained high unit costs, with a reputation for "luxury" purchasing, and with a poor track record in terms of objectives attained may well find its budget proposal under a great deal more scrutiny than if its past record had been more enviable.

Evaluation of a proposed budget may best be described as those review activities that attempt to assess whether management's plan is likely to be achieved in reality. The process by which such evaluations arrive at their conclusions is always part guesswork and is based on estimations of probability or improbability about an agency's ability to accomplish the objectives it says it will. But if some part of the evaluation of the plan is guesswork, some part of it is also based on rational analysis.

Rational appraisal of a budget request considers any or all of the following: (1) Are resource requests linked to specific activities such that the carrying out of the proposed activity is dependent on the resource package? (2) Is the action/work program given reasonable linkage and relationship to a specific problem and objective under attack? (3) Can the agency efficiently carry out its intended work program? This is especially important where proposed budgets request a large increase over the previous year, for there may be some question appropriately raised concerning time and personnel skill requirements in either initiating a new program or in significantly increasing the size of an existing one. (4) What is the agency's track record in carrying out activity, spending resources, and being able to project its attainment of objectives? (5) Are the identified objectives of high enough priority to warrant the expenditure of public funds?

The evaluation of a budget period completed (audit-evaluation) asks similar questions to those posed during the evaluation of a budget request. The difference is that the former can rely on concrete data for answers while the latter cannot. The evaluation of a completed budget period uses data on resources spent, activities undertaken, and objectives attained and the data exists as a matter of fact rather than conjecture. The basic questions for an audit-evaluation of a budget completed fall into three audit groups.

Audit Group 1—The determination of the degree to which the agency plans for resource utilization, activities to be undertaken, and objectives to be met were achieved in the course of program implementation.

Audit Group 2—The determination of the relationships among resources, activities, and objectives which resulted from program implementation.

Audit Group 3—A Comparison of Audit Group 2 relationships to some norm such as the implicit or explicit relationships proposed in the agency plan.

Figure 3

FORMS OF BUDGET AUDIT–EVALUATION

Elements Compared [19]		Minimal Budget Format Required	Audit Group	Evaluation Form
Resources Expended	Resources Authorized	Control	1	Effort
Activities Accomplished	Activities Anticipated	Management	1	Effort
Net Attained Objectives	Net Planned Objectives	PPB	1	Effect
Net Attained Objectives	Prior Level of Problem	PPB	1	Impact
Resources Expended	Activities Accomplished	Management	2	Efficiency
Resources Expended	Net Attained Objectives	PPB	2	Efficiency
Activities Accomplished	Net Attained Objectives	PPB	2	Efficiency
Resources *Expended* Activities Accomplished	Resources *Proposed* Activities Proposed	Management	3	Efficiency
Resources *Expended* Net Attained Objectives	Resources *Proposed* Net Proposed Objectives	PPB	3	Efficiency
Activities *Accomplished* Net Attained Objectives	Activities *Proposed* Net Proposed Objectives	PPB	3	Efficiency

19. Deniston *et al.*, pp. 157–162 provided me the original idea-model for comparing the data elements in this fashion.

Process evaluation, although not specifically mentioned in Figure 3, uses as its initial data base the forms of audit-evaluation listed in Figure 3. These data are a starting point for assessing what effects may be attributable to program expenditures and activities. But the heart of process evaluation involves much more than the relatively simple comparisons envisioned by Figure 3; process evaluation is a research methodology for adequately controlling for extraneous variables, and thus must include data that is only indirectly associated with agency functionings.

It is also important to note that Figure 3 audit-evaluations provide an important data base for making determinations about an agency's track record, and that these kinds of determinations will enter into the evaluation of the agency's budget request. Additionally, Audit Group 2 comparisons, with some reshaping of the elements (for example, resources requested/activities planned rather than resources expanded/activities accomplished) can offer a model for undertaking some specific evaluations of budget requests.

BENDING THEORY TO MEET CURRENT REALITY

Will Rogers once quipped that "a budget is a mythical bean bag. Congress votes mythical beans into it, and then tries to reach in and pull real beans out." PPB, as it stands now, is in a kind of mythical bean bag, because most state and local agencies lack the data and skill necessary to effectively budget under a PPB orientation. Collecting accurate data on resources, activities, and objectives, and then properly analyzing the relationships of these data sets is the most immediate problematic aspect of PPB. Although Wildavsky may ultimately be right that planning will cause data overload, the problem for most state and local criminal justice agencies may at the moment be data underload in the sense of collecting the wrong kinds of data in the first place.

The reality of criminal justice budgeting at the state and local level is that few viable PPB models are in operation. The reasons for this are many and complicated running from simple political and bureaucratic resistance on the one hand, to the lack of skilled personnel and funds to effectuate a PPB system on the other. Many, perhaps most criminal justice agencies at these levels operate under a budgeting format that is essentially line-item in nature. Under such realities there is little hope that PPB will be a pervasive, formal requirement of budgeting at the state and local levels in the foreseeable future. And even in those states and localities where some PPB format is ostensibly adopted, only a few of them will pass beyond the form and into the substance of a PPB approach to resource allocation.

The first effective step toward PPB, that of budgeting in programmatic terms, is yet to be taken by most local agencies. Line item budgeting perpetuates the view that resources are allocated to organizational divisions, units, bureaus, etc. in terms of major account categories like personnel, equipment and supplies. A far more relevant approach in terms of beginning the process of making public agencies ultimately accountable would be adoption of the view that resources are allocated to programs, and only incidentally to organizational units or to account categories. Such a programmatic orientation represents a functional approach to budgeting rather than a structural approach since the analysis of resource allocation centers about program purposes rather than agency structure. A programmatic orientation leads to the analysis, aggregation, and categorization of resources expended and activities undertaken in terms of program objectives pursued.

As a practical matter, agency personnel must become familiar with a programming approach to budgeting before they may be expected to analyze program alternatives. Thus, introducing the programming portion of PPB into an agency before introducing the planning portion is a meaningful and necessary first step. It is also a matter of practicality that the planned consideration of alternatives begins with the status quo or at least with some understanding of it. Change is usually forced by dissatisfaction with the way things are, but we must have some idea of "the way things are" if for no other reason then to avoid them in the future. We must, in other words, know what we are spending on programs before we may effectively analyze alternative modes of allocation to programs.

Programmatic budgeting, as distinguished from PPB, sets limited goals for itself. Its main concern is to relate resource expenditures (costs) to programs and not to line item expenditures. Also, programmatic budgeting is less concerned than PPB with analyzing alternatives and more concerned with determining what we are doing or propose to do in allocating resources to obtain objectives.

There is a problem in measuring such allocations, however, as program costs may not be easily aggregated. Typically, there is no one-to-one relationship between organization units and organizational goals. A specific objective (e. g. crime suppression) may be pursued by several agency units (e. g. patrol division, communications division, etc.). Thus, we may not assume that certain objectives are assigned to certain units only. Likewise, we may not assume that all of the resources accorded an agency subunit are applied simultaneously to pursue crime prevention through visibility and criminal apprehension through availability.

For example, one of the functions (programs) of law enforcement agencies may be taken to be maintenance of public order and this function may be subdivided to include, in part, civil disturbances, civil defense, parades and special events coverage, etc. Several departmental units will participate in fulfilling such functions but rarely will maintenance of public order, as defined above, be their only function. Black and white patrol units may, for example, periodically be on parade duty instead of fulfilling their "normal" function of patrolling for the specific purpose of crime prevention and criminal apprehension. Yet, while on parade duty, a programmatic approach to budgeting would dictate that man hours and materials used by the black and white units be taken as a cost and activity of maintaining public order rather than as a cost and activity of crime prevention or criminal apprehension specifically. Thus, in moving from line item to programmatic budgeting, we do not assume that a unit budget is synonymous with the costs of a single program area; rather, we assume that the costs of running most units of an agency must be divided among several programs and their associated activities.

Solving these problems in aggregating costs programmatically is one of the keys to more effective budgeting and management. And it is, by itself, a useful first step in more effective budgeting for two reasons. First, it helps to locate expenditure overlap and duplication, which is often hidden or ignored under line item and even management or performance budgeting. Second, and most important, it helps aggregate "total" program costs thereby eventually facilitating our understanding of what certain programs and their explicit or inherent objectives cost.

These advantages to programmatically aggregating costs are not limited to individual agencies but rather conveniently spread to the centralized budgetary agencies at local, state, and federal levels. Indeed, as pointed out by numerous writers, the link between appropriations and organizational units is typically crosswalk under programmatic budgeting; that is, revenues appropriated for certain programs will be found in several agencies whether we plan it that way or not and programmatic budgeting recognizes such crossing of organizational lines. Recognizing such budgeting linkage is the first step toward facilitating interagency cooperation in a given program area.

Aside from these two concrete benefits, programmatic budgeting will offer many agencies a first step toward familiarizing personnel with the need to begin thinking how resources and activities are related to program objectives. In accomplishing this, agencies begin to assemble the kind of data and skill pool that later may be used in accountability evaluation as well as in subsequent efforts at more effectively allocating public resources.

WRESTLING WITH POLICE CRIME CONTROL PRODUCTIVITY MEASUREMENT *

INTRODUCTION

Productivity is generally defined as the amount of output obtained for a given amount of input. The classic private-sector productivity measurement, that of identifying a single physical output and dividing it by the number of man-hours expended to give units per man-hour, is hardly adequate, however, for measuring such government services as police crime control activities. This report discusses a number of alternatives that have been proposed to improve police crime control productivity measurement.[1]

No one is likely to be fully satisfied by any of these approaches. Nor, I would guess, will there ever be an approach that is fully satisfying to any large number of government officials or citizens. However, my assumption is that even limited measurement improvement would help. Ultimately, individual governments will have to decide for themselves whether the added information that can be obtained is worth the added effort and resources required to obtain it.

USES FOR PRODUCTIVITY MEASUREMENT

Former Secretary of Commerce Peter G. Peterson said in 1972 that productivity improvement without productivity measurement is not possible. At the time Mr. Peterson was chairman of the National Commission on Productivity. Mr. Peterson's statement may seem extreme to many; however, he was pointing to the difficulty of knowing whether any improvement has indeed been achieved and knowing where to direct one's attention if one does not have adequate productivity measurement. A number of general uses for productivity measurement can be identified:

1. By identifying current levels of productivity, measurement can indicate the existence of particular problems.

2. When productivity is measured over time, measurement can indicate the progress or lack of progress in improving productivity.

* Source: Hatry, Harry P., "Wrestling with Police Crime Control Productivity Measurement", in *Readings on Productivity in Policing*. Edited by John F. Heaphy and Joan L. Wolfle, Washington, D.C.: © The Police Foundation 1975.

1. The works named in References 1, 2, 6, 21, 24, 26, 29, 30, 33, 40, 44, 46, 49 and 53 have been quite helpful in formulating this discussion. In addition, the following have provided helpful comments in reviews of previous drafts: Peter Bloch, Phil Shaenman, and Al Schwartz of the Urban Institute; John Quinn of the International Association of Chiefs of Police; and John Heaphy and Joseph Lewis of the Police Foundation. Of course, the opinions expressed here are solely the responsibility of the author.

3. When collected by geographical areas within a jurisdiction, productivity data can help identify areas in particular need of attention.

4. Measurement can serve as a basis for evaluating specific activities. Measurement may indicate activities that need to be modified or personnel who need special attention, e. g., training.

5. Measurements of existing productivity can provide agencies with the information necessary to set productivity targets. Actual performance can subsequently be compared to the targets to indicate degree of accomplishment.

6. Performance incentives for both managerial and nonmanagerial employees might be established. Many communities have recently been trying out various aspects of management by objectives (MBO), program budgeting, and the like. The various productivity measurements would become inputs into such procedures. (The City of Orange, in a recent controversial experiment, has linked future salaries to selected reported crime reductions.) By utilizing a larger number of the productivity measurements presented later and not relying solely on such measurements as reported crime rates, it may well be that performance incentives could be placed in a reasonably comprehensive perspective and maintain public credibility.

7. Measurement of data can be used for in-depth productivity studies on ways to improve specific aspects of productivity.

8. Productivity measurement information can be a major way to account for government operations to the public. Accountability is becoming of growing concern and refers not only to the legal use of funds but also to the broader question of what is actually being accomplished by government operations.

Any productivity improvement program will need a productivity measurement component, both to help guide where productivity improvement is needed as well as to evaluate how successful the improvements have been.

While productivity measurement thus has many uses, it should be recognized that it is not an end in itself. By itself, productivity measurement will not tell a government what is wrong or what should be done to improve the situation. It exists to help guide government in its productivity improvement efforts.

WHAT IS MEANT BY PRODUCTIVITY IN
POLICE CRIME CONTROL?

Defining the output or product of police crime control is a major problem. As noted in the introduction, for most public sector services (and certainly for police activities), what is meant by output or product can take many different forms. At least five police functions can be identified.

1.　There is general agreement that one output of crime control activity should be reduced crime. Thus, preventing or deterring crime is a principal police function. However, it is also clear—and has been said many times before—that police activity is only one of many factors (including demographic and economic conditions) affecting the amount of crime in a community. In addition, the courts, the prosecutor's office, corrections agencies, various social service programs, and other government activities also have important roles in crime reduction. Nevertheless, the police seem to share this important responsibility. By raising the probability of apprehension and by arresting criminals who are subsequently removed (at least temporarily) from the opportunity for subsequent crime, the police presumably contribute to reduced crime.[2]

2.　A related police function is helping to maintain a feeling of security in the community.

3.　A third major function of the police is to apprehend the persons responsible for crimes.

4.　In addition, the police have non-crime-related functions, such as traffic law enforcement and emergency response to non-crime citizen problems. (Handling of family quarrels is considered here to be a crime-related activity—as a means to prevent future crimes, as well as, in some cases, apprehension of offenders, maintenance of security, and the reduction of severity of the incident.)

5.　In the process of undertaking these functions, performance qualities become important. It is generally agreed that police services should be provided rapidly and in a fair, courteous, and honest manner while avoiding undue harassment and false accusation of innocent persons. These latter characteristics should apply to the treatment of victims, witnesses, bystanders, and offenders.

2.　Since there is little formal "proof" as to this and related assumptions, and since skeptics can point to such evidence as the recent Kansas City Preventive Patrol Experiment, which suggests that routine patrol car preventive patrol may not make much of a contribution to crime prevention (see Reference 25), I will avoid expressing complete certainty about the ability of the police to help in this role. Nevertheless, it is certainly a product that the public hopes will, at least partially, come from police activity, and therefore it should be a subject for measurement.

Productivity measurement in the private sector generally involves the use of a physically identifiable item as the unit of output to be related to the amount of man-hours or dollars of input.[3] The closest analogy in police services is probably the number of calls responded to by police related to the number of police man-hours. However, few have seriously suggested such a measure as being a major indicator of police productivity. This is because (a) there are many different types of calls, varying from calls about major crimes in progress to calls for assistance in getting into a locked car; (b) mere response to a call says little about what the police were actually able to accomplish by their response; and (c) responding to calls is only one part of police activity. Nevertheless, for some specific police activities, some of the more traditional types of productivity measures have been used such as the number of cases of a certain type handled per investigative man-hour, or the number of fingerprints processed per man-hour (if a jurisdiction has enough such work to make this meaningful). These primarily address the efficiency with which a certain activity is performed.

An important issue in public sector service productivity measurement is whether the term *productivity* should be used to encompass effectiveness (the extent to which the service is accomplishing its purposes) as well as efficiency (the extent to which it is undertaking its activities at minimum cost in resources). For the police crime control function, there seems to be general implicit agreement that governments cannot talk productivity without discussing the effectiveness of the service. But effectiveness, as will be discussed later, is almost never presented in the form of a ratio of output to input, as is the classical productivity measure. The position is taken here that this is primarily a definitional problem, not one of substance. In talking about productivity measurement, effectiveness and efficiency need to be considered jointly. The specific meaning of this and how it might be done will be illustrated in the following sections.

This paper will not examine the measurement of traffic control productivity (which involves not only the police but also such other government activities as traffic engineering, signs and signals, and even street maintenance and construction). Nevertheless, since traffic control and crime control activity may be undertaken by the same police officer, this does cause problems for police crime control productivity measurement. This is discussed later under Input Measurement Problems.

3. But even in the private sector quality issues are handled, if at all, with great difficulty.

WHOSE PRODUCTIVITY SHOULD BE MEASURED?

This is a basic question which must be considered in police productivity measurement. The following levels of concern can be distinguished:

1. The productivity of the individual police officer (or individual police employee, civilian or sworn).

2. The productivity of police units, such as shifts, police districts, neighborhood policing teams, or precincts.

3. The productivity of particular kinds of units, such as motorized police, foot patrols, investigative units, special tactical strike forces, canine corps, etc.

4. The productivity of the police department as a whole.

5. The productivity of the crime control system, including both police activities and private activities to reduce crime.

6. The productivity of the total community criminal justice system, including the police, the courts, the prosecutor's office, corrections and social service agencies, and private sector crime prevention activities (such as use of locks, watch dogs, etc.).

In one way or another, a community is concerned with the productivity of each of these. However, each interest group in a community —citizens, city council, mayor or city or county manager, police chief, police division heads, police employees and their associations—will have different priorities. The choice of viewpoint(s) desired by a local government will affect the set of productivity measurements that is needed. Some of the different perspectives are as follows:

- Measurements of the proportion of police time spent on "non-productive" activities are likely to be of considerably more interest and use to police department managers and employees than to citizens, who are likely to be considerably more concerned about crime rates in their neighborhoods.

- City or county officials are likely to be most interested in the productivity of the crime control system, or the total criminal justice system (although in the latter case their interest will be tempered by their lack of responsibility for the courts, prosecution, and where controlled by a different level of government, the correctional systems).

- For higher local government management levels and the council and public it probably is most important to be concerned with, on one hand, the combined effectiveness of the police operations, and secondarily, of groups or teams of police.

- For internal management purposes (i. e., internal to the police agency), periodic examination of the productivity of individual employees may be appropriate—in the same way that annual performance appraisals are provided *but* with more output-oriented measurements.

A special note of caution seems appropriate for attempts to measure the productivity of individual police employees. The measurement of individual police officer performance is discussed later. Many if not most of the important products of police services such as deterrence of crimes and successful apprehensions of offenders are generally due to the combined activities of a number of persons in the police department. For example, for a successful apprehension there may be field work by the policemen at the scene of the incident, subsequent investigation by a police investigator, often supported by numerous crime lab operations such as fingerprinting and weapon analysis techniques, and perhaps crime analysis, communications, and data processing units.

ILLUSTRATIVE PRODUCTIVITY MEASURES

The principal technical issue in productivity measurement is what specifically should be measured. This section addresses that issue and how the data might be collected.

A set of functions of police crime control was identified in a previous section. These functions suggest the major purposes, goals, or objectives of police crime control and are the basis for the measurements discussed below.

Productivity measurements can be obtained on a regular basis (e. g., weekly, monthly, annually) in order to identify problem areas and monitor progress in productivity. Measurements can also be taken at special points in time in order to evaluate specific productivity improvement projects.[4]

Some recent suggestions about specific productivity measures are listed in Exhibits 1 and 2. Exhibit 1 is taken from the National Commission on Productivity's 1973 report of its Advisory Group on Productivity and Law Enforcement. Exhibit 2 is taken from a 1972 National Commission on Productivity publication (prepared by The Urban Institute) which was one of the first to examine the produc-

4. Procedures for evaluating productivity improvement projects so as to identify the contribution of the project as distinguished from other factors is a subject of itself and is not further discussed here. Reference 25, on the Kansas City preventive patrol experiment, and Reference 52, on the District of Columbia policewoman experiment, describe examples of the more sophisticated and powerful (and most expensive) evaluation approach, that of conducting "controlled" experiments.

tivity measurement problem in crime control.   Four characteristics of
the two exhibits are particularly important:

1. Each of the exhibits lists a number of measures.   None of
    the authors believed that a single measure, or even a few
    measures, would adequately reveal productivity.

2. Each of the exhibits contains measures of the effectiveness
    or quality of police services and not merely the workload
    accomplished.

3. In each of the two exhibits are measures that are *not* in the
    form of the classic productivity measurement, i. e., an out-
    put divided by an imput.

4. A number of the proposed measurements in each exhibit re-
    quire special data collection procedures which currently are
    not in general use by local governments.

Most of the principal measures in these exhibits will be discussed
in the following sections.

Exhibit 1

POLICE PATROL MEASUREMENTS *

National Commission on Productivity Advisory
Group on Productivity in Law Enforcement, 1973

INCREASING PATROL TIME

1. Measure to help determine the ability of management to make
    manpower available for patrol:

$$\frac{\text{Patrol Officers Assigned to Street Patrol Work}}{\text{Total Patrol Officers}}$$

This measure does not indicate whether the patrol officers thus
assigned are accomplishing anything useful. It is an indication of the department's success in making sworn officers available for more directly patrol-related activity. [Author's note:
This measure also implies that patrol officers not on street patrol
are not being used as productively as those on street patrol.]

2. Measure to indicate the extent to which patrol time out in the
    field is being committed to patrol activities:

$$\frac{\text{Man-Hours of Patrol Time Spent on Activities Contributing to Patrol Objectives}}{\text{Total Patrol Man-Hours}}$$

Time can be "lost" by performing non-patrol tasks during duty
hours. Examples are filling out unnecessary forms, servicing
vehicles, running errands, and spending unnecessarily long hours
waiting for court appearances. As noted for the previous measure, this measure does not indicate whether the time made
available is put to good use. It does measure success in making more time available, which can be turned to good use.

---

* These measures and the accompanying notes are taken from Reference
29, *Opportunities for Improving Productivity in Police Services*, Report of
the Advisory Group on Productivity in Law Enforcement, National Commission on Productivity, Washington, D.C., 1973. Some minor liberties have
been taken in assembling the measures identified in that report and putting
them into the arrangement used here.

MAXIMIZING THE IMPACT OF PATROL: DETERRENCE

In the absence of a direct measure of deterrence, three types of substitutes were used:

3. Existing reported crime indices, used with discretion.

4. Victimization surveys.

5. Quantitative measurement of activities which professional judgment suggests contribute to deterrence.

MAXIMIZING THE IMPACT OF PATROL: PATROL RESPONSE TIME

3.
$$\frac{\text{Number of Calls of a Given Type Responded to in Under "X" Minutes}}{\text{Total Calls of That Type}}$$

"X" minutes is used in the numerator to indicate that different response times are appropriate for different types of calls. The value of "X" would depend on whether the call was an emergency or non-emergency call, or whether the call was about a crime in progress, suspicious activity, or previously committed crime. Additional breakouts by type of crime may also prove helpful. A call about a bank robbery, for example, may require a more rapid response than a larceny in progress. In each case the department must determine for itself what is a desirable response time ("X") for a particular kind of call, based upon the considerations noted above.

7.
$$\frac{\text{Number of Calls Responded to in Under "X" Minutes}}{\text{Resources Devoted to the Response Function}}$$

To the extent that measures 6 and 7 reveal inefficient resource use, it would help, in diagnosing the problem, to divide response time into three segments: Dispatching delay, queue delay, and travel delay.

The note under measure 6 also applies here.

8. Measure of response effectiveness in leading to arrests:

$$\frac{\text{Arrests Surviving the First Judicial Screening Resulting From a Response to a Crime Call}}{\text{Crime-Related Calls for Service}}$$

[B7203]

Again, this measure should be applied to appropriate categories of arrest (felony, etc.) and be calculated separately for each major type of call.

MAXIMIZING THE IMPACT OF PATROL: APPREHENSION OF CRIMINAL OFFENDERS

9.   Measure for apprehension productivity:

$$\frac{\text{Arrests Resulting From Patrol Surviving the First Judicial Screening}}{\text{Total Patrol Man-Years}}$$

10. An example of more detailed measures of apprehension productivity measure for each major arrest category:

$$\frac{\text{Felony Arrests Resulting from Patrol Surviving the First Judicial Screening}}{\text{Total Patrol Man-Years}}$$

This measure can be modified for consideration of different kinds of arrests, including felonies, misdemeanors that involve a particular victim, consensual crime misdemeanors as determined by local jurisdictions, and other violations.

11. Measures of the ultimate disposition of arrests, which provide an additional check on the quality of apprehensions and post-arrest activities:

$$\frac{\text{Convictions}}{\text{All Arrests Made by Patrol Force}}$$

12. $$\frac{\text{Convictions}}{\text{Arrests Resulting From Patrol That Survive the First Judicial Screening}}$$

Measures 11 and 12 also may be calculated separately for each arrest category to provide more detailed information.

PROVISION OF NON–CRIME SERVICES

13. $$\frac{\text{Number of Non-Crime Calls for Service Satisfactorily Responded To}}{\text{Man-Hours Devoted to Non-Crime Service Calls}}$$

Here the number of calls includes both emergency and non-emergency situations. (Information on quality of the response would be provided by a follow-up survey of callers.)

14. Calculating the measure separately for major categories of non-crime service calls. This would be useful. For example:

$$\frac{\text{Medical Emergency Calls That Emergency Room Personnel Evaluate as Having Received Appropriate First Aid}}{\text{Total Medical Emergencies}}$$

MANAGING HUMAN RESOURCES *

15.
$$\frac{\text{Number of Charges During the Year (perhaps only those clearly supportable)}}{\text{Total Number of Department Personnel}}$$

Several types of complaint and disciplinary actions can be lodged against officers; for example, for illegal search, illegal detention, illegal confiscation of property, and other acts of criminal and unethical conduct against the public, or for violation of departmental policies and regulations, ranging from insubordination to sleeping on duty.

16.
$$\frac{\text{Number of Man-Days Lost During the Year Due to Illness, Disciplinary Action, and Injury}}{\text{Total Number of Man-Days Served During the Year}}$$

17.
$$\frac{\text{Total Turnover During the Year}}{\text{Total Number of Department Personnel}}$$

---

* Additional measures for recruitment, selection and assignment, and training were also included in the report but are not included here.

[B7201]

Exhibit 2

PRODUCTIVITY MEASUREMENTS
FOR THE POLICE CRIME CONTROL FUNCTION * & **

(The Urban Institute, 1972)

A. CURRENTLY AVAILABLE

1. Population served per police employee and per dollar ***

2. Crime rates and changes in crime rates for reported crimes (relative to dollars or employees per capita)

3. Clearance rates of reported crimes (relative to dollars or employees per capita)

4. Arrests per police department employee and per dollar ***

5. Clearances per police department employee and per dollar ***

B. REQUIRING SIGNIFICANT ADDITIONAL
   DATA–GATHERING

1. Crime rates including estimates of unreported crimes based on victimization studies

2. Clearance rates including estimates of unreported crimes based on victimization studies

3. Percent of felony arrests that "survive" preliminary hearings in courts of limited jurisdiction

4. Percent of arrests that lead to convictions

5. Average response times for calls for service

6. Percent of crimes solved in less than "x" days

7. Percent of population indicating a lack of feeling of security

8. Percent of population expressing dissatisfaction with police services

---

* This exhibit is from Reference 30, *The Challenge of Productivity Diversity: Improving Local Government Productivity Measurement and Evaluation, Part III, Measuring Police-Crime Control Productivity,* prepared by The Urban Institute for the National Commission on Productivity, National Technical Information Service, PB223117, June, 1972. This reference suggests that the best approach to police crime control productivity measurement is to consider the *set* of measures along with the associated input data (i.e., man-hour and dollar cost data).

** These measures (except for A-1, B-7, and B-8) should be disaggregated by type of crime.

*** Data on resource inputs should, to the extent possible, exclude resources expended on non-crime functions, such as traffic control.

PROBLEMS WITH EXISTING MEASURES AND WAYS TO ALLEVIATE THESE PROBLEMS WITH NEWER MEASUREMENTS

Crime Prevention-Deterrence Measures

Communities hope crime prevention and deterrence are a major impact (if not *the* major impact) of police crime control activities. Even though the deterrent effect of visible police patrol is yet to be determined, other kinds of police work seem quite likely to deter at least some crime. If the police are more successful at the apprehension of criminals the likelihood of punishment presumably is increased and thus certain potential criminal acts are deterred. Arrests leading to the incarceration of criminals who would otherwise be free to commit new crimes also seems likely to reduce crime. Thus the police can be said to have a role in crime prevention and deterrence.

But the problem in productivity measurement, as has often been stated, is that it is extremely difficult to determine how many crimes police activity has prevented. Even very large scale, in-depth, ad hoc studies (not feasible for regular productivity measurement) are likely to find this extremely difficult.[5] Thus, what is done as a practical matter is to measure the number of crimes *that have not been deterred*.[6] By looking at changes in crime rates over time and making comparisons with similar communities a local government can obtain some idea, albeit a crude one, about the extent of crime prevention.

The traditional approach has been to count crimes reported to the police. The FBI, in its Uniform Crime Reports, has attempted to achieve some commonality of definitions on crimes and procedures. A number of objections, however, have frequently been raised about these data.[7] These objections will not be repeated here in detail, but the major problem is that a significant percentage of crimes is not reported to the police. Recent victimization surveys conducted nationally by the federal government and by local governments indicate that only about 25 to 75 percent of all crime is reported, with reporting varying by type of crime.[8]

To alleviate this problem the use of surveys in which a scientific sample of citizens is asked about their victimization has been gaining support. Victimization *rates*, the total number of estimated crimes

5. For some particularly interesting studies of tests of this relationship, see References 4, 25, 36, and 44.

6. See Reference 53 for an exposition of this point.

7. For example, see References 20, 30, 43, and 48.

8. For example, see References 13, 31, 32, and 35.

divided by the population, are then computed.[9] Victimization surveys rely on memories, and willingness to respond, of those sampled. Such surveys are therefore subject to errors other than the possible errors arising from sampling. Some studies of these problems have been made by the federal government,[10] indicating that such errors do exist and the likely direction and nature of the errors. Nevertheless, this author agrees with the many researchers who believe that the estimates obtained are a substantial improvement over reported crime rates.

The recent experience of St. Petersburg, Florida illustrates the usefulness of victimization information. Reported crimes had shown a sharp rise over a two-year period. In the second year the police had initiated a special effort to have citizens report crimes. The victimization estimates obtained from citizen surveys at the end of each of the two years indicated that *total* victimization including both reported and unreported crimes had risen less sharply than reported crimes. Thus, a considerably different picture emerged than that obtainable from only the reported crime statistics.

The data from a victimization survey can be used *directly* to give an estimate of total victimization (since respondents are asked to list both reported and unreported crimes). Alternatively, governments can multiply the ratio, obtained from the survey, of unreported crimes to reported crimes, by the official count of reported crimes; this will provide an estimate of the number of unreported crimes which, when added to the official count of reported crimes, will provide an estimate of total victimization.[11]

The victimization surveys undertaken by the federal government so far have involved a lengthy questionnaire and large samples. These give fairly precise victimization estimates but can be quite

9. Victimization rates can also be interpreted as the probability that an individual (or business establishment, if computed on a per business establishment basis) was victimized during the period. Most typically, the total estimated number of crimes is divided by the appropriate population. Perhaps a more appropriate measure of the probability of a specific person or household being victimized would be to use, as the numerator of the ratio, the number victimized one or more times.

10. See References 5, 16, 32, 35, and 45. The National Academy of Science currently has underway a new study to evaluate the National Crime Panel which will provide national victimization data by interviewing 60,000 families and 15,000 businesses each year. In addition, 10,000 families and 2,000 businesses in each of 13 cities will be surveyed each year over a three-year period.

11. However, considerable care is needed in this procedure. The survey-derived data must be applied in a compatible way to the reported crime data. For example, if the unreported crimes estimated apply solely to household crimes, they should be applied to the reported number of household crimes, not to the number of crimes against commercial establishments.

costly and therefore may not be practical on a regular basis for other than the largest cities and counties. However, some recent surveys undertaken by local governments have used shorter forms of the questionnaire, with smaller sample sizes (600–1,000 households) and using somewhat less sophisticated sampling techniques than those used by the Bureau of the Census. (Among areas recently undertaking such efforts are St. Petersburg, Florida; Nashville, Tennessee; Palo Alto, California; Randolph Township, New Jersey; and Arlington County, Virginia. The surveys in the first four covered other municipal services as well as police.[12]

The question is whether such surveys can be undertaken at a reasonable cost while retaining sufficient precision so that local governments, even smaller ones, will be able to undertake *annual* surveys in order to obtain adequate and regular comparative data. While worthwhile surveys costing less than $10,000 seem possible, some technical questions remain. Municipalities using such surveys will have to settle for less precision and less detailed questioning. The one-to-two percentage point confidence limits, possible through the larger surveys and the longer interviews, would cost many thousand of dollars more per year.[13] Fortunately, such considerable precision and detail may not be necessary, but the use of smaller surveys will mean that municipalities will have to accept the fact that small differences in victimization from one year to the next will have considerably more likelihood of being due to sampling error rather than real changes in total crime rates. Other cost savings may be achieved by using telephone (rather than in-person) interviews[14] and by using the survey to obtain information on other governmental services. (The latter would reduce the costs to the police agency.)

My tentative judgment is that these small and regular victimization surveys are probably justified. They provide information that, although not completely precise or detailed, will still be considerably better than reported crime rates. They seem likely to refine the skepticism about crime rates that citizens might otherwise have—es-

---

12. See Reference 13. Reference 46 contains the questionnaire used by St. Petersburg. Note that none of these surveyed commercial establishments.

13. To illustrate the difference between larger and smaller surveys, it can be pointed out that a random sample of 500 households, costing under $10,000 would provide statistical confidence intervals of about plus or minus 4 percentage points at the 90–95 percent confidence level.

14. Telephone surveys also have the advantage of permitting many callbacks to persons not at home and under some conditions permit more convenient access to certain households. Recent random dialing approaches have made the telephone survey professionally acceptable but still have the sometimes major problem that households without telephones cannot be reached by this means.

pecially if productivity measurement became regularly reported to the public.

Without victimization surveys, crime reports remain the only source of crime count information—probably better than nothing, but by no means ideal.

Another question is how to combine the number of incidents for each category of crime. The FBI categorizes each crime as to whether it is a Part I or Part II crime and whether it is an *Index* crime.[15] The Index is commonly used to represent the most serious crimes. The Index adds together each of a number of categories from murder to larceny. Thus, in effect, the Index counts one murder and one larceny equally. The Index is, therefore, affected to a considerable extent by changes in the more common types of Index crimes, such as larceny and burglary.[16] Critics have proposed various weighting schemes, such as the Sellin-Wolfgang weights [17] or some modification of them. Interestingly, however, one recent comparison of what the Index would look like if the Sellin-Wolfgang weight were used rather than the FBI's equal-weight approach reported that for the 1960–72 time period, the two were highly correlated for *national* totals and therefore the Sellin-Wolfgang weights provided little additional information.[18]

But this does not seem to be an important issue for productivity measurement by individual local governments. No one suggests dropping the data on the individual crime categories; a municipality will always have available the figures for the individual components of the Index as well as on the Index itself.

In sum then, the *ideal* measure of crime prevention productivity, "the number of crimes prevented per man-year," is not feasible given the current state of the measurement art. Rather it is necessary to track the actual amount of non-prevention, "the number of crimes committed," and its per capita form, "the number committed per capita," (or "per business establishment"), preferably by obtaining a more accurate figure that includes an estimate of the number of unreported crimes. Note that the classical productivity measure form, "number of crimes per man-year," does not make sense as the productivity measure. For example, a 10 percent *improvement* in both numerator and denominator would leave the ratio the same as before

15. Such distinctions as violent vs. property crimes, Index crimes, Part I vs. Part II crimes, stranger to stranger crimes, street crimes, *victimless* crimes, each have some use though these categories are often ambiguous.

16. Burglary and larceny comprise about 70 percent of all reported In-

dex crimes. If auto theft is added, these three categories comprise over 85 percent. See Reference 17.

17. See Reference 43.

18. See Reference 7.

the improvements! Even more troublesome is that it is not clear whether larger ratios would represent better or worse conditions since a larger value for the ratio, number of crimes per man-year, might represent increased crime, or it might represent increased efficiency or merely a reduction in the number of police employees.

Apprehension-of-Offenders Measures

After a crime is committed the police have the job of apprehending the perpetrator(s). Currently, the measures of output on apprehension customarily used are the number of arrests and clearance rates. Important problems exist, however, with the current definitions and data collection procedures used for each measure.

1. *Arrests.* The number of arrests per police man-year at first glance may seem to be a very attractive measure of police productivity, and it has been used as a basis for evaluating the productivity of individual patrol officers.

The mere fact that an arrest was made, however, does not mean that the person committing the crime was successfully brought to justice, nor that the person arrested was actually the guilty party. Even if the person arrested was guilty, many things can happen after an arrest which can lead to the offenders being let off without being punished (or otherwise treated in an appropriate manner, such as by probation, release to a rehabilitation program, etc.). Furthermore, some arrests are likely to be made of persons who are innocent or which are otherwise inappropriate.[19] There are many reasons for inappropriate or poor-quality arrests, some of which can be attributed to police action such as poor judgment, insufficient diligence collecting evidence, mishandling of evidence, misunderstanding of the law, and the like. Failures in the criminal justice system can also occur in the prosecution system or the courts. Some situations, such as witnesses refusing to testify, will leave unresolved the question as to where the responsibility lies. In any case, arrests which do not lead to some type of constructive action or which involve innocent persons, regardless of the reason, are inappropriate and, in a literal sense, unproductive. In examining the productivity

19. A dropped arrest does not necessarily mean that the person arrested was innocent. Also, some arrests of innocent persons or of persons who, though guilty by the letter of the law, should better not have been arrested (such as in certain family argument incidents), get by the initial judicial screening and perhaps even lead to a conviction. The arrest of innocent people is a different problem from insufficient evidence. Ideally, we would like to know as an indication of poor productivity the number of innocent people arrested. However, no feasible procedure for estimating the number of such situations seem to be available. Research on the subject of how many innocent people are arrested and convicted might be appropriate, but the measure does not at this time seem feasible for regular performance productivity measurement.

of the police department and its employees, we would ideally like to isolate those situations in which inappropriate or ineffective arrests were due to actions within the purview of the police. As a practical matter, however, this can at best be approximated.

Furthermore, the measure "arrests per police man-year" is liable to produce perverse effects if emphasis is placed by a municipality on increasing the number of arrests per man-year. If the police believe they are being evaluated on the number of arrests per policeman, they may be encouraged to make excessive, unreasonable, or at least marginal arrests.

As a step towards evaluating the quality and effectiveness of arrests, and at the same time to reduce the likelihood of encouraging undesirable arrests, Exhibits 1 and 2 each suggest the use of the measure "number or percent of arrests that pass the first judicial screening."[20] This becomes a productivity measure in the classical form when related to the number of man-years involved. Recent tests of this measure suggest that in data collection procedures the *reasons* for the dropping of all charges should be identified to the extent possible, particularly for the purpose of distinguishing reasons which are likely to be at least partly controllable by the police from those which are not controllable.[21] Also, procedures on how to count reduced charges and multiple charges on an arrest need to be specified.

The number, or percent, of arrests per man-year that lead ultimately to a conviction (at least on one charge) is another option proposed in the exhibits. However, because of the additional involvement of the court and prosecution systems, and the time span from arrest to ultimate disposition, thus making the data less timely for productivity measurement purposes, this measure may be less useful to the police. It may be a better indicator of the productivity of the criminal justice system considered as a whole, however.

Unfortunately, measures reflecting arrest dispositions have current drawbacks. First, the data are not currently generally available to police agencies. Very few police departments currently receive regular, systematic data on the disposition of arrests at the various points in the adjudication process. Collection of these data has been undertaken in such jurisdictions as the District of Columbia, Kansas City and New York City. Other preliminary tests of procedures to obtain and use court disposition data have been tried in St. Petersburg and Nashville.[22] Such data collection requires the cooperation of

20. This might be a preliminary hearing or a state prosecuting attorney's investigation. For misdemeanors, where these hearings are waived, final disposition of the case would need to be the basis for the measure.

21. See, for example, References 11 and 40 and the work of Washington, D.C., and New York City.

22. A description of these tests and data collection procedures based on them can be found in Reference 40.

the courts or what is perhaps more easily obtained, the cooperation of the prosecutor's office. Whatever the difficulties in obtaining such data, however, they may well be worth the effort, not only for productivity measurement purposes, but also by providing the police with timely operational data to keep them better informed on the disposition of persons who have been arrested.

A second problem is that the reasons for arrests not surviving the first judicial screening (or not leading to a conviction) can be quite diverse, and many of them may be unrelated to police actions. Some police departments may therefore be reluctant to use such a measure, fearing that they will be blamed unfairly for arrests that are dropped. Nevertheless, the information certainly seems appropriate, and if not used unfairly to criticize the police can be a constructive measuring yardstick.

Another difficulty with arrest disposition measures relates to the special handling of juvenile offenders.[23] Most juveniles are processed through the Juvenile Court, where they do not go through the same adjudication process as adults and where information about them is held more tightly.

This confidentiality of information on specific cases and different adjudication process are hurdles to be overcome in obtaining appropriate data. However, it seems likely that useful data collection procedures on the disposition of arrests could be worked out with Juvenile Courts that would maintain the confidentiality of individual cases.

Local governments may differ somewhat in their definitions as to what constitutes an arrest for data-gathering purposes. As with procedures for collecting any data, careful attention is needed to develop clear and comprehensive definitions for data categories and to assure that data collection procedures are properly followed. It also may be useful to distinguish the number of arrests made at the scene from those resulting from subsequent investigation. This would provide information relevant to the productivity of quick-response units, as compared to investigative units.

2. *Clearance Rates.* A number of concerns have been expressed at various times about such problems as variations in what constitutes a clearance and the variability that can occur when a police department emphasizes or does not emphasize exceptional clearances, such as making special efforts to get offenders to admit to other crimes. Two other important problems exist.

First, as with arrest rates, the counts of clearances used in most jurisdictions include incidents for which an arrest was made, regard-

---

23. Thus far, the experiences with the quality-of-arrest measure that this author is aware of have been limited to arrests of adults.

less of whether the arrests survive the initial judicial screening or do not lead to an ultimate "conviction." Thus, if a crime leads to an arrest which is subsequently thrown out of court there is no current provision to "unclear" the crime for clearance rate reporting purposes or to at least count such occurrences.

Second, a clearance (as defined by the FBI) is recorded by the arrest of any one of several criminals committing a crime even if the others are never apprehended. There is currently no measure which indicates the success of the police in identifying and apprehending *each* of the offenders involved in a single crime carried out by more than one person. A proposal made in the 1972 Urban Institute report was to measure the percentage of total known offenders who were subsequently arrested. Thus, if in an armed robbery it was known that there were three offenders, and only one eventually was apprehended, the apprehension rate for the incident would be 33.3 percent. Currently, however, the incident would be computed as fully cleared for statistical purposes. Two variations of this measure, both useful, seem appropriate. One would emphasize the total *solution* rate: the "total number of man-crimes for which someone was successfully brought to justice, including *other* crimes cleared by arrests" divided by "the total estimated number of man-crimes." The second variation would focus on the risk to the criminal (the probability of being caught in one particular incident). Here, the denominator would be the same, but the numerator would be "the number of persons arrested and successfully brought to justice," without counting other crimes that the police simultaneously are able to clear. For example, if there are two crime incidents, one involving one criminal and the second involving four, and if one of the four persons is arrested and convicted, and in the process the police also link that person to the first crime, then the *solution rate* measure would be $2/5 = .40$ but the *criminal risk* rate would be $1/5 = .20$. (As a practical matter, for many crimes, such as burglaries, it is not possible to know how many offenders actually participated. The reported number would probably need to be conservatively weighted, that is, one offender would be assumed for incidents in which no contrary information is available.)

In sum, then, police departments and their communities currently do not have full information on the number of successful apprehensions relative to the total number of those who should be apprehended.[24] Ways to provide better information are to measure both the "number of arrests that survive the initial judicial screening per man-year," and the "percent of estimated man-crimes committed leading to an apprehension that survives the initial judicial screen-

---

24. Another problem arises in comparing performance with other jurisdic-tions. Police departments may differ in their definitions of clearance.

ing." These both seem to be appropriate and feasible to measure in determining apprehension productivity.

Citizen Feedback Measures: Including Measures of Feeling of Security; Rapid, Courteous, and Fair Response; and Satisfaction with Response to Non-Crime Calls

Exhibits 1 and 2 both recommend measures that require feedback from citizens as to their perceptions of the quality of services they are receiving, such as their feeling of security and their satisfaction with crime and non-crime call response from the police. Such information is seldom, if ever, collected regularly by local governments today. Fortunately, such questions can be included at little additional cost in the same survey used to collect victimization data. Or, alternatively, these data might be collected by systematic surveys of persons who have previously called for assistance.[25] These measures are useful for detecting problem areas and improvement or worsening of conditions over time.

Certain measures based on citizen perception data can be related to man-hours expended to provide the classic form of productivity measurement. For example, measure 13 of Exhibit 1 is "number of non-crime calls for service satisfactorily responded to per man-hour," where the identification of satisfaction is obtained from a survey of persons who have called for assistance. Other possibilities would be to compute the "estimated number of persons responding that they felt reasonably safe being alone in their neighborhood at night per police man-year or per dollar." This use of citizen perception feedback is uncommon and may seem strange to many. It is analogous to the industrial practice in which only outputs that pass quality control inspection are counted when measuring output and relating it to total cost. Thus, at the very least, these measures might be more informative as far as productivity is concerned than use of the measures "number of calls responded to per police-year" or "population served per police-year or per dollar," which indicate nothing about the adequacy of the service provided.

Note that here, as with victimization survey information, the values used for the output unit have to be estimated from the results of the sample survey and thus are subject to possible sampling error as well as a variety of other problems in the sampling process (such as problems in listing all of the population from which the sample of persons to be interviewed is to be drawn, questionnaire-wording problems, possible interviewer errors, and respondent memory limitations).

25. Reference 40 discusses this procedure at greater length.

Police honesty and corruption are other important concerns to a community. Whether they should be included in examining a police department's productivity is not clear. The NCOP Advisory Committee report[26] contains a measure on the number of *charges* against the police department, such as complaints or disciplinary actions lodged against police officers (Measure 15 in Exhibit 1). If separated into charges related to supportable incidents of police dishonesty and corruption, as distinguished from other complaints, such as harassment—the measure would be relevant here. However, this is not a very satisfying measure because of the hidden nature of most incidents of corruption.

Police-community relations is a similar local issue. The quality of police relations with the community might be measured roughly through citizen surveys. A productivity measurement might be the "number of persons who express a positive attitude toward the police per police man-year," based on results of questions in the citizen survey. Such a measure, however, has the problem of possibly encouraging police to expend undue effort on *propaganda*.

Workload-Oriented Measures

Neither the NCOP Advisory Group on Productivity in Law Enforcement) Exhibit 1) nor the earlier Urban Institute report (Exhibit 2) calls for the use, for productivity measurement purposes, of the traditional measures "number of calls per man-year" or, for investigative officers, "caseloads per officer." Such measurements presumably have been used to identify the efficiency of groups of employees or individual employees. These particular measures, however, do not take into account case difficulty or workload accomplished. The latter problem can be reduced by using cases actually *closed* or completed per man-year, but cases vary widely and the quality of their handling is difficult to assess.

With the sudden recent rediscovery by local governments of the industrial engineer, there is likely to be considerable effort in many local governments on applying work measurements and work standards (such as by use of time studies) to government activities. Some of this interest is bound to flow into the police area as work measurement specialists attempt to develop standards for everything countable. Such measures as "caseloads per investigator" or its more classic form for work standards, "number of man-hours per case" for specific categories of cases, will probably once again be scrutinized. Such measures are most appropriate where the product is relatively standardized, the procedures for obtaining that product are standardized, and quality standards are clear. Major problems in the police

---

26. Reference 29.

area will continue to be the great diversity of incidents and cases, thus requiring a wide variation in the amount of effort necessary to resolve cases and the consequent difficulty in adequately specifying characteristics for case handling.

Certain routine police activities, however, such as those involving clerical or certain data processing tasks, may well be amenable to work standards which can help a department to improve the scheduling of such activities. Work measurement approaches might also help identify improved procedures that police could use for a variety of their activities. However, it does not seem likely that traditional work standards will be useful on a widespread basis in police departments.

Productivity measurement in such terms as "percent of police time spent on productive activities" is likely to be a measure of major concern to internal police management concerned with maximum efficient use of manpower. But difficulties abound in defining what are, and what are not, productive activities. The measure just named also raises a problem, in that it is not clear what the relation is between improvements in this measure and more effective crime control, i. e., crime reduction or apprehensions. Nevertheless, this measure can be useful to internal police management in evaluating certain types of productivity improvement efforts.

PROBLEMS WITH MEASURING THE APPROPRIATE INPUTS [27]

Thus far I have concentrated on problems and possibilities in measuring the output, or the impacts, of police control activities. There are also problems in calculating the amount of input—the number of man-years or dollars associated with the output. Even if output over input ratios are not always appropriate, it is always appropriate to compare resources applied against the various measures of police effectiveness.

In general it is desirable to relate outputs to both manpower and total dollars. The more traditional form of productivity measurement has been to use manpower alone as the input unit and thus determine labor productivity. However, local governments are interested in the productivity of all the resources at their disposal and thus will probably want to relate outputs to total dollars as well.

Some typical input measurement problems are listed below.

1. A major question is what to do about police resources applied to non-crime services, particularly traffic control, es-

27. Some further discussion of problems with input measurement is contained in Reference 28, page 15ff, and Reference 50, page 13ff.

pecially in the common situation where the same police officers carry out both crime and non-crime functions.

2. A similar problem exists for providing data on specific crime control activities, such as specific police units. Even more difficult to obtain is information on the resources applied to specific types of crimes, such as burglaries or robberies, where the same police employees may routinely switch from one crime to the other.

3. Overhead, support costs, and costs of equipment are also problems. Supervision, employee fringe benefits, vehicle maintenance, and equipment and vehicle purchases need to be considered when measuring output against total costs. For example, considering the use of mechanization, output per unit of manpower will rise, but when all costs are considered (including the increased equipment costs), the output per total dollar will show less of an improvement and perhaps even a worsening. Costs for facilities and equipment that are expected to last more than one year should probably be amortized in a fashion that avoids distorting the calculations for individual years. One approach is to develop an equivalent rental cost (already done in some localities, where police departments are charged for vehicles on a rental basis even though the vehicles are actually owned by the government).

Most local governments lack the cost-accounting systems necessary to provide man-hour or cost information for specific police activities. This author is reluctant to suggest extensive cost-accounting procedures, which could involve very detailed timekeeping by members of the police department. This could quickly become more costly and annoying than it is worth. However, some improvements in cost-accounting, combined with some cost *estimation* for special needs, seem generally appropriate.

In making comparisons from one year to the next on productivity measurements using dollars, adjustments for price increases should be made to provide "constant dollar" productivity comparisons.[28] However, governments are also concerned with current dollars (i. e., dollars unadjusted for price-level changes), and it seems appropriate to relate output to current dollars as well. Use of both constant and current dollar measures will permit governments to identify to what extent productivity changes are due to price increases.

---

28. A local government can readily adjust its own prices from year to year, based on its salary and wage increases for various positions. The prob-lem becomes considerably more difficult in making comparisons with other jurisdictions.

MEASUREMENT OF THE PRODUCTIVITY OF INDIVIDUAL POLICE DEPARTMENT EMPLOYEES: SHOULD IT BE DONE AND UNDER WHAT CONDITIONS?

As mentioned earlier, most major police products will represent the joint efforts of many employees. Therefore, most productivity measurement should aim at the joint product and not at the contribution of each individual employee. Nevertheless, for *internal* police management purposes periodic examination of the productivity of individuals, if undertaken properly, may be appropriate. If undertaken, great care will be needed both to avoid antagonizing the work force and to avoid a measurement system that encourages employees to pervert the basic purposes of the agency.

Of particular interest are likely to be measurements for each individual of the following:

Apprehension

1a. Arrests, especially the number that pass the preliminary judicial screening, or

1b. The number that pass or are not rejected *for a police-related reason.*

2a. Percent of arrests that pass the preliminary judicial screening, or

2b. Percent of arrests that pass or are not rejected for a police-related reason.

Patrol Time

3. Percent of patrol time spent on activities contributing to patrol objectives (see Measure 2 in Exhibit 1).

The latter measure (3) is an indicator of efficiency; the former are indicators of effectiveness—at least of apprehension effectiveness.

There are many problems in such evaluations. The evaluations should be kept within the police department and used to guide efforts to improve the work force, preferably through encouraging improved performance by lower-rated individuals, such as through added training or assistance with particular individual difficulties that may be inhibiting performance.

Comparisons should, of course, be made primarily with other individuals working in similar units and under similar conditions. It is important to look carefully for the reasons for low performance. There may be good reasons for it. The employee may have been on sick leave during much of the period, may have been assigned to an area with a very low incidence of crime during the period (incident rates will vary by both location and shift), may have worked an area where the mix of crime was such that arrests were comparatively few (assault, for example, being more likely to lead to arrest than larceny), or may have been involved in circumstances which resulted in others receiving credit for arrests in which the individual participated, etc. Demographic and economic factors, discussed in the next section, are also likely to be useful for interpreting performance individuals.

Our extensive examination of individual patrol officer performance in regard to arrests during 1971 was conducted by a police inspector in a large city police department. The study presented data on total number of felony arrests, total number of misdemeanor arrests, and total number of summonses issued for each patrol officer for each precinct and for each type of unit (e. g., motor units, scooter units, special anti-crime units, etc.)[29] Neighborhood conditions, such as crime rates and population density, were considered by persons familiar on a first-hand basis with them. Individual police officers who had low productivity were questioned as to the reasons. (Some of those reasons were fear of working on the street, lack of anyone taking them to task, couldn't work beyond formal duty hours because working on other jobs or taking care of children while wife was working a full-time job, etc.) No attempt was made in this study to determine whether the arrests were justified or not, including the disposition of arrests.

Quality-of-arrests determinations seem indispensable, however, when arrests are used as a productivity measure for individual police in order to avoid encouraging officers to make undesirable arrests.[30] The measure "number surviving the initial judicial screening" seems of considerable help here. However, a problem remains in determining whether proper judgment was exercised in those instances where the officer has discretion in making an arrest, e. g., in family arguments, fights between acquaintances, etc.[31] *Quality* here seems extremely difficult to measure quantitatively, since seldom will there be an independent, trained observer on the scene to make such ratings. For this aspect of arrest quality the judgment of the officer's supervisor seems the best, if not the only, option at this time. A possible scoring system (proposed in the recent LEAA Prescriptive Package on Neighborhood Team Policing)[32] for rating the relative arrest pro-

29. The report presents data with the names of individuals and appropriately is available only on a restricted basis.

30. In addition to References 29 and 30, see, for example, Reference 12.

31. Discussion of the discretion that police officers have in making arrests is contained in References 6, 8, 34, and 38.

32. Reference 6, pp. 96–99.

ductivity of different officers is shown in Exhibit 3.[33] This scoring
system attempts to consider several dimensions of arrest importance
and quality: general type of crime, disposition, and use of force
(such as whether it was appropriate or led to unnecessary injury).

Exhibit 3

SAMPLE ARREST PRODUCTIVITY INDEX *

ACTIVITY	POINTSCORE	COMMENT
Parking violation	1	Do not count if dismissed.
Moving violation	2	Do not count if dismissed.
Misdemeanor arrest (no prosecution)	4	
Felony arrest (no prosecution)	8	
Misdemeanor arrest resulting in a prosecution (no conviction)	8	
Felony arrest (no conviction)	16	
Misdemeanor arrest (conviction)	12	
Felony arrest (conviction)	24	
Arrest without probable cause	−4 to −24	Minus score depends on seriousness of officer's error and frequency of previous error (do *not* count any positive points for the arrest).
Arrest involving the *necessary* use of physical force	+4	In addition to other points earned for the arrest. Do not count if the arrest was without probable cause.
Arrest of a dangerous individual without the use of force	+8	In addition to other point scores for the arrest.
Arrest involving an error in judgment causing injury or death to offender	−4 to −24	Minus score depends on seriousness of officer's error and frequency of previous errors.
Arrest involving injury or death of bystander	−24 to −72	Minus score depends on seriousness of officer's error and frequency of previous errors.
Arrest of an individual for several previous offenses	—	Total points for all offenses up to a maximum score of 36, including points for prosecution or conviction. Also count points related to the use of force or avoidance of force in connection with the arrest.

* Source: *Neighborhood Team Policing,* by Peter B. Bloch and David Specht.
National Institute of Law Enforcement and Criminal Justice, December 1973.

[B7199]

---

33. See note 33 on p. 418.

Police investigative activities are likely to be particularly amenable to measurement of arrest production. I repeat here, however, that measurement of the productivity of individual employees (as with traditional performance appraisals) should be internal to the police agency, and there should be no public dissemination of names of individuals or information permitting such identification. When and if a police agency develops procedures for examining the productivity of individual police personnel, it should incorporate a procedure for careful interpretation of the reasons for apparent low productivity.

In undertaking such performance evaluation, participation by employees in developing the procedures seems necessary to alleviate the natural hostility and negative actions likely to occur if such procedures are installed unilaterally or without sufficient consideration of the interests of employees.

INTERPRETING PRODUCTIVITY MEASUREMENT DATA

There are numerous approaches and techniques to data analysis. It is beyond the scope of this paper to discuss these at length.[34] However, three aspects of analysis will be briefly addressed: (1) what a government might use for comparison to determine how "well" it is doing; (2) what other factors should be considered in assessing productivity; and (3) establishing targets for next year's productivity performance.

Appropriate Comparisons [35]

(a) *Performance can be compared among time periods.* Such information will not become available until a measure has been used for more than one time period. If comparisons are made for periods less than a year, seasonal factors will need to be considered.

(b) *Comparisons among police districts, precincts, or population groups within a jurisdiction may be used.* Governments could use districts that perform well as targets for poorer performance districts. But since differences in performance may reflect inherent differences among the districts (or population groups) rather than differences in the effectiveness of the city service, comparisons of different population groups or service districts should take such factors into account. This is discussed further in the next subsection.

---

33. Much care and consideration is needed in developing such a scoring system. For instance, the example shown in Exhibit 3 may place too much importance on parking and traffic incidents, and encourage police to emphasize strict enforcement of parking and traffic violations, which probably can be achieved easily as compared to felony arrests.

34. For some examples of related analytical approaches, see Reference 19 and Chapter 4 of Reference 30.

35. This section is adapted from Reference 46, pp. 15–16.

(c) *In some cases the performance of other governments will be available for comparison.* Such comparisons, of course, are valid only if the same measurements are used. For example, some data are available nationally on reported crime rates, clearance rates, and arrests (and recently some data have become available on victimization surveys). As more local governments undertake these measurements more information will become available for comparison. But comparisons will have to be made carefully because of the many differences between jurisdictions. Only in a few cases are national data currently available on a government-by-government basis, such as on reported crimes and number of police employees). On other measures comparisons will have to be made with aggregate figures or by obtaining data directly from other jurisdictions, if available.

(d) *Comparisons might be made with estimates of how much change in productivity was anticipated by an advance analysis.* This may be an excellent approach, but it requires in-depth analysis, such as a projection of the likely costs and effectiveness of the jurisdiction's program. Actual performance could subsequently be compared with those that had been projected. Such studies, however, are likely to be feasible only in very selective circumstances.

The above comparisons can be used individually or in combination.

External Explanatory Factors Which Should Be Considered

Many factors other than police crime control efforts will affect such productivity measurements as crime and clearance rates. Such factors can change over time, can differ in various parts of a community, and can differ among communities. These factors may therefore account for some of the apparent differences in performance over time, among parts of a jurisdiction, or among jurisdictions. Thus, wherever possible, it is desirable to make allowances for such factors in interpreting whether performance is relatively good or bad.

(a) *Crime Prevention-Deterrence Measurements.* A variety of socio-economic-demographic characteristics of the population have been studied in attempts to identify factors that have strong correlation with crime rates.[36] These studies have primarily compared different cities in the United States to determine likely explanatory factors. Researchers have frequently assumed that factors such as size [37] and location (e. g., suburban vs. central city), number unemployed, number with low incomes, and sex and age mix (e. g., males

---

36. For example, see References 4, 10, 15, 22, 23, 24, 30, 37, 39, 41, 42, and 47.

37. For example, city size may affect salary levels and other costs and result in economies, or dis-economies of scale.

between the ages of, say, 15 and 25), seem likely to be correlated with crime rates. If this is so, the performance of police agencies should be considered in the context of these factors. Crime rates in locations where existing factors were such that high crime rates should be expected, should be considered in that light, and vice versa. This is also likely to apply to different geographical areas within a single jurisdiction.

It is beyond the scope of this paper to synthesize the numerous research studies and statistical analyses in which possible correlations have been examined. My impression after examining some of these is that the results to date have been far from conclusive. Those correlations which have been discovered appear to explain only a small part of the variations in performance.[38] The results are not nearly sufficiently definitive to provide an individual government with what would be most useful, that is, norms, or a procedure for deriving them, for each jurisdiction based on its own particular characteristics.

Thus at this time the only useful suggestion I can make is for a government to continue to emphasize comparisons with other parts of the jurisdictions or other jurisdictions of roughly the same population and type and to monitor factors such as unemployment rates, disparity in income levels, racial changes, and to make judgment allowances when making these comparisons. This is unsatisfying and not very helpful, but it seems to be the only recourse until, and if, more useful findings become available that permit more definitive adjustments.

(b) *Apprehension Measurements.* Little statistical analysis, to my knowledge, has been done as to non-police factors that might help explain differences in arrest or clearances among jurisdictions or among sub-regions within a jurisdiction. One attempt is described in Reference 30. It indicates that the number of clearances per police employee was related to the number of index crimes per police employee.

Exhibit 4 illustrates graphically the finding. The rationale was that "the more cases a police officer has to solve, the more he should be expected to solve up to the point that he becomes saturated with work. This would be especially likely if it is true that a large portion of all crimes that get solved essentially solve themselves, or are easily solved by routine police work."[39]

---

38. Most such studies have had to depend on less than the most desirable data, such as having to use reported crime data rather than crime rate data derived from victimization surveys. Many studies have also been handicapped by old data on at least some of the variables considered.

39. See Reference 30, p. 57. The study included all employees of the department and not, for example, only investigative units.

The 1972 report suggested that individual jurisdictions compare their own current "number of clearances per employee" figures against a norm derived from an equation such as that shown in Exhibit 5. This equation was developed from the data shown in Exhibit 4. For example, a city with 150,000 population and 24 Index crimes per police employee could use 4.4 Index clearances per police employee as its own norm against which to compare its own performance.[40] That effort, however, was merely a preliminary analysis. If subsequent analysis indicates that this relationship generally holds, such an adjustment would seem worthy of consideration by individual communities. Of course, it only considers one of many factors (number of reported index crimes per police employee) as an explanatory variable.

Exhibit 4

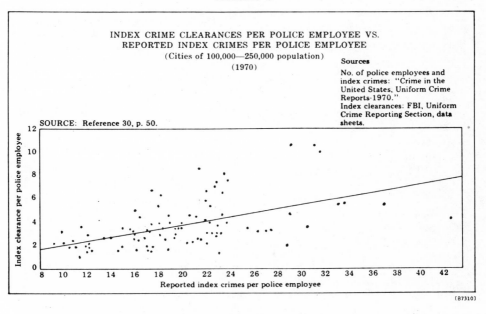

INDEX CRIME CLEARANCES PER POLICE EMPLOYEE VS.
REPORTED INDEX CRIMES PER POLICE EMPLOYEE
(Cities of 100,000—250,000 population)
(1970)

Sources

No. of police employees and index crimes: "Crime in the United States, Uniform Crime Reports-1970."
Index clearances: FBI, Uniform Crime Reporting Section, data sheets.

SOURCE: Reference 30, p. 50.

Index clearance per police employee (y-axis) vs. *Reported index crimes per police employee* (x-axis)

[87310]

40. $(.161 \times 24) + .504 = 4.368.$

Exhibit 5

RESULTS OF REGRESSION ANALYSIS CLEARANCES PER
POLICE EMPLOYEE VS. INDEX CRIMES
PER EMPLOYEE

For each case a straight line was fitted to the data using the least
squares criterion. The equation for the line was $y = mx + b$,
where:
     $y =$ index clearances per police employee (at end of year)
     $x =$ reported index offenses per police employee (at end of
     year)
     $m, b =$ contents divided from the basic data on the cities

	City Population			
	1970		1965	
	All Cities Over 100,000	100–250,000	Greater Than 250,000	Greater Than 250,000
m	.174	.161	.185	.179
b	.443	.504	.549	.889
r	.585	.493	.724	.655
r^2	.342	.242	.525	.432
No. of Cities Used in Sample	136	84	52	49
Statistical Significance	.01 level	.01 level	.01 level	.01 level

Source: Reference 30, p. 60.

[B7195]

     That same report also suggested a procedure for obtaining a
norm for suggested clearance rates based on national clearance rate
data. Clearance rates on each particular Part I crime can, of course,
be compared against the national averages reported in the FBI Uniform Crime Reports.[41] However, if a jurisdiction wants to examine
its performance in aggregate over all Part I crimes, an easy calculation can be used. Clearance rates differ significantly among crime

41. Differences among local governments in data collection and reporting, as noted earlier, put these comparisons in some question, but as
with crime rates, these national data
are probably better than nothing.

categories in the United States, ranging from clearance rates on the order of 10 to 20 percent for larceny to 50 to 80 percent for person-to-person crimes such as rape and murder.[42]   From year to year, or from jurisdiction to jurisdiction, the mix of crimes can vary considerably.   By multiplying the base-year national clearance rates (perhaps for jurisdictions in a given population range) by the specific number of reported crimes of each category in the jurisdiction for the year of interest, and then adding these, an aggregate norm is obtained for the number of clearances.   This would then be compared to the actual total number of clearances for the jurisdiction for the year of interest.   Comparisons of the two numbers would indicate to what extent the clearances for the current year were better or worse than would be expected, based on the national averages.

Similarly, a local government could also compare its current aggregative Part I crime clearance rate against its *own* performance in some prior year.   It would use the same procedure as noted above, except that the clearance rates of the *jurisdiction's base year* would be multiplied by the jurisdiction's current year's number of crimes of each category to give the aggregate norm.   Note that these procedures are only necessary when looking at aggregative clearances, not clearances for individual types of crimes.

These two examples illustrate the approaches that individual governments might undertake to develop norms or standards for their own current performance.   They are refinements over the more straight forward comparisons discussed in the section on *Appropriate Comparisons*.

Establishing Targets for Next Year's Productivity

The preceding section discussed comparisons that might be used to determine whether recent productivity has been relatively good or bad.   Here, another approach will be discussed, that of establishing targets for productivity measures for the next time period (say the next year) against which the next year's actual productivity can be compared.   A major purpose of target-setting is to encourage high-level performance.   Recent use by many local governments of Management By Objectives (MBO) is one expression of the interest in this approach.

However, setting targets on certain productivity measures, such as those involving crime rates (which can be affected by many external factors), can be hazardous.   Governments wanting to establish productivity targets should not do so casually.   Targets should be set only after careful consideration of past experiences, what is feasible in light of the resources available, and specific police programs.   It is

42.   See Reference 17.

highly desirable that targets be set with the participation of those who will be held responsible for meeting them. Targets that are too easy to meet will be of little use; targets that are unrealistic are likely to be frustrating to all concerned. With little experience thus far in the United States on setting productivity targets of the type presented here, caution will be appropriate during the early stage of the use of these productivity measurements.

It is recommended that targets not be set on an "arrests per police-year" measure, if at the same time there is no "arrest that survived the initial judicial screening" measure. As discussed earlier, without the latter, the likelihood of perverse behavior detrimental to the community becomes too high.

Target setting on productivity for *individual* police employees is likely to be a very controversial issue, and should probably not be undertaken without intensive participation by the individual employees.

Miscellaneous Productivity Analysis Approaches

A number of attempts have been made to analyze public sector productivity statistically.[43] These attempts have for the most part been aimed at identifying determinants of changes in unit costs or aggregative patterns of changing productivity. They have generally been oriented towards inter-city issues. Thus far these approaches do not seem to have yielded procedures or data significantly useful to individual local governments for measuring their own productivity.

CAN PRODUCTIVITY DATA BE DEPENDED ON?

As the use of productivity measurement data for evaluating police performance becomes more common, particularly in helping to determine future wages and benefits, special precautions will become necessary to reduce the possibility of either unintentional error or intentional manipulations of data. Recently, when evaluators undertook an early examination of the new crime reduction performance incentive system in the City of Orange California, they encountered extensive concern among many knowledgeable professionals, who believed that inevitably the police would be sorely tempted to manipulate crime report data in their favor (such as by non-reporting and alterations of crime categories in certain situations). In any case, public credibility is important for all concerned, public employees and city management alike.

43. For an excellent summary of the work to date in this direction, see Reference 51. Of particular interest to local governments is its presentation of rough approximations to identify changes in unit costs that can be attributed to (a) workload changes, (b) cost-factor increases, and (c) quality-productivity.

Two approaches seem appropriate to prevent intentional or unintentional error. These should be used by police departments both to reinforce the credibility of the data they are providing and to avoid the scorn of the inevitable skeptics of the world. These two approaches are: (1) wherever possible, to provide for collection of data by an independent, disinterested source; and (2) to provide for external auditing of data.

1. Collection of data by independent, objective means is becoming more possible in local government. A major theme in crime reporting currently is the use of the victimization survey. Since such a survey inevitably will be conducted and directed by persons outside the police department, it would be an appropriate check on reported crime data (even if the police department sponsors and funds the survey as long as reputable survey professionals are used). Other data obtainable through a survey of citizens, such as feelings of security and citizen satisfaction with police handling of incidents, would also have the advantage of being objectively gathered.

2. Periodic auditing is familiar to local governments but usually is limited to financial matters. However, as productivity measurement becomes more important, it will also be necessary to undertake periodic audits of procedures and practices. Some states already call for auditing of crime reports. The drawback here is that this can be expensive. To reduce the expense, such auditing could involve sampling techniques and not cover all procedures (and all incidents) each year. Instead, periodic, unscheduled audits, perhaps even performed by the staff of some central city staff office, might be undertaken. It is particularly important to check for misclassification or miscounting of crimes, arrests and clearances and sloppy recordkeeping or changes in classification practices. For example, one eastern police department found that a clerk was counting as cleared those cases that were routinely closed after a few years, even though no arrest had been made. (This made comparisons of past and present figures meaningless.)

SOME SUMMARY THOUGHTS

Measuring police crime control productivity is now a very unsatisfying activity. Nevertheless, substantial improvements over current general practices seem possible for local governments. The major improvements seem to be as follows:

1. Though the "number of crimes deterred" is not currently measurable, improvement in measuring the number of crimes

seems possible through victimization surveys. The key issue appears to be whether smaller, less detailed, surveys than those undertaken by the federal government are sufficient so that individual cities and counties could, on at least an annual basis, undertake such surveys. Initial experiences are encouraging but not yet by any means conclusive.

2. For measuring apprehension productivity, at least two improvements seem desirable. First, indicators of the quality of arrests seem highly desirable, perhaps in part based on arrest survival at the initial judicial screening. Secondly, all *man-crimes* should be accounted for in determining a really comprehensive and proper *clearance* rate (that is, a crime should not be counted as completely solved until all criminals involved in the crime have been apprehended and with a *satisfactory* disposition). Reasons for *non-satisfactory* disposition should be regularly examined by police for a variety of management purposes.

3. Other measures of police performance, involving citizen feedback, can be obtained from the same citizen survey used to obtain data on the number of unreported crimes. These include indications of citizen feelings of security, and citizen perception of the rapidity, courteousness, and fairness of police in response to both crime and non-crime calls.

4. Work measurement and work standards appear to be trends for local governments. Though likely to have limited applicability to most major police activities, they are likely to have some influence in helping to identify preferred procedures (on relatively routine activities). In certain activities, such as clerical activities, work standards may be appropriate.

5. Measures of the productivity of *individual* police employees are likely to increase in use but should be used very cautiously probably only as an internal management tool for constructive improvements. Indicators of the productivity of individual police employees, especially individual police officers, raise the same problems as measures of total police productivity. Arrest counts seem appropriate, but should be screened as to their quality, e. g., the number and percent that pass the initial judicial screening. Supervisors should carefully consider the circumstances surrounding arrest counts. They should consider such factors as the opportunity to make arrests each individual had and the various circumstances involved.

6. No commonly accepted standards or norms exist for interpreting how *good* current levels of productivity are. However, the following are likely to be useful: comparisons of current performance with past performance, comparisons of performance of (similar) police districts or similar units, comparisons with similar jurisdictions that collect similar performance data and, when available, comparisons with the performance projections made in in-depth analyses. Consideration, of course, should be given to external and non-controllable circumstances, such as varying demographic and economic characteristics. Unfortunately, there are few tools other than subjective judgment currently available to guide governments in adjusting to such special circumstances.

7. Measurements should be subject to periodic auditing, both to ensure the quality of the information obtained and to reinforce public credibility.

There appears to be little question that local governments can improve their productivity measurement practices. Many of the procedures noted above can readily be scaled down to be useful to even the smallest jurisdictions. However, if the government, for whatever reasons, cannot or is not interested in using productivity measurement information for making decisions regarding improvements in either the costs or outputs of police services, or has not developed the data for some future analytical purpose, the undertaking of the procedures would be a costly waste.

1. Ahern, James F. "Crime and the Police," Chapter 6 from *Police in Trouble*. New York: Hawthorn Books, Inc. 1972.
2. Albright, Ellen et al. *Criminal Justice Research: Evaluation in Criminal Justice Programs, Guidelines and Examples*. Washington, D.C.: Government Printing Office, June 1973.
3. Anderson, Ralph E., *Police Standards and Goals*. International Association of Chiefs of Police. Gaithersburg, Md. Undated.
4. Beaton, W. Patrick. "The Determinants of Police Protection Expenditures." *National Tax Journal*. Vol. XXVII, No. 2 (June 1974).
5. Biderman, Albert D. "Surveys of Population Samples for Estimating Crime Incidence." *Annals of American Academy of Political and Social Science*. Vol. 374 (November 1967).
6. Bloch, Peter B. and David Specht. *Neighborhood Team Policing*. National Institute of Law Enforcement and Criminal Justice. Washington, D.C. December 1973.
7. Blumstein, Alfred. *Seriousness Weights in an Index of Crime*. Carnegie-Mellon University Urban Systems Institute. Pittsburgh. January 1974.

8. Bozza, Charles M. "Motivations Guiding Policemen in the Arrest Process." *Journal of Police Science and Administration.* Vol. 1 (1973).

9. Chaiken, Jan M. et al. *The Impact of Police Activity on Crime: Robberies on the New York City Subway System.* New York: New York City Rand Institute. January 1974. (R–1424)

10. Chilton, Roland J. "Continuity in Delinquency Area Research Comparison of Studies for Baltimore, Detroit, and Indianapolis." *American Sociological Review.* Vol. 29, No. 1 (February 1964).

11. City of Kansas City, Missouri. *Annual Report of the Kansas City, Missouri Police Department.* 1970.

12. City of New York, New York. *City of New York Police Department Evaluation Guide.* Undated (about 1974).

13. City of St. Petersburg, Florida. *Multi-Service Citizen Survey for the City of St. Petersburg.* Office of Management and Budget, St. Petersburg, Florida. January 1974.

14. City of Sunnyvale, California. *Performance Auditing Project: Public Safety Function.* September 1974.

15. Council on Municipal Performance. "City Crime." *Municipal Performance Report.* May-June 1973, with June 1974 Supplement. Also discussed in "City Crime: Report of Council on Municipal Performance." *Criminal Law Bulletin.* Vol. 9, No. 7 (1973).

16. Dodge, Richard W. and Anthony G. Turner. "Methodological Foundations for Establishing a National Survey of Victimization." Speech presented at the 1971 American Statistical Association meeting, August 23–26, 1971.

17. Federal Bureau of Investigation. *Crime in the United States: Uniform Reports, 1973.* Published annually.

18. ——. *Uniform Crime Reporting Handbook: How to Prepare Uniform Crime Reports.* Washington, D.C. January 1974.

19. Greenwood, Peter W. *An Analysis of the Apprehension Activities of the New York City Police Department.* New York: New York City Rand Institute. September 1970. (R–529)

20. Hindlang, Michael J. "The Uniform Crime Reports Revisited." *Journal of Criminal Justice.* Vol. 2, No. 1 (Spring 1974).

21. Institute of Municipal Treasurers and Accountants. *Output Measurement Discussion Papers,* Vol. 3, "Police and Protection." London. December 1972.

22. Jones, E. Terrence. "Evaluating Everyday Policies: Police Activity and Crime Incidence." *Urban Affairs Quarterly.* Vol. 8, No. 1 (March 1973).

23. ——. "The Impact of Crime Rate Changes on Police Protection Expenditures in American Cities." *Criminology.* Vol. II, No. 4 (February 1974).

24. Kakalik, James S. and Sorrel Wildhorn. *Aids to Decisionmaking in Police Patrol.* Santa Monica: Rand Corporation. February 1971 (R–593)

25. Kelling, George L. et al. *The Kansas City Prevention Patrol Experiment: A Summary Report.* The Police Foundation. Washington, D. C. October 1974.

26. Lind, Robert C. and John P. Lipsky. "The Measurement of Police Output: Conceptual Issues and Alternative Approaches." *Law and Contemporary Problems: Police Practices.* Duke University. Vol. XXXVI (Autumn 1971).

27. Morgan, J. M., Jr. and R. Scott Fosler. "Police Productivity." *Police Chief.* Vol. XLI, No. 7 (July 1974).

28. National Commission on Productivity. *Improving Productivity and Productivity Measurement in Local Governments.* Washington, D.C. June 1971.

29. ——. *Opportunities for Improving Productivity in Police Services.* Washington, D.C. 1973.

30. The Urban Institute. *The Challenge of Productivity Diversity: Improving Local Government Productivity Measurement and Evaluation, Part III: Measuring Police-Crime Control Productivity.* National Commission on Productivity. National Technical Information Service, PB223117 (June 1972).

31. National Criminal Justice Information and Statistics Service. *Crime in Eight American Cities.* Washington, D.C. July 1974.

32. ——. *Crimes and Victims: A Report on the Dayton-San Jose Pilot Survey of Victimization.* Washington, D.C. June 1974.

33. Ostrom, Elinor, "On the Meaning and Measurement of Output and Efficiency in the Provision of Urban Police Services." *Journal of Criminal Justice.* Vol. 1, No. 2 (Summer 1973).

34. Parnas, Raymond. "Police Discretion and Diversion of Incidents of Intra-Family Violence." *Law and Contemporary Problems: Police Practices.* Duke University. Vol. XXXVI (Autumn 1971).

35. President's Commission on Law Enforcement and Administration of Justice. *The Challenge of Crime in a Free Society.* Washington, D. C.: Government Printing Office. 1967.

36. Press, S. James. *Some Effects of an Increase in Police Manpower in the 20th Precinct of New York City.* New York City Rand Institute. October 1971. (R–704)

37. Quinney, Richard. "Structural Characteristics, Population Areas, and Crime Rates in the United States." *Journal of Criminal Law, Criminology and Police Science.* Vol. 52, No. 1 (September 1966).

38. Rubenstein, Jonathan. *City Police.* New York: Farrar, Straus, and Giroux. 1973.

39. Scarr, Harry A. et al. *Criminal Justice Research: Patterns of Burglary.* 2nd ed. National Institute of Law Enforcement and Criminal Justice. Washington, D.C.: Government Printing Office. 1973.

40. Schaenman, Philip S. "Measuring Police Effectiveness in Crime Control." Draft final report to National Science Foundation. The Urban Institute, Washington, D.C. August 8, 1974.

41. Schmid, Calvin F. "Urban Crime Areas: Parts I and II." *American Sociological Review.* Vol. 25, Nos. 4 and 5 (August and October 1960, respectively).

42. Schuessler, Karl and Gerald Slatin. "Sources of Variation in U.S. City Crime, 1950 and 1969." *Journal of Research in Crime and Delinquency.* Vol. 1, No. 2 (July 1964).

43. Sellin, Johan Thorsten and Marvin E. Wolfgang. *The Measurement of Delinquency*. New York: John Wiley and Sons. 1964.

44. Shoup, Donald C. and Stephen L. Mehay. *Program Budgeting for Urban Police Services*. Institute of Government and Public Affairs, University of California-Los Angeles. Los Angeles, California. 1971.

45. Turner, Anthony G. *The San Jose Methods Test of Known Crime Victims*. Statistics Division Technical Series Report No. 1, Law Enforcement Assistance Administration. July 1971.

46. Urban Institute and International City Management Association project team *Measuring the Effectiveness of Basic Municipal Services: Initial Report*. Washington, D.C.: International City Management Association. February 1974.

47. Walzer, Norman. "Economies of Scale and Municipal Police Services: The Illinois Experience." *Review of Economics and Statistics*. Vol. 54, No. 4 (November 1972).

48. Ziesel, Hans. "The Future of Law Enforcement Statistics: A Summary View." Chapter 12 from *Federal Statistics: Report of the President's Commission*. Vol. II. Washington, D.C.: Government Printing Office. 1971.

49. Schaenman, Philip S. "Police Productivity Measurement: Initial Approaches and Practical Problems." *Proceedings of the Criminal Justice Symposium Focusing on Police Productivity*, Lehigh University. July 19, 1974. To be published.

50. Hatry, Harry P. "On Measuring Local Government Efficiency (A Preliminary Examination)." Draft final report to National Science Foundation. The Urban Institute, Washington, D.C. August 8, 1974.

51. Ross, John P. and Jesse Burkhead. *Productivity in the Local Government Sector*. Lexington, Massachusetts: Lexington Books (D.C. Health & Co.). 1974.

52. Bloch, Peter B. and Deborah Anderson. *Policewomen on Patrol Final Report*. The Police Foundation. Washington, D.C. May 1974.

53. Bloch, Peter B. *Equality of Distribution of Police Services—A Case Study of Washington, D.C.* Washington, D.C.: The Urban Institute, February 1974.

THE EVALUATION OF POLICE PROGRAMS *

Although responsible police administrators are concerned with and anxious to use evaluation as a management tool, many administrators are uncertain about the nature of evaluation. The President's Crime Commission noted that university-trained research personnel frequently approached organizational problems from an academic frame of reference or that they were almost completely unacquainted with operational problems. They used a mysterious language of "contingency coefficients" and "multiple linear regressions" and their techniques and methodologies for evaluation were equally mysterious.

* Reproduced from *The Police Chief* magazine, Robert M. Carter, November 1971 issue, with permission of the International Association of Chiefs of Police.

Conversely, administrators were generally neither trained in a social science approach to evaluation nor able to envision a continuing research and evaluation program within their agencies.

It is not surprising that this background has produced some considerable confusion and suspicion about the nature and process of evaluation. And yet, the process of evaluation is not a stranger to the police administrator. Evaluation based upon sound data is the key to decision-making, and decision-making capability is of first importance among all administrative activities. Careful assessment and evaluation mark the appropriate decision: inadequate or partial evaluation most assuredly limits the administrator's ability to make sound judgments.

At bottom, however, the process of evaluation is not especially complex—particularly when its major components or elements are dissected and analyzed. There are four identifiable parts in the spectrum of evaluation: objectives, programs, standards and methodologies. I will examine them separately and then join them together into a simple model of evaluation.[1]

Evaluation of a program or process does not begin with the program, but with a clear and explicit *identification of the objectives toward which the program is geared*. The police administrator must be able to outline his goals or purposes, not only in general terms, but also as precise, clear objectives: "Objective number one is . . . objective number two is . . .," and so on. Further, he must recognize that the objectives may be either a primary "need to achieve" objective or a secondary "nice to achieve" objective. There may be one or more of each type of objective and accordingly a priority or special emphasis may be placed upon the accomplishment of one objective rather than another. For the purposes of model construction, the objectives may be represented as a target.

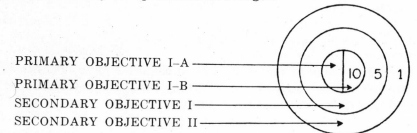

Figure 1.   Objectives

[B7193]

1. The approach outlined below has been successfully utilized for program evaluation at the Delinquency Control Institute of the University of Southern California and at the California Youth Authority Juvenile Law Enforcement Officers' Training Course. Police participants, examining police programs and following the model step-by-step, have found the procedure to be useful.

Figure 1 indicates that there are two equally important primary objectives represented by the two segments of the bull's-eye. There are also two secondary objectives, not of equal importance, assigned to the 5 and 1 rings.

It is emphasized that the administrator should be aware of the objectives and their priorities without recourse to outside consultants or experts.

The second component of the evaluation process is the explicit *identification of the program or process and its parts.* As in the case of objectives, the police administrator should be aware of most of the elements comprising a particular program. It is not sufficient to identify the program in broad terms; specifics are required. As an example, the police administrator who tells us that he has a delinquency prevention program has in fact told us very very little. To understand his program would require some considerable detail about basics like who is involved and why, how did they get involved and when, the degree of involvement, the specific nature of the program and so on.

For model construction purposes a neat, symmetrical representation of "program" is inappropriate, since all components cannot be identified. There are pieces which are elusive or hidden, and there are some whose existence is unsuspected. Accordingly, our model presentation (Figure 2) is somewhat amoeba-like with most, but not all, components identified. The unknown elements are identified by "x."

When objective and program are fused into the model, the thrust of evaluation becomes evident, as shown in Figure 3. Programs are evaluated against—or in terms of—objectives.

Evaluation cannot exist in a vacuum and be only an examination of program components and objectives. One must develop a type or types of measures to determine how well programs and objectives mesh. The third element in the process of evaluation is the *development of one or more measures or standards or criteria* for evaluation. These measures may be few or many, simple or complex; but, as was the case for objectives and programs, they should be precise, explicit and identifiable by the police administrator. Since these standards serve as the measuring device to determine the fit of program to objective, the model utilizes a simulated ruler as in Figure 4. The ruler for this model has six units representing cost, time, personnel, ease of operations, politics and effort required. The ruler, of course, may be longer or shorter with finer or coarser or different and varying units of measure.

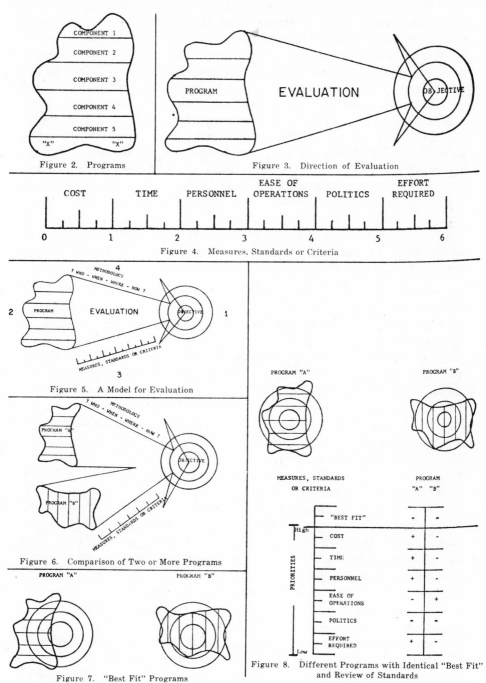

Figure 2.   Programs

Figure 3.   Direction of Evaluation

Figure 4.   Measures, Standards or Criteria

Figure 5.   A Model for Evaluation

Figure 6.   Comparison of Two or More Programs

Figure 7.   "Best Fit" Programs

Figure 8.   Different Programs with Identical "Best Fit"
and Review of Standards

[B7311]

At this point, three of the four elements of evaluation have been identified: objectives, programs and standards. It has also been pointed out that the police administrator should have fairly complete knowledge about the specific components of these three elements without recourse to experts from outside his agency. The fourth element of evaluation is methodology. *Methodology provides the techniques for evaluation* and focuses on four questions—who, when, where and how? These questions may take the following forms: "*Who* will do the evaluation—the agency itself or outside consultants?" "*When* will it be done—at the beginning, during or end of the program?" "*Where* will the evaluation be done—in the agency, in a research division or on a campus?" "*How* will the evaluation be done—by computer, subjective techniques or by tic marks drawn on a yellow tablet?" Although it is possible that the administrator will not know the answers to these and related methodological questions, he should be aware of the questions. They recur whatever the nature of the evaluation task.

Figure 5 presents the completed model for the evaluation process.

The model focuses on the evaluation of a single *program* against one or more *objectives* by a set of *standards* utilizing a specific *methodology*. The model did not assume the existence of alternative programs, but if alternatives exist, and this is the usual experience, one must determine which available program alternative is most appropriate in terms of the agency and its operations.

In comparing two or more programs, it is absolutely essential to recognize that an accurate evaluation is impossible if there are different standards or methodologies or changed objectives. Simply put, Programs "A" and "B" cannot be evaluated, one against the other, if objectives are changed or if different sets of standards or methodologies are used. One simple evaluation guideline exists for comparison of programs: Of the four variable, *only* programs may vary; all else must remain constant. In short, programs cannot be compared if we use different targets, different rulers for measurement, or different questions or methodologies. The model for this kind of evaluation appears in Figure 6. Note that only program varies.

When alternative programs are evaluated against identical objectives, using common standards and the same methodology, two criteria are used to determine which program is the most appropriate. The first is "best fit"; the second is an analysis of the alternatives by each of the standards. "Best fit" is simply determining how well each program achieves the stated objectives. Figure 7 shows how program "A" covers or achieves less than one-half of the target objectives; program "B" encompasses all of the primary objectives and some of the secondary objectives. Clearly "B" is the "best fit" of program and objectives.

If two different programs have a similar "best fit," a comparison is made by *analysis of each of the standards in order of their priority*. Using a ruler similar to that presented earlier, a priority of standards is first established, i.e., first priority is cost, second is operational ease, third is effort, and so on. Then the programs are compared against the standards. Thus, how do these programs compare in cost, in ease of implementation into current operations, in effort required? If minimum cost is the essential standard and "A" is three times that of "B," then "B" is the obvious choice. If the costs are identical, but "A" may become operational with less difficulty than "'B," and all other standards are more or less equal, "A" is the appropriate choice. If cost and operational ease are similar for both programs, we proceed to the next standard—and the one after that —until one alternative is a clear choice over the other. A simple format for such a review of standards appears in Figure 8, in which Program "A" has a clear advantage over "B."

In summary, evaluation can be examined as a process and in terms of a simple model with four major and essential components. A plan for evaluation starts with objectives and flows through programs, standards and methodologies. As a practical matter, these components may be combined in the development of a plan of evaluation, but it must be emphasized that they are independent of one another and, at some point, must be isolated and examined separately. Further, the police administrator must have first-hand knowledge about the objectives, programs and standards and should at least be aware of several basic questions relating to methodology.

Substantial funds from state and federal sources are available to law enforcement agencies for innovative crime prevention programs and other activities. Almost without exception, applications for research-based, action or demonstration grants require a plan for evaluation. The police administrator must become familiar with the process of evaluation, whether seeking grant funds or simply making decisions about ongoing or contemplated operations. Evaluation is a function of administration and a requirement for the administrator.

Areas for Discussion for Part IV

1. What are the various methods utilized in police organizations for establishing direction and internal control?

2. Since goal setting is an extremely important process within the police organization, what impact does the lack of clear-cut goals have on the management process?

3. Policy formulation is a direct result of planning and goal setting; discuss the ability or inability of police executives to establish policy in police organizations.

4. Describe the planning process and its impact upon police systems.

5. Systems analysis involves the continual observation and analysis of organizational activities; what are the implications of this process upon management?

6. Discuss the implications of goal setting and planning on the budgetary process.

7. What is the relationship between the democratic/participative organizational approach discussed in Part Two and the systems approach discussed in this section?

PART V

CHANGING THE POLICE ORGANIZATION

If an organization is to remain a viable part of society, it must constantly change. Change is as basic as the very nature of organizations. The institution of an organization in our society represents society's or some segment of society's identification and subsequent action taken toward the solution of a problem or set of problems. Society mandates that organizations be problem or goal oriented. Concomitantly, police organizations strive toward enforcing laws, apprehending criminals, maintaining order, and providing services to the community. Traditionally, police executives and other government officials have monitored public sentiments and administered their police departments accordingly. Historically, society's expectations of organizations have changed; therefore, if an organization was to continue to remain viable or even exist, it had to comply with society's contemporary expectations.

Moreover, internal problems have forced organizations to make adjustments in their structure and managerial processes. Over the last several decades there have been vast changes in the organizational expectations of organizational members. For the most part society has moved from an authoritative perception to a more democratic perception of man. Today's worker expects to be treated more democratically. Warren Bennis considers this factor as being of primary importance in causing changes in the organization.[1] If organizations are to achieve maximum effectiveness, they must secure the cooperation of their employees. Therefore, organizations must change to adopt to the changing expectations and demands set forth by employees.

Organizational change can occur in two areas, organizational structure and managerial processes and the expectations and subsequent behavior of organizational members. Basically, change in structure and managerial processes included planned restructuring of power and authority matrices, hierarchy, span of control, division of labor, and communications (these changes are, more or less, elaborated on in Part II). Changes of this nature are usually management initiated in an attempt to increase the overall effectiveness of the organization.

On the other hand, change evolving around organizational expectations and behavior constitutes an attempt to mold attitudes, norma-

---

1. See Warren G. Bennis. "Beyond Bureaucracy," in *American Bureauc-* *racy.* Chicago: Transaction Books, Inc., 1970. pp. 3–16.

tive systems, and actions to meet the needs of the organization; although, changes of this nature can and usually are attempted in conjunction with changes in organizational structure and managerial processes. Change modalities included techniques ranging from individual counseling to organization-wide therapeutic milieus.[2] The essence of this type of organization change is the attempt to create an awareness of organizational problems and needs and the importance of the organizational membership, individually and collectively. It is an attempt to bond the people to their organization.

Historically, there has been a great deal of discussion on change and police organizations.[3] However, presently there exists only sparse bits of evidence that change has been affected in policing.[4] Change tends to be more rhetorical as opposed to actual. Although, when presented, change philosophies are extremely logical and encouraging; however, change is a most complex process, and there are numerous intervening factors which frequently are neglected in planning.

To better understand the difficulty in affecting change, the fact that an organization is a system and functions within a political, social, and economic environment must be clearly understood.[5] Change agents and the organizational members are not the only primary figures involved in change. Regarding the police organization, the community, government officials and other public and private agencies impact the successfulness of any change effort. Moreover, there are many internal factors which inhibit organizational change. Generally, most people are resistant to any change. Change frequently threatens one's power in the organization.[6]

This section of the text attempts to provide the reader with a complete discussion of the issues evolving around change in the police

2. For a concise discussion of the various methods of change see Daniel Katz and Robert L. Kahn. *The Social Psychology of Organizations,* New York: John Wiley & Sons, Inc., 1966. pp. 390–451.

3. Ronald G. Lynch. *The Police Manager,* Boston: Holbrook Press, Inc., 1975. pp. 235–252.

4. See Pierce R. Brooks. "Lakewood Colorado: Change Agent in Police Administration and Organization." *Proceedings: Tenth Annual Interagency Workshop, June 2–13, 1975.* Sam Houston State University, Huntsville, Texas, 1976. And Victor I. Cizanckas and Donald G. Hanna.

Modern Police Management and Organization, Englewood Cliffs, N. J.: Prentice-Hall, Inc., 1977. And, Ronald Reams, Jack Kuykendall and David Burns, "Police Management Systems: What is an Appropriate Model?" *Journal of Police Science and Administration.* Vol. 3, No. 4, 1975. pp. 475–481.

5. Katz and Kahn, pp. 14–29.

6. See Lawrence W. Sherman, "Middle Management and Police Democratization: A Reply to John E. Angell." Criminology, (February, 1975): 363–377.

organization. We have attempted to collect those articles which concentrate on change techniques and problems. We feel that organizational change is best facilitated through a clear understanding of the organization and the change process. We attempted to provide the reader with material which provides the required insights into organizational change theory.

Objectives for Part V

1. Identify the methods of organization change and their implications to police administration.

2. Identify methods which the police administrator may utilize to determine if change is needed in the police organization.

3. Identify the state of the art of change theory in police organizations.

4. Identify the internal and external factors which inhibit change in the police organization.

5. Identify problems associated with implementing unnecessary change in the police organization.

CHANGING THE POLICE—THE IMPOSSIBLE DREAM? *

There is, today, intense interest in the American policeman. He is, at once, the darling of the Establishment, the *bete noir* of the Movement, the cause of frustration and violence, the *sine qua non* of ordered liberty, the necessary instrument of social control, the embodiment of fascist oppression, the shame and the pride of the nation.

Even though our people have perused reports of presidential commissions for 176 years (beginning with George Washington's 1794 Whiskey Rebellion commission), only recent commission reports have dealt heavily with criminal justice,(1) and prominently therein with the American policeman. The implementation of commission recommendations has been minimal, and, for the most part, recommendations have been ignored, received as suspect, given lip-service attention, or rejected by both political and police leadership.

Even though legislators, over the years, have compulsively sought to eradicate problems of crime and disorder with punitive and repressive legislation—and failed—the efforts continue. The Omnibus Crime Control Act of 1968 is questioned relative to provisions on confessions and audio-surveillance; the District of Columbia Crime Bill is questioned relative to provisions on "no-knock" entries

* Source: Germann, A. C. "Changing the Police-The Impossible Dream?", Reprinted by special permission of the Journal of Criminal Law, Criminology and Police Science, Copyright © 1971 by Northwestern University School of Law, Vol. 62, No. 3.

and preventive detention; and the Organized Crime Control Act of 1970 is questioned relative to provisions for "dangerous special offenders." Most questioning indicates grave fear that the police assault is not really being directed to murderers, rapists, and thieves, but that the police are out to stifle dissent, harass non-conformists, and contain the militant minorities. There is strong feeling that the police target is not criminality, but social, political, and cultural deviance.

It is becoming almost impossible to describe the current police scene without seeming to impart a derogatory, hostile, anti-police message. It is always difficult to suggest change without imputing some criticism of the status quo, but in the police area such phenomenon is critical, for to many police The mortal sin is for anyone, in or out of the police service, to question or criticize the police. A police-state atmosphere is highly evident within the police establishment, and policemen may question, criticize, or deviate from the police "party-line" only at their peril, with grave jeopardy of assignment, evaluation, and promotion. If Socrates were alive and curious (blue) he would immediately become anathema to most police agencies, particularly the larger ones. Police regard the critical questioner as ignorant, malicious, or subversive—period.

To continue to support the police without question or condition is to pour public monies down a rat-hole, for American communities do not have law and order with equal justice, and police today, using police statistics, are about as ineffective as they were twenty years ago in protecting the community notwithstanding great technological efficiency and sophisticated gadgetry. Perhaps it is time for the nation to re-evaluate the goals and objectives, policies and procedures, methods and techniques of social control and community policing.

People question whether police are engaged in humanitarian service or in authoritarian iron-rule; whether police are truly organs of the total community or hired guns set by one part of the community against another part. It is high time for all people to observe, experience, and judge policing at close range as it occurs in all enclaves of the community.

There are formidable obstacles to overcome if American police are to undergo necessary and massive changes for policing the 70's. Leadership—whether police or political—needs to be of a new type to draw our people together as brothers and sisters. The nation has had excessive current experience with police and political leadership that nurtures fear, resentment, hatred and violence. Police leadership decisions, today, tend to preserve the status quo and enshrine the archaic. Somehow, in the police establishment, leadership must be developed that is open, willing to listen, willing to question, willing to experiment, and willing to change even the most revered attitude or practice. Most current police leadership does not have the breadth of vision, perspective or motivation to do what must be done: *Work with all of the people to eliminate the police Neanderthal and to develop a sensitive and humane people-oriented protective service.* That is the need, desperate and immediate.

POLICE EDUCATION AND TRAINING

Much police education and training is archaic and inane. A story may illustrate: There once lived a group of Neanderthals who depended upon sloth snaring, mammoth slaying, and saber-tooth scaring for survival. These techniques were so necessary that old Flint Fist started a training program to teach the younger Neanderthals— the teacher was good, the techniques were fun, the students were eager, and the payoff was helpful to the tribe. Eons passed. Conditions changed; sloths, mammoths, and saber-tooths migrated, evolved, became extinct; the tribe became a nation; fire, wheel, lever were innovated; and new dangers developed. But, old Flint Fist and his loyal followers continued the attitudes and actions they were conditioned to and refused to change methods or training, shutting their minds firmly to the fact that the real world had changed. They were able to convince the community that they should be supported over the years, for whenever they were questioned or criticized they told horrifying tales of lurking evils, evoked memories of past brave conquests, and a frightened and grateful people sustained them. Originally, their techniques and training had some rational basis, but it was only time until the techniques and training were outmoded, and their anachronistic commitments became laughable, and obviously ineffective when utilized against the new dangers.

Much of the current police methods and training consist of sloth snaring, mammoth slaying, and saber-tooth scaring. The new social realities and the dynamics of the current scene are ignored.

Education and training for police must serve to humanize the police, enhance democratic values, and develop foundations for mutually supportive police-public partnerships. Many current education and training programs serve only to perpetuate Neanderthal attitudes and practices. Radical revision is needed to change them from isolated, closed rigidities, with uniformed "boot camp" indoctrination of automatons, to integrated, interdisciplinary programs for the preparation of sensitive criminal justice professionals who are creative, innovative, and effective change agents.

POLICE ATTITUDES AND VALUES

As with other vocational groupings, there is much police moralistic self-righteousness and ideological intolerance. But, with police, the problem is hypersensitive, for with their office goes immense authority and power, and immense potential for harm to individual and community. The motion pictures *"Z,"* *Billy Jack* and *Flap* portray a variety of police attitudes and values. The character of Rafferty in *Flap* is seen by many Americans as highly representative of the police personality. Over the years, in a variety of media presentations, the American social control agent has been presented as a handsome supercop fighting the ugly supercriminal, using a wide variety of gimmickry, proceeding in any fashion he desires, and always getting his man. Thus, our public is conditioned to seeing the criminal as some form of ugly deviant, the policeman as hero, science and technology as powerful magic, attention to due process and civility as immaterial, and order as paramount. *Flap's* Rafferty might signify a genuine change in media approach.

There is no question that police folkways give internal legitimacy to the tactics of harassment and have done so over the years. Recently, at the University of California at Los Angeles, Sociology Professor F. K. Heussenstamm "recruited five black, five white, and five Mexican-American drivers with no traffic violations within a year and asked them to sign pledges that they would obey all the rules of the road as carefully as possible. Each then affixed a Black Panther Party sticker to his car bumper. Strangely, within 17 days all 15 experimental subjects had bad driving records—amounting to 33 summonses handed out by police, with fines totaling $500." (2)

In some absurd conviction that the methods of the past will somehow suffice to solve present problems, the police Neanderthal supports obsolete and self-destructive actions, such as excessively harsh and ferocious response when unpopular groups violate a law.

"Police cities" exist in this nation—communities where, in the *name* of impartial law enforcement, police enforce their own prejudices, or the prejudices of the majority, with impunity, with immunity, with governmental support, and often with smug satisfaction.

Police attitudes, for the most part, indicate no responsibility for unnecessary or illegal police violence, or abuses of police authority. The question arises: Is the individual citizen to be held responsible for his acts, but not the agents of the government? Police often become enraged at citizen questioning of police actions, but it should be considered as an act of highest patriotism and loyalty to American ideals for any citizen to attempt to keep his government on a moral level above that of Adolf Hitler. The voices of American police leadership are strangely silent in this area. A recent issue of *The Police Chief*, official publication of the International Association of Chiefs of Police, carries an editorial relative to the recent attacks upon policemen, and suggests, as "viable preventive measures," more severe laws, defense instruction, protective equipment, bomb squads, and improvement of intelligence.(3) Nothing is said about the possible relationship of abuses of police authority and power to such attacks upon police; nothing is said about the development of a viable police-public partnership in all community enclaves. It is the judgment of this writer that "many chickens are now coming home to roost," and if police response can only consist of traditional mechanical measures it is evidence of intellectual bankruptcy or blind obstinacy at the highest leadership levels.

Even outsiders to the American police scene can sense some of the attitude and value problems of the police. One British police superintendent, speaking a few months ago about American police, said: "Their role can be likened to Jekyll and Hyde—on the one hand they are furiously promoting community relations programs to woo over their public—and on the other they are shooting, beating, and bombing their public to keep them in order."(4)

Perhaps one key to police attitudes and values is in how the policeman views himself. Narrowly, as a muscled crook-catcher? Or broadly, as an ombudsman of the poor, a protector of all the enclaves, as competent in insuring due process as in strangling out a combative drunk? It is interesting to read in the October 30, 1970, Crime Control Digest that the Los Angeles Police Department received two L.E.A.A. grants—one was for legal advisors, $15,000, and the other was for a field stress target range, $250,000. A cynical observer would opine that people put their money where their hearts lie.

There are reasons to be discouraged about the American police scene, but there are glimmerings of hope. Currently, the police Neanderthal is in the driver's seat all over the nation, and he is difficult to remove for he has immense power to frighten and damage any detractor. The police "dossier" may not only be used properly in safeguarding the community and nation, but that file may also serve as a most potent lever to neutralize anyone troublesome to the police establishment.

There are some rumblings within the police establishment, and a few of the sensitive professionals of a variety of ages, races, and ranks are engaged in serious conflict with the police Neanderthal who is also of a variety of ages, races, and ranks. These conflicts could provide some areas of possible joint action between the sensitive professional and change oriented members of the community. A benign conspiracy? An urge to needed internal revolution within the police establishment? A suggested split between the sensitive and humane and compassionate police and those who are rigid and mechanical and indifferent? Yes! Citizens can help by encouraging and supporting those police whose attitudes and values are worthy of respect, while at the same time taking issue with any police who misuse authority and power. "Off the Pig" is very expressive, but it is time that "He's a Friend of the People!" be voiced loud and strong for any American police who so deserve.

Some areas of possible mutual interest that could be explored:

Commission Recommendations. The recommendations of the recent Presidential commissions are revolutionary, yet consistent with the Constitution. If implemented, people could experience a more safe and just life, and the American dream would become more reality than myth. No audit, community by community, or state by state, has been made to determine the degree of compliance with commission recommendations. Nothing would prevent a blue-ribbon committee in any community undertaking a study of their police vis-a-vis implementation of commission recommendations.

It would be helpful if more cities volunteered to experiment with new fashions of policing and became testing grounds for radical changes in social control. It is wishful thinking to expect the precincts or subdivisions of the larger police agencies to experiment with radical change, unless top leadership is replaced. For the most part, changes of import are pioneered by smaller agencies of police. The larger agencies are mired in the glue of their own omniscience.

Organization and Operations. It would be helpful to experiment with demilitarized police organizations. This would involve elimination of military rank—stripes, bars and stars removed—with stature and respect gained by virtue of competence and integrity. This would allow more flexibility of program oriented operations.

It would be helpful to experiment with much more community involvement in police operations. Not manipulated community involvement which allows selected police buffs to volunteer as community advisors, but involvement that provides for citizen participation in decision making relative to police priorities and enforcement policies for a particular neighborhood in which the involved citizens live. Representatives of all clientele served—including former offenders —should form such advisory boards.

It would be helpful to experiment with a precinct manager who was recruited outside of the police system. While such a manager would be responsible to the chief of police, a background of other than previous police experience would bring new ideas into the ofttimes moribund police institution. Such lateral entry could provide a police leader who would reflect the ethnic and cultural qualities of his community and who would more easily bring citizen-police harmony by setting the example for the people.

Education and Training. It would be helpful to develop a model of police-university cooperation which could be emulated nationwide. There is now great animosity between the sensitive academician and the police Neanderthal, and between the sensitive police professional and the academic Neanderthal. For example, if the University of California, Irvine, working with the Irvine community, were to develop a police-community partnership, it might involve a four-year social ecology program for all policemen, graduate work in applied behavioral sciences, and continuous participation and audit by the total community. Majors in anthropology, sociology, and psychology could be urged to spend a minimum of three years as policemen—three years in the world's greatest social science laboratory. Like programs could be developed around the ghettos and barrios with police involved in Black Studies, Chicano Studies, and Asian Studies, with peripheral attention to linguistics.

It would be helpful to develop alternatives to existing training centers—F.B.I. National Academy, Southern Police Institute, Northwestern University Traffic Institute—so that totally new approaches to training could be instituted.

It would be helpful if sensitivity training—self-awareness processes—were included in every police training course.

It would be helpful if officers assigned to non-English speaking areas were first fully trained in the language of the community.

It would be helpful if the community being policed were encouraged to design and instruct in a training program for police being assigned to that community.

Personnel Management. It would be helpful to involve citizens of the community policed in the processes of recruitment, screening, and promotion. In time, this would provide for a variety of police personalities and replace the current police-controlled system that develops mirror-image counterparts of existing police.

It would be helpful to have psychiatrists, psychologists, sociologists, anthropologists, and legal experts probing into the police establishment, and reporting to the people in much greater detail than is now the case.

It would be helpful to develop alternative professional organizations, for the current bodies—International Association of Chiefs of Police, Fraternal Order of Police, Police Benevolent Associations, Police Unions—in general, are not change oriented to the needed degree, and are largely committed to the dogmas of a past age.

It would be helpful to experiment with tandem personnel systems. We now operate older manual record systems side by side with an automated system; perhaps we could do likewise with personnel.

We might develop a non-civil service group, operating under contract, in order to attract a variety of expertise.

It would be helpful to expand the process of lateral entrance for all levels of service, and make a talent-pool of sensitive professional expertise available to any mayor, city manager, city council, county board, police chief, or neighborhood committee.

It would be helpful to develop new categories of police agent, requiring advanced educational levels, and involving assignments with greater authority, flexibility, and discretion. This could result in dual channels of service so that sensitive, able people could remain in field service while receiving professional compensation. In some agencies, the sharp men are promoted; men in the field may come to be comprised of either young and inexperienced officers, or older, angry, bitter, cynical disillusioned men who are unable to advance.

Evaluation. It would be helpful to devise new methods to measure and evaluate police activities. Current evaluation processes are often repressively oriented, and the "brownie points" come with crook-catching, not general protection, counseling, referral, and service.

It would be helpful to utilize the computer processes to monitor due process throughout the criminal justice system, from first field contact to final release. This could result in re-evaluation of many police processes.

It would be helpful to allow citizens access to their own dossiers so that any incorrect or inaccurate information could be challenged and expunged. This could result in re-evaluation of the intelligence function.

It would be helpful to involve citizens in the evaluation of deployment policies. Some research, (5) for example, indicates that a particular East Los Angeles area is very comparable to the West Valley area of Los Angeles. They have about the same populations, major crime rates, and percentage of alcoholics. The West Valley area has a 95% non-Spanish surname population and a median income of about $8,500. The East L.A. area has a 50–60% Spanish surname population and a median income of about $5,500. When deployment of police is studied, it appears that there are about 3 police per square mile in the West Valley area and about 13 police per square mile in the East L.A. area. When arrests for drunk and drunk driving are compared, the West Valley area will have about 1,500 per year, and the East L.A. area about 10,000 per year. If such data are correct, the imbalance of deployment and enforcement is worthy of discussion and evaluation.

It would be helpful to compare data on accident causing traffic violations with data on traffic citations; in such manner the "duck pond" ("easy ticket" location) can be isolated and eliminated.

Police-Community Relations. It would be helpful to eliminate the mislabeling of crime prevention programs, public relations programs, youth programs, and human relations training, as "police-community relations" programs. Police-community relations carries the connotation of conflict resolution, of two-way dialog with all enclaves of the community, of open relationships between police and public — and is very rare.

Complaint Handling. It would be helpful to experiment with new methods of complaint handling. Many people believe that current procedures are long, inconsequential, and that there is no real recourse for the victim of founded police malfeasance. The suspension, dismissal, and prosecution of errant officer, with substantial award of damages for injury to person, property, or reputation, is so rare on the American police scene as to be almost nonexistent. The victim of police inhumanity can be arrested and threatened with heavy prosecutions and thus effectively neutralized and silenced; stipulations of probable cause can be demanded in exchange for dismissal of charges.

The "internal affairs" investigating units can be ferocious with respect to insubordination or violation of departmental orders, and, on the west coast, in cases of theft or bribery, but such units are almost deaf, dumb, and blind when it comes to violations of due process, to invasions of privacy, to degrading and abusive treatment. To suggest that such units can operate as the "world's greatest washing machine—everything that goes in dirty comes out clean!" is understandable. It is obvious to many people that such units fail to vigorously pursue abuses of authority (violations of due process, invasions of privacy, false arrests), abuses of power (unnecessary use of force), and arrogant bullying (harassment of the unpopular). It is very doubtful that review boards or ombudsmen will bring real change or genuine recourse; police malpractice will remain so long as it is tolerated by the police; it will be tolerated by the police so long as it is tolerated by the public—period.

It would be very helpful to develop a team, or teams, of blue-ribbon "truth-tellers" who could accompany the police on raids, observe police station house conduct, examine police operations at demonstrations, scrutinize field conduct in all parts of the community, and report to the people. Such "truth-tellers" should be selected from all enclaves and have reputations of unquestioned integrity and independence. Their reports should receive the widest possible readership.

It would be helpful to have more data on community violence that is government sponsored or commissioned. The Los Angeles *Times* editorial, "Support Your Local Police," (November 16, 1970) stated that "One officer of the Los Angeles Police Department has been killed this year (by guns). . . . Five officers of the L.A. P.D. have been wounded by gunfire this year, and 50 shot at." Every decent person is saddened and angry to hear of the death, injury, or assault of a policeman, or of any human being. It should be of interest, also, to know how many people in Los Angeles have been killed by police guns this year, or wounded by police gunfire, or shot at by police. It should be of interest to know, in any metropolitan area, how many people have been killed, injured, or assaulted by police, even though such actions be considered lawful and necessary, and it should be of interest to know their ages, races, and neighborhoods. There may be some relationship between the use of violence by the government and the use of violence by private parties.

Community Involvement. It would be very helpful to experiment with a variety of methods of community involvement, for people should understand their police, support their police, and control their police. Today's police seem to operate independently of civilian control. It may be a legitimate consideration for the people policed to participate in decisions relative to police policy.

It would be helfpul to involve people of the community in decisions that relate to police weaponry and armaments, for some people believe that police are ever more paramilitary, choosing weapons that are needlessly destructive—saps, weighted gloves, Mace, dum-dum soft-point expanding bullets, high-powered rifles, machine guns— and, therefore, at their own whim, using inhumane means. Charles Reich states, in relation to Mace, that "no procedures known to the public were utilized in the decision to start using this chemical on people, and no procedures exist for challenging or changing the decision." (6) Such a sober opinion stands in contrast to the statement of the Los Angeles County Sheriff:

> We are supplying our men with more modern and more sophisticated equipment. I do not intend to publicize where this is stored, nor precisely what the equipment is, but we are better prepared from a standpoint of weaponry to contend with our problem than we have ever been. . . . I have been asked if high-powered rifles, automatic weapons, and tear gas projectiles are available to all Los Angeles County Sheriffs Deputies at this moment. The answer is yes. When needed, they are available at a moments notice. (7).

It is suggested, very often, that only the police are capable of determining what the police should do, or how they should do it. The people are murmuring loudly in some enclaves: "Should we allow a bunch of mean, narrow-minded, bigoted mercenaries to tell free men how the community should be policed? If we have the right pay for policing, do we not also have the right to change policing?" That crude form of questioning contains the kernel of today's police problem: *Do the people who are being policed have the right to a meaningful voice in that policing?*

The police are an institution of the community and, in theory, should exist to assist the entire community form a safe and just place to live, and, in theory, it should not be up to the police, unilaterally, to decide how this will be achieved. It is correct to say that policing is too important a business to leave to the chiefs.

CONCLUSION

Change in American policing will not occur unless and until large numbers of concerned citizens from all enclaves in the community, socially aware police and criminal justice personnel, sensitive government legislators and administrators begin to address the real issues, rather than dealing with abstractions and procedural minutiae. It is correct to say that "we the people" must sit down as members of one family and hear each other. If we cannot do this, we are doomed to increasing violence in our communities, with police playing a central role.

In a viable democracy, concepts such as "Power to the People!" and "To Protect and to Serve" must be more than mere rhetoric.

(1) Wickersham, Civil Rights Commission, President's Commission on Law Enforcement and Administration of Justice, National Advisory Commission on Civil Disorders, Commission on Prevention and Control of Violence, Commission on Campus Unrest, Commission on Obscenity and Pornography.

(2) Forum Newsletter, Playboy, January, 1971, pp. 58–59.

(3) Tamm, Quinn, Editorial: *Target—The Police*, The Police Chief, November, 1970.

(4) Kennard, Superintendent J. P. de B., Warwickshire and Coventry Constabulary, in "The American Scene," an address to the Conference of the Association of Chief Police Officers of England and Wales on July 1, 1970, mimeo. p. 14.

(5) Morales, Armando, "Theories on Law Enforcement Patrol Personnel Deployment," August, 1970. Xerox.

(6) Reich, Charles A., *The Greening of America* (1970), p. 334.

(7) *Los Angeles County Sheriff's Bulletin*, No. 47, October 9, 1970.

THE DANGER FROM WITHIN: ORGANIZATION STAGNATION *

In recent years, it has been an annual or biannual practice of some groups to bring great pressure and criticism upon law enforcement units or departments. While such attacks may well be hostile and accompanied by broad and sometimes embarrassing coverage in the news media, they nevertheless typically have the salutary effect of unifying the group or department under attack. However, a far greater peril is often found within law enforcement units that have the potential to subject the organization to devastating and paralytic effects. That danger is organization stagnation.

Stagnation is a state wherein the organization fails to serve the purposes intended and expends its efforts simply maintaining its own existence. Organization stagnation is not unique to large law enforcement organizations or departments for it affects the small and large alike. Moreover, it is troublesome to diagnose because its symptoms are difficult to identify during the early stage of development.

The purpose of this article is to point to the more common symptoms of stagnation that signal the onset of organization paralysis. The symptoms are basically the same with respect to any type of law enforcement organization. Early-stage symptoms will be identified and discussed and finally an analysis made of advanced-stage symptoms. While not all stagnation symptoms are listed, those which are discussed in the analysis which follows are probably the most serious ones encountered by police administrators and members of organized law enforcement groups.

The potential elements for stagnation are present in every law enforcement organization. Moreover, there is a tendency by members of the organization to overlook and make allowances for stagnation symptoms by assuming that they will correct themselves in time. As the structural relationships deteriorate, the symptoms become more and more apparent to even the lowest members of the organization for their jobs will have changed in character, if not in function, as increased effort and demands will have been made upon them for greater efficiency. In addition, morale is often low and human relations problems abound with members of the organization openly critical of one another about the poor leadership and administrative shortcomings real or imagined in that person or group of persons. By this point, a law enforcement agency or department is in serious

---

* Source: Kaufman, Charles N. "The Danger Within: Organization Stagna- tion." *FBI Law Enforcement Bulletin,* (February, 1973) pp. 3–28.

difficulty and may require very radical changes to survive and rejuvenate itself into a dynamic institution.

EARLY–STAGE SYMPTOMS

Early-stage symptoms are both elusive and insidious. They are elusive and insidious because one can point to very little solid or hard data to verify them as being symptoms of organization paralysis. Since any tangible, undesirable effects may well be months or even years away, the immediacy of corrective action does not carry the degree of necessity for change which is involved. However, the perceptive individual is able to recognize such symptoms and take proper corrective and remedial procedures. In the early stages of stagnation the following symptoms appear to be significant indicators possessing the potential for arresting the life and activity of the organization.

LACK OF INNOVATION

There is little doubt that organization growth and development can be only as effective as the quantity and quality of its innovations. Innovations are new combinations of old ideas which allow the organization to maintain or exceed its present position with respect to a high level of services. In the area of law enforcement, this takes the form of new methods and approaches to solve and prevent crimes, as well as provide necessary public services. For law enforcement units, it can take the form of a new method of providing services more efficiently or even the providing of additional services.

The lack of innovation has a delayed effect on any organization. In many instances, it does not show up until the department or unit is unable to provide an acceptable response to problems it is expected to resolve. The response is usually a hasty, ill-planned crash program designed to catch up that seldom comes close to meeting the objective of solving the problem but does appear to satisfy the clamor by the public or governing members for someone to do something.

LEADERSHIP FAILURE

It is oftentimes stated that organizations die just like trees, from the top first and then on down into the rest of the structure. Individuals come into leadership positions in law enforcement by a variety of means; some are elected while others are appointed. Unfortunately, not all persons moved into leadership positions are capable of coping with the problems and decisions of that position. Many are either unwilling or unable to make decisions and carry them out while still others are immobilized by the fear or threat of criticism.

In its early stages, leadership failure in law enforcement is often discovered by a lack of direction—both personal and organizational.

This is difficult to identify as most people confuse effort with goal-directed activity. Some leaders quickly lose sight of their objectives and merely redouble their effort, giving everyone else the illusion that much is being accomplished. The ineffective leader is also found by noting the degree to which he is unable to initiate and influence the actions of others. If his subordinates reject him as well as his attempts to influence them, they will usually replace him with an informal leader of their own choosing. It is this informal leader to whom they will look for direction, thus creating a situation where insubordination may well take place. In some instances, the author has seen the men go to a captain with any and all problems and never go near the chief as they do not respect him as a leader.

An ineffective leader can be covered up by others around him who assume part of his work responsibilities or even by a committee that meets to make his decisions for him. In one instance, where leadership had failed at the top, one captain held training sessions where part of the time was actually devoted to working out problems which the chief had created and finding means to keep him from compounding the errors. In effect, this group of officers covered up and carried the chief for several years at which time the captain moved to a new position, the meetings were discontinued, and without that marked effort by all, the leadership deteriorated to where the chief was replaced within a year's time. In the short run, ineffective leadership seldom produces problems that cannot be patched up. This patching and makeshift covering up of errors of administrative omission and commission, while quite easy to discover, are quite something else to resolve. If allowed to persist, these errors become points of increasing friction and pressure that divert organization efforts and energies from the work and goals of the organization.

ABSENCE OF FACTUAL INFORMATION FOR PLANNING

Law enforcement organizations possess a certain inertia that allows them to continue even in the absence of planning guideposts such as programs, policies, and procedures. The absence of planning is easier to discover than the absence of innovation or a lack of leadership. While decisions based on intuition and hunch come easy, they are no substitute for hard data generated from past actions and a careful assessment of future operating conditions. It is quite surprising to many administrators that rather sizable amounts of data exist in most areas where decisions are to be made. When the quality of decisions begins to deteriorate, lack of information, or sometimes even misinformation, is usually a significant causal factor of this problem. Moreover, proposed solutions to problems may not be well thought out, and a certain panic becomes apparent in the decisions and daily efforts of all supervisory personnel.

A lack of information for budgetary planning is also one of the major reasons for a failure to obtain necessary funds for an adequate law enforcement program. The top administrator in a subdivision of a large metropolitan area never kept statistics and data for planning. Subsequently, he just took whatever his city board of governors felt like giving him for budget increases. Equipment soon was inadequate to serve a growing population, and the size of the force was far too small to provide quality law enforcement. The result was that a subordinate developed some plans and information for presentation to the governing board. The total request was granted much to the embarrassment of the chief.

LACK OF CLEAR–CUT GOALS

There are two types of goals found in every law enforcement organization: philosophical and operational. Philosophical goals give a broad general direction to administrators but seldom are applied directly to day-to-day decisionmaking. Operational goals are the day-to-day and week-to-week standards that provide the basis for work activity and motivation of officers and employees. As an organization begins to stagnate, the decisionmakers often exhibit a lack of direction as to what the objectives really are. As they search and expend departmental efforts in a variety of ways, careful methodical effort gives way to "windmilling" and inefficiency.

At this point, it is common to find coordination between departments and levels beginning to break down. This breakdown in coordination is due to a lack of common, clear-cut goals between departments. Moreover, to make matters worse, when decisions are made, they are put into effect without consulting other parts of the organization, thus creating confusion and delay in serving constituents. Goal confusion and fuzziness slow the organization response to its public, and they begin to search for other places where their needs will be served.

FAILURE TO COME TO DECISIONS

Indecision is a marked symptom of organization stagnation. While this condition normally stems from a lack of clear-cut operating goals, it can, and does, in some instances, exist independently. Some police administrators find decisionmaking difficult even when the organization has few, if any, problems. When stress is added, such individuals can become completely immobilized with the result that time and circumstances determine the destiny of the organization rather than marked and forceful actions.

In one midwestern city, the chief of police was absolutely unable to make a decision and would urge his subordinates to make the decisions. If any problems arose, he did not stand behind his subordinates and, in fact, at times joined in with harsh criticism. Needless to say, within a few years' time no one would propose new ideas or tentative solutions to old problems as they had lost their respect for their chief.

As any situation deteriorates, there is a major effort by many organization members to force decisions which begin to polarize factions into separate opposing camps, further forestalling actions to get the organization going again. There appears little to be done about the indecisive person other than to replace him if such actions are possible. Typically, replacement comes at a time so late in the stagnation period that months or years may be required to implement the major reorganization necessary to revitalize the organization.

FAILURE TO DELEGATE

In and of itself, failure to delegate authority to subordinates does not necessarily indicate organization stagnation is beginning. However, coupled with any one or more of the above early-stage symptoms, failure to delegate becomes a significant indicator of stagnation. The leader of any group that fails to delegate limits the quantity and quality of work that the organization can complete. The reason is obvious. Since he must approve everything and the hours in the day are limited, there is a level of output beyond which it is impossible to go. That level is determined directly by the amount of time the leader or supervisor is willing to give to the organization.

In one law enforcement organization where the chief demanded to make all of the decisions—even small ones—the organization was severely paralyzed. Since the chief did not delegate, his subordinates did not have a chance to make decisions and plan. As such, the organization came to a point where 30 percent of its top administrative personnel would retire in 5 years' time and few, if any, were capable of moving up, as they had not been able to develop skills in planning and decisionmaking.

Failure to delegate, as the organization begins to encounter difficulty and crisis, is reinforced by a manifold increase of problems. Lack of delegation is precisely what the organization does not need. Instead of a highly centralized, ever-tightening control by one person, it needs more authority in the hands of lower administrators for meeting and resolving the problems when they arise and where they find them.

The early-stage symptoms do not cause deterioration at any predictable rate. Moreover, a factor such as increased effort can compensate for a limited amount of organization inflexibility and stagnation. The presence of several of the early-stage factors tends to accelerate the stagnation process. While a clear demarcation point between early and advanced stages is difficult, the later stages are characterized by symptoms that generally keep the organization in disequilibrium, or an opposite extreme of severe overbureaucratization and red tape that have brought meaningful law enforcement activity to almost a standstill.

ADVANCED–STAGE SYMPTOMS

By the time a law enforcement department or unit reaches the advanced stages of stagnation, those who are served by the organization often find it difficult to get service on even routine matters. Moreover, those who are in positions of authority are either unwilling or unable to do anything about the difficulties of stagnation and final organization breakdown.

There are three major symptoms of the advanced or later stages of organization stagnation. All of the early-stage symptoms may be present, but they are, in the large part, eclipsed by three problem areas that have the attention of everyone. These major symptoms are: Management by crisis; communications breakdown; and a lack of organization adaptation.

MANAGEMENT BY CRISIS

Management by crisis is also known as "brush-fire law enforcement." It is a situation wherein the administrators are kept busy reacting to problems as they arise and are unable to take effective actions to head off problems of the future. Planning either does not exist or it is almost totally ineffective. This situation is a most critical one, for decisions are often being made in haste without regard to long-term effects.

From an operations standpoint, management by crisis is exemplified by work performed continually behind schedule, people assigned jobs for which they have few, if any, qualifications, and work often being duplicated by several departments or persons in the organization. Human relations problems are created hour after hour and, at times, seemingly without end. And, for many in administration, a certain desperation begins to pervade the decisionmaking and implementation processes.

In one community, the chief law enforcement administrator was kept so busy reacting to crisis after crisis that the lack of planning actually brought on problems that could have been avoided or prevented by some effort at preparation for the future. In this instance, the quality of effort deteriorated for officers, and their superiors suffered a morale breakdown with everyone griping about his job in particular and law enforcement in general. Attitudes became so negative that officers purposely feigned overwork to avoid answering calls. Law enforcement at an acceptable level ceased to exist in that community.

COMMUNICATIONS BREAKDOWN

Another marked characteristic of advanced organization stagnation is a breakdown in communications. The deterioration of communications does not occur suddenly but develops over time and the seriousness of its effects is not immediately discernible to everyone. However, those in the organization are usually quite well aware of them through daily interaction with one another in trying to keep the organization going.

Very commonly there is a screening of information upward. Subordinates, in such instances, are reluctant to send information upward that reflects poorly on themselves and especially on the organization's performance. The reason for this is quite obvious—disappointing or poor performance usually brings criticism from superiors, especially if the data is subject to critical review by a governing board. Such practices, while sparing the subordinates the unpleasantries of criticism, only complicate a deteriorating situation as the decisionmakers do not have an accurate picture or assessment of what is happening.

As problem after problem arises and effective solutions are not forthcoming that reverse the tide of poor performance, there is also a tendency for personnel to fragment into two or even three hard-core groups. Each group attempts to make a scapegoat of the other and subsequently blames the other for the problems of the organization. Particular individuals are singled out, and each new problem or reversal is pointed to as further evidence of that individual's incompetence. The result is that coolness and aloofness lead to less and less interpersonal communication just when increased communication is necessary. This state of affairs is most serious, and only a marked reshuffling of persons and duties will provide the atmosphere for the chance of a change in attitude on the part of organization participants.

LACK OF ADAPTATION

A lack of adaptation to changes in the need and demand for services points to stagnation more forcefully than any other symptom. As an organization begins to age, its inability to adapt becomes apparent. Many feel that the major variable for measuring the age of an organization is its ability to adapt and respond to the needs of its public and constituents.

Since by this time management is usually very busy responding to and going from crisis to crisis, there is little evidence of presence of an overall effort to adapt to the basic problems that come to plague the organization. The lack of adaptation traces back to a lack of planning, for through planning one is able to determine many problems before they arise.

Adaptation is hampered also by a lack of teamwork and confidence among the middle and top decisionmakers in the organization. Adaptation requires teamwork throughout the organization and, since strong factions have polarized around certain individuals or even issues, innovations are blocked and adaptation is thwarted.

Another stagnation factor that makes adaptation all but impossible is the lack of flexibility as found in separate departments wherein the means of operation become ends in themselves. This is a most unfortunate situation. As problems arise, the response by management is often one of tightening control in the form of rules and regulations with strict enforcement. Personnel soon come to find that it is more important to follow procedures than serve the public. The result is that to avoid criticism or discipline from superiors the rules are followed no matter what happens.

By this time, the organization is a victim of a cycle or chain of problems that not only are a cause of one another, but also reinforce one another making it all but impossible to break the chain. The management, by crisis, is a cause of the breakdown of communications, and as communications break down, it creates more crises that must be met. But it becomes less and less flexible, and with planning and adaptation at a minimum there is in turn the ever-increasing unanticipated crisis situation, and the cycle begins all over. This is a most frustrating and disheartening situation for those who must contend with the problem. When law enforcement organizations reach the point of exhibiting advanced-stage symptoms, they usually have human relations problems that make them unpleasant places to work. Seldom are such organizations rescued and brought back to life. It is regrettable when stagnation takes place, and only strong and vigorous efforts can forestall it. The problem is to be keenly aware of the symptoms and remedy them before they become serious.

SUMMARY

Organizations tend to stagnate at different rates of decline. Even so, they tend to exhibit the same symptoms of distress. The stagnation usually has two rather distinct stages, and the major differences in the stages concern the degree to which the symptoms or problems are present. Specifically, when dire problems of communications, management by crisis, and a lack of adaptation are found together, the organization is probably in a rather advanced state of stagnation, where great efforts are being made just to exist and resolve its internal problems.

An alert law enforcement administration does not allow the early-stage symptoms to become severe and critically compromise the operation and life of the organization. It is in the early stages that corrective action is most successful with the least amount of difficulty and inconvenience to the people involved. It is scarcely too much to state that the quality of administration in any law enforcement unit can be measured by the degree to which stagnation symptoms are present and causing problems. How about your own law enforcement unit—does it exhibit stagnation symptoms or is it a healthy, vigorous organization?

CHANGING URBAN POLICE: PRACTITIONERS' VIEW *

INTRODUCTION

Police administrators are responsible for providing a police operation that serves the public needs. On the surface, this responsibility appears to be simple enough; however, the realities encountered in operationalizing it are enormously complex. It is the purpose of this paper to review and analyze urban policing and suggest methods that police administrators can use to improve the effectiveness of their police organizations.

If police organizations are to fully realize their objective of addressing community needs, we believe it is important that police administrators adopt a consumer-oriented philosophy and take steps to ensure that their organizations have sufficient exposure and flexibility to align themselves with the needs of their clientele.

Our experience indicates that an administrator should consider a number of measures in preparing his organization for change. First, he should take steps to neutralize and establish support for change among his subordinates. Among the techniques that can be utilized for reducing resistance are (1) rewards and threats, (2) rationality and indoctrination, (3) cooption and replacement, and (4) camouflage and diversionary tactics.

Second, he should take steps to structure his organization to facilitate consumer-oriented change. In developing a new structure, he should consider emphasizing the following: (1) opening the organization, (2) supporting tolerance, (3) reducing organizational rigidity, (4) improving communications, (5) reducing reliance on formal authority, and (6) establishing a Centralized-Decentralized Organizational Model.

* Source: Igleburger, Robert M.; Angell, John E. and Pence, Gary, "Changing Urban Police: Practicioners View," in *Innovations in Law Enforcement* (Criminal Justice Monograph), Washington: National Institute of Law Enforcement and Criminal Justice, June, 1973. pp. 76–114.

Administrative actions to facilitate the development of dynamic police organizations will create difficult problems regardless of the approach utilized. The methods we suggest will be effective, but they will not provide a completely smooth transition from a traditional police bureaucracy to a new organizational design.

WHY CHANGE POLICE?

The basic purpose of public administration in American society is to fulfill those needs of the community that cannot be met through individual action or private enterprise. The definition of community needs is arrived at through a process referred to as politics. By responding to community needs, the government gains the consent of those who are served. However, this consent is not dependent on providing satisfactory responses for all unfulfilled citizen needs; it is also gained by the government providing an arena for controversy and conflict (Appleby, 1965, p. 334). It is through citizen interaction in this arena that the citizens arrive at the necessary cohesion to require governmental action, and the power of public officials is limited.

While the role of the police is to some extent defined by custom, culture, and law, it is constantly being redefined through the political processes. Therefore, police administrators must be cognizant of their political environments and provide organizations that are capable of making appropriate adjustments in their operations.

POLITICAL RESPONSIVENESS

Police administrators must participate in political processes because of their responsibility for ensuring police services that satisfy communities' demands for services and security. However, police officials do not have sufficient responsibility nor authority to adequately fulfill the demands of all citizens for police service and security. They share responsibility and authority with a variety of other organizations, governmental agencies, and social institutions.

Unfortunately, there are many police chiefs who display a willingness to accept total responsibility for objectives over which they have little control, such as reducing crime. It would be far more realistic to admit that the community, other governmental agencies, and a variety of social organizations share this responsibility. Such recognition would enable police administrators to legitimately involve a much broader reservoir of resources in the solution of their problems.

Aside from the preceding question of responsibility and authority, the police organizational hierarchy, which should be designed to receive and respond to community needs, has evolved to the point where the political environment has little impact on it (Tullock, 1965, pp. 137–141). A police department must be capable of accurately receiving popular demands, injecting them with considerations of prudence, perspective, principle, and concern for individual rights, and responding to them. Therefore, the police organization cannot be evaluated solely on the efficiency with which it performs rote functions. It must be assessed by its ability to reconcile diverse community needs into a response that is tempered by concerns for the individual and legitimatized by community support (Appleby, 1965, p. 335). Appropriate change within police organization will not come through piecemeal efforts designed strictly to improve operational efficiency. It will come through organizational techniques that provide continuous monitoring of the total environment of law enforcement.

THE COMMUNITY ENVIRONMENT

Over the past two decades, the urban environments within which police organizations exist have changed drastically. The changes in demographic characteristics alone have been profound enough to stagger one's imagination. For example, the racial composition of Dayton has changed from 90 percent to 70 percent white. The average income of citizens has remained constant in a period of sharp inflation. The heterogenity of our residents has increased.

The once powerful and stable middle class whites have been losing their power to a wide range of other groups. The *carte blanche* that was once given to the police to deal with social deviates has been withdrawn. The once illegitimate street people, radical groups, young people, and social deviates have become organized. These organized groups have been legitimized by such actions as the civil rights movement of the 60's, the increased attention to the demands of youth and minorities, and the reclassification of social behavior such as alcoholism and deviate sexual behavior among consenting adults as non-criminal.

Undoubtedly, the most significant influences that have changed the community environment for the police have been the Supreme Court and the educational system. For the first time in the history of society, a powerful government institution, the United States Supreme Court, actually took giant steps to guarantee both the political equality of men, as well as the subservient nature of government to men.

The educational system began to move in the same direction. Old authoritarian techniques and approaches have been replaced by individualized instruction that encourages self-motivation on the part of the student. Basic education has become universal, and continuous adult education has been accepted as a necessity. Schools have actually begun to deal with social information. They are recognizing the need to respond to students who are questioning the concepts of universal righteousness of the "American system."

The changes in community environments have caused police administrators to question themselves as to their clients, goals, organizational arrangements, strategies, and procedures. Police officials who have previously enjoyed the luxury of dealing with a well-defined power group are faced with pressure from groups that only a few years ago could not have commanded recognition from a passing police patrolman.

CONSUMER ORIENTATION

Given the circumstances that have been described, it is not surprising that many communities are demanding better and different services; what is surprising is the community's reaction to the lack of police responsiveness. Public law enforcement officials have for a number of years monopolized the service of security of persons and property. The monopoly is now being broken. In Dayton, we have experienced competition from the Republic of New Africa, a Black militant organization, which provides limited patrol service. Recently, a former Dayton policeman, who is now operating a private security agency, submitted a proposal to a Neighborhood Priority Board, formed under the auspices of the Model Cities Program, to develop a private, special police force for a white working-class area of our city.

Our experiences in Dayton are not significantly different from those of other cities. The police monopoly is being broken by volunteer citizens' groups and private police who are attempting to provide service on a neighborhood basis. We, the police, have now been placed in a situation where we can no longer "not give a damn." No longer can we count on the protection provided us by our positions as a monopoly. We must compete for citizen support.

The change process has always been crisis oriented in Dayton. Dayton is noted for originating the City Manager form of government. However, it was not originated until after the great flood of 1913 and the threat of the NCR Company to relocate unless city government became more efficient. The destruction of the police monopoly may well generate the spark that ignites the demand for change within the internal structure of police organizations. If this occurs, police administrators may realistically be able to reorganize with the necessary support base to become consumer oriented instead of product oriented. What has been described as an occupational army may through market analysis become an agent for providing service.

Professional police administrators in the United States appear to have difficulty adopting a consumer orientation because of self-imposed collusion of ignorance. However, increasingly, chiefs are attempting to modify their approaches; and their efforts are resulting in their being heralded by community leaders, and at the same time, stifled by the internal structure of the police organization. The process of implementing change is always difficult; within police agencies, it appears to be an impossible dream. The agents of change have become anathema to most police agencies. The following are a few of the characteristics of the police sub-culture that stifle change.

Blind Chauvinism

One of the areas of concern for progressive police administrators in law enforcement today is the blind chauvinism; i. e., that belief that the solution to the police problem is *esprit de corps* that permeates many police departments. Many of these chauvinistic individuals are more concerned about the length of a man's sideburns than the quality of his work. There appears to be an increasing hue and cry within some of these monolithic structures for more "spit and polish." The purpose of these comments are not to negate the importance of discipline but to place it in its proper perspective. Meaningful discipline and *esprit de corps* are the products of an organizational structure, which provides for the integration of the individual goals with the objectives of the organization. This does not mean the elimination of professional discretion or individuality.

We believe the level of chauvinism within a police department is directly related to the degree of authoritarianism present. Our value system is grounded in conservatism and dictates that crime be suppressed by whatever means necessary. Many police officers believe that the Constitution and civil liberties serve only to thwart their efforts. The work of William Vega indicated that most police officers see crime as the response of the individual, not associated with his environment. This value system of police conservatives enables them to disassociate the acts of individuals from society. Even well-read moderates find this value system difficult to accept.

A study performed by Smith, Locke, and Walker within the New York Police Department indicates that non-college police tend to be more authoritarian than college-educated police. This provides a basis for assuming that the police would be more realistic if they had a broader base of experience. However, Vega has pointed out that even liberals are coopted by police organizations. Liberals within police departments either alter their beliefs to conform, drop out, or go underground. If this is the case, most police departments do not have a significant population of resident liberals. However, there is no more reason for all police officers to be liberal than there is for them all to be conservative; but police departments need employees who are representative of the communities they serve.

Many police officers, who work in urban areas, are removed from the problems that mandate change because they have spent most of their lives in environments and cultures removed from the life-styles of modern urban citizens. They grew up in rural areas, small towns, or white middle-class neighborhoods. Their parents were blue-collar whites. After joining an urban police agency, they move to middle-class suburban communities where they do not have to con-front the problems faced by the urban people they serve. They travel into the city to spend as much of their eight hours as possible isolated from their clients by a car, an office, and bureaucratic rules and sta-tus. They socialize mainly with other police; they fight for two-man cars which ensures they will be further re-enforced by a person with values like their own.

A police organization, in order to interact with a community, should have a diverse representation within its membership. If a rule-oriented police organization does not permit any officers to wear long hair or beards, is it not saying that there is something wrong or distasteful about people who do? Will such an organization provide the same quality of service to members of the community who wear long hair and beards?

Management by Abdication

Another symptomatic problem associated area is management by abdication (MBA). This consists of rule-oriented management per-sonnel who attempt to implement change through fiat while simulta-neously abdicating responsibility for it. A MBA organization is rule-oriented as opposed to goal-oriented and responsibility for serv-ice is difficult to identify because the emphasis is on procedure as op-posed to results. The vast majority of police organizations are struc-tured along para-military lines of command and control. This ap-proach requires specialization and the development of functional re-sponsibilities which facilitates management by abdication.

Responsibility for providing police service in specific geographic areas of a city is difficult to identify in highly specialized police de-partments. Field lieutenants are normally held responsible for eight-hour time periods. Captains are responsible for bureaus such as investigation, operations, or records. Beat patrolmen share re-sponsibility for police service with many specialized technicians. The order maintenance function and crime control functions have become the responsibility of specialized public relations units and crime con-trol teams respectively, in many police departments. The only person within this type of framework who can be held directly responsible for police service is the chief of police. Thus, there is little or no im-petus within other areas of the organization for change. This has culminated in a situation in most areas where the chief of police not only makes the decision to change, but quarterbacks the entire process. Change that occurs through this type of process has been compared by McBride to hanging ornaments on a Christmas tree (1971, p. 20). These ornaments are normally removed when the Christmas season is over and change that occurs through this process has a life expectancy directly proportional to that of the chief of police. Productive change on the other hand, results from a spontaneous process which is ignited when the conditions are right for it.

The rule orientation of MBA is one of the primary defects within police management today. The vast majority of police agencies have become secure within the classical organizational structure that has been described. The operation of such an organization is mechanical. The duties of members are described in detail, and there are hard and fast rules along with a hierarchy of superior officers to make sure procedures are carried out according to rules. Such a structure was created to give and maintain status based upon an individual's ability to follow departmental rules and regulations which are in many cases of questionable value and often are not flexible enough to respond to the changing needs of a heterogeneous community. This became painfully obvious to us in Dayton when two police officers decided that they could better deal with a disorderly group by removing their firearms and placing them in the trunk of their car. Many individuals within the department reacted to this act with tremendous hostility because of a departmental policy that required police officers to carry their weapons at all times, both on and off duty. This rule has since been changed to give the individual officer the right to decide when he should not carry a weapon. The rule orientation of specialization has not only caused the police not to respond to the changing character of the community, but also in some cases to resist change which threatens the established status quo. If John Gardner (1965, p. 45) is correct in saying the last act of a dying organization is to produce a better and more comprehensive version of the rule book, then surely we are listening to the death gasp of many police organizations today.

Police chiefs are in the position of sitting on top of a giant pyramid. In this position, they are only able to cushion the police response not form it. The real power within the organization is at the operational level. The problem is that this level lacks the responsibility of direction and is not accountable to the community; therefore, it does not have to be responsive to it. The police chief, however, is normally in an appointed position and responsible to his community. The chief is in many cases attempting to direct change that operational personnel see no benefit in implementing. The change is usually goal-oriented as opposed to rule-oriented and therefore, threatening to the existing status quo and social relationships (Davis, 1968, p. 55).

The chief who attempts to bring about change is confronted by the phenomenon of MBA; i. e., rule-oriented management personnel who implement change through fiat while simultaneously abdicating responsibility for it. Change within this setting becomes damned as the child of the Ivy League Boys in Research and Development, who lack credibility and common sense, or of a starry-eyed chief, who has somehow become misdirected.

Why does this situation exist? One reason is related to efforts to insulate police departments from the spoils system (Smith, 1960, pp. 316–317). This attempt to professionalize the police has at times backfired. If we look at James Q. Wilson's paper, "The Police and Their Problems: A Theory," we note that the professional model he describes involves a legalistic approach which strives to eliminate discretion. If this is taken in conjunction with the insulation of the police from the spoils system without any mechanism to realistically replace it, then the lack of police responsiveness to the community should be expected.

Role Confusion

Role confusion is the symptom of another problem area within the police bureaucracy. Police officers at the line level have not been prepared to differentiate in response requirements. They are the product of a rule-oriented structure that provides "cookbook solutions" to problems (Fosdick, 1969, p. 313). Police officers are constantly confronted with demands from the community for varying types of service which they have not been trained to handle. This has resulted in a situation where police officers are threatened by the changing needs of the community. The status of police work is based upon law enforcement; the enforcement of the law has a certain aura of glamour associated with it. To be a public servant is to be less than an enforcer. Yet, police officers are confronted with a paradox since the community demands more service than law enforcement (Webster, 1970). Does a police officer enforce laws or provide service to the community? Since individual police officers have no direct responsibility to the community, and little or no contact with the political process, they are, in effect, free agents.

Police officers respond to the community as enforcers of the law. If there is any conflict in values, they become confused and respond in the manner in which they have been trained. They enforce the law without regard for the consequences. Enforcement of the law, in many cases, such as in Detroit in 1967, may result in disorder. However, the rule-oriented structure allows for no variance in response. Priorities are left to the individual officer and are affected by each officer's bias and values. The result is periodic chaos and an inability to understand why. The line-level officers who provide the services receive only the gut-level dissatisfaction of the street people, "The man is a pig." Yet, the "man" did his job. He enforced the law. The individual officer has not been prepared to analyze his job but has been provided with an overabundance of defense mechanisms (Vega, p. 17).

The police bureaucracy has been too effective in insulating people below the chief administrator from the conflicting changes and competing demands of the public. Seldom does a police officer below the chief have to face the demands of legislative officials, pressure groups, and private citizens with which the chief must deal. This type of conflict is normally almost entirely handled by the chief executive because of his position at the apex of the classical hierarchical structure. Given the dynamic nature of modern society, the chief is constantly subject to pressure in this position. When the chief decides that he must modify his organization to respond to his citizens, the members of the organization refuse to support him. Chiefs need not wonder why they are denied employee support; the chief has effectively insulated his subordinates, and they have not had to suffer through the confrontations and conflicts that have caused him to change. *Ex post facto* attempts by the chief to educate his subordinates to the reason for his deciding to change are usually not successful. The lower they are in the bureaucracy, the more insulated employees are from the problems faced by the chief and the less supportive they will be for significant changes that effect their behavior.

CONCLUSIONS

Obviously, without a well-defined approach to overcoming the restrictive aspects of the police sub-culture, a chief of police will not be able to ensure his citizens of an organization that will be responsive to their needs.

The characteristics of the police sub-culture and the characteristics of the police bureaucratic structure are basic reasons why the system is not satisfying community needs. An analysis of these factors suggests that the system, as it is currently arranged, will never be effective in identifying its goals and developing strategies for providing environmental security for urban peoples. The police structure itself must be changed; however, we need to recognize and admit to ourselves that speeding up the processes of justice, increasing the number of gimmicks, and improving the hardware available to the police will not produce the needed change. Such modifications are frequently used by police administrators and planners to con their potential critics into believing that progress is being made. These changes are nothing more than camouflage to conceal the real problems and diversionary tactics to keep attention off the critical shortcomings of the present system.

Most well-meaning police administrators rely on this cosmetic approach simply because they feel hopelessly hamstrung and impotent. Our experience and education have prepared us to be a cog in the police bureaucracy and defend it against all suggestions of inadequacy. We usually are not familiar with even the most superficial information about changing social organizations. Although police administrators have tried to resist and be their own men, they have been indoctrinated with the basic axiom of a police bureaucracy, "Those who do nothing do not encounter trouble as often as those who take action frequently."

The closed police sub-culture, the closed personnel system, the ambiguous nature of the community demands, and the pressure of the members of the police bureaucracy are eventually sufficient to convince a police manager of the wisdom of following the party line. As Sayre and Kaufman pointed out after observing the New York City Police Department, "In the end, whatever the dash and determination at the beginning, the commissioners yield to the necessity of being merely a spokesman and the advocate rather than the leader and the innovator" (1960, p. 292). The police executive usually decides that his personal security and comfort will be seriously affected if he pushes organizational changes that are in the best interest of society. Administrators normally yield to the pressure and relax—confident in the knowledge that they are supported by the bureaucracy and many powerful social groups.

It is imperative that we stop kidding ourselves and assume the risks associated with being change agents. We must focus on restructuring our organizations to achieve a stronger link between the environment, our constituency, and our employees. To do this, we need to evaluate the techiques available to us to obtain sufficient support from our personnel to establish an effective police organization.

ESTABLISHING SUPPORT FOR CHANGE

The traditional assumption that a chief of police has the power to make changes because he also has the formal authority is invalid. As Bernard has pointed out, the power of an administrator is restricted by what his subordinates consider legitimate (1968). Subordinates who want to restrict a manager's authority have at their disposal such techniques as work slow-downs, speed-ups, "by-the-rules" activities, communication disruption, distortion, and actual sabotage. They have the ability to accumulate support outside the organization and to focus sufficient pressure or legal attention on the administrator to neutralize or remove his authority. Therefore, the administrator has to deal with the problem of keeping his personnel from denying him the power to operate. Although desirable, their support is not absolutely essential, but an administrator who does not have employee support must be able to neutralize large-scale employee attempts to deny him the power necessary to keep the organization open and flexible.

The administrator has a variety of methods, which should be considered in developing strategies to get support or to neutralize employees' resistance to change. These techniques include rationality and indoctrination; rewards and threats; cooption and replacement; and camouflage and diversionary tactics. The ability to use these methods successfully depends on the administrator, as well as the situation. However, before employing them, a chief needs to recognize that organizations are complex in interrelations. A movement intended to achieve one purpose will inevitably have repercussions. Each action taken by the chief will be accompanied by a reaction. The chief will often be surprised by the unanticipated changes he sets in motion, and he must be prepared to absorb the heat. However, this is an occupational hazard which a police administrator must constantly face.

Rewards and Threats

These traditional tactics are used extensively by police officials, although one has to admit that the emphasis has always been on threats. From the first time a police recruit enters a training program until the day he retires from the police field, he is constantly told what will be done to him if he does not conform to the expectations of his supervisors and "superiors." This causes some people to suspect that police officers have become insensitive to other types of motivation.

The limited research available suggests that reward, particularly psychological rewards, are much more effective than threats (Argyris, 1965). Most police administrators have a variety of threatening units designed to identify undesirable organizational deviates and punish them; however, there is a need for units and procedures designed to identify desirable deviates and reward them with praise and publicity.

Rationality and Indoctrination

Police administrators have traditionally utilized indoctrination to change the behavior of their subordinates. The "training" which is designed for the indoctrination is structured to restrict criticism and questions from the "trainees" (Frost, 1959; Greenwood, 1972; Saunders, 1970). Trainees are required to submit to instructors who degrade and insult them in such a way as to damage their self-confidence. The indoctrination that is often carried out as police training is designed in a way that in many instances will destroy the individuality of police officers. This forces a new police officer to yield to being an unthinking member of a group that is dependent on its "superiors" for decisions and guidance. The counter productiveness of this approach to change is increasingly apparent. People resist this type of indoctrination; they reject conclusions that are forced on them by authorities.

People who have low opinions of themselves tend to be more closed and suspicious than people with good self-concepts. People who are constantly approached as if they are mentally retarded tend to develop behaviors that resemble that of a mental incapacitated person. Therefore, while one-way indoctrination may have a short-term impact on changing behavior, it will probably be counterproductive in the long run.

Rational discussion of problems and alternatives by all people in the organization will be more likely to establish an adequate environment for change. This approach, however, does not give the orderly appearance of efficient operations because it cannot be carried out without conflict (Coser, 1964). People who have apprehensions and questions about the changes can express their feelings and fears. All ranks argue and debate; they negotiate and compromise; and they each can have an impact on any changes that occur. At the same time, their individuality and worth is reinforced; they learn that they are important and their opinions matter. Such self-confidence and security makes them more open to change.

Although both indoctrination and rational discussion can be used to obtain support for change, we believe rational discussion is far superior to the traditional indoctrination approaches.

Cooption and Replacement

The chief administrator can consider using the two techniques of cooption and replacement to ensure that resistance to his authority does not damage his ability to keep the organization receptive to productive change. Cooption can be achieved by identifying the informal employee leaders who are critical of his efforts and placing them in positions where their responsibilities conflict with their rhetoric and actions. Once such a person is in a position where he has access to more information and is subjected to the pressures of responsibility, he will usually condition his behavior and attitudes. Even those people who are not completely coopted may have their effectiveness as critics neutralized because of their changed relationship to their peers.

Another approach that has been used often by traditional change agents involves replacing employees who have been inside the system for a long period of time with professionals from outside the organization (Bennis, 1966). This approach is not to be confused with nepotism nor amicism that in the past has been utilized by well-meaning administrators. Replacement provides at least five advantages to the change oriented administrator: (1) it reduces the number of people who refuse to support an open viable system; (2) it provides people with greater competencies than are available within the organization; (3) it increases the status of the organization in the eyes of the public; (4) it opens windows into the organization to outsiders; and (5) it provides employees who have stronger loyalties to the chief than to departmental sub-culture and its politics. Obviously, unlike amicism and nepotism, this strategy involves more than simply bringing in an outsider who will support the programs of the chief administrator.

The persons who are selected as replacements must be extensively evaluated to ensure that they are professional enough to stay above the protective devices of the old-line police bureaucrats. They must be highly competent and have adequate credentials to guard against the possibility of being discredited by those resistant to change. They must be loyal to concepts of democracy and secure in their commitment to establishing consumer-oriented police organizations that address the needs of the community.

It is important that the replacements be given positions where they can provide support for the chief administrator. A replacement who is placed as an editor of reports or an accountant has little impact on the organization and provides little support for the chief; however, an administrative assistant or a bureau commander has much more potential. It is also important to consider the organizational problems that such replacements will cause for the administrator. This approach involves changes of significant enough proportion that they may cause seriously damaging counter-reactions.

Once a replacement is within the organization, the administrator will have to support and protect him, because the bureaucracy will deal harshly with him. The old-line police bureaucrats are neither naive nor stupid; they will understand what is happening to their strength in the department, and they will attempt to discredit and destroy the interloper. The insiders have the advantages of knowing the existing system and the people who staff it; and they can use this knowledge to stifle the outsider. Insiders may deliberately complicate the paper work and restrict the channels of communication for the outsider so that many of his early efforts will have to be devoted to protecting himself rather than achieving organization goals. Therefore, while the chief administrator will reap benefits from the presence of the outsider, he must be prepared to devote considerable attention to protecting him, and accepting his advice over the objections of the tradition-bound insiders.

Camouflage and Diversionary Tactics

It appears to us that informal consensual groups, such as exist in a police department subculture, usually cannot pursue several causes at the same time. Therefore, the chief who wishes to make changes that are likely to generate hostility among his employees can time the changes to occur at a time when the employees are already engaged in an emotional battle. For example, if the police are tied up in a battle with a pressure group that is attempting to implement a police review board, the chief can take advantage of the situation and use it for cover while he strengthens internal control procedures and he may even be able to win internal support by attacking the police review board concepts as an evil conspiracy which will damage police.

Obviously, the techniques of camouflage and diversion should not be crudely manipulated in an unethical fashion. Our point is that they offer ways of using undesirable situations to the chief's advantage, but he certainly should not be identified as the instigator of the proposals which he uses to his own ends. In the past, whether intentionally or unwittingly, administrators have utilized these techniques to win support for themselves and their programs. Therefore, we have observed their effectiveness.

CONCLUSION

As with any management action, the preceding methods can be abused by an unethical administrator. Prior to a decision to use them, the chief should explore the ethical questions involved. However, they can be both effective and ethical approaches to winning support for organizational changes.

Such extensive efforts to obtain support for organizational change is probably unwise unless the chief administrator has a strong commitment to the need for making his organization more client-oriented. In the following section, we will discuss our thoughts concerning the general direction of the change needed in urban police organizations if they are to become truly consumer-oriented public agencies.

STRUCTURING FOR CHANGE

The police administrator who wants to develop a consumer-oriented police department and establish the potential for continuous change within his organization, cannot assume that once he obtains internal support for change that progress will automatically continue. Unmanaged change may be counterproductive. The world has pollution, wars, inhuman and inefficient governments, racism, and alienated people as stark testimony to the problems that can result from unmanaged change. However, at the same time, it is also important to recognize that in our society, no public administrator has the authority, power, or resources to completely control change (Katz and Kahn, 1967, pp. 390–452).

Due to past definitions of the responsibilities, roles, and boundaries of governmental agencies, a police chief constantly finds that he does not have sufficient direct control to force his department to receive and fulfill the needs and demands of the public. For example, most people are insisting that the police make their communities safe and secure places. However, community security can be more of a state of mind than a physical reality. The quality of a person's security is directly associated to his personal feelings of freedom from danger. A person who is thirsty, hungry, cold, lonely, or paranoid may never feel that his community is a safe place. Although a police department can enter into cooperative arrangements with mental health and welfare agencies to solve some of these problems, it does not have the knowledge nor the resources to eliminate all of them. Therefore, a chief will usually have to be satisfied with a somewhat less than perfect solution to community needs.

The important point is that a police administrator has to approach the problems pragmatically rather than normatively. He should attempt to define and map the limitations imposed on him and his organization. If he cannot possibly work within these limitations, he should attempt to develop techniques and plans for their elimination. And, while he cannot possibly control his organization as precisely as he can aim a rifle, he can be expected to ensure that his department generally moves in the direction of identifying and responding to the needs of the citizens in his jurisdiction. Since he does not have complete control nor a perfectly defined set of objectives and priorities, he will have to rely on gross, trial and error efforts which result in rather disjointed, lurching change rather than a mechanically smooth operation. Initially, the chief should attempt to modify the philosophy and approach to organization and management, but eventually he will have to completely restructure his organization along different lines than have traditionally been utilized. The following are modifications that chiefs should be considering.

Opening the Organization

The police sub-culture that we spoke of earlier appears to be the result of the closed, routinized nature of police organizations and their operations (McNamara, 1967). The organizational and administrative incest that has developed because of this system has resulted in a like-minded group of employees in police departments. The chief administrator can facilitate change by initiating steps to open the police department to outsiders (Bennis, 1966, pp. 113–130). He should make certain that the outsiders are not restricted exclusively to low-level, non-policy making positions where they will be without influence. They should be built into the organization as fulfledged members, helpers, observers, and advisors. To be effective as change agents, they need to be utilized in such a manner that they can interject fresh points of view at all levels of the organization, challenge existing methods and activities, and provide the public with windows into the police department.

Such an opening of the system will serve to unfreeze many of the previously unchallenged notions and procedures, and it will facilitate re-establishing the police as a part of their communities.

Supporting Tolerance

As we previously suggested, one of the major reasons why police personnel find it so difficult to change is their intolerance of deviation from what they have learned is normal (Gardner, 1965, pp. 67–75). Personnel in a bureaucracy have been taught to define their environment in simplistic terms of good or bad, black or white, right or wrong. In most police departments, they sorely need to be conditioned to accept and tolerate differences.

The chief can facilitate the conditioning of his personnel by removing the organizational obstacles to individuality such as hair policies, height requirements, clothing restrictions, etc. Assuming the organization can tolerate more substantial pressure, he might go even further and deliberately select people for employment who do not meet the stereotypes of police employees that have developed. Police departments need liberals, conservatives, blacks, whites, young, old, fat, skinny, males, females, intelligent people, average people, and shades in between. A chief who recognizes the value of tolerating differences among people and establishes conditions for the spread of such tolerant attitudes establishes the conditions necessary for moving his organization toward an effective consumer-oriented department.

Reducing Organizational Rigidity

The rules, values, habits, and customs of police organization make them stable, unyielding structures that have difficulty adopting a consumer orientation. In order for client-oriented organizational change to occur, this irrational rigidity must be loosened. Methods for modifying the restrictions that have created the problem have to be developed. By reducing the support for rigidity, police personnel can be conditioned to accept ambiguous situations (Watson, 1971, pp. 745–765). Such simple things as changes in physical layouts, procedures, rank structures, uniforms, color of equipment, and the systematic, periodic shuffling of personnel might be a part of the conditioning processes.

Sections of the rule book might be suspended. Policy-making groups consisting of representatives from all ranks of the organization and citizens could be set up to continuously up-date policies. Task forces can be utilized to handle temporary situations, and after they have completed their assignments, they could be returned to their normal assignments. Lower ranking officers or civilians could be assigned to chair temporary study groups that have representatives from all ranks of the department. Exchanges of personnel with other agencies can also be used. Although no single action will break the rigidity of a police organization, the frequent use of a variety of these techniques will have a significant impact.

Improving Communications

We have previously mentioned the communications problems in a police bureaucracy. These problems are caused by formal ranks and informal status differences, concerns for personal security, chains of command, complex communications methods, and many other reasons. However, regardless of the specific reason for the problems, a consumer-oriented organization needs numerous, open channels of communications. A chief administrator can facilitate the development of a dynamic organization by establishing new methods and channels for communications. Task forces, departmental ombudsmen, information specialists, departmental meetings, team efforts, personnel rotations, shortening the chain of command, decentralization, improved communications equipment, and less emphasis on authority and status in running the organization, are all techniques that can be used for improving communications and facilitating change.

Reducing Reliance on Formal Authority

Close supervision and autocratic methods stifle consumer-inputs and change within a police organization. Top down pressure for change is not sufficient. Participation in decision-making and the use of persuasion and negotiation are more effective than authority in up-dating organizations.

A chief should take steps to increase the participation in organizational processes and decision-making. This would entail softening his reliance on authority. He can utilize his personnel where they are competent to perform regardless of rank in supervisory and staff positions. He can systematically consult with departmental personnel of all ranks before making important decisions. He can encourage managers and supervisors to assume a teacher-student rather than a master-slave relationship with their subordinates.

ESTABLISHING A CENTRALIZED-DECENTRALIZED ORGANIZATIONAL MODEL

Obviously, the preceding techniques can be implemented by making modifications in the existing classical organizational model used by the police. However, for a truly responsive client-oriented organization, these changes alone will not be sufficient. Eventually, police administrators must make relatively drastic changes in their organizational structures. We predict that if voluntary changes are not made by police administrators, the new power groups will force change on the police departments as they are currently attempting to do in Berkeley, California.

As we have pointed out elsewhere, American cities have changed most importantly with regards to attitudes, values, expectations, and power diffusion. The increased activism and power of minority groups emphasizes the impracticability of a police department establishing one set of priorities for an entire city. Different communities have different opinions about what actions police should take in fulfilling specialized needs. Aside from the problems caused by the insulated nature of the police operations and the inflexibility of the police bureaucracy, there is no rational reason why the police cannot respond to the differences in communities within their jurisdiction.

Police agencies are governmental units. They have no sacred goals or priorities that cannot be changed if such a change better serves their citizens. Police agencies should be dedicated to the principle of the greatest good for the greatest number. It appears to us that a properly decentralized police structure with professionally oriented personnel would enable the police to provide a more responsive police service.

Proper decentralization does not entail turning over control of the police to an elected community board or commission. Obviously, this has not worked successfully in the past. We believe a need exists for a police structure, which has community participation in priority making and policy development and at the same time, is centrally coordinated to ensure a consistent quality of policing efforts throughout the jurisdiction. Centralized coordination is necessary to prevent abuses such as discrimination by the police in one community against people who live in another area and to guard against the disjointed fragmented approaches that are so common in many areas. This approach facilitates controlled decentralization through a Centralized-Decentralized Model.

This Centralized-Decentralized approach to organizing police involves centralizing all of the support and staff functions and decentralizing the operational or service delivery activities of the police.

The support activities could be arranged to facilitate the efforts of the various decentralized operational activities without rigidly dictating operational priorities or policies. In order to be effective in coordinating the field activities, the centralized support operations will need the authority to establish minimum reporting and communications standards as well as the obligation to compare the operational units that are assigned to various communities. In addition, the centralized support section could be given the responsibility for defining community needs, assigning operational personnel to the communities, providing information and intelligence to the operational teams, and assisting the community teams with training and personnel improvement.

The operational units would consist of teams of officers assigned to a well-defined geographic area with enough homogenous elements to be considered a community. Each team would be given the responsibility and authority to work closely with their community to define their problems and needs and to provide the appropriate police services. Obviously, the team would be required to observe the same ethical, legal, and financial limitations that would govern all teams. The teams would be staffed by people with complimentary skills to ensure that each team would be able to handle the variety of problems they would be expected to face. Hopefully, the members of each team would be generalists-specialists, in other words, every officer would be expected to perform all types of police work, but at the same time, have highly developed skills in one or two areas which would directly aid in eliminating problems in the specific geographical area to which he has been assigned.

Within well-defined boundaries, the internal management of each team could be left largely with the team. The procedures used by the teams could be left basically up to the members of the teams, who would be required to work them out with the community. Even the work assignments of team members could be within the authority of the team rather than a central authority. The chief and his centralized staff could evaluate the teams on the extent to which each achieved its objectives rather than the extent to which its members follow universal, internal rules or standard operating procedures developed for the entire police organization.

This type of centralized-decentralized organizational arrangement can be considered analogous to the arrangement utilized in a hospital, except it makes provisions for community input that is not utilized in the hospital model. The chief and the support section is analogous to the hospital administrators and the supportive services of the hospital. The teams of police officers are analogous to medical and surgical teams that work in the hospital. The hospital administrator coordinates the surgical teams and provides them with support personnel and equipment, but he does not become involved in the actual operations. These operational activities are the responsibility of the medical and surgical groups. Similarly, we would leave all but the broadest priorities and methods of performing the police job up to the teams of police officers and their clients; and we would organize a professional staff of technicians to provide them with high-quality support and coordination.

Obviously, this approach depends on highly competent, sensitive employees who are dedicated to serving their citizens. However, we believe that this Centralized-Decentralized Model will result in a more effective and dynamic police operation. In Dayton, we have been experimenting with this concept under an LEAA Grant. The initial evaluation of our efforts at decentralization indicates that the citizens in the Fifth District, the decentralized area, believe that their policemen are more responsive to their needs than citizens in other areas of the city. We have also found that the citizens in the Fifth District feel more secure with the police responses being provided at the community level than the citizens in our control group (Dayton, 1971). This has been accomplished while maintaining the same level of effectiveness in achieving our organizational objectives, as we have with the highly centralized operation in other areas of Dayton.

This approach seems to be the most effective in involving citizens and police officers in establishing objectives and priorities for police. The Centralized-Decentralized Model is dependent on community meetings and discussions between police officers and the citizens they serve. Through this type of interaction, an acceptable consensus concerning the police role and goals can be developed. Changes will be acceptable to the police because of their involvement in the process. Ultimately, this approach will provide a dynamic, professional, consumer-oriented police operation that will result in a higher level of service and greater security.

CONCLUSION

Police administrators are responsible for providing a police operation that serves the public needs. On the surface, this responsibility appears to be simple enough; however, the complexities involved in operationalizing it are enormous.

The democratic political process is an appropriate device for providing a police organization with information about public needs, but police organizations have become so removed and insulated from the political processes that the service they provide is at times almost totally unrelated to citizen problems. Even in those situations where the chief of police is sensitive to the problems and needs of his citizens, he alone cannot decipher sufficient information to determine the appropriate priorities for his organization to address.   In addition, due to the inherent rigidity of a modern police bureaucracy, the chief's ability to initiate organizational change is severely limited.

If police organizations are to fully realize their objective of addressing community needs, it is essential that police administrators adopt a philosophy supporting a consumer orientation and take steps to ensure that their organizations have sufficient exposure and flexibility to align themselves with the needs of their clientele.

Our experience indicates that an administrator should consider a number of factors in preparing his organization for change.   First, he should take steps to neutralize resistance and establish support for change among his subordinates.   Among the techniques that can be utilized for reducing resistance are (1) rewards and threats, (2) rationality and indoctrination, (3) cooption and replacement, and (4) camouflage and diversionary tactics.

Second, he should take steps to structure his organization to facilitate consumer-oriented change.   In developing a new structure, he should consider emphasizing the following: (1) opening the organization, (2) supporting tolerance, (3) reducing organizational rigidity, (4) improving communications, (5) reducing reliance on formal authority, and (6) establishing a Centralized-Decentralized Organizational Model.

Administrative actions to facilitate the development of dynamic police organizations will create difficult problems regardless of the approach utilized.   Outsiders may criticize the organization for its disjointed appearance.   However, as John W. Gardner has pointed out, ". . . creative organizations or societies are rarely tidy.   Some tolerance for inconsistencies, for profusion of purposes and strategies, and for conflict is the price of freedom and vitality" (1965, p. 70).

Although we believe the methods we have suggested will, in the long run, be most effective, they will not provide a completely smooth transition from a traditional police bureaucracy to a new organizational design.   They will most likely cause frustration for police officers involved.   Initially, officers will demand that they not be subjected to such threatening techniques; they will insist on stronger rules for personal security; they will plead low morale; and they may be disruptive to the organizational processes in an attempt to emphasize their dissatisfaction with the responsibilities they are asked to assume.   However, we believe that the probability that these techniques will pay off in developing a more effective, consumer-oriented police department where police can achieve a higher level of work satisfaction and professionalism, makes it reasonable for administrators to assume the risks involved.

BIBLIOGRAPHY

Appleby, Paul H. "Public Administration and Democracy." *Public Administration and Democracy.* Roscoe D. Martin, (Ed.) Syracuse, New York: Syracuse University Press, 1965.

Angell, John E. "An Alternative to Classical Police Organizational Arrangements." *Criminology*, Vol. 9, No. 2 & 3, (Aug.–Nov., 1971), pp. 185–207.

Argyris, Chris. *Organization and Innovation.* Homeward, Illinois: Richard D. Irwin, Inc., 1965.

Baldwin, James. *Nobody Knows My Name.* New York: Dial Press, 1961.

Bennis, Warren G. "A New Role for the Behavioral Sciences: Effecting Organizational Change." *Administrative Science Quarterly* (Sept., 1963).

Bennis, Warren G. *Changing Organizations.* New York: McGraw-Hill Book Co., 1966.

Bennis, Warren G., et al (Eds). *The Planning of Change.* New York: Holt, Rinehart and Winston, 1961.

Bordua, David J. *The Police: Six Sociological Essays.* New York: John Wiley and Sons, Inc., 1967.

Chapman, Samuel G. *Police Patrol Readings.* Springfield: Charles C. Thomas, Publisher, 1964, pp. 245–274.

Coch, Lester and John R. P. French, Jr. "Overcoming Resistance to Change." *Human Relations*, Vol. 1, No. 4 (1948).

Colin, J. M. "After X and Y Comes Z." *Personnel Journal* (January, 1971).

Coser, Lewis A. *The Functions of Social Conflict.* Toronto, Ontario: Free Press, March, 1968.

Davis, James A. "Authority—Flow Theory and the Impact of Chester Bernard." *California Management Review*, Vol. XIII, No. 1 (Fall, 1970).

Dayton/Montgomery County Pilot Cities Program: *Evaluation of Community-Centered Team Policing.* Dayton: Community Research, Inc., 1971.

Downs, Anthony. *Inside Bureaucracy.* Boston: Little, Brown, 1967.

Elliott, J. F. and Thomas J. Surdino. *Crime Control Team.* Springfield: Charles C. Thomas, 1971.

Etzioni, Amitai. *Modern Organizations.* Englewood Cliffs, New Jersey: Prentice-Hall, Inc., 1964.

Fosdick, Raymond B. *American Police Systems.* Montclair, New Jersey: Patterson Smith Publishing, Rev. 1969.

Gardner, John W. *Self Renewal: The Individual and the Innovative Society.* New York: Harper and Row, 1965.

Gazell, James A. "Authority—Flow Theory and the Impact of Chester Bernard." *California Management Review*, Vol. XIII, No. 1 (Fall, 1970).

Geneen, Harold S. "The Human Element in Communications." *California Management Review* (Winter, 1966).

Golembiewski, Robert T. "The Laboratory Approach to Organization Change: Scheme of a Method." *Public Administration Review* (September, 1967).

Golembiewski, Robert T. *Men, Management, and Morality.* New York: McGraw-Hill, 1965.

Goodwin, Watson. "Resistance to Change." *American Behavioral Scientist*, Vol. 14, No. 5 (May–June, 1971), pp. 745–765.

Greenwood, Noel. "Quiet Revolution Under Way in Police Training, Education." Oakland Police Department Information Bulletin. Reprinted from *Los Angeles Times* (1972).

Judson, Arnold S. *A Manager's Guide to Making Changes.* New York: John Wiley & Sons, Inc., 1966.

Katz, Daniel and Kahn, Robert L. *The Social Psychology of Organizations.* New York: John Wiley & Sons, Inc., 1966.

Katz, Daniel and Kahn, Robert L. *The Social Psychology of Organizations.* New York: John Wiley & Sons, Inc., 1967, pp. 390–452.

Leavitt, Harold J. *Managerial Psychology.* 2nd Ed. Chicago, Illinois: University of Chicago Press, 1964.

Lindblow, Charles E. *The Policy-Making Process.* Englewood Cliffs, New Jersey: Prentice-Hall, Inc., 1968.

March, James G. *Handbook of Organizations.* Rand McNally & Co., 1965.

McNamara, John H. "Uncertainties in Police Work," in *The Police* New York: John Wiley & Sons, Inc., 1967, edited by David J. Bordue, pp. 203–207.

McBride, Thomas F. Speech given at the Management Institute of the National Association of Attorneys General. Denver, Colorado, November 6, 1971.

National Advisory Commission on Civil Disorders. *Kerner Commission Report.* Washington, D. C.: U. S. Government Printing Office, 1968.

Rogers, David. *The Management of Big Cities.* Beverly Hills, California: Sage Publications, 1971.

Saunders, Charles B. *Upgrading the American Police.* The Brookings Institute, 1970.

Schein, Edgar H. *Organized Psychology.* Englewood Cliffs, New Jersey: Prentice-Hall, Inc., 1965.

Smith, Alexander B., Bernard Locke, and William F. Walker. "Authoritarianism in College and Non-College Oriented Police." *Journal of Criminal Law, Criminology, and Police Science*, Vol. 58, No. 1.

Toffler, Alvin. *Future Shock.* New York: Bantam Books, 1971.

Trojanowicz, Robert C. *A Comparison of Behavior Styles of Policemen and Social Workers.* Unpublished doctoral dissertation, Michigan State University, 1969.

Tullock, Gordon. *Politics of Bureaucracy.* Washington, D. C.: Public Affairs Press, 1965.

Vega, William. "The Liberal Policeman: A Contradiction in Terms?" *Issues in Criminology*, Vol. 4 No. 1.

Webster, John A. "Police Task and Time Study." *Journal of Criminal Law, Criminology, and Police Science* (March, 1970).

Williams, Edgar G. "Changing Systems and Behavior." *Business Horizons* (August, 1969).

Wilson, James Q. "The Police and Their Problems: A Theory." *Public Policy XII.* Carl J. Friedrick and Seymour E. Harris, (Eds.). Graduate School of Public Administration, Harvard University, 1963.

1. We undertook this paper as three practitioners who have been heavily involved in attempts to improve urban policing. The material we have developed is based on both personal experiences and our interpretation of the implications of the research findings. Although we are indebted to many people who have reacted to the ideas expressed herein, we are particularly grateful to Mr. Edward A. Lettus, a Research Associate on the Dayton/Montgomery County Pilot Cities staff. Mr. Lettus devoted a tremendous amount of his time to collecting resource material, reacting to our ideas, and editing the various drafts of the paper. We sincerely appreciate his efforts.

2. Information concerning variations on the recommendations contained under this sub-heading can be found in Samual G. Chapman, *Police Patrol Readings* (Springfield: Charles C. Thomas, Publisher, 1964), pp. 245–274; The President's Commission on Law Enforcement, *Task Force Report: The Police* (Washington, Government Printing Office, 1967), pp. 117–118; J. F. Elliott and Thomas J. Surdino, *Crime Control Team* (Springfield: Charles C. Thomas, 1971); and John E. Angell, "An Alternative to Classical Police Organizational Arrangements," *Criminology* (Vol. 9, No. 2 & 3, Aug.-Nov., 1971), pp. 185–207.

MYTHOLOGY AND THE MANAGEMENT OF CHANGE: INCONSISTENCIES IN THE BEHAVIOR OF STAFF *

An attempt to change inevitably involves personal and organizational risks and requires that we face crucial uncertainties: when we deal with human beings, we have to accept the fact that ultimately there can be no right answers. The point that we want to make in what follows is this: very often, those who are charged with respon-

* Source: Chauncey F. Bell and Donald B. Manson, "Mythology and the Management of Change: Inconsistencies in the Behavior of Staff," *The Change Process in Criminal Justice*, Criminal Justice Monograph, Washington: U. S. Government Printing Office, June 1973, pp. 1–17.

sibility for bringing about change ignore or do not sufficiently and honestly address risk and uncertainty in their efforts to induce change. In ignoring those crucial issues, very often they behave in ways which appear to have been designed to impede change rather than to support it. We are hoping to offer some alternatives to those who honestly seek change, and yet are terminally frustrated, or who are perplexed by some of the negative reactions to their efforts.

Let's begin by describing a "game" that we've seen played many times with surprising results.

The game involves a "gamesman" and eligible players. With each play, the eligible player has an equal chance of making nothing (i. e., losing his stake) or $10.00. He must put down a stake each time he plays; and he can play an indefinite number of times.

There is one other rule: not everyone is eligible to play. The gamesman determines who can play by asking each person how much he is willing to stake before the first time he plays. If he thinks the offered stakes are too low, the gamesman won't let the person play.

The game begins when the gamesman asks each person what his stake would be: $1.00, $3.00, $5.00, etc. Invariably, he hears a few low stakes ($1.50 or so), and a few high stakes ($5.50). Most people are willing to stake about $3.50.

And those are very surprising results. Why? Because the game, put more simply, is an offer of a guaranteed return of $5.00 on the stake for each play. (If there is an equal chance of making nothing or $10.00 on each play and if the player can play for an indefinite period, he will average $5.00 per play.) Most of the players staked less than $4.50. Yet anything under that amount gives a usurious return on the investment.

Because of the way the game is described, most players think that there is a real risk in playing. The gamesman could have said: how much will you give me on repeated occasions, if I will give you back $5.00 each time. As originally described, the game sounds riskier than it is. Now, why do we describe such a silly game here?

Almost daily, we see staff people go into criminal justice agencies and offer "sure things," or very risky proposals to agency heads. When they leave frustrated, they say, "why that old stick in the mud. I offered him an answer to some of his problems, and he wouldn't invest more than 5 percent of his time for it."

Most people do not like the risk and will go some distance to avoid it. The chance of loss is a powerful incentive to inaction, or at the least, hedged commitments. Our efforts in the process of change need to address risk and uncertainty directly, not as an unpleasant by-product. We cannot afford to sidestep this major impediment to change or to fall back on moral outrage, saying "Ain't it awful" that *they* aren't willing to take the actions we know they ought to take.

Most of the roles which we provide, however, create a perception of risk and uncertainty in the person to be changed, and rest upon assumptions about people which are inconsistent with attempts to accomplish change.

Notice that throughout the following discussion we draw a clear distinction between "staff" and "line" personnel, meaning the helper and the helped. This is an oversimplification, and not infrequently the roles as we draw them are reversed or confused. In addition, there are several quite different types of staff. We will continue to draw the clear distinction, however, as if it existed that way, in order to simplify our major points.

Figure 1 shows a simplified version of a negative change encounter. Note that we are not talking about encounters where the line response is positive. There, at least in theory, we have no problem.

Figure 1

A "CHANGE ENCOUNTER"

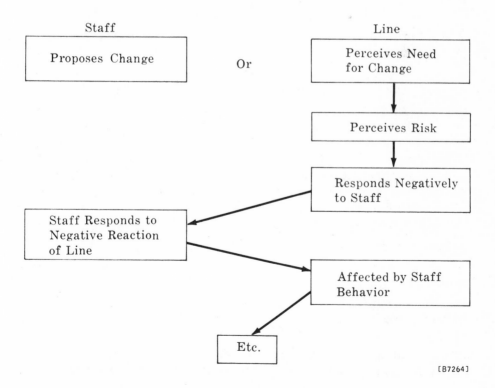

[B7264]

What role do we cast for the line official presented with an opportunity to change? The line official is a recalcitrant, bullheaded stick in the mud. He is behind the times; he is moved only by crises; and he is uninterested in improving himself or his agency. He vacillates and compromises; he indulges in patronage and politics.

Of course, under pressure, we might be forced to admit that his agency usually has managed to keep its head above water; he does survive most crises; he at least partially commands the respect of tens, hundreds, or sometimes thousands of men; and surprisingly often, he's a pretty likable guy.

But his intentions are confused; he is not a professional. He's not a well-educated man, and he makes decisions off the top of his head. He's technically unsophisticated and that cannot lead to excellence; or can it?

We give this guy a rather limited set of lines with which to respond to a suggested change. He can say:

1. "We are working on the problem already, and we don't want your assistance;" or

2. "We don't have any problems that are out of the ordinary here;" or

3. "We know what our problems are, and we know what we have to do about them. Now, if you will only give us X more personnel and Y more money, we'll stop wasting each other's time and get to work;" or

4. "We sure need a new way to go about this   .   .   .   but your idea is no damn good, because   .   .   .;" or

5. "Ain't it awful" that we are in such a sad state of affairs; that the courts don't do their job; that the personnel we have are so underqualified; that we are so overworked; that we haven't had talent such as yours available to us;" this statement to be immediately followed by, "Well, gee, it sure has been nice talking to you, and I sure hope you'll come back soon."

We don't give the guy much credit in this model, and some extremely questionable assumptions underlie this characterization.

What kinds of roles do we cast for the staff participant in the encounter?

He is most often a young, well educated, professional. He is aggressive, intelligent, full of insight, energetic, and possesses bright ideas.

Of course, under pressure, we might be forced to admit he may also be naive, nosy, and callous. His reach may exceed his grasp; or, his life experience may be limited. He may not know about the "real world."

But overall, we know that at least his intentions are good, and that he is someone who, if we can tolerate and control him, may be able to help. He is the opposite of the political hack; he abhors politics; he believes in objective data. That can only be good, can it not?

The range of roles and lines available to the staff man are more complicated than those of the line official because he is the one who is imposing himself, trying to sell himself, in an encounter designed to bring about change.

STAFF ROLES

The staff member can behave in a number of ways with regard to change activities:

1. The *professional* staff role rests upon a body of established information—that which he has learned in school and from books. The professional offers answers to problems through a collection of the right data, analyzed in the right ways. He says, "If we can resist political pressure and spend our time and money in the right ways, then we will really be able to do something about your problems," or, "If only *they* would collect the data we need, we would be able to really help them."

2. The *reformer* is following a semi-religious calling. You can see it in his eyes. If only you will follow his teachings, he will show you the way. He does not trust anyone in the existing structure, because it is always corrupt and/or incompetent. He says very little and can be arrogant and authoritarian. This is a relatively rare staff role, because in a staff position it is all but impossible to gain the real power required by the role.

3. The *manipulator* assumes that if he is just clever enough and plans carefully and properly, he can change *anything*. He seeks or develops complex power structures; the power to withhold money, to tie up essential papers, or to block access to the ears of powerful politicians. He says, "If you want our money, you will do the job our way," or with a broad smile on his face, "We really want to get your program started. Now, will you just answer a few questions?"

4. The *contractor*'s role is very simple in theory, and very complex in actual practice. As the name suggests, when implemented successfully, his role is one half of an open and honest contract between two people. The contractor agrees to

work, with a pre-agreed set of ground rules, upon his counterpart's terms. In the best sense, this is a political role; the contractor says "Scratch my back. Trust me and let me work with you on an equal basis. In return, I'll scratch yours; I'll work for you." He says, "Give me a call and I'll come—not to reform, professionalize or give you the answers, but to help in any reasonable way I can, in accordance with your instructions."

Obviously, this Dr. Jekyll can be a Mr. Hyde, and Mr. Hyde can be immoral and can contribute greatly to the problems on which he works.

The important point for the contractor role is that it is inherently amoral. There is no inherently moral or correct outcome to be expected from using the role. The staff person choosing it must explicitly acknowledge that the outcome depends upon the wisdom and morality of the user.

On the other hand, the other three roles don't guarantee, and usually don't even cause moral or good results in a change process, either.

Professionalism, in some professions, has come to mean insulation from outsiders, excessive attention to personal prestige, and the creation of a special language understood only by members of the profession. The potential for bad outcomes from the efforts of reformers and manipulators should be obvious.

We hope that these role descriptions have not been too brief, too flippant, or too oversimplified for you to see some truth in them. This business of change is an old one, and we are engaging in it with sometimes new and high-sounding words. In the process of the encounter, in the heat of a good fight, we often forget some basic things.

The frequency with which the first three roles reappear, played by different people, and the consistency from person to person of some of the words and phrasing used in change encounters, suggest to me that there are some underlying assumptions commonly held by those playing these roles.

UNDERLYING ASSUMPTIONS OF STAFF ROLES

Although the following list is not exhaustive, it is meant to be illustrative of staff assumptions that restrict staff/line cooperation.

1. We will begin with the assumption that *decision-makers do not have any ideas, or the capacity to develop ideas to get themselves out of their dilemmas.* Direct and indirect references to the assumption surround us. The word innovative

is a nemesis to agency officials. It means risk, criticism, prior incompetence, and a variety of other really troublesome things to the one who supposedly needs it. Yet how many genuinely innovative ideas or procedures have been developed in the last few years? An example came up in a recent lunch with a police chief who is working on one of the national task forces: he pointed out, from his perspective as a chief of a small department, that the basic ingredients of team policing have existed in his department for years and are essentially the same as those of the old beat cop, who we put on a centralized dispatch system, to improve efficiency, a decade or so ago.

The suggestion is not that fresh ideas aren't needed. However, we tend to make a subtle leap in logic, from the perception that we need fresh ideas, to the unstated, but entirely different assumption that we need new ideas because we don't have any ideas. On the same first assumption, notice that the term *needs*, meaning a line official's ideas, as an ingredient in a change process, is generally viewed with scorn. It is regressive. Needs are not good, unless there has been an objective survey of specific problems and a formal analysis of alternatives to these problems preceding the statement of needs.

We suggest that our underlined assumption above is most often a poor one; incorrect, insulting to its object, and a partial source of the mistrust which line officials often have for staff which hold the assumption. To believe that there are not many good ideas, hidden or otherwise, in agencies with problems, is to increase the uncertainty of decision-makers about how much they can trust those who say they wish to help.

2. A second commonly held assumption is that *the present problems in an agency result in large part from their making bad decisions, and that therefore we have to improve the quality of the decisions made, to improve the agency.* In extreme cases, all ideas from a line agency are discounted before an honest discussion about them has occurred. Ideas are discounted because, "he has always been wrong to date," or because, "they haven't done anything right in years." This assumption is based upon the premise that we are dealing with decision-makers who frequently arrive at bad decisions, and so we need to provide them with skills to make better decisions. Most of the time, this assumption is incorrect, and more importantly, it is a damaging assumption to hold as we

are working with someone who has the capacity to effect change.

Let's begin with why the assumption does damage: we believe that *you* are wrong; the decisions you have been making for years have been wrong; and your life's work is for naught. How do you feel about that? You should be feeling a certain resistance to listening to me. Only a masochist would enjoy such treatment, whether it is delivered directly, or indirectly and inferentially, as so often happens. The assumption that someone's problems result from his own bad decisions is damaging because it cannot be hidden: the line official knows what the person sitting opposite him thinks, and so the assumption impedes any honest interchange. It increases dramatically the resistance of the line official to accepting help from staff.

We also have said that the assumption was often wrong as well as being counterproductive. More often than making "wrong" decisions, decision-makers either:

A.   Postpone needed decisions because of the apparent risk involved; or,

B.   Make basic decisions but fail to follow up with a series of smaller but equally important decisions needed to implement the primary decision; or,

C.   Fall into rigid patterns of decision-making because of a complex desire to avoid risk ("It worked once, therefore it ought to work again.").

Early in his career, I am told that B. F. Skinner ran an experiment in which he provided some individuals with a lighted panel with a number of buttons. Each subject was told to find the button which most frequently lit the light. Unknown to the subjects, Skinner had wired random chance into the button-light relationships. The predominant behavior pattern among the subjects was to go back and forth across the buttons, and finding one that lit the light a couple of times, to settle upon that one and continuously push it. They moved only sporadically away from it.

One of the points that we are making here is that inaction is a far more frequent offender than poor action; and risk and uncertainty are powerful incentives to inactivity. The number of useful and productive decisions an experienced and mature decision-maker, in a supportive environment, can make off the seat of his pants is staggering. To make a decision, to take action requires the actor to take a risk, and avoiding a decision is facilitated by saying we are uncertain about it; we need more data. Such an excuse, however, ignores the fact that we will always be uncertain, even after the decision is made, if it was the best possible decision.

I have to digress here for a moment. Many of you, at this point, will be saying to yourselves, yes, but what about this guy who I have been trying to work with who really does make bad decisions; who is an obstinate S.O.B.; and who really doesn't have any productive ideas about how to help himself? There are such people, and when you come to work with them in a staff capacity, you have to make a basic decision about whether or not you like wasting your time. When such people hold real power, they cannot be changed without first wishing it themselves. It is convenient to think that no one but one's self is competent, because then we have the whole world to reform. The truth is that such people are really rather rare, and far more common are mistrustful people who have problems derived primarily from sources other than original sin.

When working for really negative people, the options open to different staff types vary considerably. A planner who works with agencies to which he does not administratively report has more options than staff working within an unyielding line agency. Job security, age, pension structures, and the lack of lateral entry in this field all act to limit options. Even the most dedicated staff people in this position sometimes have no effective choice but to wait, hope, waste their time, or give in.

3.   Our third assumption says: *There is something wrong with a less than wholehearted response to an officer of help.* The characterization we made earlier of the line official is a pretty common one; the most common response of a line official faced with a suggestion that he ought to change is suspicion, recalcitrance, and a variety of other negative signals.

The assumption that is problematic here is that there is something really wrong with someone who responds with less than complete openness in a chance encounter. The man who responds initially to outside staff with complete openness and total honesty is either a thoroughly extra-ordinary human being, or quite foolish, or he is putting the staff man on; the latter ought to be suspicious. Staff are inconsistent when upset, irate, angry, or the like with a less than wholehearted response in a change encounter. None of our commonly understood role definitions allow us to respond positively to the perceived risk and uncertainty which underlie less than open responses. Most of the common responses embody the opposite effect: Get some power over the guy so you can force him to change: "The S.O.B. doesn't want our help; he doesn't think he has a problem; he really doesn't want to do a good job."

Faced with intransigence it is all too easy to back the line official up against a wall, or bury him in data showing what a poor job he is doing. After all, the staff man usually has the correct answer in his bag of tricks, doesn't he? Far more difficult than to dig into a bag of tricks is to listen and try to help.

4. A fourth assumption is that *seat of the pants decisions are inherently inferior, even undesirable, because they are not backed up by formal objective information.* From two root problems we bring outselves to a point where we attempt to *choose* between intuitive and objective data. First, because objective data ought to reduce the uncertainty we have with our answers' correctness, and in the case of perfect data—reduce to zero the risk involved in change, we naturally gravitate to more data. And second, because intuitive judgments incorporate unclean components—politics and personal gain —we try to substitute objective information. The assumption is misleading.

We have to begin with the recognition that there are no singularly right answers in human endeavor; we will have to further recognize that the intuitive mechanism is far more sophisticated than any analytical machinery yet developed. Factual data is extremely important; we have to both acquire and use more information about what we are doing. Ultimately, however, all of our key change decisions are going to be made somewhat arbitrarily in the face of ultimate uncertainty about whether we are right or not.

It is as unreasonable to use the tools of planning and analytical research as our sole guidelines to change, as it would be to judge an architect solely by his use of dividers, ruler, and compass.

Pehaps those in staff positions need also to recognize a certain exceptional disinclination to risk and uncertainty which usually characterizes those of us who choose staff instead of line responsibilities.

We have a special problem with data in the criminal justice field. Because the business of criminal justice is so serious, we try not to guess about the arrest, trial, and prison. We carry that necessary reluctance to operate on less than complete information over to planning for the administration of justice, where more circumstantial data does less harm. Nearly everyone is developing comprehensive information packages covering all arrests, all prisoners, all trials, etc. Almost no one, however, is regularly using sampling techniques to develop planning information.

To postpone action until all the information is in may contribute to a series of basic impediments to change itself; it is easier to work on data than to work with people on their problems. We need to use data more extensively, but let's use it wisely and with an eye to its limits, rather than a wish that it were better.

5. Fifth, we assume that *duplication of effort is wasteful and to be avoided where it doesn't exist, and stamped out where it does exist.* Consolidation of police departments reduces duplication of effort; sometimes regional planning does the same; and funding a program in one community when a statewide system for the problem is being developed is duplication of effort. The assumption is not always accurate. All too often, we are failing to differentiate between duplication in routinized activities, and duplication in learning or change processes.

There are some terrible ironies in this area in the Safe Streets Act, for example. Unfortunately, but accurately, most proposal review under the program is routinized, and involves little learning for either party involved. What do we do? We have duplication of effort galore.

On the other hand, there is substantial evidence that duplication has positive, and sometimes essential value where it relates to the introduction of changes. We would like to believe that, for example, we can develop a model computer program for control of data and resources in a large criminal justice agency, which can be transferred to other agencies.

For years, in computer sales jargon, we have heard of a mythological library of prepacked basic computer programs. In the case of basic programs, however, it just doesn't work. Each agency has to develop its own, and although it can usefully build upon or use the work of others in that process, essentially the effort is always duplicative, and always new.

Finally, we want to propose for your consideration the beginning of an alternative set of working assumptions which we can use when working for change in the criminal justice field.

ALTERNATIVE WORKING ASSUMPTIONS

We now present some alternative assumptions we have used ourselves over the last two years in working with officials in the largest cities and counties in the country. They have not been evaluated and are not susceptible to objective analysis. They are really intended as working assumptions. They are neither right nor wrong. They do seem to be useful, and help to develop more productive change encounters.

1. The first working assumption we propose is that *trust between the helper and the helped is essential to almost all change processes.* Put most simply, you have the best chance of getting some of your own ideas used if those who can use them trust you. The idea is to provide support for the process of change, not to provide the particular result you desire. Unless a staff man is trusted by a line official, that staff is an unknown commodity, unpredictable, and risky to deal with; the line official will not generally talk sufficiently about what the details of his problems are, and what ideas he has about them, for the staff really to be able to help.

    Developing trust is an extremely demanding and complicated process, but absolutely necessary if support for change is the desired function or result.

2. The second assumption we have already talked about: *make an explicit, working assumption that the line officials worked with have specific ideas about what they can do to change, and that they are capable of making good decisions.* It is impossible to hide the fact that you hold the opposite assumption if you do, and it is crippling. By contrast, the contribution that can be made to a trusting relationship by a positive assumption is very exciting. Beginning with this assumption, it very often becomes possible to really help someone with an idea they haven't been able to figure out how to implement; which idea they wouldn't even mention if they didn't trust the listener.

    If it turns out to be a bad working assumption after a reasonable period of time, then change the assumption. With the changed assumption the staff man should recognize that he is then in a position where there is little or nothing that he can do unless and until the line official wishes to change.

3. The third working assumption is that *neutral, passive, or even negative or recalcitrant behavior on the part of line of-*

ficials is normal in a change encounter. The appropriate staff response is one of acceptance and honest support of the needs of the line official. Offer to help, express honest disagreements while attempting to understand risks from the line official's perspective. Above all, don't act as if there were something wrong with a line official for not offering open arms to all new ideas.

4. The fourth working assumption is that *duplication of effort is an essential ingredient of many change processes and should be designed into new programs.* Extensive on-side assistance should be provided; and people who can answer the question, "How did others do this?" should be put in contact with the line officials involved.

    We must not continue to fail to differentiate between what is genuinely wasteful duplication, and what duplication, being part of a learning process, is necessary and desirable. People must be allowed and encouraged to try things that may be mistakes. There are also places where duplication ought to be avoided, as in routinized operations. However, our definitions ought to be pretty flexible on this issue. What is routinized for one person may be chaotic and risky for another, until they have tried it.

5. Finally, let's begin to accept the fact that data doesn't provide answers, and major decisions will never be answered by the right data collected in the right ways. "Objective" data is a misnomer; there is no such thing. Observed data ought to be used in support of the intuitions of decision-makers at all levels of the heirarchies with which we work.

We will conclude by quoting a passage from R. D. Laing's book, *Knots*, which seems to me to summarize, painfully, some of the most important points we have tried to make:

There must be something the matter with him
    because he would not be acting as he does
    unless there was
    therefore he is acting as he is
    because there is something the matter with him

He does not think there is anything the matter with him because
    one of the things that is
    the matter with him
    is that he does not think that there is anything
    the matter with him

therefore
    we have to help him realize that,
    the fact that he does not think there is anything

the matter with him
is one of the things that is
the matter with him

there is something the matter with him because he thinks
there must be something the matter with us

for trying to help him to see
that there must be something the matter with him
to think that there is something the matter with us
for trying to help him to see that
we are helping him.   .   .

POLITICAL OBSTACLES TO CHANGE IN CRIMINAL JUSTICE AGENCIES: AN INTERORGANIZATIONAL PERSPECTIVE *

The problem of managing change or "putting innovations to work" is complex, a problem with many facets.   Yet, if the process of change is to be either understood or managed, the problem needs to be broken down into digestable chunks.   This paper attempts to consider such a chunk—political obstacles to change—in terms of interorganizational mechanisms, of dependence, influence, and power. "Political" is used here in the sense of factors influencing change and involving interaction among organizations.   The focus is not on partisan politics, but on small "p" politics—conflicts over the goals, methods, and activities of criminal justice agencies.

The success of innovative programs requested by administrators of police departments, courts, or correctional agencies is often influenced by a variety of outside forces—mayor's office, legislature, police benevolent association.   Conditions of dependency among organizations prescribed by law and those based on values, attitudes, or pressures both limit the flexibility, for instance, of a court administrator seeking change and provide him with opportunities to use these relationships to build support for his programs.   This paper explores interorganizational dependence relationships and their influence on change in criminal justice organizations.

SOURCES OF DEPENDENCE

The criminal justice system involves more than just a police chief, or district attorney or warden.   A complex network of formal and informal organizational interactions have been developed to deal with the criminal and the victim.   These interactions help to create conditions of dependence between a criminal justice agency and the

* Source: Paul Solomon and John Gardiner, "Political Obstacles to Change in Criminal Justice Agencies: An Interorganizational Perspective," *The* *Change Process in Criminal Justice,* Criminal Justice Monograph, Washington: U. S. Government Printing Office, 1973, pp. 171–185.

other organizations included in this network. Dependence refers to the requirements of one agency for the resources of another; a state prison, for instance, is dependent on the legislature for financial resources. The nature of a dependence relationship, however, depends upon its extent and form.

Extent of Dependence

A police department is totally dependent on a city council, if the city council is the sole source of funding for the department. In contrast, if the department has an alternative source of funding, its dependence on the city council is not complete. The police chief may find support for a project that council cannot or will not fund from another source. In short, the extent of dependence is determined by whether or not there are multiple opportunities to obtain the same resource. If there are, the extent of dependence is proportionately diminished. If revenue is confined to a single source, the agency does not have the capacity to choose among alternative resources and is limited as to the programs it can attempt to develop. (Thompson, 1967: 30)

Forms of Dependence: Legal-Authoritative

A police department or prison is embedded in a legal web of authority and responsibility that includes local, state, and federal levels of control. However, the primary level of authority and responsibility varies from agency to agency. Cities and towns, by and large, control the police. Counties bear major responsibility for the courts. The states most often operate the correctional institutions (ACIR, 1971, Chapter 4). As a result, criminal justice organizations, are entwined in an array of legal-authoritative relationships (mayor's office-police department) which determine responsibility for the activities and constrain the actions of justice organizations.

Forms of Dependence: Legal Transactional

While operating, criminal justice agencies receive their managerial direction and financial support from various levels of the government hierarchy; they interact on a transactional basis as the offender is processed from arrest through the courts into prison. A discrepancy exists, therefore, between the direct authority of the local government over the law enforcement agency and the reality of daily interaction among justice agencies. This discrepancy can create conflicting pressures involving legal-transactional and legal-authoritative forms of dependence. When a criminal justice administrator finds himself in the crossfire of these dependency relationships, he is faced with the dilemma of satisfying conflicting interests. The situation may lead to his abstaining from innovative solutions to law enforcement problems.

Forms of Dependence: Normative Influence

Normative refers to the values, norms, or views held by individuals and organizations in a community; influence refers to the exercise of pressures to conform to these views. The reference to normative influence, thus, relates to the community organizations, professional associations, reference groups, and individuals that potentially might exert pressure and influence on the policies of criminal justice agencies (Perrucci and Pilisuk, 1970). These organizations derive their influence from their ability to mobilize community support to influence the actions of partisan political organizations. The mobilization of public interest groups or community organizations occurs primarily on an *ad hoc* basis, as a response to perceived deficiencies in the justice process.

A justice organization is dependent for financial, informational, and other forms of support on a set of organizations (Evan, 1966). This organization set can be subdivided to reflect the distinguishing characteristics of its members. This analysis is useful for understanding how dependence influences change.

CONSEQUENCES OF DEPENDENCE

When one organization depends upon others to satisfy its resource needs, it loses a portion of its independence. This loss of autonomy is acute in the criminal justice area, because agencies have few alternative resource sources. This suggests that the forms of dependence characterizing an agency's relationship with other agencies affects its relative power. The agency's capability for defining and implementing changes is, thus, reduced.

Consequences: The Obstacle of Conflicting Goals

Any government unit having authority over a justice agency may control not only its purse strings but also job placement, promotions, and agency operation in general. In contrast, the transactional flow of offenders involves operating relationships among police department, district attorney's office, courts, prisons, and the probation office.

Change efforts that attempt to either reduce the incidence of crime or improve attempts at its solution have to be directed at an operating agency. Yet, justice agencies are managed by different centers of political and governmental power, which often operate to achieve contradictory ends. These contradictory ends inhibit the acceptability of change, each center of power working against innovations supported by the other. Donald Cressey's discussion of the conflicting goals of criminal justice agencies illustrates this conflict. ". . . police are charged with the duty of keeping the crime rate down and tend to look with disfavor upon prison programs which might reduce the degree of security against escapes . . . social welfare and educational groups become upset when changes in custodial routines threaten to disrupt programs of treatment and training" (Cressey, 1966: 1030). A justice organization may, then, be diverted from its crime reduction efforts by the goals of another governmental organization. Change efforts directed towards alleviating crime may be lost in political conflict. This complex system of interdependencies creates barriers to change already existing ones that are constructed to prohibit basic communication about solutions to law enforcement problems. In short, the criminal justice organization loses the flexibility and adaptability that comes from autonomy.

Consequences: Power of Community Organization

While the relationships between governmental units and criminal justice agencies may hinder innovation in operating agencies, the influence of community organizations may at times be used to facilitate change. These organizations are devices for bringing together individuals in response to some issue or problem in the community. They obtain their influence and power from their ability to motivate sufficient numbers of people to donate their time and money for the support of the "organizational viewpoint" (Perrucci and Pilisuk, 1970). Only, if sufficient resources are obtained will governmental administrators be convinced that the issues involved are politically significant. Without the resource of strength in numbers or finances, the community organization will have little power to either promote or hinder change in law enforcement agencies. Yet, the fact remains that a criminal justice administrator may turn to such community interest groups to obtain support for his programs. This strategy of informal absorption of community interests into the justice agency, cooptation, utilizes one form of a dependency relationship, normative influence, to lessen the constraints of another, legal-authoritative.

Consequences: Dependence as an Obstacle

A major problem in dealing with organizational change is that the contexts of organizations are constantly changing (Emery and Trist, 1965). All criminal justice administrators are faced with the consequences of social events, riots, supreme court decision, and elections, over which they have little control. The onslaught of crises continually facing justice agencies create obstacles to change by using resources for firefighting that might otherwise be available for creative responses to problems. These crises are not changes in the way of altering the formal structure and mode of operation of an agency. Rather they alter the character of inputs to the organization (Terreberry, 1968: 601). Since he must continually call upon his limited resources to fight fires—citizen demands to reduce robbery in a particular neighborhood, employee dissatisfaction, etc.—the administrator enthusiastic about innovation often finds few resources available to buy support for it. A dilemma results because while the agency is faced with a need to cope with its turbulent environment, it often does not have the resource capabilities necessary for responding. Because the justice agency is so highly dependent on organizations in its environment, it does not have the option of the ostrich or turtle and sooner or later must respond in some fashion.

THE MANAGEMENT OF INTERDEPENDENCE

Strategies for Interaction

All criminal justice administrators have a basic awareness of the relationships of their agencies to others. After some reflection, an administrator will probably be able to develop a complete statement of these relationships. Once this has been done, he can use his knowledge to win support for his change programs. In short, the various dependency relationships have to be understood if they are to facilitate change (Emery and Trist, 1965). A strategy may be formed that uses centers of power to either promote change or generate new ideas for attacking problems of crime. The relevant centers of power will vary from situation to situation. Most often they will include the government agency responsible for the budget and supervision of the justice agency. They may also include community organizations with influence in both government and law enforcement agencies. A justice unit, itself, may be included because of the charismatic qualities of its leader. Whatever the case, an administrator may find that he can use centers of power to get support for change. If a police chief, for example, decided upon a strategy of altering change proposals to fit the views or requirements of a city council member or the mayor, the proposal when it is accepted may by chance still substantially meet the department's requirements. If the required alterations are so substantial that the change is valueless, an indirect approach can be attempted.

As an alternative, an administrator may try to get support from both those affected by the change and those with the power to influence it. A warden can involve his guards in the development and implementation of a change. If he obtains their support, he can use it to convince the commissioner of corrections to accept the change. Employee groups such as police benevolent associations, or bar groups can be used by allowing them to participate in planning and implementing the change to pressure these centers of power (Katz and Kahn, 1966, Chapter 13). An administrator can, alternatively, attempt to develop community support for his programs. A district attorney, for instance, can publicize his suggestions for change in bail

procedures. He can also attempt to get the support of community organizations for his program by actively seeking their acceptance of it.
In any case, the support of either professional association, community
organization, or some other reference group can only be obtained by
working for it continuously. Yet, such support will only be effective
if it is sufficient to convince the leadership of controlling organizations that the change is warranted.

Facilitation of Interaction

A different set of problems faces an organization such as a state
planning agency, regional planning council, or criminal justice coordinating council. These agencies fund projects designed to improve the
ability of justice units to deter crime or apprehend offenders. Any
funding organization has the option of encouraging requests for project funding and assisting in the development of ideas for change by
local law enforcement units. If it chooses to follow this option, the
agency needs to develop a strategy for achieving these ends. The following outlines such a strategy.

All of the components of the strategy deal with the development
of mechanisms for using dependence relationships to facilitate
change. First, the channels of communication that facilitate the flow
of ideas, information, and influence from one organization to another
need to be developed (Hudson and Hudson, 1969). In order to get an
idea to these places where it will receive due consideration, mechanisms of transfer need to be established. More than the simple mailing of a letter or report is needed. A communcation channel involves
complex personal interactions that not only develop a climate for interchange of ideas, but encourage the translation of these ideas into
improvement in the operation of justice organizations (Katz and
Kahn, 1966, Chapter 9). The idea is not necessarily to formally
structure the communication channel, in the sense of a computer system; it is important, however, for the organization to develop a systematic approach for handling communication.

A unit charged with communication and other responsibilities
for managing interdependence is needed to make these communication linkages work. Persons operating this function can serve as
links in the process of change in law enforcement agencies (Merton,
1965). They can tie the resources, for instance, of a funding organization—a state law enforcement planning agency—to the needs of the
criminal justice system. This unit, thus, can function to transfer
ideas designed to attack criminal justice problems to law enforcement
agencies. In addition, the unit can work with local agencies, combining the unit members' knowledge in the technical and social sciences
with the expertise of local justice personnel, to develop solutions for
law enforcement problems (Lefton, 1970). These proposals may then

be directed to another subunit of the state planning agency for evaluation and, perhaps, funding. The important point is that those who
are affected by a change proposal in a law enforcement problem area
need to be brought into this process of planning for change (Zalezen-
ik and Jardim, 1971). This unit can manage this process.

Once a plan has been accepted, there is still the problem of implementation. The focus of the discussion has been on how to get acceptance and support for a change idea under conditions of interdependence. Once acceptance has been obtained and implementation of
the change begun, there is still a need to see how the change is altering dependence relationships. When a change effort is comprehensive enough to alter these relationships, there is a likelihood that the
affected agency will serve as an obstacle to the change. That is, unless the agency is aware of the change and has been included in efforts to plan and carry it out, its lack of involvement and knowledge
may hinder the achievement of the change goals. For instance, by
considering how change in the police department affects the operations of the district attorney's office, a police chief may be able to improve his relationships with that office on both political and operating levels. Thus, political obstacles to change may also be reduced by
the establishment of ongoing cooperative relationships among crimi
nal justice agencies (OSTI, 1967).

CONCLUSION

This discussion has dealt primarily with obstacles to change
brought about through the interdependencies of criminal justice orga-
zations with the other organizations in their contexts. This focus
was chosen because of interests in (1) how an administrator can effect change where his organization is highly dependent on other organizations for support, and (2) how a unit channelling funds to local justice agencies can use the power of its dollar to help reduce
crime and apprehend criminal offenders. The strategies suggested
for dealing with obstacles resulting from dependence are necessarily
general. The idea was not to state once and for all how to manage
change. The knowledge necessary for this sort of statement does not
exist. Besides, the individual administrator needs to develop a strategy to suit his problems. These strategies were, however, presented
to show the importance of community involvement in criminal justice
change and the participation of law enforcement personnel in any attempts, for instance, to reduce crime.

Too many discussions of obstacles to change convey the impression that change is good. In fact, change may be good or bad. The
quality of change depends on factors that are organizational as well
as political. Any discussion of change must remember that some
changes need to be slowed down, prevented, or more clearly thought

out. Efforts to understand or manage change are not directed towards implementing every change, but only at getting proposals or ideas for change to the point where they can be considered for their own merits. The proposal for change needs to get to the point where the promising idea can be developed into a plan for change by and for those it will affect. By understanding and using power and dependence relationships existing in a given law enforcement setting, political obstacles to change could possibly become facilitators of change.

REFERENCES

Advisory Commission on Intergovernmental Relations, *State-Local Relations in the Criminal Justice System.* Washington, D.C.: U.S. Government Printing Office, 1971.

Cressey, D. R., "Prison Organization," in J. G. March (ed.), *Handbook of Organizations.* Chicago: Rand-McNally, 1965: 1023–1070.

Emery, F. E. and E. L. Trist, "The Causal Texture of Organizational Environments," *Human Relations,* Vol. 18, (1965), 21–32.

Evan, W. M., "A Systems Model of Organizational Climate," in R. Tegiuri and G. H. Litwin (eds.), *Organizational Climate.* Boston: Division of Research, Harvard Graduate School of Business, Harvard University, 1968: 107–122.

Hudson, J. R. and Anne M. Hudson, "Strategies of Innovation in Public Bureaucracies," Stony Brook: State University of New York, 1969.

Katz, D. and R. L. Kahn, *The Social Psychology of Organizations,* New York: Wiley, 1966.

Lefton, M., "Client Characteristics and Structural Outcomes: Toward a Specification of Linkages," in Rosengren, W. R. and M. Lefton (eds.), *Organizations and Clients.* Columbus: Bobbs-Merril, 1970: 17–36.

Merton, R. K., "The Environment of the Innovating Organization: Some Conjectures and Proposals," in Steiner, G. A. (ed.), *The Creative Organization.* Chicago: University of Chicago Press, 1965: 50–65.

Organization for Social and Technical Innovation (OSTI), *Implementation* Submitted to the President's Commission on Law Enforcement and Administration of Justice, 1967.

Perucci, R. and M. Pilisuk, "Leaders and Ruling Elites: The Interorganizational Bases of Power," *American Sociological Review,* Vol. 35, (December, 1970), 1040–1057.

Price, J. L., *Organizational Effectiveness.* Homewood, Illinois: Irwin-Dorsey, 1968: 95–135.

Selznick, P., *TVA and the Grassroots.* Berkeley: University of California Press, 1949: 259–264.

Terreberry, Shirley, "The Evolution of Organizational Environments," *Administrative Science Quarterly,* Vol. 12, No. 4, (March, 1968), 590–613.

Thompson, J. D., *Organizations in Action.* New York: McGraw-Hill, 1967: 29–38.

Trist, E. L., "The Professional Facilitation of Planned Change in Organizations," in *Reviews, Abstracts, Working Groups: XVI International Congress of Applied Psychology*. Amsterdam: Swets and Zeithlenger, 1968: 111–120.

Turk, H., "Interorganizational Networks in Urban Society: Initial Perspectives and Comparative Research," *American Sociological Review*, Vol. 31, No. 1, (February, 1970), 1–19.

Wilson, J. Q., *Varieties of Police Behavior*. Harvard University, 1968.

Zaleznik, A. and A. Jardim, "Management," in Lazarsfeld *Uses of Sociology*. New York: Basic Books, 1967: 193–233.

OBSERVATIONS ON THE CHANGE PROCESS IN THE POLICE FIELD: AN EXTERNAL VIEW *

OBSTACLES TO CRIMINAL JUSTICE CHANGE

The transformation of innovation into operational reality first encounters the obstacle of validity. What is a successful demonstration? Possibly no demonstration is successful in any ultimate sense in the criminal justice field. Or, to put it another way, no panacea has been discovered. This means that there are arguments against most of the changes we want to adopt, especially if they have been objectively tested. This is the major obstacle of promoting change, and many worthwhile ideas have died in the face of this. The national adoption of the Manhattan Bail Project is a prime example.

A second obstacle is the cost benefit factor. Nothing motivates legislators to adopt changes more than the promise of dollar savings. The fact that many innovations, if adopted, would, might, or could substantially increase costs or appear as though they might, can serve as a giant obstacle to change.

A third obstacle is disagreement on the objective which the innovation purports to achieve. On issues ranging from "coddling-criminal-type reforms" and methadone to bail or preventive detention, the decision-makers are split into liberals, moderates, and conservatives. This is related to the validity and integrity issues mentioned previously. This disagreement among the decision-makers brings into sharp focus such conundrums as security vs. openness, police effectiveness vs. human relations, institutionalized rehabilitation vs. community residence. It doesn't help to contend that one or the other an-

* Christopher F. Edley, "Observations on the Change Process in the Police Field: An External View," *Innovation in Law Enforcement*, Criminal Justice Monograph, Washington: U. S. Government Printing Office, June 1973, pp. 48–56.

tagonist is enlightened, for the evidence supports neither.   Just to sight a few, I list the following:

—Educational level for ideal police officer.

—Automobile patrol vs. foot patrol.

—Civilian police review boards.

—Assignment of police to areas of residence.

—Guns vs. no guns.

Public opinion can be a major obstacle to change.   Its persuasive influence can support or intimidate police and other key officials. Both reformers and office holders use technicques of persuasion, such as public relations and public education devices to enhance their positions.

The ambiguities of preemption, especially among government agencies and levels of government, can also be a problem.   A program, perhaps an unfunded one, is announced in Washington, D.C.; and states and cities hold up on their own plans often ignoring a master plan.   Government agencies do the same at all levels, and it is a special type of "one upsmanship."

Jurisdictional ineffectiveness not only promotes inefficiency but also hampers reforms that require size and major expenditures.   Similarly, size can contribute to polarization if the community is not tied into the system.   Consolidation of responsibility and decentralization of accountability are suggested, but they would be innovations.

OVERCOMING OBSTACLES TO CHANGE

The pride and ambition of the key officials in local government are the strong positive factors.   Even where it appears that such persons are not professional in a formal training sense, e. g., where the person is a political appointee or the beneficiary of a seniority system, the desire to overcome shortcomings is often used to compensate for lack of complete professionalism:

1.   Most office holders recognize that changes are essential. Those in government and private philanthropy who seek to stimulate or induce innovative thinking will find a warm reception for the most part.

2.   Despite the fact that city hall has appointive power, a common alliance often occurs with the police department.

Competition for limited funds is a strong incentive for innovations.   There is a "bargain sale" mentality involved, resembling the department store sale where garments are piled in disheveled array on counters to attract bargain hunters.   The availability of block grant funds, thus, induces officials and communities to apply and in the process to stretch their own creative powers:

1. Quality control is almost impossible in the competitive format. The goal and victory are the winning of the funds and *not* whether the project is significant. The fund dispenser, more than usual, awards the best applications in a mediocre field.

2. The competitive format also attracts the greatest external pressures applied to the giving agency.

3. The competitive format, for these reasons and others, gives the lowest yield of significant innovations and experiments per dollar spent.

Negotiation and compromise will frequently permit an otherwise blocked project to continue:

1. The semantics of project goals are frequently irrelevant to the launching and execution of a well-designed project. Frequently a police project, e. g., civilian female receptionist aids in police precinct headquarters, will be perceived by the police for one purpose, improving community relations, and by the community for another, curbing abuse in the headquarters. Insistence by either that the other endorse his purpose can defeat the project.

2. Politicans are more likely to be supportive and, if need be, politically courageous when they are consulted or involved in a meaningful way. This opportunity arises when:

    a. Political clearance is required because of the police official's established working relationship.

    b. Local funding commitments are necessary.

    c. The length of the project requires it to be protected from drastic shifts in policy and leadership.

3. Preliminary studies and planning in a variety of ways can open doors for experiments and innovations otherwise blocked. This is no different from other types of government projects.

    a. Distinguished experts or citizens committees make recommendations following study.

    b. Existing recommendation, e. g., President's Commission on Violence, are adopted for action.

4. Law suits to compel action, e. g., attacking police tests, can offer opportunities for compromise settlements out of court.

Intermediary change agents, as perceived by a funding source, can often be used to advantage when their credibility is generally accepted. Hence, an application from a national police organization such as the International Association of Chiefs of Police (IACP), or a regional one such as the Southern Police Institute, or a local university may open doors otherwise closed. In an effort to carry this one step further, the Ford Foundation has created the Police Foundation as an independent $30 million organization designed to assist police departments to improve themselves. We hope that the Police Foundation will establish its identity and expertise with police and serve them better than the Ford Foundation could with comparable sums.

CREATING AN ENVIRONMENT FOR CHANGE

The President's Crime Commission was a force for enlightened constructive change and as such strongly influences private and public attitudes toward reform. On the other hand, demonstrations by minority groups, anti-war forces, and crime statistics, while occasionally stimulating constructive reform, have encouraged crackdowns and recommendations of repression, at least verbally. If I thought these opposed positions irreconcilable, then attending this conference would be futile. I do believe that most rational men can reach agreement on what to do about crime problems. Most of the mistakes made result from unilateral actions in the political arena.

The police are in an excellent position to assess certain phenomena of our criminal justice system. It appears from police spokesmen that the rank and file majority believe that stiff sentences should prevail. There are many judges who believe in giving the police what they want. But, what is the policemen's response to the fact that blacks are in prison in much larger numbers than their percentage of the population. In one southwestern state where blacks are 3 percent of the population, they are 40 percent of the prison population. In New York, blacks charge that whites are diverted after arrest through police discretion, plea bargaining, and probation with mostly Puerto Ricans and blacks staying the route to prison. No evaluation of the facts would be more interesting or valid than that of the police.

Perhaps there are better illustrations, but the point is that police can help enormously to change the atmosphere by objectively assessing the criminal justice system. The defensive and hostile positions taken by police traditionally may not serve their purpose well. An experiment the other way could be revealing.

The community, especially in the inner city, may be experiencing a slow evolution towards support for crime fighting. The inner-city population must change its own atmosphere and communicate this concern more effectively to the larger community.

Political leadership, mass media, crime statistics and other factors affecting criminal justice can be honest and supportive of constructive change or honest and/or negative change.

THE ROLE OF PUBLIC SERVICE GROUPS

Public service groups are most visible and successful when they undertake a certain mission which supplements the efforts of a criminal justice agency. This involves more than the use of private resources to accomplish criminal justice system ends, for the latter purpose could be met by providing earmarked funds to the appropriate criminal justice agency. Outsiders and experts from other walks on project staffs and studies add important and obvious dimensions.

They have the requisite flexibility to deal with the obstacles and to demand that certain ones be removed as their price of doing business. Those that cannot are doomed to failure, in my opinion.

They can establish credibility with the broad community. Critical studies, controversial positions, support for the agency, demands for funds, responsibility for demonstration failures are a few of the many ways that private service groups can serve.

Examples of Public Service Groups associated with the Ford Foundation, as well as with many other funding sources, including LEAA are as follows:

Criminal Justice Centers

Harvard University, University of Chicago, University of California (Davis), Georgetown University, Vera Institute.

Other Efforts

Southeastern Correctional Research Center, University of Pennsylvania, University of California (Berkeley).

Organizations

A sample of a few Ford-funded organizations active in change in the criminal justice system. They are as follows:

National Council on Crime and Delinquency.

American Justice Institute.

ABA Commission on Correctional Facilities and Services.

NAACP Legal Defense Fund.

American Bar Association.

Institute of Judicial Administration.

National Center for State Courts.

National Legal Aid and Defender Association.

The presence of public service groups is so evident that it is difficult to contemplate a just system without them. The system shows little capability or sensitivity for self-correction. Even the best agency heads, and some are here, are unable to beard the lion without outside support. There is a limit to the changes which can be effected solely by insiders. Indeed, performance by the best of the breed suggests a 10 to 20 percent achievement as the maximum for one administrator.

CONCLUSION

I have attempted to set down some rather obvious suggestions of how private groups, including foundations, assist the change process in the criminal justice system by stimulating innovation, overcoming obstacles within the system, and creating an environment of change. Illustrations have been used sparingly, although they exist in profusion, partly to avoid embarrassment, but also to underscore the eclectic nature of the observations drawn from my several years of experience as a lawyer, prosecutor, and professional philanthropist. No effort has been made to be exhaustive or symmetrical, and this paper should be viewed as a first effort to articulate observed factors operative in the change process.

HUMANIZING CHANGE IN THE POLICE ORGANIZATION *

As others have indicated in preceding chapters, police departments are faced with a high degree of authoritarianism, conformity, and stagnation which inhibit change, either organizationally or for individual officers. Van Maanen (1974) has even maintained that the norms implicit in this rigidity not only inhibit change, but also alter the pursuit of justice. Whether or not the "stagnation" has extended this far, there is little doubt that high levels of organizational conformity do exist in American police departments.

A natural response to this rigidity of organization in a business oriented society could be expected to be programs which have been found to work so well with similar situations in the business community. Organization Development (OD) is a rubric for a broad set of many such programs which have demonstrated their value in organizations of many types throughout the country (Bowers, 1973; Beer and Huse, 1972; Blumberg and Wiener, 1971; and Bennis, 1969). Clearly, if OD has facilitated positive integration of personnel, reduced conflict among groups and individuals, and generally raised the level of organizational effectiveness in other organizations, it merits consideration for our needs in criminal justice administration.

* Source: "Humanizing Change in the Police Organization", an original article by
   James Fox, College of Law Enforcement, Eastern Kentucky University.

It is to this question that this chapter is addressed. We do not presume to fully analyze the full range of possibilities inherent in this management tool. There are many excellent discussions of organization development available (Beckhard, 1969; Beer, 1976; Bennis, 1969; and Alderfer and Brown, 1975), though it must be admitted that they do not focus upon its application in a police department. Our focus here is more narrow, dealing with the major and more frequently used elements of OD and their possible application in police administration. We shall argue that these administrative processes included under OD *should* be used in each administrative component of the criminal justice system, *in as much as the characteristics of that component will allow*. However, the characteristics of the business organization, or other organizations referenced in OD literature, are directly contradicted in the vast majority of police departments. For this reason, we feel, rational application of these techniques to police administration calls for less ambitious goals than those to which the typical OD consultant has grown accustomed. *Within the parameters set by the police culture*, organizational changes can be facilitated through OD and, as these changes take root, further changes are made possible by imaginative utilization OD processes.

Before these points are addressed definitively, however, it is necessary to identify some elements of the setting of police administration which may limit the capability of these processes to facilitate organizational change. The effort, therefore, in the first section of our discussion is to give a brief sketch of this setting, to which the reader is encouraged to add from his or her own experience. (Perhaps the reader may even share these additions with the author in direct correspondence.) Included in this discussion of setting are the informal as well as formal social system of the organization, the social, including the normative system of the community, and the physical and geographical characteristics of the setting in which law enforcement takes place. These are viewed as possibly establishing limits to the effectiveness of the OD efforts.

The second section presents a light overview of the processes included in many OD programs. These are intended to delimit discussion for better understanding. In doing so, of course, one runs the risk of oversimplifying a complex process and may be accused of biasing the analysis. It should be understood that here we are not attempting to explain OD, there are several excellent references for that purpose (mentioned above), as well as seminars, workshops, and courses on this topic. Our intention is to argue in behalf of a carefully designed, cautiously phased organization development program for police departments, and to do so requires at least a basic common understanding of some of the OD processes.

Finally, we turn to the character of the OD processes which may best meet the needs of police administrators and the characteristics of the police organization which may best serve as a recipient of such a program.

THE SETTING FOR LAW ENFORCEMENT

For society, the importance of quality law enforcement is great indeed. Egon Bittner, a leading scholar of police in contemporary society, has stated that "It would seem reasonable that only the most gifted, the most aspiring, and the most equiposed among us are eligible for it" [that is, eligible to assume this role]. Bittner then proceeds to outline the three steps that lead to this realization. "First, when policemen do those things only policemen can do, they invariably deal with matters of absolutely critical importance, at least to the people with whom they deal. . . . Second, while lawyers, physicians, teachers, social workers, and clergymen also deal with critical problems, they have bodies of technical knowledge or elaborate schemes of norms to guide them in their respective tasks. . . . Third, the mandate to deal with problems in which force may have to be used implies the special trust that force will be used on *in extremis*" (Bittner: 1974).

With this realization, and in face of the very serious responsibility society has placed upon them as police administrators, the supervisory staff of police organizations have sought to develop an intensely dedicated and loyal cadre. In Bakke's terms, the officer is "fused" to the organization through a series of social bonds that are consciously developed by a series of socialization phases (Bakke: 1955). These processes select the most promising (i. e. those most likely to assimilate the normative patterns of the police system), apply a system of rigid training wherein recruits are introduced to the normative system, reinforce this and verify it with personal experience under the supervision of an experienced officer, and follow these experiences with a continuous series of peer and supervisor reinforcement mechanisms. Throughout these experiences, the officer develops an increasing identification of himself as a police officer, an identification by which he sees himself as distinct from other members of his society. Moreover, if Van Maanen is correct, this process proceeds to the extent that the officer defines himself in more and more narrow terms, with his watch, with his particular peers, or team, and with the territory to which he is routinely assigned (1974: 112–116).

The continuous socialization processes to which the officer is exposed, reinforced as they are by the survival dictates of street level law enforcement, develop a uniquely separate social identity. The characteristics of this identity are not unknown to police administrators, nor even to scholars of police behavior (Reiss, 1971; Skolnick, 1966; Neiderhoffer, 1967; and Wilson, 1968). Among these the foremost may well be the personal commitment to the ephemeral goal of crime reduction, the "quality arrest", which is seen as good police work, *worthy of a man*. As his socializing experiences continue, as the soldiers of Stouffer's study (1949), the officer develops the realization that it is his web of peer group friendships that protects him from the dangers of the street—not the administrative structure of the department. Thus, a characteristic of deep and intense loyalty develops among line officers that defies formal organizational processes and societal norms.

A third characteristic (i. e., in addition to the socialization processes and field experience, discussed above) to be discussed here is more complex in origin and effect. With the large mass of activities that can be defined by the officer on the street as within his jurisdiction, he is forced to choose which activity to pursue. This choice is frequently assisted by departmental policy and supervisory directions, of course, but the immediate decision is left to the officer himself. The choice is not infrequently between a clear-cut case which lends itself to resolution (e. g. traffic, vice or, less frequently, murder) and difficult cases, involving much time and little promise of success (e. g. larceny, burglary, or white collar crime). It would be surprising indeed if men dedicated to produce did not choose those crimes which led to more frequent resolution. To this is added still another aspect of the problem; that is, the handling of cases produces reports (the officer's behavior is on record) and the more difficult the case (the more the necessary contact with nonoffender citizens), the higher the probability that the report will not be favorable. Thus, the officer finds it to his advantage and to the Departments' advantage, to avoid the complex case if possible, to pursue the less complex case if available, but to be otherwise engaged. Cases requiring long detailed investigation are therefore avoided. The contradiction between this and the ideal which the officer has of his own performance only furthers his dependence upon his fellow officers who share his situation.

Thus far we have observed three of the characteristics of the officer on the street, focusing upon the individual member of this unique organization. He is the primary element in the description of the setting of law enforcement. Other elements include (1) the physical environment (2) social environment of his police activities and (3) the organizational environment within which they are conducted.

To the officer, while these elements are difficult to measure, their importance is beyond doubt. His effectiveness and his safety frequently depend upon his knowledge of the territory to which he is assigned—the uses of each building (at all hours of the day or night), the location of potential trouble, the paths over which illicit activity flow, and those points in the area wherein he can expect to find support. With experience, he is able to fuse his own activities with those working and living in the area—he develops an understanding of their behavior and *they gain sets of expectations regarding his behavior.* With this consistency of expected and manifest behavior develops a trust that enables him to work his territory. Unexpected behavior on his part, or by an officer from another area entering his jurisdiction may disrupt the balance of expected and manifest behavior and place trust in doubt. Likewise, changes in the social composition of the area, changes in the uses of buildings, throughways, or open areas, or changes in lines of demarcation are likely to lead to increased caution on the part of an alert officer. Thus, the distribution of activities throughout his territory of jurisdiction, over time, poses a critical element of the setting in which the officer functions.

The "Administration" (i. e. the things that are communicated to him by his superiors, how they are communicated, and the responses expected from him) composes a third external element in the officer's setting. The greater the frequency of contact initiated by the Administration, the less secure the officer tends to feel on his own: it leaves a sense that his abilities are in doubt. Yet, no communication can raise graver doubts: he may be considered "in pasture", or his beat may be considered expendable, or he may be taken for granted and thus ignored. Actually, consistency—predictability—here is also important, as it is between the officer and the community. This consistency of interaction between the Department and the officer is sought in most departments. It is, after all, a basic aspect of Weberian bureaucracy. However, vertical communication is often routinized to the point that its purpose—mutual understanding—is obscured in overly cautious jargon, leaving the officer on the street more and more isolated.

SUMMARY

The purpose of this first section was to identify some of the features of the organization of a police department. It is not assumed that these features describe the "average" department, for we would deny that the "average" exists. Nor do we assume that most departments are reflected here, since most are much too small to be found in these descriptions. It is, however, our hope that the majority of the "working cops" will find observations here which will strike a chord of recognition, since the majority of our local police are members of larger departments.

Another feature of the above discussion which may need comment is the lack of organizational diagrams and discussion of "chains of command" and "span of control". As important as these considerations are to an understanding of police organizations, it is our feeling that they do not have as crucial an importance for OD effectiveness as does the culture in which police activities are conducted. This rationale comes, admittedly, from the basic assumption that the objectives of police administration are ultimately met by the officer on the street—all else is supportive.

ORGANIZATION DEVELOPMENT

As we have said, OD is a combination of processes, not a single administrative activity. Nor is it a specific set of processes in a particular combination which can be dispensed as though from a pharmacy. Equally important, it should be understood that organization development *is not organizational change*—it is the term used here to identify several behavioral-science processes which are necessarily custom-designed for a *particular organization, at a particular time, to facilitate organizational change*. This will be our working definition; however, there are other definitions, and it might provide some insight into our definition if we review some of those which we are not using.

Beckhard (1969) defines organization development as "an effort (1) *planned*, (2) *organization-wide*, and (3) *managed* from the *top*, to (4) increase organization *effectiveness* and *health* through (5) *planned interventions* in the organization's "processes", using *behavior-science* knowledge." [1] Bennis (1969) defines OD as "an educational strategy employing the widest possible means of experience-based behavior in order to achieve more and better organizational choices in a highly turbulent world." [2] In his discussion of this definition Bennis makes several points of interest for us: (1) the objective is *planned organizational change*, (2) the emphasis is upon experienced behavior, (3) change agents are not part of the organization itself, (4) the *client—change agent trust* is of utmost importance, and (5) the primary value system *of the change agent* is supportive of "humanistic" management. Throughout his discussions, Bennis uses the phrases "team management", "conflict resolution", "confidence and trust", and "tension reduction"; with focus upon the group, rather than upon the individual.

Blake and Mouton (1969) focus upon a "Managerial Grid", which provides an individual the opportunity to visualize the interaction between human relations objectives in the organization and production objectives. With such a focus, it is possible to elicit interaction on specific issues evoked by less than perfect intersects of the two objective-orientations, the gap between the desired state and the

1. Beckhard, p. 9. (*Underlining his*)   2. Bennis, pp. 10–17.

realized state is identified, and methods of closing the gap are analysed. The entire process takes place in groups of managers first, then, as the upper levels become thoroughly imbued with the concept of "Corporate Excellence", they train employees on the organizational level below themselves. According to Blake and Mouton the entire organization must be involved in change, if it is to work. Among other observations relative to facilitating change, they stress (1) the need for top management to lead the change, (2) the need to be able to see and understand the concept of excellence in organizational performance, and (3) the need to deal with *every issue*—"Nothing is sacrosanct"—and then to proceed in a sequential and orderly way.[3]

Change as a social process is generally viewed as being composed of "unfreezing" the normative system of the organization, intervening in the organization's processes in a planned manner (hopefully positive), and then "refreezing" the normative system with the changed behaviors included and the antithetical processes eliminated. Organizational development is then viewed as those processes which are used to:

1. Examine the organization in its "solid state" (prior to change) to diagnose the directions and character of changes needed (Diagnostic Stage).

2. Determine the "ingredients" to be added, or altered in the organization's "liquid state" (Design Stage).

3. Increase the opportunity for the individuals within the organization to involve themselves in the change process (Initiation, or "Unfreezing" Stage).

4. Implement the changes when the organization is in this more flexible, or "open", or "liquid" state, allowing for acceptance to evolve (Implementation State).

5. Adjust the changes in response to feedback while the organization is still in "fluid state" (Adjustment Stage).

6. Encourage individualized identification with the changed organization, returning to a "solid state" (Identification Stage).

These are not presented as products of our own imagination, though they are not entirely representative of any one of the other authors in this field. We have tried to synthesize the thinking of others and our own, to describe sequential stages in OD. Hopefully, if the stages are understood, one can better understand what we mean by Organization Development.

Lawrence and Lorsch (1969) have drawn attention to the importance of the *Diagnostic Stage*, as Beckhard did in a more recent arti-

3. Blake-Mouton, pp. 10–21.

cle (1975), and Michael Beer did in his excellent chapter on the topic of organization development in *Handbook of Industrial and Organizational Psychology* (1976).   Each of these provides more depth than we can here, but the basic elements are similar.   This Diagnostic Stage is an essential stage in OD, since its purpose is to describe the present state of the organization and its environment to the end that the *need for change* is identified.   Beyond this, the direction and character of the necessary change are analysed.   At this point, also, it must be determined that the top management will support the change itself and the OD processes—without this commitment the effort cannot succeed.

Techniques of diagnosis vary considerably, depending upon the consultants employed, the nature of the organization, and the personnel of the organization.   They may include group or individual interviews, observations, records analyses, or one of a number of questionnaire surveys.   Our own preference is for a combination of techniques, since each taps a different type or different quality of information.   However, the greater the variety, the more costly this stage becomes and it is occasionally difficult for the client to remember the importance of high quality diagnosis in the success of the entire effort when faced with the budget.

When the diagnosis of the organization is completed it may be determined that there is not enough commitment to change on the part of management, or the particular changes found to be necessary are beyond the human capabilities of management to deal with, or there is not sufficient trust between the client and the consultant to proceed further.   These issues must be faced directly—and at this time!   To enter the design stage, wherein images of change are evoked at many levels of the organization, and then to halt the process can have a detrimental effect upon the organization.

The *Design Stage* is the point at which the specific techniques to be used to facilitate change are selected.   Timing for the implementation of these intervention techniques is determined.   Evaluation points and techniques are established.   Intervenors (individuals who will conduct the seminars, or T-groups, or other techniques) are selected.   Costs of all elements are determined and contracts are completed.   The client should have a clear understanding of the autonomy of the consultant in the stages to come: the consultant should have a clear understanding of the degree of client commitment (not necessarily measurable in dollars).   Both should have a clear, unambiguous understanding of the specific techniques in the design, why they are used, why the particular sequence is used, how and by whom the processes will be evaluated, and what the entire project will cost —financially and in terms of emotional energies of the personnel involved.

The *Initiation*, of "Unfreezing", *Stage* may be said to have started when individuals were asked questions in the period we identified as the diagnostic stage. Beer [4] has taken exactly this position. However, specific intervention techniques are designed for the purpose of "unfreezing" the organization and it is for this reason that we give this stage distinct identifications. Among these techniques, probably the most widely known is the training laboratory; however, the most frequently used is likely to be the review of data derived from the Diagnostic Stage by groups of employees and managers. In any case, the thrust of this stage is to increase the levels of involvement in the consideration of change possibilities. It is, therefore, essential that openness be demonstrable during this and succeeding stages: options which are not available need to be identified, but a significant range of open options must be available. It is of paramount importance that the participation of employees be totally unintimidated. Neither administrative consideration nor peer group influences should be allowed to block the free flow of ideas.

The flow into the *Implementation Stage* is then natural and self-generating. At this time more focused group activities evolve, focusing upon the characteristics of the change, its effects on the organization, its effects on the people involved, the identification of those people affected, and the identification of other, environmental, respondents. It is important at this stage also to ensure that the participants have no sense of intimidation from other elements of the organization. As one proceeds through this stage, feedback is encouraged as a means of determining the degree to which the change has had an impact upon the organization, the environment, and the people of both the environment and the organization.

In response to the feedback from the previous stage certain adjustments are inevitably called for. These may include such things as administrative adjustment of pay schedules, educational leave policies, or space allocation. They may also involve family or personal counseling for certain employees and managers. Omitting this stage, or overreacting during this stage, can lead to serious consequences for the organization. It is for this reason that feedback from the preceeding stage must be verified carefully and it is for this reason that a wide range of adjustment techniques needs to be available.

As these adjustments are made, the organization begins to return to a state of stable sets of expectations/actions wherein members identify with their roles within the changed organization. The *Identification Stage* is the point at which the organization-as-changed is

4. Beer. *Handbook of Industrial and Organizational Psychology*, pp. 945–948.

brought to a jell. Efforts in this stage are directed toward reinforcing revised expected behavior patterns.

SUMMARY

Organization development has been discussed as a series of varied processes which are purposefully designed to facilitate organization change. The purpose of this discussion has been to introduce the reader to a set of concepts related to this management tool. Variations, of course, do exist in the types of procedures or techniques utilized, whether or not combinations are used, the particular combinations considered appropriate, and the basic philosophy implicit in the program. We have presented the overview of one approach which is intended to assist the reader to conceptualize the OD program. With this background, it is hoped that application of this concept can be made to police administration.

THE USE OF ORGANIZATION DEVELOPMENT IN POLICE ADMINISTRATION

Police agencies vary in the degree to which OD programs would be feasible and, if feasible, the type of program most appropriate. Clearly, budgetary considerations may discourage the small departments from adopting a full range of processes in Organization Development. Yet, the same department may find it advantageous and feasible to participate in laboratory training programs or management grid seminars for managerial personnel. This may or may not be accompanied by a modified form of the Diagnostic Stage. It is, in our opinion, better planning to diagnose the setting of the organization prior to any intervention technique, though many businesses and educational institutions have not followed this advice.

In fact, it would appear that any criminal justice agency would do well to institute an organizational diagnosis as long as management is willing to permit information to flow freely. The time and cost of organizational diagnosis would vary with the size of the department and techniques used, of course, but the advantages to any top management would be expected to be considerable.

Beyond the Diagnostic Stage, in our opinion, attitudes, expectations, and various forms of commitment by members of the organization are stimulated to a much larger extent. Those who participate in T-Groups, Sensitivity Sessions, Grid Management Seminars, and/or other intervention techniques generally anticipate that they might use skills or knowledge they have developed. The frustration of such expectations can add to organizational problems rather than resolving them. However, as in other aspects of this issue, there are many managers who have felt that it was to their advantage to participate in a limited portion of the intervention process.

But these concerns apply to any organization. Police organizations may well have additional, unique factors to consider. Many of these were implied in the first section. Police departments are faced with objectives which can, and often are, operationalized in a variety of ways. Moreover, the objectives are not usually controlled within the organization, but they are controlled by the community through the political processes. This element alone may place the police department beyond possible help from organization development processes. On the other hand, a comprehensive program of organizational development may be just the thing that responsible political leaders are seeking from their police departments. I can be a major asset to them. Whether or not it does depends largely upon the levels of consistency which can be found in these pressures.

Another possible deterrent may be found in the heavy weight of tradition which is carried by the paramilitary organizational structure of the typical police department. Organization Development loosens the bonds of communication and depends upon an openness in communication which can exist only where there is no fear of reprisal of any type from management or from peers. Such openness is hard to find in a police department.

These are indeed formidable obstacles. They are in fact the very obstacles to good administration of a department which OD may be best able to eliminate. If there is a sincere commitment on the part of the police management and community representatives, it would appear that the very problems which would otherwise thwart a complete OD effort could be overcome and a healthier, more effective organization would result. The point to this is that an effective OD program for police administration depends upon a commitment to change which does not exclude consideration of objectives, organizational structure, traditional procedures or the community environment.

Finally, Beckhard (1975) has observed that continued change also requires conscious procedures and commitment. He points out that perhaps, "the most important single requirement for continued change is a continued feedback and information system that lets people in the system know the system status in relation to the desired goals".[5] We would add that this system must not become corrupted by politically generated distortions or omissions.

SUMMARY AND CONCLUSIONS

We have attempted to view police administration as a potential client group for the positive application of an important new managerial program Organization Development. In doing so, we explored

5. Beckhard, p. 54.

some of the characteristics of police organizations, we reviewed some of the more salient features of OD as it has been applied to other systems, and we considered some of the concerns which might be raised to the application of OD to a police department.

It is apparent that police departments present fertile ground for the effective application of Organizational Development. However, the very areas to which the techniques may be applied most effectively loom as the greatest obstacles to the acceptance of this managerial program. The key may well rest with the degree of commitment found in the crucial managerial personnel and community representatives.

Though the promise of organization change through OD is great it is by no means certain. The possibilities may be rejected as inapplicable or inappropriate, or the system may regress to "old ways" with time. Indeed, it would not be impossible that we would find ourselves attempting to fight twenty-first century crime with a nineteenth century police system. The difference rests, *not in equipment*, but in the quality of personnel and their utilization. It is our belief that properly designed programs of Organization Development offer the means by which a new thrust to the future can be made in police administration.

REFERENCES

Alderfer, Clayton P. and L. Dave Brown (1975) Learning from Changing: Organizational Diagnosis and Development. Volume 19. Beverly Hills: Sage Publications.

Bakke, E. Wright (1955) The Fusion Process. New Haven: Yale University.

Beckhard, Richard (1969) Organization Development: Strategies and Models. Reading, Massachusetts: Addison-Wesley.

Beckhard, Richard (1975) "Strategies for Large System Change." Sloan Management Review 16 (Winter): 43–55.

Beer, Michael (1976) "The Technology of Organization Development." Pp. 937–993 in Marvin D. Dunnette (ed.), Handbook of Industrial and Organizational Psychology. Chicago: Rand McNally.

Beer, Michael, and Edgar F. Huse (1972) "A Systems Approach to Organizational Development." Journal of Applied Behavioral Science 8 (January–February). 79–101.

Bennis, Warren G. (1969) Organization Development: Its Nature, Origins, and Prospects. Reading, Massachusetts: Addison-Wesley.

Bittner, Egon (1974) "Florence Nightingale in Pursuit of Willie Sutton: A Theory of the Police." Pp. 17–44 in Herbert Jacob (e) d.), The Potential for Reform of Criminal Justice. Beverly Hills: Sage Publications.

Blake, Robert R. and Jane S. Mouton (1969) Building a Dynamic Corporation Through Grid Organization Development. Reading, Massachusetts: Addison-Wesley.

Blumberg, Arthur and William Wiener (1971) "One from Two: Facilitating an Organizational Merger." Journal of Applied Behavioral Science 7 (January–February): 87–102.

Bowers, David G. (1973) "OD Techniques and Their Results in 23 Organizations: The Michigan ICL Study." Journal of Applied Behavioral Science 9 (January–February): 21–43.

Lawrence, Paul R. and Jay W. Lorsch (1969) Developing Organizations. Reading, Massachusetts: Addison-Wesley.

Reiss, Albert J. (1971) The Police and the Public. New Haven: Yale University.

Skolnick, Jerome (1966) Justice Without Trial: Law Enforcement in a Democratic Society. New York: John Wiley.

Stouffer, Samuel A., et al. (1949) The American Soldier: Combat and Its Aftermath. Princeton: Princeton University.

Van Maanen, John (1974) "Working the Street: A Developmental View of Police Behavior." Pp. 83–130 in H. Jacob (ed.), The Potential for Reform of Criminal Justice. Volume III. Beverly Hills: Sage Publications.

Wilson, James Q. (1968) Varieties of Police Behavior. Cambridge, Massachusetts: Harvard University.

POLICE INNOVATIONS *
ISSUES AND ANSWERS

Innovation in police work embraces a very broad spectrum of seemingly earnest attempts by police administrators to address issues of societal changes having direct impact on police organizations. Sophisticated patrol techniques, scientific investigative instruments, modern computerized communications systems—all contribute to a preponderant mix of police advancements that have been and continue to be examined by law enforcement practitioners for viable solutions to challenges in American society. Contemporary police administrators and their personnel, therefore, increasingly are urged to adopt attitudes which encourage creative and innovative thinking in an effort to build organizations capable of continuing change.[1] Innovative programs are natural results of such thinking.

---

* Reproduced from the *Police Chief* Magazine, December, 1975 issue, with permission of the International Association of Chiefs of Police. By Anthony Vastola.

1. Clarence M. Kelley, "Receptiveness to Change," *FBI Law Enforcement Bulletin*, 42 (Nov., 1973), p. 17.

Yet innovative programs, once adopted, often have difficulty surviving.[2] Frequently, there are controversies about whether the success or failure of a program is due to the inherent strengths or weaknesses of the original idea, the project design, general support or resistance of the police department's leadership to accept change, or some other related factors.[3] Too often these controversies go unresolved.

This paper examines issues negatively impacting police innovation and suggests some practical methods police administrators might use to resolve these issues. The author assumes that the program is solvent and worth saving, i. e., the problems therefore rest somewhere with the program's administration. The several urban police innovations described in this paper serve as practical examples, pertinent to the issues and supportive of my propositions for the subject. Three general facets of program impact will be explored: timeliness of implementation, internal implications, and external implications. Each phase is interdependent for program success; failure to administer one phase properly will have direct negative impact on the others.

TIMELINESS OF IMPLEMENTATION

Before a program is implemented, while the police administrator undergoes the basic planning process, he should stop and ask himself a very crucial question: Is it the right time for this program? Some objective diagnosis of the kind of climate (internal and external) for change is imperative.[4] Without this examination, a potentially successful venture is left almost entirely to chance for survival.

The Dayton, Ohio, Police Department, for example, chose to implement a team-policing program during a period of high-level community tension and turmoil, when attention was being focused on the police department to deal effectively with various community crises. This climate of unrest was one aspect attributed to difficulties the program encountered.[5]

2. *Opportunities for Improving Productivity in Police Services* (Washington, D.C., National Commission on Productivity, 1973), p. 67.

3. Catherine H. Milton, "Demonstration Projects as a Strategy for Change," *Innovation in Law Enforcement* (Washington, D.C., U.S. Government Printing Office, 1973), p. 115.

4. Robert B. Duncan, "The Climate for Change in Three Police Departments:

Some Implications for Action," *Innovation in Law Enforcement* (Washington, D.C., U. S. Government Printing Office, 1973), p. 39.

5. Lawrence W. Sherman, Catherine H. Milton, and Thomas V. Kelly, *Team Policing; Seven Case Studies* (Washington, D.C., Police Foundation, 1973), p. 20.

In New York City, a team-policing project was implemented during a very anxious period in the police department. An investigating commission was about to begin hearings which would publicly document police corruption in New York City. Concurrently, the police department was operating under severe budgetary limitations.[6] Despite these difficult times, the police commissioner decided to test a team-policing program that increased discretion of first-line supervisors and their officers, and removed these supervisors from ordinary patrol responsibilities.[7]

Both police departments—Dayton and New York City—embarked on bold ventures to improve police services. Each was concerned with rising crime rates and spreading community distance from the police. Each project held highly principled objectives, innovative concepts, and promise for the future of police patrol in the nation. Regrettably, neither project today enjoys nearly the attention nor the success it once hoped to attain.

While one cannot challenge the principles of these programs, one might reasonably question the timeliness of their beginnings.

What, then, does a police administrator do when the need for some organizational change is clearly indicated, when some program promises to meet that need, but, unfortunately, when some interposing factor threatens to defeat that very program from the outset? Most progressive administrators prefer chancing program implementation (and defeat) to no action at all. Often their choice is influenced by a common misconception that some good must always come from change. In fact, change may be good or bad. From this perspective, the administrator must remember that some changes need to be slowed down, prevented, or more clearly thoughtout.[8]

Of course, the realities of an administrator's office often make inaction an unpopular decision, especially when he is sitting on a program of some considerable attraction to a political official or some local pressure group.

The use of the pilot project is a viable alternative to inaction for an administrator who is under pressure to institute a new program during an inopportune period. The pilot is a very flexible organizational model. To be effective, the pilot should remain highly adaptable, apolitical in nature, and independent of local government. It should be expressed as a visitor to the community serviced, as a

6. Peter B. Bloch, and David L. Specht, *Evaluation of Operation Neighborhood* (Washington, D.C., The Urban Institute, 1973), pp. 129–133.

7. *Ibid.*, pp. 129–133.

8. Paul Solomon and John Gardiner, "Political Obstacles to Change in Criminal Justice Agencies: An Interorganizational Perspective," *The Change Process in Criminal Justice* (Washington, D.C., U. S. Government Printing Office, 1973), p. 183.

means for thoughtful analysis of a law enforcement problem.[9]   The pilot program should be allowed sufficient lead time to test and evaluate its ultimate effectiveness.

INTERNAL IMPLICATIONS

Successful change, of course, requires more than just good timing for its beginning.   Failure to gain cooperation of police department personnel can easily doom an innovative program to failure. Obviously, different programs will elicit different responses from a department's sworn members.   "A focused patrol program, for example, may create a negative reaction because officers believe it will entail more supervision than random patrol.   Some programs . . . may be extremely popular with the personnel directly involved, but are resented by other personnel."[10]   Before a program is implemented, the police manager should be reasonably sure about who will ultimately benefit and who will initially be hurt by this change.   He can then better prepare his personnel, especially those initially bothered, for the transition.

Internal cooperation can be substantially induced if the police administrator recognizes a program's potential impact on employee motivation and behavior.   His policies must be unequivocably established or else his personnel are likely to perceive them as unrealistic or irrelevant.[11]   Too often an innovative program may require idealized stereotyped officers who don't exist in the organization and cannot be hired.   Frequently, constructive change requires added innovation to redirect and intelligently motivate the people who are to be relied upon to achieve desired goals.[12]   Specialized training as an added innovation should go a long way to alleviate this problem.

This seemingly basic part of a program's methodological design can be and often is given a back seat.   When New York City implemented a team-policing program, no attempt was made to indoctrinate most organizational members in the program's concepts.   Many conflicts that later developed between officers involved in the new program and other precinct officials were clearly attributable to a lack of understanding of the new program's principles.[13]

9.   Robert C. Cushman, "The Pilot Cities Experience." *The Change Process in Criminal Justice* (Washington, D. C., U.S. Government Printing Office, 1973), pp. 44–45.

10.   *Opportunities for Improving Productivity,* p. 68.

11.   James Q. Wilson, *Varieties of Police Behavior* (New York, Atheneum, 1972), p. 66.

12.   Herbert Edelhertz, "The Research Process as a Factor in Implementation of Design for Criminal Justice Change," *The Change Process in Criminal Justice* (Washington, D.C., U. S. Government Printing Office, 1973), p. 142.

13.   Bloch.   *Operation Neighborhood,* p. 8.

A team sergeant, for example, might ask a team officer to inspect an area located a short distance from his authorized post. While on partrol, the team officer might visit that locale, only to be "caught" by a patrol supervisor and questioned about why he strayed away from his authorized post boundaries. Although the spirit of team policing might have permitted this behavior, the rules of the organization did not. A patrol supervisor, unfamiliar with team-policing principles, might therefore charge the officer with violation of a department rule.

Another example of the importance of training occurred in Kansas City, Missouri. The police administrator recognized that experimental conditions of a patrol project were not being maintained and that several problems had arisen. One problem involved violations of the project guidelines. Additional training sessions were held, and administrative emphasis was brought to bear to ensure adherence to the guidelines. The experiment was suspended until problems were corrected.[14]

Another internal issue is the notion that continuous change earmarks a progressive police manager, which has created a state of "innovative overkill" in many police organizations. Too many programs introduced almost simultaneously will tend to negatively influence each other to the point that nothing works the way it was intended. For example, New York City implemented a career paths program which was, for the most part, antithetical to the concept of a team-policing program introduced at the same time. Under career paths guidelines, officers were rotated regularly among precincts, limiting their opportunity to develop close neighborhood ties. This practice detracted from the theme of team policing and tended to disrupt team activities through high personnel turnovers.[15]

Dayton, Ohio, and Syracuse, New York, had very similar experiences with their team-policing programs. In Dayton, "the large number of programs that were being implemented at the same time created an atmosphere of instability within the department." [16] Syracuse, because of waves of reform and reorganization, engendered quiet resistance from police rank and file. Middle managers lost enthusiasm for innovation. An attitude of "this too shall pass" was held by some managers.[17]

14. George L. Kelling, et al., *Kansas City Preventive Patrol Experiment*, A Summary Report (Washington, D.C., Police Foundation, 1974), p. 10.

15. Bloch, *Operation Neighborhood*, p. 9.

16. Sherman, *Team Policing*, p. 21.

17. Ibid., p. 35.

Several criteria must be met to reduce internal strife and increase the likelihood of a program's survival. Assignment to the program must be thought desirable by participants. Often this is evidenced by high morale and elite status bestowed on program members. The program should offer some material rewards, either extra money or leave days, for participants. There should also be some intrinsic rewards, such as distinctive uniforms or equipment, or some advantages that others of similar rank are not given. Finally, and very important, nonparticipants must believe in the program's merits and themselves strive to become members.

Miami, Florida, has a Motorcycle Enforcement Unit as a traffic control program that appears to meet those criteria.[18] The assignment is considered highly desirable, morale is high, and it is a position of noted status. Officers can receive extra money through the large volume of off-duty work available to members of the unit for escort services, and members may take their motorcycles to and from home. The unit is held in high regard by other officers in the police organization and by city residents as well.

EXTERNAL IMPLICATIONS

Long experience should have made the police administrator acutely aware of factors external to a police organization which can significantly influence the success of a policing program. Such factors are generally determined by private institutions, by other government agencies, or by other parts of the criminal justice system.[19] Their influence is manifested in political pressure upon a police administrator to institute change.[20] To manage change, therefore, a police administrator must participate in political processes. He must objectively understand and accept the reciprocal role his department plays with other organizations, government agencies, and social institutions.[21]

Frequently, a police administrator will willingly accept total responsibility for objectives such as reducing crime over which his department has little control.[22] Failure to share this responsibility with others will most likely leave the police official helpless in his ef-

18. *Study of the City of Miami Police Department* (New York City Police Department, Middle Management Exchange Program, 1972), pp. 53–54.

19. Bloch, *Operation Neighborhood*, p. 3.

20. Kelly, "Receptiveness to Change," p. 17.

21. Robert M. Igleburger, John E. Angell, and Garry Pence, Changing Urban Police: Practitioners View," *Innovation in Law Enforcement* (Washington, D.C., U. S. Government Printing Office, 1973), pp. 78–79.

22. O. W. Wilson and Roy C. McLaren, *Police Administration*, 3rd ed. (New York, McGraw-Hill Book Company, 1972), p. 4.

fort to design or implement a program effectively supportive of community demands and needs. The implication here is that "a project will have a better chance of survival if it has been championed and planned by a core of police and community officials, not just by the police chief himself, who may be gone in a year."[23]

Before a police administrator fully supports a new project, he should learn public opinion of such change and its predictable consequences for his organization. In 1970, for example, the police of Puerto Rico learned from a survey of public opinion that 51 percent of the citizens rated police service as fair or poor. The same survey also indicated that specialized training in public relations and human relations was required for police officers. As a result, a community relations division was created in 1971.[24]

At times, however, public opinion alone will not be a fair indicator for rational decision making. Often there will be mixed responses to some police program or procedure. In Detroit, for example, a plainclothes unit called STRESS (stop the robbers—enjoy safe streets) aroused considerable public resentment after killing twelve persons in a year.[25] Yet, at the same time, a considerable volume of letters, petitions, and postal cards indicated public opinion favored retention of the unit.[26] Public reaction to a program may depend as much upon the character of the program as upon its proven effectiveness.[27]

When the time is right to initiate a program it is not enough simply to embark on a campaign to urge support. The prudent police administrator must demonstrate the kinds of support needed to give the project a chance for success.[28]

One project clearly demonstrates the cooperative system so necessary for a viable police program. In 1971, the Philadelphia Police Department, after a three-month study of graffiti problems in the city, created a police Graffiti Squad. The city quickly encouraged development of programs in art lessons and similar activities in hope that they would create an outlet for expression and fulfill the need for recognition of many youths who ordinarily resort to graffiti ac-

23. Milton, "Demonstration Projects," p. 126.

24. *Study of Puerto Rico Police Department* (New York City Police Department, Middle Management Exchange Program, 1974), p. 218.

25. Jonathan Rubenstein, *City Police* (New York, Ballantine Books, 1973), p. 368.

26. *Study of the Detroit Police Department* (New York City Police Department, Middle Management Exchange Program, 1972), pp. 293–294.

27. *Improving Productivity*, p. 68.

28. Gerald M. Caplan, "Concern and Choice: The Selection of Program Priorities in Criminal Justice Research," *Journal of Criminal Justice.* (Winter, 1973), p. 297.

tivity. The Graffiti Squad was involved in a program to acquire an old bus to be used by graffiti writers. Permission was also sought from several construction sites to use their temporary wooden fences for graffiti. Cooperation was also enlisted from the Police Athletic League in several clean-up drives. Public schools became involved in educational projects to teach children the costly effects of graffiti on city economy. The courts cooperated, too. Stringent fines were imposed on guilty offenders, and they were required to defray the cost of cleaning up the graffiti left by their misbehavior. The Graffiti Squad visited merchants and advised them on how to safeguard items often shoplifted by youths for tools, such as spray paints and marking pens. The squad gained public support through personal contacts with victims of graffiti offenders. Complainants were reassured that their plight would be given serious attention by the police department.[29]

These kinds of purposeful interaction undoubtedly lend positive support to a police department in successfully meeting its desired program objectives.

SUMMARY AND CONCLUSION

A police administrator, to increase the likelihood of program success, must objectively diagnose the climate for change before program implementation. The administration of internal matters has broad implications for successful innovation. The police administrator should examine the latent aspects of a new program in terms of employee perception and behavior.

Police administrators should participate in political processes and share responsibilities with others outside the police department. Public opinion and its predictable implications are important to innovation, particularly to those programs of a potentially sensitive nature.

Proper administration of change can do much to resolve issues surrounding police innovation and increase the likelihood of program success.

Areas for Discussion for Part V

1. There are several recognized methods by which to change the police organization, discuss the situations where the various change modes can best be utilized.

2. During the last several decades change in police organizations has gone through an evolutionary process, what is the disposition of change today as compared to past years?

29. *Study of Philadelphia Police Department* (New York City Police Department, Middle Management Exchange Program, 1973), pp. 147–148.

3. During the last several decades there have been significant changes in the police role, structure, and management, what were the causes of these changes, and how was change implemented?

4. What impact has internal factors (employee expectations, fiscal constraints, etc.) and external factors (societal expectations, political constraints, etc.) had upon police change?

5. How does the police administrator determine the optimal amount of change in the police organization?